THEOLOGY OF EMIL G. HIRSCH

DAVID EINHORN HIRSCH
EDITOR

WHITEHALL COMPANY
1200 So. Willis Ave.
Wheeling, Illinois 60090

Library of Congress Catalog Card No. 76-56964

Printed in the U.S.A.

0-87655-039-1 Casebound

0-87655-539-3 Paperback

Contents

CHAPT.		PAGE
	INTRODUCTION	5
I.	AGNOSTICISM	9
II.	ALBO	15
III.	ALTRUISM	23
IV.	ARTICLES OF FAITH	26
V.	ASCETICISM	39
VI.	ATHEISM	46
VII.	BODY IN JEWISH THEOLOGY	55
VIII.	COMMANDMENT	60
IX.	COMPASSION	79
X.	COSMOGONY	83
XI.	CREATION	89
XII.	CRESCAS	100
XIII.	CRUCIFIXION	109
XIV.	CRUELTY	114
XV.	DARKNESS	121
XVI.	DAY OF THE LORD	124
XVII.	DECALOGUE IN JEWISH THEOLOGY	128
XVIII.	DEISM	134
XIX.	DUALISM	138
XX.	ETHICS	140
XXI.	EVE	158
XXII.	EVOLUTION	162
XXIII.	FALL OF ANGELS	166
XXIV.	FALL OF MAN	169
XXV.	GOD	174
XXVI.	CHILDREN OF GOD	215
XXVII.	GODLINESS	218
XXVIII.	THE GOLDEN RULE	221
XXIX.	HEGEL	224

XXX.	HIGH PLACE	228
XXXI.	HIGH PRIEST	236
XXXII.	HOST OF HEAVEN	248
XXXIII.	JEHOVAH	250
XXXIV.	OPTIMISM AND PESSIMISM	252
XXXV.	PROPHETS AND PROPHECY	257
XXXVI.	PROSELYTE	274
XXXVII.	PROVIDENCE	288
XXXVIII.	PSALMS	295
XXXIX.	REFORM JUDAISM	311
XL.	RIGHT AND RIGHTEOUSNESS	326
XLI.	SABBATH	338
XLII.	SABBATH AND SUNDAY	368
XLIII.	SACRIFICE	372
XLIV.	SALVATION	406
XLV.	SELAH	411
XLVI.	SERVANT OF GOD	417
XLVII.	SHEMONEH 'ESREH	422
XLVIII.	SON OF GOD	458
XLIX.	SON OF MAN	461
L.	TABLES OF THE LAW	465
LI.	THEOCRACY	470
	INDEX	473

Introduction

Emil G. Hirsch, Ph.D.,L.L.D., was Professor of Rabbinical Literature and Philosophy at the University of Chicago for thirty years, and Rabbi of Chicago Sinai Congregation for forty-three years until his death in 1923.

In this book I have brought together that portion of his writings which reflect his own Theology and Judaism.

All of these writings are from *The Jewish Encyclopedia* (first published by Funk and Wagnalls).

I have left references to other subjects and writings so that my readers may further trace the finely spun thread of my father's thoughts.

In a few cases the subject was divided and a portion written by a second scholar. I have not included that scholar's portion in this book except in three cases....enumeration of the 613 Commandments in the chapter on *Commandment* by Isaac Broyde, Doctor of the University of Paris; the listings of the Articles at the end of the chapter on *Articles of Faith* by my uncle, Kaufmann Kohler, Ph.D., President of the Hebrew Union College; and the Biblical Data and Critical View for the chapter on *Prophets And Prophecy* by J. Frederic McCurdy, Ph.D.,L.L.D., Professor of Oriental Languages, University College, Toronto, Canada.

The two chapters on *Commandment* and on *Dualism* were coauthored with my uncle, Dr. Kaufmann Kohler; and the chapter on *Decalogue* was coauthored with Edvard Konig, Ph.D.,L.L.D., Professor Old Testament Exegesis, University of Bonn, Germany.

Since writing my biography, *Emil G. Hirsch.....The Reform Advocate,* I have received many requests from scholars and students from all religions to bring forth more writings and sermons of my father.

Theology Of Emil G. Hirsch is the first of several volumes I have planned.

According to my father....

> The purpose of human life is service now and here...
> None can be spared...
> What is ours is ours only as a means to enlarge the common life...
> It becomes the duty of the strong to look after the weak to help them to strength, in order to increase the sum total of all.

This is my purpose.

David Einhorn Hirsch
November 1, 1976

THEOLOGY
OF
EMIL G. HIRSCH

For My Grandchildren
As a Remembrance and a Heritage

I

Agnosticism

AGNOSTICISM: A term invented by Prof. Thomas H. Huxley in 1869, expressive of opposition to the claims of the Christian gnostic as "the one who knows all about God" (see Huxley in the "Nineteenth Century," February, 1889), in adaptation of the descriptive adjective found in St. Paul's mention of the altar "to the unknown God" (Acts, xvii. 23). The word agnostic with its derivative has passed into recent literature as the designation in the main of the theories of two groups of thinkers. In its original implication, corresponding to the position of its inventor, the term agnostic represented a state of suspended judgment with regard both to theism and atheism. On the ground that existing evidence does not justify either the affirmation or the denial of the being of God, God is held to be unknown. However, the word has assumed a secondary meaning. It has come to denote the theory that God is not only now unknown, but is forever unknowable, on the assumption that the nature of human knowledge is such as to preclude knowledge of ultimate things. In the former sense the agnostic position makes a reaction against the dogmatism of both the Church and of atheistic materialism. Each presumed to possess ultimate knowledge. A protest against the arrogant gnosis of these, Agnosticism represents a wholesome phase of modern thought. It is expressive of the recognized need of modesty and a higher degree of reverence. The dogmatism of the Church was neither modest nor reverent; and these, its failings, marred also the attitude of its antipode, insistent materialism.

Name and Meaning.

Not content to teach that God is, the Church proceeded to catalogue what He is. In claiming for itself this knowledge, it ignored the limitations of human thought. It confounded analogy with identity. The Church failed, furthermore, in self-consistency. It appealed to revelation, and thus conceded the position of those who insist upon the inability of human reason to arrive at a comprehensive knowledge of God. On the other hand, it assumed that the human mind, lacking the insight to attain unto the knowledge of God, may yet understand and interpret revelation, and proceeded to develop, from data beyond cognition, a theory of the Godhead and of God's relations to the world and every individual therein. This contradiction proved to be the vulnerable point which atheism was not slow to attack, but atheism in turn fell into the error of its antagonist. Refusing to acknowledge reality beyond the visible, tangible, and sensuous world, it contradicted itself in building up a theory of the universe which transcended the data of immediate experience. Its denials were as dogmatic as were the affirmations of Church theism. Agnosticism, in proclaiming a truce to the verbalism of both contestants, came upon the world of thought as a refreshing breeze after a hot and stifling sirocco. As such a protest and reaction, it helped to clarify the atmosphere and contributed to the reexamination of the foundations of belief. It emphasized the necessity of clearer statements of the basic propositions at issue. But it could be only preliminary. The metaphysical interest in man is too strong to resign itself to inactivity, and the passion for unity and harmony is too insistently interwoven in the very constitution of the human soul to respect the lines drawn by this Agnosticism of "suspended judgment" in expectancy of further and fuller evidence.

Man's Knowledge of God.

Agnosticism versus Atheism.

In its own development Agnosticism had to progress beyond its first positions. Enunciating the doctrine that God is not only unknown, but forever unknowable, the later agnostic theories recur to the metaphysical epistemology of Kant and Comte, as modified in the synthetic philosophy of Herbert Spencer. Fundamental to this phase of Agnosticism is the thesis that knowledge is confined to phenomena—that the nature of ultimate things lies beyond the reach of human thought. The radical defect of this contention has often been pointed out. If it were true that our knowledge is limited to the phenomenal, by no possibility could we ever

Development of Agnosticism.

become aware of the limitation. To affirm that things-in-themselves exist, but that man can not know them, implies the contradiction of one half of the proposition in the other. If we can not know things-in-themselves, how do we know that they exist? If we know that they exist, then they are not unknowable. The knowledge that they are includes in a certain degree also the knowledge of what they are. The argument which proves that we can not know what things are in themselves tells against the knowledge that they are.

In the Kantian system the principle of causation is relied upon to prove the existence of the things in themselves. But, if our knowledge is confined within the realm of phenomena, this principle, of necessity, will apply only to phenomenal existence. We can not take one step farther by the aid of this crutch. In knowing the limits, we have passed beyond them. This new Agnosticism controverts the position of the sensationists. It concedes that sensations must have a cause beyond themselves. Our knowledge of the outer world is regarded as an inference, depending on an act of abstract thinking. It is then conceded that we know more than the immediate data of experience, for sensations are the only states of experience. Yet we assume, on the principle of causation, the existence of a world beyond and antecedent to our sensations. In truth, the knowledge of sensations is not more direct than that of objects.

To know consists not in the act of immediate experience, but is a composite operation in which comparison and memory—that is to say, the conscious

Consciousness and Knowledge.

revivifying of experiences which have passed away and are no more—play considerable part. Self-consciousness as the basis of thought thus transcends the actual as clearly as does the inference of things beyond the phenomenal. But this world, to which our sensations, as interpreted by consciousness, point, and the knowledge of which, though beyond experience, is ours, we interpret by the data of our own consciousness. We project into the beyond our own personality. Our personal experience now, as Kant himself has pointed out, is in a certain sense out of and above time, since the conscious unity which is present in it all, and without which it could not exist, is no member of the temporal series, but is that which makes the very conception of time possible. Our own self thus asserts itself as free from the limitations of time, and, therefore, it is not proved that the reality underlying the All must, of necessity, be quite unlike what we know as human life. What we know of self we may not deny to the absolute.

The fear of falling into ANTHROPOMORPHISM AND ANTHROPOPATHISM is the fatal obsession of Agnosticism; but we think as men, and can not think otherwise. Mythopoetic construction is inherent in all mental synthesis. Science can not spare the privilege or resist the inclination. Any system of interpreting nature to man must resort to the picture language, which alone evokes response from the human mind. Confusion in the use of the term knowledge has lent a semblance of cogency to the contentions of Agnosticism. What we know, we know as human beings: that is to say, in its relations to our conscious self. Sensations, the immediate material of our consciousness, we know in no manner different from the way in which we know the unities beyond and underneath these sensations. In their relations to us we know the things-in-themselves, the existence of which need not be established for us by a process of thought, but the knowledge of which is an original datum, which is presupposed in every act of thinking. Our own personal identity and self-consciousness are of things-in-themselves. As we know ourselves, we know them. The knowledge of our Ego, which is the consciousness of our unity, leads to the knowledge of the ultimate unity underlying all that is. While we may never know what God is in Himself, we do know what He is for us. As we are a part of the All, that which we are must also be in some degree of the essence and nature of the All. The All can not be less than we, a part thereof.

Knowledge of God and the World.

Judaism has little to learn, and still less to fear, from modern Agnosticism. Conceiving of man as created in the image of God, it bases its God-knowledge on the self-knowledge of man. By looking into himself, man learns to know his God; and it is in terms of this self-cognition that Judaism expresses its God-consciousness. The early Biblical writings are naively anthropomorphic and anthropopathic. The philosophers of Judaism, beginning with PHILO, prefer to hypostasize divine manifestations and powers, such as wisdom, grace, justice, prescience, to descriptions of His entity in human terms. This tendency finds expression in the nomenclature which

Jewish Views.

borrows designations of space and locality to connote the Deity. "Being," "He who is," seem to suffice to name Him adequately. Beyond this ascription of Being, the pious disinclination to associate with Him other and less comprehensive connotations would not venture. The ḥazan who exhausted a rich vocabulary of attributive description in his zeal to magnify God was censured for his presumption (Bab. Ber. 33*b*). "The NAME" is the favorite synonym for God.

Fundamental to the theology of most of the philosophic writers among the Jews is the thesis that, while we may predicate existence of God, we can not attain unto the knowledge of His quality (Maimonides, "Moreh," i. 58). Joseph Albo reports the answer given by a "wise man" to the query, whether he knew the *what* of the Godhead: "Did I possess this knowledge, I myself would be God" ("'Iḳḳarim," ii. 30). The controversy concerning the ascription of attributes to the Deity was fanned into a high blaze in consequence of dogmatic disputes in the camp of Mohammedan theologians. Saadia devotes a series of chapters ("Emunot we-De'ot," ii. 4–9) to the discussion of the problem, and comes to the conclusion that attributes, in the strict sense of the word, can not be predicated of God. Those found in the Bible may be divided into such as indicate essence and such as connote action; the former are comprehended in God's unity and are a mere accommodation to the necessities of language, while those of activity are mere designations of God's power in nature and history.

Saadia was succeeded by a long series of thinkers, who contend that the attributes have in reality only a negative implication. They exclude their contraries, but do not affirm of God a positive reality, not included before in His Being. Maimonides, in his "Moreh Nebukim" (i. 50–60), on the whole is inclined to accept this theory. To attribute qualities to God would amount to limiting Him, and thus would degrade His Being. The attributes life, power, knowledge, and will constitute only a seeming exception. But while in man life and knowledge, thought and power are separate and divided, in God, the One and Indivisible, they are one. God's thought is not of the order of human thought. It is spontaneous. Why, then, adds Maimonides, in view of the essential difference of implication in the terms, use them in connection with God? From the very beginning, he adds, Jews had a dread of pronouncing the name of the Deity. The priests alone at certain times and in holy places could presume to

Qualification by Negation.

utter the Ineffable Appellation. Others had to paraphrase it. Adonai and Elohim designate God as cognized from His works. Still Maimonides' thesis has also its positive side. The more we know what God is not, the nearer, says he, we draw by this road of negation to the perception of what is involved in the concept of the Deity as the One and Indivisible Unity.

In all essentials, modern Judaism shares the position of Maimonides. It regards all attempts at descriptive connotations of the Godhead as anthropomorphic makeshifts to find words for a thought which in reality is beyond the power of human tongue adequately to convey. God is. In Himself, He is unknowable. In so far as He is in relation to our own self, the life of Israel, the human family, and the world, He is known. Up to a certain point, then, Judaism is agnostic. It parts company with Agnosticism at the point where the certitude of our own immediate consciousness of the reality beyond the limited range of sensational experience is called into doubt. By the light of this consciousness, which is an immediate datum, by the facts of his own identity and persistency as a conscious entity in time and space—yet withal above time and space, and constituted into a moral personality by the additional data of Israel's history and the guidance of the world and humanity—the Jew, in accordance with Judaism's doctrine, draws the warrant for predicating in his faltering human language the existence of that "power not ourselves making for righteousness," paraphrasing attributes which agnostic metaphysics, in its confusion of the implications and the limitations of knowledge, refuses to admit. The Unknowable God, through the medium of human cognition, is apprehended as the God who is, and, as existing, is known by analogy and brought nearer to man by symbolism rooted in human experience and human self-consciousness.

Modern Jewish Views.

II
Albo

ALBO, JOSEPH: Spanish preacher and theologian of the fifteenth century; known chiefly as the author of the work on the fundamentals of Judaism "'Iḳḳarim" (Principles). Little is known of the details of his life. Monreal, a town in Aragon, is generally assumed to have been his birthplace; but this surmise rests upon doubtful evidence. Astruc, in his report of the prolonged religious debate held at Tortosa in 1413–14, mentions Albo as one of the Jewish participants, and says that he was the delegate of the congregation of Monreal. But in the Latin account of the great verbal battle no reference is made to this locality; and there is, consequently, good ground for doubting the correctness of the assertion. Graetz believes that Albo could not have been less than thirty years of age when he was sent to take part in the disputation referred to, and he accordingly places the date of Albo's birth not later than 1380. It seems to be certain that he died in 1444, although some have been of the opinion that his death occurred in 1430. He is mentioned, however, as preaching at Soria in 1433.

The use Albo makes of medical illustrations creates the presumption that he was an adept in medical science, which suggests that he may have practised medicine, thus emulating the excellent tradition of earlier Jewish writers on philosophical subjects. He shows himself also fairly well versed in the systems of Arabic Aristotelians, though his knowledge of their works was in all probability only second-hand and obtained through Hebrew translations. His teacher was Ḥasdai Crescas, the well-known author of a religio-speculative book, "Or Adonai." Whether Crescas was still living when Albo published his "'Iḳḳarim" has been one of the disputed points among the recent expounders of his philosophy. Albo's latest critic, Tänzer ("Die Religionsphilosophie des Joseph Albo," Presburg, 1896), clearly establishes the fact that the first part of the work must have been composed before the death of Albo's master.

The opinions of modern students of medieval Jewish philosophy are divided as to the intrinsic worth of Albo's expositions. Munk, while conceding that "'Iḳḳarim" marks an epoch in Jewish theology, is exceedingly careful to accentuate its lack of value as a philosophical production (see Munk, "Mélanges," p. 507). Graetz is still more pronounced in his refusal to credit the book with signal qualities calling for recognition. He charges the author with shallowness and a fondness for long-spun platitudes, due to his homiletic idiosyncrasies, which would replace strict accuracy of logical process by superabundance of verbiage (Grätz, "Gesch. d. Juden," viii. 157). Ludwig Schlesinger, who wrote an introduction to his brother's German translation of the "'Iḳḳarim" (Frankfort-on-the-Main, 1844), avers that Albo did little more than schedule, on a new plan, the articles of faith of Maimonides. On the other hand, S. Back, in his dissertation on Joseph Albo (Breslau, 1869), places him on a high pedestal as "the first Jewish thinker who had the courage to coordinate philosophy and religion, or even to make both identical." "Albo," says Back, "did not merely give the Jewish religion a philosophical foundation; he made philosophy preeminently religious in its contents." The purpose of the book was neither to coordinate religion and philosophy nor to build up a strictly logical system of dogmatics. Much fairer to the vital intentions of the author is the theory developed by Tänzer, that the "'Iḳḳarim" constitutes in reality a well-conceived contribution to the apologetics of Judaism.

His Significance.

The work was not composed in its entirety at once. The first part was published as an independent work. It develops the gist of Albo's thought; and it was only when its publication brought down upon him a perfect deluge of abuse and criticism that he felt impelled to add to it three more sections—by way, as it were, of amplification and commentary on the views advanced in the first. In his preface to the second part Albo delivers himself of a vigorous sermon on the subject of his censors: "He that would criticize a book should, above all, know the method employed by its author, and should judge all the passages on a certain subject as a whole." He castigates the hasty and careless procedure of those who will pass judgment on an author without remembering this fundamental requirement of sound criticism. Albo's opponents certainly did not handle him delicately. He was accused, among other things,

His "'Iḳḳarim."

of plagiarism. It was maintained that he appropriated the thoughts of his teacher Crescas especially, without giving him due credit. This accusation has been repeated, even in modern times, by no less a scholar than M. Joël. Examination of the incriminating evidence, however, does not substantiate the indictment. Crescas having been Albo's teacher, the similarities are only such as might be reasonably expected in the writings of both preceptor and disciple.

Popular as the loose statement is, that Albo was actuated to write his "'Iḳḳarim" by a desire to reduce to a more handy number the thirteen articles of faith drawn up by Maimonides, it must be dismissed as erroneous. The enumeration of fundamental dogmas or principles of religion is an incidental result of Albo's inquiry, not the primary and essential motive. It is an open question how far the claim may be pressed that Judaism has produced an independent philosophy of religion. But whatever labor was devoted to this field by Jewish thinkers was, in every case, primarily prompted and inspired by the ardent desire to defend the citadel of Jewish faith against the assaults of its enemies. Taking a broad survey of the whole field, it may safely be said that at four different periods Judaism must have been under the stress of this duty. When, in Alexandria, Greek thought laid siege to the fortress of Judaism, the consequent urgency of a sufficient resistance produced Philo's system. The second reasoned exposition of Judaism was produced at the time of the controversies with Karaism and under the influence of the polemics of the Mohammedan schools. Maimonides, in turn, represents the reaction exerted by the Arabic Aristotelian schoolmen. And, finally, Albo enters the lists as Judaism's champion under the challenge of Christian doctrine. This characteristic element, in the genesis of whatever system of philosophical dogmatics Judaism evolved, must be constantly borne in mind in judging any phase or feature of the system, and especially in forming an estimate of Albo's method.

Philosophy and Apologetics.

Times of controversy concerning spiritual things call, naturally, for the systematization of one's own fund of philosophy. Much has been written on the subject of the dogmatic or undogmatic nature of Judaism. Certain it is that the inclination for elaborating creeds has tempted the Jewish theologians to frame dogmas only in critical times of heated controversy. Albo had many predecessors in this field, both among the Rabbinites and the Karaites. But, strange as it may seem, he only followed the example of Abba Mari ben Moses ben Joseph of Lunel, one of the most outspoken leaders of the anti-Maimonists (in his "Minḥat Ḳenaot"), and of Simon ben Ẓemah Duran (in his "Magen Abot"), in limiting the fundamental "roots" to three—namely, the belief in the existence of God; in revelation; and in divine retribution, or, if it be preferred, in immortality. In the formulation of other articles of faith the controversies to which the compilers had been exposed, and in which they had taken part, influenced, to a large extent, both the selection of the specific principles to be accentuated and the verbal dress in which they were arrayed. Similarly in the case of Albo, his selection was made with a view to correct the scheme of Maimonides in those points where it seemed to support the contentions of the Christian dogmatists and controversialists. Maimonides himself had been influenced by a desire to obviate certain Christian and Mohammedan contentions. His emphasis upon the absolute incorporeality of God only finds its true light when the doctrine of the incarnation is borne in mind. His Messianic expectation, with the stress upon the constancy with which its future fulfilment is to be looked for, had also an anti-Christian bearing. But this very point, the Messianic dogma, had in turn—soon after Maimonides—become a source of grave anxiety to the Jews, forced, as they were, to meet in public disputations the champions of the regnant and militant Church. Among the spokesmen of the Church not a few were converts from Judaism. These were not slow to urge this Messianic dogma of Maimonides as far as they might, to embarrass the defenders of Judaism.

Distinctive Features of Albo's Scheme.

Before Maimonides the question of the corporeality of the Messiah appears not to have been among the problems discussed and debated in the polemics between the Church and the Synagogue. But half a century after him, when his Messianic doctrine had been accepted as one of the essential articles of the faith, it is this very point that is pushed into the foreground of the discussions. Having participated in one of these public disputations, Albo must have become conscious of the embarrassment which the Maimonidean position could not but occasion to the defenders of Judaism. In his scheme, therefore, the Messiah is eliminated as an integral part of the Synagogue's faith. In its stead he lays stress upon the doctrine of divine retribution. Graetz has argued that Albo was prompted by a desire to Christianize Judaism. The contrary is the truth. In order to deprive the Christian disputants of their favorite weapon, and with the clear purpose of neutralizing Maimonides in this respect, Albo ignores the Messianic hope.

This apologetic interest marks his disquisition in its entirety. The title of his book indicates his method at the very outset. Basic to his investigation is the recognition that "human happiness is conditioned by knowledge [עיון] and conduct." But "human intellect can not attain unto perfect knowledge and ethical conduct, since its power is limited and soon exhausted in the contemplation of the things the truth of which it would find; therefore, of necessity, there must be something above human intellect through which knowledge and conduct can attain to a degree of excellence that admits of no doubt." The insufficiency of human intellect postulates the necessity of divine guidance; and thus it is the duty of every man to know the God-given law. But to know it is possible only if one has established the true principles, without which there can be no divine law. Seeing that on this vital theme there are so much divergence, confusion, and shallowness, Albo resolves to erect a structure for the true religion.

His great criterion in this his search is the question, What principles are indispensable to a religion that is both divine and true? All revealed religions—and it is in behalf of revealed religion that he sets out on his excursion—recognize three fundamental principles. But would the identity of these three principles in revealed religions not entitle the devotees of each to claim their own as the one true religion? No, replies Albo: these three principles may be alike indispensable to the so-called revealed religions, and, therefore, basic to any religion claiming to be revealed; but only that religion is the true one that understands these basic thoughts correctly. And the test for this correctness of understanding he holds to be the further recognition of certain other truths and inferences that must follow logically from the acknowledgment of the three fundamentals. Unless a revealed religion accept all of these inferences, it is not to be recognized as the one true religion. Now Judaism is not only based upon the three fundamental principles, but it acknowledges also the binding force of the inferences from them. As a consequence, Judaism is the true revealed religion. Having drawn this conclusion, Albo has attained the end for which he undertook his investigation. His purpose, as this analysis of

Fundamental Principles.

his introduction shows, was not to place Judaism upon a solid philosophical foundation, but to vindicate for Judaism, as opposed to the other revealed religions, the right to the distinction of being the true revealed religion. His argument may be open to serious objection. It is certainly true that he starts with a *petitio principii*. He assumes that religion is revealed; and writes as a theologian, not as a philosopher. But his theology is triumphant. Granting his premises, one can not but concede the consistency of his deductions.

Albo's terminology is probably original with him. The three fundamentals he designates *'iḳḳarim*, or roots (*'iḳḳar shorashim*; Dan. iv. 12 [15], 20 [26]). Hence the title of his work. The (eight) derived and necessary truths—upon the recognition and correct application of which depends whether the revealed religion prove itself to be the true religion—he calls *shorashim*, or secondary roots. Both of these—the 'iḳḳarim and the shorashim—are indispensable to the subsistence of the trunk of the tree. The branches, however, are not in this category. Traditional customs and other outgrowths, of which there are a great number in every religion—the *'anafim* (twigs), as he calls them—are not absolutely necessary to the life of religion. They may be removed or may die off, and still the trunk will subsist. Since the three 'iḳḳarim are the same in all religions, Albo calls them also the *'iḳḳarim kolelim* (the universal principles or roots; see Tänzer's work quoted above). The eight shorashim he styles sometimes *'iḳḳarim peraṭiyim*, as well as, in some cases, *'iḳḳarim meyuḥadim* (specialized or particular roots). But his terminology is not consistent throughout the work.

His Peculiar Terminology.

In the elaboration of his scheme Albo finds ample opportunity to criticize the opinions of his predecessors. He seems to be anxious to keep all heresy-hunting within proper bounds. Accordingly, he endeavors to establish the boundary-lines between which Jewish skepticism may be exercised without risk of forfeiture of orthodoxy. His canon for distinguishing heterodoxy from orthodoxy is the recognition of the truth of the Torah. But a remarkable latitude of interpretation is allowed; so much so, that it would indeed be difficult under Albo's theories to impugn the orthodoxy of even the most liberal. He rejects the assumption that creation *ex nihilo* is an essential implication of the belief in the Deity; and criticizes with a free hand the articles of faith by Maimonides, and also the six that Crescas had evolved. He shows that neither Maimonides nor Crescas keeps in view his own fundamental criterion; namely, the absolute indispensability of a principle without which the trunk of the tree could not subsist; and on this score he rejects most of their creed.

According to Albo, the first of his fundamental root-principles—the belief in the existence of God—embraces the following shorashim, or secondary radicals: (1) God's unity; (2) His incorporeality; (3) His independence of time; and (4) His perfection: in Him there can be neither weakness nor other defect. The second root-principle—the belief in revelation, or the communication of divine instruction by God to man—leads him to derive the following three secondary radicals: (1) The appointment of prophets as the mediums of this divine revelation; (2) the belief in the unique greatness of Moses as a prophet; and (3) the binding force of the Mosaic law until another shall have been divulged and proclaimed in as public a manner (before six hundred thousand men). No later prophet has, consequently, the right to abrogate the Mosaic dispensation. Finally, from the third root-principle—the belief in divine retribution—he derives one secondary radical: the belief in bodily resurrection. According to Albo, therefore, the belief in the Messiah is only a twig or branch. It is not necessary to the soundness of the trunk. It is, hence, not an integral part of Judaism. Nor is it true that every law is binding. Though every single ordinance has the power of conferring happiness in its observance, it is not true that every law, or that all of the Law, must be observed, or that through the neglect of one or the other law, or of any part of the Law, the Jew violates the divine covenant. The anti-Paulinian drift and point of this contention are palpable.

The style of Albo's work is rather homiletic. His phraseology suffers from prolixity; and his argumentation is at times exceedingly wearisome. Nevertheless, his book has come to be a standard popular treatise, and notwithstanding the severe polemics against Albo, made by Isaac Abravanel and others, it has wielded considerable influence in shaping the religious thoughts and confirming the religious beliefs of the Jews.

[The first edition of the "'Iḳḳarim" appeared at Soncino, 1485; it was published with a commentary under the title of "Ohel Ya'aḳob," by Jacob ben Samuel Koppelman ben Bunem, of Brzesc (Kuyavia), Freiburg, 1584, and with a larger commentary ("'Eẓ Shatul") by Gedeliah ben Solomon Lipschitz, Venice, 1618. From the later editions the passages containing criticisms on the Christian creed, in Book III. chaps. xxv., xxvi., have been expunged by the censor, while Gilbert Genebrard wrote a refutation of the same with valuable notes. This refutation was published with his own remarks by the renegade Jew Claudius Mai, Paris, 1566 (see Schlesinger's translation, notes on p. 666). The "'Iḳḳarim" has been translated into German by Dr. W. Schlesinger, rabbi of Sulzbach, and his brother, L. Schlesinger, wrote an introduction to the same, Frankfort-on-the-Main, 1844.

A very favorable view of Albo's work is expressed by L. Löw, "Ha-Mafteaḥ" (Gross-Kanizsa), pp. 266–268; Karpeles, "Gesch. der Jüd. Lit." pp. 815–818; Brann, "Gesch. der Juden," ii. 208, and Bloch, in Winter and Wünsche, "Gesch. der Jüd. Lit." ii. 787–790. As to Albo's dependence on Crescas, Simon Duran, and others, see M. Joël, "Don Chasdai Crescas' Religionsphilosophische Lehren," pp. 76–78, 81, Breslau, 1866; Jaulus, in "Monatsschrift," 1874, pp. 462 *et seq.*; Brüll, in his "Jahrbücher," iv. 52; and Schechter, in "Studies in Judaism," pp. 167, 171, 352, and notes 19 and 24. K.]

BIBLIOGRAPHY: Tänzer, *Die Religionsphilosophie des Joseph Albo*, Presburg, 1896; Munk, *Mélanges*, p. 507; Grätz, *Gesch. d. Juden*, 2d ed., viii. 115 *et seq.*, 157–167; M. Eisler, *Vorlesungen über die Jüd. Philosophen des Mittelalters*, iii. 186 *et seq.*; Kaufmann, *Gesch. der Attributenlehre*, index, *s.v.*; idem, *Die Sinne*, index, *s.v.*; S. Back, *Joseph Albo*, Breslau, 1869; Schechter, *The Dogmas of Judaism*, in *Jew. Quart. Rev.* i. 120 *et seq.*

III

Altruism

ALTRUISM: A term derived from the late Latin *alter hic* ("this other"); dative, *alteri huic*, contracted to *alteruic*. It seems to have been first used by Comte (1798–1857), to designate conduct impelled by motives utterly unselfish and inspired by the sole desire to bring about the happiness of another without regard to, or even at the expense of, one's own. As such it is opposed to egoism. It stands to reason that there is no equivalent of it in ancient or modern Hebrew. The very idea which it connotes, exaggerated self-obliteration, is not indigenous to Judaism. An analysis of the basic idea of Jewish ethics will reveal the reason why. Both Altruism and its contrary, egoism, belong to ethical systems founded on the concept of happiness as the ultimate motive of conduct and the *summum bonum.* According as the happiness of the individual self or that of the individual other or others is projected into dominant importance, hedonistic (*i.e.*, happiness) ethics becomes either egoistic or altruistic. And even those systems, largely theological, that seemingly have harmonized Altruism with egoism have done this by accentuating that self-happiness will only be attained through conduct leading to the increase or the establishment of the happiness of another.

In this sense both the ethics of Christianity and Buddhism were at one and the same time egoistic and altruistic. Self-obliteration in this life assures self-realization in the other. Self-realization being, according to Buddhism, the mother of all evil, self-obliteration is the road to permanent happiness. Buddhistic as well as Christian Altruism are thus founded on other-worldliness, which in the Christian scheme flowers in the assurance of personal felicity in a higher state, whereas in that of Buddhism it promises release from all evil of self-existence in the blissful and happy Nirvana.

Ethics of Christianity and Buddhism.

The non-theological systems of ethics, almost without exception, have failed to establish a higher harmony between egoism and Altruism. In the more recent writings on evolutionary ethics—the school of Herbert Spencer—the endeavor is made. Upon psychological grounds it is maintained that every altruistic act is, if not in its motives, always in its effects egoistic. Maternal love, for example, leads to the happiness of the mother through her own self-sacrifice. The pre-Spencerian (hedonistic) schools have posited either self or the other as the fountain-head of moral conduct. Comte virtually reverted to the fundamental thought of the English moralists of the seventeenth and eighteenth centuries, according to whom the sympathies rooted in human nature are the mainsprings of morality (Cumberland, Shaftesbury, Hutcheson, Butler, Paley, Adam Smith). Modern Altruism is a reaction against the exaggerated egoism of the philosophy of the French Revolution, leading to the exaltation of such figments and abstractions as the economic man—a being supposed to act upon one sole motive to the exclusion of any other; viz., unmitigated or even enlightened selfishness. Modern liberalism in politics, religion, and economics having taken its cue from the writings of Rousseau, Voltaire, and the encyclopedists, it was but natural that the pendulum of thought should swing back to the opposite pole and posit as the secret of all true life an equally excessive love for the fellow, in which the self of man failed to receive its legitimate due. This one-sided emphasis upon altruistic conduct in turn evoked the counter-revolution culminating in the apotheosis of the selfish, desocialized man, the "overman" of Nietzsche's doctrine, as before him Max Stirner had developed the theory of the selfish man's supremacy and autocracy.

This fatal antithesis beween self and others is avoided in the ethics of Judaism. The fundamental motive of the moral life is, according to Judaism, not the quest for happiness. Morality is summed up in service. The purpose of human life is service now and here. In the creation narrative man is destined to be ruler over every being and thing created. In this purpose all that live and breathe in the wide sweep of human fellowship have a part. None can be spared. He who should efface himself would commit as grievous a breach of the covenant as he who should crush another. The measure of the service which is upon us is contingent upon the strength, talent, possession, and power which have come to us. The ethical ambition on this basis

Morality Summed up in Service.

runs to the desire for increase of strength, knowledge, possession, and power. Weakness is not a virtue. The stronger the man the better able he is to render service. Therefore, the appeal of Judaism is that each shall become a self and strive for the realization of the fullest possible measure of self. Self-realization is the realization of a part of the service placed upon all. But, on the other hand, and flowing from the same concept of service, what is ours is ours only as a means to enlarge the common life. We are stewards of our talents and property, trustees thereof in the service of all. As the weakness of one diminishes the sum of service rendered, it becomes the duty of the strong to look after the weak; to help them to strength, in order thus to increase the sum total of strength at the disposal of all.

In this way Judaism overcomes the opposition of egoism to Altruism and finds the higher synthesis on the basis of the community of service. Self-assertion flowers into the sympathy and help extended to others struggling for fuller self-realization. In the Jewish view of life as a service both *ego* and *alter* find their higher harmony. Hillel's maxim, "If I am not for myself, who will be? If I am only for myself, what am I? If not now, when then?" epitomizes this concordance of self and the others. Egoism is limited to its legitimate field, that developing every man into as strong a self as is possible with a view to more perfect service; and even so is Altruism saved from exaggeration. Self-effacement is contrary to the moral law of life. The highest aim in the economy of society and of creation is self-assertion in the service of all. Not egoism which feeds self at the expense of others, nor Altruism which effaces self while thinking of others, but mutualism as implied in the words, "Love thy neighbor as thyself," is the guiding principle of Jewish ethics.

IV

Articles Of Faith

ARTICLES OF FAITH: In the same sense as Christianity or Islam, Judaism can not be credited with the possession of Articles of Faith. Many attempts have indeed been made at systematizing and reducing to a fixed phraseology and sequence the contents of the Jewish religion. But these have always lacked the one essential element: authoritative sanction on the part of a supreme ecclesiastical body. And for this reason they have not been recognized as final or regarded as of universally binding force. Though to a certain extent incorporated in the liturgy and utilized for purposes of instruction, these formulations of the cardinal tenets of Judaism carried no greater weight than that imparted to them by the fame and scholarship of their respective authors. None of them had a character analogous to that given in the Church to its three great formulas (the so-called Apostles' Creed, the Nicene or Constantinopolitan, and the Athanasian), or even to the "Kalimat As-Shahādat" of the Mohammedans. The recital of this "Kalimah" is the first of the five pillars of practical religion in Islam, and every one converted to Islam must repeat it verbatim; so that among the conditions required of every believer with reference to confession is the duty to repeat it aloud at least once in a lifetime. None of the many summaries from the pens of Jewish philosophers and rabbis has been invested with similar importance and prominence. The reasons for this relative absence of official and obligatory creeds are easily ascertained. The remark of

No Fixed Dogmas.

Leibnitz, in his preface to the "Essais de Théodicée," that the nations which filled the earth before the establishment of Christianity had ceremonies of devotion, sacrifices, libations, and a priesthood, but that they had no Articles of Faith and no dogmatic theology, applies with slight modification to the Jews. Originally race—or perhaps it is more correct to say nationality—and religion were coextensive. Birth, not profession, admitted to the religio-national fellowship. As long as internal dissension or external attack did not necessitate for purposes of defense the formulation of the peculiar and differentiating doctrines, the thought of paragraphing and fixing the contents of the religious consciousness could not insinuate itself into the mind of even the most faithful. Missionary or proselytizing religions are driven to the definite declaration of their teachings. The admission of the neophyte hinges upon the profession and the acceptance on his part of the belief; and that there may be no uncertainty about what is essential and what non-essential, it is incumbent on the proper authorities to determine and promulgate the cardinal tenets in a form that will facilitate repetition and memorizing. And the same necessity arises when the Church or religious fellowship is torn by internal heresies. Under the necessity of combating heresies of various degrees of perilousness and of stubborn insistence, the Church and Islam were forced to define and officially limit their respective theological concepts. Both of these provocations to creed-building were less intense in Judaism. The proselytizing zeal, though during certain periods more active than at others, was, on the whole, neutralized, partly by inherent disinclination and partly by force of circumstances. Righteousness, according to Jewish belief, was not conditioned on the acceptance of the Jewish religion. And the righteous among the nations that carried into practise the seven fundamental laws of the covenant with Noah and his descendants were declared to be participants in the felicity of the hereafter. This interpretation of the status of non-Jews precluded the development of a missionary attitude. Moreover, the regulations for the reception of proselytes, as developed in course of

No Need for Creeds in Judaism.

time, prove the eminently practical—that is, the non-creedal—character of Judaism. Compliance with certain rites—baptism, circumcision, and sacrifice—is the test of the would-be convert's faith. He is instructed in the details of the legal practise that manifests the Jew's religiosity, while the profession of faith demanded is limited to the acknowledgment of the unity of God and the rejection of idolatry (Yoreh De'ah, Gerim, 268, 2). Judah ha-Levi ("Cuzari," i. 115) puts the whole matter very strikingly when he says: "We are not putting on an equality with us a person entering our religion through confession alone [Arabic original, *bikalamati* = by word]. We require deeds, including in that term self-restraint, purity, study of the Law, circumcision, and the performance of the other duties demanded by the Torah." For the preparation of the convert, therefore, no other method of instruction was employed than for the training of one born a Jew. The aim of teaching was to convey a knowledge of the Law, obedience to which manifested the acceptance of the underlying religious principles; namely, the existence of God and the holiness of Israel as the people of His covenant.

The controversy whether Judaism demands belief in dogma, or inculcates obedience to practical laws alone, has enlisted many competent scholars. Moses Mendelssohn, in his "Jerusalem," defended the non-dogmatic nature of Judaism, while Löw among others (see his "Gesammelte Schriften," i. 31–52, 433 *et seq.* 1871) took the opposite side. Löw made it clear that the Mendelssohnian theory had been carried beyond its legitimate bounds. The meaning of the word for faith and belief in Hebrew (אמונה) had undoubtedly been strained too far to substantiate the Mendelssohnian thesis. Underlying the practise of the Law was assuredly the recognition of certain fundamental and decisive religious principles culminating in the belief in God and revelation, and likewise in the doctrine of retributive divine justice. The modern critical view of the development of the Pentateuch within the evolution of Israel's monotheism confirms this theory. The controversy of the Prophets hinges on the adoption by the people of Israel of the religion of YHWH, that excluded from the outset idolatry, or certainly the recognition of any other deity than YHWH as the legitimate Lord of Israel; that, in its progressive evolution, associated with YHWH the concepts of holiness, justice, and righteousness; and that culminated in the teaching of God's spirituality and universality. The historical books of the Bible, as recast in accordance with these latter religious ideas, evince the force of a strong and clearly apprehended conviction concerning the providential purpose in the destinies of earth's inhabitants, and more especially in the guidance of Israel. The Psalms and Wisdom books manifest the predominance of definite religious beliefs. To say that Judaism is a barren legalistic convention, as Mendelssohn avers, is an unmistakable exaggeration. The modicum of truth in his theory is that throughout Biblical Judaism, as in fact through all later phases of Jewish religious thinking and practise, this doctrinal element remains always in solution. It is not crystallized into fixed phraseology or rigid dogma. And, moreover, the ethical and practical implications of the religion are never obscured. This is evidenced by the Biblical passages that, in the opinion of many, partake of the nature of Articles of Faith, or are of great value as showing what, in the opinion of their respective authors, constitutes the essence of religion. Among these the most noteworthy are Deut. vi. 4; Isa. xlv. 5–7; Micah vi. 8; Ps. xv.; Isa. i. 16, 17; xxxiii. 15.

Evolution of Judaism.

Whatever controversies may have agitated Israel during the centuries of the Prophets and the earlier postexilic period, they were not of a kind to induce the defining of Articles of Faith to counteract the influences of heretical teaching. Dogmatic differences manifest themselves only after the Maccabean struggle for independence. But even these differences were not far-reaching enough to overcome the inherent aversion to dogmatic fixation of principles; for, with the Jews, acceptance of principles was not so much a matter of theoretical assent as of practical conduct. Though Josephus would have the divisions between the Pharisees and Sadducees hinge on the formal acceptance or rejection of certain points of doctrine—such as Providence, resurrection of the body, which, for the Pharisees, was identical

Discussions and Dogmatism Disfavored.

with future retribution — it is the consensus of opinion among modern scholars that the differences between these two parties were rooted in their respective political programs, and implied in their respectively national and anti-national attitudes, rather than in their philosophical or religious dogmas.

If the words of Sirach (iii. 20–23) are to be taken as a criterion, the intensely pious of his days did not incline to speculations on what was beyond their powers to comprehend. They were content to perform their religious duties in simplicity of faith. The Mishnah (Ḥag. ii. 1) indorsed this view of Sirach, and in some degree discountenanced theosophy and dogmatism. Among the recorded discussions in the schools of the Rabbis, dogmatic problems commanded only a very inferior degree of attention ('Er. 13*b*: controversy concerning the value of human life; Ḥag. 12*a*: concerning the order of Creation). Nevertheless, in the earliest Mishnah is found the caution of Abtalion against heresy and unbelief (Ab. i. 11 [12]); and many a Baraita betrays the prevalence of religious differences (Ber. 12*b*; 'Ab. Zarah 17*a*). These controversies have left their impress upon the prayer-book and the liturgy. This is shown by the prominence given to the Shema'; to the Messianic predictions in the Shemoneh-'Esreh (the "Eighteen Benedictions"), which emphasized the belief in the Resurrection; and, finally, to the prominence given to the Decalogue—though the latter was again omitted in order to counteract the belief that it alone had been revealed (Tamid v. 1; Yer. Ber. 6*b*; Bab. Ber. 12*a*). These expressions of belief are held to have originated in the desire to give definite utterance and impressiveness to the corresponding doctrines that were either rejected or attenuated by some of the heretical schools. But while these portions of the daily liturgy are expressive of the doctrinal contents of the regnant party in the synagogue (see Landshuth, in Edelman's "Hegyon Leb"; and LITURGY), they were not cast into the form of catalogued Articles of Faith.

The first to make the attempt to formulate them was Philo of Alexandria. The influence of Greek thought induced among the Jews of Egypt the reflective mood. Discussion was undoubtedly active on the unsettled points of speculative belief; and such discussion led, as it nearly always does, to a stricter definition of the doctrines. In his work, "De Mundi Opificio," lxi., Philo enumerates five articles as embracing the chief tenets of Mosaism: (1) God is and rules; (2) God is one; (3) the world was created; (4) Creation is one; (5) God's providence rules Creation. But among the Tannaim and Amoraim this example of Philo found no followers, though many of their number were drawn into controversies with both Jews and non-Jews, and had to fortify their faith against the attacks of contemporaneous philosophy as well as against rising Christianity. Only in a general way the Mishnah Sanh. xi. 1 excludes from the world to come the Epicureans and those that deny belief in resurrection or in the divine origin of the Torah. R. Akiba would also regard as heretical the readers of ספרים החצונים —certain extraneous writings (Apocrypha or Gospels)—and persons that would heal through whispered formulas of magic. Abba Saul designated as under suspicion of infidelity those that pronounce the ineffable name of the Deity. By implication the contrary doctrine and attitude may thus be regarded as having been proclaimed as orthodox. On the other hand, Akiba himself declares that the command to love one's neighbor is the fundamental principle of the Law; while Ben Asai assigns this distinction to the Biblical verse, "This is the book of the generations of man" (Gen. v. i.; Gen. R. xxiv.). The definition of Hillel the elder, in his interview with a would-be convert (Shab. 31*a*), embodies in the golden rule the one fundamental article of faith. A teacher of the third Christian century, R. Simlai, traces the development of Jewish religious principles from Moses with his 613 commands of prohibition and injunction, through David, who, according to this rabbi, enumerates eleven; through Isaiah, with six; Micah, with three; to Habakkuk, who simply but impressively sums up all religious faith in the single phrase, "The pious lives in his faith" (Mak., toward end). As the Halakah enjoins that one shall prefer death to an act of idolatry, incest, unchastity, or murder, the inference is plain that the corresponding positive principles were held to be fundamental articles of Judaism.

Philo and Akiba.

From Philo down to late medieval and even modern writers the Decalogue has been held to be in some way a summary of both the articles of the true faith and the duties derived from that faith. According to the Alexandrian philosopher (see "De Vita Mosis") the order of the Ten Words is not accidental. They divide readily into two groups: the first five summarizing man's relations to the Deity; the other five specifying man's duties to his fellows. Ibn Ezra virtually adopts this view. He interprets the contents of the Decalogue, not merely in their legal-ritual bearing, but as expressive of ethico-religious principles. But this view can be traced to other traditions. In Yer. Ber. 6*b* the Shema' is declared to be only an epitome of the Decalogue. That in the poetry of the synagogal ritual this thought often dominates is well known. No less a thinker than Saadia Gaon composed a liturgical production of this character (see AZHAROT); and R. Eliezer ben Nathan of Mayence enriched the prayer-book with a piyyuṭ in which the six hundred and thirteen commands are rubricated in the order of and in connection with the Decalogue. The theory that the Decalogue was the foundation of Judaism, its article of faith, was advocated by Isaac Abravanel (see his Commentary on Ex. xx. 1); and in recent years by Isaac M. Wise of Cincinnati in his "Catechism" and other writings.

The Decalogue as a Summary.

The only confession of faith, however, which, though not so denominated, has found universal acceptance, forms a part of the daily liturgy contained in all Jewish prayer-books. In its original form it read somewhat as follows: "True and established is this word for us forever. True it is that Thou art our God as Thou wast the God of our fathers; our King as [Thou wast] the King of our fathers; our Redeemer and the Redeemer of our fathers; our Creator and the Rock of our salvation; our Deliverer and Savior—this from eternity is Thy name, and there is no God besides Thee." This statement dates probably from the days of the Hasmoneans (see Landshuth, in "Hegyon Leb").

In the stricter sense of the term, specifications in connected sequence, and rational analysis of Articles of Faith, did not find favor with the teachers and the faithful before the Arabic period. The polemics with the Karaites on the one hand, and, on the other, the necessity of defending their religion against the attacks of the philosophies current among both Mohammedans and Jews, induced the leading thinkers to define and formulate their beliefs. Saadia's "Emunot we-Deot" is in reality one long exposition of the main tenets of the faith. The plan of the book discloses a systematization of the different religious doctrines that, in the estimation of the author, constitute the sum total of his faith. They are, in the order of their treatment by him, the following: (1) The world is created; (2) God is one and incorporeal; (3) belief in revelation (including the divine origin of tradition); (4) man is called to righteousness and endowed with all necessary qualities of mind and soul to avoid sin; (5) belief in reward and punishment: (6) the soul is created pure; after death it leaves the body; (7) belief in resurrection; (8) Messianic expectation, retribution, and final judgment. Judah ha-Levi endeavored, in his "Cuzari," to determine the fundamentals of Judaism on another basis. He rejects all appeal to speculative reason, repudiating the method of the Motekallamin. The miracles and traditions are, in their supernatural character, both the source and the evidence of the true faith. With them Judaism stands and falls. The book of Baḥya ibn Paḳuda ("Ḥobot ha-Lebabot"), while remarkable, as it is, for endeavoring to give religion its true setting as a spiritual force, contributed nothing of note to the exposition of the fundamental articles. It goes without saying that the unity of God, His government of the world, the possibilities of leading a divine life—which were never forfeited by man—are expounded as essentials of Judaism.

Saadia's, Judah ha-Levi's, and Baḥya's Creed.

More interesting on this point is the work of R. Abraham ibn Daud (1120) entitled "Emunah Ramah" (The High Faith). In the second division of his treatise he discourses on the principles of faith and the Law. These principles are: The existence of God; His unity; His spirituality; His other attributes; His power as manifested in His works; His provi-

Ibn Daud and Ḥananel ben Ḥushiel.

dence. Less well known is the scheme of an African rabbi, Ḥananel b. Ḥushiel, about a century earlier, according to whom Judaism's fundamental articles number four: Belief in God; belief in prophecy; belief in a future state; belief in the advent of the Messiah.

The most widely spread and popular of all creeds is that of Maimonides, embracing the thirteen articles. Why he chose this particular number has been a subject of much discussion. Some have seen in the number a reference to the thirteen attributes of God. Probably no meaning attaches to the choice of the number. His articles are: (1) The existence of God; (2) His unity; (3) His spirituality; (4) His eternity; (5) God alone the object of worship; (6) Revelation through His prophets; (7) the preeminence of Moses among the Prophets; (8) God's law given on Mount Sinai; (9) the immutability of the Torah as God's Law; (10) God's foreknowledge of men's actions; (11) retribution; (12) the coming of the Messiah; (13) Resurrection. This creed Maimonides wrote while still a very young man; it forms a part of his Mishnah Commentary, but he never referred to it in his later works (see S. Adler, "Tenets of Faith and Their Authority in the Talmud," in his "Ḳobeẓ 'al Yad," p. 92, where Yad ha-Ḥazaḳah, Issure Biah, xiv. 2, is referred to as proof that Maimonides in his advanced age regarded as fundamentals of the faith only the unity of God and the prohibition of idolatry). It did not meet universal acceptance; but, as its phraseology is succinct, it has passed into the prayer-book, and is therefore familiar to almost all Jews of the Orthodox school.

The Thirteen Articles of Maimonides.

The successors of Maimonides, from the thirteenth to the fifteenth century—Naḥmanides, Abba Mari ben Moses, Simon ben Ẓemaḥ Duran, Albo, Isaac Arama, and Joseph Jaabez—reduced his thirteen articles to three: Belief in God; in Creation (or revelation); and in providence (or retribution). Others, like Crescas and David ben Samuel Estella, spoke of seven fundamental articles, laying stress also on freewill. On the other hand, David ben Yom-Ṭob ibn Bilia, in his "Yesodot ha-Maskil" (Fundamentals of the Thinking Man), adds to the thirteen of Maimonides thirteen of his own—a number which a contemporary of Albo (see "'Iḳḳarim," iii.) also chose for his fundamentals; while Jedaiah Penini, in the last chapter of his "Beḥinat ha-Dat," enumerated no less than thirty-five cardinal principles (see Löw, "Jüdische Dogmen," in "Gesammelte Werke," i. 156 *et seq.*; and Schechter, "Dogmas of Judaism," in "Studies of Judaism," pp. 147–181).

In the fourteenth century Asher ben Jehiel of Toledo raised his voice against the Maimonidean Articles of Faith, declaring them to be only temporary, and suggested that another be added to recognize that the Exile is a punishment for the sins of Israel. Isaac Abravanel, in his "Rosh Amanah," took the same attitude toward Maimonides' creed. While defending Maimonides against Ḥasdai and Albo, he refused to accept dogmatic articles for Judaism, holding, with all the cabalists, that the 613 commandments of the Law are all tantamount to Articles of Faith.

In liturgical poetry the Articles of Faith as evolved by philosophical speculation met with metrical presentation. The most noted of such metrical and rimed elaborations are the "Adon 'Olam," by an anonymous writer—now used as an introduction to the morning services (by the Sephardim as the conclusion of the *musaf* or "additional" service), and of comparatively recent date; and the other known as the "Yigdal," according to Luzzatto, by R. Daniel b. Judah Dayyan.

Modern Catechisms.

The modern catechisms abound in formulated Articles of Faith. These are generally intended to be recited by the candidates for confirmation, or to be used for the reception of proselytes (see Dr. Einhorn's "'Olat Tamid"). The Central Conference of American Rabbis, in devising a formula for the admission of proselytes, elaborated a set of Articles of Faith. These modern schemes have not met with general favor—their authors being in almost all cases the only ones that have had recourse to them in practise. The points of agreement in these recent productions consist in the affirmation of the unity of God; the election of Israel as the priest people; the Messianic destiny of all humanity. The declaration of principles by the

Pittsburg Conference (1885) is to be classed, perhaps, with the many attempts to fix in a succinct enumeration the main principles of the modern Jewish religious consciousness.

The Karaites. The Karaites are not behind the Rabbinites in the elaboration of Articles of Faith. The oldest instances of the existence of such articles among them are found in the famous work by Judah ben Elijah Hadassi, "Eshkol ha-Kofer." In the order there given these are the articles of the Karaite faith: (1) God is the Creator of all created beings; (2) He is premundane and has no peer or associate; (3) the whole universe is created; (4) God called Moses and the other Prophets of the Biblical canon; (5) the Law of Moses alone is true; (6) to know the language of the Bible is a religious duty; (7) the Temple at Jerusalem is the palace of the world's Ruler; (8) belief in Resurrection contemporaneous with the advent of the Messiah; (9) final judgment; (10) retribution. The number ten here is not accidental. It is in keeping with the scheme of the Decalogue. Judah Hadassi acknowledges that he had predecessors in this line, and mentions some of the works on which he bases his enumeration. The most succinct cataloguing of the Karaite faith in articles is that by Elijah Bashyatzi (died about 1490). His articles vary but little from those by Hadassi, but they are put with greater philosophical precision (see Jost, "Geschichte des Judenthums," ii. 331).

BIBLIOGRAPHY: Schlesinger, German translation of '*Ikkarim* (especially introduction and annotations), xvi-xliii. 620 *et seq.*, 640 *et seq.*; Löw, *Gesammelte Werke*, i. 31-52, 133-176; Jost, *Gesch. des Judenthums und Seiner Sekten*; Hamburger, *Realencyclopädie*, s.v. *Dogmen*; Rapoport, *Biography of Hananel*; Schechter, *The Dogmas of Judaism*, in *Studies in Judaism*, pp. 147-181; J. Aub, *Ueber die Glaubens-Symbole der Mosaischen Religion*; Frankel's *Zeitschrift für die Religiösen Interessen des Judenthums*, 1845, 409, 449; Creizenach, *Grundlehren des Israelitischen Glaubens*, in Geiger's *Wissensch. Zeitschrift für Jüd. Theologie*, i. 39 *et seq.*, ii. 68, 255.

The Articles: The thirteen Articles of Faith formulated according to Maimonides in his Mishnah Commentary to Sanhedrin, introduction to ch. ix. —which have been accepted by the great majority of Jews and are found in the old prayer-book—are as follows:

1. I firmly believe that the Creator—blessed be His name!—is both Creator and Ruler of all created beings, and that He alone hath made, doth make, and ever will make all works of nature.

2. I firmly believe that the Creator—blessed be His name!—is one; and no Unity is like His in any form; and that He alone is our God who was, is, and ever will be.

3. I firmly believe that the Creator—blessed be His name!—is not a body; and no corporeal relations apply to Him; and that there exists nothing that has any similarity to Him.

4. I firmly believe that the Creator—blessed be His name!—was the first and will also be the last.

5. I firmly believe that the Creator—blessed be His name!—is alone worthy of being worshiped, and that no other being is worthy of our worship.

6. I firmly believe that all the words of the Prophets are true.

7. I firmly believe that the prophecy of Moses, our master—peace be upon him!—was true; and that he was the chief of the Prophets, both of those that preceded him and of those that followed him.

8. I firmly believe that the Law which we possess now is the same that hath been given to Moses our master—peace be upon him!

9. I firmly believe that this Law will not be changed, and that there will be no other Law [or dispensation] given by the Creator—blessed be His name!

10. I firmly believe that the Creator—blessed be His name!—knoweth all the actions of men and all their thoughts, as it is said: "He that fashioneth the hearts of them all, He that considereth all their works" (Ps. xxxiii. 15).

11. I firmly believe that the Creator—blessed be He!—rewardeth those that keep His commandments and punisheth those that transgress His commandments.

12. I firmly believe in the coming of the Messiah; and although He may tarry, I daily hope for His coming.

13. I firmly believe that there will take place a revival of the dead at a time which will please the Creator—blessed be His name, and exalted His memorial for ever and ever!

According to Maimonides he that rejects any of these articles is an unbeliever, and places himself outside of the Jewish community.

Joseph Albo reduces the articles to three fundamental principles:

1. *Existence of God:* Comprehension of God's unity, His incorporeality, His eternity, and of the fact of His being the object of man's worship.

2. *Revelation:* Comprehension of prophecy, of Moses as supreme authority, of the divine origin and immutability of the Law.

3. *Retribution:* Comprehension of the divine judgment and of Resurrection.

These three principles have, in the main, been adopted also by modern theologians, both conservative and liberal, as the fundamentals of Judaism in the religious instruction of children as well as in the confession of faith to be recited by proselytes; some (*e.g.*, Büdinger) laying especial stress on the immortality of the soul, others (*e.g.*, Stein) on the priestly mission of Israel, or the Messianic hope.

Einhorn posits the following five Articles of Faith:

1. God the Creator.
2. Man in His image.
3. Revelation (through Moses).
4. God the Judge.
5. Israel His priest-people.

The Central Conference of American Rabbis, in 1896, at Milwaukee, Wis., adopted the following four (or five) articles in the "Proselyte Confession":

1. God the Only One.
2. Man His image.
3*a*. Immortality of the soul.
3*b*. Retribution.
4. Israel's mission.

K.

V

Asceticism

ASCETICISM: A term derived from the Greek verb ἀσκέω, meaning "to practise strenuously," "to exercise." Athletes were therefore said to go through ascetic training, and to be ascetics. In this usage the twofold application—to the mode of living and the results attained—which marks the later theological implication of the term is clearly discernible. From the arena of physical contests the word easily passed over to that of spiritual struggles; and pre-Christian writers speak of the "askesis" of the soul or of virtue—the discipline of the soul, or the exercise in virtue. But the physical idea, no less than the moral, underlies the meaning of the term in medieval Christian parlance. The monastery, as the place where the required life of abstemiousness is lived under rigorous regulation and discipline, becomes the "asketerion," a word which to the classical Greek conveyed only the notion of a place reserved for physical exercise; while the monks were the "ascetikoi," the ascetics, under discipline attaining unto the perfect practise.

Non-Jewish.

It is thus seen that both the term and the idea which the term expresses are of non-Jewish origin and implications. Judaism can not be said to encourage Asceticism, even in the restricted sense of discipline. Rationalists have indeed affected to construe the ritual legalism of both the Pentateuch and the later rabbinical codes as a disciplinary scheme, devised by God or man with the view of bringing men under rigid restriction of freedom of action, in the satisfaction of the appetites and the control of the passions, to a higher degree of moral perfection. But even before comparative studies had shown that most, if not all, of the so-called disciplinary contrivances of the Mosaic scheme rest on notions altogether other than those assumed, the rigorous constructionists among Jewish theologians put themselves on record as utterly inimical to the ascription of utility, either moral or material, to the divine laws. They were simply divine commandments, and to inquire into their origin or their purpose was forbidden—"Ḥuḳḳah ḥaḳḳaḳti; we'en attem reshuyim leharher aḥareha" (I have decreed the statute; but you are not permitted to inquire into its reasons; Yoma 67*b*; Sifra, Aḥare, xiii.).

At all events, Judaism is of a temper which is fatal to asceticism; and the history of both Judaism and the Jews is, on the whole, free from ascetic aberrations. Fundamental to the teachings of Judaism is the thought that the world is good. Pessimism has no standing-ground. Life is not under the curse. The doctrine of original sin, the depravity of man, has never had foothold within the theology of the synagogue. It never held sway over the mind and the religious imagination of the Jews. In consequence of this the body and the flesh were never regarded by them as contaminated, and the appetites and passions were not suspected of being rooted in evil. The appeal to mortify the flesh for the sake of pleasing Heaven could not find voice in the synagogue.

Asceticism is indigenous to the religions which posit as fundamental the wickedness of this life and the corruption under sin of the flesh. Buddhism, therefore, as well as Christianity, leads to ascetic practises. Monasteries are institutions of Buddhism no less than of Catholic Christianity. The assumption, found in the views of the Montanists and others, that concessions made to the natural appetites may be pardoned in those that are of a lower degree of holiness, while the perfectly holy will refuse to yield in the least to carnal needs and desires, is easily detected also in some of the teachings of Gautama Buddha. The ideal of holiness of both the Buddhist and the Christian saint culminates in poverty and chastity; *i.e.*, celibacy. Fasting and other disciplinary methods are resorted to to curb the flesh. Under a strict construction of the meaning of Asceticism, it is an error to assume that its history may be extended to embrace also certain rites in vogue among devotees to fetishism and nature-worship. Mutilations, the sacrifice of the hair, dietary observances and prohibitions, which abound in all forms of religion at a certain stage of development, do not spring from the notion of the sinfulness of the natural instincts and of life. Nor is the sacrificial scheme in any way connected with Asceticism. The idea of privation is foreign to it. If the offering was a gift to the Deity and as such entailed upon the offerer the parting with something of value, the expectation which animated him was invariably that of receiving rich return. But whatever theory must be accepted in explanation of the various rites of mutilation, and of the sacrificial ritual, certain it is that Judaism from the beginning set its face most sternly against the one, and materially restricted the other. Mutilations for whatever purpose and of whatever character were absolutely prohibited. Funeral horrors and superstitions were not tolerated. The Levitical code restricted sacrifices to one place. The priests only were entrusted with the office at the altar. And, if the Prophets are the truest expounders of the ideals and ideas of the religion of Israel, even the sacrificial and sacerdotal system, with its implications of extraordinary and precautionary cleanliness and physical abstemiousness, was of little vital moment.

Torture of the Flesh.

Fasting, which plays so essential a part in the practises of ascetics, found official recognition only in the development of the Day of Atonement. The Prophets, again, had little patience with fasting. There are some obscure allusions to fast days of popular observance; but the Prophets of exilic and post-exilic days insist on the futility of this custom. Isaiah (lviii.), while appealing for a broader charity and deeper sense of justice, maintains that these, and not fasting, are the expression of a will sanctified unto God. It is characteristic of the attitude of later Judaism that this very chapter has been assigned for the Hafṭarah for the Day of Atonement, the one penitential fast-day of the synagogue.

Nevertheless, fasting among the Jews was resorted to in times of great distress. The Book of Esther, of late date, illustrates this for the period included in the Biblical canon. Rabbinical sources prove the growing tendency to abstain from drink and food whenever memories of disaster marked the days of the synagogal calendar, or instant danger threatened the community. In the scheme of the synagogue the one fast-day of the Bible received no less than twenty-two as companions (compare FASTING). Still, it may be doubted whether this multiplication of fast-days can be taken as a sign of an increased tendency to Asceticism. Probably the theory of Robertson Smith ("The Religion of the Semites," p. 413) still holds good to a large extent in explanation of many of the fast-observances of later Judaism, as undoubtedly it does for the voluntary and occasional fast-days mentioned in the historical books of the Bible; namely, that Oriental fasting is merely a preparation for the eating of the sacrificial meal. The rabbinical injunction, not to eat too late a meal on the eve of the Sabbath-day, so as to enjoy all the more that of the Sabbath, tends to corroborate the theory. Perhaps this also underlies the rabbinical report that some examples of rabbinical piety fasted every Friday (in preparation for the Sabbath).

Fasting.

Among the Rabbis some are mentioned as great and consistent fasters. Rabbi Zeira especially is remembered for his fondness of this form of piety. Yet to make of him an ascetic would transcend the bounds of truth. He fasted that he might forget his Babylonian method of teaching before emigrating to Palestine (B. M. 85*a*). The story continues that he abstained from drink and food for the period of one hundred days, in order that hell-fire might later have no power over him. Simon ben Yoḥai is depicted as an ascetic in the traditions preserved in rabbinical literature. But exposed to persecutions under the Hadrian régime, and often in danger of his life, his whole mind was of an exceptionally somber turn for a Jewish teacher. Moreover, his ascetic practises were not inspired by a consciousness of the futility of this life and its sinfulness, but by the anxiety to fulfil to

Ascetics in Talmud.

the letter the Law, to ponder on the Torah day and night. He begrudged the hours necessary for the care of the body as so many precious moments stolen from the study of the holy Law. He envied the generation of the desert who had been fed on heavenly manna, and were thus absolved from the care for their daily bread; an echo of this sentiment may be detected in the petition of Jesus for daily bread (on Simon b. Yoḥai, see Bacher, "Ag. Tan." ii. 70–149).

Still, with all these seeming leanings to ascetic conduct, these rabbis did not encourage individual fasting. The community in distress did indeed proclaim a public fast; and it was the duty of the loyal member to participate. For he who would not share in the distress would have no part in the consolation of the people (Ta'an. 11*a*). The habitual faster was called a sinner (*ib.*). This judgment was enforced by an appeal to the Biblical text in connection with the "Nazir's" (Nazarite's) expiatory sacrifice (Num. vi. 11). Rabbi Zeira would not permit his disciples to indulge in extraordinary practises of self-restraint, if they presumed thereby to reflect on the piety of others saner than they. The title applied to such an adept at saintly practises is characteristically deprecatory for his attitude of mind: his conduct is declared to smack of conceit, if not of hypocrisy (Yer. Ber. ii. 5*d*).

The attempt has been made to explain the Biblical Nazarites as forerunners of monastic orders addicted to the practise of ascetic discipline. Pentateuchal legislation concerning them shows them to have been merely tolerated. Modern criticism explains their peculiarities as arising from motives other than those that determine the conduct of ascetics. The Biblical Nazirs, forerunners of the Nebi'im (Prophets), were protestants against the adoption of the customs and the religious rites of the Canaanites. In their dress and mode of life they emphasized their loyalty to YHWH, enthroned on the desert mountain. Wine and the crown of hair were sacred to the gods of the land. Their very appearance emphasized their rejection of the new deities. And in later days the number of those that took the Nazarite vow was exceedingly small. One is inclined to the opinion that no case occurred in which the Pentateuchal provisions became effective.

Nor may the Essenes be classed among the order of ascetics. While some of their institutions, notably celibacy, appear to lend support to the theory that would class them as such, their fundamental doctrines show no connection with the pessimism that is the essential factor in Asceticism. They were political indifferentists; they were but little, if at all, under the sway of national aspirations. They stood for a universal fellowship of the pure and just. They set but little store by the goods of this earth, and were members of a communistic fraternity. But it is inadmissible to construe from these elements of their hopes and habits the inference that in them is to be found a genuine Jewish order of monks and ascetics.

Essenes not Ascetics.

A stronger case against the theory that Judaism is a very uncongenial soil for the growth of Asceticism might be made out by an appeal to the later Jewish mystics, the Ḥasidim and Cabalists of various forms, all ecstatic fantastics, and—this is a point that must not be overlooked—more or less strongly under the influence of distinctly non-Jewish conceits.

Looking upon this life as essentially good, according to Gen. i. 31; upon the human body as a servant of the spirit, and therefore not corrupt; upon the joys of earth as God-given and therefore to be cherished with gratitude toward the divine giver; having a prayer for every indulgence in food and drink; a benediction for every new experience of whatever nature, gladsome or sad—the Jew partook with genuine zest of the good cheer of life, without, however, lapsing into frivolity, gluttony, or intemperance. His religion, that taught him to remember his dignity as one made in the image of God, and to hold his body in esteem as the temple of God's spirit within, a dwelling of the Most Holy, "a host," as Hillel put it, "for the guest, the soul," kept the Jew equidistant from the pole of self-torturing pessimism, from the mortification of the flesh under the obsession of its sinfulness and foulness, and from the other pole of levity and sensuousness. Never intemperate in drink or food, he sought and found true joy in the consecration of his life and all of its powers and opportunities to the service of his God, a God who had caused the fruit of the vine to grow and the earth to give forth the bread, a God who created the light and sent the darkness, a God who, as a Talmudical legend—one of the many with Elijah for their subject—has it, reserves paradise "for them that cause their fellows to laugh" (Ta'an. 22*a*). The most beautiful saying of the rabbis about Asceticism is: "Man will have to give account in the future for every lawful enjoyment offered to him which he has ungratefully refused" (Rab in Yer. Ḳid., at the close); compare Tanḥ., end, "The wicked in his life is considered as one dead," etc.

BIBLIOGRAPHY: Lazarus, *Ethics of Judaism*, §§ 246–256.

VI

Atheism

ATHEISM: A term derived from the Greek, meaning literally the "disbelief in a God." As originally used in the writings of the people that coined it, it carried the implication of non-recognition of the God or the gods acknowledged as supreme, and therefore entitled to worship by the state. It was in this sense that Socrates was accused and convicted of Atheism. The same note is dominant in the oft-quoted dictum attributed to Polybius, that reverence for the gods is the foundation of all public order and security.

The Hebrew dictionary has no word of exactly similar import. The reasons for this are not difficult to establish. Atheism, in the restricted sense of the Greek usage, could not find expression among the Hebrews before they had come into contact and conflict with other nations. As long as their tribal consciousness was strong and supreme among them, recognition on the part of all members of the clan or tribe of the god to whom the family clan or tribe and people owed allegiance was spontaneous. Recent researches in this field have established beyond the possibility of doubt that this sense of family or tribal or national affinity is focal to all primitive religion. Sacrifice and all other features of private or public cult center in this all-regulating sentiment. The deity is entertained by the members of the family at the sacrificial meal. Even some institutions of the Israelitish cult, such as the Pesaḥ meal, reflect the mental mood of

Impossible in Ancient Israel.

this original conviction. Denial of the family or tribal or national deity would have amounted to relinquishment of one's family or people; and such abandonment is a thought of which man is incompetent before a long stretch of historical experience has changed his whole mental attitude.

In the development of the Jewish God-idea, as traced by modern Biblical criticism, the conflict between the Prophets and their antagonists pivots not so much around the controversy whether God be or be not, but around the recognition of YHWH as the only and legitimate God of Israel. Even they who opposed the Prophets were not atheists in the modern acceptation of the word. They may be so styled, if the implications of the term be restricted to the original Greek usage. According to prophetic preachment, Israel owed allegiance to YHWH alone. This is the emphasis of their oft-repeated statement that it was YHWH who led the people of Israel out of Egypt. The first statement of the Decalogue is not a protest against Atheism in the modern sense. It posits positively the prophetic thesis that no other God but YHWH brought about Israel's redemption from Egyptian bondage. The force of this prophetic contention is well illustrated by the counter or corresponding claim advanced in behalf of the deities nationalized by Jeroboam at Dan and Beth-el (I Kings xii. 28). With all the strenuousness of their insistence upon the sole supremacy and legitimacy of YHWH as Israel's God, the Prophets never went the length to call their opponents atheists. That the gods whom the followers of the false prophets worshiped were not gods is a conviction that appears only in later prophets, and then not in a very violent emphasis. Jeremiah resorts to mild sarcasm (Jer. ii. 27, 28). The second Isaiah is more pronounced in his ridicule heaped upon the worshipers of idols. Yet the quarrel is not because some or many deny God. Their censure is evoked by the fact that some or many worship gods that have no claim upon the recognition of Israel, the people of YHWH.

Again, Atheism always is the result of criticism and skepticism. Both in the individual and in the race it is, as it were, an afterthought. No people starts out with Atheism. The original religiousness of man is always spontaneously theistic in one form or another. And as long as the religious consciousness of man is in its prime vigor, there is no provocation for critical analysis of its contents. Periods of decline in religiousness produce skepticism, which, in turn, breeds Atheism. Up to the Exile the conditions for Atheism—in this sense—were lacking in Israel. Even the Exile, though fatal to the religious fervor of a great number—as is apparent by a study of the "'Ebed YHWH" hymns, portraying as they do the indignities and ridicule to which a pious minority were exposed at the hands of their compatriots—brought to bear upon the minds of the Jews influences much more potent in the opposite direction. Contact with the Babylonian-Assyrian, and shortly after with the Persian, civilization had a pronounced tendency to develop an abiding predisposition toward mysticism, which is always fatal to sober Atheism. In this connection it is well to remember that Jewish angelology and demonology took their rise in the Captivity; and certainly an age susceptible to suggestions of the order vocalized in the belief in angels and their counterparts is not very propitious for the cultivation of atheistic proclivities. The literature assigned to the Exile evidences the prevalence of the very opposite inclination. It is safe to hold that anterior to the Greek period there was but little cause among the Jews to pay attention to atheistic enunciations. This fact accounts for the absence of a term to denote both the professor and the system of Atheism.

Atheism the Result of Skepticism.

Psalm liii., preserved in a double version (in Ps. xiv.), mentions the speech of one who maintains that there is no God. The professor of this belief is styled "nabal," and in the context is contrasted with the "maskil" (verse 3); wherefore the word was understood to be "fool," or, as Ibn Ezra has it in his commentary, the contrary of "ḥakam" (wise). This meaning the Targum to Psalm xiv. also accepts, rendering it by "shaṭya." Other commentators hold that the psalm does not register a general proposition, but records the utterances of some definite person—Titus or Nebuchadnezzar. From the character of these men it may be inferred that the interpreters who refer the expression in the Psalm to them, took the word "nabal" in the secondary sense of "knave," implying that foolishness which always characterizes a corrupt or pervert mind. "Nabal" would thus be a synonym of "rasha'" or "zed."

The nearest approach to a phrase which might be considered the equivalent of our modern "atheist" is the rabbinical "kofer be'iḳḳar," one who denies a fundamental tenet of the Jewish religion; namely, the existence and then the unity of God. Of all the other designations applied in rabbinical writings to heretics, none other seems so directly to suggest or to stand for avowed and open negation of the Deity's existence and supremacy (B. B. 15*b*; Pesiḳ. p. 163). Atheism is included among the heresies charged against the "minim" (Shab. 116*b*; and Maimonides, Yad ha-Ḥazaḳah, Teshubah, iii., where he enumerates among the heretics "minim," "those that declare that there is no God and that the world has neither governor nor leader").

Talmudic Designations.

But as in the case of the Biblical "nabal," so in the descriptions of the atheist by the Rabbis it would appear that Atheism was much more a matter of perverse and immoral conduct than of formulated philosophical or metaphysical assertion and conviction. At least it is from the conduct of man that his Atheism is inferred. Observance of the Sabbath was regarded as evidence of belief in the Creator; while neglect to keep the day of rest holy gave point to the presumption of atheistic leanings. The passage in Sifra, Beḥuḳḳotai, iii. 2, shows that the observance or the rejection of the "laws and ordinances" was the decisive factor in the attribution of Atheism, according to rabbinical understanding. Adam is said to have been an atheist; for in hiding himself to escape, he gave proof of his belief that God was not omnipresent (Sanh. 38*b*).

How far the term "Epicurean," אפיקורוס (see Apiḳoros), served to denote an atheist, is not very clear. It is patent that by this name were designated men who denied the doctrine of resurrection and revelation. As both of these may be said to be involved in the (rabbinical) doctrine concerning the Godhead, the appellation "Epicurean" may in a loose way have been synonymous with the latter-day atheist. Connecting this Greek word with the Aramaic root "paḳar" (to free oneself), the rabbinical sources—even Maimonides—assumed as the characteristic trait of an Epicurean's conduct disregard of all that made for reverence and decency. "Scoffer" might, therefore, be suggested as the best rendering in English. As one that would scoff at the words of the learned and wise, of the God-fearing and pious (Ned. 23*a*; Sanh. 99*b*), the Epicurean naturally created the impression by his conduct that he shared the views of the "nabal" and was under suspicion that in his insolence he would go so far as to deny the existence of God and to stand in no awe of His providential guidance of life and the world. Hence the advice always to be ready to refute the arguments of the Epicurean (Abot ii. 14).

Strange to say, the Jews often had to defend themselves against the charge of being atheists, though, in the conception of the Prophets, Israel's history was the convincing proof of God's providence. Israel was chosen to be His witness. The prime solicitude of Moses (Ex. xxxii. 12, 13) lest the "Egyptians" should put a wrong construction on the events of Israel's career and become confirmed in their false conceptions of Israel's God, is also, as it were, the "leitmotif" of the theology of later Biblical writers. The appeal of the Seventy-ninth Psalm is for God to manifest Himself in His avenging splendor, lest, from the weakness of Israel, the "nations" might infer that He had abdicated in favor of their idols. Psalm cxv. 2 *seq.*—undoubtedly of the Maccabean period—expresses the same anxiety but on a higher and more spiritual plane. It reflects the arguments and conceits of even the enlightened among the Greeks. The invisible God of the Jews was beyond the range of the ancient world's intelligence. A visible God alone was entitled to recognition.

Jews Accused of Atheism.

Greek thought may not have gone so far as Pharaoh did—according to the Midrash (Ex. R. v.), reflecting certainly the anti-Jewish attitude of the Greco-Roman period—in refusing to recognize YHWH for the reason that his name was not included in the official list of deities, yet it did erect an altar to "the unknown God" (Acts xvii. 23), as, in fact, the hospitality of the Pantheon was elastic enough to admit every new deity. Still, two considerations dominated the judgment of the Greek world on the religion, or, according to them, irreligion, of the Jews. The Jews believed in an invisible God; therefore, according to the Greek mode of thinking, in no God. Secondly, the Jews refused to join them in their worship, though the Greeks were prepared to pay honor to the gods of other nations. These two complaints are at the bottom of the accusation of Atheism against the Jews which is very frequent and violent in the writings of Alexandrian detractors and Roman historians. The philosophers among the Greeks, indeed, furnished many an argument in defense of the excellence of Jewish monotheism; but the vast multitude was still addicted to the grosser notions. If the Jews were citizens of the towns where they resided, as they claimed to be, why did they not join in worshiping the communal gods? This was the burden of the popular prejudice against them; and Apion (Josephus, "Contra Ap." ii. § 6), Posidonius, and Apollonius Molo made themselves the willing mouthpieces of popular distrust. Here was proof that the Jews were really atheists. In the Roman empire they refused to pay religious honors to the statues of the emperors. This fact sufficed, in the eyes of Tacitus and Pliny, to accuse them of despising the gods and to describe them as atheists, as a people void of all virtue (Tacitus, "Historiæ," v. 5; see Schürer, "Gesch." 3d ed., iii. 417).

The same feeling that led the Greek and Roman enemies of the Jews to accuse them of irreligion is potent in the modern charge brought against them of unbelief. Atheism is indeed a relative term. The Mohammedan regards both the Christian and the Jew as infidels; and the Christian is not slow to return the compliment to the follower of the Prophet. Refusing to accept the construction of his history that Christian theology puts on it, and declining to subscribe to many of the Christological interpretations of his Bible, the Jew is under the suspicion of irreligion and Atheism. The "amixia," the stubborn defense of his historical identity, and his right to maintain his religious distinctness, which puzzled and angered the Greeks (compare Haman's argument in Esther iii. 8, the precipitate of the Maccabean era), is still a pretext for denying to the Jew genuine religious feeling, and a provocation to class him among the wanton deniers of God.

The attitude toward the Jews in the Koran illustrates the same fact. Mohammed, incensed at the refusal of the Jews to acclaim him as the expected final prophet, pours out over them the vials of his wrath and abuse. Though "the people of the book," they have falsified it. They claim to believe, and still are unbelievers. They disavow him, simply because he believes in God and they do not (Koran, suras ii. 70–73, 116; v. 48, 49, 64–69; ix. 30).

Attitude of Mohammed and Philo.

That there were atheists among the Jews stands to reason, and is made evident among other things by the tenor of the Book of Ecclesiastes, which, without the later addition of the saving concluding verses, is really an exposition of the skepticism that had impregnated the minds of the higher classes during the Greek fever preceding the Maccabean rebellion. In Alexandria, too, Jews must have been openly or tacitly inclined to accept the philosophy of negation. Philo takes occasion to discuss Atheism. He quotes the arguments advanced in its defense by those who maintain that nothing exists but the perceptible and visible universe, which had never come into being and which would never perish, but which, though unbegotten and incorruptible, was without pilot, guardian, or protector ("De Somnis," ii. 43). He does not state that they who advance these theories are Jews; but as he mentions others who embrace a pantheistic interpretation, and describes them as Chaldeans ("De Migratione Abrahami," p. 32), it is not improbable that "the others" may have been of his people. To Atheism he opposes the doctrine of Moses, "the beholder of the invisible nature, and seer of God" ("De Mutatione Nominum," § 2), according to which the Divine exists, and is neither the cosmos nor the soul of the cosmos, but is the supreme God.

The religious philosophy of the Middle Ages has no occasion to deal directly with formulated Atheism. Its preoccupation is largely apologetic, not so much against the attacks of formal and formidable Atheism as against certain theistic or semitheistic schools or other controverts: first Karaite, then Arabic, and, still later, Christian theologians. But in their discussions of the fundamentals of faith the problem of theism versus Atheism in one way or another is involved. The contentions of the Dahri, Mohammedan atheists, believing in the eternity of matter, and the duration of the world from eternity, and denying resurrection and final judgment, as well as the theories of the Motazilites, the Mohammedan freethinkers, rejecting all eternal attributes of God, furnish the text for a large portion of the speculation of the Jewish philosophers. The one objective point of all medieval Jewish philosophy is the clarification of the concept of the Godhead by the removal of every form of anthropomorphism and anthropopathism, and to vindicate to human reason concordance with the true intents of the revealed word of God. The question which Mohammedan Atheism raised regarding the eternity of matter is in the very center of polemic debate. But in the later speculation, the system of Crescas, for instance the eternity of matter, is admitted without reservation.

This throws light at once on the problem whether Spinoza should be classed among the *atheoi*. From the Jewish point of view this must be denied. Under close analysis, Spinoza does not go beyond the positions maintained on some points by Maimonides, on more by Crescas. He carries to its furthest consequences the Jewish solicitude to divest the idea of the Godhead of anthropomorphic associations (on this point see Joel, "Zur Genesis der Lehre Spinoza's," Breslau, 1871).

In modern Judaism, as is evinced by printed sermons and other publications, Atheism of every kind has found voice and adherents. The influence of the natural sciences, and the unwarranted conclusions now recognized as such by none more readily than by the thinkers devoted to the exploration of nature's domain, have also left their mark on Jewry. Both the idle Atheism of conceit and the more serious Atheism of reaction against the dogmatism of anterior days have had exponents in the circles grouped around the synagogues. As elsewhere, evolution was invoked to dethrone God, and therefore, departing from the methods of scholasticism, the arguments based on evolution were not ignored by the defenders of theism in the pulpit. In the discussion two lines were more especially followed. Atheism was tested as to its rationality, and was found of all irrational theories of the world and life the most irrational.

Mind presupposes mind. The gap between thought and matter has not been bridged by natural selection or by evolution. Du Bois-Reymond's agnosticism left the domain of faith to religious cultivation. Whatever difficulties from a materialistic point of view the doctrine of God as the Creator and guide of world and of man, as the Author of life, and as the Ultimate Reality underlying the All may present and must present—for to know God as He is man would have to be God—the divine element in man, his conscience and self-consciousness, his moral power and experiences, are inexplicable and unreadable riddles to the materialist. Materialism has no key for their solution. History, especially the history of the Jews, witnesses to a will which is not ours, but may be made ours; to the potency of purposes which are not ours, but may be followed by us; to laws in harmony with which alone man can attain unto happiness and preserve his dignity. To these facts and factors the Jewish theist has pointed in defense of his theistic interpretation of life and its phenomena, while always ready to modify the symbolism into which he would cast the supreme thought. The old demonstrations of God's existence indeed, after Kant, can not be said to be cogent. But the moral proof of theism in refutation of Atheism has taken on new strength in the very searching by Kant's master criticism. The theism of Israel's religion has been verified by the facts and forces of Israel's history, as the "witness to YHWH."

BIBLIOGRAPHY: S. Hirsch, *Die Humanität als Religion*, lecture ii, Trier 1858; I. M. Wise, *The Cosmic God*, Cincinnati, 1876.

VII

Body In Jewish Theology

BODY IN JEWISH THEOLOGY: In Hebrew the idea of "body" is expressed by the term "basar" (Assyrian, "bishru"), which, commonly translated "flesh," originally denoted blood-relation, clan (see Gen. ii. 23, 24), the physical appearance being regarded as the evidence of consanguinity, and only secondarily the "body," and hence the general state or condition of man, or man as a creature of flesh, and finally mankind, "all flesh" (Isa. lxvi. 23). A less frequently employed term is "gewiyāh," which with rare exceptions is used to designate not the living body, but the corpse. The Greek translators employ *σάρξ*, or, rarely, *σῶμα*, the former, in accordance with Greek usage, generally in the plural. In later Hebrew the words "geshem," "gushma," and "guph" were used, or the combination "basar wa dam" (*σάρξ καὶ αἷμα*). This latter phrase implies the distinction between God and man, as, for instance, in contexts contrasting "the Holy One, blessed be He!" with "the king of flesh and blood," which contrast is rooted neither in the thought of man's sinfulness over and against the perfection of the Creator nor in the opposition of the material to the spiritual—the antithesis posited by Philo between the *ψυχή* or the *νοῦς* on the one hand, and the *σῶμα*, the "dead nature of ours," on the other—but in the conception of man as a weak, dependent, and mortal creature.

According to Gen. ii. 7 the body is formed of dust and is, therefore, frail and mortal. It will return to dust, whence it was taken (*ib.* iii. 19). It lives because the spirit of life was breathed into it (*ib.* ii. 7; Ezek. xxxvii. 8).

The defiling character of the dead or the diseased body, which is so prominently referred to in the purity laws in the Levitical code, has, by the modern critical school, been recognized as belonging to a range of ideas universally found in all religions at a certain stage of their development, and as being an adaptation of observances pertaining to an anterior phase of religious thought and practise. Speculations on the nature of sin, and its seat in the body of man, do not lie within the plane of the unreflected religious consciousness which is characteristic of Old Testament literature and life.

The following may be accepted as representing the rabbinical views on the nature, the function, and the destiny of the body.

Rabbinic Conception.

In accordance with the Book of Genesis, man is considered to be created of two originally uncombined elements, soul and body; the former coming from the higher world, and the latter taken from the lower (Gen. R. viii. 14; Ḥag. 16a). The destiny of the latter is to serve the former, and it is organized to fulfil the Torah. The dust of which the body of man (Adam) was formed was composed of contributions from all the regions of the earth (Sanh. 38a; Rashi to Gen. ii. 7).

A shapeless body ("golem") came from the hand of the Creator (Gen. R. xiv.), and filled the whole earth, or, according to another version, reached from earth to the sky. Bisexed, this creature had also two faces until, through the later differentiation according to sex, man found in woman his counterpart. This (ultimate) body of man retains (in the nails) traces of an original coat of light (Rashi on Gen. ii. 21), but as now constructed it consists of 248 members (bones) and 365 nerves (compare Targum Yer. to Gen. i. 27), which numbers are assumed to correspond to the number of the mandatory and prohibitive commandments of the Law (see ANATOMY).

The psychology of the times connecting certain functions of the soul with certain organs of the body is recognized in the rabbinical writings; while symbolism in reference to the various purposes of the organs and the processes of physical life also holds a place in the anatomical science of the Talmudical teachers. As to the relation which the body holds to the soul, and the questions when the soul enters the body, whether the soul is preexistent, and whether for every newly created body there is also a newly created soul, opinions differ; though the majority are in favor of the preexistence of the soul.

The body is *not* regarded as impure. The adjective "ṭamé" (impure), used of the body in contrast to the pure soul (Mek., Beshallaḥ, Shirah, 2; compare Sanh. 91a, b), refers rather to the physical process through which the body is produced from a "malodorous" drop (Abot iii. 1). To strain the meaning of the word "saruḥah," used to convey this idea, as does Weber ("Alt-Synagogale Theologie," p. 229), is inadmissible. The body is the seat of the "yeẓer hara'" (evil inclination). This latter is natural and necessary; it is not in itself a manifestation of congenital sinful depravity (Gen. R. ix.).

Body and Soul.

Body and soul are alike responsible for deeds committed (Tan., Wayiḳra, 6) (see YEẒER HARA'). Aaron ben Elijah, the Karaite ("Eẓ Ḥayyim," cxii.), bases upon this responsibility of the body an argument in favor of resurrection (compare the parable of the blind and the lame in Rabbi Judah ha-Nasi's argument before the emperor Antoninus, Sanh. 91b).

To provide food and drink and dress in proper quantity and becoming style is a religious duty (Maimonides, "Yad," De'ot, v.). Mutilations of the body are prohibited (Lev. xix. 27, 28; Deut. xxiii. 3).

Even after death the body was regarded as demanding respectful treatment. Once the "temple" (tabernacle) of the soul and its servant, the cerement of dust was to be guarded against sacrilegious dissection (Ḥul. 11b). Hence the Levitical laws rendering impure the persons touching the dead body, according to the explanation of R. Johanan ben Zakkai (Yad. iv. 6; Num. R. xix.; see also Einhorn, "Ner Tamid," pp. 83 *et seq.*, Philadelphia, 1866).

The body decays; but it will rise again at the time of the resurrection. The bodies of the risen are reproductions of those which they tenanted while living: cripples and the deformed will rise with the old deformities (Gen. R. xiv., xcv.) (see LUZ and RESURRECTION). Early Talmudic conceits ascribe feeling to the body even after death (Shab. 152b; see ḤIBBUṬ HA-ḲEBER; Wolff, "Muhamed. Eschatologie," p. 62, Leipsic, 1872).

Post-Talmudic Judaism virtually accepts the foregoing views, as does, for instance, Saadia, "Emunot we-De'ot," vi., where he controverts the idea that the soul is abused by being made to reside in the body. The latter is the soul's necessary agent, and this body is the one best suited for the ends of man. The body is not impure. The Law declares certain secretions of the body to be unclean, but only after they have left, not while they are in, the body (Baḥya ben Joseph, "Ḥobot ha-Lebabot"). The human body evidences the Creator's wisdom (see BAḤYA BEN JOSEPH).

Later Views.

Like a red thread through the speculations of the medieval Jewish and Arabic thinkers runs the doctrine of the four elements. Man being the microcosm, and the world the macrocosm, the effort is made to establish a correspondence between the body of the former and that of the latter. The four elements are discovered in the four humors of man's body. Israeli's work on the elements, based upon the "Sefer Yeẓirah," influenced all subsequent thinkers in this direction. In Donolo and in Ibn Gabirol there is the theory that the blood in man corresponds to the air; the white humor, to the water; the black humor, to the earth; and the red bile, to the fire. The five senses of man are also very prominent in the symbolic and allegorical interpretation of the Biblical texts. Ethics and poetry as well borrowed instruction and inspiration from the five senses (Kaufmann, "Die Sinne," Leipsic, 1884) (see ADAM). The body of man was thus studied from many points of view, but was always regarded as a marvelous construction witnessing to the wisdom of the Creator, whose praise was sung in benediction (Ber. 60a). The latter, after dwelling on the wonderful adaptability of the bodily organs to their functions, names God as "the Healer of all flesh and the wonderful Artificer."

It may be noticed that Reform Judaism has relinquished the belief in the resurrection of the body. The catechisms and prayer-books of the modern synagogues, however, teach that "the body is intended by the Creator to be the servant of the immortal soul, and as such is not congenitally depraved." "This very body—woven of dust—Thou hast dignified to be a dwelling-place of Thine, a minister unto Thy spirit. Even it issued pure from Thine hand. Thou hast implanted in it the capacity for sin, but not sin itself" (David Einhorn's "Prayer-Book," 2d Eng. ed., Chicago, 1896, part ii. 207).

VIII

Commandment

COMMANDMENT: The rendering in the English Bible versions of the Hebrew מצוה, which, in its technical sense, is used in the Bible of a commandment given either by God or by man (I Kings ii. 43). According to the critical schools, it is a word of comparatively late coinage, as it does not occur in documents earlier than D and JE. In the singular it sometimes denotes the "code of law" (II Chron. viii. 13; Ezra x. 3; Ps. xix. 9), or even "Deuteronomy" alone (Deut. vi. 25, viii. 1); and as such is parallel to "Torah" (Ex. xxiv. 12). In the plural it designates specific commands contained in the code, which are as a rule expressed in sentences beginning with "Ye shall" or "Ye shall not," and is sometimes combined with "ḥuḳḳim," "ḥuḳḳot" (statutes), "mishpaṭim" (ordinances), and even "'edut" (testimonies). E. G. H.

In rabbinic terminology "miẓwah" is the general term for a divinely instituted rule of conduct. As such, the divine commandments are divided into (1) mandatory laws known as מצות עשה, and (2) those of a prohibitory character, the מצות לא תעשה. This terminology rests on the theological construction that God's will is the source of and authority for every moral and religious duty.

In due logical development of this theology, the Rabbis came to assume that the Law comprised 613 commandments (see COMMANDMENTS, THE 613), of which 611 are said to have been given through Moses (Deut. xxxiii. 4, תורה being numerically equal to 611); the first two commandments of the Decalogue were given by the mouth of God Himself (R. Joshua b. Levi, in Pes. R. xxii.; compare Mak. 24b–25a; Hor. 8a; Pirḳe R. El. xli.). According to

R. Ismael only the principal commandments were given on Mount Sinai, the special commandments having been given in the Tent of Meeting. According to R. Akiba they were all given on Mount Sinai, repeated in the Tent of Meeting, and declared a third time by Moses before his death (Soṭah 37b; compare Mek., Mishpaṭim, xx. to Ex. xxiii. 19, and Sifre, Debarim, 104). All divine commandments, however, were given on Mount Sinai, and no prophet could add any new one (Sifra to Lev. xxvii. 34; Yoma 80a). Many of these laws concern only special classes of people, such as kings or priesthood, Levites or Nazarites, or are conditioned by local or temporary circumstances of the Jewish nation, as, for instance, the agricultural, sacrificial, and Levitical laws.

The Biblical commandments are called in the Talmud "miẓwot de oraita"; commandments of the Law in contradistinction to the rabbinical commandments, "miẓwot de rabbanan." Among the latter are: (1) the benediction, or thanksgiving for each enjoyment; (2) ablution of the hands before eating; (3) lighting of the Sabbath lamp; (4) the 'Erub, on preparation for Sabbath transfer; (5) the Hallel liturgy on holy days; (6) the Ḥanukkah lights; and (7) the reading of the Esther scroll on Purim. These seven rabbinical commandments are treated like Biblical commandments in so far as, previous to the fulfilment of each, this Benediction is recited: "Blessed be the Lord who has commanded us . . . ," the divine command being implied in the general law (Deut. xvii. 11, xxxii. 7; Shab. 23a). Many of the Biblical laws are derived from the Law only by rabbinical interpretation, as, the reading of the Shema' (Deut. vi. 4–7), the binding of the tefillin and the fixing of the mezuzah (*ib.* 8–9), and the saying of grace after meals (*ib.* viii. 10). "While reciting the Shema' every morning the Israelite takes upon himself the yoke of the kingdom of heaven; while reciting the chapter 'We-hayah im shamoa'' [Deut. xi. 13–22] he takes upon himself the yoke of the divine commandments" (Ber. ii. 1). "In fulfilling a divine commandment one must do it with the intention of thus fulfilling God's will" (Ber. 13a, b; Naz. 23a, b). A hundred miẓwot ought to be fulfilled by the Israelite each day (see Benediction), and seven ought to surround him constantly like guardian spirits (R. Meïr, in Yer. Ber., end; Tosef., Ber., end). "Also, the commonest Israelite is as full of merit by fulfilment of divine commandments as the pomegranate is of seed" (Cant. R. iv. 3). The fulfilment of a divine commandment is a merit ("miẓwah"); the neglect, a transgression ("'aberah"). These are weighed against each other in the balance on the day of judgment to decide whether a man belongs to the righteous or to the wicked to be accordingly rewarded or punished ('Ab. Zarah 2a, 3a; Ḳid. 39b).

The sons of Noah were also considered to be under the obligation to obey the will of God as revealed in direct specific orders or miẓwot promulgated for them. These are variously enumerated as five, six, and ten. In Tos. 'Ab. Zarah viii. 4 seven Noachian commandments are enumerated: (1) to establish courts of justice, (2) to abstain from idolatry, (3) from blasphemy, (4) from incest, (5) from murder, (6) from robbery, (7) from eating flesh cut from living animals. In Gen. R. xvi.–xxiv. (compare *ib.* xxiv.; Lev. R. xiii.), only six are mentioned as having been given to the first man. In Sanh. 56a, 57a, seven Noachian commandments are spoken of, and derived partly as Adamitic, from Gen. ii. 16, and partly from Gen. ix. 4 *et seq.* To these some tannaim add three: the prohibition of blood from living animals, of castration, and of witchcraft. In Ḥal. 92a thirty commandments are mentioned as having been accepted, but not observed, by the sons of Noah (compare Gen. R. xcviii.; Midr. Teh. Ps. ii. 5; Yer. 'Ab. Zarah ii. 40c). In the Book of Jubilees (vii. 21) only the three capital sins are specified (see NOACHIAN LAWS).

"Miẓwah," in the parlance of the Rabbis, came to express any act of human kindness, such as the burial of the body of an unknown person ("met miẓwah"; compare Bernays, "Gesammelte Schriften," 1885, i. 278 *et seq.*, on the Buzygian laws mentioned by Philo in connection with these "commandments" of humanity; Sifre, Naso, 26; Naz. 47b). A miẓwah which can be fulfilled only by the transgression of another law is considered unlawful ("miẓwah ha-bo'ah ba'aberah, 'aberah"; Suk. 30a; Yer. Shab. xiii. 14a). The proselyte on being initiated into Judaism must be familiarized with commandments both of great and of small import (Yeb. 47b). This rule seems to be directed against the older practise followed by the Christian Church (see DIDACHE). The fulfilment of a commandment is a protection against evil powers (Ber. 31a; Pes. 8a; Soṭah 21a; Ḳid. i. 10), and becomes a guardian angel pleading for reward in the future life (Soṭah 3b).

According to the teachings of Judaism, all moral laws are virtually and in their ultimate analysis divine commandments. Obedience to the Divine Will is the first requisite of the moral life (see DUTY). This is the meaning of the Biblical account of Adam's offense. The first commandment was intended to test his obedience and thus to awaken his moral consciousness (see SIN; ORIGINAL SIN, DOGMA OF). In the Pentateuch the Ten Commandments are not designated as "Miẓwot," but are called the "Ten Words" (עשרת הדברים). In Jewish literature they are spoken of as the עשרת הדברות (see DECALOGUE).

E. G. H. K.—E. G. H.

COMMANDMENTS, THE 613: That the law of Moses contains 613 commandments is stated by R. Simlai, a Palestinian haggadist, who says (Mak. 23b): "Six hundred and thirteen commandments were revealed to Moses; 365 being prohibitions equal in number to the days of the year, and 248 being mandates corresponding in number to the bones of the human body." The number 613 is found as early as tannaitic times—*e.g.*, in a saying of Simon ben Eleazar (Mek., Yitro, Baḥodesh, 5) and one of Simon ben Azzai (Sifre, Deut. § 76, Friedman's ed., p. 90b)—and is apparently based upon ancient tradition (see Tan., Ki Teẓe, ed. Buber, 2; Ex. R. xxxii.; Num. R. xiii., xviii.; Yeb. 47b; Shab. 87a; Ned. 25a; Shebu. 29a; comp. Bacher, "Ag. Tan." i. 413, ii. 436). The authenticity of the statements attributed to R. Simlai, however, has been questioned by authorities such as Naḥmanides and Abraham ibn Ezra (see M. Bloch, in "Rev. Et. Juives," i. 197, 210; v. 27 *et seq.*; Weiss, "Dor," p. 74, note 50). The first to undertake the task of identifying the commandments was Simeon Kahira, in his "Halakot Gedolot." He begins with the prohibitions, which he classes in the order of the gravity of the punishments incurred by their transgression, while in regard to the mandates he follows the order of the parashiyyot, beginning with the Decalogue.

Kahira was followed by Saadia, Gabirol, and many others, who enumerated the 613 commandments in liturgical poems (see AZHAROT). In order to make up the number 613, Kahira and the poets just mentioned were compelled to incorporate many rabbinical laws. This method was criticized by Maimonides, who published a work entitled "Sefer ha-Miẓwot," laying down fourteen guiding principles for the identification of the commandments, which he enumerates accordingly. Some of these principles were attacked by Naḥmanides and others, who showed that Maimonides himself had not always been consistent. New identifications were therefore proposed by Moses ben Jacob of Coucy, author of the "Sefer Miẓwot ha-Gadol" (SeMaG), and Isaac ben Joseph of Corbeil, author of the "Sefer Miẓwot ha-Ḳaton" (SeMaḲ). The following is a list of the 613 commandments of Maimonides:

MANDATORY COMMANDMENTS.

1. To know that the Lord God exists. Ex. xx. 2.
2. To acknowledge His unity. Deut. vi. 4.
3-4. To love and fear Him. Deut. vi. 5, 13.
5. To pray to Him. Ex. xxiii. 25.
6. To cleave to Him. Deut. x. 20.
7. To swear by His name. Deut. vi. 13, x. 20.
8. To resemble Him in His ways. Deut. xxviii. 9.
9. To sanctify His name. Lev. xxii. 32.
10. To read the Shema' each morning and evening. Deut. vi. 7.
11. To learn and to teach others the Law. Deut. vi. 7.
12-13. To bind tefillin on the forehead and arm. Deut. vi. 8.
14. To make ẓiẓit. Num. xv. 38.
15. To fix a MEZUZAH. Deut. vi. 9.
16. To assemble the people to hear the Law every seventh year. Deut. xxxi. 12.
17. To write a copy of the Law for oneself. Deut. xxxi. 19.
18. That the king write a special copy of the Law for himself. Deut. xvii. 18.
19. To bless God after eating. Deut. viii. 10.
20. To build the Temple. Ex. xxv. 8.
21. To reverence the sanctuary. Lev. xix. 30.
22. To watch the sanctuary perpetually. Num. xviii. 2.
23. That Levites shall serve in the sanctuary. Num. xviii. 23.
24. That at services the priests wash their hands and feet. Ex. xxx. 19.
25. That the priests kindle the lights in the sanctuary. Ex. xxx. 19.

26. That the priests bless Israel. Num. vi. 23.

27. To set showbread and incense before the Lord on Sabbath. Ex. xxv. 30.

28. To burn incense twice each day. Ex. xxx. 7.

29. To keep fire continually upon the altar. Lev. vi. 13.

30. To remove the ashes daily from the altar. Lev. vi. 10.

31. To put the impure out of the holy place. Num. v. 2.

32. That the Aaronites have the place of honor. Lev. xxi. 8.

33. To clothe the Aaronites with priestly garments. Ex. xxviii. 2.

34. That the Kehathites carry the Ark upon their shoulders. Num. vii. 9.

35. To anoint high priests and kings with oil. Ex. xxx. 31.

36. That the priests officiate by turns. Deut. xviii. 6, 8.

37. That the priests pay due honors to the dead. Lev. xxi. 3.

38. That the high priest take a virgin to wife. Lev. xxi. 13.

39. To sacrifice twice a day. Num. xxviii. 3.

40. That the chief priest offer an oblation daily. Lev. vi. 20.

41–3. To offer an additional oblation every Sabbath, on the first of every month, and on the Feast of Passover. Num. xxviii. 9, xxviii. 11; Lev. xxiii. 36.

44. To offer a sheaf of the first barley on the second day of Passover. Lev. xxiii. 10.

45. To add an oblation on the day of the Feast of Shebu'ot. Num. xxviii. 26.

46. To offer two loaves of bread on Shebu'ot. Lev. xxiii. 17.

47. To add an offering on the first of Tishri. Num. xxix. 1.

48. To add an offering on the Day of Atonement. Num. xxix. 7.

49. To observe the service on the Day of Atonement. Lev. xvi. 3.

50. To add an offering on the Feast of Sukkot. Num. xxix. 13.

51. To offer a special sacrifice on the eighth day of Sukkot. Num. xxix. 35.

52. To keep the festival at the three seasons of the year. Ex. xxiii. 14.

53. That every male appear at the feast. Deut. xvi. 16.

54. To rejoice at the feasts. Deut. xvi. 14.

55–6. To slay the paschal lamb and eat the flesh roasted, on the fifteenth night of Nisan. Ex. xii. 6, xii. 8.

57–8. To observe the second Passover and eat the paschal lamb with maẓẓah and maror. Num. ix. 11, 13; ix. 11.

59. To blow the trumpets over the sacrifices, and in time of tribulation. Num. x. 10.

60. That cattle, when sacrificed, be eight days old or more. Lev. xxii. 27.

61. That all cattle sacrificed be perfect. Lev. xxii. 21.

62. That all offerings be salted. Lev. ii. 13.

63. To bring a burnt offering. Lev. i. 3.

64–7. To bring a sacrifice for sin, for trespass, a peace-offering, and a meat-offering. Lev. ii. 1, vi. 25, vii. 1, 11.

68. That the Sanhedrin bring a sin-offering if they have erred in doctrine. Lev. iv. 13.

69. That one who has by error transgressed a KARET prohibition bring a sin-offering. Lev. iv. 27, v. 1.

70. That one in doubt whether he has transgressed a prohibition bring a sin-offering. Lev. v. 17, 18.

71. That a trespass-offering be brought for having sworn falsely and the like. Lev. v. 15, 21; xix. 20.

72. To offer a sacrifice according to one's means. Lev. v. 7, 11.

73. That confession of sins be made before the Lord. Num. v. 7.

74–5. That a man or woman having an issue offer a sacrifice. Lev. xv. 13, 28.

76. That a leper after being cleansed bring an offering. Lev. xiv. 10.

77. That a woman offer a sacrifice after childbirth. Lev. xii. 6.

78. To tithe the cattle. Lev. xxvii. 32.

79. To sacrifice the first-born of clean cattle. Deut. xv. 19.

80. To redeem the first-born of man. Num. xviii. 15.

81–2. To redeem the firstling of an ass, and to break its neck if the animal be not redeemed. Ex. xiii. 13.

83. To bring all offerings to Jerusalem. Deut. xii. 5, 6.

84. To offer all sacrifices in the Temple. Deut. xii. 14.

85. To bring to the Temple also the offerings from beyond the land of Israel. Deut. xii. 26.

86. To redeem holy animals that have blemishes. Deut. xii. 15.

87. That a beast exchanged for an offering is holy. Lev. xxvii. 10.

88. That the remainder of the meat-offerings be eaten. Lev. vi. 16.

89. That the flesh of sin- and trespass-offerings be eaten. Ex. xxix. 33.

90–1. To burn consecrated flesh that has become unclean; also the remainder of the consecrated flesh not eaten. Lev. vii. 17, 19.

92–3. That the Nazarite suffer his hair to grow during his separation, and shave it at the close of his Nazariteship. Num. vi. 5, 9.

94. That a man keep his vow. Deut. xxiii. 23.

95. That the judge act according to the Law in annulling vows. Num. xxx. 3.

96. That all who touch a carcass are unclean. Lev. xi. 34.

97. That eight species of animals contaminate. Lev. xi. 39.

98. That food is contaminated by contact with unclean things. Lev. xi. 34.

99. That a menstruous woman contaminates. Lev. xv. 19.

100. That a lying-in woman is unclean. Lev. xii. 2.

101. That a leper is unclean and contaminates others. Lev. xiii. 3.

102–3. That a leprous garment and a leprous house contaminate. Lev. xiii. 47, xiv. 35.

104–6. That a man or woman having a running issue contaminates, as does the seed of copulation. Lev. xv. 2, 16, 28.

107. That a corpse contaminates. Num. xix. 14.

108. That the water of separation contaminates the clean, cleansing only the unclean from the pollution of the dead. Num. xix. 26.

109. To cleanse from uncleanness by washing in running water. Lev. xv. 16.

110–12. That leprosy be cleansed with cedar-wood, etc.; that the leper shave all his hair, rend his raiment, and bare his head. Lev. xiii. 45; xiv. 2, 9.

113. To burn a red heifer and preserve its ashes. Num. xix. 9.

114. To pay the equivalent of a "singular" vow. Lev. xxvii. 2.

115–7. That one who vows an unclean beast, or his house, or his field, shall pay the appointed sum, or as the priest shall direct. Lev. xxvii. 11, 14, 16.

118. That he shall make restitution who trespasses through ignorance in things holy. Lev. v. 16.

119. That plantations in their fourth year shall be holy. Lev. xix. 24.

120–4. To leave to the poor the corners of the field unreaped, the gleanings of the harvest, the forgotten sheaf, the gleanings in the vineyard, and the residue of the grapes. Lev. xix. 9, 10; Deut. xxiv. 19.

125. To bring the first-fruits into the sanctuary. Ex. xxiii. 19.

126. To give the great heave-offering to the priest. Deut. xviii. 4.

127. To separate the tithe of corn for the Levites. Num. xviii. 24; Lev. xxvii. 30.

128. To separate a second tithe and eat it in Jerusalem. Deut. xiv. 22.

129. That the Levites shall give a tithe of the tithe to the priest. Num. xviii. 26.

130. To separate the tithe for the poor in the third and sixth years instead of in the second. Deut. xiv. 28.

131–2. To recite the chapter on the tithe and read it over the first-fruit. Deut. xxvi. 5, 13.

133. To separate for the priest a cake of the first of the dough. Num. xv. 20.

134–5. To let the field rest fallow every seventh year, and to cease from tilling the ground. Ex. xxiii. 11, xxxiv. 21.

136–8. To hallow the year of jubilee by resting, to sound the trumpet in the year of jubilee, and to grant a redemption for the land in that year. Lev. xxv. 9, 10, 24.

139. To allow a house sold in a walled city to be redeemed within the year. Lev. xxv. 29.

140. To number the years of jubilee yearly and septennially. Lev. xxv. 8.

141. To release all debts in the seventh year. Deut. xv. 2.

142. To exact the debt of a foreigner. Deut. xv. 3.

143. To give to the priest his share of the cattle sacrifices. Deut. xviii. 3.

144. To give the first of the fleece to the priest. Deut. xviii. 4.

145. To discriminate between what belongs to the Lord and what to the priest. Lev. xxvii. 21, 28.

146. To perform the right mode of slaughtering beasts. Deut. xii. 23.

147. To cover the blood of wild beast and bird. Lev. xvii. 13.

148. To set free the parent bird when taking a nest. Deut. xxii. 7.

149–52. To search diligently for the marks in clean beasts, fowl, locusts, and fish. Lev. xi. 2; Deut. xiv. 11; Lev. xi. 9.

153. That the Sanhedrin sanctify the new moon and reckon the years and months. Ex. xii. 2.

154–5. To rest on and hallow the Sabbath. Ex. xx. 8 and xxiii. 12.

156. To remove the leaven. Ex. xii. 15.

157–8. To relate the story of the Exodus and to eat unleavened bread on Passover night. Ex. xii. 18, xiii. 8.

159–60. To rest on the first and seventh days of Passover. Ex. xii. 16.

161. To reckon forty-nine days from the time of the cutting of the first sheaf. Lev. xxiii. 15.

162–3. To rest on Shebu'ot and on the first day of Tishri. Lev. xxiii. 24.

164–5. To fast and rest on the Day of Atonement. Lev. xvi. 29, xxiii. 32.

166–7. To rest on the first and eighth days of Sukkot. Lev. xxiii. 35, 36.

168. To dwell in booths seven days. Lev. xxiii. 42.

169. To take the four kinds of branches of trees. Lev. xxiii. 40.

170. To hear the sound of the trumpet on the first of Tishri. Num. xxix. 1.

171. To give half a shekel each year as ransom. Ex. xxx. 13.

172. To obey the prophet of each generation if he neither adds nor takes away from the statutes. Deut. xviii. 15.

173. To appoint a king. Deut. xviii. 15.

174. To obey the authority of the Sanhedrin. Deut. xvii. 11.

175. To yield to the majority in case of division. Ex. xxiii. 2.

176. To appoint judges in every town. Deut. xvi. 18.

177. To administer judgment impartially. Lev. xix. 15.

178. That whoever possesses evidence shall testify in court. Lev. v. 1.

179. To examine witnesses diligently. Deut. xiii. 14.

180. To do unto false witnesses as they themselves designed to do unto others. Deut. xix. 19.

181. To decapitate the heifer as commanded. Deut. xxi. 4.

182. To establish six cities of refuge. Deut. xix. 3.

183. To give cities to the Levites for habitations. Num. xxxv. 2.

184. To make battlements on the housetops. Deut. xxii. 8.

185–6. To destroy idolaters and to burn their city. Deut. xii. 2, xiii. 16.

187. To destroy the seven Canaanite nations. Deut. xx. 17.

188–9. To blot out the remembrance of Amalek. Deut. xxv. 17, 19.

190. To observe a certain procedure in voluntary battle. Deut. xx. 10.

191. To anoint the priest for war. Deut. xx. 2.

192–3. To keep the camp pure and in a sanitary condition. Deut. xxiii. 12, 13.

194. To restore plunder. Lev. vi. 4.

195. To give alms. Deut. xv. 8, 11.

196. To give liberal gifts to a freed Hebrew servant. Deut. xv. 14.

197. To lend to the poor. Deut. xv. 8.

198. To lend on usury to idolaters. Deut. xxiii. 21.

199. To restore a pledge to its owner. Deut. xxiv. 13.

200–1. To pay a hireling his hire when due, and to permit him to eat during work. Deut. xxiv. 15, 24, 25.

202–3. To help a neighbor's beast. Ex. xxiii. 5; and Deut. xxii. 4.

204. To restore lost property. Deut. xx. 1.

205. To rebuke the sinner. Lev. xix. 17.

206. To love the children of the covenant. Lev. xix. 18.

207. To love the stranger. Deut. x. 19.

208. To have just balances and weights. Lev. xix. 36.

209. To honor the wise. Lev. xix. 32.

210. To honor parents. Ex. xx. 12.

211. To fear parents. Lev. xix. 3.

212. To perpetuate the human species by marriage. Gen. i. 28.

213. To lead a pure married life. Deut. xxiv. 5.

214. That the bridegroom rejoice for a year with his wife. Deut. xxiv. 1.

215. To circumcise the males. Gen. xvii. 10; Lev. xii. 3.

216–7. To marry the wife of a deceased brother, and give ḤALIZAH in case of declining to do so. Deut. xxv. 5, 9.

218–9. That the violator of a virgin shall marry her, and he may not put her away all his days. Deut. xxii. 29.

220. That the seducer pay a penalty. Ex. xxii. 16.

221. That beautiful female captives must not be sold, etc. Deut. xxi. 11.

222. To divorce by a written contract. Deut. xxiv. 1.

223. That the suspected adulteress be subjected to trial of jealousy. Num. v. 30.

224. To beat the wicked. Deut. xxv. 2.

225. To exile the homicide through ignorance. Num. xxxv. 25.

226-30. That executions be effected by means of the sword, strangling, fire, stoning, and hanging. Ex. xxi. 20; Lev. xx. 14; Deut. xxi. 22, xxii. 24.

231. To bury on the same day one put to death. Deut. xxi. 23.

232. To deal with a Hebrew servant according to the Law. Ex. xxi. 2.

233-4. To redeem a betrothed Hebrew maid servant. Ex. xxi. 8.

235. To make the non-Hebrew slave serve for ever. Lev. xxv. 46.

236. That he who wounds another pay a fine. Ex. xxi. 18.

237-8. To judge of injuries to a beast by a pitfall. Ex. xxi. 33.

239. To punish the thief with death or to compel him to make restitution. Ex. xxi. 16, xxii. 1.

240-2. To give judgment in cases of trespass by cattle, of injuries by fire, or of robbery of money or goods left in charge of an unpaid keeper. Ex. xxii. 5-7.

243-4. To judge as to the injuries caused by the hireling or by the borrower. Ex. xxii. 10, 14.

245-6. To judge in disputes between buyer and seller or between plaintiff and defendant. Lev. xxv. 14; Ex. xxii. 9.

247. To rescue the persecuted, even at the cost of the life of the oppressor. Deut. xxv. 12.

248. To judge in disputes concerning inheritances. Num. xxvii. 8.

Prohibitive Commandments.

1. Belief in the existence of any but the one God. Ex. xx. 3.

2-4. The making of images. Ex. xx. 3, 4; xxxiv. 17.

5-6. The worship of stars and planets. Ex. xx 5.

7. The sacrifice of children to Moloch. Lev. xviii. 21.

8-9. Necromancy and familiar spirits. Lev. xix. 31.

10. Showing regard for the service of the stars and planets. Lev. xix. 4.

11. The erection of pillars. Lev. xxvi. 1.

12. The erection of pillars of stone. Lev. xxvi. 1.

13. Planting of trees in the sanctuary. Deut. xvi. 21.

14-16. Swearing by idols, or leading any Israelite toward idolatry. Ex. xxiii. 13; Deut. xiii. 11.

17-19. To show mercy to the seducer. Deut. xiii. 8.

20-21. Defense or concealment of the seducer by the seduced. Deut. xiii. 8.

22. The use of ornaments of idols. Deut. vii. 25.

23-4. To rebuild a city destroyed on account of its idolatry or to use its wealth. Deut. xiii. 16, 17.

25. The use of things belonging to idols or idolaters, or of the provisions and libations offered to idols. Deut. vii. 26.

26. Prophesying in the name of idols. Deut. xviii. 20.

27. False prophecies. Deut. xviii. 20.

28. Listening to prophecies in the name of idols. Deut. xiii. 3.

29. Fear of a false prophet or hindering any one from killing him. Deut. xviii. 22.

30. Walking in the manner of the idolaters, and practising their rites. Lev. xx. 23.

31–8. Enchantment, augury, and consultation of familiar spirits, etc. Lev. xix. 26; Deut. xviii. 10, 11.

39–40. The use of male attire by women, and vice versa. Deut. xxii. 5.

41. Tattooing the body after the manner of idolaters. Lev. xix. 28.

42. The use of garments made of both linen and wool. "Sha'aṭnez," Deut. xxii. 11.

43–4. Rounding "the corners of the head" or of the beard. Lev. xix. 27.

45. Lacerating oneself for the dead. Deut. xiv. 1.

46. To return to Egypt to dwell permanently there. Deut. xvii. 16.

47. Indulgence in impure thoughts and sights. Num. xv. 39.

48–9. Covenanting with, and preservation of, the seven nations. Ex. xxiii. 32.

50–2. To show mercy to or to intermarry with idolaters or to allow them to dwell in the land. Ex. xxiii. 33; and Deut. vii. 2, 3.

53. The marriage of a daughter of Israel with an Ammonite or Moabite. Deut. xxiii. 3.

54–5. To refuse admission to the congregation to a descendant of Esau or to an Egyptian after the third generation. Deut. xxiii. 7.

56. To offer peace to the Ammonites and Moabites in time of war. Deut. xxiii. 6.

57. The destruction of fruit-trees in time of war. Deut. xx. 19.

58. Fear of the enemy by warriors. Deut. iii. 22, vii. 21, xx. 3.

59. To forget the evil wrought by Amalek. Deut. xxv. 19.

60. Blasphemy of the Holy Name. Ex. xxii. 28.

61. To violate an oath, however rash. Lev. xix. 12.

62. Taking the name of the Lord in vain. Ex. xx. 7.

63. Profaning the name of the Holy One. Lev. xxii. 32.

64. To tempt the Lord. Deut. vi. 16.

65. Destruction of the sanctuary, synagogues, or schools, and erasure of the Holy Name and Holy Writings. Deut. xii. 2, 4.

66. To suffer the body of one hanged to remain on the tree. Deut. xxi. 23.

67. To cease watching the sanctuary. Num. xviii. 5.

68–71. The entrance of the priests into the sanctuary at certain times; priests with a blemish may not go beyond the altar nor serve in the sanctuary. Lev. xvi. 2, 23; xxi. 17, 21.

72. The ministry of Levites in the service of priests, and vice versa. Num. xviii. 3.

73. The entrance of intoxicated persons into the sanctuary, and the teaching of the Law by the same. Lev. x. 9.

74–6. Service in the sanctuary by strangers or by unclean priests, etc. Lev. xxii. 2; Num. xviii. 4.

77–8. Entrance into the court or the camp of the Levites by unclean priests. Num. v. 3; Deut. xxiii. 10.

79. The erection of an altar of hewn stone. Ex. xx. 25.

80. Ascension by steps to the altar. Ex. xx. 26.

81. To burn incense, or to offer it on the golden altar. Ex. xxx. 9.

82. To extinguish the fire on the altar. Lev. vi. 13.

83–5. Misuse of the holy oil, the anointing oil, or the holy incense. Ex. xxx. 32, 37.

86. Removal of the staves from the ark. Ex. xxv. 15.

87–8. To loosen the breastplate from the ephod or to tear the upper garment. Ex. xxviii. 32.

89–90. The killing and offering of sacrifices without the Temple. Deut. xii. 13; Lev. xvii. 3, 4.

91–5. The sanctification and use of blemished things for sacrifice. Lev. xxii. 22, 24; Deut. xvii. 1.

96. The offering of blemished animals from Gentiles. Lev. xxii. 25.

97. The offering of imperfect animals in sacrifice. Lev. xxii. 21.

98–100. To offer in sacrifice leaven or honey, an unsalted oblation, the hire of a harlot, or the price of a dog. Lev. ii. 11, 13; Deut. xxiii. 18.

101. To kill an animal and its young on the same day. Lev. xxii. 28.

102–5. The use of olive-oil or frankincense in the sin-offering or the jealousy-offering. Lev. v. 11; Num. v. 15.

106–7. To exchange sacrifices. Lev. xvii. 26, xxvii. 10.

108. The redemption of the first-born of clean cattle. Num. xviii. 17.

109. The sale of the tithe of the herd. Lev. xxvii. 33.

110–11. The sale or redemption of a dedicated field. Lev. xxvii. 28.

112. The division of the head of the bird in a sin-offering. Lev. v. 3.

113–4. Working with or shearing the first-born. Deut. xv. 19.

115–7. To kill the paschal lamb while there is leaven, or leave its fat or any part of its flesh over night. Ex. xii. 10, xxiii. 18.

118. To leave any of the festal offering until the third day. Deut. xvi. 4.

119. To leave part of the second Passover lamb until the morning. Num. ix. 12.

120. The preservation of any part of the thank-offering until the morning. Ex. xii. 10.

121–2. To break a bone of the paschal lamb or of the second Passover lamb. Ex. xii. 46; Num. ix. 12.

123. To carry of the flesh of Passover out of the house. Ex. xii. 46.

124. To allow the remnants of the meat-offering to become leavened. Lev. vi. 17.

125–8. To eat the paschal lamb raw or sodden, or to allow it to be eaten by a foreigner, by one uncircumcised, or by an apostate Israelite. Ex. xii. 9, 43, 45, 48.

129–32. An unclean person may not eat of holy things, nor of holy things polluted; nor of that which is left of sacrifices; nor of sacrifices which are polluted. Lev. vii. 18, 19, 20; xix. 8.

133–6. A stranger may not eat of the heave-offering, nor a sojourner with the priest, nor an hired servant, nor an uncircumcised person, nor an unclean priest. Lev. xxii. 4, 10.

137. A priest's daughter married to a stranger may not eat of the holy things. Lev. xxii. 12.

138–40. To eat the meat-offering of the priest, or the flesh of the sin-offering, or holy things which have been defiled. Lev. vi. 23, 30; Deut. xiv. 3.

141–4. To eat the second tithe of corn, or of the vintage, or of the oil, or the pure firstling without Jerusalem. Deut. xii. 17.

145–7. The consumption by the priest outside the courts of the sin- or trespass-offering, of the flesh of the burnt offering, or of lighter sacrifices before the blood has been sprinkled. Deut. xii. 17.

148. A stranger may not eat of the flesh of the most holy things. Ex. xxix. 33.

149. The priest may not eat of the first-fruits before they are brought into the court. Deut. xii. 17.

150–1. To eat the second tithe in mourning or in impurity, even in Jerusalem, until it be redeemed. Deut. xxvi. 14.

152. Use of the money of the second tithe except for eating or drinking. Deut. xxvi. 14.

153. Eating the corn before the heave-offerings and tithes have been separated. Lev. xxii. 15.

154. Changing the order regarding the wave-offering, the first-fruits, and the first and second tithes. Ex. xxii. 29.

155. The delay of vows and free-will offerings. Deut. xxiii. 21.

156. Attendance at the feast without an offering. Ex. xxiii. 15.

157. The violation of vows. Num. xxx. 2.

158–60. The marriage of a priest with a harlot, a "profane" woman ("ḥalalah"), or a divorcee. Lev. xxi. 7.

161–2. The marriage of a high priest with a widow, nor may he take her as his concubine. Lev. xxi. 14.

163–4. Priests may not enter the sanctuary with uncovered head or with torn garments. Lev. x. 6.

165. Priests may not leave the court during service. Lev. x. 7.

166–8. The pollution of priests and of the high priest. Lev. xxi. 1, 11.

169–70. The participation of the tribe of Levi in the holy land and in the spoils. Deut. xviii. 1.

171. To make oneself bald for the dead. Deut. xiv. 1.

172–9. The eating of unclean cattle, unclean fish, unclean fowl, creeping things that fly, things that creep upon the earth, or reptiles ("remesh"), etc. Lev. xi. 4, 13, 42–44; Deut. xiv. 19.

180–2. The eating of beasts in a dying condition, or torn animals ("ṭerefah"), or a member of a living animal. Ex. xxii. 31; Deut. xii. 21, 23.

183–5. The eating of the sinew which shrank, of blood, or of fat. Gen. xxxii. 32; Lev. vii. 23, 26.

186–7. The boiling of flesh in milk and the eating of flesh with milk. Ex. xxiii. 19, xxxiv. 26; Deut. xiv. 21.

188. The eating of the flesh of an ox that has been stoned. Ex. xxi. 28.

189–91. The eating of bread made of the new corn, or roasted grain, or green ears of the new corn, before the Passover offering has been brought. Lev. xxiii. 14.

192. The use of the fruit of a young tree before the fourth year. Lev. xix. 23.

193. The eating of mixed seeds of the vineyard. Deut. xxii. 9.

194. The use of libations to idols. Deut. xxxii. 38.

195. Gluttony and drunkenness. Deut. xxi. 20; Lev. xix. 26.

196. Eating on the Day of Atonement. Lev. xxiii. 29.

197–9. The eating of anything leavened on Passover, or of leavened bread after the middle of the fourteenth day. Ex. xii. 20; Deut. xiii. 3, xvi. 3.

200–1. The exposure of leaven and leavened bread. Ex. xiii. 7, 19.

202-6. A Nazarite may not drink wine or any liquor made from grapes, nor may he eat grapes or any part thereof. Num. vi. 3-5.

207-9. A Nazarite may not pollute himself for the dead, nor enter into the tent of the dead, nor shall he shave his hair. Num. vi. 5-7.

210-4. To reap the whole of the field, to gather the fallen ears of corn in harvest, to cut off all the clusters of the vineyard, to gather every grape of the vineyard, or to return to take a forgotten handful. Lev. xix. 9-10; Deut. xxiv. 19, 20.

215-6. The sowing of different kinds of seed together, or of corn and herbs in a vineyard. Lev. xix. 19; Deut. xxii. 9.

217. The gendering of cattle with those of diverse species. Lev. xix. 19.

218. The use of two different kinds of cattle together. Deut. xxii. 10.

219. The prevention of an animal working in the field from eating. Deut. xxv. 4.

220-3. To till the ground, to prune trees, to reap spontaneously grown corn, or to gather the fruit of trees, in the seventh year. Lev. xxv. 4-5.

224-6. To till the earth, to prune trees, to reap what grows spontaneously, or to gather fruit, in the jubilee year. Lev. xxv. 11.

227. The permanent sale of a field in the land of Israel. Lev. xxv. 23.

228. To change the suburbs of the Levites or their fields. Lev. xxv. 34.

229. To leave the Levite without support. Deut. xii. 19.

230. To demand the amount of a debt after the lapse of the seventh year. Deut. xv. 2.

231. To refuse to lend to the poor on account of the release year. Deut. xv. 9.

232. To refuse to lend to the poor the things which he requires. Deut. xv. 7.

233. Sending a Hebrew slave away empty-handed. Deut. xv. 13.

234. Exaction with regard to loans to the poor. Ex. xxii. 25.

235-6. Loans to or by an Israelite upon usury. Lev. xxv. 37.

237. Usury, or participation therein either as surety, witness, or writer of contracts. Ex. xxii. 25; Deut. xxiii. 19.

238. Delay in the payment of wages. Lev. xix. 13.

239-42. The exaction of a pledge from a debtor by violence; the retention of a pledge from the poor when he requires it; the receipt of a pledge from a widow, and the exaction of a pledge when it is such that one obtains by it a living. Deut. xxiv. 6, 10, 17.

243. To kidnap a man of Israel. Ex. xx. 15.

244. To steal. Lev. xix. 11.

245. To rob by violence. Lev. xix. 13.

246. To remove the landmark. Deut. xix. 14.

247. To defraud. Lev. xix. 13.

248. To defraud one's neighbor. Lev. xix. 11.

249. To swear falsely with regard to a neighbor's property. Lev. xix. 11.

250. To injure any one in bargaining. Lev. xxv. 14.

251-3. To oppress or injure any one. Ex. xxii. 21; Lev. xxv. 17.

254-5. To deliver a fugitive slave to his master, or to vex him. Deut. xxiii. 15, 16.

256. To afflict the widow and orphan. Ex. xxii. 22.

257-9. To use a Hebrew servant as a slave, to sell him as a bondman, or to treat him cruelly. Lev. xxv. 39, 42-43.

260. To permit a heathen to treat a Hebrew servant cruelly. Lev. xxv. 53.

261. To sell a Hebrew maid servant. Ex. xxi. 8.

262. To withhold from a betrothed Hebrew slave food, raiment, or conjugal rights. Ex. xxi. 10.

263. To sell as a slave a beautiful captive. Deut. xxi. 14.

264. To humble a beautiful woman. Deut. xxi. 14.

265. To covet a man's wife. Ex. xx. 17.

266. Covetousness. Deut. v. 21.

267-8. A hireling may not cut down standing corn during his labor, nor take more fruit than he can eat. Deut. xxiii. 24.

269. To hide when a thing lost is to be returned to the owner. Deut. xxii. 3.

270. To refrain from helping an animal fallen under its burden. Deut. xxii. 4.

271-2. Fraud in weights and measures. Lev. xix. 35; Deut. xxv. 13, 14.

273. Unrighteousness in judgment. Lev. xix. 35.

274. The acceptance of bribes. Ex. xxiii. 8.

275-6. Partiality or fear in a judge. Lev. xix. 15; Deut. i. 17.

277. To pity the poor in judgment. Ex. xxiii. 3.

278. To pervert the judgment of a sinner. Ex. xxiii. 6.

279. To spare the offender in matters of fines. Deut. xix. 13.

280. To pervert the judgment of strangers or orphans. Deut. xxiv. 17.

281. To hear one litigant except in the presence of the other. Ex. xxiii. 1.

282. To decide by a majority of one in capital cases. Ex. xxiii. 2.

283. Having first pleaded for a man in a capital case, one may not afterward plead against him. Ex. xxiii. 2.

284. The appointment as judge of one who is not learned in the Law. Deut. i. 17.

285. False witness. Ex. xx. 16.

286. The acceptance of testimony from a wicked person. Ex. xxiii. 1.

287. The testimony of relatives. Deut. xxiv. 16.

288. To pronounce judgment upon the testimony of only one witness. Deut. xix. 15.

289. To kill the innocent. Ex. xx. 13.

290. To convict on circumstantial evidence only. Ex. xxiii. 7.

291. To condemn to death on the evidence of only one witness. Num. xxxv. 30.

292. To execute before conviction one charged with a crime. Num. xxxv. 12.

293 To pity or spare the persecutor. Deut. xxv. 12.

294. To punish the victim in a case of rape. Deut. xxii. 26.

295-6. The acceptance of ransom for a murderer or for a manslayer. Num. xxxv. 31, 32.

297. The toleration of bloodshed. Lev. xix. 16.

298-9. To leave a stumbling-block in the way, or to cause the simple to stumble on the road. Deut. xxii. 8; Lev. xix. 14.

300. To exceed the number of stripes assigned to the guilty. Deut. xxv. 3.

301. Calumny. Lev. xix. 16.

302. To bear hatred in one's heart. Lev. xix. 17.

303. To cause the face of an Israelite to blush. Lev. xix. 17.

304–5. To bear a grudge. Lev. xix. 18.

306. To take the dam with the young. Deut. xxii, 6.

307–8. To shave the hair of the scall, or to pluck out the marks of leprosy. Lev. xiii. 33; Deut. xxiv. 8.

309. To plow or sow in a valley in which a slain body has been found. Deut. xxi. 4.

310. To suffer a witch to live. Ex. xxii. 18.

311. To force a bridegroom to perform military service. Deut. xxiv. 5.

312. Rebellion against the Sanhedrin. Deut. xvii. 11.

313–4. To add to or detract from the precepts of the Law. Deut. xii. 32.

315–6. To curse the judges, a prince, or a ruler. Ex. xxii. 28.

317. To curse any Israelite. Lev. xix. 14.

318–9. To curse or smite father or mother. Ex. xxi. 15, 17.

320–1. To work or to go beyond the city limits on the Sabbath. Ex. xx. 10.

322. To punish on the Sabbath. Ex. xxxv. 3.

323–9. To work on the first or the seventh day of Passover, or on the Feast of Shebu'ot, or on the first day of the seventh month, or on the Day of Atonement, or on the first or the eighth day of the Feast of Tabernacles. Ex. xii. 16; Lev. xxiii. 7, 16, 20, 25, 28, 35, 36.

330–45. The various marriages constituting incest. Lev. xviii. 7–18.

346. To have intercourse with a menstruous woman. Lev. xviii. 19.

347–53. Adultery, sodomy, etc. Lev. xviii. 7, 14, 20, 22, 23.

354. The marriage of a bastard with a daughter of Israel. Deut. xxiii. 2.

355. Harlotry. Deut. xxiii. 17.

356. The remarriage of a divorcee with her first husband. Deut. xxiv. 4.

357. The marriage of a widow with any one but the brother of her deceased husband. Deut. xxv. 5.

358. Divorcing of a victim of rape by the offender. Deut. xxii. 29.

359. Divorcing of a wife upon whom an evil name has been brought. Deut. xxii. 9.

360. The marriage of a eunuch with a daughter of Israel. Deut. xxiii. 1.

361. The castration of any male whatsoever. Lev. xxii. 24.

362. The election of a stranger as king over Israel. Deut. xvii. 15.

363–5. The possession by a king of an excessive number of horses and wives, or of an unduly large quantity of silver and gold. Deut. xvii. 16, 17.

Of the mandates Naḥmanides rejected Nos. 5, 7, 63, 64, 65, 66, 67, 85, 89, 95–108 (inclusive), 149, 150, 151, 198, 227, 228, 237, and 299, substituting for them the following:

5. To eat the first-born of cattle and the second tithe in Jerusalem. Deut. xiv. 23.

7. To eat the wave-offering only when it is without blemish. Deut. xv. 22.

63. To eat the fruit of the seventh year, and not to trade with it. Lev. xxv. 6.

64. To possess the land of Israel. Num. xxxiii. 53.

65. To leave open one side in besieging a town. Num. xxxi. 7 (see Sifre *ad loc.*).

66. To remember what God did to Miriam. Deut. xxiv. 9.

67. To be perfect with the Lord. Deut. xviii. 13.

85. To select the wave-offering from the best. Num. xviii. 29.

89. To bring an offering of cattle only. Lev. i. 1.

95. To offer all the sacrifices between the two oblations. Lev. vi. 5.

96. To eat the paschal lamb in the night only. Ex. xii. 8.

97. That the avenger of blood pursue the murderer. Num. xxxv. 19.

98. To avoid the garments of the leprous. Lev. xiii. 51.

99. To recite the blessing over the Torah before reading it. Deut. xxxii. 2.

100. To sustain the sojourning stranger. Lev. xxv. 49.

101. To return usury taken from an Israelite. Lev. xxv. 35.

102. To renounce profit from the Nazarite's hair. Num. vi. 5.

103. To make an ark and a mercy-seat. Ex. xxv. 15.

104. To keep an oath or vow. Deut. xxiii. 24.

105. To reckon months and years. Deut. xvi. 1.

106. To bring an offering morning and evening. Num. xxviii. 4.

107. To offer incense morning and evening. Ex. xxx. 7, 8.

108. To read the Shema' morning and evening. Deut. vi. 17.

149. To recognize unconditionally the first-born son. Deut. xxi. 17.

150. To liberate the slave whose tooth or eye has been knocked out by his master. Ex. xxi. 27.

151. To execute him who has incurred capital punishment. Deut. xvii. 7.

198, 227, 228. That the priest shall serve in the sanctuary all the sacrifices; to separate the wave-offering, a cake of the dough, and give it to the priest. Num. xviii. 7: Deut. xviii. 7; Num. xv. 21.

237. To separate the first tithe and give it to the Levite, and give the poor's tithe to the poor. Num. xviii. 24.

299. To consult the Urim and the Thummim for the king. Num. xxvii. 21.

Of the prohibitions Naḥmanides rejects Nos. 2, 3, 5, 14, 28, 58, 69, 70, 92, 93, 94, 95, 143, 150, 152, 177, 178, 179, 190, 191, 199, 201, 294, 307, 319, 321, 353, substituting for them the following:

2–3. Forgetfulness of the law of God and of the sojourn on Mount Sinai. Deut. iv. 9, viii. 11.

5. Alteration of the order of the vessels in the Temple. Ex. xxiii. 13 (see Mekilta *ad loc.*).

14, 28. The offering of sacrifices with the intention of eating them in other than the prescribed time and place, and the eating of sacrifices so offered. Lev. vii. 18; Deut. xvii. 1.

58. Eating the bird slain for the cleansing from leprosy. Lev. xiv. 14.

69. Selection of the heave-offering by the Levites. Num. xviii. 32.

70. The acceptance of shekels from heathens. Lev. xxii. 25.

92. The condemnation on the testimony of only one witness. Deut. xvii. 6.

93. Allowing the faint-hearted to go to war. Deut. xx. 8.

94. To cause the Shekinah to depart from the camp by reason of any impurity. Deut. xxiii. 15.

95. Depriving the first-born of his birthright. Deut. xxi. 16.

143. Clemency to a murderer. Deut. xix. 21.

150. Marriage of the deceased brother's wife after "ḥalizah." Deut. xxv. 9.

152. Cohabitation with a wife who has committed adultery. Deut. xxiv. 4.

177. Regretting the poing of charity and the freeing of a Hebrew slave in the seventh year. Deut. xv. 10, 18.

178. Robbery of vessels of the sanctuary. Num. iv. 20.

179. The Levite may not carry the holy vessels after the fiftieth year. Num. viii. 25.

190. The divorced wife when married to another may not be taken back. Deut. xxiv. 4.

191. Disputing the priesthood. Num. xvii. 5.

199. Deriving profit from the beheaded heifer. Num. xxxv. 34.

201. To marry a daughter to one who is forbidden to her. Lev. xix. 9.

294. Profanation of the Holy Land.

307. Leaving the sanctuary during the service.

Two prohibitions are contained in each of the following verses, by which the number of the remaining rejected prohibitions is made up: Lev. xxiii. 4; Lev. ii. 11; Deut. xxiii. 19; Ex. xii. 9; Ex. xxii. 21; Ex. xxviii. 7; Deut. xxiv. 5; Deut. xxi. 18; Deut. ii. 9.

Moses of Coucy rejects Maimonides' mandates Nos. 142, 193, 198, substituting the following:

142. To justify the decision of the Lord. Deut. viii. 5.

193. To reckon the solstices and constellations. Deut. iv. 6.

198. To keep far from a false matter. Ex. xxiii. 7.

Of the prohibitions he rejects Nos. 14, 26, 67, 70, 78, 95, 140, 150, 152, 165, 177, 178, 199, 266, 278, 283, 291, substituting the following:

14. Abandonment of the Torah. Deut. iv. 9.
26. The kissing of idols. Ex. xxiii. 24.
67. The making of idols. Lev. xxvi. 1.
70. Pride. Deut. viii. 14.
78. Prostitution of a daughter of Israel. Lev. xix. 29.
95. Cursing oneself. Deut. iv.
140. A priest may not make himself unclean for the dead. Lev. xxi. 1.

There are two prohibitions in each of the following verses, by which the number of the remaining rejected prohibitions is made up: Ex. xii. 9; Lev. ii. 11; Deut. xxiii. 1, 13, 18; xxiv. 6.

Joseph of Corbeil has the following mandates not found in the lists of Maimonides, Naḥmanides, and Moses of Coucy:

To gaze upon the fringes. Num. xv. 39.

To show kindness toward the needy, both in feeling and in deed; to bury the dead; and to show forbearance. Ex. xviii. 20.

To practise modesty in privacy. Deut. xxiii. 15.

To remember the Exodus from Egypt. Deut. xvi. 3.

To love admonition. Deut. x. 16.

To teach. Lev. x. 11.

To cleanse soiled vessels with boiled water and to immerse vessels. Num. xxxi. 23.

To give to the stranger meat forbidden to Israelites. Deut. xiv. 21.

To sanctify the first-born of clean cattle. Deut. xv. 19.

That men shall live with their wives, but keep from them at certain times. Deut. xxiv. 5; Lev. xv. 31.

To blot out the names of idols, to break down their pillars, and hew down the "asherim." Deut. vii. 5, xii. 3.

To burn the asherah, demolish the places of idolatrous worship, break down the altars, and destroy the vessels used for idolatry. Deut. xii. 3; Num. xxx. 52; Deut. vii. 5; xii. 2, 3.

The prohibitions not included by the other compilers, but found in the Semaḳ, are:

Intolerance of admonition. Deut. x. 16.

Self-righteousness. Deut. ix. 4.

Delay in attending to the natural needs. Deut. xxiii. 15.

Sodomy. Ex. xx. 14.

Bibliography: M. Bloch, *Les 613 Lois*, in *Rev. Et. Juives*, i. 197 *et seq.*, v. 25 *et seq.*; Michael Creizenach, *Thoriag*, 1833; M. Brueck, *Das Mosaische Judenthum*, 1837; D. Rosin, *Ein Compendium der Jüdischen Gesetzeskunde*, Breslau, 1871; Jellinek, *Ḳonteris Taryag*, Vienna, 1878; Schechter, *Studies in Judaism*, 1896, p. 248.

K. I. Br.

IX

Compassion

COMPASSION: Sorrow and pity for one in distress, creating a desire to relieve, a feeling ascribed alike to man and God; in Biblical Hebrew, רחם ("riḥam," from "reḥem," the mother, womb), "to pity" or "to show mercy" in view of the sufferer's helplessness, hence also "to forgive" (Hab. iii. 2); חמל, "to forbear" (Ex. ii. 6; I Sam. xv. 3; Jer. xv. 15, xxi. 7); חוס, "to spare" (Deut. vii. 16, xiii. 8; Ezek. vii. 4, xx. 17); חנן and חסד, "to be gracious" and "kind" (Isa. xxii. 23 [if the text is correct]; Prov. xx. 28; Job vi. 14; Num. xiv. 19; Gen. xxx. ii. 10; Isa. lxiii. 7). The Rabbis speak of the "thirteen attributes of compassion," י״ג מדות של רחמים (Ex. xxxiv. 6; Pesiḳ. 57a; R. H. 17a). Later a distinction is made between attributes of compassion and those of love (חסד; see Asher ben David in his commentary on the Thirteen Attributes, where he classifies them under "justice," "love," and "compassion").

The Biblical conception of compassion is the feeling of the parent for the child ("pitieth"; Ps. ciii. 13). Hence the prophet's appeal in confirmation of his trust in God figures the feeling of a mother for her offspring (Isa. xlix. 15), and Pharaoh's daughter, moved by maternal sympathy, has compassion on the weeping babe (Ex. ii. 6).

But this feeling should mark the conduct of man to man (I Sam. xxiii. 21); its possession is a proof that men are among those deserving recognition as "blessed unto Yhwh"; and in Zech. vii. 9 it is included among the postulates of brotherly dealings. Inversely, the lack of compassion marks a people as "cruel" (אכזרי; Jer. vi. 23). The Chaldeans are without compassion in that they slay the young and helpless (II Chron. xxxvi. 17); and Edom is censured for having cast away all "pity" (Amos i. 11). The poor are especially entitled to compassion (A. V. "pity"; Prov. xix. 17). The repeated injunctions of the Law and the Prophets that the "widow," the "orphan," and the "stranger" shall be protected show how deeply rooted was the feeling of compassion in the hearts of the righteous in Israel. It can not be admitted that the provisions for the extermination of the seven original Palestinian tribes (Deut. vii. 3, 16) indicate the absence of kindly sympathy for aliens. Even if these provisions do not, as the critical school insists, represent merely pious wishes, they are at least entitled to be regarded as war measures, and, as such, were exceptional. They rank with similar provisions to cover the cases of the murderer and the false prophet (Deut. xiii. 8; xix. 13, 21). The very horror with which the conduct of the Chaldees and Edom (see above) was regarded proves the contrary. Even the "enemy" was within the sweep of Jewish compassion. And so was the dumb animal, as the humane provisions of the Pentateuch against cruelty to them demonstrate (see CRUELTY TO ANIMALS).

Seat of Compassion.

The physiological psychology of the Bible places the seat of the sympathetic emotions in the bowels. But the eyes were credited with the function of indicating them. Hence the frequent use of the expression "the eye has," or "has not," pity. The "length of the breath"—that is, in anger or wrath (ארך אפים)—is another idiomatic expression for compassionate forbearance.

God is full of compassion (Ps. ciii. 11, cxlv. 3); and this compassion is invoked on men (Deut. xiii. 17), and promised to them (Deut. xxx. 3). "His compassions fail not, being new every morning" (Lam. iii. 22). Repeatedly He showed His compassion (II Kings xiii. 23; II Chron. xxxvi. 15). His "mercy [or "compassion"] endureth forever." He loveth the "poor," the "widow," the "orphan," and the "stranger." He is named חנון ורחום ("gracious and full of compassion"; Ex. xxxiv. 6, *passim*). To obtain His "compassion," as the quality that pardons, sinners must first repent and return to Him (II Chron. xxx.). But when they do this, even non-Jews will experience His compassion (Book of Jonah). For God "pitieth" like a father those "that fear him" (Ps. ciii. 13).

These Biblical ideas become the foundation of the ethical and theological teachings of the Rabbis. Israel especially should be distinguished for its compassionate disposition (Yeb. 79a), so that one who is merciful falls under the presumption of being of the seed of Abraham (Beẓ. 32b). One who is not prone to pity and forbearance is cruel (B. Ḳ. 92a), and this though to be compassionate has the tendency to rob life of its savor (Pes. 113b). The thoughtlessly frivolous is like a cruel man, but one who is compassionate experiences the lot of the poor man (B. B. 145b). Compassion shown to fellow man will win compassion from on high (Shab. 151a). Eyes without pity will become blind, and hands that will not spare will be cut off (Ta'an. 21a). Women are recognized as prone to pity (Meg. 14b). In fact, this trait of its women was one of the glories of Jerusalem (B. B. 104b). To praise God meant to become merciful like unto Him (Shab. 133b; Ex. xv.). Strangers certainly came within the scope of the rabbinical ideas of compassion. Their dead were buried with the dead of Israel; their poor were assisted; their sick were visited (Giṭ. 61a, Tos. v. 4, 5). The angels when about to celebrate in song Israel's victory over Egypt were hushed by God with the rebuke: "The works of My hands have been drowned, and you would intone jubilant pæans!" (Meg. 10b).

The peculiar interdiction of the explanation of Pentateuchal laws as manifestations of divine compassion for dumb creatures (Ber. 33b) proves that this explanation was popular (see CRUELTY TO ANIMALS). But the Rabbis often lay stress on the fact that the Torah takes great care to "spare" (חסה) the property of man (Soṭah 14b; Nega'im xii.).

God is recognized as the "Compassionate" (רחמן; compare the frequent use of "raḥman" in the Koran). He is invoked as the אב הרחמים (Father of Compassion). So close is this association with Him that "Raḥmana" becomes the usual designation for His revealed word. He suffers with His people (Rabbi Meïr: "The Shekinah exclaims with the suffering patient, 'Oh, my head! Oh, my arm!'"

Sanh. iv. 46a; but see Levy, *s.v.* קל). He mourns with His people (Lam. R. to i. 1). The relation which God's "compassion" sustains to His "justice" is also a subject of rabbinical inquiry, as it was among the early Christian sects. When the shofar is sounded "God's quality of compassion mounts the throne" (Pesiḳ. 151b, 155a; Lev. R. xxix.; compare also Abraham's prayer [Yer. Ta'an. 65d]). The name "Elohim" designates God's justice (מדת הדין), and the name YHWH God's compassion (מדת הרחמים; Ex. R. vi.). Even while God is preparing to inflict punishment, God's compassion is bestirring itself (Yer. Ta'an. 65b, bottom; Pesiḳ. 161b; Midr. Teh. to Ps. 86; Pes. 87b). Philo says "God's pity is older than His judgment" ("Quod Deus Sit Immutabilis," 16). The name YHWH is repeated twice in Ex. xxxiv. 6 to allay the fears of Moses. As before the sin of the golden calf had been committed God dealt with Israel according to His compassion, so even now, after their sinning, will He deal with them in mercy (Pesiḳ. R. 5; Num. R. xii.).

X

Cosmogony

COSMOGONY.—Biblical Data: A theory concerning the origin ("begetting") of the world; the mythological or ante-scientific view, as preserved in the traditions, oral or written, and the folk-poetry of primitive and ancient peoples.

Curiosity concerning the origin of the visible universe and the manner and order in which the various forms of life came into being, manifested itself at a comparatively early period. Cosmogonies are, therefore, found among nearly all races, and form a large part of their mythologies, preserved as tribal or national traditions. Old as they are, they reflect climatic and cultural conditions of various localities; and these differences, often unharmonized, appear in the later literary and religious versions. The original cosmogonies are spontaneous productions of folk-fancy, and are therefore unsystematic, forming as a rule only a chapter in the theogonies or genealogies of the gods. Systematization is a sign that primitive notions have been subjected to treatment in the interest of a certain theology or advanced religious consciousness. By those who ascribe to the Hebrew mind the same process of development and to Hebrew literature the same manner of growth as are observed among other peoples, the cosmogony—or, to be more exact, the cosmogonies—of the Bible must be viewed and analyzed according to the light derived from comparison with similar conceits among non-Hebrews. By analogy, then, with other ancient peoples, the form in which the Hebrew cosmogony presents itself in the Bible is not the original. The literary documents are later than the material incorporated. They exhibit the influences of a developed theology as well as the effect of a blending of different accounts that are at variance with one another in their radical versions.

The comparatively late date of the literary documents—according to the critical schools—has misled most of the modern commentators into the assumption that the early Hebrews were without cosmogonies. Rénan's denial to the Semites of the mythopeic faculty seemed thus to be borne out by the results of Pentateuchal analysis and of literary criticism of the other Biblical books. This inference, however, can not be maintained (see Gunkel, "Schöpfung und Chaos"; *idem*, "Genesis"). The Hebrews must have had the same impulse toward speculation on the origin of things as had other groups of men; and as this impulse manifests itself always at a very early period in the evolution of mind (the tribal or national consciousness), one is safe in the a priori ascription to the Hebrews of the production and possession of cosmogonic legends at a very remote epoch. This conclusion from analogy is corroborated by the study of the literary documents bearing on this point. Gunkel (*l.c.*) has demonstrated that the cosmogonic accounts or allusions thereto (technical archaic terms, like "tohu wabohu"; the use of words in an unusual sense, for instance רוח אלהים; and mythological personifications, like Rahab) display easily discernible signs of incorporated old material (Gen. i., ii.; Job xxvi. 12, xl. 25, xli. 26; Ps. xl. 5, lxxiv. 12–19, lxxxvii. 4, lxxxix. 10; Isa. xxvii. 1, li. 9). That Gen. i. belongs to the later strata of the Pentateuch (P) is conceded by all except those scholars that reject higher criticism altogether. Dillmann, for instance, and Delitzsch (in the last edition of his commentary) do not hesitate to assign it to the Priestly Code, though they would have it be pre-exilic. It certainly has the appearance of a systematic presentation, but nevertheless *it is not a free invention.*

Early Hebrew Cosmogony.

It has long been recognized that Biblical cosmogony bears certain similarities to that of other peoples; *e.g.*, the Phenicians (who speak of πνεῦμα and dark χαός originally existent; through their union, πόθος ["desire"], μῶτ ["primordial mud"] is generated;

but of this μῶτ come the egg, etc. [for other versions see Damascius, "De Primis Principiis," p. 125]; the wife of the first man is Βαθυ [= בהו]), or the Egyptians (who spoke of primeval water ["nun"] and the primeval egg [see Dillmann, Commentary on Genesis, p. 5, and De la Saussaye, "Religionsgeschichte," 2d ed., i. 146 *et seq.*]). The notion of the primeval egg seems to be a universal one (see Dillmann, *l.c.* p. 4; "Laws of Manu," i. 5 *et seq.*).

Strikingly similar to the Biblical cosmogony is that of the Babylonians (Friedrich Delitzsch, "Babylonischer Weltschöpfungsepos"; Jensen, "Kosmologie der Babylonier," pp. 263-364; Zimmern, in Gunkel, "Schöpfung und Chaos," pp. 401 *et seq.*; Schrader, "K. B." vi.). Its birthplace is betrayed by its reflection of the climatic conditions of Babylonia. In winter, floods and darkness prevail. With the advent of spring the waters "divide" and are "subjugated" through the power of the winds that blow. Applying to primeval days this yearly phenomenon of the conquest of the flood and darkness, the Babylonian fancy assumes as self-existent in the beginning the great expanse of water (and unlit darkness). The former is conceived of as a monstrous dragon, Tiamat (= תהם), which, in the epitome given by Berosus, is represented as the "primeval woman," with whom Bel cohabits, splitting her into two halves, one of which becomes the earth and the other the sky, in characteristic reflection of Babylon's climate, and of the spring sun piercing the waters at the end of the winter's rainy season. Stories about Tiamat have been found as far back as the fourth millennium B.C. The narrative, as recovered from the tablets, begins by recording that "long since, when above the heaven had not been named, and earth was also without name [*i.e.*, non-existent] there was only primeval ocean-flood." This is personified as a male (Apsu) and a female (Tiamat). The gods, which had not yet arisen, were then made: Tiamat was their mother. Hatred of the new-born light causes her to rebel against the higher deities. Some of the gods side with her,

Babylonian Cosmogony.

Babylonian Accounts.

and to aid her in her fight she produces huge monsters. Marduk offers to punish her, on condition that the supreme rule over heaven and earth be accorded him after the victory. He rides to the combat in his war-chariot, and, meeting Tiamat, kills her by forcing open her mouth, which he fills with the hurricane that cuts her in two from within, and puts her crew in chains. He then divides her carcass: out of one part he makes heaven; out of the other, earth. The following is the order in which Creation is said to have been successively called forth by Marduk: (1) the heaven; (2) the heavenly bodies; (3) the earth; (4) the plants; (5) the animals; (6) man.

It is plain that not only in Gen. i., but in other Biblical cosmogonic descriptions (notably in Ps. civ. 5-9; also in Job xxxviii. 10; Ps. xxxiii. 6, lxv. 8; Prov. viii. 29; Jer. v. 22, xxxi. 35; the Prayer of Manasses), traits and incidents abound that suggest this Babylonian myth. In the main, four theories have been advanced to account for this: (1) Both the Babylonian and the Hebrew are varied versions of an originally common Semitic tradition. (2) The Hebrews carried an originally Babylonian tradition with them when emigrating from Ur-Kasdim. (3) They adopted the Babylonian epos during the Babylonian captivity. (4) This tradition, originally Babylonian, as the background shows, had long before the Hebrew conquest of Palestine been carried to Canaan through the then universal domination of Babylon; and the Hebrews gradually appropriated it in the course of their own political and religious development. This last theory (Gunkel's) is the most plausible. Gen. i. marks the final adaptation and recasting under the influence of theological ideas (*i.e.*, monotheism; six days for work and the seventh day for rest). As now found in Gen. i., it seems to be a composite of two, if not more, ancient myths. Besides those Babylonian elements indicated above, it contains reminiscences of another Babylonian tradition of a primitive (golden) age without bloodshed (vegetarianism), and recalls notions of non-Babylonian cycles ("the egg idea" in the brooding of the רוח, the Phenician בהו).

The allusions to this ancient (Babylonian) cosmogony are really much fresher and fuller in mythological conceits in the other passages quoted above. These, then, represent a cosmogony anterior to the reconstruction on monotheistic lines now incorporated in Genesis. In them the Dragon myth ("Tiamat," "Rahab") is of frequent recurrence; but while it points to a cosmogonic source, it may in some cases (Job xxvi. 13, for instance) have sprung from a natural celestial phenomenon such as an eclipse. So also in eschatological descriptions and apocalyptic visions these incidents of the old tradition recur (Ps. xviii., lxxvii., xciii. 3 *et seq.*; Nahum i.; Hab. iii.). See DRAGON; LEVIATHAN.

Earlier Versions.

On the other hand, the Bible has preserved cosmogonies, or reminiscences of them, that are not of Babylonian origin. Gen. ii. 4 *et seq.*, belonging, according to critics, to the Jahvistic source, starts with *dry* earth, and makes the sprouting of vegetation depend on man's previous creation; that is, on his labor. This exhibits Palestinian coloring. The dry, parched, waterless soil without rain is taken from a Palestinian landscape (see, however, Cheyne in "Encyc. Bibl." i. 949). Again, Ps. xc. 2 speaks of the time before the birth of the mountains and the parturition of earth and world. In Job xxxviii. it is said that God laid the foundations of the earth "when the morning stars sang together," and all the "sons of God" broke forth in glee. In Ps. xxiv. 2 there is a reference to the mystery involved in God's grounding the earth on the waters so that it can not be moved. These are not mere poetic explications of Gen. i. They are derived from other cosmogonic cycles, which a tone time may even have included, as among all other ancient peoples, a theogony (notice the "sons of God"; see Gunkel, "Genesis," p. 119).

The value of the cosmogony of Genesis lies in its *monotheistic* emphasis. Though the plural "Elohim," the words "let us make," and the view of man being "the image of God" reflect polytheistic and mythological conceptions of a previous stage, the stress is laid on the thought that one God made the all by His will, and made it "good." The Sabbath—originally not a part of the Babylonian epos—is the crowning glory of this cosmogony, notwithstanding the strong anthropomorphism of the concept that the Creator Himself rested. The attempt to establish a concordance between Genesis and geology seems to do an injustice to science and religion both. The ancient Hebrews had a very imperfect conception of the structure of the universe. Gen. i. was not written to be a scientific treatise. It was to impress and to express the twin-doctrine of God's creative omnipotence and of man's dignity as being destined on earth to be a creator himself.

With the Babylonians, the Hebrews believed that in the beginning, before earth and heaven had been separated ("created," ברא), there were primeval ocean ("tehom," always without the article) and darkness (חשך). From this the "word of God" (compare such passages as, God "roars" [נער], Ps. xviii. 16; civ. 7) called forth light. He divided the waters: the upper waters he shut up in heaven, and on the lower He established the earth. In older descriptions the combat against the tehom is related with more details. Tehom (also Rahab) has helpers, the תנין and the Leviathan, Behemot, the "Naḥash Bariaḥ." The following is the order of Creation as given in Gen. i.: (1) the heaven; (2) the earth; (3) the plants; (4) the celestial bodies; (5) the animals; (6) man. The Hebrews regarded the earth as a plain or a hill figured like a hemisphere, swimming on water. Over this is arched the solid vault of heaven. To this vault are fastened the lights, the stars. So slight is this elevation that birds may rise to it and fly along its expanse.

Bibliography: Gunkel, *Schöpfung und Chaos in Urzeit und Endzeit*; Idem, *Genesis*; Holzinger, *Genesis*, pp. 17 *et seq.*; Jensen, *Kosmologie der Babylonier*.

XI

Creation

CREATION: The bringing into existence of the world by the act of God. Most Jewish philosophers find in בריאה (Gen. i. 1) creation *ex nihilo* (יש מאין). The etymological meaning of the verb בריאה, however, is "to cut out and put into shape," and thus presupposes the use of material. This fact was recognized by Ibn Ezra and Naḥmanides, for instance (commentaries on Gen. i. 1; see also Maimonides, "Moreh Nebukim," ii. 30), and constitutes one of the arguments in the discussion of the problem.

Whatever may be the nature of the traditions in Genesis (see COSMOGONY), and however strong may be the presumption that they suggest the existence of an original substance which was reshaped in accordance with the Deity's purposes (see DRAGON; DARKNESS), it is clear that the Prophets and many of the Psalms accept without reservation the doctrine of creation from nothing by the will of a supermundane personal God (Ps. xxxiii. 6–9, cii. 26, cxxi. 2; Jer. x. 12; Isa. xlii. 5, xlv. 7–9): "By the word of the Lord were the heavens made; and all the host of them by the breath of his mouth." To such a degree has this found acceptance as the doctrine of the Synagogue that God has come to be designated as "He who spake and the world sprang into existence" (see BARUK SHE-AMAR and 'Er. 13b; Meg. 13b; Sanh. 19a, 105a; Ḳid. 31a; Ḥul. 63b, 84b; Sifre to Num. § 84; Gen. R. 34b; Ex. R. xxv.; Shab. 139a; Midrash Mishle, 10c). God is "the author of creation," עושה בראשית ("bereshit" having become the technical term for "creation"; Gen. R. xvi.; Ber. 54a, 58a; Ḥag. 12a, 18a; Ḥul. 83a; Ecclus. [Sirach] xv. 14).

The belief in God as the author of creation ranks first among the thirteen fundamentals (see ARTICLES OF FAITH) enumerated by Maimonides. It occurs in the YIGDAL, where God is called קדמון לכל דבר אשר נברא, "anterior [because Himself uncreated] to all that was created"; in the ADON 'OLAM; and it is taught in all modern Jewish catechisms.

Difficulties of the Conception.

Nevertheless, Jewish literature (Talmudic, pseudo-epigraphic, and philosophical) shows that the difficulties involved in this assumption of a creation *ex nihilo* (יש מאין) and in time, were recognized at a very early day, and that there were many among the Jews who spoke out on this subject with perfect candor and freedom. Around the first chapter of Genesis was waged many a controversy with both fellow Jews and non-Jews. The influence of Greek ideas is clearly discernible in various Midrashic homilies on the subject—*e.g.*, those dealing with the mode of divine creation (Gen. R. i., "God looked into the Torah, and through it He created"—a Platonic idea; *ib.* x.); with the view of God as architect (*ib.* i.; Ḥag. 12; compare Philo, "De Opificiis Mundi," iv.); with the creative word or letter (Gen. R. i.; Midr. ha-Gadol, ed. Schechter, pp. 10 *et seq.*; Pesiḳ. R. xxi.; Yer. Ḥag. ii. 77c); with the original elements (Gen. R. x.; Ex. R. xiii., xv.; Yer. Ḥag. ii. 77a); with the order of creation, the subject of the well-known controversy between the schools of Hillel and Shammai (compare Ḥag. 12a; Ta'an. 32a; Pirḳe R. El. xxxvi.); with the various acts of creation assigned to various days (Charles, "Book of Jubilees," 1902, pp. 11 *et seq.*); with the time consumed in creation (Ber. R, xii.); with successive creations (Pes. 54a; Gen. R. i.; Ab. R. N. xxxvii.); and, finally, with the purpose of creation (Abot vi.; Sanh. 98b; Ber. 6b, 61b; see also Bacher, "Ag. Tan." and "Ag. Pal. Amor.," Indices, *s.v.* "Weltschöpfung," etc.). The Slavonic Enoch (xxiii.–xxxv.) contains an elaborate presentation of old Jewish cosmogonic speculations, apparently under Egyptian Orphic influences (see N. Bonwetsch, "Das Slavische Henochbuch," Berlin, 1896; "The Book of the Secrets of Enoch," ed. by W. R. Morfill and R. H. Charles, Oxford, 1896).

The danger lest speculation on creation might lead to Gnosticism underlies the hesitancy to leave the study of Gen. i. open to all without restriction (Sanh. 37a; Deut. R. ii.; Ḥag. 19b; Midr. Teh. to Ps. cxxxvi.; Midr. ha-Gadol, ed. Schechter, p. 4). That such speculation is of no consequence to the practical religiosity which Judaism means to foster is well expressed in the caution not to "inquire into what was before the world was" (Mishnah Ḥag. ii.; Yer. Ḥag. ii.). See CABALA.

The Alexandrian Jews, under the sway of Platonic and Neoplatonic ideas, conceived of creation as carried into effect through intermediate agencies, though still an act of divine will, while the relation of the agencies to the Godhead is not always clearly defined, so that it is possible to regard them almost as divine hypostases—subdeities, as it were, with independent existence and a will of their own (ALEXANDRIAN PHILOSOPHY). The divine *σοφία* ("wisdom") has a cooperative part in creation (Wisdom ix. 9). While the Palestinian (II Macc. vii. 28) insists that all was made by God "out of nothing" (*'εζ οὐκ ὄντων*), Wisdom (xi. 17) posits a formless arch-matter (*ὕλη*), which the Creator simply brought into order.

Philo proceeds to fully develop this idea. The Mosaic account of creation is not to be accepted literally (see Drummond, "Philo Judæus," i. 293). Creation was not in time. "It is folly to suppose that the universe was made in six days, or in time at all." The expression "six days" merely indicates the most perfect arrangement ("De Allegoriis Legum," i. 2; "De Opificiis Mundi," i. 3; "Quod Deus Sit Immutabilis," i. 277). To the question whether the world had no real beginning, he gives, though inconsistent with himself, a negative answer. There was a time when the parts of the cosmos "deified by the heathen" were not; God alone was never non-existent ("Dec. Orac." ii. 190). "For the genesis of anything," he says, "many things must combine: that by which, that out of which, that through which, that on account of which" (= cause, material, instrument, purpose). God is the cause of the cosmos, while the four elements are the material ("De Cherubim," i. 161, 162).

Views of Philo.

Nothing suggests that he regarded this material as other than uncreated. It was there when God arranged the new order of things. God is the demiurge ("De Eo Quod Deterius Potiori Insidiatur," i. 220; "De Plantatione Noe," i. 320; his expressions are *δημιουργός, κοσμοπλάστης, τεχνίτης*). As in other points, so on this, Philo is not rigidly consistent. There are passages again from which a belief in the creation of matter out of nothing might be assumed. He speaks of matter as corruptible, and "corruptible" is, in his theory, a correlative of "created" ("Quis Rerum Divinarum Heres Sit," i. 495).

It was not matter, but form, that God praised as good, and acknowledged thus as His creative work. Yet Philo protests that God is "not a demiurge, but a creator." What before was not, He made (*οὐ δημιουργός μόνον, ἀλλὰ καὶ κτίστης αὐτὸς ὤν*, "De Somniis," i. 632; see Siegfried, "Philo von Alexandrien," p. 232). Drummond argues, against Siegfried, that God is here styled Creator only of the ideal, intelligible world, not of matter in the visible world (*l.c.* i. 304). In regard to Philo's Logos and the Memra of the Targum see LOGOS.

In the writings of the Jewish philosophers of the Middle Ages, creation is one of the problems most earnestly discussed. It belonged to the "four questions" (Maimonides, "Moreh," i. 71) which were regarded as fundamental. The alternative was between חדוש העולם, Ar. חדת אלעאלם ("creation"), and קדמות העולם, Ar. קדם אלעאלם ("eternity of matter"). The Arabian thinkers and schoolmen were perplexed by the same problem (Munk, "Mélanges," p. 421). They had been moved to discuss the subject by their studies (at second hand) of Plato and Aristotle. The Greek mind could not conceive of creation out of nothing—"Ex nihilo nihil fit."

In Medieval Jewish Philosophy.

Plato's *ὕλη* (consult his "Timæus") was eternal. Aristotle, too, maintained the eternity of matter ("De Cœlo," i. 10–12; "Phys." ii. 6–9). God is the source of the order of things predestined by Himself ("De Mundo," ii.), though Maimonides and Judah ha-Levi argue for the possibility of claiming for Aristotle the contrary view ("Moreh Nebukim," ii. 15; "Cuzari," i. 65).

Is the doctrine of the eternity of matter compatible with the Jewish conception of God? On three grounds this has been negatived: (1) It limits God's omnipotence and freedom. (2) It is in conflict with the Biblical account, and denies the possibility of miracles, though the Talmudic theory of miracles would not be affected. "God, when He created the sea, imposed the condition that it should divide itself before Moses' staff" (Ab. v. 9). (3) Great men, such as Moses and the Messiah, would be utterly impossible (Albo, "'Iḳḳarim," i. 12). The first point may be considered cogent, but the two others are not very profound.

In two ways do those of the Jewish philosophers who maintain the *creatio ex nihilo* attempt to prove their thesis: (1) by demonstrating the necessity of the Creation, and (2) by showing that it is impossible that the world was not created ("Cuzari," v. 18; "Moreh Nebukim," ii. 30). But in order to achieve this, they had first to disprove the arguments of their opponents. These were the same as those with which Mohammedan theologians (see Shahrastani, ii. 199 *et seq.*) had been confronted. Maimonides (*l.c.* ii. 14; compare also Aaron b. Elijah, "'Eẓ Ḥayyim," vi., vii.) arranges them into two groups: (1) מצד העולם עצמו (cosmological, Schmiedl's terminology), and (2) מצד האל ית' (theological).

In the first group there are the arguments: (*a*) Motion must be eternal, without beginning. Time is an accident of motion; "timeless (*i.e.*, changeless) motion" and "motionless (*i.e.*, changeless) time" are self-contradictory conceptions; therefore, time has no beginning. (*b*) The prime arch-matter underlying the four elements must be eternal. "To become" implies taking on form. But primal matter, according to its own presupposition, implied in the concept "prime," has no form; hence it has never "become." (*c*) Decay and undoing are caused by contradictory elements. But spherical motion excludes contradictory principles, and is without beginning and end. (*d*) Suppose the world had a beginning; then either its creation was necessary—that is, eternal—or its previous existence was impossible (and thus it might not be now); but if it was possible, then possibility (potentiality) presupposes a subject carrying attributes involving the possibility. This subject could not but be eternal.

In the second group there are the arguments (*a*) God could not have been a creator in potentia without suffering change in Himself from potentia to reality. What caused this change? (*b*) The world created in time presupposes some exciting cause for God's will to create. Either God did not previously will to create, or, if He did, He had not the power. The world can not be thought eternal unless we admit defects in God. (*c*) The world is perfect, the product of God's wisdom. God's wisdom and His essence are coincident. God being eternal, His work must also be eternal. (*d*) What did God do before the world was?

How did Jewish thinkers meet these positions? They followed in the paths of the Arab Motekallamin. Especially did they lay emphasis on the proof of free determination," which the Arabic logicians had developed (דרך התיחד, Ar. "al-takhṣiṣ"). Admitting no "law of nature," they posited the principle of limitless possibility. Things are as they are, not because they must be so, but because a free Being outside of them wills them to be so. He might also have willed them to be otherwise. He who determines is also He who creates; that is, produces from nothing. The world is as it is because a Being determined its being, preferring its being to its non-being. Matter dependent for form upon another, even if eternal, can not exist. God is by inherent necessity. The fact that matter is as it is, shows that it was created to be as it is by the preference of the Creator.

In historical succession Saadia was the first to take up the problem, especially in his "Emunot" (i. 1–5). He argues for the creation from the irrationality of an endless limitless quantity—a favorite theme among the Motekallamin. His argumentation is extremely obscure. He enumerates thirteen theories concerning creation; among them, first, the Biblical; then that of the atomists; next the theory of emanation and dualism; finally, that in which the four elements are held to be eternal, a theory which he says had many adherents among the Jews.

Ibn Gabirol devotes a large part of his "Meḳor Ḥayyim" to the problem. He does not rely upon Biblical texts. His creation theory is as follows: The prime substance emanated out of itself Will, or the creative Word. This Will mediates between God and the world. From the Will emanated universal matter (element) יסוד כללי, from which came all beings. His position is a sort of pantheism, not altogether Biblical.

Baḥya ibn Pakuda, in "Ḥobot ha-Lebabot," maintains that (1) nothing is self-created; (2) there must be a highest first cause; (3) composition proves generation or creation.

Judah ha-Levi invokes the testimony of tradition in his "Cuzari" (i. 43–68; see also Maimonides' "Moreh," iii. 50; Abravanel, in his שמים חדשים, p. 34). He pleads for the authenticity of the Mosaic account as being corroborated by tradition; by the facts of human speech, which show the common descent of all men; by the identity of the system for counting time; etc.

Abraham bar Ḥiyya Albargeloni is another defender of creation. His "Sefer Hegyon ha-Nefesh" tries to explain the Biblical tradition on mathematical grounds. "Ὕλη" and "form" had potential existence until God called them into reality through His will in combination. But when we speak of time and the like with reference to God, we use human similes. Time is only a measurer. Therefore before the world was, there was nothing to measure and consequently no time. Ὕλη = "Tohu," and form = "Bohu"; both were preexistent, as the text shows by its use of the expression "the earth had been" (היתה. "Form" = בו הוא).

Maimonides is most timid in his defense of creation. He concedes that it can not be proved. The most that can be attempted is to weaken the arguments of the opposition schools ("Moreh," i. 67, 71; see Gersonides to Gen. i.). He endeavors to disprove the eternity of the world as far as he may, and to strengthen whatever seems to favor the contrary theory ("Moreh," i. 13–30). He makes much of Aristotle's indecision concerning the point at issue. He advances "arguments that approximate demonstrations" (see MAIMONIDES, MOSES). They have contributed nothing to the solution of the perplexity.

Views of Maimonides.

Of his successors, Albalag, Gersonides, and Naḥmanides either reject creation *ex nihilo* or seriously modify it. Ḥasdai Crescas (in "Or Adonai," iii. 1, 4) criticizes most severely Gersonides' assumptions that matter and God are equally absolute; while the former is void of everything, even of form, the latter is highest perfection. Why should equally absolute and necessary matter submit to the will of God? He charges Gersonides with inconsistencies in denying special providence while assuming the power of God over and in the special particulars of arch-matter. His pupil Albo regards the denial of creation *ex nihilo* as tantamount to the denial of God's perfection ("'Iḳḳarim," i. 23).

The Karaites as a rule accept *creatio ex nihilo.* It is one of their articles of faith (see "'Eẓ Ḥayyim," xii.).

Bibliography: Schmiedl, *Studien zur Religionsphilosophie*, Vienna, 1869; J. Guttmann, *Die Scholastik des Dreizehnten Jahrhunderts*, Breslau, 1902; idem, *Das Verhältniss des Thomas von Aquino zum Judentum*, Göttingen, 1891.

——In the Koran and Mohammedan Literature: The Koran does not contain a descriptive and detailed account of the Creation; but it abounds in allusions to God's power as manifested therein, and in appeals to it in refutation of heretical assumptions (Polytheism; sura xvi.), or in support of certain dogmas (Resurrection; *ib.* xxii. 1–7). On the whole, these various references show that Mohammed had a general, vague, hearsay acquaintance with both the Biblical and Talmudical traditions of the Jews. "It is God," according to sura xi. 9, "that created the heavens and the earth in six days." Before creation "His throne [compare כסא הכבוד] was upon the water" (see Gen. i. 2; suras l. 37, lvii. 4). Special emphasis is laid on the forming of the mountains, which are said to give stability to the earth (suras xxi. 22, xxxi. 9, xli. 9, lxxviii. 6). In this a reminiscence of the Biblical זרועות עולם (Deut. xxxiii. 27; compare Ps. xc. 2) is suggested, while the popular conceit of the Arabs has it that the earth, when first created, was smooth and flat, which induced the angels to ask who could stand on so tottering a frame. Thereupon God next morning threw the mountains on it (Sale, "Koran," p. 215, note g, Philadelphia ed., 1876). In the space of four days God distributed nourishment to all that asked (sura xli. 9). The earth and the heavens are said to have been originally a compact mass which God divided, while water is said to be the life-giving element (sura xxi. 9, 31). Things were created after a certain preestablished measure (sura liv. 49; the word "ḳadr" may also be rendered "decree"; but see Baiḍawi, *ad loc.*). "One word" alone brought the world into being "like the twinkling of an eye" (sura liv. 50). As Baiḍawi remarks, this word was "Kun" (Let there be!), though the statement is also explained to imply that God accomplished His work very easily and quickly, without manual labor or assistance (compare sura l. 37, and Talmudic בלא עמל ובלא יגיעה, Ber. R. xii.; see Baiḍawi, *ad loc.*). Nor did He create in sport (compare rabbinical לא לבטלה), but in truth, and for a definite term, to last until the day of final judgment (suras xliv. 35, xlvi. 2; Baiḍawi, *ad loc.*). With scant consistency, however, Mohammed speaks in another passage of a creation not in six but in two days. Baiḍawi (sura xli. 8) interprets "days" as "turns."

In Mohammedan Tradition.

Mas'udi ("Prairies d'Or," ed. Meynard and Courteille, i. 36 *et seq.*) gives in detail the following traditional order: "First water, which carried the divine throne, was created. From this primal water God caused a vapor to arise and form the sky. Then He dried the liquid mass, transforming it into one earth, which He split up later into seven. This earth was completed in two days—Sunday and Monday. The earth was placed on a fish that supported it [sura lxviii. 1; compare Pirḳe R. El. ix., and Ginzberg "Die Haggada bei den Kirchenvätern," p. 19, where it is shown that by this fish is meant the leviathan]. This fish and the earth God propped on blocks of stone, resting on the back of an angel, this again on a rock, and this finally on the wind. But the motions of the fish shook the earth mightily, so God put the mountains in place and rendered it stable. The mountains furnished food for earth's tenants. The trees were created during two days—Tuesday and Wednesday. Then God mounted up to the vaporous sky and made of it one heaven, which, in two more days—Thursday and Friday—He split up into seven. Hence the name for Friday,

'Jum'ah' (joining together), 'union' or 'assembly,' because on it the creation of the heavens was united to that of the earth. Then God filled the heavens with angels, seas, icebergs. Creation thus completed, God peopled the earth with the jinn, made of purest fire [sura lv. 14], among them being Iblis, the Devil. When about to create man (Adam), He informed the angels of His intention to make him His vicegerent on earth. The angels made objections [as in the rabbinical legend, Gen. R. viii.]. Gabriel was sent to bring clay from the earth, but the earth refused to supply it. Michael, also sent on the same errand, was unsuccessful. Finally the angel of death went forth, vowing that he would succeed. He brought back earth of various colors, hence the various colors among men. Adam was made of the surface ["adim"] soil. Forty years a portion of such soil was hung up to become a compact mass, and then left for another period of forty years, until the clay became corrupt. To this God then gave human shape, but left it without a soul for one hundred and twenty years. Finally, after enduring many indignities at the hand of Iblis, and being an object of terror to the angels, and at last causing Iblis' banishment, Adam was endowed with divine breath, according to some gradually; and when he was entirely permeated with this divine breath, he sneezed; whereupon God taught him to say: 'Praise be to God! may thy Master have mercy on thee, O Adam!'"

An altogether different account is found in the "Kitab Aḥwal al-Ḳiyamah," edited by Wolff ("Muhammadanische Eschatologie," Leipsic, 1872). The first object created was a tree with four thousand branches—the tree of knowledge; the second, the light of Mohammed—a pearl in the shape of a peacock, which was placed on the tree. Then God made the mirror of shame, placing it so that the peacock saw his reflected image; whereupon shame seized him and he prostrated himself five times before God. The light of Mohammed, too, blushed before God, and in consequence perspired. From the beads of perspiration taken from various parts of the body were created the angels, the upper and lower thrones of God, the tablet of revelation or of decree, the pen,

Paradise and Gehenna, sun, moon, and stars, the dividing interval between heaven and earth, the Prophets, the Sages, the martyrs, the pious, the celestial and the terrestrial Ka'bah, the Temple in Jerusalem, the places for the mosques, the Moslems—men and women, the souls of the Jews, the Christians, the Magi, and, finally, the earth from east to west, and all that it contains. This apocalyptic account is comparatively late [but echoes rabbinical traditions concerning the light of the Messiah (Gen. R. i.), the כסא הכבוד, Paradise and Gehinnon (Pes. 54a); compare also Slavonic Enoch, xxv.—xxvi.—K.].

BIBLIOGRAPHY: Munk, *Mélanges*, Paris, 1859; Maimonides, *Moreh Nebukim*, ed. Munk, *passim;* Dieterici, *Ichwan Es-safa*, Leipsic, 1896; Steiner, *Die Mutaziliten*, Leipsic, 1865; Houtsma, *De Strijd over het Dogma*, Leyden, 1875.

XII

Crescas

CRESCAS, ḤASDAI BEN ABRAHAM (or **BEN JUDAH**; misreading of חסדאי בן אברהם קרשקש): Religious philosopher; born in Barcelona, Spain, 1340; died 1410. He was of an illustrious and learned family, in "Ḳore ha-Dorot" falsely designated as of the family עמשי (the abbreviation of על משכבם שלום יבוא, found at the end of the genealogy in his own preface to his great work). He was a disciple of the Talmudist and philosopher NISSIM BEN REUBEN (RaN), and, following in the footsteps of both his ancestors and his teacher, he became a Talmudic authority and a philosopher of great originality (Joël, "Don Chasdai Creskas," p. 78, note 2, Breslau, 1866), important in the history of modern thought for his deep influence on SPINOZA. While he did not occupy an official position as rabbi, he seems to have been active as a teacher. Among his fellow students and friends, Isaac ben Sheshet (RIBaSH), famous for his responsa, takes precedence. ALBO is the best known of his pupils, but at least two others have won recognition—R. Mattathias of Saragossa (see "He-Ḥaluẓ," vii. 94), and R. Zechariah ha-Levi, the translator of Al-Ghazzali's "Refutation of the Philosophers" (see Steinschneider, in "Oẓar ha-Neḥmad," ii. 231). Crescas was a man of means. As such he was appointed sole executor of the will of his uncle Vitalis (Ḥayyim) Azday by the King and the Queen of Aragon in 1393 (Jacobs, "Sources of Spanish-Jewish History," pp. 134–137). Still, though enjoying the high esteem even of prominent non-Jews, he did not escape the common fate of his coreligionists. Imprisoned upon a false accusation in 1378, he suffered personal indignities because he was a Jew (Grätz, "Gesch." viii., ch. 4). His only son died in 1391, a martyr for his faith (see Crescas' pathetic words in Wiener's edition of "Shebeṭ Yehudah," Appendix), during the persecutions of that period. Nevertheless he kept his "eyes turned to the Father in heaven." How deep his faith was is shown by the circumstance that, notwithstanding this bereavement, his mental powers were unbroken; for the works that have made him immortal are all posterior to that terrible year. Another episode of his life worthy of note is connected with the appearance of the pseudo-Messiah of Cisneros, one of whose adherents he became. In 1401–02 he visited Joseph Orabuena at Pamplona at the request of the King of Navarre, who paid the expenses of his journey to various Navarrese towns (Jacobs, *l.c.* Nos. 1570, 1574). He was at that time described as "Rab of Saragossa."

Of his writings three have become known: (1) His letter to the congregations of Avignon, published as an appendix to Wiener's edition of "Shebeṭ Yehudah" (see above), in which he relates the incidents of the persecution of 1391. (2) An exposition and refutation of the main doctrines of Christianity. This "tratado" was written in Spanish in 1398. The Spanish original is no longer extant; but a Hebrew translation by Joseph ibn Shem-Ṭob, with the title בטול עקרי הנוצרים ("Refutation of the Cardinal Principles of the Christians"), has been preserved. The work was composed at the solicitation of Spanish noblemen (Grätz, "Gesch." viii. 411, note 2), and this explains the use of the vernacular. Crescas' object in writing what is virtually an apologetic treatise on Judaism was to present the reasons which held the Jews fast to their ancestral faith. He does this in a dispassionate, dignified manner, by contrasting the reasonableness of Jewish doctrines with the unintelligible perplexities of the Christian dogma. Crescas may also have had in mind, while thus defending Judaism, the many apostates who tried to demonstrate the genuineness of their Christian convictions by attacking their native religion. He was a lifelong combatant in the ranks of those who would expose the falsehoods of these apostates.

His main contribution to literature is (3) a work entitled "Or Adonai" (Light of the Lord). In it he develops his philosophy and proves himself master in the realm of thought. He had intended this work for the first part of a complete presentation of the contents of Judaism. It was to be followed by a second, to be known as the "Ner Adonai" (Lamp of the Lord), in which he desired to treat of duties and ceremonies. But this second part was never written. He doubtless had in mind the example of Maimonides. The "Or Adonai," as a philosophical treatment of Jewish dogma, corresponds to Maimonides' "Moreh Nebukim"; the "Ner Adonai" was to have been written on the lines of Maimonides' "Yad ha-Ḥazaḳah."

Crescas' "Or Adonai," notwithstanding its signal merit as the production of an independent and original thinker, met with scant attention. The much less meritorious elaboration of his pupil Albo (the "'Iḳḳarim") found its way into the libraries and minds of innumerable readers, and was republished time and again, though its strong points are mostly purloined from Crescas; but the master and teacher suffered from neglect and even eclipse. (Munk, in his "Mélanges," forgets to mention him.) Only the haggadic commentaries which, always strikingly clear, embroider occasionally the text of his rigid speculations, were frequently quoted in "'En Ya'aḳob," by Jacob ibn Ḥabib, who characterizes them as "sweeter than honey." "Or Adonai" is found in manuscript in almost every extensive Hebrew collection, but the editions have been few and faulty. The first print is that edited at Ferrara in 1556, which edition is disfigured by intolerable carelessness. Other editions are the Johannisberg quarto and the Vienna (1860) octavo. Both have added to the old mistakes a considerable number of new ones (Philipp Bloch, "Die Willensfreiheit von Chasdai Kreskas," pp. ii., iii., Munich, 1879).

The "Or Adonai."

Neither the style of the author nor the inherent difficulties of the subject are sufficient to explain this lack of interest in the work. His vocabulary is precise, and the presentation concise. The book offers no insurmountable difficulties for earnest students. The matter is attractive enough, and not beside the range of the philosophical interests of the Jews. And yet those who read and commentated Maimonides and Albo passed Crescas by. It is the position taken by the author, the boldness with which he strikes at the very roots of the Maimonidean-Aristotelian thesis, that produced this indifference. In this he failed of the sympathy even of such as were glad to honor him as "the Ḥasid" (Joël, *l.c.* p. 2), Characteristic of the attitude and feeling of the more numerous class which idolized Aristotle as represented by Maimonides, are the words of Shem-Ṭob in his commentary to part ii. of the "Moreh Nebukim": "Perverted fool" and "without comprehension" are among the words employed, and he characterizes Ḥasdai's objection to Aristotle as "impudent [הזיות] nonsense" (Joël, *l.c.* p. 2, note 1). In other words, Crescas met the fate always in store for the iconoclast. Among the Arab philosophers Al-Ghazzali's experience is similar.

Object of the Work.

Crescas' avowed purpose was to liberate Judaism from the bondage of Aristotelianism, which, through Maimonides, influenced by Ibn Sina, and Gersonides (Ralbag), influenced by Ibn Roshd (AVERROES) threatened to blur the distinctness of the Jewish faith, reducing the doctrinal contents of Judaism to a surrogate of Aristotelian concepts. Abu-Ḥamid al-Ghazzali wrote the "Tehafat al-Falasifa" (Destruction of the Philosophers; see Munk, "Mélanges," pp. 373 *et seq.*) with a like aim — namely, to defend orthodox belief as far as it was menaced first by the doctrines of the philosophers which teach that matter is eternal and indestructible, that the world is indestructible and permanent, and that God is merely a demiurge, and further by their efforts at demonstrating God's existence, their inability to disprove the possibility of dualism, and their denial of God's attributes.

Crescas makes no concealment of his purpose to vindicate orthodoxy against the liberalism of Maimonides and Gersonides. Of these two the former especially had endeavored to harmonize revelation and faith with philosophy. While, in those instances where this harmony could not be established, Maimonides refused to follow Aristotle to the exclusion of Moses, his successors seemed bent upon the opposite course. For them Aristotle was infallible. His concepts of God's providence, of creation, matter, and immortality were theirs. They had often enough been attacked by orthodoxy, but excommunications and invectives were then, as always, powerless to suppress thought. Crescas met them as a philosopher who recognized the right of philosophical speculation. He did not agree with those Christian and Mohammedan theologians who in their speculations were advocates of a twofold truth—one for the theologian and the other for the philosopher, the former not cognizable by natural man, because supernatural and irrational, the latter open to the intelligence of natural man (compare Isaac ALBALAG's מצד העיון, "philosophical," as opposed to מצד האמונה, "theological").

Well versed in philosophical literature, Crescas then proceeds to show that Aristotle is far from infallible. He is, as the Jewish anti-Aristotelian, of one intention with Giordano Bruno, and the precursor of Spinoza. He deplores that Maimonides, whose scholarship and honesty he admires, should have made of the fragile theses of Greek philosophy props for Jewish doctrine, saying that the example proved pernicious for his imitators. He believes it is high time to probe the proofs of "the Greek [Aristotle] who darkens the eyes of Israel in these days." This is his task. After having shown the untenability of the Aristotelian propositions, he would "establish the roots and the cornerstones upon which the Torah [= Jewish religion] is propped, and the pivots upon which it turns" (Preface). He does not denounce heretics, but exposes the weakness of the ground on which rest what he considers to be heterodox views. He desires to set forth the contents of Judaism and the limitations in respect to them of the scope of philosophy.

His book comprises four main divisions ("ma'-amar"), subdivided into "kelalim" and chapters ("peraḳim"): the first treating of the foundation of all belief—the existence of God; the second, of the fundamental doctrines of the faith; the third, of other doctrines which, though not fundamental, are binding on every adherent of Judaism; the fourth, of doctrines which, though traditional, are without obligatory character, and which are open to philosophical construction.

The first main division opens with a thorough criticism of the twenty-five (twenty-six) Aristotelian propositions ("haḳdamot") which Maimonides accepts as axiomatic, and out of which he constructs his idea of God. In the first section he presents all the demonstrations for these theorems, especially those adduced by Tabrizi; in the second, he shows the inadequacy of these ontological and physical propositions, and thus demolishes Maimonides' proofs for his God-concept. Crescas, admitting that the existence of a first cause is susceptible of

The First Cause.

philosophic proof, but only by contingence (he rejects the Aristotelian assumption that an endless chain of causes is unthinkable; *i.e.*, the first cause of all that is must be regarded as existent), holds philosophy to be incompetent to prove God's absolute unity, as does Ghazzali. The first cause may be philosophically construed to be simple, for if it were composite another would have to be assumed for the compounding. Still, this would not necessitate the positing of God's unity. Other deities might with other functions still be in existence, even if our God were thought to be omnipotent. Therefore revelation alone is competent to establish God's unity. Without the "Shema' Yisraael," philosophy fails to be a trusty guide. He introduces a new element into his God-idea. His predecessors contended that God's highest happiness—the divine essence, in fact—was His knowledge. He rejects this as inadequate, and posits instead God's love, always intent upon communicating itself and doing good. He argues against Maimonides for the admissibility of divine attributes. From the human subjective point of view, attributes may appear to posit differences in God; but this does not mean that they do so in God objectively. In Him, in the Absolutely Good, they merge as identical unity; predicates, especially of only logical or conceptual significance, are incompetent to cause real multiplicity or composition.

In the second division he enumerates those six fundamental doctrines as presupposed by revealed faith, without which Judaism would fall: God's omniscience, providence, and omnipotence; the belief in prophecy, freedom of the will, and that the world was created for a purpose. God's omniscience embraces all the innumerable individual beings; He has knowledge of what is as yet not in existence; He knows what of all possibilities will happen, though thereby the nature of the possible is not altered. God's knowledge is different from that of man: inferences from one to the other are not valid. (Here he sides with Maimonides against Gersonides.) God's providence embraces directly and indirectly all species and individuals. It rewards and punishes, especially in the hereafter. Crescas rejects the theories of Maimonides and Gersonides on this point. Love, not knowledge (intellectual), is the bond between God and man. From God's love proceeds only what is good, and punishment is also inherently good. God's omnipotence is not merely infinite in time, but also in intensity. Revelation, and it alone ("creatio ex nihilo"), makes it clear. Natural law is no limitation for God, but whatever is irrational proves neither God's omnipotence nor His lack of power; that is, God acts reasonably. Prophecy is the highest degree of human mentality. Maimonides makes it dependent upon certain conditions. While Crescas admits this, he differs from Maimonides in that he will not admit the refusal of the prophetic gift when these conditions are fulfilled. Connection and communion with God are not brought about by knowledge, but by love and reverence, leading us to Him if we keep His commandments. Very extensive is his presentation of the freedom of the will. He inclines toward its rejection; at all events, to its limitation. The law of causality is so all-pervasive that human conduct can not withdraw itself from its operations. Moreover, God's omniscience anticipates our resolutions. But the Torah teaches the freedom of choice and presupposes our self-determination. Thus he concludes that the human will is free in certain respects, but determined in others. Will operates as a free agent when considered alone, but when regarded in relation to the remote cause, it acts by necessity; or, will operates in freedom, both per se and in regard to the provoking cause, but is bound if analyzed with reference to the divine omniscience. Man feels himself free; therefore he is responsible and must be rewarded or punished. The accompanying sentiment (readiness or disinclination to act) makes the deed our own.

In the sixth section of this division, Crescas displays characteristic originality. Maimonides rejected as futile and unwarranted all inquiry into the ultimate purpose of the world. Crescas posits such an ultimate purpose and assumes it to be the happiness of the soul. In this life the soul is intently striving after union with the divine; the laws of the Torah help to realize this, the soul's, never quiescent yearning. After death, the soul will enter upon greater possibilities of love, in the higher existence. Former thinkers made immortality depend on knowledge. This is contrary to the teachings of religion, and also utterly unreasonable. Love brings about the soul's happiness of eternal duration in the hereafter and the communion with God thereupon ensuing. "The soul is the form and essence of man, a subtle spiritual substance, capacitated for knowledge, but in its substance not yet cognizant." By this definition he establishes the soul's independence of knowledge. Knowledge does not produce the soul. Man's highest perfection is not attained through knowledge, but principally through love, the tendency to, and longing for, the fountainhead of all good. Man's last purpose, his highest good, is love, manifested in obedience to God's laws. God's highest purpose is to make man participate in the eternal bliss to come.

The Purpose of the World.

The third main division devotes much attention to the theories concerning CREATION. Whatever theory, however, be accepted, the belief in miracles and revelation is not affected. Religious tradition is so preponderatingly in favor of the assumption that the world and matter are created, and Gersonides' counter-reasoning is so inconclusive, that Crescas regards the denial of creation as heterodox. Immortality, punishment, reward, resurrection (a miracle, but not irrational), the irrevocability and eternal obligation of the Law, the belief in urim and thummim and Messianic redemption, are the other tenets treated as doctrines which should be accepted, but which are not, strictly speaking, basic.

In the fourth division thirteen opinions are enumerated as open to speculative decision, among them the questions concerning the dissolution of the world. (Crescas holds the earth will pass away while the heavens will endure.) Have there been other worlds besides our own? Are the heavenly bodies endowed with soul and reason? Have amulets and incantations any significance? What are the "Shedim"? What about metempsychosis?

An opponent of Maimonides on philosophical grounds, Crescas was also dissatisfied with the method of the "Mishneh Torah," for reasons often adduced by others as well; namely, the absence of indications of the sources, the rare mention of divergent opinions, and the lack of provision to meet new cases, owing to its neglect to establish general principles of universal application ("Or Adonai," Preface).

If among Jews he exercised for a long time only through Albo any perceptible influence, though he was studied, for instance, by Abravanel, who controverts especially his Messianic theories, and by Abram Shalom in his "Neveh Shalom," Crescas' work was of prime and fundamental importance through the part it had in the shaping of Spinoza's system. Spinoza's distinction between attributes and properties is identical with Crescas' distinction between attributes subjectively ascribed and their objective reality in God. The connection between Spinoza's views on creation and free will, on love of God and of others, and those of Crescas has been established by Joël in his "Zur Genesis der Lehre Spinoza's" (Breslau, 1871).

BIBLIOGRAPHY: Joël, *Zur Genesis der Lehre Spinoza's*, Breslau, 1871; Philipp Bloch, *Die Jüdische Religionsphilosophie*, in Winter and Wünsche, *Jüdische Litteratur*, Trier, 1894; idem, *Die Willensfreiheit von Chasdai Kreskas*, Munich, 1879; Grätz, *Gesch.* viii. ch. 4; Hamburger, *R. B. T.* Supplement, iii. 5, 6; Schmiedel, *Jüdische Religionsphilosophie*, Vienna, 1869; Bernfeld, *Da'at Elohim*, pp. 465, 476; P. J. Müller, *Die Godsleer der Joeden*, Groningen, 1898.

XIII

Crucifixion

CRUCIFIXION: The act of putting to death by nailing or binding to a cross. Among the modes of CAPITAL PUNISHMENT known to the Jewish penal law, crucifixion is not found; the "hanging" of criminals "on a tree," mentioned in Deut. xxi. 22, was resorted to in New Testament times only after lapidation (Sanh. vi. 4; Sifre, ii. 221, ed. Friedmann, Vienna, 1864). A Jewish court could not have passed a sentence of death by crucifixion without violating the Jewish law. The Roman penal code recognized this cruel penalty from remote times (Aurelius Victor Cæsar, 41). It may have developed out of the primitive custom of "hanging" ("arbori suspendere") on the "arbor infelix," which was dedicated to the gods of the nether world. Seneca ("Epistola," 101) still calls the cross "infelix lignum." Trees were often used for crucifying convicts (Tertullian, "Apologia," viii. 16). Originally only slaves were crucified; hence "death on the cross" and "supplicium servile" were used indiscriminately (Tacitus, "Historia," iv. 3, 11). Later, provincial freedmen of obscure station ("humiles") were added to the class liable to this sentence. Roman citizens were exempt under all circumstances (Cicero, "Verr." i. 7; iii. 2, 24, 26; iv. 10 *et seq.*). The following crimes entailed this penalty: piracy, highway robbery, assassination, forgery, false testimony, mutiny, high treason, rebellion (see Pauly-Wissowa, "Real-Encyc." *s.v.* "Crux"; Josephus, "B. J." v. 11, § 1). Soldiers that deserted to the enemy and slaves who denounced their masters ("delatio domini") were also punished by death on the cross.

Mode of Execution.

The crosses used were of different shapes. Some were in the form of a **T**, others in that of a St. Andrew's cross, **X**, while others again were in four parts, ✝. The more common kind consisted of a stake ("palus") firmly embedded in the ground ("crucem figere") before the condemned arrived at the place of execution (Cicero, "Verr." v. 12; Josephus, "B. J." vii. 6, § 4) and a cross-beam ("patibulum"), bearing the "titulus"—the inscription naming the crime (Matt. xxvii. 37; Luke xxiii. 38; Suetonius, "Cal." 38). It was this cross-beam, not the heavy stake, which the condemned was compelled to carry to the scene of execution (Plutarch, "De Sera Num. Vind." 9; Matt. *ib.*; John xix. 17; see Cross). The cross was not very high, and the sentenced man could without difficulty be drawn up with ropes ("in crucem tollere, agere, dare, ferre"). His hands and feet were fastened with nails to the cross-beam and stake (Tertullian, "Adv. Judæos," 10; Seneca, "Vita Beata," 19); though it has been held that, as in Egypt, the hands and feet were merely bound with ropes (see Winer, "B. R." i. 678). The execution was always preceded by flagellation (Livy, xxxiv. 26; Josephus, "B. J." ii. 14, § 9; v. 11, § 1); and on his way to his doom, led through the most populous streets, the delinquent was exposed to insult and injury. Upon arrival at the stake, his clothes were removed, and the execution took place. Death was probably caused by starvation or exhaustion, the cramped position of the body causing fearful tortures, and ultimately gradual paralysis. Whether a foot-rest was provided is open to doubt; but usually the body was placed astride a board ("sedile"). The agony lasted at least twelve hours, in some cases as long as three days. To hasten death the legs were broken, and this was considered an act of clemency (Cicero, "Phil." xiii. 27). The body remained on the cross, food for birds of prey until it rotted, or was cast before wild beasts. Special permission to remove the body was occasionally granted. Officers (carnifex and triumviri) and soldiers were in charge.

This cruel way of carrying into effect the sentence of death was introduced into Palestine by the Romans. Josephus brands the first crucifixion as an act of unusual cruelty ("Ant." xiii. 14, § 2), and as illegal. But many Jews underwent this extreme penalty (*ib.* xx. 6, § 2; "Vita," § 75; "B. J." ii. 12, § 6; 14, § 9; v. 11, § 1; Philo, ii. 529).

During the times of unrest which preceded the rise in open rebellion against Rome (about 30–66 B.C.), "rebels" met with short shrift at the hands of the oppressor. They were crucified as traitors. The sons of Judas the Galilean were among those who suffered this fate.

The details given in the New Testament accounts (Matt. xxvii. and parallels) of the crucifixion of Jesus agree on the whole with the procedure in vogue under Roman law. Two modifications are worthy of note: (1) In order to make him insensible to pain, a drink (ὄξος, Matt. xxvii. 34, 48; John xix. 29) was given him. This was in accordance with the humane Jewish provision (see Maimonides, "Yad," Sanh. xiii. 2; Sanh. 43a). The beverage was a mixture of myrrh (קורט של לבונה) and wine, given "so that the delinquent might lose clear consciousness through the ensuing intoxication." (2) Jesus' legs were broken to shorten his agony, and his body was removed and buried, the latter act in keeping with Jewish law and custom. These exceptions, however, exhaust the incidents in the crucifixion of Jesus that might point to a participation therein, and a regulation thereof, by Jews or Jewish law. The mode and manner of Jesus' death undoubtedly point to Roman customs and laws as the directive power.

From the Jewish point of view, the crime of which Jesus was convicted by the Jewish priests is greatly in doubt (see Jesus). If it was blasphemy, lapidation should, according to Jewish law, have been the penalty, with suspension from the gallows after death (Mishnah Sanh. iii. 4; Sifre, iii. 221). Nor were any of the well-known measures taken (Sanh. vi.) which provide before execution for the contingency of a reversal of the sentence. Neither was the "cross"—*i.e.*, the gallows for hanging—constructed as usual after lapidation, and as ordained in Sanhedrin vi. 4. His hands were not bound as prescribed; the "cross" was not buried with his body (Maimonides, "Yad," Sanh. xv. 9). Whether the Jewish law would have tolerated a threefold execution at one and the same time is more than uncertain (Sanh. vi. 4; Sifre, ii. 221).

The greatest difficulty from the point of view of the Jewish penal procedure is presented by the day and time of the execution. According to the Gospels, Jesus died on Friday, the eve of Sabbath. Yet on that day, in view of the approach of the Sabbath (or holiday), executions lasting until late in the afternoon were almost impossible (Sifre, ii. 221; Sanh. 35b; Mekilta to Wayaḳhel). The Synoptics do not agree with John on the date of the month. According to the latter he died on the 14th of Nisan, as though he were the paschal lamb; but executions were certainly not regular on the eve of a Jewish holiday. According to the Synoptics, the date of his death was the 15th of Nisan (first day of Passover), when again no execution could be held (Mishnah Sanh. iv. 1; and the commentaries; Yer. Sanh. ii. 3; Yer. Beẓ. v. 2; Ket. i. 1). This discrepancy has given rise to various attempts at rectification. That by Chwolson is the most ingenious, assuming that Jesus died on the 14th, and accounting for the error in Matthew by a mistranslation from the original Hebrew in Matt. xxvi. 17 (קרב וקרבו, due to the omission of the first קרב; see his "Das Letzte Passamahl Christi," p. 13). But even so, the whole artificial construction of the law regarding Passover when the 15th of Nisan was on Saturday, attempted by Chwolson, would not remove the difficulty of an execution occurring on Friday = eve of Sabbath and eve of holiday; and the body could not have been removed as late as the ninth hour (3 P.M.). Bodies of delinquents were not buried in private graves (Sanh. vi. 5), while that of Jesus was buried in a sepulcher belonging to Joseph of Arimathea. Besides this, penal jurisdiction had been taken from the Sanhedrin in capital cases "forty years before the fall of the Temple."

Date of Jesus' Crucifixion.

These facts show that the crucifixion of Jesus was an act of the Roman government. That it was customary to liberate one sentenced to death on account of the holiday season is not corroborated by Jewish sources. But many of the Jews suspected of Messianic ambitions had been nailed to the cross by Rome. The Messiah, "king of the Jews," was a rebel in the estimation of Rome, and rebels were crucified (Suetonius, "Vespas." 4; "Claudius," xxv.; Josephus, "Ant." xx. 5, § 1; 8, § 6; Acts v. 36, 37). The inscription on the cross of Jesus reveals the crime for which, according to Roman law, Jesus expired. He was a rebel. Tacitus ("Annales," 54, 59) reports therefore without comment the fact that Jesus was crucified. For Romans no amplification was necessary. Pontius Pilate's part in the tragedy as told in the Gospels is that of a wretched coward; but this does not agree with his character as recorded elsewhere (see Schürer, "Gesch." Index, *s.v.*). The other incidents in the New Testament report—the rending of the curtain, darkness (eclipse of the sun), the rising of the dead from their graves—are apocalyptic embellishments derived from Jewish Messianic eschatology. The so-called writs for the execution (see Mayer, "Die Rechte der Israeliten, Athener, und Römer," iii. 428, note 27) are spurious.

BIBLIOGRAPHY: Ludwig Philipson, *Haben die Juden Jesum Gekreuzigt?* 2d ed., reprint, 1902; Hirsch, *The Crucifixion from the Jewish Point of View*, Chicago, 1892; Chwolson, *Das Letzte Passamahl Christi*, St. Petersburg, 1892; works of Jewish historians, as Grätz, Jost, etc.; Schürer, *Gesch.*; commentaries on the Gospels.

XIV

Cruelty

CRUELTY: The disposition to inflict pain and to gloat over suffering. Widely prevalent among, if not characteristic of, savages and barbarians, it has influenced their treatment of strangers, enemies, and evildoers. Primitive races, however, are strongly inured to pain, being early in life trained to endure it unflinchingly, as the various initiatory rites at puberty in universal vogue among them show (see Heinrich Schurtz, "Altersklassen und Männerbunde," pp. 92 *et seq.*, Berlin, 1902). Moreover, lack of imagination incapacitates them for measuring the suffering entailed on others (Tylor, "Anthropology," p. 408, New York, 1897). Again, among them, as also among civilized nations of antiquity, religious notions sanctify the passion for revenge, nearly always an element of cruelty. Abel's "blood cries to heaven" (Gen. iv. 10, Hebr.). The deity itself is injured and offended, and the land is defiled by bloodshed (see Schneider, "Die Naturvölker," 1886, i. 86; Leopold Schmidt, "Die Ethik der Alten Griechen," ii. 309 *et seq.*, Berlin, 1882; Tiele, "Verglijkende Geschiedenis von de Egypt. en Mesopotam. Godsdienster," p. 160; "Tr. Soc. Bibl. Arch." viii. 12 *et seq.*).

The "lex talionis," universally observed by savage and semi-civilized peoples, illustrates this principle. Injury had to be requited by corresponding injury. "Eye for eye, tooth for tooth, hand for hand" (Ex. xxi. 24). Literally construed at first, the provisions of this law in course of time, and with the refinement of feeling accompanying progressing civilization, were translated into pecuniary assessments in compensation of injuries.

"Lex Talionis."

Cruel practises connected with the observances of religion, such as mutilations, the cutting of gashes (see CUTTINGS), the burning of children to propitiate Moloch, and human sacrifice generally, rest originally upon a similar idea.

The ancient Hebrews in their primitive state were in disposition little different from their neighbors and cognates. In the period of "ignorance" the pre-Mohammedan Arabs deemed "revenge to be the twin brother of gratitude," and not to visit an offense upon the offender was considered cowardly and ignoble (see Goldziher, "Muhammedanische Studien," 1889, i. 15 *et seq.*). The books of Judges and Samuel prove that the Israelitish invaders of Canaan displayed in their dealings with their enemies the temper of their day. The bodies of those slain in battle were stripped of everything valuable. Occasionally their heads were cut off as trophies (I Sam. xvii. 51, 54; xxxi. 9; II Sam. xx. 22). Among the Assyrians this was the rule (compare II Kings x. 6 *et seq.*). In later times, however, decent burial was accorded to dead enemies (Ezek. xxxix. 11), or they were cremated (Isa. xxx. 33).

Captives were shown little leniency. To mark them as conquered, they were subjected to the humiliation of being trodden under foot (Joshua x. 24; compare Ps. cx. 1). This was also the custom among the Assyrians and Egyptians. Still, excessive cruelties are only reported in cases where fury had been aroused by the length of the pursuit (Judges i. 6 *et seq.*). The most atrocious instance of cruelty in requital of previous insult is afforded, if the text is correct, by David's dealing with the Ammonites (see Klostermann's commentary on II Sam. xii. 31). Amaziah is reported to have hurled ten thousand captive Edomites from a rock (II Chron. xxv. 12). As a rule, however, the Hebrews did not go to such extremes, and, compared with the Assyrians, were merciful. The latter impaled their prisoners, or flayed them alive, or tore out their tongues (see, for the case of the Elamite prisoners, Koyundjik Collection, slabs 48–50; Kaulen, "Assyrien und Babylonien," 5th ed., p. 265). The Philistines put out Samson's eyes (Judges xvi. 21). Nahash, the king of the Ammonites, threatened the Jebusites with

Treatment of Captives.

the blinding of their right eyes (I Sam. xi. 2). King Zedekiah was blinded by the Chaldeans (II Kings xxv. 7). Among the Chaldeans and Persians, and even now in Eastern countries, this procedure is not exceptional. Ezek. xxiii. 25 alludes to the cutting off of the noses and ears of captives. Rings were put through the under lips of captured kings to fasten the chain to (חחים, "S. B. O. T." Ezekiel, p. 133). Atrocious barbarities against women big with child are mentioned as having occurred in the ferocious civil wars of the Northern Kingdom (II Kings xv. 16), but these, as well as the dashing to pieces of children, seem to have been common among Syrians, Ammonites, Assyrians, and Chaldeans (II Kings viii. 12; Amos i. 13; Ps. cxxxvii. 9 *et seq.*). If not killed, the captives were led away "naked" (see COAT) and fettered, to be sold into slavery (Num. xxxi. 26; Deut. xx. 14; Isa. xx. 4).

The country of the enemy was devastated; its trees were cut down, its wells wrecked, its cities and hamlets sacked and razed; tribute was levied and hostages demanded (II Kings iii. 19, 25; xiv. 14).

In the earlier civil code of the Hebrews, the "book of the Covenant" (Ex. xxi.–xxiv.), the law of retaliation is still fundamental. Mutilations were thus legalized. The Deuteronomic legislation applies this principle in the case of false witnesses (Deut. xix. 16 *et seq.*). A woman guilty of a certain indecent act lost her hand (Deut. xxv. 11 *et seq.*). Similar and severer provisions are also found in the recently discovered code of Hammurabi (see Winckler, "Die Gesetze Hammurabi," Leipsic, 1902); and the punishments provided by the laws of other ancient and modern Oriental nations show still greater cruelty. Adulterous women had their noses cut off, while the co-respondent was condemned to a thousand stripes (Diodorus Siculus, i. 78). The statement of Josephus ("Vita," §§ 33, 34) that rebels and traitors suffered the loss of one or both hands reflects the ferocity of the civil war.

Stages of Progress.

The primitive severity of the earlier practise, however, was tempered by clemency. This appears clearly in the provisions for carrying out the punishment of stripes. The number of stripes must not exceed forty (Deut. xxv. 1–4; in Hammurabi's code the maximum is fixed at fifty), and they must be administered before a proper court officer. As also among the Egyptians (see Wilkinson, "Ancient Egypt," ii. 41 *et seq.*), the stripes were applied to the back of the delinquent, not, as is the cruel Eastern practise, to the soles of the feet. The instrument employed was in early times a rod or switch (Prov. x. 13). The later rabbinical authorities prescribe the use of a plaited leather strap, construing "biḳoret," in Lev. xix. 20, to indicate this (see Gesenius, "Th." i. 234), and limit the number of stripes to thirty-nine (Mak. iii. 10; Josephus, "Ant." iv. 8, § 21). The use of "scorpions" ("'aḳrabim"), mentioned in I Kings xii. 11, 14; II Chron. x. 11, 14, was, as the context shows, regarded as excessively cruel, and must have been rare. They were pointed and knotty rods, or whips with sharp iron points (Gesenius, *l.c.* ii. 1062). Beating with bags filled with sand and pointed pieces of iron was another method of punishment (Ephraem Syrus). The Syrians seem to have had recourse to similar instruments of torture (II Macc. vii. 1). Later, the Romans adopted the use of whips weighted with rough, heavy stones, or lead balls (Cicero, "Cluent." 63). Thorny rods or switches were also occasionally used (Judges viii. 7, 16; compare Prov. xxvi. 3).

Treatment of Slaves.

Other indications of the gradual refinement of feeling are revealed in the fact that the slave ultimately acquired a right to protection against bodily injury, and that the master who caused his death by cruel beating was punished (Ex. xxi. 21, 26–27). If, however, death was not immediate, the owner was considered to have injured his own property. Philo regards the provision which grants freedom to the maimed slave as based less upon the principle of compensation than upon the desire to protect the slave against further insult, the master naturally finding a constant cause of irritation in the slave incapacitated for full work in consequence of his rash or cruel treatment The law also modified to a considerable extent the rights of vengeance and Asylum (Ex. xxi. 13, 14), and provided for the protection of those guilty of manslaughter.

With what abhorrence the Prophets viewed the atrocities committed in the spirit of the savage in earlier times is clear from the opening chapters of Amos. They denounced the cruel rites—mutilations, human sacrifices—sanctioned by the religion of Canaan, and modified barbarity through the potent leaven of mercy and humanity. As a punishment the invasion of a "cruel" people is announced, and the detailed description shows that the Jewish people had outgrown the temper which regarded such atrocities as natural (Jer. vi. 23, 24; Deut. xxxii. 32, 33).

In the later books cruelty is expanded to include unfriendly and unnatural conduct (Prov. xi. 17) on the part of one from whom, by reason of friendship or consanguinity, consideration is to be expected (Job xxx. 21). As symptoms of cruelty, anger and jealousy are enumerated (Prov. xxvii. 4).

Attitude of Later Judaism.

Later Judaism, in interpreting the Mosaic legislation, proceeded upon the theory that any unnatural act was cruel. The seething of the kid in the milk of its mother, the wearing of wool and linen together, the yoking of ox and ass together, the sowing of different seeds in one field, were so regarded (Philo, "De Specialibus Legibus"). Humanity, therefore, was declared to be the sister of piety, and was inculcated in many injunctions of the Mosaic code; it is befitting the king (*idem*, "De Vita Moysis," ii. 1, 2); it is to be shown to strangers as readily and fully as to fellow countrymen; it is due to the demented and to dumb creatures (*idem*, "De Caritate"). The "lex talionis" was modified (Mek., Mishpaṭim, 8). Capital punishment was virtually abolished in all cases where malice prepense was not established beyond all doubt.

Judges who pronounced the death sentence too frequently were stigmatized as shedders of blood (Mak. 7a), and this in spite of the conviction that "misapplied clemency leads to unjustifiable cruelty" (Lam. R. vii. 16). And when the sentence of death was carried into effect tender regard was extended to the body of the executed (Sanh. v. 3; Babli 55b). Decapitation by the sword was for this reason declared to be an indignity (ניוול, B. B. 8b). Needless exposure of the body was looked upon with the same disfavor; a woman undergoing lapidation was not uncovered (Yer. Soṭah iii. 19b, end). This consideration was shown the dead in all cases, the view prevailing that until the body is inhumed, or, according to others, until decomposition sets in, the soul hovering over the abandoned frame feels whatever insult or injury is offered (see BODY IN JEWISH THEOLOGY). R. Akiba inhibited exhumation as an act of cruelty (B. B. 154a).

Philo ("In Flaccum") gives a vivid account of the outrages perpetrated by the Romans upon the living as well as upon the dead. Some cruelties commonly practised by the Romans seem never to have been known to the Hebrews. The exposure of children, and the burying alive of undesired daughters, common among pre-Mohammedan Arabs, were quite unknown to the Hebrews.

In rabbinical Judaism the idea of "cruelty" includes also an unforgiving temper. It thus came to signify what has been termed "the cruelty of civilized men" (Lazarus, "Ethik des Judentums," i. 308), such as calumny, slander, putting to shame, calling men by nicknames, slighting their honor. Characteristic of the one not cruel was the readiness to "forego one's due" (מעביר על מדותיו), and this disposition is deemed essential to the attainment of forgiveness of one's own sins (Yoma 23a). One that in public puts a man to shame is likened to the murderer (B. M. 58b, 59a). One that will not forgive his fellow is cruel: מנין שאם לא מחל שהוא אכזרי (B. Ḳ. 92a; see also Maimonides, "Yad," De'ot, vi. 6; Teshubah, ii. 10). Nimrod, Goliath, Haman, Cain, and others are remembered as examples of cruelty (Pesiḳ. ix. 78b). Tax-gatherers are typically cruel, as also among the Mohammedans (B. Ḳ. x. 1–2; Goldziher, *ib.* i. 19, note; Philo, "De Specialibus Legibus"; see PUBLICANS). Prophetic and rabbinical Judaism, in thus enlarging the scope of "cruelty" to embrace not merely the infliction of physical, but also of mental and moral suffering, and in denouncing a haughty, heartless, unforgiving, grasping disposition as "cruel," has discarded utterly the principle of retaliation. The Deuteronomic laws (Deut. xx. 7; Josh. vi. 21) concerning the annihilation of the seven aboriginal nations of the land, if they were ever carried out to the letter, were written in the spirit of holy warfare against idolatry (see BAN) at a time when cruel temper was universally prevalent.

Later Judaism condemns cruelty in whatever form. Its abhorrence of barbarity is illustrated also by the prohibition against cutting out a piece of flesh from a living animal (אבר מן החי), which mutilation was a well-established practise among the Romans and many other ancient peoples (Ḥul. 101b *et seq.*). This prohibition does not rest upon ritual grounds, but is based on moral repugnance; the Noachides are also under this prohibition. The "pound of flesh" in Shakespeare's "Merchant of Venice" is an impossibility according to Jewish law, though the Roman Law of the Twelve Tables legalizes such security. The whole "Shylock" story originated in old Aryan mythology.

That evil-doers were not treated without cruelty is apparent from the frequent allusions in the Biblical books to the terrors and sufferings incidental to imprisonment (II Sam. iii. 34; Job. xiii. 27; Ps. lxxxviii. 7, cv. 18, cvii. 10; Isa. xxiv. 22; Zech. ix. 11). Though prisons existed (Jer. xxxvii. 15, 20), abandoned cisterns filled with mire were used for the detention of men that had incurred the displeasure of the mighty (Jer. xxxviii. 6). Ill fed (I Kings xx. 27), the prisoners were often bound with chains and ropes (Job xxxvi. 8; Ps. cxlix. 8); the feet especially were fastened together with brass (Judges xvi. 21; II Sam. iii. 34; Jer. lii. 11) or iron links (Ps. cv. 18; Prov. vii. 22). Often the feet were put into the stocks or blocks ("sad," Job xiii. 27, xxxiii. 11), while in other cases a veritable instrument of torture was used, the "mahpeket," a wooden contrivance so arranged as to force the body into unnatural contortions. The neck, too, was constrained by a ring ("ẓinoḳ") or iron collar (Jer. xx. 2; Sirach vi. 30).

The Romans, however, were past-masters in the art of applying these various expedients. Under the non-Hebrew designation קולר, the Latin "collare," the rabbinical books recall a neck-ring largely in use to render prisoners helpless (Eḥa Rabb. Proem. xxxiv.). Characteristic in this connection as showing the dread of the inhumanities of non-Jewish tormentors is the prohibition (Tosef., 'Ab. Zarah, ii. 4) "not to sell them either weapons or these devices for restraining prisoners"; *i.e.*, קולרין (ed. Zuckermann wrongly, כבלין (קוללין; סדין and שלשלאות של ברזל (iron chains).

XV

Darkness

DARKNESS: The rendering in the English versions of the Hebrew חשך and its synonyms אפל, אפלה, ערפל, צלמות. At one time darkness was regarded as something substantial, and not merely as the absence of light. This is apparent from the frequent juxtaposition of "darkness" with "light." God forms light and darkness (Isa. xlv. 7); light and darkness are consumed or confined (Job xxvi. 10). In the Creation-story, darkness is said to have been over primitive chaos, Abyss. In this opening sentence traces or reminiscences of an early mythological personification have been detected (see Cosmogony). Darkness antedates creation. It has also been noticed that it is not called good, as are the other works of the Creator. The absence of the definite article before חשך in Gen. i. 1 points in the same direction.

Something of this mythological notion is present in Job's imprecation (Job iii. 4, 5), where both "Ḥoshek" and "Ẓalmut" (or "Ẓalmawet") are invoked as though ravenous monsters lying in wait for prey (the verb recalls the blood-avenger, the "goel"). They are in parallelism with a phrase—"Let all that maketh black the day" [R. V.]—which is now recognized by nearly all commentators to describe mythological beasts (see Dragon). In ordinary speech, of course, the Hebrew mind did not revert to this personification of darkness and its underlying antecedent mythological conceits. Darkness is simply the night, as light is the day (Gen. i. 5, 18). The sun grows dark; the day is darkened; and the like. In mines and other subterranean regions darkness has its realm, which the searcher for the precious metals invades, and thus forces upon it the establishment of new boundaries (Job xxviii. 3). This impression of substantiality goes with the descriptions of Egyptian darkness (Ps. cv. 28; Ex. x. 23). Darkness is also likened to a pillar of cloud (Ex. xiv. 20), as something almost palpable, if not personal. It is a frequent circumstance of theophany (II Sam. xxii. 12 = Ps. xviii. 12); and is associated with "She'ol" in such a way as to make it plausible that this place of the ingathering of the shades was a domain ruled over by twin demons, Ḥoshek and Ẓalmut (darkness and thick darkness). The double form, masculine and feminine, "ḥoshek" and "ḥashekah," also goes back to mythology.

In figurative speech, for reasons that are apparent, darkness was used for a secret hiding-place (Isa. xlv. 3; Job xxxiv. 22; Ps. cxxxix. 11, 12). As the effect of sorrow is to dim the eyes by tears, or as grief or sin injects darkness into the world (compare 'Ab. Zarah 8a), the Hebrew speaks of distress as darkness (Isa. v. 30, xxix. 18; Ps. cvii. 10–14, again "Ḥoshek" and "Ẓalmut").

Darkness is uncanny. It may be the hiding-place of evil spirits; this, at all events, was the notion in post-Biblical times (compare Demonology); therefore darkness expresses fear, dread, terror. As such it is one of the equipments of the Day of the Lord, a circumstance of judgment (Amos v. 18, 20; Zeph. i. 15; Nahum i. 8). This eschatological idea underlies also the darkness which ensues upon the Crucifixion (Matt. xxvii. 45). According to the theory advanced by Gunkel ("Schöpfung und Chaos"), that in eschatological visions primitive mythology finds its expression, the underlying idea is that darkness is an attendant on final judgment or punishment (Matt. viii. 12, xxii. 13, and frequently in N. T.).

Darkness is also the emblem of mysterious afflictions, of ignorance and frailty (Job xix. 8, xxiii. 17; Isa. ix. 2), of sin and evil (Isa. v. 20; Prov. ii. 13), of mourning (Isa. xlvii. 5), of doubt and vexation (Job v. 14, xii. 25), and of confusion (Ps. xxxv. 5). As wisdom is light, so ignorance is darkness (Job xxxvii. 19; Eccl. ii. 14).

Darkness was the ninth of the ten Egyptian plagues (Ex. x. 21 *et seq.*). What caused the darkness has been a subject of much unsatisfactory discussion. Some reminiscence based upon observation of natural phenomena is always involved in the other plagues. What the reminiscence is in this case has not been determined; a storm of dust has been suggested by some commentators.

XVI

Day Of The Lord

DAY OF THE LORD (יום ה׳): An essential factor in the prophetic doctrine of divine judgment at the end of time (see ESCHATOLOGY), generally, though not always, involving both punishment and blessing. It is identical with "that day" (היום ההוא· Isa. xvii. 7, xxx. 23, xxxviii. 5; Hos. ii. 18; Micah ii. 4, v. 10; Zech. ix. 16; xiv. 4, 6, 9), "those days" (Joel iii.1), "that time" (העת ההיא: Jer. xxxi. 1, R. V.; xxx. 25, Hebr.; Zeph. iii. 19, 20), or simply "the day" (Ezek. vii. 10), or "the time." On the supposition that Genesis reflects the nation's earliest hopes—denied by the critical schools—the promises given to the Patriarchs of ultimate blessings upon Israel and, through Israel, upon mankind (Gen. xii. 2, 3; xvii. 2, 4, 5, 6; xxvi. 3, 4; xxvii. 29; xxxii. 12), may be taken for the primitive germ of the idea. The original conception was probably that of the day on which YHWH manifests Himself as the wielder of thunder and lightning, as the devastator who shatters the powers opposing Him; and this was in historical times transformed into the day when He would smite Israel's foes (compare Isa. xiii. 6; Ezek. xxx. 3). But in the eighth century B.C. Amos is found sounding a decided warning against his people's expectation that simply because they are YHWH's people the "day of YHWH" will bring requitement on Israel's enemies alone. It will be an occasion of visiting wrong-doing both within and without Israel. "I will cause the sun to go down at noon, and I will darken the earth in the clear day" (Amos v. 18; viii. 9).

In Amos the punitive aspect of "the day" is dominant; ix. 8–15 is held to be exilic by most modern commentators; but see Driver, "Joel and Amos," pp. 119–123 (Amos iii. 2, v. 18, viii. 9). The day is "darkness and not light" (v. 18). Amos' contemporary Hosea does not use the phrase, but he expresses the idea of a judgment to come along lines identical with those found in Amos (Hosea x. 8, xiii. 16). Isaiah, too, strikes in the main the note of gloom. Israel and Judah both feel the weight of divine wrath provoked by their unrighteousness (Isa. i. 10–17, 21–26; ii. 19–21; iii. 1–15; v. 8–24). But this will show YHWH's power. He will be exalted (ii. 11–17). The judgment cometh suddenly with earthquakes and thunder and tempest and whirlwind and the flame of a devouring fire (xxix. 6). Still through this terrible process, like the purifying of silver, the nation will be restored on a basis of righteousness (i. 24–26). Isaiah's horizon is national. The foreign nations, too, will be judged, but only in relation to Israel. The kingdom is Israel's alone (this is on the theory that the Messianic passages, except Isa. i. 24–26, are of a later age; see Cheyne, Duhm, Hackmann, G. A. Smith, and others; Hastings, "Dict. Bible," ii. 488). Micah, too, emphasizes the doom of Jerusalem as *the* feature of the end-time (iii. 12).

In the latter half of the seventh century B.C. (Nahum, Habakkuk, and Zephaniah) the idea that "that day" will see the punishment of wicked Assyria in behalf of righteous Israel finds expression. This view thus contains a new ethical element; it is not, as formerly in the popular conception (see above), the *natural* relation of Israel and YHWH that brings wrath upon Israel's enemies, but it is because Israel is righteous (צדיק), and Assyria, or non-Israel, is wicked (רשע; Hab. i. 4, 13). Judgment and consequent destruction fall on the "Gentiles," not on Israel. There is here the first intimation of a world-judgment in connection with "the day," an aspect that becomes thenceforth more and more prominently emphasized. Zephaniah, indeed, puts it strongly, but with the significant addition that a righteous remnant of Israel will survive the day ("judgment" on Jerusalem—i. 8–13; on Philistia, Ethiopia, Assyria—ii. 1–6; "on the nations"—iii. 8;

on the earth's inhabitants—i. 2, 3). The day of YHWH is a day of trouble, distress, and desolation; of supernatural terrors and of darkness and thick darkness (i. 14–18). The assembled nations are destroyed by YHWH's anger (iii. 8). The enemies of Israel who are to be punished are, in Zephaniah's conception, no longer definite peoples, as they were for Isaiah (see above); they are the גויים generally, and the instruments of God's punitive power are a mysterious if not mythical people—the "invited guests" of YHWH (קראיו, i. 7).

During the Exile.

In the Exile the conception underwent further amplifications. Judgment is held to deal with individuals. As a result a righteous congregation (not nation) was to emerge to form the nucleus of the Messianic kingdom. This kingdom was to have its prelude in the day of YHWH, meting out individual retribution (Jer. i. 11–16; xxiii. 7, 8; xxiv. 5, 6; xxv. 15–24, 27–33; xxxvi. 6–10), which will lead to change of heart (xxiv. 7; compare xxxii. 39); a new heart and a new covenant (xxxi. 33, 34). The blessings of the new conditions will be participated in by the nations (iii. 17; xii. 14, 15; xvi. 19). Only the impenitent will be destroyed (xii. 16, 17).

Ezekiel's vision enlarges on details. A universal uprising of the nations under GOG is one of the incidents (compare Ezek. xxxviii., xxxix.; Zeph. i. 7). With this the climax in the development of the idea of the day of YHWH seems to have been reached. Henceforth the thought of judgment (= day of YHWH) disappears almost entirely, and is succeeded by a universal Messianic kingdom, preceded not by a day of wrath, but by the missionary zeal of righteous Israel and the spontaneous conversion of the nations (see MESSIAH).

After the Exile.

Of the post-exilic prophets only Malachi lays great stress on the element of judgment. The Temple is central to his religious construction. To it YHWH will come suddenly, but a messenger will prepare for His coming for judgment. Before that "great and dreadful day" ELIJAH will "turn the heart of the fathers to the children, and the heart of the children to their fathers" (Mal. iv. 23, 24 [A. V. 5, 6]). This judgment (in Hag. ii. 21–23, it is destructive for the nations) is only on Israel (*ib.* ii. 17; Mal. iii. 3, 5, 13 *et seq.*). The day "burns as a furnace"; it destroys "all the proud and the workers of iniquity."

In apocalyptic writings, however, the day of YHWH reappears. Joel (400 B.C.) reverts to it. The valley of Jehoshaphat is the place of judgment. The nations are gathered, judged, and annihilated (Joel iii. 1, 2, 12). YHWH is Israel's defender (iii. 2). Israel is justified, but it is Israel purified (ii. 25–27, 28, 29; iii. 16, 17). Before "the day" all Israel is filled with the spirit of God (ii. 28, 29). Nature announces its approach (ii. 30, 31). As in Joel, so in all apocalyptic visions the idea is prominent that the day of YHWH (= of judgment) marks evil's culmination, but that Israel and the righteous will be supernaturally helped in their greatest need. Faintly foreshadowed in Ezekiel, this thought is reproduced in various ways, until in Daniel (vii. 9, 11, 12, 21, 22; xii. 1) it finds typical expression, and is a dominant factor in Jewish apocalyptic writings and Talmudic eschatology.

BIBLIOGRAPHY: The commentaries to the prophetical passages quoted; R. H. Charles, *A Critical History of the Doctrine of a Future Life*, London, 1899; Smith, *The Day of the Lord*, in *American Journal of Theology*, 1900.

XVII

Decalogue In Jewish Theology

DECALOGUE, THE, IN JEWISH THEOLOGY: The Ten Words are designated by Philo as κεφαλαῖα νόμων = "the heads of the law," the title of the chapter "De Decem Oraculis." The second table Philo, contrary to the usual order, begins with the commandment against adultery, describing adultery as the greatest of all violations of the Law, since it corrupts three houses—that of the adulterer, that of the wronged husband, and that of the adulterer's wife. The fourth commandment refers to all festivals, and, according to Philo, embraces all the laws conducive to the spread of kindness and gentleness and fellowship and the feeling of equality among men (with reference to Sabbatical year and the jubilee). Under the fifth commandment he ranges all laws in regard to family life, the honor due to old people, the duties of the old to the young, the ruler to his subjects, the benefactor to the needy, the master to his servants, etc.

Philo's exposition of the preeminence and original character of the Decalogue, both in its general tenor and in many of its particular details, reflects the teachings of the Mishnaic period, as indeed it also anticipates some of the positions of later Rabbis. The fact that the recital of the Ten Words constituted a salient feature of the daily liturgy in the morning service (Tamid v. 1; Ber. 3c) indicates that they were regarded as the essential parts of divine revelation. This practise was discontinued as a protest against the unwarranted inference drawn therefrom by sectaries that the Decalogue alone had been revealed by God on Sinai (Ber. 11a). The Shema' ("Hear, O Israel," Deut. vi. 4) and the selections from Deut. vi. 4–9, xi. 13–22; Num. xv. 37 *et seq.*, which follow the Shema' in the order of the liturgy, and form as it were a part thereof, were believed to contain in essence the Decalogue.

The new Pesiḳta (Bet Ham. vi. 41; comp. Bacher, "Die Agada der Palästin. Amoräer," ii. 183) holds the reading of the Shema' every morning as tantamount to the keeping of the Ten Commandments, because they, too, had been proclaimed "in the morning" (Ex. xix. 16). Again, Sifre to Deut. i. 3 controverts the assumption that the Decalogue alone had been revealed through Moses. Like the Shema', Num. xix., looked upon by R. Ḥiyya as fundamental, is construed by R. Levi as a cryptogram of the Decalogue (see DIDACHE).

According to Hananiah, the son of Joshua's brother, the Decalogue contains all the laws of the Torah (Yer. Sheḳ. 46d, bottom; Soṭah 22d; Cant. Rabbah to v. 14), his words, "parashiyyoteha we-diḳduḳeha shel Torah," recalling Philo's view that the Decalogue contains the capital, the rest of the Pentateuch the special, laws. Berechiah is credited with a similar opinion (Bacher, *l.c.* iii. 356). The Decalogue is compared with a rare jewel of ten pearls (Exod. R. xliv.; Tan. [Ki] Tissa, end). The Patriarchs had been loyal to the principles of the Decalogue long before they had been revealed to Moses. (Attention is called to Yalḳ. Shim'oni, i. 276, end.) The universality of the Decalogue is accentuated by the fact of its being offered in turn to all the nations (Deut. xxxiii. 2, 3; Hab. iii. 3; Ta'an. 25a; 'Ab. Zarah 2a) in the desert territory ("hefḳer") which belonged to none exclusively (Mek., Yitro, 1). and of its proclamation in all the (seventy) languages of the world (Shab. 88b).

The first and second commandments are rated as preeminent (Sifre to Num. xv. 31), both on account of their doctrine and also because they alone, as is indicated by the use of the first person singular, were spoken to the people by God Himself (Macc. 24a; Sanh. 99a; Hor. 8a; compare Geiger, "Jüd. Zeit." iv. 113 *et seq.*). On the other hand, the tenth commandment is also held fundamentally to include the others; at least its violation amounted to transgressing the seven "nots" (לאוין) of the Decalogue (Pesiḳ. R. 22). As the tenth forbids the coveting of a neighbor's wife, the foregoing statement of its scope agrees with the similar valuation placed upon the seventh (against adultery: Tan., Naso). Adultery is a violation of the first commandment, according to Jer. v. 7, 8, 12; of the second, according to Num. v. 14 (וקנא = Ex. xx. 5); of the third, because adultery is denied, as is generally the case, with an oath; of the fifth, inasmuch as the child of such a union can not honor its parents; of the sixth, because adulterers are always prepared to kill if caught in the act; of the seventh, which directly forbids adultery; of the eighth, as the adulterer is virtually a thief (see Prov. ix. 17); of the ninth, because the adulteress gives false testimony against her husband; of the tenth, in that the adulterer makes his son another man's heir. In regard to the fourth (concerning the Sabbath), the eventuality is assumed that the issue of an adulterous intimacy between a non-priest and a woman of the priestly caste might become a priest. The arrangement of the two tables whereby one is opposite six indicates that murder includes the denial of God (Mek. to Ex. xx. 17). The last six commandments are also regarded as the basis of all morality (Tosef., Shebu. iii. 6).

The Seventh Commandment.

As a statue is seen by a thousand, and its eye covers them all, so, R. Levi says, every single person heard the words as though personally addressed (Pesiḳ. 110a; Tan., ed. Buber, to Yitro 17; compare Pesiḳ. xxi., where Jochanan is credited with this simile, while Levi points to one sound heard by many). The fact that the versions of Ex. and Deut. present textual discrepancies was explained by the theory that both were divinely given בדיבור אחד, in one act of divine speech (Sheb. 20b; R. H. 27a; Mek. xx. 8; Sifre, Deut. xxii. 11), which "would be impossible for men," and "which the human ear could not hear"; but, according to Ps. lxii. 12, the one speech of God was apprehended as two by men. In fact, the Ten Words were all proclaimed at once ("bedibbur eḥad," Mek. xx. 1). The first set of tables did not contain, in the fifth, the words "that it may be well with thee," because they were predestined to be broken (B. Ḳ. 55a). Interesting is the report that R. Ḥiyya was ignorant of this difference between Deut. and Ex. (B. Ḳ. 54b).

The Decalogue often appears as a subject of controversy with non-Jews, a circumstance which goes far to demonstrate the fundamental value attached to it (see Pesiḳ. R. xxiii.). One such controversy is with Hadrian (Pesiḳ. R. xxi.). The subjects discussed are such as why is circumcision not in the Decalogue? (Pesiḳ. R. xxiii.; Tan. to Lek Leka, Agad. Bereshit xvii.); or why does not the Torah begin with the Decalogue? (Mek. to xx. 2). The "Ten Words" are even a "pleader" for Israel (Pesiḳ. R. xi.; Midr. Teh. to Ps. xvii. 4).

How the Ten Words were distributed between the tables is also a subject of rabbinical inquiry. The prevailing opinion is that there were five on each; but it has also been maintained that each had the whole ten (see Decalogue; Yer. Sheḳ. 49d; Yer. Soṭah 22d; Cant. Rabbah v. 14; Mek. xx. 27): even twice—once on each side (Yer. Sheḳ. vi. 1). Simai argues that the Ten Words were inscribed on each table four times (*τετράγωνον*; *ib.*).

Tables of the Law.

The dimensions of the tables furnish a fruitful subject for exegetical ingenuity. The objection that they were too heavy for one man to carry (raised even by modern Bible critics) is met by ascribing to the letters engraved thereon miraculous powers. They virtually carried the tables; only when they began to fly away did Moses feel the weight of the stones (Yer. Ta'an. iv.; Tan., Ki Teẓe *et al.*). The first set given with pomp attracted the "evil eye," and hence were broken (Tan., Ki Teẓe). According to some, Moses was ordered by God to break the tables, and received God's thanks for the act (Ab. R. N. ii.: see note of Schechter on the passage; Yalḳ. 363, 640). According to another version, when Moses noticed that the script began to fly off, he became alarmed and threw the tables down, whereupon he was struck dumb (Yalḳ., Ki Teẓe). By the use of "anoki" ("I am," an Egyptian word: Pesiḳ. R. xxi.), which God had employed in His conversations with Abraham, Isaac, and Jacob (Gen. xv. 1, xxvi. 24, xxxi. 13), He convinced the people that it was the God of their fathers who spoke to them (Tan., ed. Buber, to Yitro 16).

In post-Talmudic literature and liturgy the Decalogue is also expounded and expanded as the fountainhead whence all other laws flow. Shebu'ot being the day of the revelation (Shab. 86a), this idea was prominently utilized in the piyyuṭim and Azharot for the holiday. Saadia adopts the numeration of the letters of the Decalogue given in Num. Rabbah xviii. as 613, a number likewise fixed by Naḥshon Gaon ('Aruk, under תפל). Eliezer ben Nathan has the same number in the "Ma'arib" for Pentecost, Eleazar b. Judah the same in the "Sefer ha-Ḥayyim." In reality, the Decalogue contains 620 letters, the mnemotechnic word for which is כתר ("crown": "the CROWN of the Law"), which number, according to its expounders, corresponds to the 613 COMMANDMENTS, one for each letter, the seven others, auxiliary vowel-consonants, indicating the seven Noachian commandments (see beginning of "Bet" in the "Sha'ar ha-Otiyyot").

Many "poetic" elaborations of the Decalogue are in existence, but the plan was also carried out by writers on legal matters (Zunz, "Literaturgesch." p. 95; Steinschneider, "Hebr. Bibl." vi. 125). The philosophical writers of the tenth to thirteenth centuries occasionally emphasized the fundamental nature of the Decalogue. Judah ha-Levi, in his "Cuzari" (ii. 28), remarks: "The root of knowledge was placed in the Ark, which is like the innermost chamber of the heart, and this [root] was the Ten Words and their derivatives; that is, the Torah." BAḤYA BEN JOSEPH, in his "Ḥobot ha-Lebabot," gate i., urges the importance of the Decalogue, and connecting therewith the Shema', construes the latter as laying down ten main principles corresponding to the Ten Words. ALBO, in his "'Iḳkarim" (iii. 26), develops in extenso the idea of the Decalogue's fundamentality, calling attention to the difference between the "words" on the first table as theological, and those on the second as ethical, both together covering the whole field of religion. Of Bible commentators following on the same line may be mentioned Rashi to Ex. xxiv. 12: "The first word of the Decalogue is the fountainhead of all."

The Decalogue Fundamental.

Naḥmanides makes the first one of the mandatory commands ("miẓwot 'aseh"). The whole people heard all ten, but understood only commandments one and two as perfectly and thoroughly as Moses. From three on, however, they did not comprehend, and therefore Moses was forced to explain them. Maimonides, desirous of removing all anthropomorphic conceptions, reiterates Philo's idea, that it was not God's voice that was heard, but an impersonal voice created especially for the enunciation of the Decalogue ("Moreh," i. 65; compare Saadia, "Emunot we-De'ot," ii. 8; "Cuzari," i. 89). The writing on the tables was also a "creation" ("Moreh," i. 66). The Karaites entertain the same view (see Japhet Abu-Ali on Ex. xx.; Munk, "Guide," i. 290, note 2; Aaron ben Elia, "Eẓ Ḥayyim," ch. 55, 98). On the effect of the second Commandment see ART.

The third commandment, interpreted to prohibit swearing, led, in unconscious appreciation of its original meaning—a caution against pronouncing divine names or imparting them to persons other than the properly initiated—to a reverent avoidance of the mention of the Shem ha-Meforash (Soṭah 38a; Sifre to Num. vi. 27, and elsewhere), and to extreme caution even in writing not to expose "the Name" to disrespect or thoughtless disregard.

Many of the modern catechisms have summarized both the doctrines and the duties of Judaism to correspond with the ten ideas of the Decalogue:

(1) The unity and personality of God.

(2) His incorporeality.

(3) Against profanation of the Name.

(4) Sabbath and festivals; cruelty to animals; slavery.

(5) Family relations.

(6) Rights and duties of life.

(7) Marriage and chastity.

(8) Rights and duties of property; interest and usury; begging.

(9) Duties to the state.

(10) Covetousness; other personal virtues and vices. For modern expansions of the Decalogue see Gerson Lasch ("Die Göttlichen Gesetze," 1857). In Dr. Samuel Hirsch's "Catechismus" the third commandment is made the basis of the discussion of prayer, inasmuch as prayers expressive of wishes and hopes no longer entertained violate the commandment. Isaac M. Wise, among modern Reform rabbis, declared the Decalogue to be "the Torah," which alone was divinely revealed. According to him, Reform Judaism has in the Decalogue its legal basis, and finds in it its limitations (see "Hebrew Review," i., Cincinnati, 1880; Isaac M. Wise, "The Law").

XVIII

Deism

DEISM: A system of belief which posits God's existence as the cause of all things, and admits His perfection, but rejects Divine revelation and government, proclaiming the all-sufficiency of natural laws. The Socinians, as opposed to the doctrine of the Trinity, were designated as deists (F. Lichtenberger, "Encyclopédie des Sciences Réligieuses," iii. 637). In the seventeenth and eighteenth centuries deism became synonymous with "natural religion," and deist with "freethinker."

Deism in England.

England and France have been successively the strongholds of deism. Lord Herbert, the "father of deism" in England, assumes certain "innate ideas," which establish five religious truths: (1) that God is; (2) that it is man's duty to worship Him; (3) that worship consists in virtue and piety; (4) that man must repent of sin and abandon his evil ways; (5) that divine retribution either in this or in the next life is certain. He holds that all positive religions are either allegorical and poetic interpretations of nature or deliberately organized impositions of priests. Hobbes (d. 1679) may be mentioned next (see Lange, "Gesch. des Materialismus," i. 245; F. Toennies, "Hobbes," in "Klassiker der Philosophie," Stuttgart, 1896). John Locke (d. 1704; see Jodl, "Gesch. der Ethik," i. 149 *et seq.*), in "The Reasonableness of Christianity as Delivered in the Scriptures" (1695), declares that "the moral part of the law of Moses is identical with natural or rational law." John Toland (d. 1722), the forerunner of the modern criticism of the N. T., in "Christianity Not

Mysterious" (1696), says: "Revelation is no reason for assuming the truth of any fact or doctrine; it is a means of information." Anthony Collins (d. 1729), author of "Discourse on Freethinking" (1713) and "Discourses on the Grounds and Reasons of the Christian Religion" (1724), asserts that "Christianity is mystical Judaism." He applies the comparative method, and utilizes the Mishnah to show the affinity of N. T. theological allegorizing to that of the Rabbis. Tindal (d. 1733), in "The Gospel a Republication of the Religion of Nature" (1730), avers that "Revelation, both Jewish and Christian, is only a repetition of the *lex naturæ.*"

In France, Voltaire, Diderot, and, above all, Rousseau, were exponents of deism, on the whole illustrating the intellectual moralism of the school. In Germany it is the "Aufklärungsphilosophie" that to a certain extent is under the influence of the deistic theses, and as Moses MENDELSSOHN is one of the prophets of the "Aufklärung," deism may be said through him to have had a part in the shaping of modern Jewish thought. Reason and common sense are, according to Mendelssohn, identical ("Werke," ii. 265, 283, 315). Religion is, according to him, natural and eminently practical. To "do," not to "believe," is the chief care of the religious man. Natural theology is as accurately certain as mathematics. That God is, is a fact, not a belief. Mendelssohn parts company with deism by modifying the doctrine of divine retribution. According to him, happiness and the doing of right are coincidental. The virtuous man is happy. However, Mendelssohn is not consistent throughout, as he admits repeatedly that, without the assumption of immortality, morality can not stand, nor can God's Providence be established (Phædon). Revelation for him is not necessary to religion; but the national law of Judaism, which is not natural, had to be revealed ("Schriften," iii. 311–319, 348–356; v. 669, Leipsic, 1843).

Mendelssohn's Deism.

The Mendelssohnian arguments left their imprint on the Jewish theology of the nineteenth century (see L. Löw, in "Ben Chananja," i.). His "deistic" moralism on the one hand, and his "national legalism" on the other, have not been without influence on the theories of the Reform rabbis (see HOLDHEIM, SAMUEL), which differentiated the moral—that is, the universal and eternal—injunctions and principles of the Law from the national and temporal; while the distinction made between moral and ceremonial laws (see CEREMONIES), though recognized by Saadia and others, received a new emphasis through Mendelssohn's views. The relations of deism to Judaism, however, have not been made the subject of systematic inquiry, though non-Jewish controversial writers have often argued that Judaism, positing a transcendental God, virtually stood for deism. This contention must be allowed if deism connotes anti-Trinitarianism. Judaism has always been rigorously Unitarian. Deism, as the denial of original sin and the soteriology built thereon, also harmonizes with Jewish doctrine. But the doctrine of deism which relegates God, after creation, to the passive rôle of a disinterested spectator, is antipodal to the teachings of Judaism. God directs the course of history and man's fate (Ex. xix. 4, xx. 2; Deut. xxxii. 11, 12; xxxiii. 29; Ps. xxxiii. 13, cxlv. 16; Jer. xxxii. 9). God neither slumbers nor sleeps. He is Israel's guardian (Ps. cxxi.). Nations may plot and rage, but God's decrees come to pass (Ps. ii.).

The question as to what God has been occupied with since the creation is the subject of rabbinical speculations (Lev. R. iii., viii.; Gen. R. lxviii.; Pesiḳ. 11b; compare Midr. Sam. v.; Tan., ed. Buber, Bemidbar, xviii.; Tan., ed. Buber, Maṭṭot, end; Tan., Ki Teẓe, beginning). God presides over the births of men (Nid. 31a; Lev. R. xiv.; Tan., Tazria'). He takes care that the race shall not die out (Pes. 43b; Pesiḳ. R. xv.). Even the instinctive actions of animals are caused by God, and so is He the power and will behind the acts of terrestrial governments (Eccl. R. x. 11). None wounds a finger without God's will (Ḥul. 7b). God sends the wind that the farmer may have wherewith to live (Pesiḳ. 69a; Lev. R. xxviii.; Eccl. R. i. 3; Pesiḳ. R. xviii.). God assigns the fate of the nations and of individuals (R. H. i. 2). Man's life is in the hand of God (Lam. R. iii. 39). Not alone the creation of the world, but also its preservation (Gen. R. xiii.; Eccl. R. i. 7, iii. 11; Gen. R. ix.; Midr. Teh. to Ps. ix.), as well as the destiny of man and man-

Talmud and Midrash.

kind, is subject to God's constant guidance. In fact, creation was never considered finished (Ḥag. 12a). As the daily morning prayer has it: "[God] createth a new creation every day, everlastingly" (compare Reḳanati, "Ta'ame ha-Miẓwot," p. 37, and "Aḳedat Yiẓḥaḳ," gate iv.). Albo ("'Iḳḳarim," iii. 26) calls attention to the distinctive element of the Jewish God-conception which associates Him not merely, "as some philosophers do," with the creation, but also with the direction of the world after creation.

These ideas of God's government are expressed in the Jewish prayer-books (especially for Rosh ha-Shanah), and are in one way or another put forth by the philosophers. The question how God's government is compatible with human freedom has kept the Jewish thinkers on the alert; but, whatever their answer, none disputes God's supremacy and government (Saadia, "Emunot we-De'ot," iv.). Ibn Gabirol assumes that God's direction is carried into effect through "mediating forces." Judah ha-Levi's discussion of the names of the Deity (Elohim and YHWH) proves his antideistic convictions. "Ehyeh asher ehyeh" indicates God's constant presence in Israel and His help ("Cuzari," iv. 1, ii. 7). Maimonides' discussion of Providence ("Moreh," iii. 17) is also antideistic, though largely influenced by the pseudo-Aristotelian doctrine that Providence does not extend to the care of individuals.

Deism posits the moral freedom of man, his predisposition to virtue: so does Judaism (Ber. 33b). "All is in the hands of God save the fear of God" is the Talmudical formula for a doctrine resting on Biblical teachings, and accepted by Jewish theology. Judaism is theistic, not deistic.

XIX

Dualism

DUALISM: The system in theology which explains the existence of evil by assuming two coeternal principles—one good, the other evil. This dualism is the chief characteristic of the religion of Zoroaster, which assigns all that is good to Ahuramazda (Ormuzd), and all that is evil to Angromainyush (Ahriman; see ZOROASTRIANISM). Against this dualism, which may have some basic elements in Chaldean mythology, the seer of the Exile protests when accentuating the doctrine that the Lord "formed the light and created darkness," that He "is the Maker of peace and the Creator of evil" (Isa. xlv. 7). The verse has found a place in the daily liturgy (see LITURGY), but with the change of the word "ra'" (evil) into "ha-kol" (all), prompted by an aversion to having "evil" directly associated with the name of God (see Ber. 11b; compare Num. R. xi. 16). The same idea occurs in Lam. (iii. 38, Hebr.): "Out of the mouth of the Most High cometh there not evil and good?" No less emphatic are the Rabbis in their opposition to the dualistic views of Parseeism when they teach that both death and the evil desire ("yeẓer ha-ra'") are agencies working for the good (Gen. R. ix.; compare Sanh. 39a, 91b; Shab. 77b; Maimonides' preface to Mishnah commentary; see SIN).

Zeller ("Gesch. der Philosophie," 2d ed., iii. 250) mistakenly ascribes dualistic notions to the Essenes (Hilgenfeld, "Ketzergesch. des Urchristenthums," 1884, p. 109; see ESSENES). On the contrary, Philo ("Quod Omnis Probus Liber," § 12) says that according to them "God only produces what is good, and nothing that is evil." They beheld in life only certain contrasts—opposing tendencies of purity and impurity, of good and evil—and, following ancient Chaldean traditions, placed the one to the right (toward the light) and the other to the left (toward the night) (Josephus, "B. J." ii. 8, § 9; "Clementine Homilies," ii. 15, 33; xix. 12; "Recognitiones," iii. 24)—views which are found also among the Gnostics and the Cabalists (see JEW. ENCYC. iii. 458, *s.v.* CABALA). Of course, the tendency toward evil was found by them, as well as by Philo, in matter—the things of the senses—in contradistinction to the spiritual world (Zeller, *l.c.* p. 348; see PHILO); but this does not contradict the belief in God as Creator of the visible world. There were, however, Gnostics who would ascribe the creation of the visible world to the demiurge ("artificer"), an inferior god mentioned in Plato's "Timæus" (§ 29); and this doctrine of "two powers" (שתי רשויות), frequently alluded to in Talmud and Midrash (Ḥag. 15a; Gen. R. i.; Eccl. R. ii. 12; see ELISHA BEN ABUYAH), actually led its followers to the dualistic view ascribing evil to the inferior god. Thus dualism became the chief doctrine, on the one hand, of the Manicheans, a sect founded on Zoroastrianism, and, on the other hand, of the anti-Judean Christian Gnostics, who opposed the Old Testament as recording the dispensation of an inferior god, the author of evil (Hilgenfeld, *l.c.* pp. 192, 209, 332, 383, 526; see GNOSTICISM; GOD; MANICHEANS).

Among Jewish philosophers Saadia ("Emunot we-De'ot," ii.) takes especial pains to demonstrate the untenability of dualistic definitions of the Godhead. Were there two creators, it must be assumed that only with the help of the other could each create, and that therefore neither is omnipotent. Light and darkness do not prove the contrary, for darkness is only a negation of light (see SAADIA). In the Maimonidean system the difficulty of reconciling the existence of evil with God's unity is solved by the assumption that evil is only negative ("Moreh," iii. 8).

K.—E. G. H.

XX

Ethics

ETHICS (ἦθος = "habit," "character"): The science of morals, or of human duty; the systematic presentation of the fundamental principles of human conduct and of the obligations and duties deducible therefrom. It includes, therefore, also the exposition of the virtues and their opposites which characterize human conduct in proportion to the extent to which man is under the consecration of the sense of obligation to realize the fundamental concepts of right conduct. Ethics may be divided into general, or theoretical, and particular, or applied. Theoretical ethics deals with the principles, aims, and ideas regulating, and the virtues characterizing, conduct—the nature, origin, and development of conscience, as attending and judging human action. Applied ethics presents a scheme of action applicable to the various relations of human life and labor, and sets forth what the rights and duties are which are involved in these relations. Ethics may also be treated descriptively; this method includes a historical examination, based upon data collected by observation, of the actual conduct, individual or collective, of man, and is thus distinct from ethics as dynamic and normative, as demanding compliance with a certain standard resulting from certain fundamental principles and ultimate aims. Philosophical ethics embraces the systematic development of ethical theory and practise out of a preceding construction (materialistic or idealistic) of life and its meaning (optimistic or pessimistic). Religious ethics finds the principles and aims of life in the teachings of religion, and proceeds to develop therefrom the demands and duties which the devotee of religion must fulfil.

Jewish ethics is based on the fundamental concepts and teachings of Judaism. These are contained, though not in systematized formulas, in Jewish literature. As it is the concern of Jewish theology to collect the data scattered throughout this vast literature, and construe therefrom the underlying system of belief and thought, so it is that of Jewish ethics to extract from the life of the Jews and the literature of Judaism the principles recognized as obligatory and actually regulating the conduct of the adherents of Judaism, as well as the ultimate aims apprehended by the consciousness of the Jew as the ideal and destiny set before man and humanity (see Lazarus, "Die Ethik des Judenthums," pp. 9 *et seq.*). This entails resort to both methods, the descriptive and the dynamic. Jewish ethics shows how the Jew has acted, as well as how he ought to act, under the consecration of the principles and precepts of his religion. Jewish ethics may be divided into (1) Biblical, (2) Apocryphal, (3) rabbinical, (4) philosophical, (5) modern; under the last will be discussed the concordant, or discordant, relation of Jewish ethics to ethical doctrine as derived from the theories advanced by the various modern philosophical schools.

——**Biblical Data:** The books forming the canon are the sources whence information concerning the ethics of Bible times may be drawn. These writings, covering a period of many centuries, reflect a rich variety of conditions and beliefs, ranging from the culture and cult of rude nomadic shepherd tribes to the refinement of life and law of a sedentary urban population, from primitive clan henotheism to the ethical monotheism of the Prophets. The writings further represent two distinct types, the sacerdotal theocracy of the Priestly Code and the universalism of the Wisdom series—perhaps also the apocalyptic Messianism of eschatological visions. It would thus seem an unwarranted assumption to treat the ethics of the Bible as a unit, as flowing from one dominant principle and flowering in the recognition of certain definite lines of conduct and obligation. Instead of one system of ethics, many would have to be recognized and expounded in the light of the documents; for instance, one under the obsession of distinctively tribal conceptions, according to which insult and injury entail the obligation to take revenge (Gen. iv. 23, 24; Judges xix.–xx.), and which does not acknowledge the right of hospitality (Gen. xix.; Judges xix.); another under the domination of national ambitions (Num. xxxi. 2 *et seq.*), with a decidedly non-humane tinge (Deut. xx. 13, 14, 16, 17). But it must be remembered that the ultimate outcome of this evolution was ethical monotheism, and that under the ideas involved in it Biblical literature was finally canonized, many books being worked over in accordance with the later religious conviction, so that only a few fragmentary indications remain of former ethical concepts, which were at variance with those sprung from a nobler and purer apprehension of Israel's relation to its God and His nature.

The critical school, in thus conceding that the canon was collected when ethical monotheism had obliterated all previous religious conceptions, is virtually at one, so far as the evidential character of the books concerning the final ethical positions of the Bible comes into play, with the traditional school, according to which the monotheism of the Bible is due to divine revelation, from which the various phases of popular polytheism are wilful backslidings. It is therefore permissible in the presentation of Biblical ethics to neglect the indications of anterior divergences, while treating it as a unit, regardless of the questions when and whether its ideal was fully realized in actuality. The treatment is more difficult on account of the character of the Biblical writings. They are not systematic treatises. The material which they contain must often be recast, and principles must be deduced from the context that are not explicitly stated in the text.

With these cautions and qualifications kept in view, it is safe to hold that the principle underlying the ethical concepts of the Bible and from which the positive duties and virtues are derived is the unity and holiness of God, in whose image man was created, and as whose priest-people among the nations Israel was appointed. A life exponential of the divine in the human is the "summum bonum," the purpose of purposes, according to the ethical doctrine of the Biblical books. This life is a possibility and an obligation involved in the humanity of every man. For every man is created in the image of God (Gen. i. 26). By virtue of this, man is appointed ruler over all that is on earth (Gen. i. 28). But man is free to choose whether he will or will not live so as to fulfil these obligations. From the stories in Genesis it is apparent that the Bible does in no way regard morality as contingent upon an antecedent and authoritative proclamation of the divine will and law. The "moral law" rests on the nature of man as God's likeness, and is expressive thereof. It is therefore autonomous, not heteronomous. From this concept of human life flows and follows necessarily its ethical quality as being under obligation to fulfil the divine intention which is in reality its own intention. Enoch, Noah, Abraham, and other heroes of tradition, representing generations that lived before the Sinaitic revelation of the Law, are conceived of as leading a virtuous life; while, on the other hand, Cain's murder and Sodom's vices illustrate the thought that righteousness and its reverse are not wilful creations and distinctions of a divinely proclaimed will, but are inherent in human nature. But Israel, being the people with whom God had made His covenant because of the Patriarchs who loved Him and were accordingly loved by Him—having no other claim to exceptional distinction than this—is under the obligation to be *the* people of God (עם סגלה, Ex. xix. 5 *et seq.*) that is to illustrate and carry out in all the relations of human life, individual and social, the implications of man's godlikeness. Hence, for Israel the aim and end, the "summum bonum," both in its individuals and as a whole, is "to be holy." Israel is a holy people (Ex. xix. 6; Deut. xiv. 2, 21; xxvi. 19; xxviii. 9), for "God is holy" (Lev. xix. 2, *et al.*). Thus the moral law corresponds to Israel's own historic intention, expressing what Israel knows to be its own innermost destiny and duty.

Autonomous in Sanction.

Israel and God are two factors of one equation. The divine law results from Israel's own divinity. It is only in the seeming, and not in the real, that this law is of extraneous origin. It is the necessary complement of Israel's own historical identity.

God is the Lawgiver because He is the only ruler of Israel and its Judge and Helper (Isa. xxxiii. 22). Israel true to itself can not be untrue to God's law. Therefore God's law is Israel's own highest life. The statutory character of Old Testament ethics is only the formal element, not its essential distinction. For this God, who requires that Israel "shall fear him and walk in all his ways and shall love and serve him with all its heart and all its soul" (Deut. x. 12, Hebr.), is Himself the highest manifestation of ethical qualities (Ex. xxxiv. 6, 7). To walk in His ways, therefore, entails the obligation to be, like Him, merciful, etc. This holy God is Himself He that "regardeth not persons, nor taketh reward: He doth execute the judgment of the fatherless and widow, and loveth the stranger" (Deut. x. 17–18), qualities which Israel, as exponential of His unity and power and love, must exhibit as the very innermost ambitions of its own historical distinctness (Deut. x. 19 *et seq.*).

Hence great stress is laid on reverence for parents (Ex. xx. 12; Lev. xix. 3). Central to the social organism is the family. Its head is the father; yet the mother as his equal is with him entitled to honor and respect at the hands of sons and daughters. Monogamy is the ideal (Gen. ii. 24). Marriage within certain degrees of consanguinity or in relations arising from previous conjugal unions is forbidden (Lev. xviii. 6 *et seq.*); chastity is regarded as of highest moment (Ex. xx. 14; Lev. xviii. 18–20); and abominations to which the Canaanites were addicted are especially loathed. The unruly and disrespectful son (Ex. xxi. 17) is regarded as the incarnation of wickedness. As virtue and righteousness flow from the recognition of the holy God, idolatry is the progenitor of vice and oppression (Ex. xxiii. 24 *et seq.*). For this judgment history has furnished ample proof. Hence the ethics of the Pentateuch shows no tolerance to either idols or their worshipers. Both being sources of contamination and corruption, they had to be torn out by the roots (Lev. xix. 4; Ex. xx. 3 *et seq.*; Deut. iv. 15–25 *et seq.*). Marriages with the aboriginal tribes were therefore prohibited (Deut. vii. 3), for Israel was to be a "holy" people. To the family belonged

Family Ethics.

also the slaves (Deut. xvi. 14). While slavery in a certain sense was recognized, the moral spirit of the Pentateuchal legislation had modified this universal institution of antiquity (see CRUELTY; SLAVERY). The Hebrew slave's term of service was limited; the female slave enjoyed certain immunities. Injuries led to manumission (Ex. xxi. 2–7, 20, 26). Man-stealing (slave-hunting) entailed death (Ex. xxi. 16). The stranger, too, was within the covenant of ethical considerations (Ex. xxii. 20 [A.V, 21]; Lev. xix. 33). "Thou shalt love him as thyself," a law the phraseology of which proves that in the preceding "thou shalt love thy neighbor as thyself" (Lev. xix. 18) "neighbor" does not connote an Israelite exclusively. There was to be one law for the native and the stranger (Lev. xix. 34; comp. Ex. xii. 49). As was the stranger (Ex. xxiii. 9), so were the poor, the widow, the orphan, commended to the special solicitude of the righteous (see INTEREST; POOR LAWS; USURY; Lev. xix. 9 *et seq.*; Ex. xxii. 24 *et seq.*, xxiii. 6).

Altruistic Virtues.

In dealings with men honesty and truthfulness are absolutely prerequisite. Stealing, flattery, falsehood, perjury and false swearing, oppression, even if only in holding back overnight the hired man's earnings, are under the ban; the coarser cruelties and dishonesties are forbidden, but so are the refined ones; and deafness and blindness entitled to gentle consideration him who was afflicted by either of these infirmities (Lev. xix. 11–14). The reputation of a fellow man was regarded as sacred (Ex. xxiii. 1). Talebearing and unkind insinuations were proscribed, as was hatred of one's brother in one's heart (Lev. xix. 17). A revengeful, relentless disposition is unethical; reverence for old age is inculcated; justice shall be done; right weight and just measure are demanded; poverty and riches shall not be regarded by the judge (Lev. xix. 15, 18, 32, 36; Ex. xxiii. 3). The dumb animal has claims upon the kindly help of man (Ex. xxiii. 4), even though it belongs to one's enemy. This epitome of the positive commandments and prohibitions, easily enlarged, will suffice to show the scope of the ethical relations considered by the Law. As a holy nation, Israel's public and private life was under consecration; justice, truthfulness, solicitude for the weak, obedience and reverence to those in authority, regard for the rights of others, strong and weak, a forgiving and candid spirit, love for fellow man and mercy for the beast, and chastity appear as the virtues flowering forth from Pentateuchal righteousness.

It has often been urged that the motive of ethical action in the Pentateuch is the desire for material prosperity and the anxiety to escape disaster. This view confounds description of fact with suggestion of motive. The Pentateuchal lawgiver addresses himself always to the nation, not to the individual. In his system Israel is under divine discipline, intended to make it in ever greater measure worthy and fit to be a holy nation exponential of the holy God. The physical and political disasters which, from the point of view of modern critics, were actual experiences in the time of the Deuteronomist, were consequences of Israel's disloyalty. Only repentance of its evil ways and adoption of ways concordant with its inner historic duty would put an end to the divinely appointed and necessary punitive discipline. The motive of Israel's ethical self-realization as the "holy people," nevertheless, is not desire for prosperity or fear of disaster. It is to be true to its appointment as the priest-people. From this historical relation of Israel to God flows, without ulterior rewards or penalties, the limpid stream of Pentateuchal morality.

Motive of Morality.

For the Prophets, too, the distinct character of Israel is basic, as is the obligation of all men to lead a righteous life. The ritual elements and sacerdotal institutions incidental to Israel's appointment are regarded as secondary by the preexilic prophets, while the intensely human side is emphasized (Isa. i. 11 *et seq.*, lviii. 2 *et seq.*). Israel is chosen, not on account of any merit of its own, but as having been "alone singled out" by God; its conduct is under more rigid scrutiny than any other people's (Amos iii. 1–2). Israel is the "wife" (Hosea), the "bride" (Jer. ii. 2–3). This covenant is one of love (Hosea vi. 7); it is sealed by righteousness and loyalty (Hosea ii. 21–22). Idolatry is adulterous abandoning of God. From this infidelity proceed all man-

Prophetic Ethics.

ner of vice, oppression, untruthfulness. Fidelity, on the other hand, leads to "doing justly and loving mercy" (Micah vi. 8). Dissolution of the bonds of confidence and disregard of the obligation to keep faith each man with his fellow characterize the worst times (Micah vii. 5). Falsehood, deceitfulness, the shedding of blood, are the horrors attending upon periods of iniquity (Isa. lix. 3–6; Jer. ix. 2–5). Truth and peace shall men love (Zech. viii. 16–17). Adultery and lying are castigated; pride is deprecated; ill-gotten wealth is condemned (Jer. xxiii. 14, ix. 22–23, xvii. 11; Hab. ii. 9–11). Gluttony and intemperance, greed and frivolity, are abhorred (Isa. v. 22; Jer. xxi. 13–14; Amos vi. 1, 4–7). The presumptuous and the scoffers are menaced with destruction (Isa. xxix. 20–21; Ezek. xiii. 18–19, 22). But kindness to the needy, benevolence, justice, pity to the suffering, a peace-loving disposition, a truly humble and contrite spirit, are the virtues which the Prophets hold up for emulation. Civic loyalty, even to a foreign ruler, is urged as a duty (Jer. xxix. 7). "Learn to do good" is the key-note of the prophetic appeal (Isa. i. 17); thus the end-time will be one of peace and righteousness; war will be no more (Isa. ii. 2 *et seq.*; see MESSIAH).

In Psalms and Wisdom Literature.

In the Psalms and the Wisdom books the national emphasis is reduced to a minimum. The good man is not so much a Jew as a man (Ps. i.). The universal character of the Biblical ethics is thus verified. Job indicates the conduct and principles of the true man. All men are made by God (Job xxix. 12–17, xxxi. 15). The picture of a despicable man is that given in Prov. vi. 12–15, and the catalogue of those whom God hates enumerates the proud, the deceitful, the shedder of innocent blood, a heart filled with intrigues, and feet running to do evil; a liar, a false witness, and he who brings men to quarrel (Prov. vi. 16–19). The ideal of woman is pictured in the song of the true housewife (Prov. xxxi. 8 *et seq.*), while Psalms xv. and xxiv. sketch the type of man Israel's ethics will produce. He walketh uprightly, worketh righteousness, speaketh truth in his heart. He backbiteth not.

The motive of such a life is to be permitted "to dwell in God's tabernacle," in modern phraseology to be in accord with the divine within oneself. The priesthood of Israel's One God is open to all that walk in His ways. The ethics of the Bible is not national nor legalistic. Its principle is the holiness of the truly human; this holiness, attainable by and obligatory upon all men, is, however, to be illustrated and realized by and in Israel as the holy people of the one holy God.

The temper of the ethics of the Bible is not ascetic. The shadow of sin is not over earth and man. Joy, the joy of doing what "God asks," and what the law of man's very being demands, willingly and out of the full liberty of his own adaptation to this inner law of his, is the clear note of the Old Testament's ethical valuation of life. The world is good and life is precious, for both have their center and origin in God. He leads men according to His purposes, which come to pass with and without the cooperation of men. It is man's privilege to range himself on the side of the divine. If found there, strength is his; he can not fall nor stumble; for righteousness is central in all. But if he fails to be true to the law of his life, if he endeavors to ignore it or to supersede it by the law of selfishness, which is the law of sin, he will fail. "The way of the wicked He turneth upside down" (Ps. i.). Ethics reaches thus beyond the human and earthly, and is related to the eternal. Ethics and religion are in the Bible one and inseparable.

——Modern: Under this heading it is proposed to treat of the agreements and differences between the concepts and theories and the resulting practises of Jewish ethics and those of the main ethical schools of modern times. The fundamental teachings of Judaism base ethics on the concept that the universe is under purpose and law—that is, that it constitutes a moral order, created and guided by divine will, a personal God, in whom thought, will, and being are identical and coincident, and who therefore is the All-Good, his very nature excluding evil. Man, "created in the image of God," is a free moral agent, endowed (1) with the perception which distinguishes right from wrong, right being that which harmonizes with the moral order of things and serves its purposes, wrong being that which is out of consonance with this order and would conflict with and oppose it; and (2) with the will and the power to choose and do the right and eschew and abandon the wrong.

The moral law, therefore, is autonomous; man finds it involved in his own nature. Man being composed of body and soul, or mind, moral action is not automatic or instinctive. It has to overcome the opposition arising from the animal elements (appetites, selfishness), which are intended to be under the control, and serve the purposes, of the mind and soul. Recognition of right, the resolve to do it, and the execution of this resolve, are the three moments in the moral act. The impelling motive is not what outwardly results from the act (reward or punishment), but the desire and intention to be and become what man should and may be. Man thus is a moral personality, as such able to harmonize his conduct with the purposes of the All, and through such concordance lift his individual self to the importance and value of an abiding force in the moral order of things. Every man is and may act as a moral personality; the "summum bonum" is the realization on earth of conditions in which every man may live the life consonant with his dignity as a moral personality. This state is the "Messianic kingdom" (מלכות שמים). The assurance that this kingdom will come and that right is might has roots in the apprehension of the universe and the world of man as a moral cosmos. Israel, by virtue of being the historic people whose genius flowered (1) in the recognition of the moral purposes underlying life and time and world (see God), and the ultimate (באחרית הימים) triumph of right over wrong, as well as (2) in the apprehension of man's dignity and destiny as a moral personality, derives from its history the right, and is therefore under obligation, to anticipate in its own life the conditions of the Messianic fulfilment, thus illustrating the possibility and potency of a life consonant with the implications of the moral order of things, and by example influencing all men to seek and find the aim of human life in the ambition to establish among men the moral harmonies resulting from the recognition that man is a moral personality, and that the forces of the universe are under moral law.

In-tuitional.

I. Jewish ethics, then, differs from the Christian in insisting that man, now as in the beginning, still has the power to discern between right and wrong and to choose between them. The consciousness of sin, and the helplessness of the sinner, are not taught or recognized. Therefore Jewish ethics is not tinged with quietism or Asceticism. Resignation and submission are not among the tendencies it fosters or justifies. Resistance to evil, and its discomfiture by remedial and positive good, is the key-note of Jewish morality, individual as well as social. Pessimism and optimism alike are eliminated by a higher synthesis; the former as negative of the inherent godliness (or morally purposed creation) of the universe and the essential worthiness of human life, the latter as ignoring the place assigned to man in the economy of things, and, with its one-sided insistence that "whatever is, is right," paralyzing man's energies. Meliorism, the conscious effort at improvement, perhaps expresses the character of Jewish ethics.

II. Neither is Jewish ethics on the same plane as the common-sense moralism of Shaftesbury and Hutcheson, or that of Wolff and the school of the "Aufklärungsphilosophie." Theirs is a system of moral hedonism, which reduces the moral life to an equation in happiness, gross or refined, sensual or spiritual. The desire for happiness is not the true basis of ethics. Nor is it true, as insisted on by this school, that happiness, except in the sense of the feeling of inner harmony with the implications and obligations of human personality, attends moral action as does effect follow upon cause. Like all hedonism, that of the moralists, too, verges on utilitarianism, the theory that what is useful (to oneself, or to the greater number) is moral. In the modification of the original equation between utility and morality, which makes the "happiness of the greater number" the test of goodness and the motive of moral action, utilitarianism has virtually abandoned its main contention without explaining why, in cases of conflict between individual interest and the welfare of the greater number, the individual should forego his immediate or ultimate advantage; for the contention that egotism always is shortsighted, reaching out for immediate and cheaper pleasure at the loss of remoter but more precious advantages, virtually denies the efficiency of utilitarianism as normative of human conduct and relations. Jewish ethics does not deny that spiritual pleasure is a concomitant of moral action, nor that moral conduct leads to consequences redounding to the welfare of society. But, contrary to the doctrine of hedonism and utilitarianism, Jewish ethics does not regard these attending feelings or resulting consequences as other than morally inconsequential. They are not proposed as motives or aims. In other words, worthiness (holiness) is the aim and the test of moral conduct, according to Jewish ethical teaching.

Autonomous.

This reveals how far Jewish ethics agrees with that of Kant, who more than any other has left his impress upon modern ethical thought. Kant, in insisting that no ulterior purpose should determine human action—going even to the extreme of holding that the degree of repugnance which must be overcome, and the absence of pleasure and delight, alone attest the moral value of a deed—was moved, on the one hand, by his dissent from the shallow "hedonism" of the "moralists" (intuitionalists), and on the other by a psychology still under the influence of the Christian dogma of original sin. Nothing is good but the "good will." But man's will is not naturally good. The "good" man, therefore, must struggle against his natural inclination. The absence of gratification, the amount of the unwillingness overcome, are indicative of the goodness of the will. Christian and hedonistic predications of rewards and punishments (temporal or eternal), for good and evil conduct respectively, led Kant to the demand that purpose be eliminated altogether from the equation of moral conduct. Jewish ethics shares with Kant the insistence that consequences, temporal or eternal, shall not determine action. But the psychology upon which Jewish ethics is grounded recognizes that while pleasure and delight, or social utility, are not to be lifted into the potencies of motives, they are possible results and concomitants of moral action. As with Kant, Jewish ethics is based on the solemnity and awfulness of the moral "ought," which it regards as the categorical imperative, implied and involved in the very nature of man.

But Jewish ethics sees in this immediate fact of human consciousness and reason a relation, beyond the human, to the essential force of the universe (God). Because man is created in the image of God he has, with this consciousness of obligation, "conscience," the sense of harmony, or the reverse, of his self with this essential destiny of man. The fundamental maxim of Jewish as of Kantian ethics insists upon such action as may and should be imitated by all. But in Jewish ethics this applicability is grounded on the assurance that every man, as God's image, is a moral personality, therefore an agent, not a tool or a thing. Equally with Kant, Jewish ethics insists on the autonomy of the moral law, but it does this because this moral law is in God and through God; because it is more inclusive than man or humanity, having in itself the assurance of being the essential meaning and purpose of all that is realizable. It is not a mere "ought" which demands, but a certainty that man "can" do what he "ought to do," because all the forces of the universe are attuned to the same "ought" and are making for righteousness. This view alone gives a firm basis to the moral life. It gives it both reality and content. The categorical imperative as put by Kant is only formal. Jewish ethics fills the categorical imperative with positive content by holding that it is man's duty as determined by the ultimate destiny of the human family, and as purposed in the moral order of things, to establish on earth the Messianic kingdom, or, in Christian ethics, "the community of saints," the "kingdom of God."

III. Jewish ethics deduces and proclaims its demands from the freedom of man's will. Determinism in all its varieties denies human freedom for the following reasons:

(1) Because the "soul" is dependent upon, and therefore controlled and limited by, the body. The contention of the determinists has not been proved.

Free Will. The material elements are substrata of the human person; as such they are factors of his being. But the "soul" or "will" nevertheless has the power to resist and neutralize the effects of the material factors. The latter, within certain extent, hamper or help; but whether increasing the difficulties or not, which the "will" encounters in asserting itself, the material elements may be and are under the will's control, even to their destruction (*e. g.*, in suicide). The materialistic constructions have not weakened the foundations of Jewish ethics.

(2) Because empirically invariable regularity of human action has been established by moral statistics. At most the tables of moral statistics prove the influence of social conditions as brakes or stimuli to human will-power; but, confronted by the crucial question, Why does one individual and not another commit the (irregular) act? the theory fails ignominiously. It does not prove that social conditions are permanent. Man has changed them at his own will under deeper insight into the law of his moral relations to other men. Hence the arguments derived from moral statistics do not touch the kernel of the Jewish doctrine of the moral freedom of man.

(3) Because will is determined by motives, and these arise out of conditions fixed by heredity and environment. The utmost this contention establishes is that men are responsible for the conditions they bequeath to posterity. These conditions may render difficult or easy the assertion of the will in the choice of motives, but they can not deprive the will of the power to choose. Environment may at will be changed, and the motives arising from it thereby modified. Jewish ethics is not grounded on the doctrine of absolute free will, but on that of the freedom of choice between motives. Man acts upon motives; but education, discipline, the training of one's mind to recognize the bearing which the motives have upon action and to test them by their concordance with or dissonance from the ideal of human conduct involved in man's higher destiny, enable man to make the better choice and to eliminate all baser motives. Even conceding the utmost that the theory of determining motives establishes,

Jewish ethics continues on safe ground when predicating the freedom of the human will.

(4) Because human freedom has been denied on theological grounds as incompatible with the omnipotence and prescience of God (see LUTHER; MANICHEANS; PREDESTINATION; comp. Koran, sura xvii.; D. F. Strauss, "Die Christliche Glaubenslehre," i. 363: Spinoza's "immanent" God). The difficulties of the problem have been felt also by Jewish philosophers (see Stein, "Das Problem der Willensfreiheit"). Still, the difficulties are largely of a scholastic nature. Jewish ethics gives man the liberty to range himself on the side of the divine purposes or to attempt to place himself in opposition to them. Without this freedom moral life is robbed of its morality. Man can do naught against God except work his own defeat; he can do all with God by working in harmony with the moral purpose and destiny underlying life.

Relation to Evolutionist Ethics.

IV. Jewish ethics is not weakened by the theories that evolution may be established in the history of moral ideas and practise; that the standards of right and wrong have changed; and that conscience has spoken a multitude of dialects. Even the theory of Spencer and others that conscience is only a slow accretion of impressions and experiences based upon the utility of certain acts is not fatal to the main principles of the Jewish ethical theory. Evolution at its best merely traces the development of the moral life; it offers no solution of its origin, why man has come to develop this peculiar range of judgments upon his past conduct, and evolve ideals regulative of future conduct. Human nature, then, in its constitution, must have carried potentially from the beginning all that really evolved from and through it in the slow process of time. Man thus tends toward the moralities, and these are refined and spiritualized in increasing measure. Jewish ethics is thus untouched in its core by the evolutional method of treatment of the phenomena of the moral life of man.

V. Jewish ethics and Jewish religion are inseparable. The moral life, it is true, is not dependent upon dogma; there are men who, though without positive dogmatic creeds, are intensely moral; as, on the other hand, there are men who combine religious and liturgical correctness, or religious emotionalism, with moral indifference and moral turpitude. Furthermore, the moral altitude of a people indicates that of its gods, while the reverse is not true (Melkarth, Astarte, Baal, Jupiter, reflect the morality of their worshipers). Nevertheless, religion alone lifts ethics into a certainty; the moral life under religious construction is expressive of what is central and supreme in all time and space, to which all things are subject and which all conditions serve. God is, in the Jewish conception, the source of all morality; the universe is under moral destiny. The key to all being and becoming is the moral purpose posited by the recognition that the supreme will of the highest moral personality is Creator and Author and Ruler of All. In God the moral sublimities are one. Hence the Jewish God-concept can best be interpreted in moral values (see God's thirteen MIDDOT). Righteousness, love, purity, are the only service man may offer Him. Immorality and Jewish religiosity are mutually exclusive. The moral life is a religious consecration. Ceremonies and symbols are for moral discipline and expressive of moral sanctities (see M. Lazarus, "Jüdische Ethik"). They appeal to the imagination of man in a way to deepen in him the sense of his moral dignity, and prompt him to greater sensitiveness to duty.

Based on Religion.

VI. The ethical teachings of religion alone, and especially the Jewish religion, establish the relation of man to himself, to his property, to others, on an ethical basis. Religion sets forth God as the Giver. Non-religious ethics is incompetent to develop consistently the obligations of man to live so that the measure of his life, and the value and worth of all other men, shall be increased. Why should man not be selfish? Why is Nietzsche's "overman," who is "beyond good and evil," not justified in using his strength as he lists? Religion, and it alone, or a religious interpretation of ethics makes the social bond something more comprehensive than an accidental and natural (material) compact between men, a policy, a pruden-

Religious Basis Necessary.

tial arrangement to make life less burdensome; religion alone makes benevolence and altruism something loftier than mere anticipatory speculations on possible claims for benefits when necessity shall arise, or the reflex impulse of a subjective transference of another's objective misery to oneself, so that pity always is shown only to self (Schopenhauer). Religion shows that as man is the recipient of all he is and has, he is the steward of what was given him (by God) for his use and that of all his fellow men.

On this basis Jewish ethics rests its doctrines of duty and virtue. Whatever increases the capacity of man's stewardship is ethical. Whatever use of time, talent, or treasure augments one's possibilities of human service is ethically consecrated. Judaism, therefore, inculcates as ethical the ambition to develop physical and mental powers, as enlargement of service is dependent upon the measure of the increase of man's powers. Wealth is not immoral; poverty is not moral. The desire to increase one's stores of power is moral provided it is under the consecration of the recognized responsibility for larger service. The weak are entitled to the protection of the strong. Property entails duties, which establish its rights. Charity is not a voluntary concession on the part of the well-situated. It is a right to which the less fortunate are entitled in justice (צדקה). The main concern of Jewish ethics is personality. Every human being is a person, not a thing. Economic doctrine is unethical and un-Jewish if it ignores and renders illusory this distinction. Slavery is for this reason immoral. Jewish ethics on this basis is not individualistic; it is not under the spell of otherworldliness. It is social. By consecrating every human being to the stewardship of his faculties and forces, and by regarding every human soul as a person, the ethics of Judaism offers the solution of all the perplexities of modern political, industrial, and economic life. Israel as the "pattern people" shall be exponential, among its brothers of the whole human family, of the principles and practises which are involved in, pillared upon, and demanded by, the ethical monotheism which lifts man to the dignity of God's image and consecrates him the steward of all of his life, his talent, and his treasure. In the "Messianic kingdom," ideally to be anticipated by Israel, justice will be enthroned and incarnated in institution, and this justice, the social correlative of holiness and love, is the ethical passion of modern, as it was of olden, Judaism.

XXI

Eve

EVE (חוה).—Biblical Data: The wife of Adam. According to Gen. iii. 20, Eve was so called because she was "the mother of all living" (R. V., margin, "Life" or "Living"). On the ground that it was not "good for man to be alone" God resolved to "make him an help meet for him" (*ib.* ii. 18), first creating, with this end in view, the beasts of the field and the fowl of the air and then bringing them unto Adam. When Adam did not find among these a helpmeet for himself, YHWH caused a deep sleep to fall upon him, and took one of his ribs, from which He made a woman, and brought her unto the man (*ib.* ii. 22). Upon seeing her, Adam welcomed her as "bone of my bones, and flesh of my flesh" (*ib.* ii. 23), declaring that she should be called "ishshah" because she was taken out of "ish" (man.)

Dwelling in the Garden of Eden with Adam, Eve is approached and tempted by the serpent. She yields to the reptile's seductive arguments, and partakes of the forbidden fruit, giving thereof to her husband, who, like her, eats of it. Both discover their nakedness and make themselves aprons of fig-leaves. When God asks for an accounting Adam puts the blame on Eve. As a punishment, the sorrows of conception and childbirth are announced to her, as well as subjection to her husband (*ib.* iii. 16). Driven out of Eden, Eve gives birth to two sons, Cain and Abel; herself naming the elder in the obscure declaration "I have gotten a man with the help of YHWH" (*ib.* iv. 1, R. V.). Later, after the murder of Abel, she bears another son, to whom she gives the name "Seth," saying that he is given to her by YHWH as a compensation for Abel (*ib.* iv. 25).

——**In Rabbinical Literature:** Eve was not created simultaneously with Adam because God foreknew that later she would be a source of complaint. He therefore delayed forming her until Adam should express a desire for her (Gen. R. xvii.). Eve was created from the thirteenth rib on Adam's right side and from the flesh of his heart (Targ. Pseudo-Jonathan to Gen. ii. 21; Pirḳe R. El. xii.). Together with Eve Satan was created (Gen. R. xvii.). God adorned Eve like a bride with all the jewelry mentioned in Isa. iii. He built the nuptial chamber for her (Gen. R. xviii.). According to Pirḳe R. El. xii., as soon as Adam beheld Eve he embraced and kissed her; her name אשה, from איש, indicates that God (יה) joined them together (see also Ab. R. N. xxxviii.). Ten gorgeous "ḥuppot" (originally, "bridal chambers"; now, "bridal canopies"), studded with gems and pearls and ornamented with gold, did God erect for Eve, whom He Himself gave away in marriage, and over whom He pronounced the blessing; while the angels danced and beat timbrels and stood guard over the bridal chamber (Pirḳe R. El. xii.).

Samael, prompted by jealousy, picked out the serpent to mislead Eve (Yalḳ., Gen. xxv.; comp. Josephus, "Ant." i. 1, § 4; Ab. R. N. i.), whom it approached, knowing that women could be more easily moved than men (Pirḳe R. El. xiii.). Or, according to another legend, the serpent was induced to lead Eve to sin by desire on its part to possess her (Soṭah 9; Gen. R. xviii.), and it cast into her the taint of lust (זוהמא; Yeb. 103b; 'Ab. Zarah 22b; Shab. 146a; Yalḳ., Gen. 28, 130). Profiting by the absence of the two guardian angels (Ḥag. 16a; Ber. 60b), Satan, or the serpent, which then had almost the shape of a man (Gen. R. xix. 1), displayed great argumentative skill in explaining the selfish reasons which had prompted God's prohibition (Pirḳe R. El. *l.c.*; Gen. R. xix.; Tan., Bereshit, viii.), and convinced Eve by ocular proof that the tree could be touched (comp. Ab. R. N. i. 4) without entailing death. Eve thereupon laid hold of the tree, and at once beheld the angel of death coming toward her (Targ. Pseudo-Jon. to Gen. iii. 6). Then, reasoning that if she died and Adam continued to live he would take another wife, she made him share her own fate (Pirḳe R. El. xiii.; Gen. R. xix.); at the invitation of the serpent she had partaken of wine; and she now mixed it with Adam's drink (Num. R. x.). Nine curses together with death befell Eve in consequence of her disobedience (Pirḳe R. El. xiv.; Ab. R. N. ii. 42).

Eve became pregnant, and bore Cain and Abel on the very day of (her creation and) expulsion from Eden (Gen. R. xii.). These were born full-grown, and each had a twin sister (*ib.*). Cain's real father was not Adam, but one of the demons (Pirḳe R. El. xxi., xxii.). Seth was Eve's first child by Adam. Eve died shortly after Adam, on the completion of the six days of mourning, and was buried in the Cave of Machpelah (Pirḳe R. El. xx.).

——**Critical View:** The account of the creation of woman—she is called "Eve" only after the curse—belongs to the J narrative. It reflects the naive speculations of the ancient Hebrews on the beginnings of the human race as introductory to the history of Israel. Its tone throughout is anthropomorphic. The story was current among the people long before it took on literary form (Gunkel, "Genesis," p. 2), and it may possibly have been an adaptation of a Babylonian myth (*ib.* p. 35). Similar accounts of the creation of woman from a part of man's body are found among many races (Tuch, "Genesis," notes on ch. ii.); for instance, in the myth of Pandora. That woman is the cause of evil is another wide-spread conceit. The etymology of "ishshah" from "ish" (Gen. ii. 23) is incorrect (אשה belongs to the root אנש), but exhibits all the characteristics of folk-etymology. The name חוה, which Adam gives the woman in Gen. iii. 20, seems not to be of Hebrew origin. The similarity of sound with חי explains the popular etymology adduced in the explanatory gloss, though it is W. R. Smith's opinion ("Kinship and Marriage in Early Arabia," p. 177) that Eve represents the bond of matriarchal kinship ("ḥayy"). Nöldeke ("Z. D. M. G." xlii. 487), following Philo ("De Agricultura Noe," § 21) and the Midrash Rabbah (*ad loc.*), explains the name as meaning "serpent," preserving thus the belief that all life sprang from a primeval serpent. The narrative forms part of a culture-myth attempting to account among other things for the pangs of childbirth, which are comparatively light among primitive peoples (compare ADAM; EDEN, GARDEN OF; FALL OF MAN). As to whether this story inculcates the divine institution of MONOGAMY or not, see Gunkel, "Genesis," p. 11, and Dillmann's and Holzinger's commentaries on Gen. ii. 23–24.

XXII

Evolution

EVOLUTION: The series of steps by which all existing beings have been developed by gradual modification; term generally applied to the theory concerning the origin of species and the descent of man connected with the names of Charles Darwin and Herbert Spencer, and defended and amplified by Ernst Haeckel and Thomas Huxley, though to a certain degree anticipated by Goethe, Lamarck, Kant, and even Heraclitus. According to this hypothesis all animal and vegetable life may be traced to one very low form of life, a minute cell, itself possibly produced by inorganic matter. This development, according to Darwin, is due to the struggle for existence, and to the transmission through natural (and sexual) selection of those qualities which enable the possessors to carry on the struggle, in which only the fittest survive. Herbert Spencer and others have applied the theory of evolution to every domain of human endeavor—civilization, religion, language, society, ethics, art, etc., tracing the line of development from the homogeneous to the heterogeneous, though recrudescences of and lapses into older forms and types (degeneration, atavism) are by no means excluded. The relation of the teachings of Judaism to this theory is not necessarily one of hostility and dissent.

Judaism and Evolution.

Evolution not only does not preclude creation, but necessarily implies it. Nor are purpose and design (teleology) eliminated from the process. Natural selection in strict construction is teleological. Mechanical design alone is precluded. In its stead the hypothesis of evolution operates with a teleology that is, both in intensity and in extent, much more adequate to the higher conceptions of God. Mechanical teleology is anthropomorphic. Jewish theism, not being anthropomorphic, does not defend mechanical teleology.

The development of life from inorganic matter, the rise of consciousness from preceding unconscious life, the origin of mind, of conscience, are not accounted for by the theory of evolution; and as at the beginning of the chain, so at these links it fails. Jewish theism, while admitting that on the whole the theory throws light on the methods pursued in the gradual rise and unfolding of life, is justified in contending that it does not eliminate the divine element and plan and purpose from the process. Evolution gives answer to the *how*, never to the *what*, and only inadequately to the *why*. Belief in miracles, in catastrophical interruptions of the continuity of nature's processes, indeed, is not compatible with the acceptance of the doctrine of evolution. The Jewish (Talmudical) view of MIRACLES, as a condition involved in the original design of nature, however, is not inherently irreconcilable with the hypothesis of evolution, while modern (Reform) Jewish theology is not concerned to defend the belief in miracles based on literal constructions of Biblical passages.

Judaism, having never taught the doctrine of the FALL OF MAN, is not obliged to reject the evolutional theory on the ground that it conflicts with the dogma which demands the assumption of man's original perfection, and which thus inverts the process and sequence posited by the evolutionists.

The theory of evolution has also been applied to the history of religion. Following the positivists, the writers on this subject from the point of view of the evolutionary school have argued that some species of animism (ancestor-worship) was the lowest form of religion, which, developing and differentiating successively into gross and then refined fetishism (totemism), nature-worship, polytheism, tribal henotheism, and national monolatry, finally flowered into universal ethical monotheism. The history of Israel's religion has also been traced from this point of view, according to which it exhibits vestiges

Evolution of Religion.

of antecedent animism and totemism, but appears in its earlier historic forms as tribal henotheism of a largely stellar and lunar (agricultural) cast; it then grew, under the influences of environment and historical experiences (national consolidation and Canaanitish contamination), into national monolatry (YHWHISM), which gradually, under Assyro-Babylonian influences, deepened and clarified into prophetic or universal ethical monotheism, again to be contracted into sacerdotal and legalistic Judaism. This theory of the rise and development of religion in general and of that of Israel in particular conflicts with (1) the assumption of an original monotheism and the subsequent lapse of man into idolatry, which, however, is a phase of the doctrine of the FALL OF MAN; and with (2) the conception of revelation as an arbitrary, local, temporal, and mechanical process of communicating divine truth to man, or to Israel.

The view, however, which looks upon revelation as a continuous, growing, and deepening process, through which divine truth unfolds itself and thus leads man to an ever fuller realization of the divine purposes of human life and the higher moral law of human existence, and Israel to an ever more vital appreciation of its relations to the divine and its destiny and duty in the economy of things and purposes human, is not inherently antagonistic to the evolutional interpretation of the rhythm of religious life.

(1) Evolution confirms religion as a necessary outcome and a concomitant of the development of human life. Thus evolution negatives the theories of the rationalists that regard religion as a benevolent or as a malevolent invention. (2) Evolution does not deny the part played by the great men (prophets) in this process of developing religious consciousness and views. (3) The rise and activity of these great men evolution can not account for. (4) In the history of Israel's religion, evolution has not explained and can not explain how, from original (Kenite) YHWHISM, void of all moral content and all original ,"holiness" (= "taboo" ["ḳodesh"]) ascribed to the Deity, could have sprung the ethical monotheism of the Prophets and the idea of moral holiness ("ḳadosh"). The power of origination

Evolution and Monotheism.

vested in genius (prophecy) is thus not eliminated as the main factor from the factors involved in the religious evolution of Israel. Babylonian influences (Delitzsch, "Babel und Bibel") did not, among the Babylonians themselves, develop the higher monotheism. It is thus beyond the range of possibility that what failed of development among its own originators should have evolved into monotheism among the Israelites, unless Israel had a peculiar and distinctive genius for monotheism. This power of originating monotheistic ideals and transmuting other ideals into monotheistic concepts, a power which the Prophets had in a high degree, and which the nation also, as a whole, gradually displayed in the development of its national genius, is the one factor for which evolution can not account. This factor may be rightly denominated "revelation." (5) The evolution theory overthrows Renan's dictum that monotheism is "the minimum of religion." None of the essential contentions of Judaism is vitally affected by the propositions of the evolution school. The philosophy of the Reform wing within Judaism, regarding Judaism as a growth, not a fixed quantity or a rigid law, and as still in the process of developing (tradition being its vital element), has even found corroboration in the theory of evolution.

XXIII

Fall Of Angels

FALL OF ANGELS: The conception of fallen angels—angels who, for wilful, rebellious conduct against God, or through weakness under temptation, thereby forfeiting their angelic dignity, were degraded and condemned to a life of mischief or shame on earth or in a place of punishment—is wide-spread. Indications of this belief, behind which probably lies the symbolizing of an astronomical phenomenon, the shooting stars, are met with in Isa. xiv. 12 (comp. Job xxxviii. 31, 32; see CONSTELLATIONS). But it is in apocalyptic writings that this notion assumes crystallized definiteness and is brought into relations with the theological problem of the origin and nature of evil and sin. That Satan fell from heaven with the velocity of lightning is a New Testament conception (Luke x. 18; Rev. xii. 7–10). Originally Satan was one of God's angels, Lucifer, who, lusting for worldly power, was degraded. Samael (Yalḳ., Gen. 25), originally the chief of the angels around God's throne, becomes the angel of death and the "chieftain of all the Satans" (Deut. R. xi.; comp. Matt. xxv. 41).

In Apocalyptic Writings.

But it is especially Samhazai and Azael of whom the fall is narrated. In Targ. Pseudo-Jonathan to Gen. vi. 4 they appear as the "nefilim" (A. V. "giants"), undoubtedly in consequence of an incorrect interpretation of this word as "those that fell from heaven." The story of these two angels is found in brief form in Yalḳ., Gen. 44; it has been published by Jellinek ("B. H." iv. 127; originally in Midrash Abkir; comp. Rashi, Yoma 67b; Geiger,

"Was Hat Mohammed aus dem Judenthume Aufgenommen?" p. 107).

As in the case of man, so in that of the angels woman was the cause of the lapse. Naamah, the wife of Noah (Gen. R. xxiii. 3), was one of the women whose great beauty tempted the angels to sin (Naḥmanides to Gen. iv. 22). As regards Azazel and Samḥazai, mentioned above, it was a young woman named איסטהר ("Isṭar," "Esther") that proved fatal to their virtue. These angels, seeing God's grief over the corruption of the sons of men (Gen. vi. 2–7), volunteered to descend to earth for the purpose of proving their contention that, as they had foretold at the creation of Adam, the weakness of man (Ps. viii. 5) was alone responsible for his immorality. In their new surroundings they themselves yielded to the blandishments of women. Samḥazai especially became passionately enamored of Isṭar. She, however, would yield to his importunities only on the condition that he tell her the name of YHWH (see GOD, NAMES OF), by virtue of which he was enabled to return to heaven. As soon as she was possessed of the secret, she rose to heaven herself, and God rewarded her constancy by assigning her a place in the constellation of Kimah. Samḥazai and his companion thereupon took to themselves wives and begat children (comp. the bene Elohim, Gen. vi. 4). Meṭaṭron soon after sends word to Samḥazai concerning the approaching flood. This announcement of the world's and his own children's impending doom brings Samḥazai to repentance, and he suspends himself midway between heaven and earth, in which penitent position he has remained ever since. Azazel, who deals in rich adornments and fine garments for women, continues in his evil ways, seducing men by his fanciful wares (hence the goat sent to Azazel on the Day of Atonement).

Woman the Cause of Fall.

Variants of this story are not rare. According to Pirḳe R. El. xxii., "the angels that fell from heaven," seeing the shameless attire of the men and women in Cain's family, had intercourse with the women, and in consequence were deprived of their garment of flaming fire and were clothed in ordinary material of dust. They also lost their angelic strength and stature. Samael was the leader of a whole band of rebellious angels (*ib.* xiii.).

In the Book of Enoch eighteen angels are named (Enoch, vi. 7) as chief participators in the conspiracy to mate with women. Samiaza is the leader, and Azael is one of the number (but see Charles, "Book of Enoch," p. 61, note to vi.-xi.). Azael, however, imparts to men all sorts of useful as well as secret knowledge and the art of beautifying eyes (Enoch, viii. 1; comp. Targ. Pseudo-Jon. to Gen. vi. 4). For other versions of the story or reminiscences thereof, see Book of Jubilees, v. 1, 6–11; vii. 21, 25; Test. Patr., Reuben, 5, and Naphtali, 31; Josephus, "Ant." i. 3, § 1; Philo, "De Gigantibus."

Later Jewish Tradition.

The later Jewish tradition, shocked at the notion of the angels' fall, insisted upon interpreting the bene Elohim of Gen. vi. 1–4 as referring to men (Gen. R. xxvi.: "sons of judges"; comp. Tryphon in Justin, "Dial. cum Tryph." p. 79). The Samaritan version reads בני שלטניה; Onḳelos, רברביא. The "Sefer ha-Yashar" ("Bereshit," end) ascribes the shameful conduct to magistrates and judges (see Charles, "Book of Jubilees," p. 33, note).

The cabalists give the older view. In the Zohar (iii. 208, ed. Mantua) Aza and Azael fall and are punished by being chained to the mountains of darkness. According to another passage (i. 37), these two rebelled against God and were hurled from heaven, and they now teach men all kinds of sorcery (for other quotations from cabalistic commentaries on the Pentateuch see Grünbaum, "Gesammelte Aufsätze zur Sprach- und Sagenkunde," p. 71).

Allusions to these fallen angels occur also in the Koran (sura ii. 96); but their names are there given as "Harut" and "Marut." Their fate in Arabic tradition is identical with that of Samḥazai and Azael (Geiger, *l.c.* p. 109). The refusal to worship Adam (suras ii. 32, vii. 11, xv. 29, xxxviii. 73) brings on the Fall, just as it does in the Midrash Bereshit Rabbati of R. Moses ha-Darshan (see Grünbaum, *l.c.* p. 70).

BIBLIOGRAPHY: Grünbaum, *Gesammelte Aufsätze zur Sprach- und Sagenkunde*, Berlin, 1901.

XXIV
Fall Of Man

FALL OF MAN: A change from the beatific condition, due to the alleged original depravity of the human race. The events narrated in Gen. iii. leading up to the expulsion of Adam and Eve from Eden are held to support the doctrine of the fall of man and to be the historical warrant for its assumption. According to this doctrine, man (and woman) was first created perfect and without sin. Placed by God in the Garden of Eden, he found his wants provided for. In a state of innocence, he was not aware of his nudity, since, not having sinned, he was without the consciousness of sin and the sense of shame had not yet been aroused in him. Man could have continued in this blissful condition and would never have tasted either the bitterness of guilt or that of death had he not disobeyed the divine command, according to which he was not to partake of the fruit of the tree of life, under penalty of immediate death. (See ADAM; EDEN; EVE.) Expelled from the garden under the curse which their disobedience brought upon them, Adam and Eve were doomed to a life of labor and pain which was the prelude to death. Happiness, innocence, and deathlessness were forever forfeited. And in their fall were involved all of their descendants, none of whom in consequence was exempt from the corruption of death and from sin.

This theological construction of the narrative in Genesis assumes the historical authenticity of the account; and finds corroborative evidence in the many stories current among various races positing at the beginning of human history a similar state of blissful perfection which, through the misdeeds of man, came irretrievably to an end, giving way to conditions the reverse of those hitherto prevailing. Among these stories, that of Zoroastrian origin, concerning Yima, the first man, presents a striking parallel to Genesis. Having committed sin, he is cast out of his primeval paradise into the power of the serpent, which brings about his death. In a later version concerning the first pair, Masha and Mashyana, is introduced the incident of eating forbidden fruit at the instigation of the lying spirit. For other parallels see J. Baring-Gould, "Legends of Old Testament Characters"; Tuch, "Genesis," on Gen. iii.

Views of the Critical School.

The critical school views these parallels in the light of non-Hebrew attempts to solve the problem with which Gen. iii. is also concerned, viz., the origin of evil. This problem at a comparatively early period of human thought impressed itself upon the minds of men, and, owing to the fundamental psychic unity of the human race, found similar solution. Sin and suffering, the displeasure of the gods and human misery, are correlatives in all early religious conceits. As actual man suffered, struggled, and died, this fate must have been brought upon him by disobedience to the divine will and by disregard of divine commands. Under tribal organization and law, combined responsibility on the part of the clan for the deeds of its component members was an axiomatic proposition. The guilt of the father necessarily involved all his descendants in its consequences. These two factors—the one psychological and religious, the other sociological—are the dominant notes in the various stories concerning the forfeiture of pristine happiness and deathlessness by man's sin.

Biology and anthropology are in accord in demonstrating that the assumed state of perfection and moral innocency is never found in the beginning of human civilization. There is no proof of a fall either physical or moral. The reverse is, on the whole, true: all evidence points to a rise from primitive imperfection.

The story in Gen. iii. belongs, in all probability, like the other incidents related in the Book of Genesis up to the twelfth chapter, to a cycle of adaptations from Assyro-Babylonian creation- and origin-myths (see COSMOGONY; EDEN), though the exact counterpart of the Biblical narrative of the temptation and expulsion has not as yet been found in the tablets. Two human figures, with a serpent behind them, stretching out their hands toward the fruit of a tree, are depicted on a Babylonian cylinder; but the rendering of the third creation-tablet is so much in doubt that no conclusion may safely be based on this representation (see Sayce, "Ancient Monuments"; Schrader, "K. A. T." 2d ed., p. 37; Davis, "Genesis and Semitic Traditions").

The Biblical myth elaborates also culture-elements. It reflects the consciousness that in remote days man was vegetarian and existed in a state of absolute nudity, fig-leaves and other foliage furnishing the first coverings when advancing culture aroused a certain sense of shame, while subsequently hides and skins of animals came to be utilized for more complete dress.

The story of the fall of man is never appealed to in the Old Testament either as a historical event or as supporting a theological construction of the nature and origin of sin. The translation in the Revised Version of Job xxxi. 33 and Hosea vi. 7 ("Adam" for the Hebrew אדם), even if correct, would not substantiate the point in issue, that the Old Testament theology based its doctrine of sin on the fall of Adam.

Relation to Old Testament Theology.

The Garden of Eden is not even alluded to in any writings before the post-exilic prophets (Ezek. xxviii. 13, xxxi. 9; Isa. li. 3; but comp. Gen. xiii. 10, and even in these no reference is found to the Fall. The contention that, notwithstanding this surprising absence of reference to the story and the theme, the Hebrews of Biblical times nevertheless entertained the notion that through the fall of the first man their own nature was corrupted, is untenable. Ps. li. 5, the classic passage of the defenders of the theory, is, under a fair interpretation, merely the avowal of the author that when he or the Israel of whom he speaks was born, Israel was unfaithful to YHWH; and Ps. xiv. 3 does not give a general statement applicable to the human race, but depicts a condition existing at a certain period in Israel.

The fall of man, as a theological concept, begins

to appear only in the late Apocrypha and pseudepigrapha, probably under Essenic (if not Judæo-Christian) influences. In II Esd. iii. 7 it is stated that when Adam was punished with death, his posterity also was included in the decree (the variants in the versions, Ethiopic, Armenian, Syriac, and Latin, all point to a Hebrew דורות). II Esd. iii. 21 has: "For on account of his evil will the first Adam fell into sin and guilt, and, like him, all that were born of him." This view is again stated in ch. vii. 48: "O Adam, what hast thou done! When thou sinnest, thy fall did not come over thee alone, but upon us, as well, thy descendants" (comp. Ecclus. [Sirach] xxv. 24, "from woman was the beginning of sin; on her account must we all die"). Similarly, in the Apocalypse of Baruch (xvii. 3) Adam is blamed for the shortening of the years of his progeny. Yet it would be hasty to hold that in these books the doctrine is advanced with the rigidity of an established dogma. Even in II Esd. iii. 9 the thesis is suggested that the consequence of the Fall came to an end with the Flood, when a generation of pious men sprang from Noah, and that it was only their descendants who wantonly brought corruption again into the world.

Philo's Views.

Philo's allegorical interpretation ("De Mundi Opificio," § 56), making of the Biblical incidents typical occurrences (*δείγματα τύπων*), represents a phase of Jewish thought on the whole more in accord with the teachings of Judaism on the Fall and on sin than is the quasi-dogmatic position of II Esdras. According to Philo, Adam typifies the rational, Eve the sensuous, element of human nature; while the serpent is the symbol of carnal lust and pleasure. After Philo, Samuel Hirsch, among modern expounders, treats the fall of man as a typical exposition of the psychological processes which precede sin (temptation) and gradually (through self-deception) culminate in actual sin (see his Catechism, ch. ii.).

The sin of Adam, according to the Rabbis, had certain grievous results for him and for the earth. The Shekinah left earth after his fall (Gen. R. xix.; Tan., Peḳude, 6). He himself lost his personal splendor, deathlessness, and gigantic stature (see ADAM).

All men were doomed thenceforth to die; none, not even the most just, might escape the common fate: the old temptation of the serpent suffices to bring on death (B. B. 17a; Shab 55b). Adam wished, therefore, to refrain from procreating children; but, learning that the Torah would be given to Israel, was induced to change his mind (Gen. R. xxi.). Through the illicit intercourse of Eve with the serpent, however, the nature of her descendants was corrupted, Israel alone overcoming this fatal defect by accepting the Torah at Sinai, which had been offered to and rejected by all other nations (Shab. 146a; 'Ab. Zarah 22b; Yeb. 103b). If Israel had not made the golden calf, death would have been removed from the midst of Israel (Shab. 88a; comp. 'Ab. Zarah 5a).

Views of the Rabbis.

Pious men and women overcame, at least partially, the consequences of Adam's fall. Abraham, Isaac, Jacob, Moses, Aaron, and Miriam did not suffer death at the hand of the angel of death; they died through God's kiss (בנשיקה), and even their bodies were not consumed by worms (B. B. 17a; M. Ḳ. 28a; Derek Ereẓ Zuṭa i.). Jacob and others entered into paradise while living (Ta'an. 5b; Derek Ereẓ Zuṭa i.). While thus it is not altogether true that the fall of man had no place in the theology of the Talmudists (against Nager, "Die Religionsphilosophie des Talmud," § 9) it is a fact that for the most part the foregoing notions were mere homiletical speculations that never crystallized into definite dogmas. R. Ammi's thesis (Shab. 55a) founded on Ezek. xviii. 20, that every death is caused by an actual sin, is entitled to recognition as clearly as the opinion held by his disputant, Simeon b. Eleazer, who contends that death is the result of the Fall.

In modern Jewish thought the fall of man is without dogmatic importance (see ORIGINAL SIN; consult, however, Benamozegh, "Morale Juive et Morale Chrétienne," p. 117; David Castelli, "Il Messia Secondo gli Ebrei," p. 179, Florence, 1874).

XXV
God

GOD: The Supreme Being, regarded as the Creator, Author, and First Cause of the universe, the Ruler of the world and of the affairs of men, the Supreme Judge and Father, tempering justice with mercy, working out His purposes through chosen agents—individuals as well as nations—and communicating His will through prophets and other appointed channels.

——**Biblical Data:** "God" is the rendering in the English versions of the Hebrew "El," "Eloah," and "Elohim." The existence of God is presupposed throughout the Bible, no attempt being anywhere made to demonstrate His reality. Philosophical skepticism belongs to a period of thought generally posterior to that covered by the Biblical books, Ecclesiastes and some of the Psalms (xiv., liii., xciv.) alone indicating in any degree in Biblical Israel a tendency toward ATHEISM. The controversies of the Earlier Prophets never treat of the fundamental problems of God's existence or non-existence; but their polemics are directed to prove that Israel, ready at all times to accept and worship one or the other god, is under the obligation to serve YHWH and none other. Again, the manner of His worship is in dispute, but not His being. The following are the main Biblical teachings concerning God:

Relation to Nature.

God and the world are distinct. The processes of nature are caused by God. Nature declares the glory of God: it is His handiwork (Gen. i.; Ps. viii., xix.; Isa. xl. 25 *et seq.*). God is the Creator. As such, He is "in heaven above and upon the earth beneath" (Deut. iv. 39). His are the heavens, and His is the earth (Ps. lxxxix. 12

[A. V. 11]; compare Amos iv. 13). He created the world by the word of His mouth (Ps. xxxiii. 6, 9). Natural sequences are His work (Jer. v. 22, 24; Ps. lxxiv. 15–17). He maintains the order of nature (Ps. cxlvii. 8–9, 16–18; Neh. ix. 6). He does not need the offerings of men, because "the earth is the Lord's and the fulness thereof" (Ps. xxiv. 1, 4, 7–13; compare Isa. i. 11; Jer. vii. 21–23; Micah vi. 6–8).

Nothing is affirmed of His substantial nature. The phrase "spirit of God" ("ruaḥ Elohim") merely describes the divine energy, and is not to be taken as equivalent to the phrase "God is a spirit," viz., an assertion concerning His incorporeality (Zech. iv. 6; Num. xiv. 22; Isa. xl. 13). He can not, however, be likened to any thing (Ex. xx. 4–5; Isa. xl. 18) or to any person (Jer. x. 6–7). No form is seen when God speaks (Deut. iv. 15). He rules supreme as the King of the nations (Jer. x. 6–7). His will comes to pass (Isa. viii. 9, 10; lv. 10, 11; Ps. xxxiii. 10–12, lxviii. 2–4). He is one, and none shares with Him His power or rulership (Deut. vi. 4; Isa. xliv. 6, xlvi. 10 [A. V. 9]). He is unchangeable, though he was the first and will be the last (Isa. xli. 4; Mal. iii. 6). All that is, is perishable: God is everlasting (Isa. xl. 7–8, 23–25; li. 12–13). Hence His help is always triumphant (Ps. xx. 8–9, xliv. 4, xlvi. 1–8). He is in all things, places, and times (Ps. cxxxix. 7–12). He is not, like man, subject to whim (Num. xxiii. 19; Deut. vii. 9). He is the Judge, searching the innermost parts of man's being, and knowing all his secrets (Jer. xvi. 17, xvii. 10, xxiii. 24; Ps. cxxxix. 1–4). His knowledge is too high for man (Ps. cxxxix. 6, 15, 16). God's wisdom, however, is the source of human understanding (Ps. xxxvi. 10). He is "merciful and gracious, longsuffering, and abundant in goodness and truth" (Ex. xxxiv. 6–7). But He can not hold the sinner guiltless (*ib.*). He manifests His supreme lordship in the events of history (Deut. xxxii. 8–12; Ps. xxii. 28, 29; lxxviii. 2–7). He is the ever-ruling King (Jer. x. 10). He punishes the wicked (Nahum i. 2); He turns their way upside down (Ps. i. 6). Appearances to the contrary are illusive (Hab. i. 13, ii. 2; Jer. xii. 1-2; Ps. x. 13–14, xxxvii. 35–39, lii. 3–9, lxii. 11–13, xcii. 7–8; Job xxi. 7–9, xxvii. 8–11, xxxv. 14).

The Biblical theodicy culminates in the thought that the end will show the futility and deceptive

Relation to Man. nature of the prosperity of the wicked (Ps. lxxvii. 17). The mightiest nations do not prevail against God (Jer. xviii. 7–10, xxv. 30–31; Ps. vii. 8–9; xxxiii. 13, 19). He judges the world in righteousness (Ps. ix. 9, 16; lxxvi. 9–10; xcv. 10–13). I Chron. xxix. 11–12 may be said to be a succinct epitome of the Biblical doctrine concerning God's manifestations in nature and in history (compare I Sam. ii.). Yet God does not delight in the death of the sinner: He desires his return from his evil ways (Ezek. xviii. 21–22, xxxviii. 10–11). Fasting is not an adequate expression of repentance (Isa. lviii. 3–8; compare Jonah ii. 10; Joel ii. 13; Zech. vii. 5). God hath demanded of man "to do justly, and to love mercy" (Micah vi. 8); hence redress for wrongs done is the first step toward attaining God's forgiveness (Ezek. xxxiii. 15), the "forsaking of one's evil ways" (Lam. iii. 37–40).

It is characteristic of the Biblical conception of God that He is with those of contrite heart (Isa. lvii. 15). He loves the weak (Deut. x. 17–18). He is the father (Isa. lxiii. 16, lxiv. 7); and like a father He taketh pity on His children (Ps. ciii. 13; see COMPASSION). Therefore, love is due to Him on the part of His children (Deut. vi. 4–5). The demand to fear Him, in the light of the implications of the Hebrew original, is anything but in conflict with the insistence that the relations between God and man are marked by parental and filial love. The God of the Bible is not a despot, to be approached in fear. For "yir'ah" connotes an attitude in which confidence and love are included, while the recognition of superiority, not separation, is expressed (Nietzsche's "pathos of distance"). Reverence in the modern sense, not fear, is its approximate equivalent. They that confide in Him renew their strength (Isa. xl. 30–31). God is holy (compare Isa. vi. 3); this phrase sums up the ultimate contents of the Bible conception of God (see FEAR OF GOD).

He is Israel's God. Not on account of any merits of its own (Deut. vii. 7–8, ix. 4–7), but because of

Relation to Israel. God's special designs, because the fathers loved Him (Deut. x. 11–16), Israel was chosen by God (Ex. xix. 4–6; Deut. iv. 20, xxxii. 9; Isa. xli. 8–9, xliii. 21; Jer. ii. 2, and often elsewhere).

Hence, in Israel's experience are illustrated God's power, love, and compassion, as, in fact, it is Israel's sole destiny to be the witness to God (Isa. xliv. 8). For Israel, therefore, God is a jealous God. He can not tolerate that Israel, appointed to be His portion (Deut. xxxii. 9), His servant (Isa. xliv. 21), His people joined unto Him for His name and glory and ornament (Jer. xiii. 11, A. V., "for a name, and for a praise, and for a glory"), should worship other gods. Israel's task is to be holy as He is holy (Lev. xix. 2; Deut. xxvi. 19). Israel itself does not fully recognize this. God sends prophets again and again to instruct and admonish His people (Jer. vii. 25, xi. 7, xxxv. 15; Isa. xxix. 13–14).

In Israel God's judgments are purposed to impress upon His people the duty placed upon it. Greater suffering He metes out to Israel (Lev. xxvi. 40; Deut. iv. 30–31; viii. 5, 19; xi. 16–17; xxxii. 15; Isa. i. 19–20, iv. 3–4, xlii. 24–xliii. 1, xlviii. 9–11; Jer. ii. 19, v. 18–19; Amos iii. 2), but He will not permit Israel to perish (Isa. xli. 10–14; xlv. 17; li. 7–8; liv. 10, 17; Jer. xxxi. 36). And Israel, brought to faithfulness, will be instrumental in winning the whole earth to God (Isa. ii. 2–4, xi. 9, xlv. 23, lxv. 25; Micah iv. 1–4; Jer. iii. 17; see MESSIAH).

God is Israel's lawgiver. His law is intended to make Israel holy. That Israel serve God, so as to win all people to the truth, is God's demand (Lev. xx. 26; Deut. iv. 6). God's unity is indicated in the one sanctuary. But legalism and sacerdotalism are withal not the ultimate (Ps. l. 7–13; I Sam. xv. 22: "to obey is better than sacrifice"; Isa. i. 11; Jer. vii. 21–23; Hosea vi. 6: "I desired love [A. V. "mercy"] and not sacrifice").

Nor is the law a scheme of salvation. Nowhere in the Old Testament is the doctrine taught that God must be satisfied (see FALL OF MAN; SIN). Sin is impotent against God, and righteousness does not benefit Him (Job xxxv. 6–8). God is omnipotent (Ps. x. 3–4). At one with Him, man is filled with joy and with a sense of serene security (Ps. xvi. 5–6, 8–9; xxvii. 1–4). Without this all else is sham (Ps. xlix. 7–13). Happy, therefore, the man who heeds God's instruction (Ps. xciv. 12; Prov. iii. 11–12). Sin never attains its aims (Ps. xxxiv. 22; Prov. xi. 19; I Sam. xxiv. 14; Job viii. 13–14, xv. 20–31). It is thus that God documents His supremacy; but unto man (and Israel) He gives freedom to choose between life and death (Deut. xxx. 15–20). He is near to them that revere Him (Ps. lxxxv. 9–14). Though His ways are not man's ways, and His thoughts not man's thoughts (Isa. lv. 8), yet to this one certainty man may cleave; namely, that God's word will come to pass and His purposes will be carried out (*ib.* verses 9, 10, 11).

The God of the Bible is not a national God, though in the fate of one people are mirrored the universal facts of His kingship and fatherhood, and the truth is emphasized that not by might, nor by power, but by God's spirit are the destinies of the world and of man ordered (Zech. iv. 6; Mal. i. 11; Ps. cxiii., cxv.). The God of the Bible is a person; *i.e.*, a being self-conscious, with will and purpose, even though by searching man can not find Him out (Job xi. 7; Ps. xciv. 7, 8, 9, 10, 11; Isa. xl. 28; Ps. cxlv. 3).

——**In Post-Biblical Literature:** In the Apocrypha of Palestinian origin the Biblical teachings concerning God are virtually reaffirmed without material modifications. In some books anthropomorphic expressions are avoided altogether; in the others they are toned down. The "hand of God," for instance (Ecclus. [Sirach] xxxiii. 3), is in the parallel distich explained as "His might." The "eyes of God" symbolize His knowledge and providence (Baruch ii. 17); the "voice of God" is synonymous with His will (*ib.* ii. 22, iii. 4).

His unity, postulating Him as the absolute, omnipresent, and therefore as the omniscient, eternal, and living God, is accentuated; while in His relations to the world and its inhabitants He is manifest as the Creator, Ruler, the perfectly righteous Judge, requiting evil and rewarding good, yet, in His mercy, forgiving sin. To Him all nature is subject, while He executes His designs according to His inscrutable wisdom. The history of former generations is cited in proof of the contention that they who confide in Him have never been disappointed (Ecclus. [Sirach] ii. 10); for God is full of mercy, pardoning sins, and is the great Helper (*ib.* verse 11).

In the Palestinian Apocrypha.

Good and evil proceed from God, as do life and death (*ib.* xi. 14). Yet sin is not caused by God, but by man's own choice (*ib.* xv. 11 *et seq.*). God is omnipresent. Though He is on high, He takes heed of men's ways (*ib.* xvi. 17, xvii. 15–16). Mountains and the ocean are in His power (*ib.* verses 18 *et seq.*).

Being the Creator, He planned the eternal order of nature (*ib.* verses 26 *et seq.*). He also fashioned man (*ib.* xvii. 1 *et seq.*). Whatever strength man has is from Him (*ib.* verse 3). The eyes of men are enabled by Him to see "the majesty of His glory," and their ears to hear "His glorious voice" (*ib.* verse 13). He liveth in all eternity and judgeth all things. None may search out His wondrous might (*ib.* xviii. 1–2), or describe His grace (*ib.* verse 3). To Him naught may be added, and from Him nothing may be taken away (*ib.* verse 6, xlii. 21). Even the "holy ones" are not competent to relate the marvels of His works (*ib.* xlii. 17). He announces that which was and that which is to be and all hidden things (*ib.* verses 19–20). He is one from all eternity (*ib.* verse 21). He is the Living God (*ib.* verse 23). Among all the varieties of things He has created nothing without purpose (לבטלה, *ib.* verse 24).

The "wisdom of God" is spoken of and exalted in the same strains as in the Biblical books (Prov. vii., viii.). All wisdom is from God and is with Him forever (Ecclus. [Sirach] i. 1). It came forth from the mouth of the Most High (*ib.* xxiv. 3); but it was created before all things (*ib.* i. 4). It is subject to the will of Him who alone is "wise, and greatly to be feared," seated on His throne (*ib.* i. 8). God "poured it out over all His works" (*ib.* i. 7; comp. xxiv. 31). However close this description of wisdom may come to a personification, it is plain that it is free from any element which might be construed as involving a departure from the Biblical position regarding God's absolute unity.

It is in the Alexandrian Apocrypha that modifications of the Biblical doctrine appear; but even here are to be found books whose theology is a reiteration of the Biblical teachings. The so-called Third Book of the Maccabees, in the prayer of the high priest Simon, invokes "God as the King of the Heavens, the Ruler of all creatures, the most Holy, the sole Governor, the Omnipotent," declaring Him to be "a just ruler,"

In Alexandrian Apocrypha.

and appeals to the events of past days in support of the faith in God's supremacy and in Israel's appointment to glorify Him (III Macc. ii. 1–20) who is all-merciful and the maker of peace.

The third book of the "Oracula Sibyllina," also, reiterates with great emphasis and without equivocation the unity of God, who is alone in His superlative greatness. God is imperishable, everlasting, self-existent, alone subsisting from eternity to eternity. He alone really is: men are nothing. He, the omnipotent, is wholly invisible to the fleshly eye. Yet He dwells in the firmament (Sibyllines, i. 1, 7–17, 20, 32; ii. 1–3, 17, 36, 46). From this heavenly abode He exercises His creative power, and rules over the universe. He sustains all that is. He is "all-nourishing," the "leader of the cosmos," the constant ruler of all things. He is the "supreme Knower" (*ib.* i. 3, 4, 5, 8, 15, 17, 35; ii. 42). He is "the One God sending out rains, winds, earthquakes, lightnings, famines, pestilences, dismal sorrows, and so forth" (*ib.* i. 32–34). By these agencies He expresses His indignation at the doings of the wicked (*ib.* ii. 19–20); while the good are rewarded beyond their deserts (*ib.* ii. 1–8). God's indwelling in man (πᾶσι βροτοῖσιν ἐνών) "as the faculty of judgment" is also taught (*ib.* i. 18). This indwelling of God, which has been claimed as an indication of the book's leaning toward a modification of the transcendentalism of the Biblical idea of God may perhaps rest on a faulty reading (comp. Drummond, "Philo Judæus," i. 173).

In the Septuagint, also, the treatment of anthropomorphic statements alone exhibits a progress beyond the earlier Biblical conceptions. For example, in Gen. vi. 6–7 "it repented the Lord" is softened into "He took it to heart"; Ex. xxiv. 9–10, "They [Moses, Aaron, and the others mentioned] saw the place where the God of Israel stood" is rendered "They saw the God of Israel"; Ex. xv. 3, instead of "The Lord is a man of war," has "The Lord is one who crushes wars"; Josh. iv. 24, "the power" for "the hand." In Isa. vi. 1, the "train of his [God's] robe" is changed into "his glory" (see Zeller, "Die Philosophie der Griechen," iii., part ii., 254). As the Targumim, so the Septuagint, on account of a more spiritualized conception of God, takes care to modify the earlier and grosser terminology; but even the phrase ὁ Θεὸς τῶν δυνάμεων (Isa. xlii. 13) does not imply the recognition of powers self-existent though under the control of God. The doctrine of the unity of God is put forth as the central truth also in the Septuagint.

Hellenistic Influences.

Nor is this theology toned down in other Hellenistic writings. While in style and method under the influence of Greek thought, the fragments of Demetrius, Pseudo-Artapanus, Pseudo-Phocylides, Ezekielus' tragedy on Exodus, and the so-called Fourth Book of Maccabees can not be said to put forth notions concerning God at variance with the Palestinian theology. The Wisdom of Solomon, the Letter of Aristeas, and the fragments of Aristobulus, however, do this. In the first of these three, Israel's God is pronounced to be the only God. He lives in solitary supremacy, responsible to Himself alone (Wisdom xii. 12–14). He IS (τόν ὄντα; *ib.* xiii. 1). He is the "eternal light" (*ib.* vii. 26). He is the Artificer (Τεχνίτης) who created or prepared (both verbs are used) the various things in nature (*ib.* xviii. 1–5). This uncertainty in the verb descriptive of God's part in creation suggests that the old Biblical conception of the Creator's functions is in this book attenuated to the bringing into order of formless primeval matter (comp. *ib.* xi. 17). Matter is compared to a lump of wax which, originally devoid of attributes, owes its qualities to divine agency (Drummond, *l.c.* p. 188).

But, while the cosmos is an expression and the result of the greatness, power, and beauty of God, He remains transcendent above it. Nevertheless, He continues to administer all things (Wisdom xii. 15, 18; xv. 1). It is His providence that acts as a pilot or rudder (*ib.* xiv. 3). In this is manifested His truth, justice, mercy, loving-kindness, and long-suffering (*ib.* xi. 23; xii. 15, 18; xv. 1). It is among His holy ones that His grace and mercy are conspicuous; but evil-doers are punished (iii. 9, 10). The pious are those who dwell with wisdom (vii. 28). God possesses immediate knowledge of men's secrets, of their speech, feelings, and thoughts (*ib.* i. 6). He foreknows but does not foreordain the future. Necessity and right (ἀνάγκη and δίκη) are both postulated. The former blinds the judgment of the impious. If they continue in their impenitence, they will be overtaken by their punishment (*ib.* i. 15; ii. 6–22; iii. 2–17; iv. 3–14; xii. 2, 10, 20; and more especially xix. 1–5). The avenging Right is, however, not hypostatized or personified to any great degree (*ib.* i. 8, xi. 20, xiv. 31, xviii. 11). God is not the creator of evil (*ib.* i. 12–14); therefore in evil He is confronted with a tendency that He can not tolerate. Hence He or His is the avenging justice.

God is neither unknown nor unknowable. The external universe reveals Him. It implies the existence of a primal source greater than it (*ib.* xiii. 1–9); and, again, through wisdom and "the spirit" sent from on high, God is found by them who do not disobey Him (*ib.* i. 2–4, ix. 13–17). Yet man can never attain unto perfect knowledge of the divine essence (see Gfrörer, cited by Drummond, *l.c.* p. 198). Notwithstanding God's transcendence, anthropopathic phraseology is introduced (Wisdom iv. 18, "God shall laugh"; "His right hand" and "arm," v. 16; "His hand," vii. 16, x. 20, xi. 17, xix. 8). This proves that the doctrine of intermediate agents is not fully developed in the book, though in its presentation of God's wisdom elements appear that root in this conception. Certainly the question had begun to force itself upon the writer's mind: How is it that God enthroned on high is yet omnipresent in the universe? Like the Stoics, the author assumes an all-penetrating divine principle which appears as the rational order of the cosmos and as the conscious reason in man. Hence God's spirit is all-pervasive (*ib.* i. 6–7). This spirit is, in a certain sense, distinct from God, an extension of the Divine Being, bringing God into relation with the phenomenal world. Still, this spirit is not a separate or subordinate person. "Wisdom" and this "spirit" are used interchangeably (*ib.* ix. 17); "wisdom is a spirit that is" a lover of mankind (*ib.* i. 4–6); wisdom is "a vapor of the power of God," a reflection of eternal light (*ib.* vii. 25–26).

"Wisdom" of God.

This wisdom has twenty-one attributes: it is "an understanding spirit, holy, alone in kind, manifold, subtile, freely moving, clear in utterance, unpolluted, distinct, unharmed, loving what is good, keen, unhindered, beneficent, loving toward man, steadfast, sure, free from care, all-powerful, all-surveying, and penetrating through all spirits that are quick of understanding, pure, most subtile" (*ib.* vii. 22–24). Wisdom is a person, the "assessor" at God's throne (*ib.* ix. 4); the chooser of God's works (*ib.* viii. 3–4). She was with God when He made the cosmos (*ib.* ix. 9). She is the artificer of all things (*ib.* vii. 21). As all this is elsewhere predicated of God also, it is plain that this "wisdom" is regarded only as an instrument, not as a delegate of the Divine. The Wisdom of Solomon speaks also of the "Logos" (*ib.* ii. 2–3, ix. 1–2, xvi. 12, xviii. 14–16); and this, taken in connection with its peculiar conception of wisdom, makes the book an important link in the chain leading from the absolute God-conception of Palestinian Judaism to the theory of the mediating agency of the Word (Λόγος, "Memra") in Philo. The Aristeas Letter does not present as clear a modification of the God-conception (but see Eleazar's statement therein, "there is only one God and 'His power' is through all things"). Aristobulus, in the Orphic verses, teaches that God is invisible (verse 20), but that through the mind He may be beheld (verses 11, 12). Maker and Ruler of the world, He is Himself the beginning, middle, and end (verses 8, 34, 35, 39). But wisdom existed before heaven and earth; God is the "molder of the cosmos" (verse 8)—statements which, by no means clear enough to form the basis of a conclusion, yet suggest also in Aristobulus' theology a departure from the doctrine of God's transcendence and His immediate control of all as the Creator ex nihilo.

Philo is the philosopher who boldly, though not always consistently, attempts to harmonize the supramundane existence and majesty of the one God with His being the Creator and Governor of all. Reverting to the Old Testament idiom, according to which "by the word of YHWH were the heavens made" (Ps. xxxiii. [xxxii.] 6)—which passage is also at the root of the Targumic use of MEMRA (see ANTHROPOMORPHISM)—and on the whole but not consistently assuming that matter was uncreated (see CREATION), he introduces the Logos as the mediating agent between God on high and the phenomenal world.

Philo is also the first Jewish writer who undertakes to prove the existence of God. His arguments are of two kinds: those drawn from nature, and those supplied by the intuitions of the soul. Man's mind, also invisible, occupies in him the same position as does that of God in the universe ("De Opificio Mundi," § 23). From this one arrives at a knowledge of God. The mind is the sovereign of the body. The cosmos must also have a king who holds it together and governs it justly, and who is the Supreme ("De Abrahamo," § 16; "De Migratione Abrahami," § 33). From a ship man forms the idea of a ship-builder. Similarly, from the cosmos he must conceive the notion of the Father and Creator, the great and excellent and all-knowing artist ("De Monarchia," i. 4; "De Præmiis et Pœnis," § 7). For a first and an efficient cause man must look outside of the material universe, which fails in the points of eternity and efficiency ("De Confusione Linguarum," §§ 21, 25; "De Somniis," i. 33). This cause is mind. But man has the gift of immortal thoughts ("De Eo Quod Deterius Potiori Insidiatur," § 24): these culminate in the apprehension of God; they press beyond the limits of the entire phenomenal world to the Unbegotten ("De Plantatione Noe," § 5). This intuition of God was the especial prerogative of the Prophets, of Abraham, and of Jacob.

Philo's Logos.

The essence of God is unknown to man, whose conceptions are colored through the medium of his own nature. Anthropopathisms and anthropomorphisms are wicked. God is incorporeal. He is without any irrational affections of the soul. God is a free, self-determining mind. His benevolence is due not to any incapacity of His for evil, but to His free preference for the good (*ib.* § 20).

Man's personality lifts him above the rest of the creatures. In analogy therewith, Philo gives God the attributes of personality, which are not restrictive, but the very reverse (Drummond, "Philo Judæus," ii. 15). Efficiency is the property of God; susceptibility, that of the begotten ("De Cherubim," § 24). God, therefore, is not only the First Cause, but He is the still efficient ground of all that is and comes to pass. He never pauses in His creative activity ("De Allegoriis Legum," i. 3). The feebleness of the human mind precludes the possibility of man's knowing God as He is in Himself (*ib.* iii. 73). God is without qualities (*ib.* i. 13). God is transcendent. He contains, but is not contained (περιέχων οὐ περιεχόμενος); yet He is also within the universe. He is omnipresent (comp. "De Confusione Linguarum," § 27; "De Posteritate Caini," § 5); still He is above the conditions of space and time ("De Posteritate Caini," § 5; "Quod Deus Sit Immutabilis," § 6). He is complete in Himself, and contains within His own being the sum of all conceivable good ("De Mutatione Nominum," § 4). He is perfect; He is omniscient ("De Eo Quod Deterius Potiori Insidiatur," § 42); He is omnipotent; He is free from evil and, therefore, can not be its source ("De Profugis," § 15); He is without passion as the most perfectly reasonable being, as the efficient and not the susceptible. God cares for the world and its parts (see PROVIDENCE) ("De Opificio Mundi," § 61). He is the "Archon of the great city," "the pilot managing the universe with saving care" ("De Decem Oraculis," § 12).

It is in the development of his theory of the divine powers that Philo injects into his theology elements not altogether in concordance with antecedent Jewish thought. These intelligible and invisible powers, though subject to God, partake of His mystery and greatness. They are immaterial. They are uncircumscribed and infinite, independent of time, and unbegotten ("Quod Deus Sit Immutabilis," § 17). They are "most holy" ("Fragmenta," ii. 655), incapable of error ("De Confusione Linguarum," § 23). Among these powers, through which God works His ends, is the Logos. "God is the most generic Thing; and His Logos is second" ("De Allegoriis Legum," ii. 21). "This Logos is the divine seal of the entire cosmos" ("De Somniis," ii. 6). It is the archetypal idea with which all things were stamped ("De Mutatione Nominum," § 23). It is the law of and in all things, which is not corruptible ("De Ebrietate," § 35). It is the bond of the universe, filling a function analogous to that of the soul in man ("Quis Rerum Divinarum Heres Sit," § 48). It is God's son (see LOGOS; PHILO).

Vacillating though it was, the theory of the divine powers and the Logos, as elaborated by Philo, certainly introduced views into the theology of

Judaism of far-reaching consequences in the development of the God-idea if not of the Synagogue at least of the Church. The absolute unity and transcendence of God were modified materially, though the Biblical notion of the likeness of man to God was in the system developed in a manner adopted again by the modern Jewish theologians (see below). Talmudic and medieval Judaism were only indirectly affected by this bold attempt to save the transmundane and supramundane implications of the God-concept and still find an explanation for the immanence of the divine in man and in the world. The Pharisaic Psalms of Solomon, for instance, echo without the least equivocation the theological constructions of the Biblical books (see ii. 15–18, 32–37); and the other apocalyptic writings (Enoch; Book of Jubilees; Testaments of the Twelve Patriarchs) present no essentially new points of view or even any augmentations.

——**In Talmudic Literature:** The Hellenistic modifications of the Biblical God-concept were further developed in the propositions of the heretical sects, such as the Minim or Gnostics, and of the Judæo-Christians and Christians. To controvert their departures from the fundamental positions of Judaism, the Palestinian synagogue, as did all later Judaism with the exception of the cabalists (see CABALA), laid all the greater stress on the unity of God, and took all the greater precaution to purge the concept from any and all human and terrestrial similarities. The Shema' (Deut. vi. 4 *et seq.*) was invested with the importance of a confession of faith. Recited twice daily (Ber. i. 1), the concluding word "eḥad" was given especial prominence, emphatic and prolonged enunciation being recommended ("kol ha-ma'arik be-eḥad"; Ber. 19a). Audible enunciation was required for the whole sentence (Sifre, Deut. 31: "Mi-kan amru: ha-ḳore et shema' welo-hishmia' le-ozno lo yaẓa"). Upon Israel especially devolved the duty of proclaiming God's unity ("le-yaḥed shemo beyoter"). The repetition of "YHWH" in the verse is held to indicate that God is one both in the affairs of this world and in those of

The Shema'.

the world to come (Yalḳ., Deut. 833). "The Eternal is Israel's portion" (Lam. iii. 24, Hebr.) demonstrates Israel's duty in the Shema' to proclaim God's unity and imperishability over against the sun-, moon-, and star-worship of the heathen (Lam. R. iii. 24; comp. Deut. R. ii., end). The "eḥad" is also taken in the sense of "meyuḥad," *i.e.*, unique, unlike any other being (Meg. 28). Two powers ("reshuyot"), therefore, can not be assumed, as Deut. xxxii. 39 proves (Tan., Yitro; Jellinek, "B. H." i. 110); and the opening sentence of the Decalogue confirms this (Mek., Yitro, v.; comp. Yalḳ., Ex. 286). In the historical events, though God's manifestations are varied and differ according to the occasion, one and the same God appears: at the Red Sea, a warrior; at Sinai, the author of the Decalogue; in the days of Daniel, an old, benignant man (Yalḳ. *l.c.*). God has neither father, nor son, nor brother (Deut. R. ii.).

Pains are taken to refute the arguments based on the grammatical plurals employed in Biblical texts when referring to God. "Elohim" does not designate a plurality of deities. The very context shows this, as the verbs in the predicate are in the singular. The phrase "Let us make man in our image" (Gen. i. 26) is proved by the subsequent statement, "so God created man in his own image" (*ib.* verse 27), to refer to one God only (Yer. Ber. ix.; Gen. R. viii., xix.). Nor, according to R. Gamaliel, is the use of both "bara" and "yaẓar," to connote God's creative action, evidence of the existence of two distinct divine powers (Gen. R. i.). The reason why in the beginning one man only was fashioned was to disprove the contention of those that believe in more than one personality in God (Sanh. 38a). God had neither associate nor helper (Sanh. 38b; Yer. Shab. vi. 8d; Eccl. R. iv. 8). The ever-recurrent principle throughout haggadic theological speculations is that there is only one "Reshut" ("Reshut aḥat hu" = "personality").

One "Reshut."

From this emphasis upon the unity and immutability of God, Weber, among others (see his "Jüdische Theologie," p. 153, Leipsic, 1897), has drawn the inference that the Jewish God was apprehended as the Absolute, persisting in and for Himself alone —supramundane and therefore extramundane also.

Between Him and the world and man there is no affinity and no bond of union. This view, however, neglects to take into account the thousand and one observations and interpretations of the Rabbis in which the very reverse doctrine is put forth. The bond between this one God—supreme, and in no way similar to man—and His creatures is very close (comp. the discussion of the effect of the Shema' taken from Yer. Ber. in Yalḳ., Deut. 836). It is not that subsisting between a despot and his abject, helpless slaves, but that between a loving father and his children. The passages bearing on the point do not support Weber's arbitrary construction that the implications of the names "Elohim" as "middat ha-din" (justice) and "YHWH" as "middat ha-raḥamim" (mercy) merely convey the notion of a supreme despot who capriciously may or may not permit mercy to temper revengeful justice (Weber, *l.c.*). In the rabbinical as in the Biblical conception of God, His paternal pity and love are never obscured (see COMPASSION).

Nor is it true, as Weber puts it and many after him have repeated, that the Jewish conception of God lacks that "self-communicating love which . . . presupposes its own immanence in the other" (Weber, *l.c.*). R. Johanan's parable of the king and his son certainly demonstrates the very reverse. "A king's son was made to carry a beam. The king, upon seeing this, commanded that the beam be laid on his own shoulders. So does God invite sinners to lay their sins upon Him" (Midr. Teh. to Ps. xxii. 6). The anti-Pauline point of the parable is patent. The convenient restriction of the term "abinu she-ba-shamayim" (our father which art in heaven) to mean, when used in a Jewish prayer, "the father of the nation," while when found in a supposedly non-Jewish prayer (see LORD'S PRAYER) it is interpreted to express the filial relation of every human soul to the Father, rests on no proof. The Rabbis denationalized and individualized their conception of God as clearly as did the Jewish compilers of the Gospels. "God used the phrase 'I am YHWH, thy God' advisedly because He was the God of every individual man, woman, or child" (*thy* God, not *your* God) (Yalḳ., Deut. 286).

In the quaint presentation of their views on God's providence, the haggadists strike this note as well.

"God chooses His own. Him whose deeds He is pleased with, He brings near unto Himself" (Midr. Shemuel, viii.; Num. R. iii.). "God is busy making marriages" (see DEISM; Lev. R. viii., lxviii.; Pesiḳ. 11b; Midr. Shemuel v.; Tan., Bemidbar, ed. Buber, 18). "God builds ladders for some to ascend [become rich], for others to descend [become poor]" (Tan., Maṭṭot and Ki Tissa, ed. Buber, and passages quoted in the foregoing sentence). "God does not provide for Israel alone, but for all lands: He does not guard Israel alone, but all men" (Sifre, Deut. 40). "None will wound as much as a finger here below unless this is the divine decree concerning him from above" (Ḥul. 7b). These passages, which might easily be indefinitely multiplied, are illustrative of the thought running through haggadic theology; and they amply demonstrate the fallacy of the view denying to the God-concept of rabbinical Judaism individualistic and denationalized elements.

In the Targumim.

The care with which anthropomorphisms are avoided in the Targumim is not due to dogmatic zeal in emphasizing the transcendental character of the Godhead, but to the endeavor not to use phraseology which might in the least degree create the presumption of God's corporeality. Hence the introduction of the particle "ke-'illu" (as it were) in the paraphrasing of passages that might suggest similarity between God and man's sensuous nature (Yer. Targ. to Gen. xviii. 8); the suppression altogether of verbs connoting physical action ("God descended," Gen. xi. 5, becomes "God revealed Himself"); the recourse to "ḳodam" (before), to guard against the humanizing of the Godhead. The MEMRA ("Word"; "Logos") and the SHEKINAH, the divine effulgent indwelling of God (see NAMES OF GOD), are not expedients to bridge the chasm between the extramundane and supramundane God and the world of things and man, as Weber claims; they are not hypostases which by being introduced into the theology of the rabbinical Synagogue do violence to the strenuous emphasis on God's unity by which it is characterized; but they owe their introduction into the phraseology of the Targumim and Midrashim respectively to this anxiety to find and use terms distinctively indicative of God's superlative sublimity and exaltedness, above and differentiated from any terrestrial or human similitude. These two terms prove, if anything, the apprehension on the part of the haggadists of God's relations to the world as the one supreme, all-directing, omnipresent, and all-pervading Essence, the all-abiding, ever-active and activizing Principle, unfolding Himself in time and space.

Equally one-sided is the view according to which the rabbinical conception of God is rigidly and narrowly legal or nomistic. Weber (*l.c.*) and many after him have in connection with this even employed the term "Judaized conception of God." In proof of the contention, after Bartolocci, Eisenmenger, and Bodenschatz, rabbinical passages have been adduced in which God is represented as "studying the Law" ('Ab. Zarah 3b; Yalḳ., Isa. 316; or, more particularly, the section concerning the red heifer, Num. R. xix., parashah "Parah Adummah"); as "teaching children" (Yalḳ., Isa. *l.c.*); as "weeping over the destruction of the Temple" (Yer. Ḥag. i. 5b; Yalḳ., Lam. 1000); as "roaring like a lion" and "playing with the LEVIATHAN" (Yalḳ., Isa. *l.c.*); as "no longer on His throne, but having only 'arba' ammot shel halakah,' the four ells of the halakah in the world for His own" (Ber. 11a); as "being under the ban, 'ḥerem'" (Pirḳe R. El. xxxviii.); as "being Levitically unclean, owing to His having buried Moses" (Sanh. 39a); as "praying" (Yalḳ., Ps. 873; Ber. 7a); as "laying tefillin and wearing a ṭallit" (Ber. 6a; R. H. 17b); as "blowing the shofar"; as "having a vow released according to the provisions of the Law" (Num. xxx. 2 *et seq.*; Ex. R. xliii.; Lev. R. xix.); and as "rising before a hoary head" (Lev. R. xxxv.). Upon examination, all these passages are seen to be homiletical extravagances, academic exercises, and mere displays of skill and versatility in the art of interpreting Biblical texts ("Schulweisheit"), and therefore of no greater importance as reflecting the religious consciousness of either their authors or the people at large than other extravagances marked as such by the prefacing of "kibbe-yakol" (if it is permitted to say so; "sit venia verbo"), or "ilmale miḳra katub e efshar le-omro" ('Er. 22a; Yer. Ber. 9d; Lev. R. xxxiv.).

The exaltation of the Torah is said to have been both the purpose and the instrument of creation: it is preexistent (Gen. R. i.), the "daughter" of Yhwh (Tan., Ki Tissa, 28; *ib.* Peḳude, 4), and its study even engages God (B. M. 86a). Differentiated from the "kabod" of God, it was given to man on earth, while the "splendor" (כבוד, also שכינה) has its abode in the higher regions (Midr. Teh. to Ps. xc. 17, xci. 9). It is praised as the one panacea, healing the whole of man ('Er. 54a). This idea is not, as has been claimed by Weber and after him by others, evidence either of the nomistic character of the "Judaized" conception of God or of the absolute transcendence of God. In the first place, the term "Torah" in most of the passages adduced in proof does not connote the Law (Pentateuch). For it "religion" might be with greater exactness substituted (see Bacher, "Die Aelteste Terminologie der Jüdischen Schriftauslegung," *s.v.* תורה). In the second, if not a restatement of the doctrine of wisdom ("ḥokmah"; see above), these ecstasies concerning the Torah have a marked anti-Pauline character. The Torah is the "sam ḥayyim" (life- [salvation-] giving drug; Sifre, Deut. § 45; Ḳid. 30b; Yoma 72b; Lev. R. xvi.).

The Law of God.

The following haggadic observations will illustrate the views formulated above:

God's omnipresence (with reference to Jer. xxiii. 24) is illustrated by two mirrors, the one convex, the other concave, magnifying and contracting respectively the image of the beholder (Gen. R. iv.). God's "mercy" will always assert itself if man repents (Pesiḳ. 164a). God's "justice" often intentionally refuses to take account of man's misdeeds (Gen. R. xxxvi.; Lev. R. v.). God requites men according to their own measure ("middah ke-neged middah"; Sanh. 90a, b; Tosef., Soṭah, iii.; Yer. Soṭah 17a, b); but the measure of good always exceeds that of evil and punishment ("middat ṭobah merubbah mi-middah pur'aniyyot"; Mek., Beshallaḥ, x. 49a). God forgives the sins of a whole community on account of the true repentance of even one man (Yoma 86b). "Ṭob" (the good) is God's main attribute (Yer. Ḥag. 77c; Eccl. R. vii. 8; Ruth R. iii. 16; comp. Matt. xix. 17). The anthropomorphic representation of God as suffering pain with men merely illustrates His goodness (Sanh. vi. 5). God fills the world; but the world does not fill or exhaust Him (Gen. R. lxviii.; Yalḳ., Hab. 563). God's "hand" is extended underneath the wings of the beings that carry the throne, to receive and take to Himself the sinners that return, and to save them from punishment (Pes. 119a). Man is in the clutches of anger; but God masters wrath (Gen. R. xlix.; Midr. Teh. to Ps. xciv. 1). God removes the "stumbling-block" (sin) (Pesiḳ. 165a; Yalḳ., Hosea, 532).

God knows all. He is like an architect who, having built a palace, knows all the hiding-places therein, and from whom, therefore, the owner can not secrete anything (Gen. R. xxiv.). God is the architect of the world (Gen. R. i.); the "Torah" is the plan. God's signet-ring is truth, אמת (the Alpha and Omega of the New Testament; Gen. R. lxxxi; Shab. 55a; Yoma 69b; Sanh. 64a; Yer. Tan. 18a; Deut. R. i.). All that confess "two God-heads" will ultimately come to grief (Deut. R. ii.). In a vast number of haggadic disquisitions on God, attention is called to the difference between the action of man and that of God, generally prefaced by "Come and see that 'shelo ke-middat basar we-dam middat ha-Ḳodesh baruk hu'" (not like the motive and conduct of flesh and blood is God's manner). For instance, man selling a precious article will part with it in sorrow; not so God. He gave His Torah to Israel and rejoiced thereat (Ber. 5a). In others, again, God is likened to a king; and from this comparison conclusions are drawn (Gen. R. xxviii. and innumerable similar parables).

Talmudic Views.

Sometimes attention is called to the difference between God and an earthly monarch. "When a king is praised, his ministers are praised with him, because they help him carry the burden of his government. Not so when God is praised. He alone is exalted, as He alone created the world" (Yalḳ., Deut. 835; Midr. Teh. to Ps. lxxxvi. 10; Gen. R. i. 3). God exalteth Himself above those that exalt themselves ("mitga'ah hu 'al ha-mitga'im; Ḥag. 13b; Mek., Beshallaḥ, 35b). In His hand is everything except the fear of Him (Ber. 33b; Meg. 25a; Niddah 16b).

Among the descriptive attributes, "mighty," "great," and "fearful" are mentioned. After Moses had formulated these (Deut. x. 17), and the last had been omitted by Jeremiah (xxxii. 18) and the first by Daniel (ix. 4), in view of the apparent victory of the heathen the "men of the Great Synagogue" (Neh. ix. 32) reinstituted the mention of all three, knowing that God's might consisted in showing indulgent long-suffering to the evil-minded, and that His "fearfulness" was demonstrated in Israel's wonderful survival. Hence their name "Great Synagogue" for having restored the crown of the divine attributes (Yoma 69b; Yer. Ber. 11c; Meg. 74c).

These attributes may not be arbitrarily augmented; however many attributes man might use, he could not adequately express God's greatness (Ber. 33b; see AGNOSTICISM); but man is bound to praise the Creator with his every breath (Gen. R. xiv.).

Stress is laid in the Talmudic theology on the resurrection of the dead. God is "meḥayyeh ha-metim," the one who restores the dead to life. The key to the resurrection is one of the three (or four) keys not given, save in very rare cases, to any one else, but is in the hands of God alone (Ta'an. 2a, b; Gen. R. lxxiii.; see ESCHATOLOGY).

God and Israel.

Israel is God's people. This relation to Him can not be dissolved by Israel (Num. R. ii.). This is expressed in the definition of God's name as "ehyeh asher ehyeh." The individual has the liberty to profess God or not; but the community, if refractory, is coerced to acknowledge Him (Ex. R. iii. 14). As a king might fasten the key of his jewel-casket by a chain lest it be lost, so God linked His name with Israel lest the people should disappear (Yer. Ta'an. 65d). Israel's love for God, evidenced when in the desert, became a great treasure of divine grace, stored up for the days of Israel's troubles (Midr. Teh. to Ps. xxxvi. 11). Upon Israel's fidelity to God even the earth's fertility is dependent (Lev. R. xlv.). God's punishments are therefore very severe for disloyal Israel, though in His grace He provides the cure always before the blow (Meg. 13b). As a father prefers himself to discipline his son rather than to have another beat him, so God Himself is Israel's judge (Midr. Teh. to Ps. lxxviii. 41). God is toward Israel, however, like that king who, incensed at his son's conduct, swore to hurl a stone at him. In order not to break his oath, but being anxious not to destroy his child, he broke the stone into pieces, which one after another he threw at him (*ib.* to Ps. vi. 4; comp. Lev. R. xxxii.). Israel's disloyalty to God involves in its consequences even the other peoples (after Haggai i. 10; Midr. Teh. to Ps. iv. 8; comp. Matt. xv. 26; Mark vii. 27; Bacher, "Ag. Pal. Amor." i. 146).

The prayer-book of the Synagogue is the precipitate of the teachings concerning God held by the Rabbis. An analysis of its contents reveals that God was adored as the Creator, the Preserver of the world ("Yoẓer Or," the first benediction before the Shema'). He is the Great, the Mighty, the Fearful, the Highest, the Loving, the All-Sustaining, Reviving the Dead (in the SHEMONEH 'ESREH), the King, Helper, Deliverer, the Support of the Weak, the Healer of the Sick. He sets free the captives, faithful even to them that sleep in the dust. He is holy. Knowledge and understanding are from Him, a manifestation of His grace ("Attah Ḥonen la-Adam"; Meg. 17b; the "Birkat Ḥokmah," Ber. 33). He forgives sin ("Ha-Marbeh li-Saloaḥ"). In His mercy He sends relief to those that suffer ("Birkat ha-Ḥolim"; 'Ab Zarah, 8a; comp. Meg. 17b). To Israel He continually shows His love and abundant grace ("Ahabah Rabbah" and "Ahabat 'Olam," the second benediction before the Shema'; Ber. 11b). Man's physical perfection is God's work ("Asher Yaẓar"; Ber. 60b). In the prayer "Modim" (the "Hoda'ah" [Meg. 18; Ber. 29, 34; Shab. 24; Soṭah 68b; Sifre, Deut. 949]; see ARTICLES OF FAITH), God's immutability is accentuated, as well as His providential care of the life and soul of every man. He is "ha-ṭob," the good one whose mercies are boundless; while in the version given in the Siddur of Rab Amram and the Maḥzor of Rome the statement is added that "God has not abandoned Israel." God is also hailed as the maker of peace. The thought of God's unity, it is needless to remark, dominates throughout. The "'Alenu," with which, according to the Kol Bo (§§ 11 and 77; Ṭur Oraḥ Ḥayyim, § 133), every service must conclude, is a résumé of the implications of Israel's conception of God. He is the Lord of the universe; the Creator. Israel by His grace was called to know Him as the King of Kings, the Holy One. He alone is God. It concludes with the fervent prayer for the coming of the day when idolatry shall be no more, but God shall be acknowledged as the one and only God.

——**In Philosophical Literature:** The rise of Karaism marks an epoch in Jewish philosophical thought concerning God. The ensuing controversies induced Jewish Rabbinite thinkers to turn their attention to the speculative problems involved in the Jewish conception of God. Mohammedan theology, under the influence of Greek philosophy, which came to it by way of Syria through the Christian Nestorians, had developed various schools, among them the Motekallamin or schoolmen, occupying a middle position between the orthodox believers in the dogmas of the Koran and the Freethinkers or Philosophers. According to Shahrastani (ed. Cureton, German transl. by Haarbrücker), they were the defenders of the fundamental truths of the Koran. They did not appeal solely to the wording of the book, but formulated a rational system, that of the Kalam (hence their name, = Hebrew "Medabberim" = "loquentes"), in which through speculation the positions of the Koran were demonstrated as logically and intellectually necessary.

Motekallamin and Motazilites.

An offshoot from the Motekallamin were the Motazilites, who differed from the former in their doctrines concerning the divine attributes. Designating themselves as the proclaimers of the unity of God, they contended that the divine attributes were in no way to be regarded as essential; they thus emphasized God's absolute unity, which was regarded by them even as numerical. Over and against them the Ash'ariya urged deterministic views in opposition to the ascription of freedom to man, and pleaded for the reality of the divine attributes. These three schools were in so far orthodox as they all regarded the Koran as the source of truth and did not intend to abandon its fundamental authority. The Philosophers alone, though in externals observant of the religious ritual, ventured to take their stand on points other than those fixed by the text of the Koran; and they did not care whether their conclusions agreed with or differed from the positions of current theology.

Jewish philosophers in the Middle Ages (900–1300) display, on the whole, the methods and intentions of these orthodox Mohammedan schools. The same problems engage their interest. The attributes of God—His unity, His prescience, the freedom of human action—are the perplexities which they attempt to solve. That the teachings of the Bible and the theology of the Synagogue are true, they assume at the very outset. It is their ambition to show that these fundamental truths are rational, in conformity with the postulates of reason. Aristotelians for the most part, they virtually adopt the propositions of Al-Kindi, Alfarabi, and Al-Ghazali, as far as they are adherents of the Kalam; while those who are not resort to the Neoplatonic elements contained in Arabic Aristotelianism to sharpen their weapons. Ibn Sina (AVICENNA) and Ibn Roshd (AVERROES), also, must be remembered among the tutors of the Jewish Aristotelians.

The first of the Jewish writers to treat of the Jewish faith from the philosophical point of view was SAADIA, the great anti-Karaite (see his controversies with Anan, Nahawandi, Ibn Sakawai, and Ben Jeroham), in his famous work "Kitab al-Amanat wal-I'tiḳadat" (Hebrew, "Sefer Emunot we-De'ot"). He shows his familiarity with the positions of the Motazilites as well as with Greek philosophy and even with Christian theology. His purpose in composing the treatise was to set forth the harmony between the revealed truths of Judaism and the reason of man. In its controversial chapters he attacks the theology of Christianity with greater vehemence than that of Islam (see Geiger, "Wiss. Zeit. Jüd. Theol." i. 192). His philosophical point of view has rightly been characterized as eclectic, though strongly influenced by Aristotelianism. He prefaces his presentation of the God-concept with a discussion of the theory of human knowledge, which latter, according to him, proceeds from the perception of the grossly sensual elements common to men and animals. But when a man perceives an object, merely the accidents come to his vision. By comparison, however, he learns to know the quantity of bodies, thus forming the notion of space; while through the observation of motion he arrives at the perception of time ("Sefer Emunot we-De'ot," ed. Amsterdam, ii.). In this way man, through continued reflection, attains to ever finer and higher degrees of knowledge, discovering the relation of cause to effect. Many men, says Saadia, reject the existence of God on the ground that the knowledge of Him is too subtle and too abstract. But this is easily met by the assertion of the graduation of knowledge, which in its ascent always

Saadia.

"Sefer Emunot we-De'ot."

reaches finer degrees, and develops into the faculty of apprehending the less concrete and more abstract.

The final cause some philosophers have held to be material, an atom. But in going one degree higher, and in assuming the existence of a creator, man must know him as the highest; that is to say, God is the noblest but also the most subtile goal of speculative reflection. Many represent God as corporeal, because they do not push their ascending knowledge far enough beyond the corporeal to the abstract and incorporeal. The Creator being the originator of all bodies, He of necessity must be apprehended as supramundane, supercorporeal. Those that ascribe to God motion and rest, wrath and goodness, also apperceive Him as corporeal. The correct conception culminates in the representation of God as free from all accidents (*ib.*). If this conception be too abstract, and is to be replaced by one more material and concrete, reflection is forced to recede. The final cause must be, by the very postulates of reason, an abstract being. God-perception is thus the rise from the sensual to the supersensual and highest limits of thought.

But the Creator has revealed Himself to His Prophets as the One, the Living, the Almighty, the All-Wise, the Incomparable. It is the philosopher's part to investigate the reality of these attributes, and to justify them before the tribunal of reason (*ib.* ii. 24b, 25a). The unity of God includes His being absolutely one, as well as His uniqueness, and is necessarily postulated by the reflection that He is the Creator of all. For if He were not one, He would be many; and multiplicity is characteristic of corporeality. Therefore, as the highest thinking rejects His corporeality, He must be one. Again, human reason postulates one creator, since for creation a creator is indispensable; but, as one creator satisfies all the implications of this concept, reason has no call to assume two or more. If there were more than one creator, proof would have to be adduced for the existence of every one; but such proof could not be taken from creation, to account for which one creator suffices. That Scripture uses two names for God is merely due to linguistic idiomatic peculiarities, as "Jerubbaal" is also named "Gideon."

God is living because He, the Creator of the world, can not be thought of as without life (*i.e.*, self-consciousness and knowledge of His deeds). His omnipotence is self-evident, since He is the Creator of the all: since creation is perfectly adjusted to its ends, God must be all-wise. These three attributes human reason discovers "at one stroke" ("pit'om," "beli maḥshabah," "mebi'ah aḥat"; *ib.* ii. 26a). Human speech, however, is so constituted as not to be able to express the three in one word. God's being is simple, not complex, every single attribute connoting Him in His entirety. Abstract and subtle though God is, He is not inactive. The illustration of this is the soul and its directive function over the body. Knowledge is still more subtile than the soul; and the same is again exemplified in the four elements. Water percolates through earth; light dominates water; the sphere of fire surrounds all other spheres and through its motion regulates the position of the planets in the universe. The motion of the spheres is caused by the command of the Creator, who, more subtile than any of the elements, is more powerful than aught else.

The Living God.

Still, Saadia concedes that no attribute may in strict construction be ascribed to God (*ib.* ii. 28b). God has also created the concept attribute; and created things can not belong to the essence of the Creator. Man may only predicate God's existence ("yeshut"). Biblical expressions are metaphorical. The errors concerning God are set forth in ten categories. Some have thought God to be a substance; some have ascribed to Him quantity; others quiddity (*ποιόν* in Aristotle); others have assigned to Him relations and dependency (*πρός τι*). The Eternal can not be in relation to or dependent upon anything created. He was before creation was. God is in no space (*ποῦ* in Aristotle). He is timeless (*ποτέ*). God can not be said to possess (*ἔχειν*): all is His. He lacks nothing. Possession, however, includes lack as its negative. God is incorporeal; therefore, He can not be apprehended as conditioned by status (*κεῖσθαι*). Nor does God work (*ποιεῖν*). In the common sense of the term, work implies motion; and motion, in the subject, can not be in God. His will suffices to achieve His purposes; and, moreover, in work matter is an element, and place and time are factors—all considerations inapplicable to God.

Nor does God suffer (πάσχειν). Even God's seeing is not analogous to human sight, which is an effect by some exterior object. Saadia controverts trinitarianism more especially, as well as DUALISM. He is most emphatic in rejecting the corporeality of God, His incarnation, involved in the Christian doctrine. For his views concerning creation see JEW. ENCYC. iv. 339, *s.v.* CREATION.

But according to Saadia, man is the ultimate object of creation ("Emunot we-De'ot," iv. 45a). How is human freedom reconcilable with God's omnipotence and omniscience? That the will of man is free Saadia can not doubt. It is the doctrine of Scripture and of tradition, confirmed by human experience and postulated by reason. Without it how could God punish evil-doers? But if God does not will the evil, how may it exist and be found in this world of reality? All things terrestrial are adjusted with a view to man; they are by divine precept for the sake of man declared to be good or evil; and it is thus man that lends them their character. God's omniscience Saadia declares to be not necessarily causal. If man sins, God may know it beforehand; but He is not the cause of the sinful disposition or act.

Ibn Gabirol's theology is more profound than that of Saadia. In his "Meḳor Ḥayyim," he shows himself to be a follower of Plotinus, an adherent of the doctrine of emanation; yet, notwithstanding this pantheistic assumption, he recognizes the domination of a supreme omnipotent will, a free, personal God. He views the cognition of the final cause as the end and goal of all knowledge. "Being" includes: (1) form and matter; (2) primal substance, the cause (God); and (3) will, the mediator between the other two. Between God the Absolute and the world of phenomena, mediating agents are assumed. Like (God) can not communicate with unlike (the world); but mediating beings having something of both may bring them into relation. God is on the uppermost rung of the ladder of being; He is the beginning and cause of

Solomon ibn Gabirol.

all. But the substance of the corporeal world is the lowest and last of all things created. The first is essentially different from the last; otherwise, the first might be the last, and vice versa. God is absolute unity; the corporeal world, absolute multiplicity and variety. Motion of the world is in time; and time is included in and is less than eternity. The Absolute is above eternity; it is infinitude. Hence there must be a mediating something between the supereternal and the subeternal. Man is the microcosm ("'olam ha-ḳaṭon"), a reflection of the macrocosm. The mind ("sekel") does not immediately connect itself with the body, but through the lower energies of the soul. In like manner in the macrocosm the highest simple substance may only join itself to the substance of the categories through the mediation of spiritual substances. Like only begets like. Hence, the first Creator could have produced simple substances only, not the sensual visible world which is totally unlike Him.

Between the First Cause and the world Gabirol places five mediators ("emẓa'ot"): (1) God's will ("ha-raẓon"); (2) general matter and form; (3) the universal mind ("sekel ha-kelali"); (4) the three world-souls ("nefashot"), vegetative, animal, and thinking souls; and (5) nature ("ha-ṭeba'"), the mover of the corporeal world.

The Divine Will.

The divine will has a considerable part in this system. It is the divine power which creates form, calls forth matter, and binds them together. It pervades all, from the highest to the lowest, just as the soul pervades the body ("Meḳor Ḥayyim," v. 60). God may be apprehended as will and as knowledge; the former operating in secret, invisibly; the latter realizing itself openly. From will emanates form, but from the oversubstance matter. Will, again, is nothing else than the totality comprehending all forms in indivisible unity. Matter without form is void of reality; it is non-existent; form is the element which confers existence on the non-existent. Matter without form is never actual ("be-fo'al"), but only potential ("be-koaḥ"). Form appears in the moment of creation, and the creative power is will; therefore, the will is the producer of form.

Upon this metaphysical corner-stone Ibn Gabirol bases his theological positions, which may be summed up as follows:

God is absolute unity. Form and matter are ideas in Him. Attributes, in strict construction, may not be predicated of Him; will and wisdom are identical with His being. Only through the things which have emanated from God may man learn and comprehend aught of God. Between God and the world is a chasm bridged only by mediatorial beings. The first of these is will or the creative word. It is the divine power activated and energized at a definite point of time. Creation is an act of the divine will. Through processes of successive emanations, the absolute One evolves multiplicity. Love and yearning for the first fountain whence issued this stream of widening emanations are in all beings the beginning of motion. They are yearning for divine perfection and omnipotence.

Ibn Gabirol may rightly be styled the Jewish speculative exponent of a system bordering on theosophy, certainly approaching obscurity and the mystic elimination of individuality in favor of an all-encompassing all-Divinity (pantheism). His system is, however, only a side-track from the main line of Jewish theological thought.

Baḥya ibn Paḳuda.

Baḥya ben Joseph ibn Paḳuda, in the treatise introducing his exposition of the "Duties of the Heart" ("Ḥobot ha-Lebabot," chapter "Ha-Yiḥud"), reverts in the main to the method of Saadia. According to Baḥya, only the prophet and the wise can serve God in truth. All others revere in God something utterly out of consonance with the exalted, sublime conception of God (*ib.* § 2). It is therefore every one's duty to arrive at a proper conception of God's unity by means of speculative reflection, and to be thus enabled to differentiate true unity ("eḥad ha-emet") from pseudo-unity ("eḥad ha-'ober"). In consequence Baḥya develops the following seven demonstrative arguments in support of God's unity:

(1) The universe is like a pyramid sloping upward from a very broad base toward the apex; or it resembles an infinite series of numbers, of which the first is one, and the last comprises so many figures as to baffle all efforts to form a conception of it. The individual beings in the world are numerically infinite; when these individuals are classified in groups according to species, etc., the number of these groups becomes smaller. Thus by

proceeding in his classifications to always more comprehensive groups, man reduces the number ever more and more until he arrives at the number five, *i.e.*, four elements plus motion. These, again, are really two only: matter and form. Their common principle, more comprehensive than either, must thus be smaller than two, *i.e.*, ONE.

(2) The harmony and concordance prevailing in creation necessitate the apprehension of the world as the work of one artist and creator.

(3) Without a creator there could be no creation. Thus reason and logic compel the assumption of a creator; but to assume more than one creator is irrational and illogical.

(4) If one believes in the existence of more than one God, one of two alternatives is suggested: (*a*) One God was potent enough to create the all; why, then, other gods? They are superfluous. (*b*) One God alone had not the power; then God was limited in power, and a being so limited is not God, but presupposes another being through which He Himself was called into existence.

Proofs of Unity.

(5) The unity of God is involved in the very conception of Him. If there were more gods than one, this dilemma would be presented: (*a*) These many gods are of one essence; then, according to the law of absolute identity, they are identical and therefore only one. Or (*b*) these gods are differentiated by differences of essential qualities: then they are not gods; for God, to be God, must be absolute and simple (non-composite) being.

(6) God connotes being without accidence, *i.e.*, qualities not involved in being. Plurality is quantity, and, therefore, accidence. Hence plurality may not be predicated of God.

(7) Inversely, the concept unity posits the unity of God. Unity, according to Euclid, is that through which a thing becomes numerically one. Unity, therefore, precedes the number one. Two gods would thus postulate before the number one the existence of unity. In all these demonstrations Baḥya follows the evidential argumentations of the Arabic schoolmen, the Motekallamin. In reference to God's attributes, Baḥya is of those who contend that attributes predicated of God connote in truth only negatives (excluding their opposites), never positives (*ib.* § 10).

This view is shared also by Judah ha-Levi, the author of the "Cuzari," probably the most popular exposition of the contents of Israel's religion, though, as Grätz rightly remarks ("Geschichte," vi. 157), little calculated to influence thinkers. He regards CREATION as an act of divine will ("Cuzari," ii. 50). God is eternal; but the world is not. He ranges the divine attributes into three classes: (1) practical, (2) relative, and (3) negative. The practical are those predicated of God on the ground of deeds which, though not immediately, yet perhaps through the intervention of natural secondary causes, were wrought by God. God is in this sense recognized as gracious, full of compassion, jealous, and avenging.

Judah ha-Levi.

Relative attributes are those that arise from the relations of man, the worshiper, to God, the one worshiped. God is holy, sublime, and to be praised; but though man in this wise expresses his thoughts concerning God, God's essence is not thereby described and is not taken out of His unity ("me-aḥaduto").

The third class seemingly express positive qualities, but in reality negative their contraries. God is living. This does not mean that He moves and feels, but that He is not unmoved or without life. Life and death belong to the corporeal world. God is beyond this distinction. This applies also to His unity; it excludes merely the notion that He is more than one. His unity, however, transcends the unity of human conceptual construction. Man's "one" is one of many, a part of a whole. In this sense God can not be called "One." Even so, in strict accuracy, God may not be termed "the first." He is without beginning. And this is also true of the designation of God as "the last." Anthropopathic expressions are used; but they result from the humanward impression of His works. "God's will" is a term connoting the cause of all lying beyond the sphere of the visible things. Concerning Ha-Levi's interpretation of the names of God see NAMES OF GOD.

In discussing the question of God's providential government and man's freedom Ha-Levi first controverts FATALISM; and he does this by showing that even the fatalist believes in possibilities. Human will, says he, is the secondary cause between man and the purpose to be accomplished. God is the First Cause: how then can there be room for human freedom? But will is a secondary cause, and is not under compulsion on the part of the first cause. The freedom of choice is thus that of man. God's omnipotence is not impugned thereby. Finally, all points back to God as the first cause of this freedom. In this freedom is involved God's omnipotence. Otherwise it might fail to be available. The knowledge of God is not a cause. God's prescience is not causal in reference to man's doings. God knows what man will do; still it is not He that causes man's action. To sum up his positions, Judah ha-Levi posits: (*a*) The existence of a first cause, *i.e.*, a wise Creator always working under purpose, whose work is perfect. It is due to man's lack of understanding that this perfection is not seen by him in all things. (*b*) There are secondary causes, not independent, however, but instrumentalities. (*c*) God gave matter its adequate form. (*d*) There are degrees in creation. The sentient beings occupy higher positions than those without feelings. Man is the highest. Israel as the confessor of the one God outranks the polytheistic heathen. (*e*) Man is free to choose between good and evil, and is responsible for his choice.

Controverts Fatalism.

Abraham ibn Daud, in his "Emunah Ramah," virtually traverses the same ground as his predecessors; but in reference to God's prescience he takes a very free attitude (*ib.* p. 96). He distinguishes two kinds of possibilities: (1) The subjective, where the uncertainty lies in the subject himself. This subjective possibility is not in God. (2) The objective, planned and willed by God Himself. While under the first is the ignorance of one living in one place concerning the doings of those in another, under the second falls the possibility of man's being good or bad. God knows beforehand of this possibility, but not of the actual choice. The later author RaLBaG advances the same theory in his "Milḥamot ha-Shem" (iii. 2). Ibn Daud also argues against the ascription of positive attributes to God ("Emunah Ramah," ii. 3).

Abraham ibn Daud.

Moses ben Maimon's "Moreh Nebukim" ("Dalalat al-Ḥa'irin") is the most important contribution to Jewish philosophical thought on God. According to him, philosophy recognizes the existence and perfection of God. God's existence is proved by the world, the effect whence he draws the inference of God's existence, the cause. The whole universe is only one individual, the parts of which are interdependent. The sublunar world is dependent upon the forces proceeding from the spheres, so that the universe is a macrocosm ("Moreh," ii. 1), and thus the effect of one cause.

Maimonides.

Two gods or causes can not be assumed, for they would have to be distinct in their community: but God is absolute; therefore He can not be composite. The corporeal alone is numerical. God as incorporeal can not be multiple ("Yad," Yesode ha-Torah, i. 7). But may God be said to be one? Unity is accidence, as is multiplicity. "God is one" connotes a negative, *i.e.*, God is not many ("Moreh," i. 57). Of God it is possible only to say that He is, but not what He is (*ib.*; "hayuto bi-lebad lo mahuto"; in Arabic "anniyyah" = ὅτι ἔστι [quodditas]). All attributes have a negative implication, even existence. God's knowledge is absolute (*ib.* iii. 19). God's knowledge is never new knowledge. There is nothing that He does not know. In His knowledge He comprehends all, even infinitude (*ib.* iii. 20). God's knowledge is not analogous to man's. Evil is merely negation or privation (*ib.* iii. 8). God is not its author; for God sends only the positive. All that is, save God, is only of possible existence; but God is the necessarily existent (*ib.* i. 57). In Him there is no distinction between essence ("'eẓem") and existence ("ha-meẓi'ut"), which distinction is in all other existing things. For this reason God is incorporeal, one, exalted above space and time, and most perfect (*ib.* ii., Preface, 18, 21, 23, 24).

By the successors of Maimonides, Albo, Ralbag (Levi ben Gershon), and Crescas, no important modifications were introduced. Albo contends that only God may be designated as one, even numerical oneness being not exclusive connotation of unity ("'Iḳḳarim," ii. 9, 10; comp. Ibn Ẓaddiḳ, "'Olam Ḳaṭon," p. 49: "eḥad ha-mispar eno ka-eḥad haelahut"). He, too, emphasizes God's incorporeality, unity, timelessness, perfection, etc. ("'Iḳḳarim," ii. 6).

Crescas pleads for the recognition of positive attributes in God. He concedes that the unity of God can not be demonstrated by speculation, but that it rests on the "Shema'" alone. It may be noticed that Aaron ben Elijah ("'Eẓ ha-Ḥayyim," ch. lxxi.) also argues in favor of positive attributes, though he regards them in the light of homonyms.

The precipitate of these philosophical speculations may be said to have been the creed of Maimonides (see ARTICLES OF FAITH). It confesses that God is the Creator, Governor of all. He alone "does, has been and will be doing." God is One; but His unity has no analogy. He alone is God, who was, is, and will be. He is incorporeal. In corporeal things there is no similitude to Him. He is the first and the last. Stress is also laid on the thought that none shares divinity with Him. This creed is virtually contained in the ADON 'OLAM and the YIGDAL.

The cabalists (see CABALA) were not so careful as Maimonides and others to refrain from anthropomorphic and anthropopathic extravagances and ascriptions (see SHI'UR ḲOMAH). Nevertheless their efforts to make of the incorporeality of God a dogma met with opposition in orthodox circles. Against Maimonides ("Yad," Teshubah, iii. 7), denying to the believers in God's corporeality a share in the world to come, ABRAHAM BEN DAVID OF POSQUIÈRES raised a fervent protest. Moses Taku is another protestant ("Oẓar Neḥmad," iii. 25; comp. Abraham Maimuni, "Milḥamot," p. 25).

BIBLIOGRAPHY: Schmiedl, *Studien über Jüdische Religionsphilosophie*, Vienna, 1869; P. J. Muller, *De Godsleer der Middeleeuwsche Joden*, Groningen, 1898; D. Kaufmann, *Attributenlehre*, Leipsic, 1880; Guttmann, *Die Religionsphilosophie des Saadia*; idem, *Die Religionsphilosophie Abraham Ibn Dauds*; M. Joël, *Zur Gesch. der Jüdischen Religionsphilosophie*, Leipsic, 1872; Munk, *Mélanges*.

——**The Modern View:** On the whole, the modern Jewish view reproduces that of the Biblical books, save that the anthropomorphic and anthropopathic terminology is recognized as due to the insufficiency of human language to express the superhuman. The influence of modern philosophers (Kant and Hegel) upon some sections of Jewish thought has been considerable. The intellectual elements in the so-called demonstrations of God's existence and the weakness of the argument have been fully recognized. The Maimonidean position, that man can not know God in Himself (מהותו), has in consequence been strengthened (see AGNOSTICISM). The human heart (the practical reason in the Kantian sense) is the first source of knowledge of God (see Samuel Hirsch, "Catechismus," *s.v.* "Die Lehre"). The experience of man and the history of Israel bear witness to God's existence, who is apprehended by man as the Living, Personal, Eternal, All-Sustaining, the Source of all life, the Creator and Governor of the universe, the Father of all, the Righteous Judge, in His mercy forgiving sins, embracing all in His love. He is both transcendental and immanent. Every human soul shares to a certain degree in the essence of the divine. In thus positing the divinity of the human soul, Judaism bridges the chasm between the transcendental and the immanent elements of its conception of God. Pantheism is rejected as one-sided; and so is the view, falsely imputed to Judaism, which has found its expression in the absolute God of Islam.

The implications of the Jewish God-idea may be described as "pan-monotheism," or "ethical monotheism." In this conception of God, Israel is called to the duty, which confers no prerogatives not also within the reach of others, of illustrating in life the godliness of the truly human, through its own "holiness"; and of leading men to the knowledge of the one eternal, holy God (see DEISM; EVOLUTION).

BIBLIOGRAPHY: Samuel Hirsch, *Die Religionsphilosophie der Juden*, Leipsic, 1843; Formstecher, *Die Religion des Geistes*; see also CATECHISM; Rülf, *Der Einheitsgedanke*.

——**Critical View**: Biblical historiography presents the theory that God revealed Himself successively to Adam, Noah, Abraham and his descendants, and finally to Moses. Monotheism was thus made known to the human race in general and to Israel in particular from the very beginning. Not ignorance but perverseness led to the recognition of other gods, necessitating the sending of the Prophets to reemphasize the teachings of Moses and the facts of the earlier revelation. Contrary to this view, the modern critical school regards monotheism as the final outcome of a long process of religious evolution, basing its hypothesis upon certain data discovered in the Biblical books as well as upon the analogy presented by Israel's historical development to that of other Semitic groups, notably, in certain stages thereof, of the Arabs (Wellhausen, "Skizzen und Vorarbeiten," iii. 164; Nöldeke, in "Z. D. M. G." 1887, p. 719).

The primitive religion of Israel and the God-concept therein attained reflected the common primitive Semitic religious ideas, which, though modified in Biblical times, and even largely eliminated, have left their traces in the theological doctrines of the Israel of later days. Renan's theory, formulated in his "Precis et Système Comparé des Langues Semitiques" (1859), ascribing to the Semites a monotheistic instinct, has been abandoned because it was found to be in conflict with facts. As far as epigraphic material, traditions, and folk-lore throw light on the question, the Semites are shown to be of polytheistic leanings. Astral in character, primitive Semitic religion deified the sun, the moon, and the other heavenly bodies. The storm-clouds, the thunder-storms, and the forces of nature making for fertility or the reverse were viewed as deities. As long as the Semites were shepherds, the sun and the other celestial phenomena connected with the day were regarded as malevolent and destructive; while the moon and stars, which lit up the night—the time when the grass of the pasture was revived—were looked upon as benevolent. In the conception of YHWH found in the poetry of the Bible, speaking the language of former mythology and theology, the element is still dominant which, associating Him with the devastating cloud or the withering, consuming fire, virtually accentuates His destructive, fearful nature (Wellhausen, *l.c.* iii. 77, 170; Baethgen, "Beiträge zur Semitischen Religionsgeschichte," p. 9, Berlin, 1888; Smend, "Lehrbuch der Alttestamentlichen Religionsgeschichte," p. 19, Leipsic, 1893).

Polytheistic Leanings of the Semites.

The intense tribal consciousness of the Semites, however, wielded from a very early period a decisive influence in the direction of associating with each tribe, sept, or clan a definite god, which the tribe or clan recognized as its own, to the exclusion of others. For the tribe thought itself descended from its god, which it met and entertained at the sacrificial meal. With this god it maintained the blood covenant. Spencer's theory, that ancestral animism is the first link in the chain of religious evolution, can not be supported by the data of Semitic religions. Ancestral animism as in vogue among the Semites, and the "cult of the dead" (see Witch of ENDOR) in Israel point rather to individual private conception than to a tribal institution. In the development of the Israelitish God-idea it was not a determining factor (Goldziher, "Le Culte des Ancêtres et des Morts chez les Arabes," in "Revue de l'Histoire des Religions," x. 332; Oort, in "Theologisch Tijdschrift," 1881, p. 350; Stade, "Geschichte des Volkes Israel," i. 387).

Characteristic, however, of the Semitic religions is the designation of the tribal or clan deity as "adon" (lord), "melek" (king), "ba'al" (owner, fructifier). The meaning of "el," which is the common Semitic term, is not certain. It has been held to connote strength (in which case God would = "the strong"), leadership ("the first"), and briliancy (Sprenger, in his "Das Leben und die Lehre des Mohammad," in which God = "sun"). It has also been connected with "elah," the sacred tree (Ed. Meyer, in Roscher's "Ausführliches Lexikon der Griechischen und Römischen Mythologie," *s.v.* "El"; and Smend, *l.c.* p. 26, note 1). Equally puzzling is the use of the plural "Elohim" in Hebrew (אלם in Phenician; comp. Ethiopic "amlak"). The interpretation that it is a "pluralis majestatis" with the value of an abstract idea ("the Godhead"), assumes too high a degree of grammatical and philosophical reflection and intention to be applicable to primitive conditions. Traces of an original polytheism might be embodied in it, were it not for the fact that the religion of Israel is the outgrowth of tribal and national monolatry rather than of polytheism.

Each tribe in Israel had its tribal god (see, for instance, DAN; GAD; ASHER). Nevertheless from a very remote period these tribes recognized their affinity to one another by the fact that above their own tribal god they acknowledged allegiance to YHWH. This YHWH was the Lord, the Master, the Ruler. His will was regarded as supreme. He revealed Himself in fire or lightning.

Tribal Gods.

In Ex. vi. 2 YHWH is identified with El-Shaddai, the god of the Patriarchs. What the latter name means is still in doubt (see Nöldeke in "Z. D. M. G." 1886, p. 735; 1888, p. 480). Modern authorities have argued from the statement in Exodus that YHWH was not known among the Hebrews before Moses, and have therefore insisted that the name at least, if not the god, was of foreign origin. Delitzsch's alleged discovery of the name "YHWH" on Babylonian tablets has yet to be verified. Moses is held to have identified a Midianite-Kenite deity with the patriarchal El-Shaddai. However this may have been, the fact remains that from the time of the Exodus onward Israel regarded itself as the people of YHWH, whose seat was Sinai, where he manifested Himself amidst thunder and lightning in His unapproachable majesty, and whence He went forth to aid His people (Judges v. 4; Deut. xxxiii. 2). It was YHWH who had brought judgment on the gods of Egypt, and by this act of His superior power had renewed the covenant relation which the fathers of old had maintained with Him.

From the very outset the character of YHWH must have been of an order conducive to the subsequent development of monotheistic and ethical connotations associated with the name and the idea. In this connection it is noteworthy that the notion of sex, so pernicious in other Semitic cults, was from the outset inoperative in the worship of YHWH. As Israel's God, He could not but be jealous and intolerant of other gods beside Him, to whom Israel would pay honor and render homage. Enthroned in the midst of fire, He was unapproachable ("ḳodesh"); the sacrificial elements in His cult were of a correspondingly simple, pastoral nature. The jealousy of YHWH was germinal of His unity; and the simplicity and austerity of His original desert worship form the basis of the moralization of the later theology.

With the invasion of the land, Israel changed from a pastoral into an agricultural people. The shepherd cult of the desert god came into contact and conflict with the agricultural deities and cults of the Canaanites. YHWH was partly worshiped under Canaanitish forms, and partly replaced by the Canaanitish deities (Baalim, etc.). But YHWH would not relinquish His claim on Israel. He remained the judge and lawgiver and ruler and king of the people He had brought out from Egypt. The Nazarites and the Prophets arose in Israel, emphasizing by their life and habits as well as by their enthusiastic and indignant protest the contrast of Israel with the peoples of the land, and of its religion with theirs (comp. the YHWH of ELIJAH; He is "Ha-Elohim"). With Canaanitish cults were connected immoralities as well as social injustice. By contrast with these the moral nature of YHWH came to be accentuated.

Change of Social Conditions.

During the first centuries of Israel's occupation of Palestine the stress in religious life was laid on Israel's fidelity to YHWH, who was Israel's only God, and whose service was to be different from that offered unto the Baalim. The question of God's unity was not in the center of dispute. YHWH was Israel's only God. Other peoples might have other gods, but Israel's God had always shown His superiority over these. Nor was umbrage taken at this time at the representations of YHWH by figures, though simplicity still remained the dominant note in His cult. A mere stone or rock served for an altar (Judges vi. 20, xiii. 10; I Sam. vi. 14); and natural pillars (holy trees, "maẓebot") were more frequent than artificial ones (see Smend, *l.c.* pp. 40 *et seq.*). The EPHOD was perhaps the only original oracular implement of the YHWH cult. Teraphim belonged apparently to domestic worship, and were tolerated under the ascendency of the YHWH national religion. "Massekah" was forbidden (Ex. xxxiv. 17), but not "pesel"; hence idols seem not to have been objected to so long as YHWH's exclusive supremacy was not called into doubt. The Ark was regarded as the visible assurance of YHWH's presence among His people. Human sacrifices, affected in the Canaanitish Moloch cult, were especially abhorred; and the lascivious rites, drunkenness, and unchastity demanded by the Baalim and their consorts were declared to be abominations in the sight of YHWH.

These conceptions of God, which, by comparison with those entertained by other peoples, were of an exalted character, even in these early centuries, were enlarged, deepened, refined, and spiritualized by the Prophets in proportion as historical events, both internal and external, induced a widening of their mental horizon and a deepening of their moral perceptions. First among these is Amos. He speaks as the messenger of the God who rules all nations, but who, having known Israel alone among them, will punish His people all the more severely. Assyria will accomplish God's primitive purpose. In Amos' theology the first step is taken beyond national henotheism. Monotheism begins through him to find its vocabulary. This God, who will punish Israel as He does the other nations, can not condone social injustice or religious (sexual) degradation (Amos iv.). The ethical implications of YHWH's religion are thus placed in the foreground. Hosea introduces the thought of love as the cardinal feature in the relations of Israel and God. He spiritualizes the function of Israel as the exponent of divine purposes. YHWH punishes; but His love is bound ultimately to awaken a responsive love by which infidelity will be eliminated and overcome.

The God of the Prophets.

Isaiah lays stress on God's holiness: the "ḳodesh," unapproachable God, is now "ḳadosh," holy (see Baudissin, "Der Begriff der Heiligkeit im Alten Testament," in "Studien zur Semitischen Religionsgesch."). It is Israel's duty as God's people to be cleansed from sin by eschewing evil and by learning to do good. Only by striving after this, and not by playing at diplomacy, can the "wrath of God" be stayed and Jerusalem be saved. The remnant indeed will survive. Isaiah's conception of God thus again marks an advance beyond that of his predecessors. God will ultimately rule as the arbiter among the nations. Peace will be established, and beasts as well as men will cease to shed blood.

Jeremiah and his contemporaries, however, draw near the summit of monotheistic interpretations of the Divine. The cultus is centralized; Deuteronomic humanitarianism is recognized as the kernel of the God-idea. Israel and Palestine are kept apart from the rest of the world. YHWH ceases to be localized. Much greater emphasis than was insisted on even by Isaiah is now laid on the moral as distinct from the sacrificial involutions of the God-idea.

The prophets of the Exile continue to clarify the God-concept of Israel. For them God is One; He is Universal. He is Creator of the All. He can not be represented by image. The broken heart is His abiding-place. Weak Israel is His servant ("'ebed"). He desires the return of the sinner. His intentions come to pass, though man's thoughts can not grasp them.

After the Exile a double tendency in the conceptions of God is easily established. First, He is Israel's Lawgiver; Israel shall be holy. Secondly, He is all mankind's Father. In the Psalms the latter note predominates. Though the post-exilic congregation is under the domination of national sacerdotalism (represented by P), in the Wisdom literature the universal and ethical implications of Israel's God-belief came to the forefront. In the later books of the Biblical canon the effort is clearly traceable to remove from God all human attributes and passions (see ANTHROPOMORPHISM and ANTHROPOPATHISM). The critical school admits in the final result what the traditional view assumes as the starting-point. The God whom Israel, through the events of its history, under the teachings of its men of genius, the Prophets, finally learned to proclaim, is One, the Ruler and Creator of all, the Judge who loveth righteousness and hateth iniquity, whose witness Israel is, whose true service is love and justice, whose purposes come and have come to pass.

Post-Exilic Conception.

BIBLIOGRAPHY: Kuenen, *The Religion of Israel* (Eng. transl. of *Godsdienst van Israel*, Haarlem, 1869–70); idem, *National Religions and Universal Religion* (Hibbert Lectures, 1882); Knappert, *The Religion of Israel*; Duhm, *Die Theologie der Propheten*, Bonn, 1875; Wilhelm Vatke, *Die Religion des A. T.* Berlin, 1835; Ewald, *Die Lehre der Bibel von Gott*, Göttingen, 1871–76; Wellhausen, *Prolegomena zur Gesch. Israels*, 3d ed., 1886; idem, *Skizzen und Vorarbeiten*, i.–vi., 1882–1903; Baudissin, *Studien zur Semitischen Religionsgesch.* Leipsic, 1876, 1878; W. Robertson Smith, *Rel. of Sem.* Edinburgh, 1885; Ed. König, *Grundprobleme der Alttest. Religionsgesch.* 1885; idem, *Der Offenbarungsbegriff*, etc.; Friedrich Baethgen, *Beiträge zur Semit. Religionsgesch.* Berlin, 1888; Smend, *Lehrbuch der Alttestamentlichen Religionsgesch.* 1893; Budde, *Vorlesungen über die Vorexilische Religion Israels*, 1901; Kayser-Dillmann, *Alt. Test. Theologie.*

XXVI

Children Of God

GOD, CHILDREN OF ("bene ha-Elohim," perhaps = "sons of the gods"): The "sons of God" are mentioned in Genesis, in a chapter (vi. 2) which reflects preprophetic, mythological, and polytheistic conceptions. They are represented as taking, at their fancy, wives from among the daughters of men. For the interpretations given to this statement see FALL OF ANGELS, and FLOOD IN RABBINICAL LITERATURE. As there stated, the later Jewish and Christian interpreters endeavored to remove the objectionable implications from the passage by taking the term "bene ha-Elohim" in the sense of "sons of judges" or "sons of magistrates." In the introduction to the Book of Job (i. 6, ii. 1) the "bene ha-Elohim" are mentioned as assembling at stated periods, SATAN being one of them. Some Assyro-Babylonian mythological conception is held by the critical school to underlie this description of the gathering of the "sons of God" to present themselves before YHWH. Another conception, taken from sidereal religion, seems to underlie the use of the phrase in Job xxxv. 7.

The Israelites are addressed as "the children of the Lord your God" (Deut. xiv. 1). When Israel was young, he was called from Egypt to be God's son (Hosea xi. 1). The Israelites are designated also "the children of the living God" (*ib.* ii. 1 [R.V. i. 10]; comp. Jer. iii. 4). They are addressed as "backsliding children" (Jer. iii. 14) that might and should call God their father (*ib.* iii. 19). Deut. xxxii. 5, though the text is corrupt, seems to indicate that through perverseness Israel has forfeited this privilege. Isaiah, also, apostrophizes the Israelites as "children [of God] that are corrupters," though God has reared them (Isa. i. 4). As a man chastises his son, so does God chastise Israel (Deut. viii. 5); and like a father pities his children, so does God show pity (see COMPASSION).

The critical school refers this conception to the notion commonly obtaining among primitive races, that tribes and families as well as peoples are descended from gods regarded by them as their physical progenitors; community of worship indicating community of origin, or adoption into the clan believed to be directly descended from the tutelary god through the blood covenant. Hence the reproach, "Saying to a stock, Thou art my father; and to a stone, Thou hast begotten me" (Jer. ii. 27). Even in Deutero-Isaiah (li. 2) this notion is said to prevail ("Look unto Abraham your father," in correspondence with verse 1: "the rock whence ye are hewn").

That this view was deepened and spiritualized to signify a much sublimer relation between the gods and their physical descendants than that which the old Semitic conception assumed, the following passages demonstrate: "Surely they are my people, children that will not lie" (Isa. lxiii. 8). "In all their affliction he was afflicted" (*ib.* verse 9). "Thou art our father, for Abraham knows us not" (*ib.* verse 16, Hebr.). "Thou art our father; we are the clay" (*ib.* lxiv. 8). "Have we not all one father?" (Mal. ii. 10).

The relation of God to the individual man is also regarded as that of a parent to his child. "For my father and my mother have forsaken me, but YHWH taketh me up" (Ps. xxvii. 10, Hebr.; comp. II Sam. vii. 14). That other peoples besides Israel are God's children seems suggested by Jer. iii. 19, the rabbinical interpretation of the verse construing it as implying this (בנים=אומות העולם, Tan., Mishpaṭim, ed. Buber, 10; Yalḳ., Jer. 270; Bacher, "Ag. Pal. Amor." ii. 34, note 1).

Israel as the "first-fruits" (ראשית תבואתה) is the "bekor," or first-born, in the household of God's children (Jer. ii. 3; Ex. iv. 22). In the interpretation of the modern Synagogue this means that Israel shall be an exemplar unto all the other children of God (see Lazarus, "Der Prophet Jeremias," pp. 31, 32). According to the teachings of Judaism, as expounded in the CATECHISMS, every man is God's child, and, therefore, the brother of every other man. Mal. ii. 10 is applied in this sense, though the prophet's appeal was addressed solely to the warring brothers of the house of Israel. In this, modern Judaism merely adopts the teachings of the Apocrypha and of the Rabbis. See Ecclus. (Sirach) xxiii. 1, 4; li. 10; Wisdom ii. 13, 16, 18; xiv. 3 (comp. xviii. 13; III Macc. v. 7; Jubilees, i. 24); Job xiii. 4; Enoch lxii. 11; Psalms of Solomon, xvii. 30; Sifre, Deut. 48 (ed. Friedmann, 84b); Ab. iii. 14; R. H. iii. 8; Yer. Ma'as. 50c; Sifra (ed. Weiss), 93d; Midr. Teh. xii. 5 (comp. Bacher, "Ag. Tan." ii. 437). See SON OF GOD.

BIBLIOGRAPHY: Dalman, *Die Worte Jesu*, pp. 150 *et seq.*, Leipsic, 1898; Taylor, *The Sayings of the Fathers*, to *Ab.* iii. 14; Schreiner, in *Jahrbuch*, 1899, pp. 61–62; idem, *Die Jüngsten Urteile*, etc., in *Jahrbuch*, 1902, pp. 21, 22; Perles, *Bousset's Religion des Judentums*, pp. 127 *et seq.*, Berlin, 1903.

XXVII

Godliness

GODLINESS : The quality of being godly, *i.e.*, godlike, manifested in character and conduct expressive of the conscious recognition and realization of man's divine origin and destiny, and in the discharge of the duties therein involved. Regarding man as fashioned in the likeness of God (Gen. i. 26, 27), Judaism predicates of every man the possibility, and ascribes to him the faculty, of realizing godliness. According to its anthropology, this faculty was never vitiated or weakened in man by original sin.

In the Authorized Version "godly" corresponds to the Hebrew "ḥasid" (Ps. iv. 3, xii. 2 [A. V. 1]); but the term "ẓaddiḳ" (righteous; Ps. i. 5, 6) equally connotes the idea. The characteristics of the godly may best be derived from the fuller account given of their antonyms. The ungodly ("resha'im"; Ps. i. 1, 5) are described as men compassed about with pride, clothed in violence, speaking loftily and corruptly, denying God's knowledge, prospering by corruption in this world, and wrongfully increasing their riches (Ps. lxxiii.). They are those that make not God their strength (*ib.* lii. 7). Godliness is thus also the antithesis to the conduct and character of the wicked ("mere'im"), the workers of iniquity ("po'ale owen"; *ib.* lxiv.), "who whet their tongue like a sword"; who encourage themselves to do evil, denying that God will see them.

The godly, by contrast, is he whose delight is in the Torah of YHWH (*ib.* i. 2), or who, to use Micah's phrase, does justly, loves mercy, and walks humbly with his God (Micah vi. 8). The godly may be said to be actuated by the desire to learn of Yhwh's way, to walk in His truth, and to keep his heart in singleness of purpose to fear His name (Ps. lxxxvi. 11). "To walk in God's ways" (Deut. xiii. 5; "halok aḥare middotaw shel ha-ḳadosh baruk hu": Soṭah 14a) is the definition of "godliness," with the explanation that man shall imitate God's attributes as enumerated in Ex. xxxiv. 6, 7a (comp. Yalḳ., Deut. 873). As God is merciful, man also should be merciful; and so with respect to all other characteristics of godliness.

According to the Rabbis, the beginning and the conclusion of the Torah relate deeds of divine benevolence. God clothed the naked; He comforted the mourners; He buried the dead (Soṭah 14a; B. Ḳ. 99a; B. M. 30b based on Mek., Yitro, 2 [ed. Weiss, 68a; ed. Friedmann, 59b]; comp. the second "berakah" in the Shemoneh 'Esreh). Godliness thus involves a like disposition and readiness on the part of man to come to the relief of all that are in distress and to be a doer of personal kindness to his fellow men ("gomel ḥasadim"; comp. Ned. 39b, 40a). Thus, whatever is involved in "gemilut ḥasadim" (see Charity) is characteristic of godliness. Matt. xxv. 31 *et seq.* is an enumeration of the implications of Jewish godliness, the context ("then shall he sit upon the throne of his glory"; *ib.* xxv. 31) indicating that this catalogue was derived from a genuinely Jewish source (comp. Midr. Teh. to Ps. cxviii. 20, ed. Buber, p. 486). Jewish godliness also inculcates modesty and delicate consideration of the feelings of one's fellow man. According to Eleazar ben Pedat, "to do justly" (Micah vi. 8) refers to judgments rendered by judges; "to love mercy [love]," to the doing of acts of love ("gemilut ḥasadim"); "to walk humbly," to quiet, unostentatious participation in burying the dead and the providing of dowries for poor girls about to be married. "If," he continues, "for the prescribed acts the Torah insists on secrecy and unostentatiousness, how much more in the case of acts which of themselves suggest the propriety of secrecy" (Suk. 49b; Mak. 24b). He who is charitable without ostentation is greater than Moses (B. B. 9b). Greater is he that induces others to do kindly deeds than one that

Charity the Essence.

thoughtlessly or improperly performs them himself (B. B. 9a). He who does justly and loves mercy fills as it were the whole world with divine love (Ps. xxxiii. 5; Suk. 49b). Jewish godliness is not an "opus operatum," as is so often held by non-Jewish theologians. Charity without love is unavailing ("en ẓedaḳah meshallemet ela lefi ḥesed she-bah"; Suk. 49b). It comprises more than accurate justice, insistence being laid on "exceeding" justice (Mek., Yitro, 2, cited above).

Godliness also comprehends the sense of dependence upon divine grace and of gratitude for the opportunity to do good. "Prayer is greater than good works" (Ber. 32b). The question why God, if He loves the poor, does not Himself provide for them, is answered by declaring it to be God's intention to permit man to acquire the higher life (B. B. 10a). Jewish godliness is careful not to put another to shame (Ḥag. 5a, on public boastful charity); God's consideration for the repentant sinner (Hosea xiv. 2) is commended to man for imitation (Pesiḳ. 163b). He who gloats over the shame of his fellow man is excluded from the world to come (Gen. R. i.). "Better be burned alive than put a fellow man to shame" (Soṭah 10b).

Consideration for Others' Feelings.

It is ungodly to remind the repentant sinner of his former evil ways; as is it to remind the descendant of non-Jews of his ancestors (B. M. 58b). There is therefore no forgiveness for him who puts another to shame or who calls him by an offensive name (B. M. 58b). Godliness includes the forgiving disposition (Prov. xvii. 9; Ab. i. 12, v. 14; R. H. 17a). To be beloved of God presupposes to be beloved of men (Ab. iii. 13). Slander and godliness are incompatible (Pes. 118a). Pride and godliness are absolute contraries (Prov. vi. 16–19; Ta'an. 7a; Soṭah 4b, 5a, b; 'Ab. Zarah 20b: humility is the greatest virtue). To be among the persecuted rather than among the persecutors is characteristic of the godly (Giṭ. 36b). "God says, 'Be like unto me. As I requite good for evil, so do thou render good for evil'" (Ex. R. xxvi.; comp. Gen. R. xxvi.).

XXVIII

The Golden Rule

GOLDEN RULE, THE: By this name is designated the saying of Jesus (Matt. vii. 12): "All things therefore whatsoever ye would that men should do unto you, even so do ye also unto them." In James ii. 8 it is called "the royal law." It has been held to be the fundamental canon of morality. In making this announcement, Jesus is claimed to have transcended the limitations of Jewish law and life. The fact is, however, that this fundamental principle, like almost if not quite all the "logia" attributed to Jesus in the Sermon on the Mount, had been proclaimed authoritatively in Israel. In the instructions given by Tobit to his son Tobias (Book of Tobit, iv.), after admonishing him to love his brethren, the father proceeds to urge upon the son to have heed of all his doings and to show himself of good breeding ("derek ereẓ") in all his conduct. "And what is displeasing to thyself, that do not unto any other" (verse 15). Again, there is the well-known anecdote in which Hillel explains to a would-be proselyte that the maxim "not to do unto one's fellow what is hateful to oneself" is the foundation of Judaism, the rest being no more than commentary (Shab. 31a). See BROTHERLY LOVE and DIDACHE.

Meaning of "Ḥaber."

It has been argued (by Hilgenfeld, Siegfried, and recently by Bousset) that the maxim of Hillel applied, like the Biblical command "Thou shalt love thy neighbor as thyself" (Lev. xix. 18), only to fellow Jews. In proof of the contention, the word "ḥaber" used by Hillel is noted. As in a technical sense ḤABER designates a member of the Pharisaic fraternity of learned pious men, so here, according to the scholars referred to above, it has a restricted significance. The circumstances under which Hillel was speaking preclude the possibility of his having thought of the technical meaning of the word. He addresses himself to a non-Jew who at best could not for years hope to be a ḥaber. "Ḥaber" is the usual rendering for the Hebrew "rea'" (neighbor). Much philological hair-splitting has been used to restrict the meaning of this word to "compatriot," but the context of Lev. xix. 18 makes it plain that "rea'," as interpreted by these "holiness laws" themselves (see ETHICS), embraces also the stranger. Tobit's admonition proves the same. After speaking of "brothers," *i.e.*, men of his race and people, the father proceeds to give his son advice regarding his conduct to others, "the hired man," for instance; and in connection with this, not in connection with the subject of his marriage, he enjoins the observance of the Golden Rule.

Love of one's friends and hatred of one's enemies are nowhere inculcated in Jewish literature, despite the fact that Bousset ("Religion des Judenthums," p. 113), referring to Matthew v. 43, calls this verse the comprehensive statement of Jewish ethical belief and doctrine. Either the second half of the sentence is an addition by a later hand, or, what is more likely, it resulted from a misapprehension of a rabbinical argumentative question. According to Schechter the statement should read as follows: "You have heard that ["ettemar" = ἐρρέθη] it has been said [in the Law] 'Thou shalt love thy neighbor.' Does this now mean ["shomea' ani"] love thy neighbor [friend] but hate thine enemy?" No. Nevertheless while Jewish ethics has never commanded and paraded love for an enemy, it has practised it (Chwolson, "Das Letzte Passahmahl Christi," p. 80). Hillel in another of his sayings speaks of love for all creatures ("ha-beriyyot"), which term certainly embraces all humanity. Nor is it true that the seeming universalism of this sentence (Abot i. 12) is restricted by the addition "bring them toward the Torah," as Bousset, following Hilgenfeld, would have it appear. "Torah" is the equivalent of the modern "religion," and if Jesus in the Golden Rule declares it to be "the law and the prophets," he puts down merely the more specific, for the wider implications of the word "torah." R. Akiba ascribed the wider application to the command "Thou shalt love thy neighbor as thyself" (Lev. xix. 18; Sifra Ḳedoshim to the verse [ed. Weiss, p. 89b]; comp. Gal. v. 14; Rom. xiii. 8; Yer. Ned. 41c; Gen. R. xxiv.; and Kohler in ETHICS, RABBINICAL). The needy or the dead of non-Jews were never outside the range of Jewish brotherly love (Tosef., Giṭ. v. 4–5; Giṭ. 61a). The phrase "mi-pene darke shalom" (on account of the ways of peace), which motivates Akiba's injunction, does not inject a non-ethical, calculating element into the proposition, but introduces the principle of equity into it.

Negative Jewish Form.

The negative form of the Golden Rule marks if anything a higher outlook than the positive statement in which it is cast in Matthew. "What you would have others do unto you," makes self and possible advantages to self the central motive; "what is hateful to you do not unto another," makes the effect upon others the regulating principle. But be this as it may, the Golden Rule is only an assertion of the essentially Jewish and rabbinical view that "measure for measure" should be the rule regulating any one man's expectation from others (rights), while more than measure should be the rule indicating one's services to others (duties). The former is phrased "middah keneged middah" (Nedarim 32b), and "ba-middah sheadam moded modadin lo" (Soṭah 8b); the latter is "li-fenim mishshurat ha-din" (B. Ḳ. 99b), or to be "ma'abir 'al middotaw," that is, of a forgiving, yielding disposition.

BIBLIOGRAPHY: Jacob Bernays, *Gesammelte Abhandlungen*, i. 274–276; L. Lazarus, *Zur Charakteristik der Talmudischen Ethik*; Herm. Cohen, *Die Nächstenliebe im Talmud*, Marburg, 1888; *idem*, in *Jahrbuch für Jüd. Geschichte und Litteratur*, 1900; L. Löw, *Ges. Schriften*, i. 45; Chwolson, *Das Letzte Passahmahl Christi*, p. 60, St. Petersburg, 1892; Güdemann, *Nächstenliebe*, in *Oesterreichische Wochenschrift*, 1900; idem, *Neutestamentliche Studien*, in *Monatsschrift*, 1893, pp. 1 *et seq.*; Bacher, *Ag. Tan.* i. 7 (2d ed., p. 4); Felix Perles, *Bousset's Religion des Judenthums*, Berlin, 1903; Hirsch, *The Times and Teachings of Jesus*, Chicago, 1894.

XXIX

Hegel

HEGEL, GEORG WILHELM FRIEDRICH: German philosopher; born at Stuttgart 1770; died at Berlin 1831. After studying at the University of Tübingen he became tutor at Bern and Frankfort-on-the-Main, and lecturer (1801) and professor (1805) of philosophy at Jena. In 1808 he became director of a gymnasium at Nuremberg; in 1816, professor at Heidelberg; and in 1818, professor at Berlin.

Hegel may be said to have been the founder of a school of thought dominant in Germany until the rise of modern natural sciences in the beginning of the later half of the nineteenth century; even now, though discredited in the land of his birth, it is to a certain extent represented by prominent thinkers in England and America. His system has been described as "logical idealism." According to him, all that is actual or real is the manifestation of spirit or mind; metaphysics is coincident with logic, which develops the creative self-movement of spirit as a dialectic and necessary process. God is this self-unfolding spirit, and in the course of the self-realizing, free process of unfolding, creation leaps into being. The world is a development of the principles that form the content of the divine mind.

His Philosophy of History.

The influence of Hegel's system was especially potent in giving the first impulse toward the elaboration of a philosophy of history. From his point of view history is a dialectic process, through which the divine (the absolute mind), in ever fuller measure, is revealed and realized. This absolute is the unlimited and as such, in the fate of the various nations which represent successive limited and finite objectifyings of certain particular phases of the dialectic movement, exercises His highest right, and thus operates in history as the Supreme Judge. This interpretation of history has since become fundamental in the theology of some of the leaders of the Jewish Reform movement. It has been made the basis for assigning to Israel a peculiar task, a mission. Furthermore, it has helped to enlarge and modify the concept of revelation. Applying these principles to Jewish history, the Jewish Hegelians (Samuel HIRSCH especially) have discovered in that history also the principle of development, a succession of fuller growths, of more complete realizations in form and apprehension of the particular spirit or idea represented by Israel in the economy of progressive humanity.

His Philosophy of Religion.

Hegel was also the first seriously to develop a philosophy of religion. In his lectures on this subject he treats first of the concept of religion, then of the positive religion, and finally of the absolute religion. Religion is defined as "thinking the Absolute," or "thinking consciousness of God"; but this thinking is distinct from philosophy in so far as it is not in the form of pure thought, but in that of feeling and imaginative representation ("Vorstellung"). The Godhead reveals Himself only to the thinking mind, therefore only to and through man. Religion, in the main, is knowledge of God, and of the relation of man to God. Therefore, as rooted in imaginative representation, not in pure idea, religion operates with symbols, which are mere forms of empirical existence, but not the speculative content. Yet this content of highest speculative truth is the essential, and is expressed in the absolute religion. Through the "cultus" (worship) the Godhead enters the innermost parts ("das Innere") of His worshipers and becomes real in their self-consciousness. Religion thus is "the knowledge of the divine spirit [in Himself] through the medium of the finite mind." This distinction between symbol and content, as well as the conception of religion as the free apprehension, in an ever fuller degree, of the divine through the finite (human) mind, was utilized by Samuel Hirsch in his rejection of the view that Judaism is Law, and that the ceremonies, regarded by him as mere symbols, are divinely commanded, unchangeable institutions. The idea (or "Lehre") is the essential. This idea realizes itself, imperfectly at first, in symbol, but with its fuller unfolding the symbols become inadequate to convey the knowledge of God. It was in this way that Hegel's philosophy of religion became of importance for modern Jewish thought.

Hegel himself, when treating of positive or definite ("bestimmte") religion, dealt with Judaism as only one of the temporary phases through which the knowledge of God passed in the course of its evolution into the absolute religion—Christianity. He divides "bestimmte Religion" into (*a*) natural religions and (*b*) the religion of "spiritual ["geistigen"] individuality." In the first group are included, besides the lowest, called by him the "immediate" religions, or "religions of magic," the Oriental religions—the Chinese "religion of measure"; the Brahman "religion of fantasy"; the Buddhistic "religion of inwardness" ("Insichsein"). Midway between this group and the second he places Zoroastrianism, which he denominates the "religion of good," or "of light," and the Syrian religion, designated as the "religion of pain." In the second group he enumerates the "religion of sublimity" (Judaism), the "religion of beauty" (the Greek), and the "religion of utility" ("Zweckmässigkeit"), or "of intellect" (the Roman).

Hegel's View of Judaism.

In thus characterizing Judaism, Hegel practically restates, in the difficult, almost unintelligible, technical phraseology of his own system, the opinion common to all Christian theologians since Paul. The unity (of God) as apprehended by Judaism is altogether transcendental. God is indeed known as "Non-World," "Non-Nature"; but He is merely cognized as the "Master," the "Lawgiver." Israel is the particular people of this particular God. Israel is under the Law; yea, Israel is forever indissolubly bound up with a particular land (Palestine).

The influence of Hegel is discernible in the writings of Samson Raphael Hirsch, who turned Hegel's

His Influence on Jewish Thinkers.

system to good account in defense of Orthodoxy. Samuel Hirsch, on the other hand, was induced to write his "Religionsphilosophie der Juden" by the desire to show that his master Hegel had misunderstood Judaism. He showed that the central thought in Hegel's system, that man is God's image and that through him the divine is realized on earth, is fundamental also to Judaism. The universal implications of the God-consciousness, vindicated by Hegel for Christianity alone, were certainly before that Jewish, in the dialectic process through which the God-consciousness finally rose to the climactic harmonizing of Nature and God (the transcendental and the natural) in the "absolute religion" (Christianity). The Jewish God-idea is not barrenly transcendental. The antithesis between God and non-God is overcome in the concept of Man (not merely one God-Man) as combining the divine and the natural (see God).

The theory of Hegel that Judaism is Law, that its motive is fear, that the holiness and wisdom of God as cognized by it are attributes merely of the sublime, unapproachable Sovereign, and as such are beyond the reach of man, as well as the other view that Judaism is definitively Palestinian, is contrary to the facts of Jewish history. Even the Bible shows that religion as reflected by it had progressed beyond this stage. The Hegelian method of regarding man and mind as under the law of growth, and God, not as a fact, but as a force, prepared the way for modern theories of evolution and the science of comparative religion.

BIBLIOGRAPHY: *Hegel's Werke*, especially *Vorlesungen über die Philosophie der Religion*, Berlin, 1832; Samuel Hirsch, *Die Religionsphilosophie der Juden*, Leipsic, 1843; Pfleiderer, *Gesch. der Religionsphilosophie*, Berlin, 1883; Prinjer, *Gesch. der Religionsphilosophie*, Brunswick, 1880, 1883; Windelband, *History of Philosophy* (transl.), New York, 1898; Zeller, *Gesch. der Deutschen Philosophie seit Leibnitz*, 2d ed., Munich, 1875.

XXX

High Place

HIGH PLACE (Hebrew, "bamah"; plural, "bamot"): A raised space primitively on a natural, later also on an artificial, elevation devoted to and equipped for the sacrificial cult of a deity. The term occurs also in the Assyrian ("bamati"; see Friedrich Delitzsch, "Assyrisches Handwörterb." p. 177); and in the Mesha inscription it is found (line 3) as במת, which leaves the grammatical number doubtful. Etymologically the long ā (ָ) indicates derivation from a non-extant root, בום. The meaning is assured. The only point in doubt is whether the bamah originally received its name from the circumstance that it was located on a towering elevation or from the possible fact that, independently of its location, it was itself a raised construction. The latter view seems the more reasonable.

Etymology of "Bamah."

The use in Assyrian of "bamati" in the sense of "mountains" or "hill country," as opposed to the plains, as well as similar implications in Hebrew (II Sam. i. 19, "high places" parallel to the "mountains" in II Sam. i. 21; comp. Micah iii. 12; Josh. xxvi. 18; Ezek. xxxvi. 2; Num. xxi. 28), is secondary. Because the bamah was often located on a hilltop, it gave its name to the mountain. The reverse is difficult to assume in view of the fact that the bamah is often differentiated from the supporting elevation (Ezek. vi. 3; I Kings xi. 7, xiv. 23), and that bamot were found in valleys (Jer. vii. 31, xix 5, xxxii. 35; Ezek. *l.c.*) and in cities (I Kings xiii. 32; II Kings xvii. 9, xxiii. 5) at their gates (II Kings xxiii. 8).

Though in many passages the term may rightly be taken to connote any shrine or sanctuary without reference to elevation or particular construction (see Amos vii. 9, where "high places" = "sanctuaries"), yet there must have been peculiarities in the bamah not necessarily found in any ordinary shrine. At all events, altar and bamot are distinct in II Kings xxiii. 13; Isa. xxxvi. 7; II Chron. xiv. 3. The distinguishing characteristic of the bamah must have been that it was a raised platform, as verbs expressing ascent (I Kings ix. 3, 19; Isa. xv. 2) and descent (I Kings x. 5) are used in connection therewith. It was, perhaps, a series of ascending terraces like the Assyro-Babylonian "zigurat" (the "tower" of Babel; Jacob's "ladder"), and this feature was probably not absent even when the high place was situated on a mountain peak. The law concerning the building of the ALTAR (Ex. xx. 24) indicates that the base was of earth—a mound upon which the altar rested—primitively a huge rough, unhewn stone or dolmen, though Ewald's theory ("Gesch." iii. 390), that the understructure at times consisted of stones piled up so as to form a cone, is not without likelihood. These high places were generally near a city (comp. I Sam. ix. 25, x. 5).

Formation and Location.

Near the bamah were often placed "maẓẓebot" and the ASHERAH (see also GROVES). The image of the god was to be seen at some of the high places (II Kings xvii. 29). EPHOD and TERAPHIM were also among their appointments (Judges xvii. 5; I Sam. xxi. 9; comp. Hosea iii. 4). Buildings are mentioned, the so-called "houses of high places" (I Sam. ix. 22 *et seq.*; I Kings xii. 31, xiii. 32); and Ezek. xvi. 16 suggests the probability that temporary tents made of "garments" were to be found there.

Further proof that the bamah was not the hill or mountain elevation, but a peculiar structure placed on the peak or erected elsewhere, is furnished by the verbs employed in connection with the destruction of the bamot: אבד (Ezek. vi. 3; II Kings xxxi. 3), השמיד (Lev. xxvi. 30), נתץ (II Kings xxiii. 8, 15; II Chron. xxxi. 1), and שרף (II Kings xxiii. 15). If "ramah" (Ezek. xvi. 24, 31) is an equivalent for "bamah," as it seems to be, the verbs denoting its erection (עשה and בנה) offer additional evidence. Moreover, the figurative value of the term in the idioms "tread upon high places" (*e.g.*, in Deut. xxxiii. 29), "ride on high places" (*e.g.*, Deut. xxxii. 13), where "fortress" is held to be its meaning, supports the foregoing view. The conquest of any city, the defeat of any tribe, included in ancient days the discomfiture of the deities, and hence the destruction or the disuse of their sanctuaries. Even in Ps. xviii. 34 (Hebr.) the word has this implication. "To place one on one's bamot" signifies to give one success (comp. Hab. iii. 19; Amos iv. 13; Micah i. 3; Job ix. 8; Isa. xiv. 14, lviii. 14), or to recognize or assert one's superiority. Attached to these high places were priests ("kohanim": I Kings xii. 32; xiii. 2, 23; II Kings xvii. 32, xxiii. 20; called also "kemarim"; II Kings xxiii. 5), as well as "ḳedeshot" and "ḳedeshim" = "diviners" (Hosea iv. 13, xi.) and "prophets" (I Sam. x. 5, 10; xi. 22). There is strong probability that the term "Levite" originally denoted a person "attached" in one capacity or another to these high places (לוי from לוה in nif'al, "to join oneself to"). At these bamot joyous festivals were celebrated (Hosea ii. 13 [A. V. 15], 15 [17]; ix. 4) with libations and sacrifices (*ib.* ii. 5 [7], iii. 1); tithes were brought to them (Gen. xxviii. 20–22; Amos iv. 4); and clan, family, or individual sacrifices were offered at them (I Sam. ix. 11; Deut. xii. 5–8, 11; the prohibition proving the prevalence of the practise). It was there that solemn covenants were ratified (Ex. xxi. 6, xxii. 8 [7]) and councils held (I Sam. xxii. 6, LXX.).

Origin of the Bamah.

That the high places were primitively sepulchral sanctuaries and thus connected with ancestral worship—this connection accounting for their peculiar form and their favorite location on mountains, where the dead were by preference put away (*e.g.*, Aaron's grave on Hor, Num. xx. 20; Miriam's in Kadesh-barnea, Num. xx. 1; Joseph's in Shechem, Josh. xxiv. 32; Moses' on Nebo, Deut. xxxiv.)—has been advanced as one theory (see Nowack, "Hebräische Archäologie," ii. 14 *et seq.*; Benzinger, "Arch." Index, *s.v.* "Bamah"). In greater favor is another theory ascribing the origin of the bamot to the prevalent notion that the gods have their abodes "on the heights" (see Baudissin, "Stu-

bamot to the prevalent notion that the gods have their abodes "on the heights" (see Baudissin, "Studien zur Semitischen Religionsgesch." ii. 232 *et seq.*).

The Old Testament documents abound in evidence that this notion was held by the Canaanites and was prevalent among the Hebrews (Deut. xii. 2; Num. xxxiii. 52). The Moabites worshiped Peor (Baal-peor) on the mountain of that name (Num. xxiii. 28; xxv. 3, 5, 18; xxxi. 16; Deut. iii. 29 ["Beth-peor"], iv. 3; Hosea ix. 10; Ps. cvi. 28), and had bamot (Isa. xv. 2, xvi. 12; Jer. xlviii. 35; comp. "Bamoth-baal," Josh. xiii. 17). "Baal-hermon" (I Chron. v. 23) points in the same direction. Carmel was certainly regarded as the dwelling-place of Baal (or YHWH; I Kings xviii.). The Arameans are reported to have believed the God of Israel to be a mountain god (I Kings xx. 23, 28). The Assyrian deities held assemblies on the mountains of the north (Isa. xiv. 13). Non-Hebrew sources complete and confirm the Biblical data on this point (see Baudissin, *l.c.* p. 239). Patriarchal biography (the mention of Moriah in Gen. xxii. 2; of Gilead ["the mount"] in Gen. xxxi. 54 [comp. Judges xi. 29]; of Ramath-mizpeh in Josh. xiii. 26; of Ramath-gilead in I Kings iv. 13), the story of Moses (see Sinai, "the mount of God," in Ex. iii. 1, iv. 27, xxiv. 13; I Kings xix. 8; the hill in connection with the victory over Amalek in Ex. xvii. 9; Mount Hor in Num. xx. 25; Mount Ebal in Deut. xxvii.; Josh. viii. 30), and the accounts of the Earlier Prophets (see Carmel in I Kings xviii.; Micah vii. 14; Tabor in Judges iv. 6, xii. 14; Hosea v. 1; Mount Olive in II Sam. xv. 32; I Kings xi. 7) illustrate most amply the currency of the same conception among the Hebrews, who must have believed that mountain peaks were especially suitable places for sacrifices and ceremonies, or—what amounts to the same thing (Schwally, "Semitische Kriegsaltertümer," i., Leipsic, 1901)—for the gathering of the armed hosts. This conception, therefore, is at the bottom of both the plan of construction—in the shape of a sloping, terraced elevation—and the selection of natural heights for the locating of the bamot. W. R. Smith ("Rel. of Sem." Index), however, contends that the selection of a hill near the city was due to practical considerations, and came into vogue at the time when the burning of the sacrifice and the smoke had become the essential features of the cult. Even so,

Home of the Gods.

the fact that a hill above all other places was chosen points back to an anterior idea that elevations are nearer the seat of the deity.

How far the connotation of "holiness" as "unapproachableness," "aloofness" influenced the plan and location of the bamah can not be determined, though the presumption is strong that this was the factor which determined the location of graves and sanctuaries on high peaks and the erection of shrines in imitation of such towering slopes.

Of bamot the following are especially mentioned:

The bamah of Gibeon (I Kings iii. 4; I Chron. xvi. 39, xxi. 29; II Chron. i. 3, 13); the bamah at Ramah, where Saul and Samuel met (I Sam. ix. 12, 13, 14, 19, 25); that at Gibeah, where Saul fell in with the howling dervishes or prophets (I Sam. x. 5, 13); that founded by Jeroboam at Beth-el (II Kings xxiii. 15); that built by Solomon in honor of CHEMOSH (I Kings xi. 7); one at a place not named (Ezek. xx. 29; comp. Jer. xlviii. 35; Isa. xvi. 12). The following places must have been bamot, though not always explicitly so denominated in the text: Bochim (Judges ii. 5); Ophrah (*ib.* vi. 24, viii. 27); Zorah (*ib.* xiii. 16–19); Shiloh (*ib.* xviii. 31); Dan (*ib.* xviii. 30); Beth-el (see above and Judges xx. 18 [R. V.], 23, 26 [R. V.], xxi. 2, 4); Mizpah (*ib.* xx. 1; I Sam. vii. 9); Ramah (see above and I Sam. vii. 17, ix. 12); Gibeah (see above and I Sam. xiv. 35); Gilgal (*ib.* x. 8, xi. 15, xiii. 9, xv. 21); Beth-lehem (*ib.* xvi. 2; xx. 6, 29); Nob (*ib.* xxi. 2); Hebron (II Sam. xv. 7); Giloh (*ib.* xv. 12); the thrashing-floor of Araunah (*ib.* xxiv. 25).

Some of these were of ancient origin, being associated with events in patriarchal days (*e.g.*, Hebron [Shechem and Beer-sheba] and Beth-el, Gen. xii. 8, xiii. 4, xxviii. 22). This list, which might easily be enlarged, shows that the theory which regards the introduction of the high places as due to the pernicious example of the Canaanites and which would regard all bamot as originally illegitimate in the cult of YHWH is inadmissible. YHWH had His legitimate bamot as the "Chemosh" and "ba'alim" had theirs. Only in the latter days of the Judean kingdom, and then in consequence of the prophetic preachment, were the high places put under the ban. The redactor of the books of Kings even concedes the legitimacy of the high places before the building of the Solomonic Temple (I Kings iii. 2), and the books of Samuel make no effort to conceal the fact that Samuel offered sacrifices (I Sam. vii. 9) at places that the later Deuteronomic theory would not countenance. That the kings, both the good

Originally Legitimate.

and the evil ones (Solomon, I Kings iii. 3, 4; Rehoboam, *ib.* xiv. 23; Jeroboam, *ib.* xii. 31, xiii.; Asa, *ib.* xv. 14; Jehoshaphat, *ib.* xxii. 43; Jehoash, II Kings xii. 3; Amaziah, *ib.* xiv. 4; Azariah, *ib.* xv. 4; Jotham, *ib.* xv. 25; Ahaz, *ib.* xvi. 4), tolerated and patronized high places is admitted. Elijah is represented as bitterly deploring the destruction of these local shrines of YHWH (I Kings xix. 10, 14), though Manasseh (II Kings xxi. 3) and even good kings are censured for having patronized them; and the catastrophe of the Northern Kingdom is attributed, in part at least, to the existence of these sanctuaries (*ib.*).

The cause for this change of attitude toward the bamot, of which the Deuteronomic and Levitical law was, according to the critics, the result, not the reason, was the corruption that grew out of the coexistence of Canaanitish and of YHWH's high places, the former contaminating the latter. The foreign wives of the kings certainly had a share in augmenting both the number and the priesthood of these shrines to non-Hebrew deities. The lascivious and immoral practises connected with the Phenician cults —the worship of the baalim and their consorts, of Molech, and of similar deities—must have reacted on the forms and atmosphere of the YHWH high places. An idea of the horrors in vogue at these shrines may be formed from the denunciations of the Earlier Prophets (*e.g.*, AMOS and HOSEA) as well as from Ezekiel (xvi. 24, xxv. 31). To destroy these plague-spots had thus become the ambition of the Prophets, not because the primitive worship of YHWH had been hostile to local sanctuaries where YHWH could be worshiped, but because while nominally devoted to YHWH, these high places had introduced rites repugnant to the holiness of Israel's God. This may have been more especially the case in the Northern Kingdom, where there were bamot at Dan and Beth-el—with probably a bull or a phallic idol for YHWH (I Kings xiv. 9; II Kings xvii. 16) and with bamot priests (I Kings xii. 32; xiii. 2, 33; Hosea x. 5; see also Amos iii. 14; Micah i. 5, 13)—and in all cities, hamlets, and even the least populous villages (II Kings xvii. 9 *et seq.*). Some of these bamot continued to exist after the destruction of Samaria (*ib.* xvii. 29).

Josiah is credited with demolishing all the bamot-houses in Samaria (*ib.* xxiii. 19), killing the priests, and burning their bones on the altar (comp. *ib.* xxiii. 15), thus fulfilling the prediction put into the mouth of the Judean prophet under Jeroboam (I Kings xiii. 32) and of Amos (vii. 5).

In Judea the high places flourished under Rehoboam (I Kings xiv. 23). His grandson Asa, though abolishing the foreign cults (*ib.* xv. 12; II Chron. xv. 8), did not totally exterminate the high places (I Kings xv. 14; II Chron. xv. 17); for his successor, Jehoshaphat, still found many of them (II Chron. xvii. 6; I Kings xxii. 47; see also I Kings xxii. 44; II Chron. xx. 33). Under Ahaz non-Hebrew bamot again increased (II Chron. xxviii. 24; comp. Tophet in Jer. vii. 31, xix. 5). Jerusalem especially abounded in them (Micah i. 5) Hezekiah is credited with having taken the first step toward remedying the evil (see HEZEKIAH, CRITICAL VIEW). Still under his successors, Manasseh and Amon, these high places were again in active operation. Josiah made an effort to put an end to the evil, but not with complete success (II Kings xxii. 3; II Chron. xxxiv. 3). There was opposition to his undertaking (see Jer. xi.), and after his death the Prophets had again to contend with the popularity of those old sanctuaries. Even after the Exile traces are found of a revival of their cult (Isa. lvii. 3, lxv. 1–7, lxvi. 17). After Josiah their priests, not all of whom were killed or transported to Jerusalem (II Kings xxiii. 5, 8), probably contrived to keep up these old local rites even at a late day, a supposition by no means irrational in view of the attachment manifested by Mohammedans to just such "maḳam" (= "meḳomot," Deut. xii. 2; Clermont-Ganneau, "The Survey of Western Palestine," p. 325, London, 1881; Conder, "Tent Work in Palestine," 1880, pp. 304–310).

Destruction of the High Places.

The critical analysis of the Law gives the same result as the foregoing historical survey. The Book of the Covenant (Ex. xx. 34) legitimates local altars; Deuteronomy (xii. 2, 3, 12; comp. xiv. 23–25; xv 20; xvi. 2, 6, 15, 16; xvii. 8; xviii. 6) orders their destruction and the centralization of the cult at Jerusalem. In the Priestly Code (P) the centralization is tacitly assumed.

The later rabbis recognize the discrepancies between the Deuteronomic law and the actions re-

Rabbinic Attitude.

ported of such saintly men as Samuel and Elijah, as well as of the Patriarchs. They solve the difficulties by assuming that up to the erection of the Tabernacle bamot were legitimate, and were forbidden only after its construction. But at Gilgal they were again permitted; at Shiloh, again prohibited. At Nob and Gibeon they were once more allowed; but after the opening of the Temple at Jerusalem they were forbidden forever (Zeb. xiv. 4 *et seq.*). The rabbinical explanations have been collected by Ugolino in his "Thesaurus" (x. 559 *et seq.*). A distinction is made between a great ("gedolah") bamah for public use and a small one for private sacrifices (Meg. i. 10; comp. Zeb. xiv. 6). The bamah was called "menuḥah" (= "temporary residence of the Shekinah"); the Temple at Jerusalem, "naḥalah" (= "permanent heritage") (Meg. 10a). A description of a small bamah is found in Tosef., Zeb., at end.

XXXI

High Priest

HIGH PRIEST (Hebrew: "kohen ha-gadol," II Kings xii. 11; Lev. xxi. 10; "kohen ha-mashiaḥ" = "the anointed priest," Lev. iv. 3; "kohen ha-rosh," II Chron. xix. 11; once, simply "ha rosh," II Chron. xxiv. 6; Aramaic: "kahana rabba" [the *ἀναραβάχης* of Josephus, "Ant." iii. 7, § 1; see Wellhausen, "Gesch. Israels," p. 161]; LXX.: *ἱερεὺς μέγας* = "the chief of the priests" [except Lev. iv. 3, where *ἀρχιερεὺς*, as in the N. T.]).—**Biblical Data**: Aaron, though he is but rarely called "the great priest," being generally simply designated "as ha-kohen" (the priest), was the first incumbent of the office, to which he was appointed by God (Ex. xxviii. 1, 2; xxix. 4, 5). The succession was to be through one of his sons, and was to remain in his own family (Lev. vi. 15; comp. Josephus, "Ant." xx. 10, § 1). Failing a son, the office devolved upon the brother next of age: such appears to have been the practise in the Maccabean period. In the time of Eli, however (I Sam. ii. 23), the office passed to the collateral branch of Ithamar (see Eleazar). But Solomon is reported to have deposed Abiathar, and to have appointed Zadok, a descendant of Eleazar, in his stead (I Kings ii. 35; I Chron. xxiv. 2, 3). After the Exile, the succession seems to have been, at first, in a direct line from father to son; but later the civil authorities arrogated to themselves the right of appointment. Antiochus IV., Epiphanes, for instance, deposed Onias III. in favor of Jason, who was followed by Menelaus (Josephus, "Ant." xii. 5, § 1; II Macc. iii. 4, iv. 23).

Herod nominated no less than six high priests; Archelaus, two. The Roman legate Quirinius and his successors exercised the right of appointment, as did Agrippa I., Herod of Chalcis, and Agrippa II. Even the people occasionally elected candidates to the office. The high priests before the Exile were, it seems, appointed for life (comp. Num. xxxv. 25, 28); in fact, from Aaron to the Captivity the number of the high priests was not greater than during the sixty years preceding the fall of the Second Temple.

Age and Qualifications.

The age of eligibility for the office is not fixed in the Law; but according to rabbinical tradition it was twenty (II Chron. xxxi. 17; Maimonides, "Yad," Kele ha-Miḳdash, v. 15; Ḥul. 24b; 'Ar. 13b). Aristobulus, however, was only seventeen when appointed by Herod ("Ant." xv. 3, § 3); but the son of Onias III. was too young (νήπιος) to succeed his father (*ib.* xii. 5, § 1). Legitimacy of birth was essential; hence the care in the keeping of the genealogical records (Josephus, "Contra Ap." i., § 7) and the distrust of one whose mother had been captured in war ("Ant." xiii. 10, § 5; Jellinek, "B. H." i. 133–137; Ḳid. 66a; see John Hyrcanus). The high priest might marry only an Israelitish maiden (Lev. xxi. 13–14). In Ezek. xliv. 22 this restriction is extended to all priests, an exception being made in favor of the widow of a priest. He was not permitted to come in contact with the bodies of the dead, even of his parents; and he was not permitted, as a sign of mourning, to leave his hair disheveled, to expose it, or to rend his garments (Lev. xxi. 10 *et seq.*). According to Josephus ("Ant." xv. 3, § 1), birth on foreign soil was not a disqualification; but the disqualifications of Lev. xxi. 17 *et seq.* applied to the high priest as well as to other priests.

The ceremonial of consecration, extending through an entire week (Ex. xxviii.; Lev. viii.), included certain rites which all priests were required to undergo: purification; the sacrifices; the "filling" of the hands; the smearing with blood. But Aaron the high priest was anointed with sacred oil, hence the title of the "anointed priest"; other passages have it that all priests were anointed (Ex. xxviii. 41, xxx. 30; Lev. vii. 36, x. 7; Num. iii. 3). The high priest's vestments of office, which he wore, during his ministrations, above those prescribed for the common priests, were: the "me'il," a sleeveless, purple robe, the lower hem of which was fringed with small golden bells alternating with pomegranate tassels in violet, red, purple, and scarlet; the EPHOD, with two onyx-stones on the shoulder-piece, on which were engraved the names of the tribes of Israel; the breastplate ("ḥoshen"), with twelve gems, each engraved with the name of one of the tribes: a pouch in which he probably carried the URIM AND THUMMIM. His HEAD-DRESS was the "miẓnefet," a tiara, or, perhaps, a peculiarly wound turban, with a peak, the front of which bore a gold plate with the inscription "Holy unto YHWH." His girdle seems to have been of more precious material than that of the common priests.

His Costume.

The first consecration was performed by Moses; the Bible does not state who consecrated subsequent high priests. Lev. xxi. 10 states emphatically that every new high priest shall be anointed; and Ex. xxix. 29 *et seq.* commands that the official garments worn by his predecessor shall be worn by the new incumbent while he is anointed and during the seven days of his consecration (comp. Num. xx. 28; Ps. cxxxiii. 2).

The distinguished rank of the high priest is apparent from the fact that his sins are regarded as belonging also to the people (Lev. iv. 3, 22). He was entrusted with the stewardship of the Urim and Thummim (Num. xxvii. 20 *et seq.*). On the Day of Atonement he alone entered the Holy of Holies, to make atonement for his house and for the people (Lev. xvi.); on that occasion he wore white linen garments instead of his ordinary and more costly vestments. He alone could offer the sacrifices for the sins of the priests, or of the people, or of himself (Lev. iv.); and only he could officiate at the sacrifices following his own or another priest's consecration (Lev. ix.). He also offered a meal-offering every morning and evening for himself and the whole body of the priesthood (Lev. vi. 14–15, though the wording of the law is not altogether definite). Other information concerning his func-

Sanctity and Functions.

tions is not given. He was privileged, probably, to take part at his own pleasure in any of the priestly rites. Josephus ("B. J." v. 5, § 7) contends that the high priest almost invariably participated in the ceremonies on the Sabbath, the New Moon, and the festivals. This may also be inferred from the glowing description given in Ecclus. (Sirach) i. of the high priest's appearance at the altar.

——**In Rabbinical Literature:** The high priest is the chief of all the priests; he should be anointed and invested with the pontifical garments; but if the sacred oil is not obtainable (see Hor. 13a; "Semag," 173, end), investiture with the additional garments (see BIBLICAL DATA) is regarded as sufficient (Maimonides, "Yad," Kele ha-Miḳdash, iv. 12). A high priest so invested is known as "merubbeh begadim." This investiture consists of arraying him in the eight pieces of dress and in removing them again on eight successive days, though (the anointing and) the investiture on the first day suffices to qualify him for the functions of the office (*ib.* iv. 13). The only distinction between the "anointed" and the "invested" high priest is that the former offers the bull for an unintentional transgression (Hor. 11b).

The Great Sanhedrin alone had the right to appoint, or confirm the appointment of, the high priest. His consecration might take place only in the daytime. Two high priests must not be appointed together. Every high priest had a "mishneh" (a second) called the Segan, or "memunneh," to stand at his right; another assistant was the "catholicos" ("Yad," *l.c.* 16–17). The right of succession was in the direct, or, the direct failing, the collateral, line, provided the conditions concerning physical fitness were fulfilled (*ib.* 20; Ket. 103b; Sifra, Ḳedoshim). For offenses which entailed flagellation the high priest could be sentenced by a court of three; after submitting to the penalty he could resume his office ("Yad," *l.c.* 22). The high priest was expected to be superior to all other priests in physique, in wisdom, in dignity, and in material wealth; if he was poor his brother priests contributed to make him rich (Yoma 18a; "Yad," *l.c.* v. 1);

His Powers.

but none of these conditions was indispensable. The high priest was required to be mindful of his honor. He might not mingle with the common people, nor permit himself to be seen disrobed, or in a public bath, etc.; but he might invite others to bathe with him (Tosef., Sanh. iv.; "Yad," *l.c.* v. 3). He might not participate in a public banquet, but he might pay a visit of consolation to mourners, though even then his dignity was guarded by prescribed etiquette (Sanh. 18–19; "Yad," *l.c.* v. 4).

The high priest might not follow the bier of one in his own family who had died, nor leave the Temple or his house during the time of mourning. The people visited him to offer consolation; in receiving them, the Segan was at his right, the next in rank and the people at his left. The people said: "We are thy atonement." He answered: "Be ye blessed from heaven" ("Yad," *l.c.* v. 5; and Mishneh Kesef, *ad loc.*). During the offering of consolation he sat on a stool, the people on the floor; he rent his garments, not from above, but from below, near the feet, the penalty for rending them from above being flagellation (Semag, Lawin, 61–62). He could not permit his hair to be disheveled, nor could he cut it ("Yad," *l.c.* v. 6). He had one house attached to the Temple (Mid. 71b), and another in the city of Jerusalem. His honor required that he should spend most of his time in the Sanctuary ("Yad," *l.c.* v. 7). The high priest was subject to the jurisdiction of the courts, but if accused of a crime entailing capital punishment he was tried by the Great Sanhedrin; he could, however, refuse to give testimony (Sanh. 18).

Restrictions.

The high priest must be married; to guard against contingencies it was proposed to hold a second wife in readiness immediately before the Day of Atonement (Yoma i. 1); but polygamy on his part was not encouraged (ביתו = "one wife"; Yoma 13a; "Yad," *l.c.* v. 10). He could give the "ḥaliẓah," and it could be given to his widow, as she also was subject to the LEVIRATE; his divorced wife could marry again (*l.c.*; Sanh. 18). When entering the Temple ("Hekal") he was supported to the curtain by three men (Tamid 67a; this may perhaps have reference to his entering the Holy of Holies; but see "Yad," *l.c.* v. 11, and the Mishneh Kesef *ad loc.*). He could take part in the service whenever he desired ("Yad," *l.c.* v. 12; Yoma i. 2; Tamid 67b; see Rashi *ad loc.*). On the Day of Atonement he wore white garments only, while on other occasions he wore his golden vestments (Yoma 60a; comp. 68b, בגדי בוץ). The seven days preceding the Day of Atonement were devoted to preparing for his high function, precautions being taken to prevent any accident that might render him Levitically impure (Yoma i. 1 *et seq.*). The ceremonial for that day is described in detail in Mishnah Yoma (see also Haneberg, "Die Religiösen Alterthümer der Bibel," pp. 659–671, Munich, 1869). For other regulations concerning the high priest see "Yad," Biat ha-Miḳdash, ii. 1, 8; for details in regard to the vestments see "Yad," Kele ha-Miḳdash, viii. 2–4, 5 (in reference to soiled vestments: the white could be worn only once); *l.c.* vii. 1 ("ẓiẓ"), vii. 3 ("me'il"), vii. 6 ("ḥoshen"), vii. 9 (ephod), ix. 1 (order of investiture).

List of High Priests.

1. Aaron	4. Abishua
2. Eleazar	5. Bukki
3. Phinehas	6. Uzzi (I Chron. vi. 3-5)

With Eli the high-priesthood passes from the line of Eleazar to that of Ithamar:

Old Testament.	*Josephus.*
7. Eli	Eli
8. Ahitub (I Chron. ix. 11)	Ahitub
9. Ahiah (I Sam. xiv. 3)	Ahiah
10. Ahimelech (I Sam. xxi. 1)	Ahimelech
11. Abiathar (I Sam. xxxiii. 6)	Abiathar ("Ant." v. 11, § 5)

From Solomon to the Captivity.

(With Zadok the line of Eleazar reappears.)

Old Testament.	*Josephus.*	*Seder 'Olam Zuta.*
12. Zadok (I Kings ii. 35)	Zadok	Zadok
13. Ahimaaz (II Sam. xv. 36)	Ahimaaz	Ahimaaz
14. Azariah (I Kings iv. 2)	Azariah	Azariah
15.	Joran	Joash
16. Jehoiarib (I Chron. ix. 10)	Jesus	Joarib
17.	Axiomar	Jehoshaphat
18. Jehoiada (II Kings xi. 4)	....	Joiada
19.	Phideas	Pedaiah
20.	Sudeas	Zedekiah
21. Azariah II. (II Chron. xxvi. 17)	Joel	Joel
22.	Jotham	Jotham
23. Urijah (II Kings xvi. 10)	Uriah	Uriah
24. Azariah III. (II Chron. xxxi. 10)	Neriah	Neriah
25.	Odeas	Hoshaiah
26. Shallum (I Chron. vi. 12)	Shallum	Shallum
27. Hilkiah (II Kings xxii. 4)	Hilkiah	Hilkiah
28. Azariah IV. (I Chron. vi. 13)	"	Azariah
29. Seraiah (II Kings xxv. 18)	Sareas	Zeraiah
30. Jehozadak (I Chron. vi. 14)	Josedek	Jehozadak

From the Captivity to Herod.

Old Testament.	*Josephus.*
31. Jeshua (Hag. i. 1)	Jesus ("Ant." xi. 3, § 10)
32. Joiakim (Neh. xii. 10)	Joiakim ("B. J." xi. 5, § 1)
33. Eliashib (Neh. iii. 1)	Eliashib ("B. J." xi. 5, § 5)
34. Joiada (Neh. xii. 10, 22)	Judas ("Ant." xi. 7, § 1)
35. Johanan (Neh. xii. 22)	Joannes ("Ant." xi. 7, § 1)
36. Jaddua (Neh. xii. 22)	Jaddus ("Ant." xi. 7, § 2)
37.	Onias I. ("Ant." xii. 2, § 5)
Apocrypha.	*Josephus* ("Antiquities").
38. Simon I. (Ecclus. [Sirach] 4, 1)	Simon the Just (xii. 2, § 5)
39.	Eleazar (xii. 2, § 5)
40.	Manasseh (xii. 4, § 1)
41.	Onias II. (xii. 4, § 1)
42.	Simon II. (xii. 4, § 10)
43. Onias (I Macc. xii. 7)	Onias III. (xii. 4, § 10)
44. Jason (II Macc. iv. 7)	Jesus (xii. 5, § 1)
45. Menelaus (II Macc. iv. 27)	Onias, called Menelaus (xii. 5, § 1)
46. Alcimus (I Macc. vii. 5)	Alcimus (xii. 9, § 7)
47. Jonathan (I Macc. ix. 28)	Jonathan (xiii. 2, § 2)
48. Simon (the Prince) (I Macc. xiv. 46)	Simon (xiii. 6, § 7)
49. John (I Macc. xvi. 23)	John Hyrcanus (xiii. 8, § 1)
50.	Aristobulus I. (xiii. 9, § 1)
51.	Alexander Jannæus (xiii. 12, § 1)
52.	Hyrcanus II. (xiii. 16, § 2)
53.	Aristobulus II. (xv. 1, § 2)
54.	Hyrcanus II. (restored) (xiv. 4, § 4)
55.	Antigone (xiv. 14, § 3)
56.	Hananeel (xv. 2, § 4)

FROM HEROD TO THE DESTRUCTION OF THE TEMPLE.

Josephus ("Antiquities").

(Under Herod.)

56. Hananeel
57. Aristobulus III. (xv. 3, §§ 1, 3)
(Hananeel reappointed; xv. 3, § 3)
58. Jesus, son of Phabet (xv. 9, § 3)
59. Simon, son of Bœthus (perhaps Bœthus **himself; xv. 9, § 3; xvii. 4, § 2)**
60. Mattathias, son of Theophilus (xvii. 6, § 4)
Joseph, son of Ellem (one day; xvii. **6, § 4; see Grätz in "Monatsschrift,"** 1881, pp. 51 *et seq.*)
61. Joazar, son of Bœthus (xvii. 6, § 4)

(Under Archelaus.)

62. Eleazar, son of Bœthus (xvii. 13, § 1)
63. Jesus, son of Sie (Σιε; xvii. 13, § 1)
(**Joazar reappointed**; xviii. 1, § 1; 2, § 1)

(Under Quirinius.)

64. Ananus, son of Seth (xviii. 2, § 2; Luke iii. 2)

(Under Valorius Gratus.)

65. Ismael, son of Phabi (xviii. 2, § 2)
66. Eleazar, son of Ananus (xviii. 2, § 2)
67. Simon, son of Camithus (xviii. 2, § 2)
68. Joseph (called "Caiaphas" (xviii. 2, § 2; 4, § 3; **Matt. xxvi. 3, 57)**

(Under Vitellius.)

69. Jonathan, son of Ananus (xviii. 4, § 3; "B. J." ii. 12, §§ 5–6; 13, § 3)
70. Theophilus, son of Ananus (xviii. 5, § 3)

(Under Agrippa.)

71. Simon, or Cantheras, son of Bœthus (**xix. 6, § 2; see Grätz**, "Gesch." 4th ed., iii. 739–746)
72. Mattathias, son of Ananus (xix. 6, § 4)
73. Elioneus, son of Cantheras (xix. 8, § 1; **Parah iii. 5**)

(Under Herod of Chalcis.)

74. Joseph, son of Cainus (xx. 1, § 3)
[Perhaps Ishmael (iii. 15, § 13) should be placed here.]
75. Ananias, son of Nebedeus (xx. 5, § 2; Derenbourg, "Hist." p. 233)
(Jonathan restored; xx. 8, § 5)

(Under Agrippa II.)

76. Ishmael, son of Fabi (xx. 8, §§ 8, 11; Parah iii. 5; Soṭah ix. 5; Derenbourg, "Hist." pp. 232–235)
77. Joseph Cabi, son of Simon (xx. 8, § 11)
78. Ananus, son of Ananus (xx. 9, § 1)
79. Jesus, son of Damneus (xx. 9, § 1; "B. J." vi. 2, § 2)
80. Jesus, son of Gamaliel (xx. 9, §§ 4, 7; Yeb. vi. 4; an instance in which a priest betrothed to a widow before his elevation was permitted to marry her afterward; Derenbourg, "Hist." p. 248)
81. Mattathias, son of Theophilus (xx. 9, § 7; "B. J." vi. 2, § 2; Grätz, in "Monatsschrift," 1881, pp. 62–64; *idem*, "Gesch." 4th ed., iii. 750 *et seq.*)
82. Phinehas, son of Samuel, appointed by the people during the war (xx. 10, § 1; "B. J." iv. 3, § 8; see Derenbourg, "Hist." p. 269)
[A man altogether unworthy.]

Josephus enumerates only fifty-two pontificates under the Second Temple, omitting the second appointments of Hyrcanus II., Hananeel, and Joazar.

——**Critical View:** The foregoing regulations concerning the office, title, and prerogatives of the high priest are given in P (Priestly Code) and the "Holiness Code" combined with it; the other Pentateuchal sources do not mention a dignitary of this order. The only seeming exception is the reference to Eleazar as the successor of Aaron "the priest" (Josh. xxiv. 33; comp. Deut. x. 6). Deuteronomy (xvii. 8 *et seq.*) speaks of "the" priest (הכהן) as entrusted with judgment, and as possessing a rank equal to that of the judge. This has been taken to indicate that the office was known to exist and was sanctioned in the days of the composition of Deuteronomy (but see Steuernagel *ad loc.*). Yet this very juxtaposition of judge and priest suggests quite a different conception of the office than that prevailing in P and detailed above. Furthermore, in Ezekiel's ideal reconstitution (Ezek. xl.–xlviii.), though much attention is given to the status of the priests, the high priest is consistently ignored. Perhaps הכהן ("the" priest), referring to the person entrusted with the purification of the Sanctuary on the two days annually set apart for this purpose (Ezek. xlv. 19 *et seq.*), designates the high priest; but it is significant that the special title is omitted and that no further particulars are given.

Only Known to Priestly Code.

The historical and prophetical books lend probability to the theory, based on the facts above, that in pre-exilic days the office had not the prominence P ascribed to it. Jehoiada (II Kings xi. 10), Urijah (*ib.* xvi. 10), and Hilkiah (*ib.* xxii. 14) are each referred to by "ha-kohen," though "ha-kohen ha-gadol" is also used, while "kohen ha-rosh" occurs in connection with Seraiah. Many have contended that this enlarged title is to be considered a later amplification of the simple הכהן, a view largely resting on II Sam. xv. 27 ("Ẓadoḳ ha-kohen"). The title כהן משנה ("the second priest"; Jer. lii. 24; II Kings xxv. 18), however, proves the recognition of a chief priest. Yet this chief priest in pre-exilic times must have been regarded in quite a different light from that presupposed in P. Under David and Solomon there were two priests, Abiathar and Zadok, who simultaneously bore the title "ha-kohen" (II Sam. viii. 17, xix. 12; I Kings i. 7, iv. 4).

Zadok is represented as officiating both at Gibeon (I Chron. xvi. 39) and at Jerusalem (II Sam. xv. 24 *et seq.*). The fact that Solomon deposed Abiathar and put Zadok in his place has been invoked to remove these difficulties; but the fact that a king could control the office is proof that it was of a character other than that assumed in P. If the conclusion is warranted that every shrine had its own chief priest (Eli at Shiloh; Ahimelech in Nob) before the complete centralization of the cult at Jerusalem, the restriction of the number of high priests to one is out of the question (see HIGH PLACE).

After the Exile, Joshua appears vested with such prominence as P ascribes to the high priest (Zech. iii.; Hag. vi. 13). In Ezra and Nehemiah, again, but little consideration is shown for the high priest. The post-exilic high priests traced their pedigree back to Zadok, appointed as chief priest at Jerusalem by Solomon (I Kings ii. 35), and Zadok was held to be a descendant of Eleazar, the son of Aaron (II Chron. v. 34). Immediately after the return from the Captivity, as is clearly to be inferred from Zechariah and Haggai, political authority was not vested in the high priest. Political (Messianic) sovereignty was represented by, or attributed to, a member of the royal house, while religious affairs were reserved to the high-priesthood, represented in the Book of Zechariah by Joshua. But in the course of time, as the Messianic hope, or even the hope of autonomy under foreign (Persian, Greek, Egyptian, or Syrian) suzerainty, became weaker, the high priest grew to be more and more also the political chief of the congregation, as much, perhaps, through the consideration shown him by the suzerain powers and their viceroys as through the effect of the increasingly thorough acceptance of the Levitical code by pious Judeans. In this connection the report (I Macc. vii. 14) that the rigorists received Alcimus, the high priest, with confidence because he was "a priest of the seed of Aaron" is significant. The author of the Book of Daniel regards the period from 536 to 171 B.C. (Joshua to Jason) as inaugurated by the first, and closed by the last, "anointed"; that is, Jason, deposed in 171, was for the writer in Daniel the last of the line of legitimate high priests.

Post-Exilic Conditions.

Ecclus. (Sirach) l. is another evidence of the great reverence in which the high priest was held. The assumption of the princely authority by the Maccabean high priests (the HASMONEANS) was merely the final link in this development, which, beginning with the death of Zerubbabel, was to combine the two ideals, the politico-Messianic and the religio-Levitical, in one office. But after the brief heyday of national independence had come to an inglorious close, the high-priesthood changed again in character, in so far as it ceased to be a hereditary and a life office. High priests were appointed and removed with great frequency (see above). This may account for the otherwise strange use of the title in the plural (ἀρχιερεῖς) in the New Testament and in Josephus ("Vita," § 38; "B. J." ii. 12, § 6; iv. 3, §§ 7, 9; iv. 4, § 3). The deposed high priests seem to have retained the title, and to have continued to exercise certain functions; the ministration on the Day of Atonement, however, may have been reserved for the actual incumbent. This, however, is not clear; Hor. iii. 1–4 mentions as distinctive the exclusive sacrifice of a bull by the high priest on the Day of Atonement and the tenth of the ephah (that is, the twelve "ḥallot"; comp. Meg. i. 9; Macc. ii. 6). But even in the latest periods the office was restricted to a few families of great distinction (probably the bene kohanim gedolim; Ket. xiii. 1–2; Oh. xvii. 5; comp. Josephus, "B. J." vi. 2, § 2; see Schürer, "Gesch." 3d ed., ii. 222).

Political Aspects.

The high priest was the presiding officer of the SANHEDRIN. This view conflicts with the later Jewish tradition according to which the Pharisaic tannaim (the ZUGGIM) at the head of the academies presided over the great Sanhedrin also (Ḥag. ii. 2). However, a careful reading of the sources ("Ant." xx. 10; "Contra Ap." ii., § 23; comp. "Ant." iv. 8, § 14; xiv. 9, §§ 3–5 [Hyrcanus II. as president]; xx. 9, § 1 [Ananus]), as well as the fact that in the post-Maccabean period the high priest was looked upon as exercising in all things, political, legal, and sacerdotal, the supreme authority, shows it to be almost certain that the presidency of the Sanhedrin was vested in the high

Connection with Sanhedrin.

priest (see Isidore Loeb in "R. E. J." **1889, xix.** 188–201; Jelski, "Die Innere Einrichtung des Grossen Synhedrions," pp. 22–28, according to whom the "nasi" was the high priest, while the "ab bet din" was a Pharisaic tanna).

BIBLIOGRAPHY: Grätz, *Gesch.* 4th ed., vol. iii.; Derenbourg, *Hist.* Paris, 1868; Schürer, *Gesch.* 3d ed., Leipsic, 1898; H. Lesètre, in Vigouroux, *Dict. de la Bible*, Paris, 1903; Buhl, in Herzog-Hauck, *Real-Encyc.*; Baudissin, *Gesch. des A. T. Priestertums*, 1889.

XXXII

Host Of Heaven

HOST OF HEAVEN (צבא השמים): Term occurring several times in the Bible, but not always with a definite meaning. The word "ẓaba" usually designates an army, and thus connotes a vast body of organized and officered men; it conveys, however, also the meaning of a numerous throng actually engaged in warfare. The singular "ẓaba" has a different meaning from the plural as used in the expression "YHWH of hosts," a frequent though comparatively late name for the God of Israel. In this expression it is most likely that the reference is to the armies of Israel, at whose head YHWH is marching to battle. All the more probable is it that the phrase "host of heaven" originally covered the idea of stars arrayed in battle-line (comp. Judges v. 20), with a mythological background, perhaps going back to remote Assyro-Babylonian conceptions (see Zimmern in Schrader, "K. A. T." 3d ed., p. 421).

The "host of heaven" is mentioned as the recipient of idolatrous veneration (Deut. iv. 19, xvii. 3; II Kings xvii. 16, xxi. 3, 5; xxiii. 4; Jer. viii. 2, xix. 13; Zeph. i. 5). The express mention of sun, moon, and stars as forming the "host of heaven" in this connection leaves no doubt that astral bodies and their cult are referred to. Sidereal worship was practised among the Canaanites, as many old names of cities (*e.g.*, Jericho = "moon city") indicate, and the astral character of the Assyro-Babylonian religion is well authenticated. The cult of the "host of heaven" was in favor among the Hebrews, but whether in imitation of the customs of their neighbors or as expressing their own original polytheistic religion (as suggested by Hommel) remains a matter for conjecture. Certain kings are mentioned as especially devoted to this form of idolatry (*e.g.*, Manasseh and Ahaz; II Kings xxiii. 3, 5, 12). It is an open question whether מלכת השמים (Jer. vii. 18, xliv. 17–19, 25) should be read "queen of heaven" or "kingdom of heaven." If the latter reading be accepted, "host of heaven" is synonymous; and even if the pointing indicating "queen of heaven" is preferred, the phrase throws light on the connotations of the other phrase (Stade's "Zeitschrift," vi. 123 *et seq.*, 289 *et seq.*; Schrader, "Sitzungsberichte der Berliner Akademie," 1886, pp. 477–491; "Zeit. für Assyr." iii. 353–364, iv. 74–76).

Connected with this meaning as the gathering or muster of the stars, to which, singly or collectively, divine honors are paid, is the implication of the phrase in other passages, in which it has been held to designate "angels" (I Kings xxii. 19; II Chron. xviii. 18). The great stars (= gods; *e.g.*, Ishtar) "muster" their retinue of smaller stars, who attend them. This passes over naturally into the phraseology of the purer and later YHWH religion. YHWH is attended by his "host," and the originally polytheistic term is retained in poetic expression (Ps. ciii. 21, cxlviii. 2). The original star-deities having been looked upon as warriors marshaling their forces for the fray (even YHWH is a "man of war"), the implications of an orderly army under command of a chief are naturally involved in the phrase "host of heaven" (comp. Josh. v. 14; Dan. viii. 10). In Isa. xxiv. 21 (Hebr.) "host of the height" is used, the term conveying the same idea as "host of heaven"; the context shows that this variant, too, is rooted in some mythological conception, perhaps apocalyptically employed, as is the case also in Isa. xxxiv. 4. The "host of the stars" (gods) is in the later religion conceived of as the assembly of angels.

BIBLIOGRAPHY: Smend, *Alttest. Religionsgesch.* Index; Ewald, *Die Lehre von Gott*, Index; Stade, *Gesch. des Volkes Israel*, ii. 236–238; Montefiore, *Hibbert Lectures*, p. 425, London, 1892; Baudissin, *Studien*, Leipsic, 1876.

XXXIII

Jehovah

JEHOVAH: A mispronunciation (introduced by Christian theologians, but almost entirely disregarded by the Jews) of the Hebrew "YHWH," the (ineffable) name of God (the TETRAGRAMMATON or "Shem ha-Meforash"). This pronunciation is grammatically impossible; it arose through pronouncing the vowels of the "ḳere" (marginal reading of the Masorites: אֲדֹנָי = "Adonay") with the consonants of the "ketib" (text-reading: יהוה = "YHWH")—"Adonay" (the Lord) being substituted with one exception wherever YHWH occurs in the Biblical and liturgical books. "Adonay" presents the vowels "shewa" (the composite ֲ under the guttural א becomes simple ְ under the י), "ḥolem," and "ḳameẓ," and these give the reading יְהֹוָה (= "Jehovah"). Sometimes, when the two names יהוה and אדני occur together, the former is pointed with "ḥatef segol" (ֱ) under the י —thus, יֱהֹוִה (= "Jehovah")—to indicate that in this combination it is to be pronounced "Elohim" (אֱלֹהִים). These substitutions of "Adonay" and "Elohim" for YHWH were devised to avoid the profanation of the Ineffable Name (hence יהוה is also written ה׳, or even ד׳, and read "ha-Shem" = "the Name").

The reading "Jehovah" is a comparatively recent invention. The earlier Christian commentators report that the Tetragrammaton was written but not pronounced by the Jews (see Theodoret, "Question. xv. in Ex." [Field, "Hexapla," i. 90, to Ex. vi. 3]; Jerome, "Præfatio Regnorum," and his letter to Marcellus, "Epistola," 136, where he notices that "PIPI" [= ΠΙΠΙ = יהוה] is presented in Greek manuscripts; Origen, see "Hexapla" to Ps. lxxi. 18 and Isa. i. 2; comp. concordance to LXX. by Hatch and

Redpath, under ΠΙΠΙ, which occasionally takes the place of the usual *κύριος*, in Philo's Bible quotations; *κύριος* = "Adonay" is the regular translation; see also AQUILA).

"Jehovah" is generally held to have been the invention of Pope Leo X.'s confessor, Peter Galatin ("De Arcanis Catholicæ Veritatis," 1518, folio xliii.), who was followed in the use of this hybrid form by Fagius (= Büchlein, 1504–49). Drusius (= Van der Driesche, 1550–1616) was the first to ascribe to Peter Galatin the use of "Jehovah," and this view has been taken since his days (comp. Hastings, "Dict. Bible," ii. 199, *s.v.* "God"; Gesenius-Buhl, "Handwörterb." 1899, p. 311; see Drusius on the tetragrammaton in his "Critici Sacri," i. 2, col. 344). But it seems that even before Galatin the name "Jehovah" had been in common use (see Drusius, *l.c.* notes to col. 351). It is found in Raymond Martin's "Pugio Fidei," written in 1270 (Paris, 1651, iii., pt. ii., ch. 3, p. 448; comp. T. Prat in "Dictionnaire de la Bible," *s.v.*). See also NAMES OF GOD.

The pronunciation "Jehovah" has been defended by Stier ("Hebr. Lehrgebäude") and Hölemann ("Bibelstudien," i.).

The use of the composite "shewa" "ḥatef segol" (ֱ) in cases where "Elohim" is to be read has led to the opinion that the composite "shewa" "ḥatef pataḥ" (ֲ) ought to have been used to indicate the reading "Adonay." It has been argued in reply that the disuse of the "pataḥ" is in keeping with the Babylonian system, in which the composite "shewa" is not usual. But the reason why the "pataḥ" is dropped is plainly the non-guttural character of the "yod"; to indicate the reading "Elohim," however, the "segol" (and "ḥirek" under the last syllable, *i.e.*, יְהֹוִה) had to appear in order that a mistake might not be made and "Adonay" be repeated. Other peculiarities of the pointing are these: with prefixes ("waw," "bet," "min") the voweling is that required by "Adonay": "wa-Adonay," "ba-Adonay," "me-Adonay." Again, after "YHWH" (= "Adonay") the "dagesh lene" is inserted in בגדכפת, which could not be the case if "Jehovah" (ending in ה) were the pronunciation. The accent of the cohortative imperatives (שׁוּבָה , קוּמָה), which should, before a word like "Jehovah," be on the first syllable, rests on the second when they stand before יהוה, which fact is proof that the Masorites read "Adonay" (a word beginning with "a").

BIBLIOGRAPHY: Schrader-Schenkel, *Bibellexikon*, iii. 147 *et seq.*; Köhler, *De Pronunciatione Tetragrammatis*, 1867; Driver, *Recent Theories on the . . . Pronunciation*, etc., in *Studia Biblica*, i., Oxford, 1885; Dalman, *Der Gottesname Adonaj und Seine Gesch.* 1889; Dillmann, *Kommentar zu Exodus und Leviticus*, p. 39, Leipsic, 1897; Herzog-Hauck, *Real-Encyc.* viii., s.v. *Jahve*.

XXXIV

Optimism And Pessimism

OPTIMISM AND PESSIMISM: Philosophical and theological systems according to which this world and human life are considered as essentially good or essentially evil. Plato, Cicero, Thomas Aquinas, Nicolaus Cusanus, and especially Leibnitz, Wolf, and Mendelssohn, are among the exponents of optimism, while Buddhism may be said to be the religion of pessimism and Schopenhauer's system its philosophical exposition.

Judaism must be said to be fundamentally optimistic. Gen. i. proclaims that all that God made was good, very good. Man alone of all creatures is not so described. He is endowed with the freedom to choose evil or good. Hence the evils of life are not inherent in the nature of things, but are consequent upon man's conduct. This is the theory worked out in Gen. ii. These two basic concepts—the essential goodness of Creation and man's moral liberty, in which is involved his freedom to sin and thus to bring upon himself both physical and moral suffering as the wage of sin—recur, though in various forms, in the successive developments of Jewish thought. According to this theory happiness and goodness must be coincident. This simple faith was rudely shaken by abundant observation of both public and private experiences to the contrary (Hab. i. 3–4; Isa. xlix. 4; Jer. xii. 1–3; Mal. ii. 17, iii. 13–15; Ps. xliv. and lxxiii.; comp. Ber. 7a). The Messianic hope, however, or the ultimate manifestation of the all-harmonizing retributive power of God, was urged as the solution of the perplexity (Ps. xxxvii. 10–22, xcii. 13–16; Isa. ii. 2–4, xi. 9; Mal.

iii. 18, iv. 1–3). It is characteristic of these Biblical attempts at a theodicy that no reference is made to retribution or recompense in the hereafter (but see Ibn Ezra on Ps. lxxiii.).

The Book of Job is devoted to an exposition of the problem. The poem positively rejects the equation between suffering and sin, but has no explanation to offer for the often unhappy lot of the righteous. Moreover, the vanity of human life finds frequent enunciation (Job vii. 1–9, xiv. 1–2), a thought which is also a favorite theme of the Psalms (lxii. 10, lxxxix. 45 *et seq.*, xc. 9–10). This idea is dominant in Ecclesiastes—a work of post-exilic origin, and it is by no means clearly established that its author points to divine retribution in the hereafter as the solution of the problem (comp. iii. 17, xii. 7). Yet, even in Ecclesiastes optimism is not silent; the world is good even if life is vain (iii. 11; comp. Shab. 30b).

Job and Ecclesiastes.

During and after the Exile the idea of immortality led to a modification of the relations between optimism and pessimism. In Ecclesiasticus (Sirach), for example, a practical pessimism is joined to the fundamentally optimistic assurance that ultimately harmony will result. Moral evil is not caused by God, but is involved in man's freedom (x. 21–22, xv. 14 *et seq.*). Physical evil is purposed by God for the undoing of the wicked (ii. 5, xi. 14, xxxix. 33–36). Yet God's work is good (xxxix. 33 *et seq.*).

Optimism is the fundamental note in Philo's theology. God's goodness is more original than His power. Evil originates in matter, which, he declares, is not created by God. See PHILO.

The question of life's worth and the inherent value of the world as it confronted post-Biblical Judaism under the stress of persecution and suffering had not merely a speculative interest. The contrast between the other-worldliness of the nascent Church and that of the Synagogue is significant for the latter's optimism. Of discussions on the problem of life's value only those between the schools of Hillel and Shammai have been reported ('Er. 13b). The conclusion is given that, abstractly, it would have been better for man not to have been born; but as he has life he should strive after moral perfection.

In the Talmud.

In the darkest days of national or individual affliction the Jews sought and found solace in the study of the Law, which they made the one abiding aim and interest of life. Nahum of Gimzo's motto, "Gam zu le-ṭobah," is characteristic of the irrepressible optimism of the Jewish world-conception (Ta'an. 21a). That the future will bring about a compensating readjustment of present ills is the conviction of such books as the Apocalypse of Baruk (comp. ch. xiv.) and the Fourth Book of Ezra (iii., iv. 2 *et seq.*, and especially vi. 6, vii. 1 *et seq.*, 15–16), while the Book of Tobit argues that evil, in truth, is unreal and always turns out to be good for the righteous.

R. Akiba's contention that whatever God does is done for good (Ber. 60b) may be said to be the summing up of what was Israel's belief in his time. Suffering is disciplinary (Sifre, Deut. 32; Ber. 5b); "Man must bless God for evil as well as for good" (Ber. 54a, 60b). R. Meïr advances the same doctrine (Ber. 60b, "ṭob me'od" = "ha-mawet"; Gen. R. ix.). This position may be said to be that of the medieval Synagogue. The Messianic hope and the belief that divine judgment will bring about justice "in the world to be," giving to its doctrine the character of transcendental optimism, though practical pessimism in view of life's deceptiveness (Eccl. R. ii.; Ber. 61b; *et al.*), is never altogether absent.

Among the Medieval Philosophers.

Among the Jewish philosophers this optimism reappears as the theme of argumentation and demonstration. Saadia argues that evil is negative as far as God is concerned; it arises from man's liberty ("Emunot we-De'ot," ii.). This life is incomplete (*ib.* x.). Hence evil is a mighty lever to influence man to strive after the completer, purer life (*ib.* vi., ix.). Suffering may be the consequence of sin, but it may also be disciplinary (*ib.* v.). The seeming prosperity of the wicked is not an argument against God's justice or His goodness. On the contrary, God is long-suffering, and even rewards the wicked for any good deeds he may have done. Saadia's theodicy culminates in the doctrine of future retribution.

Joseph ben Jacob ibn Zaddiḳ inclines toward pessimism. He denies teleological intentions to be determinant of Creation. Evil is caused by God, though Creation is an emanation from God's goodness. But evil is disciplinary. Still, he who takes cognizance of this world must hate and despise it and strive for that (other) world which is of eternal duration. For good is something exceptional in this world; this world is only endurable as preliminary to another and a better (see his "'Olam Ḳaṭan," *passim*).

Judah ha-Levi, in his "Cuzari," states very clearly the difficulties of the optimistic view (comp. iii., § 11, for instance), but he takes refuge in the direct statement of revelation that God's doings are perfect. Human mental limitations are at the bottom of the assumed imperfections in God's work (v., § 20). The fulfilment of God's Law is Israel's destiny. In this, life's contrasts will be adjusted. This life, if well lived, prepares for the higher world.

Abraham ibn Daud proceeds from the position that evil can not originate in God ("Emunah Ramah," Introduction). God is not, like man, a composite being. As a composite being man is able to do both good and evil, but good issues from reason and evil from desire or passion. The simplicity of God precludes His being the source of two antithetical forces; He can produce only the good. Evil in the world is due to matter, which is antipodal to God. But as matter is largely the negative principle, so in evil inheres for the most part no positive quality. Negations are; they are not produced. Hence God, the Creator, has no share in the being of evil. Moreover, the proportion of evil to good in Creation is so small as scarcely to be worth noticing; and even as such, evil proves to be but good in disguise (see "Emunah Ramah," *passim*).

Views of Maimonides.

Maimonides also contends that from God only the perfect can emanate. Evil is caused by matter, and as such it is privative, not positive. Evil is found only in sublunar things and is always accidental. Man's soul is free from evil. How far this ascription of evil to matter serves to establish a theodicy depends upon the view taken of matter. If it, too, is ultimately the work of the Creator (and this is Maimonides' opinion), evil still is the creation of God. Another difficulty is apparent. Metaphysically evil may be nonentity, a privative negation; but physically it is fraught with suffering. Even so, according to Maimonides, evil is an infinitesimal quantity compared with the preponderating good in the world ("Moreh," iii. 12); and, besides, moral evil, rooted in the freedom of man, is the parent of most of the physical ills, but it is bound to diminish in measure as the active reason is put in control; and this ever-enlarging dominion of reason is preordained in the nature of things. The deeper the wisdom of men becomes, the less ardent will be their (foolish) desires; and wisdom is as inherent in man as the power to see in the eye. With the wider and fuller spread of truth, hatred and discord will vanish from among men (*ib.* iii. 11). Man is only a small part of the universe, not its main and only end. Even if it were proved that in human life evil and suffering exceed the good, this would not demonstrate the essential evilness of Creation. Most ills to which man is heir are either beneficial to his race or are directly traceable to his own conduct, and therefore are accidental and avoidable.

In Crescas' system evil is not regarded as something negative. It is apprehended as real, but still relative, that is, as something which, from the higher point of view, is seen to be good. Later Jewish thinkers have added but little to the elucidation of the problem. In modern theological literature the question has not been extensively discussed. Samuel Hirsch ("Catechismus," p. 100) contends that, in reality, evil has only the power to deceive and destroy itself, while the physical or moral suffering entailed by evil on the doer or on others is to be regarded as probationary and disciplinary. Man's relation to things decides their characterization as "evil" or "good." For the righteous even pain is a blessing.

Judaism, therefore, never advised passive resignation, or the abandonment of and withdrawal from the world. It rejects the theory that the root of life is evil, or that man and life and the world are corrupt as a consequence of original sin. Its optimism is apparent in its faith in the slow but certain uplifting of mankind, in the ultimate triumph of justice over injustice, and in the certain coming of a Messianic age.

XXXV

Prophets And Prophecy

PROPHETS AND PROPHECY.—Biblical Data and Critical View: Though many ancient peoples had their prophets, the term has received its popular acceptation from Israel alone, because, taken as a class, the Hebrew prophets have been without parallel in human history in their work and influence. This brief article will consider, first, the historical development of prophecy, and, second, the extant utterances of the Prophets.

I. Historical Development of Prophecy: The name "prophet," from the Greek meaning "forespeaker" (πρὸ being used in the original local sense), is an equivalent of the Hebrew נביא, which signifies properly a delegate or mouthpiece of another (see Ex. vii. 1), from the general Semitic sense of the root, "to declare," "announce." Synonymous to a certain degree was the word "seer" (רואה, חוזה), which, as I Sam. ix. 9 indicates, was an earlier designation than "prophet," at least in popular speech. The usage of these words gives the historical starting-point for inquiring as to the development of true prophetism in Israel.

Terms Used for the Prophetic Function.

But there is an earlier stage still than that of "seeing," for it may be observed that while Samuel was currently called "the seer," a prominent part of his manifold work was divining. There are several Hebrew terms for divination of one kind or another; but none of these is used as a synonym for "prophesying." Moreover, the words for "seer" are used quite rarely, the probable explanation being that the bulk of the canonical writings proceed from a time when it was considered that the special function of declaring or announcing characterized prophecy in Israel better than the elementary offices of divining or seeing. At the same time it must be remembered that "seeing" is always an essential condition of true prophecy; hence the continued use of the term "vision" to the last days of prophetic history, long after the time when seeing had ceased to be the most distinctive function of the prophet.

The historic order of Hebrew prophecy begins with Moses (*c.* 1200 B.C.). He was not a mere prototype of the canonical prophets, but a sort of comprehensive type in himself, being the typical combination of civil and religious director in one. His claim to be considered the first and greatest of the Prophets is founded upon the fact that he introduced the worship of YHWH among his people, and gave them the rudiments of law and a new sense of justice wider and deeper than that of the tribal system. By him "direction" (Torah) was given to Israel; all later true prophets kept Israel in the same right course along the line of religious and moral development.

Moses and Samuel.

Samuel (*c.* 1050 B.C.) was the first legitimate successor of Moses. He was, it is true, characteristically a "seer" (I Sam. ix.), but the revelation which he gave referred to all possible matters, from those of personal or local interest to the announcement of the kingdom. Like Moses, he was a political leader or "judge." That he was also a priest completes his fully representative character.

But there was a new development of the highest significance in the time of Samuel. There were bands, or, more properly, gilds of "prophets" (doubtless in large part promoted by him), and these must be considered as the prototypes of the professional prophets found all through the later history. They seem to have been most active at times of great national or religious peril. Thus, after the critical age of the Philistine oppression, they are most prominent in the days of the Phenician Ba'al-worship, the era of Elijah and Elisha. They are not merely seers and diviners, but ministers and companions of leading reformers and na-

Prophetic Gilds.

tional deliverers. That they degenerated in time into mere professionals was inevitable, because it is of the very nature of true prophetism to be spontaneous and, so to speak, non-institutional; but their great service in their day is undeniable. The view is probably right which traces their origin to the necessity felt for some organized cooperation in behalf of the exclusive worship of YHWH and the triumph of His cause.

After the establishment of the kingdom under David no prophet was officially a political leader, and yet all the existing prophets were active statesmen, first of all interested in securing the weal of the people of YHWH. Naturally, they watched the king most closely of all. Nathan and Gad to David and Solomon, and Ahijah of Shiloh to Jeroboam, were kingly counselors or mentors, to whom these monarchs felt that they had to listen, willingly or unwillingly.

The next new type of prophecy was realized in its first and greatest representative, Elijah, who is found maintaining not merely a private, but a public attitude of opposition to a king displeasing to YHWH, ready even to promote a revolution in order to purify morals and worship. In Elijah is seen also the first example of the preaching prophet, the prophet par excellence, and it was not merely because of religious degeneracy, but mainly because of the genuinely and potentially ethical character of prophecy, that a firmer and more rigorous demand for righteousness was made by the Prophets as the changing times demanded new champions of reform.

Elijah, Reformer and Preacher.

But the final and most decisive stage was reached when the spoken became also the written word, when the matter of prophecy took the form of literature. It was no mere coincidence, but the result of a necessary process that this step was taken when Israel first came into relation with the wider political world, with the oncoming of the Assyrians upon Syria and Palestine. Many things then conspired to encourage literary prophecy: the example and stimulus of poetical and historical collections already made under prophetic inspiration; the need

Written Prophecy. of handbooks and statements of principles for the use of disciples; the desire to influence those beyond the reach of the preacher's voice; the necessity for a lasting record of and witness to the revelations of the past; and, chief of all, the inner compulsion to the adequate publication of new and all-important truths.

Foremost among such truths were the facts, now first practically realized, that God's government and interests were not merely national, but universal, that righteousness was not merely tribal or personal or racial, but international and world-wide. Neither before nor since have the ideas of God's immediate rule and the urgency of His claims been so deeply felt by any body or class of men as in the centuries which witnessed the struggle waged by the prophets of Israel for the supremacy of YHWH and the rule of justice and righteousness which was His will. The truths then uttered are contained in the writings of the Later Prophets. They were not abstractions, but principles of the divine government and of the right, human, national life. They had their external occasions in the incidents of history, and were thus strictly of providential origin; and they were actual revelations, seen as concrete realities by the seers and preachers whose words both attest and commemorate their visions.

II. Utterances of the Prophets: The first of the literary prophets of the canon was Amos. His brief work, which may have been recast at a later date, is one of the marvels of literature for comprehensiveness, variety, compactness, methodical arrangement, force of expression, and compelling eloquence.

Amos. He wrote about 765 B.C., just after northern Israel had attained its greatest power and prosperity under Jeroboam II., and Israel had at last triumphed over the Syrians. In the midst of a feast at the central shrine of Beth-el, Amos, a shepherd of Tekoah in Judah, and not a member of any prophetic gild, suddenly appeared with words of denunciation and threatening from YHWH. He disturbed the national self-complacency by citing and denouncing the sins of the people and of their civil and religious rulers, declaring that precisely because God had chosen them to be His own would He punish them for their iniquity. He rebuked their oppression of the poor, their greed, their dishonesty, as sins against YHWH Himself; assured them that their excessive religiousness would not save them in the day of their deserved punishment; that, as far as judgment was concerned, they stood no better with Him than did the Ethiopians, or the Arameans, or the Philistines. The most essential thing in his message was that the object of worship and the worshipers must be alike in character: YHWH is a righteous God; they must be righteous as being His people. The historical background of the prophecy of Amos is the dreadful Syrian wars. His outlook is wider still; it is a greater world-power that is to inflict upon Israel the condign punishment of its sins (v. 27).

Hosea.

Hosea, the next and last prophet of the Northern Kingdom, came upon the scene about fifteen years after Amos, and the principal part of his prophecy (ch. iv.–xiv.) was written about 735 B.C. Amos had alluded to the Assyrians without naming them. Hosea is face to face with the terrible problem of the fate of Israel at the hands of Assyria. To him it was beyond the possibility of doubt that Israel must be not only crushed, but annihilated (ch. v. 11, x. 15, etc.). It was a question of the moral order of YHWH's world, not merely a question of the relative political or military strength of the two nationalities. To the masses in Israel such a fate was unthinkable, for YHWH was Israel's God. To Hosea, as well as to Amos, any other fate was unthinkable, and that also because YHWH was Israel's God. Everything depended upon the view taken of the character of YHWH; and yet Hosea knew that God cared for His people far more than they in their superstitious credulity thought He did. Indeed, the love of YHWH for Israel is the burden of his discourse. His own tragic history helped him to understand this relation. He had espoused a wife who became unfaithful to him, and yet he would not let her go forever; he sought to bring her back to her duty and her true home. There was imaged forth the ineradicable love of YHWH for His people; and between the cries and lamentations of the almost broken-hearted prophet can be heard ever and anon strains of hope and assurance, and the divine promise of pardon and reconciliation. Thus while prophecy in Northern Israel came to an end with this new and strange lyrical tragedy, the world has learned from the prophet-poet that God's love and care are as sure and lasting as His justice and righteousness.

The career of the next great prophet, Isaiah, is connected with the kingdom of Judah. Here the historical conditions are more complex, and the prophetic message is therefore more profound and many-sided. Isaiah deals much with the same themes as did Amos and Hosea: the sins of luxury, fashion, and frivolity in men and women; land-grabbing; defiance of YHWH (ch. ii., iii., v.). To his revelation he adds the great announcement and argument that YHWH is supreme, as well as universal, in His control and providence. Ahaz makes a dexterous alliance with Assyria, against the prophetic counsel, for the sake of checkmating Samaria and Damascus. Let him beware; YHWH is supreme; He will dissolve the hostile combination; but Judah itself will ultimately fall before those very Assyrians (ch. vii.). The Ethiopian overlord of Egypt sends an embassy to the Asiatic states to incite them against Assyria. Isaiah gives the answer: God from His throne watches all nations alike, and in His good time Assyria shall meet its fate (ch. xviii.). The great revolt against Assyria has begun. The Assyrians have come upon the land. Again the question is taken out of the province of politics into that of providence. Assyria is God's instrument in the punishment of His people, and when it has done its work it shall meet its predestined doom (ch. x.). So the trumpet-tone of providence and judgment is heard all through the prophetic message till Jerusalem is saved by the heaven-sent plague among the host of Sennacherib.

Isaiah.

While in the next century written prophecy was not entirely absent, another sort of literary activity —whose highest product is seen in Deuteronomy— was demanded by the times and occasions. Assyria had played its rôle and had vanished. The Chaldean empire had just taken its place. The little

Habakkuk and Jeremiah.

nations, including Israel, become the prey of the new spoiler. The wondrous seer Habakkuk (*c.* 600 B.C.) ponders over the situation. He recognizes in the Chaldeans also God's instrument. But the Chaldeans are even greater transgressors than YHWH's own people. Shall they escape punishment? Are militarism and aggressive warfare to be approved and rewarded by the righteous God? (ch. i.). Climbing his watch-tower, the prophet gains a clear vision of the conditions and a prevision of the issue. The career and fate of Chaldea are brought under the same law as the career and fate of Israel, and this law is working surely though unseen (ch. ii.). Habakkuk thus proclaims the universality of God's justice as well as of His power and providence.

In Jeremiah (626–581) prophecy is at its highest and fullest. His long and perfectly transparent official life full of vicissitudes, his protracted conferences and pleadings with YHWH Himself, his eagerness to learn and do the right, his more than priestly or military devotion to his arduous calling, his practical enterprise and courage in spite of native diffidence, make his word and work a matchless subject for study, inspiration, and imitation. The greatest religious genius of his race, he was also the confessor and martyr of the ancient Covenant, and he still wields a moral influence unique and unfailing. What then did his life and word stand for and proclaim? Among other things, these: (1) the nature and duty of true patriotism: oppose your country's policy when it is wrong; at the peril of liberty and life, set loyalty to God and justice above loyalty to king and country; (2) the spirituality of God and of true religion (ix. 23 *et seq.*, xxxi. 31); (3) the perpetuity and continuity of YHWH's rule and providence (xvi. 14, 15; xxiii. 7, 8); (4) the principle of individual as opposed to tribal or inherited responsibility (xxxi. 29, 30).

These are a selection of the leading truths and principles announced by the Prophets. It will be observed: (1) that they are the cardinal truths of Old Testament revelation; (2) that they were given in the natural order of development, that is, according to the needs and capacities of the learners; (3) that they were evoked by certain definite, historical occasions. From the foregoing summary it may also be learned how the function as well as the scope of the prophet was diversified and expanded. In the most rudimentary stage are found traces of the primitive arts and practises of soothsaying and divination; and yet in the very beginnings of the prophetic work in Israel there can be discerned the essential elements of true prophecy, the "seeing" of things veiled from the common eye and the "declaring" of the things thus seen. If Israel presents the only continuous and saving revelation ever vouchsafed to men, the decisive factor in the unique revelation is the character of the Revealer. It was the privilege of the Prophets, the elect of humanity, to understand and know YHWH (Jer. ix. 24), and it still remains profoundly true that "Adonai YHWH doeth nothing unless He has revealed His secret to His servants the Prophets" (Amos iii. 7, Hebr.).

BIBLIOGRAPHY: Besides the standard introductions and commentaries to the Old Testament and the prophetic literature: Knobel, *Prophetismus der Hebräer*, 1837; Tholuck, *Die Propheten und Ihre Weissagungen*, 1860; Baur, *Gesch. der Alttest. Weissagung*, 1860; Oehler, *Das Verhältniss der Alttest. Prophetie zur Heidnischen Mantik*, 1861; Kuenen, *Prophets and Prophecy in Israel*, 1877; Duhm, *Theologie der Propheten*, 1875; F. E. König, *Der Offenbarungsbegriff des A. T.* 1882; W. R. Smith, *The Prophets of Israel*, 1882; C. G. Montefiore, *The Religion of Israel* (the Hibbert Lectures for 1892); Darmesteter, *Les Prophètes d'Israël*, 1892; Kirkpatrick, *The Doctrine of the Prophets*, 1892; Smend, *Lehrbuch der Alttest. Religionsgesch.* 1893; Cornill, *Der Israelitische Prophetismus*, 1894; McCurdy, *History, Prophecy, and the Monuments*, 1894–1901; Kittel, *Profetie und Weissagung*, 1899.

E. G. H. J. F. McC.

——**In Post-Biblical Literature:** The first to reflect upon the phenomena of prophecy and to suggest that certain states, either mental or moral, are prerequisite to the reception or exercise of the prophetic gift was Philo of Alexandria. As in many others of his conceptions and constructions, so in his explanation of prophecy, he follows the lead of Plato, accepting his theory concerning mantic enthusiasm ("Phædrus," p. 534, ed. Stephanus). In order that the divine light might rise in man the human must first set altogether. Under the complete emigration of the mortal or human spirit and the inpouring of the immortal or divine spirit the Prophets become passive instruments of a higher power, the voluntary action of their own faculties

Views of Philo.

being entirely suspended (Philo, "Quis Rerum Divinarum Hæres Sit," § 53). The prophet "utters nothing of his own": he speaks only what is suggested to him by God, by whom, for the time, he is possessed. Prophecy includes the power of predicting the future; still the prophet's main function is to be the interpreter of God, and to find out, while in the state of ecstasy, enthusiasm, or inspired frenzy in which he falls, things that the reflective faculties are incompetent to discover (Philo, *l.c.* §§ 52–53; "De Vita Mosis," ii. 1; "Duo de Monarchia," i. 9; "De Justitia," § 8; "Præmiis et Pœnis," § 9; Drummond, "Philo Judæus," ii. 282; Hamburger, "R. B. T." ii. 1003, *s.v.* "Religionsphilosophie").

Yet this inspiration is held not to be the effect of a special and arbitrary miracle. Communion between God and man is permanently possible for man. Every truly good and wise man has the gift of prophecy: the wicked alone forfeit the distinction of being God's interpreters. The Biblical writers were filled with this divine enthusiasm, Moses possessing it in a fuller measure than any others, who are not so much original channels of inspired revelation as companions and disciples of Moses (Drummond, *l.c.* i. 14–16).

As might be expected from the method of the Tannaim and the Amoraim, no systematic exposition of the nature of prophecy is given by any of the Talmudic authorities. Still, mixed with the homiletic applications and interpretations of Biblical texts, there are a goodly number of observations concerning the Prophets and prophecy in general. Of these the following seem to be the more noteworthy.

Talmudic Views.

The prophetic gift is vouchsafed only to such as are physically strong, mentally wise and rich (Shab. 92a; Ned. 38a). In fact, all the Prophets were "rich" (Ned. 38a). Prophets are distinguished by individual traits. In their language, for instance, they display the influence of environment. Ezekiel is like a rural provincial admitted to the royal presence, while Isaiah resembles the cultured inhabitant of the large city (Ḥag. 13b). Moses, of course, occupies an exceptional position. He beheld truth as if it were reflected by a clear mirror; all others, as by a dull glass (Yeb. 49b). This thought is present in the observation that all other prophets had to look into nine mirrors, while Moses glanced at one only (Lev. R. i.). With the exception of Moses and Isaiah none of the Prophets knew the content of their prophecies (Midr. Shoḥer Ṭob to Ps. xc. 1). The words of all other prophets are virtually mere repetitions of those of Moses (Ex. R. xlii.; see also Bacher, "Ag. Pal. Amor." i. 164, 500); in fact, but one content was in all prophecies. Yet no two prophets reproduced that content in the same manner (Sanh. 89a). Unanimity and concordance of verbal expression betray the false prophet (*ib.*). The Prophets, however, are worthy of praise because they employ phraseology that is intelligible, not even shrinking from using anthropomorphic similes and comparisons drawn from nature (Midr. Shoḥer Ṭob to Ps. i. 1; Pesiḳ. 36a; J. Levy, "Ein Wort über die Mekilta von R. Simon," pp. 21–36; Bacher, *l.c.* iii. 191, note 4).

All prophecies were included in the revelation at Sinai (Ex. R. xxviii.; Tan., Yitro). Still, the "holy spirit" that descended upon individual prophets was not the same in degree in each case; some prophets received sufficient for one book, others enough for two books, and others only so much as two verses (Lev. R. xv.; comp. Bacher, *l.c.* ii. 447, note 1). Prophecy was sometimes contingent upon the character of the generation among whom the potential prophet lived (Sanh. 11a; Ber. 57a; Suk. 28a; B. B. 134a). All written prophecies begin with words of censure, but conclude with phrases of consolation (Yer. Ber. 8d; Midr. Shoḥer Ṭob to Ps. iv. 8; Pesiḳ. 116a; Jeremiah is in reality no exception to the rule). Only those prophecies were published that were valid for future days; but God will at some time promulgate the many prophecies which, because dealing only with the affairs of their day, remained unpublished (Cant. R. iv. 11; Meg. 14a; Eccl. R. i. 9). In connection with this the statement is made that in Elijah's time there lived in Israel myriads of prophets and as many prophetesses (Cant. R. *l.c.*). The prediction of peace must come true if made by a true prophet; not so that of evil, for God can resolve to withhold punishment (Tan., Wayera, on xxi. 1).

Mingled Censure and Consolation.

Judah ben Simeon attributes to Isaiah the distinction of having received immediate inspiration, while other prophets received theirs through their predecessors (Pesiḳ. 125b *et seq.*; Lev. R. xiii.); and, referring to such repetitions as "Comfort ye, comfort ye," he ascribes to him a double portion of prophetic power. A very late midrashic collection (Agadat Bereshit xiv.) designates Isaiah as the greatest, and Obadiah as the least, of the Prophets, and imputes to both the knowledge of all spoken languages. The prophetic predictions of future blessings were intended to incite Israel to piety; in reality, however, only a part of future glory was shown to the Prophets (Yalḳ. ii. 368; Eccl. R. i. 8). Where the prophet's father is mentioned by name, the father also was a prophet; where no place of birth is given, the prophet was a Jerusalemite (Meg. 15a). A chaste bride is promised that prophets shall be among her sons (*ib.* 10b). It is reckoned that forty-eight prophets and seven prophetesses have arisen in Israel. On the other hand, the statement is made that the number of prophets was double the number of those that left Egypt (*ib.* 14a). Eight prophets are said to have sprung from Rahab (*ib.*). Fifty is the number given of the prophets among the exiles returning from Babylon (Zeb. 62a). Every tribe produced prophets. With the death of the Former Prophets the urim and thummim ceased in Israel (Suk. 27a; Soṭah 48a).

Since the destruction of the Temple prophecy has passed over to the wise, the semidemented (fools), and the children, but the wise man is superior to the prophet (B. B. 12a). Eight prophets are mentioned as having filled their office after the destruction of the First Temple, Amos being among them. In the same passage Joel is assigned a post-exilic date (Pesiḳ. 128b). The elders are, like the ḥakamim (see B. B. 12a), credited with superiority over the Prophets (Yer. Ber. 3b; Yer. Sanh. 30b).

Prophecy was not regarded as confined to Israel. The "nations of the world" had seven prophets (B. B. 15b; comp. Eccl. R. iii. 19). Before the building of the Tabernacle, the nations shared the gift with Israel (Lev. R. i.; Cant. R. ii. 3). The restriction of prophecy to Israel was due to Moses' prayer (Ex. xxxi. 16; Ex. R. xxxii.;

"Prophets of the Nations."

Ber. 7a). To "the nations" the prophets come only at night (Gen. R. lii.; Lev. R. i.) and speak only with a "half" address (Lev. R. ix.); but to Israel they speak in open daylight. The distinction between the manner in which God speaks to the prophets of Israel and those of the "nations" is explained in a parable about a king who spoke directly to his friend (Israel), but to strangers only from behind a curtain (Gen. R. lii.). Again, to the "prophets of the nations" God discloses His will only as one stationed afar off; to those of Israel as one standing most close (Lev. R. i.). Balaam is regarded as the most eminent of the non-Jewish prophets (see Geiger's "Jüd. Zeit." vol. i.).

Under the stress of controversy Saadia was compelled to take up the problem of prophecy more systematically than had the Rabbis of the Talmudic period. As the contention had been raised that prophecy in reality was unnecessary, since if the message was rational reason unaided could evolve its content, while if it was irrational it was incomprehensible and useless, Saadia argued that the Torah contained rational and revealed commandments. The latter certainly required the intervention of prophecy, otherwise they could not be known to men. But the former? For them prophecy was needed first because most men are slow to employ their reason, and secondly because through prophecy knowledge is imparted more rapidly ("Emunot we-De'ot," p. 12, ed. Berlin). The third argument is that reason can not evolve more than general principles, leaving man dependent upon prophecy for details. Men can, for instance, reason out the duty of thankfulness, but can not know, through mere reason, how to express their gratitude in a way that would be acceptable in God's sight. Hence the Prophets supplied what human reason could not supply when they established the order of prayers and determined the proper seasons for prayer. The same applies to questions of property, marriage, and the like.

Views of Saadia.

But what is the criterion of true prophecy? The miracles which the prophet works and by which he attests the truth of his message (*ib.* iii. 4), though the degree of probability in the prophet's announcement is also a test of its genuineness, without which even the miracle loses its weight as evidence. The Prophets, indeed, were men, not angels. But this fact renders all the more obvious the divine wisdom. Because ordinary men and not angels are chosen to be the instruments of God's revelation, what of extraordinary power they exhibit must of necessity arouse their auditors and the witnesses of the miracles wrought to a realization that God is speaking through them. For the same reason the ability to work miracles is temporary and conditioned, which again demonstrates that the Prophets do not derive their power from themselves, but are subject to a will other and higher than their own.

To meet the difficulties involved in the assumption that God speaks and appears, so as to be heard and seen, Saadia resorts to the theory that a voice specially created ad hoc is the medium of inspiration, as a "light creation" is that of appearance (*ib.* ii. 8). This "light creation," in fact, is for the prophet the evidence of the reality of his vision, containing the assurance that he has received a divine revelation. It is thus apparent that Saadia denies the cooperation of the mental and moral qualifications of the prophet in the process of prophecy.

Baḥya repeats, to a certain extent, the arguments of Saadia in proof of the insufficiency of reason and the necessity of prophecy. Human nature is twofold, and the material elements might not be held in due control were prophecy not to come to the rescue. Thus reason alone could not have arrived at complete truth.

Baḥya and Ibn Gabirol.

That miracles are the evidence of prophecy Baḥya urges with even greater emphasis than did his predecessor ("Ḥobot ha-Lebabot," iii. 1, 4). Nevertheless, he contends that purity of soul and perfection of rational knowledge constitute the highest condition attainable by man, and that these make one "the beloved of God" and confer a strange, superior power "to see the sublimest things and grasp the deepest secrets" (*ib.* x.; Kaufmann, "Die Theologie des Bachya," p. 228, Vienna, 1875).

Solomon ibn Gabirol regards prophecy as identical with the highest possible degree of rational knowledge, wherein the soul finds itself in unity with the All-Spirit. Man rises toward this perfect communion from degree to degree, until at last he attains unto and is united with the fount of life (see Sandler, "Das Problem der Prophetie," p. 29, Breslau, 1891).

Judah ha-Levi confines prophecy to Palestine. It is the אדמת הנבואה and the הארץ המסגלת ("Cuzari," i. 95). Prophecy is the product of the Holy Land (*ib.* ii. 10), and Israel as the people of that land is the one people of prophecy. Israel is the heart of the human race, and its great men, again, are the hearts of this heart (*ib.* ii. 12). Abraham had to migrate to Palestine in order to become fit for the receiving of divine messages (*ib.* ii. 14). To meet the objection that Moses, among others, received prophetic revelations on non-Palestinian soil, Judah gives the name of Palestine a wider interpretation: "Greater Palestine" is the home of prophecy. But this prophecy, again, is a divine gift, and no speculation by philosopher can ever replace it. It alone inspires men to make sacrifices and to meet death, certain that they have "seen" God and that God has "spoken" to them and communicated His truth to them. This is the difference between "the God of Abraham and the God of Aristotle" (*ib.* iv. 16). The prophet is endowed by God with a new inner sense, the עין נסתרה (= "hidden [inner] eye"), and this "inner eye" enables the prophet to see mighty visions (*ib.* iv. 3). The test of the truth is the unanimity of the Prophets, who alone can judge of prophetic truth. The agreement of the "seers" as against the "blind" is the finally decisive factor. Judah ha-Levi demands of the prophet, lest he mistake mere imagination for genuine vision, purity of conduct, freedom from passion, an equable temperament "of identical mixture," a contemplative life, an ardent yearning toward the higher things, and a lasting, almost complete, absorption in God. Upon such as fulfil these conditions in their entirety the divine spirit of prophecy is poured out (*ib.* v. 12). This "outpouring" or "irradiation" is meant by the Prophets when they speak of "God's glory," "God's form," the "Shekinah," "the fire-cloud," etc. (*ib.* iii. 2). It is called also the "divine" or "effulgent" Light (*ib.* ii. 14). So inspired, the prophet is "the counselor, admonisher, and censor of the people"; he is its "head"; like Moses, he is a lawgiver (*ib.* ii.

Judah ha-Levi.

28). Joseph ben Jacob ibn Ẓaddiḳ ("'Olam Ḳaṭôn") regards prophecy as an emanation of the divine spirit, of which all, without distinction, may become recipients.

The philosophers so far presented consider prophecy a gift from without. Abraham ibn Daud was the first among Jewish schoolmen to insist that prophecy is the outgrowth of natural predispositions and acquired knowledge. He links prophecy to dreams (see Ber. 57b). An Aristotelian, he invokes the "active intellect" to connect the natural with the supernatural. He also attributes to "imagination" a share in the phenomena of prophecy. He assumes two degrees of prophetic insight, each with subdivisions: the visions given in dreams, and those imparted to the prophet while he is awake. In dreams imagination predominates; when the prophet is awake the "active intellect" is dominant ("Emunah Ramah," ed. Weil, pp. 70–73). Soothsaying as distinct from prophecy results in accordance with the extent to which the "intellect" is under the control of imagination. Imagination produces the sensuous similes and allegories under which the prophet conceives the content of his message. As the intellect succeeds in minimizing imagination, revelation is imparted in clearer words, free from simile and allegory. Inner reflection is potent in prophecy grasped by the waking mind. Palestine is for Abraham the land of prophecy, Israel its predestined people. In Israel they attain this power who lead a morally pure life and associate with men of prophetic experience. Otherwise prophecy is within the reach of all, provided God consents to bestow it.

Abraham ibn Daud's theories are, with characteristic modifications, restated by Maimonides. He enumerates three opinions: (1) that of the masses, according to which God selected whom He would, though never so ignorant; (2) that of the philosophers, which rates prophecy as incidental to a degree of perfection inherent in human nature; (3) that "which is taught in Scripture and forms one of the principles of our religion." The last agrees with the second in all points except one. For "we believe that, even if one has the capacity for prophecy and has duly pre-

The Maimonidean View of Prophecy.

pared himself, he may yet not actually prophesy. The will of God" is the decisive factor. This fact is, according to Maimonides, a miracle.

The indispensable prerequisites are three: innate superiority of the imaginative faculty; moral perfection; mental perfection, acquired by training. These qualities are possessed in different degrees by wise men, and the degrees of the prophetic faculty vary accordingly. In the Prophets the influence of the active intellect penetrates into both their logical and their imaginative faculties. Prophecy is an emanation from the Divine Being, and is transmitted through the medium of the active intellect, first to man's rational faculty and then to his imaginative faculty. Prophecy can not be acquired by a man, however earnest the culture of his mental and moral faculties may be. In the course of his exposition, in which he discusses the effect of the absence, or undue preponderance, of one of the component faculties, Maimonides analyzes the linguistic peculiarities of the Biblical prophecies and examines the conditions (*e.g.*, anger or grief) under which the prophetic gift may be lost. He explains that there are eleven ascending degrees in prophecy or prophetic inspiration, though Moses occupies a place by himself; his inspiration is different in kind as well as in degree from that of all others ("Moreh," ii., xxxii.–xlviii.; "Yad," Yesode ha-Torah, vii. 6). For the controversies that were aroused by Maimonides' views the articles ALFAKAR, MOSES BEN MAIMON, and MOSES BEN NAḤMAN should be consulted (see also Naḥmanides on Gen. xviii. 1).

Isaac ben Moses ARAMA ("Aḳedat Yiẓḥaḳ," xxxv.) declares Maimonides' view that the prophetic gift is essentially inherent in human faculties, and that its absence when all prerequisite conditions are present is a miracle, to be thoroughly un-Jewish. Precisely the contrary is the case, as prophecy is always miraculous.

Later Views.

Joseph ALBO ("'Iḳḳarim," iii. 8), though arguing against Maimonides, accepts (*ib.* iii. 17) Maimonides' explanation that Moses' prophecy is distinct and unique because of the absence therefrom of imagination.

Isaac ABRAVANEL (on Gen. xxi. 27) maintains the reality of the visions of the Prophets which Maimonides ascribed to the intervention of the imaginative faculties. Among the writers on prophecy Gersonides (LEVI BEN GERSHON) must be mentioned. Dreams, for this writer, are not vain plays of fancy; neither are the powers of soothsayers fictitious; the latter merely lack one element essential to prophecy, and that is wisdom. Moreover, prophecy is always infallible. It is an emanation from the all-surveying, all-controlling, universal active intellect, while the soothsayer's knowledge is caused by the action of a "particular" spheric influence or spirit on the imagination of the fortune-teller ("Milḥamot ha-Shem," ii.).

Ḥasdai CRESCAS regards prophecy as an emanation from the Divine Spirit, which influences the rational faculty with as well as without the imaginative faculty ("Or Adonai," ii. 4, 1).

Modern Jewish theologians have contributed but little to the elucidation of the phenomenon of prophecy. Most of the catechisms are content to repeat Maimonides' analysis (so with Einhorn's "Ner Tamid"); others evade the question altogether. Maybaum ("Prophet und Prophetismus im Alten Israel") has not entered into a full discussion of the psychological factors involved. The views of the critical school, however, have come to be adopted by many modern Jewish authors.

BIBLIOGRAPHY: A. Schmidl, *Studien über Jüdische Religionsphilosophie*, Vienna, 1869; Neumann Sandler, *Das Problem der Prophetie in der Jüdische Religionsphilosophie*, Breslau, 1891; Emil G. Hirsch, *Myth, Miracle, and Midrash*, Chicago, 1899.

J. E. G. H.

XXXVI
Proselyte

PROSELYTE (προσήλυτος, from προσέρχεσθαι): Term employed generally, though not exclusively, in the Septuagint as a rendering for the Hebrew word "ger," designating a convert from one religion to another. The original meaning of the Hebrew is involved in some doubt. Modern interpreters hold it to have connoted, at first, a stranger (or a "client," in the technical sense of the word) residing in Palestine, who had put himself under the protection of the people (or of one of them) among whom he had taken up his abode. In later, post-exilic usage it denotes a convert to the Jewish religion. In the Septuagint and the New Testament the Greek equivalent has almost invariably the latter signification (but see Geiger, "Urschrift," pp. 353 *et seq.*),

The "Ger."

though in the Septuagint the word implies also residence in Palestine on the part of one who had previously resided elsewhere, an implication entirely lost both in the Talmudical "ger" and in the New Testament προσήλυτος. Philo applies the latter term in the wider sense of "one having come to a new and God-pleasing life" ("Duo de Monarchia," i. 7), but uses another word to express the idea of "convert" —ἔπηλυς. Josephus, though referring to converts to Judaism, does not use the term, interpreting the Biblical passages in which "ger" occurs as applying to the poor or the foreigner.

Whatever may have been the original implication of the Hebrew word, it is certain that Biblical authors refer to proselytes, though describing them in paraphrases. Ex. xii. 48 provides for the proselyte's partaking of the paschal lamb, referring to him as a "ger" that is "circumcised." Isa. xiv. 1 mentions converts as "strangers" who shall "cleave to the house of Jacob" (but comp. next verse). Deut. xxiii. 8 (Hebr.) speaks of "one who enters into the assembly of Jacob," and (Deutero-) Isa. lvi. 3–6 enlarges on the attitude of those that joined themselves to Yhwh, "to minister to Him and love His name, to be His servant, keeping the Sabbath from profaning it, and laying hold on His covenant." "Nokri" (ξένος = "stranger") is another equivalent for "proselyte," meaning one who, like Ruth, seeks refuge under the wings of Yhwh (Ruth ii. 11–12; comp. Isa. ii. 2–4, xliv. 5; Jer. iii. 17, iv. 2, xii. 16; Zeph. iii. 9; I Kings viii. 41–43; Ruth i. 16). Probably in almost all these passages "converts" are assumed to be residents of Palestine. They are thus "gerim," but circumcised. In the Priestly Code "ger" would seem to have this meaning throughout. In Esther viii. 17 alone the expression "mityahadim" (= "became Jews") occurs.

According to Philo, a proselyte is one who abandons polytheism and adopts the worship of the One God ("De Pœnitentia," § 2; "De Caritate," § 12). Josephus describes the convert as one who adopts the Jewish customs, following the laws of the Jews and worshiping God as they do—one who has become a Jew ("Ant." xx. 2, §§ 1, 4; comp. xviii. 3, § 5; for another description see the Apocalypse of Baruch, xli. 3, 4; xlii. 5). By many scholars the opinion is held that the phrase "yir'e Adonai" denotes either proselytes in general or a certain class ("ger toshab"; see below). This interpretation is that of the Midrash (Lev. R. iii.; Shoḥer Ṭob to Ps. xxii. 22). While this construction is borne out by some passages (Ps. cxv. 11–13, cxviii. 4, cxxxv. 20), in others the reference is clearly to native Israelites (Ps. xv. 4, xxii. 23–25, xxv. 12–14, *et al.*). For the value of the term in the New Testament (in the Acts) see Bertholet, "Die Stellung der Israeliten und der Juden zu den Fremden" (pp. 328–334), and O. Holtzmann, "Neutestamentliche Zeitgesch." (p. 185). According to Schürer ("Die Juden im Bosporanischen Reiche," in "Sitzungsberichte der Berliner Akademie," 1897), the phrase "those who fear the Most High God" designates associations of

Greeks in the first post-Christian centuries, who had taken their name and their monotheistic faith from the Jews, but still retained many of the elements of Greek life and religion (see Jacob Bernays, "Die Gottesfürchtigen bei Juvenal," in his "Gesammelte Schriften," ii. 71–80).

The attitude of ancient Israel to proselytes and proselytism is indicated in the history of the term "ger" as sketched above, which, again, reflects the progressive changes incidental to the development of Israel from a nation into a religious congregation under the priestly law. (For the position of strangers see GENTILE.) Ezra's policy, founded on the belief that the new commonwealth should be of the holy seed, naturally led to the exclusion of those of foreign origin. Still, the non-Israelite could gain admittance through circumcision (see Ex. xii.).

Historic Conditions.

Pre-exilic Israel had but little reason to seek proselytes or concern itself with their status and reception. The "strangers" in its midst were not many (II Chron. ii. 16 is certainly unhistorical). As "clients," they were under the protection of the community. Such laws as refer to them in pre-exilic legislation, especially if compared with the legislative provisions of other nations, may justly be said to be humane (see DEUTERONOMY; GENTILE). That the aboriginal population was looked upon with suspicion was due to their constituting a constant peril to the monotheistic religion. Hence the cruel provisions for their extermination, which, however, were not carried into effect.

During the Exile Israel came in contact with non-Israelites in a new and more intimate degree, and Deutero-Isaiah reflects the consequent change in Israel's attitude (see passages quoted above). Even after the restoration Ezra's position was not without its opponents. The books of Jonah and Ruth testify to the views held by the anti-Ezra pleaders for a non-racial and all-embracing Israel. Not only did Greek Judaism tolerate the reception of proselytes, but it even seems to have been active in its desire for the spread of Jewish monotheism (comp. Schürer, *l.c.*). Philo's references to proselytes make this sure (comp. Renan, "Le Judaïsme en Fait de Religion et de Race").

According to Josephus there prevailed in his day among the inhabitants of both Greek and barbarian cities ("Contra Ap." ii., § 39) a great zeal for the Jewish religion. This statement refers to Emperor Domitian's last years, two decades after Jerusalem's fall. It shows that throughout the Roman empire Judaism had made inroads upon the pagan religions. Latin writers furnish evidence corroborating this. It is true that Tacitus ("Hist." iv. 5) is anxious to convey the impression that only the most despicable elements of the population were found among these converts to Judaism; but this is amply refuted by other Roman historians, as Dio Cassius (67, 14, 68), Cicero ("Pro Flacco," § 28), Horace ("Satires," i. 9, 69; iv. 142), and Juvenal (xiv. 96).

Among converts of note are mentioned the royal family of Adiabene—Queen Helena and her sons Izates and Monobazus ("Ant." xx., ch. 2–4), Flavius Clemens (Dio Cassius, *l.c.*), Fulvia, the wife of Saturninus, a senator (Philo, "Contra Flaccum," ed. Mangey, ii., § 517; "Ant." xiii. 9, § 1; 11, § 3). Women seem to have predominated among them (Josephus, "B. J." ii. 20, § 2; "Ant." xviii. 3, § 5; Suk. 23; Yer. Suk. ii. 4; 'Ab. Zarah 10; comp. Grätz, "Die Jüdischen Proselyten im Römerreiche," Breslau, 1884; Huidekoper, "Judaism in Rome").

Roman Proselytes.

In Palestine, too, proselytes must have been both numerically and socially of importance. Otherwise the Tannaim would have had no justification for discussing their status and the conditions of their reception. Common prejudice imputes to Phariseeism an aversion to proselytes, but perhaps this idea calls for modification. That aversion, if it existed, may have been due to the part taken in Jewish history by Herod, a descendant of the Idumeans whom John Hyrcanus had compelled to embrace Judaism —a fate shared later by the Itureans ("Ant." xiii. 9, § 1; xv. 7, § 9; comp. xiii. 9, § 3). The "proselyte anecdotes" in which Hillel and Shammai have a central part (Shab. 31a) certainly suggest that the antipathy to proselytes was not shared by all, while R. Simeon's dictum that the hand of welcome should be extended to the proselyte (Lev. R. ii. 8), that he might be brought under the wings of the Shekinah, indicates a disposition quite the reverse. In this connection the censure of the Pharisees in Matt. xxv.

15 is significant. Grätz (*l.c.* p. 30), it is true, argues that the verse refers to an actual incident, the voyage of R. Gamaliel, R. Eliezer b. Azariah, R. Joshua, and R. Akiba to Rome, where they converted Flavius Clemens, a nephew of Emperor Domitian. But the more acceptable interpretation is that given by Jellinek ("B. H." v., p. xlvi.), according to which the passionate outburst recorded in the Gospel of Matthew condemns the Pharisaic practise of winning over every year at least one proselyte each (comp. Gen. R. xxviii.). There is good ground also for the contention of Grätz (*l.c.* p. 33) that immediately after the destruction of the Second Temple Judaism made many conquests, especially among Romans of the upper classes. Among the proselytes of this time a certain Judah, an Ammonite, is mentioned. Contrary to the Biblical law prohibiting marriage between Jews and Ammonites, he is allowed to marry a Jewess, the decision being brought about largely by Joshua's influence (Yad. iv. 4; Tosef., Yad. ii. 7; comp. Ber. 28a).

Other cases in which Biblical marriage-prohibitions were set aside were those of Menyamin, an Egyptian (on the authority of R. Akiba; Tosef., Ḳid. v. 5; Yer. Yeb. 9b; Sifre, Ki Tissa, 253; Yeb. 76b, 78a; Soṭah 9a), Onḳelos, or Akylas (Aquila), from Pontus (Tosef., Dem. vi. 13; Yer. Dem. 26d), Veturia Paulla, called Sarah after her conversion (see Schürer, "Die Gemeindeverfassung der Juden in Rom," p. 35, No. 11, Leipsic, 1879).

At this epoch, too, the necessity for determining the status of the "half-converts" grew imperative. By "half-converts" is meant a class of men and women of non-Jewish birth who, forsaking their ancestral pagan and polytheistic religions, embraced monotheism and adopted the fundamental principles of Jewish morality, without, however, submitting to circumcision or observing other ceremonial laws. They have been identified with the "yir'e Adonai" (the *σηβόμενοι τὸν Θεόν*). Their number was very large during the centuries immediately preceding and following the fall of Jerusalem; Ps. xv. has been interpreted as referring to them.

In order to find a precedent the Rabbis went so far as to assume that proselytes of this order were recognized in Biblical law, applying to them the term "toshab" ("sojourner," "aborigine," referring to the Canaanites; see Maimonides' explanation in "Yad," Issure Biah, xiv. 7; see Grätz, *l.c.* p. 15), in connection with "ger" (see Ex. xxv. 47, where the better reading would be "we-toshab"). Another name for one of this class was "proselyte of the gate" ("ger ha-sha'ar," that is, one under Jewish civil jurisdiction; comp. Deut. v. 14, xiv. 21, referring to the stranger who had legal claims upon the generosity and protection of his Jewish neighbors). In order to be recognized as one of these the neophyte had publicly to assume, before three "ḥaberim," or men of authority, the solemn obligation not to worship idols, an obligation which involved the recognition of the seven Noachian injunctions as binding ('Ab. Zarah 64b; "Yad," Issure Biah, xiv. 7).

Semi-Converts.

The application to half-converts of all the laws obligatory upon the sons of Jacob, including those that refer to the taking of interest, or to retaining their hire overnight, or to drinking wine made by non-Jews, seems to have led to discussion and dissension among the rabbinical authorities.

The more rigorous seem to have been inclined to insist upon such converts observing the entire Law, with the exception of the reservations and modifications explicitly made in their behalf. The more lenient were ready to accord them full equality with Jews as soon as they had solemnly forsworn idolatry. The "via media" was taken by those that regarded public adherence to the seven Noachian precepts as the indispensable prerequisite (Gerim iii.; 'Ab. Zarah 64b; Yer. Yeb. 8d; Grätz, *l.c.* pp. 19–20). The outward sign of this adherence to Judaism was the observance of the Sabbath (Grätz, *l.c.* pp. 20 *et seq.*; but comp. Ker. 8b).

The recognition of these quasi-proselytes rendered it obligatory upon the Jews to treat them as brothers (see 'Ab. Zarah 65a; Pes. 21a). But by the third century the steady growth of Christianity had caused these qualified conversions to Judaism to be regarded with increasing disfavor. According to Simeon b. Eleazar, this form of adoption into Judaism was valid only when the

Influence of Christianity.

institution of the jubilee also was observed, that is, according to the common understanding of his dictum, during the national existence of Israel ('Ar. 29a). A similar observation of Maimonides ("Yad," Issure Biah, xiv. 7–8; *ib.* 'Akkum, x. 6) is construed in the same sense. It seems more probable that Maimonides and Simeon ben Eleazar wished to convey the idea that, for their day, the institution of the ger toshab was without practical warrant in the Torah. R. Johanan declares that if after a probation of twelve months the ger toshab did not submit to the rite of circumcision, he was to be regarded as a heathen ('Ab. Zarah 65a; the same period of probation is fixed by Ḥanina bar Ḥama in Yer. Yeb. 8d).

In contradistinction to the ger toshab, the full proselyte was designated as "ger ha-ẓedeḳ," "ger ha-berit" (a sincere and righteous proselyte, one who has submitted to circumcision; see Mek., Mishpaṭim, 18; Gerim iii.). The common, technical term for "making a convert" in rabbinical literature is "ḳabbel" (to accept), or "ḳareb taḥat kanfe ha-Shekinah" (to bring one near, or under the wings of, the Shekinah). This phrase plainly presupposes an active propaganda for winning converts (comp. Cant. R. v. 16, where God is referred to as making propagandic efforts). In fact, that proselytes are welcome in Israel and are beloved of God is the theme of many a rabbinical homily (Ruth R. iii.; Tan., Wayiḳra [ed. Buber, 3]; see also Mek., Mishpaṭim, 18; Tosef., Demai, ii. 10; Bek. 32a).

Eleazar b. Pedat sees in Israel's dispersion the divine purpose of winning proselytes (Pes. 87b). Jethro is the classical witness to the argument of other proselytes that the "door was not shut in the face of the heathen" (Pesiḳ. R. 35). He is introduced as writing a letter to Moses (Mek., Yitro, 'Amaleḳ, 1) advising him to make the entry into Judaism easy for proselytes. Ruth and Rahab are quoted as illustrating the same lesson (Shoḥer Ṭob to Ps. v. 11).

Views Concerning Proselytes.

Emperor Antoninus also is mentioned as a proselyte (Yer. Meg. 72b, 74a) whose conversion illustrates the desirability of making converts. The circumstance that Nero (Giṭ. 56a), and, in fact, most of the Biblical persecutors of

Israel, are represented as having finally embraced Judaism (Sanh. 96b), the further fact that almost every great Biblical hero is regarded as an active propagandist, and that great teachers like Shemaiah and Abtalion, Akiba and Meïr, were proselytes, or were regarded as proselytes or as descendants of proselytes (see Bacher, "Ag. Tan." i. 5–6), go far to suggest that proselytes were not always looked upon with suspicion. According to Joshua ben Hananiah, "food" and "raiment" in Deut. x. 18 refer to the learning and the cloak of honor which are in store for the proselyte (Gen. R. lxx.). Job xxxi. 32 was explained as inculcating the practise of holding off applicants with the left hand while drawing them near with the right (Yer. Sanh. 29b). Modern researches have shown positively that Judaism sent forth apostles. Jethro was a type of these propagandists (see Bacher, "Ag. Tan." i. 210; Harnack, "Die Mission und Ausbreitung des Christentums," pp. 237–240, Leipsic, 1902; Grätz, "Gesch." 3d ed., vol. iv., note 21; S. Krauss, "Die Jüdischen Apostel," in "J. Q. R." xvii. 370).

Sincerity of motive in the proselyte was insisted upon. Care was taken to exclude those who were prompted to embrace Judaism by the desire to contract an advantageous marriage, by the hope of wealth or honor, by fear or superstitious dreams (R. Nehemiah, in Yeb. 24b; comp. 76a). The midrashic amplification of the conversation between Naomi and Ruth (Ruth R. i. 16; Yeb. 47b) reveals the kind of conduct the Rabbis dreaded in proselytes and what admonitions, with the penalties for disregarding them, they thought wise to impress upon the candidates. Attendance at theaters and circuses, living in houses without mezuzot, and unchastity were among the former. The same spirit of caution is apparent in a midrashic illustration to the story of Adam and Eve, in which the proselyte wife is warned by her husband against eating bread with unclean hands, partaking of untithed fruit, or violating the Sabbath or her marriage vow (Ab. R. N. i.). From Ruth's experience the rule was derived that proselytes must be refused reception three times, but not oftener (Ruth R. ii.).

The details of the act of reception seem not to have been settled definitely before the second Christian century. From the law that proselyte and native Israelite should be treated alike (Num. xv. 14 *et seq.*) the inference was drawn that circumcision, the bath of purification, and sacrifice were prerequisites for conversion (comp. "Yad," Issure Biah, xiii. 4). The sacrifice was to be an "'olat behemah" (a burnt offering of cattle; *ib.* xiii. 5; Ker. ii. 1; 8b, 9a); but to lessen the hardship an offering of fowls was accepted as sufficient. Neglect to bring this offering entailed certain restrictions, but did not invalidate the conversion if the other conditions were complied with. After the destruction of the Temple, when all sacrifices were suspended, it was ordained that proselytes should set aside a small coin in lieu of the offering, so that in case the Temple were rebuilt they might at once purchase the offering. Later, when the prospect of the rebuilding of the Temple grew very remote ("mi-pene ha-taḳḳalah"), even this requirement was dropped (comp. Ker. 8a; R. H. 31b; Gerim ii.; Tosef., Sheḳalim, iii. 22).

Mode of Reception.

Nor was it, at one time, the unanimous opinion of the authorities that circumcision was absolutely indispensable. R. Eliezer ben Hyrcanus carried on a controversy on this subject with R. Joshua, the latter pleading for the possibility of omitting the rite, the former insisting on its performance (Yeb. 46a). The point seems to have remained unsettled for the time (see Grätz, "Die Jüdischen Proselyten," p. 13). For Rabbi Joshua the "ṭebilah" (bath of purification) was sufficient, while his antagonist required both circumcision and bath.

The bitterness engendered by the Hadrianic persecution undoubtedly prompted the Rabbis to make conversion as difficult as possible. It is more than a mere supposition that both at that period and earlier Jews suffered considerably from the cowardice and treachery of proselytes, who often acted as spies or, to escape the "fiscus Judaicus" (see Grätz, *l.c.* pp. 7 *et seq.*), denounced the Jews to the Romans. An instance of this kind is reported in connection with Simeon ben Yoḥai's sufferings (Shab. 33b). This circumstance explains the reasons that led to the introduction into the daily liturgy of a prayer against the "denunciators and slanderers" ("mesorot," "minim"; see Joël, "Blicke in die Religionsgesch." i. 33). Yet the true proselytes were all the more highly esteemed; a benediction in their behalf was added to the eighteen of the Shemoneh 'Esreh, and later was incorporated with that for the elders and pious (Tosef., Ber. iii.; Yer. Ber. 8a; Ta'an. 85c; comp. Grätz, *l.c.* p. 11).

After the Hadrianic rebellion the following procedure came into use. A complete "court," or "board," of rabbinical authorities was alone made competent to sanction the reception. The candidate was first solemnly admonished to consider the worldly disadvantages and the religious burdens involved in the intended step. He, or she, was asked, "What induces thee to join us? Dost thou not know that, in these days, the Israelites are in trouble, oppressed, despised, and subjected to endless sufferings?" If he replied, "I know it, and I am unworthy to share their glorious lot," he was reminded most impressively that while a heathen he was liable to no penalties for eating fat or desecrating the Sabbath, or for similar trespasses, but as soon as he became a Jew, he must suffer excision for the former, and death by stoning for the latter. On the other hand, the rewards in store for the faithful were also explained to him. If the applicant remained firm, he was circumcised in the presence of three rabbis, and then led to be baptized; but even while in the bath he was instructed by learned teachers in the graver and the lighter obligations which he was undertaking. After this he was considered a Jew (Yeb. 47a, b). The presence of three men was required also at the bath of women converts, though due precautions were taken not to affront their modesty. This procedure is obligatory at the present time, according to the rabbinical codes (see Shulḥan 'Aruk, Yoreh De'ah, 268; "Yad," Issure Biah, xiv.). The ceremony should be performed by a properly constituted board of three learned men, and in the daytime; but if only two were present and the ceremony took place at night, it would not therefore be invalid. The ceremony of conversion could not take place on the Sabbath or on a holy day (*ib.*). Proper evidence of conversion was required before the claimant was recognized as a proselyte, though to a certain extent

Influence of the Hadrianic Persecution.

piety of conduct was a presumption in his favor. If the convert reverted to his former ways of living, he was regarded as a rebellious Israelite, not as a heathen; his marriage with a Jewess, for instance, was not invalidated by his lapses. The conversion of a pregnant woman included also the child. Minors could be converted with their parents, or even alone, by the bet din, but they were permitted to recant when of age.

The proselyte is regarded as a new-born child; hence his former family connections are considered as ended, and he might legally marry his own mother or sister; but lest he come to the conclusion that his new status is less holy than his former, such unions are prohibited (see Shulḥan 'Aruk, Yoreh De'ah, 269; "Yad," Issure Biah, xiv. 13). This conception of the proselyte's new birth (Yeb. 62a; Yer. Yeb. 4a) and of his new status with reference to his old family is the subject of many a halakic discussion (Yeb. xi. 2; Yer. Yeb. *l.c.*; *et al.*) and has led to certain regulations concerning marriages contracted either before or after conversion ("Yad," *l.c.* xiv. 13 *et seq.*; with reference to the first-fruit offering see Yer. Bik. 64a; Tosef., Bik. i. 2). That many of the earlier rabbis were opposed to proselytes is plain from observations imputed to them.

Unfavorable View.

R. Eliezer is credited with the opinion that the nature of proselytes is corrupt, and that hence they are apt to become backsliders (Mek., Mishpaṭim, 18; B. Ḳ. 59b; Gerim iv.). Jose ben Judah insists that any candidate should be rejected unless he binds himself to observe not only every tittle of the Torah but all the precepts of the scribes, even to the least of them (Tosef., Dem. ii. 5; Sifra 91a, to Lev. xix. 34).

Sad experience or personal fanaticism underlies the oft-cited statement—in reality a play upon Isa. xiv. 1—that proselytes are as burdensome to Israel as leprosy (Yeb. 47b, 109b; Ḳid. 70b; 'Ab. Zarah 3b; Ket. 11a; Niddah 13b); or the dictum that proselytes will not be received during the days of the Messiah ("Yad," Issure Biah, xiii.–xiv.; *ib.* 'Abadim, ix.; Yoreh De'ah, 268). While evil upon evil is predicted for the "meḳabbele gerim" (propagandists; Yeb. 109b), the proselytes themselves, notwithstanding their new birth, are said to be exposed to intense suffering, which is variously explained as due to their ignorance of the Law (Yeb. 48b), or to the presence of an impure motive in their conversion (*e.g.*, fear instead of love), or to previous misconduct (Yeb. 68b). Nevertheless, once received, they were to be treated as the peers of the Jew by birth.

According to R. Simeon b. Laḳish, proselytes are more precious at Sinai than Israel was, for the latter would not have taken the "kingdom" upon himself had not miracles accompanied revelation, while the former assume the "kingdom" without having seen even one miracle. Hence an injury to a proselyte is tantamount to an injury to God (Tan., Lek Leka, beginning; Ḥag. 5a). The proselyte might marry without restriction ("Yad," Issure Biah, xii. 17). The descendants of Ammon, Moab, Egypt, and Edom formed an exception: the males of Ammon and Moab were excluded forever, though no restriction existed against marriage with their women. Descendants of Egyptians and Edomites of either sex were proscribed in the first and second generations; the third enjoyed full connubial rights. But these restrictions were assumed to have been rendered inoperative by Sennacherib's conquest, and therefore as having no authority in later times ("Yad," *l.c.* xii. 17–24).

Besides the proselytes already mentioned, all belonging to the Roman period, there are records of others later. Among these were the kings of the Jewish Himyarite empire; Arab tribes (before the 6th cent.); Dhu Nuwas; Ḥarith ibn 'Amr; the Kenites; Waraḳah ibn-Naufal; the Chazars. Many also must have come from the ranks of the Christians; this would be the natural inference from the prohibition of conversion to Judaism issued by the Councils of Orleans, repeating previous prohibitions by Emperor Constantine. The code of Alfonso X. made conversion to Judaism a capital crime (Graetz, "Hist." ii. 562; iii. 37, 595).

In Modern Times.

In modern times conversions to Judaism are not very numerous. Marriage is, in contravention of the rabbinical caution, in most instances the motive, and proselytes of the feminine sex predominate. In some of the new rituals formulas for the reception of proselytes are found—for instance, in Einhorn's "'Olat Tamid" (German ed.). Instruction in the Jewish religion precedes the ceremony, which, after circumcision and baptism, consists in a public confession of faith, in the main amounting to a repudiation of certain Christian dogmas, and concluding with the reciting of the Shema'. Some agitation occurred in American Jewry over the abrogation of circumcision in the case of an adult neophyte ("milat gerim"). I. M. Wise made such a proposition before the Rabbinical Conference at Philadelphia (Nov., 1869), but his subsequent attitude (see "The Israelite" and "Die Deborah," Dec., 1869, and Jan., 1870) on the question leaves it doubtful whether he was in earnest in making the proposition. Bernard Felsenthal ("Zur Proselytenfrage," Chicago, 1878) raised the question about ten years later, arguing in favor of the abrogation of the rite and quoting R. Joshua's opinion among others. The Central Conference of American Rabbis finally, at the suggestion of I. M. Wise, resolved not to insist on milat gerim, and devised regulations for the solemn reception of proselytes. I. S. Moses has proposed the establishment of congregations of semiproselytes, reviving, as it were, the institution of the ger toshab.

Female Proselytes.

Certain restrictions regulating the status of women proselytes are found in the Mishnah. Girls born before the conversion of their mothers were not regarded as entitled to the benefit of the provisions concerning a slanderous report as to virginity set forth in Deut. xxii. 13-21 (see Ket. iv. 3); and if found untrue to their marriage vows, their punishment was strangulation, not lapidation. Only such female proselytes as at conversion had not attained the age of three years and one day, and even they not in all cases, were treated, in the law regulating matrimony, as was the native Jewish woman (*ib.* i. 2, 4; iii. 1, 2). Proselytes were not allowed to become the wives of priests; daughters of proselytes, only in case one of the parents was a Jew by birth (Yeb. vi. 5; Ḳid. iv. 7; see Cohen). R. Jose objects to the requirement that one parent must be of Jewish birth (Ḳid. *l.c.*). On the other hand, proselytes could contract marriages with men who, according to Deut. xxii. 3, were barred from marrying Jewish women (Yeb. viii. 2). While a proselyte woman was deemed liable to the ordeal of jealousy described in Num. v. 11. ('Eduy. v. 6), the provisions of the Law regarding the collection of damages in the case of injury to pregnant women were construed as not applicable to her (B. Ḳ. v. 4, but consult Gemara; "R. E. J." xiii. 318).

In these passages the strict interpretation of the Pentateuchal texts, as restricted to Israel, prevails, and in a similar spirit, in the order of PRECEDENCE as laid down in Hor. iii. 8, only the manumitted slave is assigned inferior rank to the proselyte, the bastard and the "natin" taking precedence over him. On the other hand, it should not be overlooked that it was deemed sinful to remind a proselyte of his ancestors or to speak in disrespectful terms of them and their life (B. M. iv. 10).

BIBLIOGRAPHY: Hastings, *Dict. Bible*; Hamburger, *R. B. T.*; Grätz, *Gesch.*; Kalisch, *Bible Studies*, vol. ii. (the Book of Jonah), London, 1878.

XXXVII

Providence

PROVIDENCE (πρόνοια): The term occurs only in the Apocryphal books (Wisdom xiv. 3, xvii. 2), and has no equivalent in Biblical Hebrew, the later philosophical writers employing "hashgaḥah" as a translation for the Arabic "'inayah." "Providence" is employed to connote (1) God's "actio æterna" (His foreknowledge and His dispositions for the realization of His supreme will [πρόγνωσις and πρόθεσις]), and (2) God's "actio temporis" (His power to preserve and to control the universe and all that is therein). Most theologians use the term solely in the latter sense, to which, therefore, the following discussion is confined.

Two Senses of the Term.

The doctrine of the providential care and government of the world is found among non-Jewish and, perhaps, non-monotheistic authors (comp. Cicero, "De Natura Deorum," ii. 30 *et seq.*; Seneca, "De Providentia"). Socrates argues that a beneficent providence is manifest in the construction of the human organs (Xenophon's "Memorabilia," i. 4, § 2). The faith in providence, YHWH's all-sustaining and directing care, more especially manifest in His relations to His people Israel, is variously, but always clearly, expressed in Hebrew Scriptures. Though nowhere presented in coherent systematic form, the Biblical belief in providence reflects the spontaneous religious consciousness of humble and confident believers rather than the reasoned deductions of strenuous thinkers.

Disregarding questions concerning chronological sequence, and other questions involved in the critical school's assumption of an evolutionary process in Israel's religion, the following collection of Biblical statements will serve to illustrate the views of Scripture on providence:

From heaven the Eternal looks down; He sees all the sons of man (Ps. xxxiii. 13, 14). In the heavens the Eternal has His throne, but His government encompasses all (Ps. xi. 4). God's realm embraces all the worlds (eons), still His rule extends over every generation (Ps. cxlv. 13). God is King (מלך) and Shepherd (Ps. xxiii. 1). God is the Record-Keeper (Ps. cxxxix. 16). Nature is constantly the object of divine sustaining solicitude, and always under divine direction (Job xxxvi. 27, xxxviii. 25; Isa. xl., xli.; Jer. xxxiii. 31–35; Ps. lxvi. 8 *et seq.*; civ. 13, 29, 30; cxlvii. 14–18). God provides food in due season for all (Ps. cxlv. 16). Man is uninterruptedly under divine care (Ps. xxii. 10; Job xiv. 5). God directs the course of human affairs, the fate and fortune of the peoples (Ps. xxxvii. 5, xlvi. 10, lxvi. 7, xci. 1–7, civ. 13–16; Prov. xvi. 4; Dan. ii. 21, iv. 14; Isa. x. 5–10; Jer. v. 24, xviii. 7–8; Job xxxvii. 2–7; Amos iv. 7).

In the life of the Biblical heroes the reality of this divine guidance and protection is prominently brought out (Gen. xxiv. 7; xlviii. 4, 15, 20). But it is Israel that is eminently the beneficiary of divine solicitude, witnessing in its own fortunes God's providence (comp. Deut. xxxii.). Essentially interwoven with the Biblical doctrine of the Messianic kingdom is the thought that the providence of God, the Ruler, is effective in the conflicts and relations of the various peoples. A necessary corollary of this faith in providence was the optimism which characterizes the Biblical world-conception. Evil was either caused by man, who had the freedom of choosing, or was disciplinary and punitive; in either case it served the end of divine providence. The sinner was, perhaps, the dearest object of divine watchfulness and love (see OPTIMISM AND PESSIMISM). The simple faith of the Biblical writers never stopped to inquire how providence and human freedom could be shown to be congruous.

Talmudic Views.

The position of the Tannaim and Amoraim is not essentially different from that taken in the Biblical books. Their opinions may be gathered from scattered homiletical and exegetical comments, from parables and anecdotes; but no systematic presentation may be reconstructed from these detached observations of theirs. The following quotations may throw light on the underlying theology: All that God does is for a good purpose (Ber. 60b). According to R. Akiba, every event is predetermined, though liberty is given. The world is judged in goodness, yet the decision is rendered in accordance with the predominating character of man's conduct (Ab. iii. 24; Ab. R. N. xxxix.). All is determined and all is finally made plain. Even in the seeming irrationality of the prosperity of evil-doers and of the suffering of the righteous, God's purpose is effective (Ab. iii. 16; Yoma 86b). God is pictured as making ladders, on which He causes some to ascend and others to descend; in other words, God is the Arbiter of men's fate and fortune (Lev. R. viii.; Gen. R. lxviii.; Pesiḳ. 11b; Midr. Shemu'el, v.; Tan., Bemidbar, 18). Moses, praying for insight into God's ways, learns why evil-doers prosper and the righteous suffer (Ber. 7a). God protects Palestine and, on its account, all other lands also. He guards Israel and other nations as well (Sifre, Deut. 40). None may wound a finger unless it be so decreed above (Ḥul. 7b).

God's protection is not like that extended by man to man. Royal servants watch in the streets over the safety of the king in the palace. God's servants remain in their houses while He, the King, watches over them from without (Men. 33b; 'Ab. Zarah 11a, with reference to the mezuzah). God's providential care is especially extended to those that "go down the sea in ships," to travelers in the desert, and to those that are recovering from illness (Jellinek, "B. H." i. 110). Rain and the miracle of human birth are often adduced as evidences of divine providence (Ta'an. 2; Lev. R. xiv. 2–3). Serpents, lions, even governments, work harm only under God's decrees (Eccl. R. x. 11). Deut. xxxi. 15 is invoked to prove that man's physical condition and moral and mental qualifications are predetermined by providence before birth, though freedom of choice is allowed to him (Tan., Piḳḳude; Yalḳ. ii. 716). The actions of the leaders in history were predetermined in God's council at Creation ("B. H." i. 1; Pirḳe R. El. xxxii.).

In the Liturgy.

The old prayers affirm this doctrine; God's creative activity is uninterrupted (so in "Yoẓer Or": "He creates anew every day the works of the beginning"). His governing providence is manifest in Israel's history (see Ahabah Rabbah). He helps and sustains the living, resurrects the dead, supports the falling, heals the sick, delivers the captive (second benediction of the SHEMONEH 'ESREH). In the New-Year liturgy (Rosh ha-Shanah, Netanneh Toḳef) God's kingship ("malkuyot") is especially emphasized, as well as His predetermination of the fate of individuals and nations—a conception occurring also in a baraita, Beẓah 15b, 16a, with reference to man's sustenance and nourishment. God's wise foresight is manifest even in the creation of the wind, which makes profitable man's labor in plowing, hoeing, planting, harvesting, and mowing (Pesiḳ. 69a; Lev. R. xxviii. 2). God provides food for every man (Lev. R. xiv. 2).

As in the Bible, in the Talmud the moral liberty of man and God's providential rulership are taught together, without further endeavor to show their compatibility. "Everything is in the control of God save the fear of God" (Ber. 33b; Meg. 25a; Niddah 16b).

If the doctrine was, for the Talmudists, partly the expression of spontaneous religious feeling, partly the result of their labored exegesis of Biblical passages, Philo's presentation is that of the trained, systematic thinker. God being the benevolent author of the world, He must continue to exercise providential care over the whole and every part of it, for it is natural for parents to provide for their children ("De Opificio Mundi," § 61). God holds the reins of the cosmos by an autocratic law ("De Migratione Abrahami," § 33). He is the "archon of the great city, the pilot who manages the universe with saving care" ("De Confusione Linguarum," § 33). In the exercise of this providential care God's goodness is poured forth with unrestricted lavishness ("De Allegoriis Legum," i. 13). His judgments are tempered with mercy ("Quod Deus Sit Immutabilis," § 16). The recipients of God's bounties being of limited capacity, God measures His gifts accordingly ("De Opificio Mundi," § 6).

Philo does not conceal the objections to the faith in providence. He endeavors to meet them, more especially in a treatise entitled "De Providentia" (see Drummond, "Philo Judæus," ii. 58). The existence of pain he endeavors to explain on the ground that God can not be held to be its author in all cases, as well as on the ground that often evil is good in disguise. Evil is prophylactic at times, disciplinary at others. Men who are righteous in our eyes may perhaps be sinners, and deserving of punishment (Drummond, *l.c.*).

The rise of Islam and the disputes engendered in its household concerning predestination and free will had the effect of stimulating Jewish thinkers in the Middle Ages to make a more profound analysis of the doctrine. How was human liberty reconcilable with God's foreseeing, foreknowing, omnipotence? The question constituted the crux of their disquisitions. Saadia discusses it in the fourth chapter of his "Emunot we-De'ot." Arguing that God's knowledge of things does not necessarily result in their reality and existence, Saadia proceeds to maintain that God's prescience is due to His knowing the ultimate outcome of human conduct, though it is not He that brings it about. But in a case in which God wills that a certain one be killed and employs another as the instrument of His will, is the murderer to be accounted responsible or not? Saadia would have the murderer adjudged accountable. He might have refused to do the act, in which case God would have employed other means to bring about the death of the sinner. The weakness of Saadia's argumentation is apparent.

Views of the Philosophers.

Judah ha-Levi conceives of divine providence as, in the main, divine government, and before showing that it and human freedom are mutually consistent, he denounces fatalism, largely by an appeal ad hominem exposing the inconsistencies of the fatalists. He agrees that, in the last analysis, all things are caused by God, but that they are not necessarily directly so caused; in many cases God is a remote cause. To the class of secondary or intermediate causes human free will belongs; it is not under constraint, but is at liberty to choose. God knows what a man's ultimate choice will be, but His knowledge is not the cause of a man's choice. In relation to man, God's prescience is accidental, not causative ("Cuzari," v.).

Abraham ibn Daud, in writing his "Emunah Ramah," purposed to reconcile the existence of evil with the providence of God. Evil can not be caused by God, who is benevolent ("Emunah Ramah," ed. Weil, p. 94). God produces only reality and positivity. Evil has no positive existence; it is the negation of good. As such, it has no author. God and matter are at opposite poles. God is absolute essence. Matter is non-existence; it is the cause of all imperfection. Some imperfections, however, are not evils. God's providence manifests itself in that every creature is endowed with that degree of perfection which corresponds to its nature. Seeming imperfections apparent in certain individuals are seen to be perfections in view of the larger ends of the community: for example, some men are born with limited mental capacities in order that they might profit society by their manual labor. In reference to man's freedom of will in its relation to providential prescience, Abraham ibn Daud assumes—in view of his introduction of the concept of potential possibilities—that God Himself has left the outcome of certain actions undecided, even as regards His own knowledge, that man's will might have the opportunity to assert itself in freedom. As an Aristotelian, Ibn Daud is, in this as in many other positions, the precursor of Maimonides.

In Maimonides' "Moreh," part iii., a lengthy exposition of providence is found. He rejects the view of providence entertained by the Epicureans, according to whom accident rules all. Next he criticizes Aristotle's theory, which assigns providence to the lunar sphere and almost excludes it from the sublunar sphere. Providence has no care for individuals, only for the species. The Aristotle against whom Maimonides here wages battle is the pseudo-Aristotelian author of "De Mundo." In the "Ethica Nicomachea" passages are found that plead for the recognition of a special ("hashgaḥah peraṭit") as well as a general ("hashgaḥah kelalit") providence. Again, Maimonides disputes the position of the Ash'ariyyah (fatalists), according to whom all is determined by God's will and power, necessarily to the complete exclusion and denial of freedom of human action. Next he takes up the theory of the Motazilites, who, on the one hand, refer everything to God's wisdom, and, on the other, attribute freedom of action to man. His objection to their doctrine arises from their failure to recognize that it involves contradictory propositions.

Views of Maimonides.

Maimonides then proceeds to expound the theory of the Jewish religion. Man is free and God is just. Good is given man as a reward, evil as a punishment. All is adjusted according to merit. Providence, practically, is concerned only about man. The relation of providence is not the same to all men. Divine influence reaches man through the intellect. The greater man's share in this divine influence, the greater the effect of divine providence on him. With the Prophets it varies according to their prophetic faculty; in the case of pious and good men, according to their piety and uprightness. The impious are become like beasts, and are thus outside the scope of providence. God is for the pious a most special providence.

God's prescience is essentially unlike any knowledge of ours. His knowledge comprehends all, even the infinite. God's knowledge does not belong to time; what He knows, He knows from eternity. His knowledge is not subject to change; it is identical with His essence. It transcends our knowledge. God knows things while they are still in the state of possibilities; hence His commands to us to take precautions against certain possibilities (*e.g.*, placing a guard around the roof, etc.). Maimonides' theory has been well described (Muller, "De Godsleer der Joden," p. 151, Gröningen, 1898) as showing that man knows what liberty is better than what providence is. Maimonides' theodicy, which culminates in the assertion that as evil is negative and privative, God can not be its author—that, in fact, it has no author—is certainly mere sophistry and word-juggling (Maimonides, "Dalalat al-Ḥa'irin," iii. 17 *et seq.*; see also "Yad," Teshubah, v.).

God's Prescience.

For the theories of Joseph Albo and Levi ben Gershon see the former's "'Iḳḳarim" (iv. 1) and the latter's "Milḥamot Adonai" (iii. 2). For Baḥya ben Joseph's view see his "Ḥobot ha-Lebabot" (iii. 8). Modern Jewish theology has not advanced the subject beyond Maimonides. In catechisms, of whatever religious bias, the doctrine of providence is taught as well as the moral responsibility of man.

It may be worth noting that, according to Josephus, one of the points in controversy among the Pharisees, the Sadducees, and the Essenes was the adoption or rejection of the doctrine of providence ("Ant." xviii. 1, § 2).

XXXVIII
Psalms

PSALMS: Name derived from the Greek ψαλμός (plural ψαλμοί), which signifies primarily playing on a stringed instrument, and secondarily the composition played or the song accompanied on such an instrument. In the Septuagint (Codex Alexandrinus) ψαλτήριον is used, which denotes a large stringed instrument, also a collection of songs intended to be sung to the accompaniment of strings (harp). These terms are employed to translate the Hebrew "mizmor" and "tehillim." The exact derivation and meaning of the former are uncertain. It would seem that, etymologically denoting "paragraph," it owes its signification of "psalm," "song," or "hymn" to the circumstance that it is found prefixed to the superscriptions of a number of psalms. The word "tehillim" is a plural, not occurring in Biblical Hebrew, from the singular "tehillah" = "song of praise." It is thus a fitting title for the collection of songs found in the "Ketubim" or Hagiographa (the third main division of the Hebrew canon), and more fully described as "Sefer Tehillim," or the "Book of Psalms." "Tehillim" is also contracted to "tillim" (Aramaic, "tillin").

——**Biblical Data:** In the printed Hebrew Bible the Book of Psalms is the first of the Ketubim; but it did not always occupy this position, having formerly been preceded by Ruth (B. B. 14b; Tos. to B. B. *l.c.*). Jerome, however ("Prologus Galeatus"), has another order, in which Job is first and the Psalms second, while Sephardic manuscripts assign to Chronicles the first and to the Psalms the second place (comp. 'Ab. Zarah 19a). The Book of

Psalms is one of the three poetic books denoted as ת"מ"א (EMaT = Job [Iyyob], Proverbs [Mishle], and Psalms [Tehillim]) and having an accentuation (see ACCENTS IN HEBREW) of their own.

The Sefer Tehillim consists of 150 psalms divided into five books, as follows: book i. = Ps. i.–xli.; ii. = Ps. xlii.–lxxii.; iii. = Ps. lxxiii.–lxxxix.; iv. = Ps. xc.–cvi.; v. = Ps. cvii.–cl., the divisions between these books being indicated by doxologies (Ps. xli. 14 [A. V. 13]; lxxii. 19 [18–19]; lxxxix. 53 [52]; cvi. 48). The conclusion of book ii. is still further marked by the gloss כלו תפלות דוד בן ישי = "The prayers of David, the son of Jesse, are ended." Of the 150 psalms 100 are ascribed, in their superscriptions, to various authors by name: one, Ps. xc., to Moses; seventy-three to David; two, lxxii. and cxxvii., to Solomon; twelve, l. and lxxiii. to lxxxiii., to Asaph; one, lxxxviii., to Heman; one, lxxxix., to Ethan; ten to the sons of Korah (eleven if lxxxviii., attributed also to Heman, is assigned to them). In the Septuagint ten more psalms are credited to David. Sixteen psalms have other (mostly musical) headings. According to their contents, the Psalms may be grouped as follows: (1) hymns of praise, (2) elegies, and (3) didactic psalms.

Hymns of Praise: These glorify God, His power, and His loving-kindness manifested in nature or shown to Israel, or they celebrate the Torah, Zion, and the Davidic kingdom. In this group are comprised the psalms of gratitude, expressing thankfulness for help extended and refuge found in times of danger and distress. The group embraces about one-third of the Psalter.

Elegies: These lend voice to feelings of grief at the spread of iniquity, the triumph of the wicked, the sufferings of the just, the "humble," or the "poor," and the abandonment of Israel. In this category are comprehended the psalms of supplication, the burden of which is fervent prayer for the amelioration of conditions, the restoration of Israel to grace, and the repentance of sinners. The line of demarcation between elegy and supplication is not sharply drawn. Lamentation often concludes with petition; and prayer, in turn, ends in lamentation. Perhaps some of this group ought to be considered as forming a distinct category by themselves, and to be designated as psalms of repentance or penitential hymns; for their key-note is open confession of sin and transgression prompted by ardent repentance, preluding the yearning for forgiveness. These are distinct from the other elegies in so far as they are inspired by consciousness of guilt and not by the gnawing sense of unmerited affliction.

Didactic Psalms: These, of quieter mood, give advice concerning righteous conduct and speech, and caution against improper behavior and attitude. Of the same general character, though aimed at a specific class or set of persons, are the imprecatory psalms, in which, often in strong language, shortcomings are censured and their consequences expatiated upon, or their perpetrators are bitterly denounced.

Most of the 150 psalms may, without straining the context and content of their language, be assigned to one or another of these three (or, with their subdivisions, seven) groups. Some scholars would add another class, viz., that of the king-psalms, *e.g.*, Ps. ii., xviii., xx., xxi., xlv., lxi., lxxii., and others. Though in these king-psalms there is always allusion to a king, they as a rule will be found to be either hymns of praise, gratitude, or supplication, or didactic songs. Another principle of grouping is concerned with the character of the speaker. Is it the nation that pours out its feelings, or is it an individual who unburdens his soul? Thus the axis of cleavage runs between national and individual psalms.

In form the Psalms exhibit in a high degree of perfection charm of language and wealth of metaphor as well as rhythm of thought, *i.e.*, all of the variety of parallelism. The prevailing scheme is the couplet of two corresponding lines. The triplet and quatrain occur also, though not frequently. For the discussion of a more regular metrical system in the Psalms than this parallelism reference is made

Literary Form.

to J. Ley ("Die Metrischen Formen der Hebräischen Poesie," 1866; "Grundzüge des Rhythmus der Hebräischen Poesie," 1875), Bickell ("Carmina V. T. Metrice," 1882; and in "Z. D. M. G." 1891–94), Grimme ("Abriss der Biblisch-Hebräischen Metrik," *ib.* 1896–97), and Ed. Sievers ("Studien zur

Hebräischen Metrik," Leipsic, 1901; see also "Theologische Rundschau," 1905, viii. 41 *et seq.*). The refrain may be said to constitute one of the salient verbal features of some of the psalms (comp. Ps. xlii. 5, 11; xliii. 5; xlvi. 7, 11; lxxx. 3, 7, 19; cvii. 8, 15, 21, 31; cxxxvi., every half-verse of which consists of "and his goodness endureth forever"). Several of the psalms are acrostic or alphabetic in their arrangement, the succession of the letters of the Hebrew alphabet occurring in various positions —the beginning of every verse, every hemistich, or every couplet; in the last-mentioned case the letters may occur in pairs, *i.e.*, in each couplet the two lines may begin with the same letter. Ps. cix. has throughout eight verses beginning with the same letter. Occasionally the scheme is not completely carried out (Ps. ix.–x.), one letter appearing in the place of another (see also Ps. xxv., xxxvii., cxi., cxii.).

Religious and Ethical Content.

The religious and ethical content of the Psalms may be summarized as a vivid consciousness of God's all-sustaining, guiding, supreme power. The verbal terms are often anthropomorphic; the similes, bold (*e.g.*, God is seated in the heavens with the earth as His footstool; He causes the heavens to bow down; He scatters the enemies of His people; He spreads a table). God's justice and mercy are the dominant notes in the theology of the Psalms. His loving-kindness is the favorite theme of the psalmists. God is the Father who loves and pities His children. He lifts up the lowly and defeats the arrogant. His kingdom endures for ever. He is the Holy One. The heavens declare His glory: they are His handiwork. The religious interpretation of nature is the intention of many of these hymns of praise (notably Ps. viii., xix., xxix., lxv., xciii., civ.). Man's frailty, and withal his strength, his exceptional position in the sweep of creation, are other favorite themes. Sin and sinners are central to some psalms, but even so is the well-assured confidence of the God-fearing. Repentance is the path-pointer to the forgiving God. Ps. l., for instance, rings with an Isaianic protest against sacrificial ritualism. The sacrifices of God are a broken spirit. Often the nation is made to speak; yet the "I" in the Psalms is not always national. Individualization of religion is not beyond the horizon. Nor is it true that the national spirit alone finds expression and that the perfect man pictured is always and necessarily conceived of as a son of Israel. The universalistic note is as often struck. The imprecations of such psalms as cix. are not demonstrations of the vindictiveness of narrow nationalism. Read in the light of the times when they were written (see PSALMS, CRITICAL VIEW), these fanatical utterances must be understood as directed against Israelites—not non-Jews. Ps. xv. is the proclamation of an ethical religion that disregards limitations of birth or blood. Again, the "poor" and the "meek" or "humble," so often mentioned—"poverty" or humility being found even among God's attributes (xviii. 35)—are Israelites, the "servants of YHWH," whose sufferings have evoked Deutero-Isaiah's description (Isa. liii.). The "return of Israel" and the establishment of God's reign of justice contemporaneously with Israel's restoration are focal in the eschatology of the Psalms, treated as a whole. But perhaps this method of regarding the Psalms as virtually reflecting identical views must be abandoned, the reasons for which are detailed in PSALMS, CRITICAL VIEW.

——**In Rabbinical Literature:** The richest in content and the most precious of the three large Ketubim (Ber. 57a), the Sefer Tehillim is regarded as a second Pentateuch, whose virtual composer was David, often likened to Moses (Midr. Teh. ch. i.). "Moses gave [Israel] the five books of the Torah, and to correspond with them [כנגדם] David gave them the Sefer Tehillim, in which also there are five books" (*ib.*). Its sacred character as distinct from such books as the "Sifre Homerus" (works of Hermes, not Homer) is explicitly emphasized (Midr. Teh. *l.c.*; Yalḳ. ii. 613, 678). The Psalms are essentially "songs and laudations" (שירות ותושבחות). According to Rab, the proper designation for the book would be "Halleluyah" (Midr. Teh. *l.c.*), because that term comprehends both the Divine Name and its glorification, and for this reason is held to be the best of the ten words for praise occurring in the

Psalms. These ten words, corresponding in number to the ten men who had a part in composing the Psalms, are: "berakah" (benediction); HALLEL; "tefillah" (prayer); "shir" (song); "mizmor" (psalm); "neginah" (melody); "nazeaḥ" (to play on an instrument); "ashre" (happy, blessed); "hodot" (thanks); "halleluyah" (*ib.*).

Ten men had a share in the compilation of this collection, but the chief editor was David (B. B. 15a; Midr. Teh. i.). Of the ten names two variant lists are given, namely: (1) Adam, Moses, Asaph, Heman, Abraham, Jeduthun, Melchizedek, and three sons of Korah; (2) Adam, Moses, Asaph, Heman, Abraham, Jeduthun, David, Solomon, the three sons of Korah counted as one, and Ezra (B. B. 14b; Cant. R. to verse iv. 4; Eccl. R. to vii. 19; sometimes for Abraham, Ethan ha-Ezraḥi is substituted). Adam's psalms are such as refer to cosmogony, creation. Ps. v., xix., xxiv., xcii. (Yalḳ. ii. 630) were said to have been written by David, though Adam was worthy to have composed them.

Composition of the Psalter.

The division into five books known to the Rabbis corresponded with that observed in modern editions. The order of the Psalms was identical with that of modern recensions; but the Rabbis suspected that it was not altogether correct. Rabbi Joshua ben Levi is reported to have desired to make alterations (Midr. Teh. xxxvii.). Moses was credited with the authorship of eleven psalms, xc.–c. (*ib.* xc.). They were excluded from the Torah because they were not composed in the prophetic spirit (*ib.*). Ps. xxx. ("at the dedication of the house") was ascribed to David as well as to Ezra (*ib.* xxx.). Twenty-two times is "ashre" found in the Psalms; and this recalls the twenty-two letters of the Hebrew alphabet (*ib.* i.). "Barki nafshi" occurs five times in Ps. ciii., recalling the analogy with the Pentateuch (*ib.* ciii.). Ps. xxix. names YHWH eighteen times, in analogy with the eighteen benedictions of the SHEMONEH 'ESREH (*ib.* xxix.). Ps. cxxxvi. is called "Hallel ha-Gadol" (Pes. 118a), to which, according to some, the songs "of degrees" also belong. The ordinary "Hallel" was composed of Ps. cxiii.–cxviii. (Pes. 117a).

The Masorah divides the book into nineteen "sedarim," the eleventh of these beginning with Ps. lxxviii. 38 (see Masoretic note at end of printed text).

One Palestinian authority, R. Joshua b. Levi, counts only 147 psalms (Yer. Shab. 15). According to Grätz ("Psalmen," p. 9), this variance was due to the effort to equalize the number of psalms with that of the Pentateuchal pericopes according to the triennial cycle. Ps. i. and ii. were counted as one in Babylon (Ber. 9b, 10a; as in the LXX.). Ps. x. 15 belonged to ix. (Meg. 17b). The concluding verse of Ps. xix. was added to Ps. xviii. (Ber. 9b); xlii. and xliii. were counted as one (see Fürst, "Kanon," p. 71). Ps. lxxviii. was divided into two parts comprising verses 1 to 37 and 38 to 72 respectively (Ḳid. 30a). Ps. cxiv. and cxv. were united (see Ḳimḥi, commentary on Ps. cxiv.), and cxviii. was divided into two. Psalms whose authors were not known, or the occasion for whose composition was not indicated, were described as "orphans" (מזמורא יתומא; 'Ab. Zarah 24b).

According to Talmudic tradition, psalms were sung by the Levites immediately after the daily libation of wine; and every liturgical psalm was sung in three parts (Suk. iv. 5). During the intervals between the parts the sons of Aaron blew three different blasts on the trumpet (Tamid vii. 3). The daily psalms are named in the order in which they were recited: on Sunday, xxiv.; Monday, xlviii.; Tuesday, lxxxii.; Wednesday, xciv.; Thursday, lxxxi.; Friday, xciii.; and Sabbath, xcii. (Tamid *l.c.*).

Liturgical Songs.

This selection shows that it was made at a time when Israel was threatened with disaster (see Rashi on Suk. 55a). The fifteen "Songs of Degrees" were sung by the Levites at the Feast of Tabernacles, at the festive drawing of water. Ps. cxxxv. and cxxxvi. were recited antiphonally by the officiating liturgist and the people. As New-Year psalms, lxxxi. and the concluding verses of xxix. were used (R. H. 30b). Those designated for the semiholy days of Sukkot are enumerated in Suk. 55a. Massek. Soferim xviii. 2 names those assigned for Passover. At New Moon a certain psalm (number not given in the Talmud) was sung in the Temple (Suk. 55a); Soferim names Ps. cv. with the concluding verses of civ. For Ḥanukkah Ps. xxx. is reserved (Soferim xviii. 2). From Soṭah ix. 10 (see Tosefta *ad loc.*) it is apparent that at one time Ps. xliv. constituted a part of the Temple morning liturgy, while xxx. was sung during the offering of the FIRST-FRUITS. The same psalm, as well as iii. and xci., was sung to the accompaniment of musical instruments on the occasion of the enlargement of Jerusalem (Shebu. 14a).

——**Critical View:** The Book of Psalms may be said to be the hymn-book of the congregation of Israel during the existence of the Second Temple, though not every psalm in the collection is of a character to which this designation may apply.

Hymn-Book of Second Temple.

By earlier critics advancing this view of the nature of the Psalms it was held that they were hymns sung in the Temple either by the Levites or by the people. Later scholars have modified this opinion in view of the circumstance that the participation of the people in the Temple ritual was very slight and also because the contents of many of the psalms are such that their recitation at sacrificial functions is not very probable (*e.g.*, Ps. xl. and l., which have a certain anti-sacrificial tendency). While B. Jacob (in Stade's "Zeitschrift," 1897, xvii.) insists that the Psalter is a hymn-book for the congregation assisting at or participating in the sacrificial rite, and as such must contain also liturgical songs intended for individuals who had to bring offerings on certain occasions, others maintain that, while a number of the hymns undoubtedly were of sacerdotal import and, consequently, were intended to be sung in the Temple, many were written for intonation at prayer in the synagogue. In this connection the determination of the reference in the so-called "I" psalms is of importance.

The discovery of the Hebrew text of Ecclesiasticus (Sirach) has caused Nöldeke (Stade's "Zeitschrift," 1900, xx.), on the strength of the observation that in Ecclus. (Sirach) li. 2–29 the "I" refers to Ben Sira, to urge that the "I" psalms must similarly be construed as individual confessions. The traditional view was that David, the reputed author of most of these "I" psalms, was in them unbosoming his own feelings and relating his own experiences. It is more probable, however, that, while the "I" in some instances may have its individual significance, on the whole this personal pronoun has reference to the "congregation of Israel" or to a circle or set of congregants at prayer, the "pious," the "meek," the "righteous." The metrical reconstruction of the Psalms (see Baethgen, "Commentar," 3d ed.) promises to throw light on this problem, as the assumption is well grounded that hymns written for or used on public liturgical occasions had a typical metrical scheme of their own (comp. "Theologische Rundschau," viii., Feb., 1905). At all events, some of the psalms must have served at private devotion (*e.g.*, Ps. cxli.), as, indeed, the custom of hymn-singing at night-time by some of the pious is alluded to (*ib.* lix., xcii., cxix., cxlix.).

Didactic Psalms.

On the other hand, many of the didactic psalms remind one of the general type of gnomic anthologies. It seems more likely that these were recited, not sung, and were learned by heart for ethical instruction and guidance. That the "alphabetical" psalms were not intended originally for liturgical uses may be inferred at least from Ps. cxi. Most of this class reflect the study-room of the scholar, and lack entirely the spontaneity of the worshipful spirit. There are good reasons for regarding Ps. i. as a prologue, prefaced to the whole collection by its latest editors, who were not priests (Sadducees), but scribes (Pharisees) interested in the rise and establishment of synagogal worship as against the sacerdotal liturgy of the Temple. If so regarded, Ps. i. reveals the intention of the editors to provide in this collection a book of instruction as well as a manual of prayer.

The existing Psalter is a compilation of various collections made at various times. The division into several parts was not in every case altogether due to a desire to imitate the structure of the Pentateuch. Books i. (Ps. i.-lxi.), ii. (Ps. lxii.-lxxii.), and iii. (Ps. lxxiii.-lxxxix.) are marked as separate collections by doxologies, a fact which points to their separate compilation. The doxology which now divides books iv. and v. after Ps. cvi. has the appearance of being the beginning of another psalm (comp. I Chron. xvi., where it occurs at the close of the interpolation verses 8 to 36). It is impossible to determine the date at which these older collections may have been put together. Book i., containing "David" psalms (originally without Ps. i. and ii.), may have been the first to be compiled. In books ii. and iii. (Ps. lxii.-lxxxix.) several older and smaller compilations seem to be represented, and that, too, in some disorder. The (*a*) "David" hymns (*ὕμνοι* =תהלות; *ib.* li.-lxxii.) are clearly distinct from the (*b*) songs of the sons of Korah (xlii.-xlix.), (*c*) "Asaph" songs (l., lxxiii.-lxxxiii.), and (*d*) later supplements of promiscuous psalms (lxxxiv.-lxxxix.). It is noteworthy that in the "David" hymns duplicates of psalms are found, incorporated also in book i. (Ps. liii. = xiv.; lxx. = xl. 14-18; lxxi. 1-3 = xxxi. 2-4), while lvii. 8 *et seq.* is duplicated in book v. (cviii. 2-6). Another peculiarity of this book is the use of "Elohim" for "Yhwh," except in the supplement (lxxxiv.-lxxxix.).

Comparison of the texts of the duplicate psalms, as well as the circumstance that these duplicates occur, indicates the freedom with which such collections were made, and suggests that many collections were in existence, each with variant content. Book iv. is distinct in so far as it contains, with the exception of three psalms (xc. "of Moses"; ci., ciii. "of David"; but in the Septuagint nine more), only anonymous ones. The character of the doxology (see above) suggests that this book was separated from the following only to carry out the analogy with the Pentateuch. Books iv. and v. are characterized by the absence of "musical" superscriptions and instructions. In book v. the group comprising cvii. to cix. is easily recognized as not organically connected with that composed of cxx.-cxxxiv. It is possible that the liturgical character and use of cxiii. to cxviii. (the [Egyptian] "Hallel") had necessitated the redaction of the "Hallel" psalms separately. The "Songs of Degrees" (see below) must have constituted at one time a series by themselves. The metrical arrangement is the same in all, with the exception of cxxxii. The rest of book v. is composed of loose "Halleluyah" psalms, into which have been inserted "David" psalms (cxxxviii.-cxlv.) and an old folk-song (cxxxvii.).

As to who were the compilers of these distinct collections it has been suggested that an inference might be drawn in the case of the psalms marked "to the sons of Korah" or "to Asaph, Heman, Ethan, Jeduthun," respectively. But the ל prefixed to the superscription in these cases is plainly not a "lamed auctoris," the names being those of the leaders of the choir-gilds (established, according to Chronicles, by David). The headings in which

The "Lamed Auctoris."

ל occurs merely indicate that the hymns were usually sung by the choristers known as "sons of Korah," etc., or that the psalm constituting a part of the repertoire of the singers so named was to be sung according to a fixed melody introduced by them. These choir-masters, then, had collected their favorite hymns, and, in consequence, these continued to be named after their collector and to be sung according to the melody introduced by the gild. It has also been urged as explaining the terms לדוד, למשה ("unto David," "unto Moses") that a certain melody was known by that term, or a collection happened to be labeled in that way. It is, however, manifest that in some instances the superscription admits of no other construction than that it is meant to name the author of the psalm (Moses, for instance, in Ps. xc.), though such expressions as "David song," "Zion song" = "YHWH song" may very well have come into vogue as designations of sacred as distinguished from profane poems and strains. Still, one must not forget that these superscriptions are late additions. The historical value of the note לדוד· (= "unto David") is not greater than that of others pretending to give the occasion when and the circumstances under which the particular psalm was composed. The variants in these superscriptions in the versions prove them to be late interpolations, reflecting the views of their authors.

By tradition David was regarded as the writer of most of the psalms, even the other names occurring in the captions being construed to be those of singers under his direction (David Ḳimḥi, Commentary on Psalms, Preface). He was held to be also the editor of the Biblical Book of Psalms. But this ascription of authorship to him is due to the tendency to connect with the name of a dominating personality the chief literary productions of the nation. Thus Moses figures as the lawgiver, and the author of the Pentateuch; Solomon, as the "wise" man and, as such, the writer of the Wisdom books; David, as the singer and, in this capacity, as the composer of hymns and as the collector of the Psalms as far as they are not his own compositions.

Date of Psalter.

When the Book of Psalms first assumed its present form is open to discussion. Certain it is that the New Testament and Josephus presuppose the existence of the Biblical Psalter in the form in which it is found in the canon. This fact is further corroborated by the date of the so-called "Psalms of Solomon." These are assigned to about 68 B.C.; a fact which indicates that at that period no new psalms could be inserted in the Biblical book, which by this time must have attained permanent and fixed form as the Book of Psalms of David. It is safest then to assign the final compilation of the Biblical book to the first third of the century immediately preceding the Christian era.

Concerning the date of the two psalms lxxix. and cxlvi., I Maccabees furnishes a clue. In I Macc. vii. 17, Ps. lxxix. 2 is quoted, while cxlvi. 4 is utilized in I Macc. ii. 63. These psalms then were known to a writer living in the time of the Hasmonean rulers. He construed Ps. lxxix. as applying to the time of Alcimus. As remarked above, the historical superscriptions are worthless for the purpose of fixing the chronology, even if the concession be made that some of these pretendedly historical notes antedate the final compilation of the Psalter and were taken from the historical romances relating the lives of the nation's heroes, in which, according to prevailing ancient literary custom, poetry was introduced to embellish prose (comp. Ex. xv.; I Sam. ii.), as indeed Ps. xviii. is found also in II Sam. xxii.

By comparison with what is known of the events of Jewish internal and external history during the last centuries before the destruction of the Second Temple, critical scholars have come to the conclusion that the political and religious circumstances and conflicts of these turbulent times are reflected in by far the greater number of psalms. Most of the 150 in the Biblical book, if not all of them, are assigned a post-exilic origin. Not one among competent contemporaneous scholars seriously defends the Davidic authorship of even a single psalm; and very few of the recent commentators maintain the pre-exilic character of one or the other song in the collection. Of exilic compositions Ps. cxxxvii. is perhaps the only specimen. To the Persian period some psalms might be assigned, notably the "nature" psalms (*e.g.*, viii., xix.), as expressive of monotheism's opposition to dualism. But there is no proof for this assumption. Still a goodly number of psalms must have been composed in pre-Maccabean years. Some psalms presuppose the existence and inviolability of the Temple and the Holy City (for instance, xlvi., xlviii., lxxvi.). Ps. iii., iv., xi., and lxii. might reflect the confidence of pious priests before the Maccabean disturbances.

Reflection of History.

But it is obvious that other psalms refer to the trickery and treachery of the house of Tobias (Ps. lxii.). The Maccabean revolution—with its heroism on the one hand, its cowardice on the other, its victories, and its defeats—has supplied many a hymn of faith and defiance and joy. The חסידים and צדיקים—the "faithful," the "righteous," the "meek"—find voice to praise God for His help and to denounce the "wicked," the foreign nations that have made common cause with Syria (see lxxiv., lxxxiii., cxviii., and cxlix.). Ps. xliv. and lxxvii. point to events after the death of Judas Maccabeus; Ps. lv. and others seem to deal with Alcimus. The establishment of the Hasmonean dynasty on the throne and the conflicts between PHARISEES (nationalists and democrats) and SADDUCEES (the representatives of aristocratic sacerdotalism) have left their impress on other hymns (Ps. cx. 1–4, "Shim'on" in acrostic). Some of the psalms are nothing less than the pronunciamentos of the Pharisees (ix., x., xiv., lvi., lviii.). Dates can not be assigned to the greater number of psalms, except in so far as their content betrays their character as Temple or synagogal hymns, as eschatological constructions, or as apocalyptic renderings of ancient history or of mythology.

Reflex of Politics.

Synagogal liturgy and strictly regulated Temple ceremonial are productions of the Maccabean and post-Maccabean conflicts. Apocalyptic ecstasy, didactic references to past history, and Messianic speculations point to the same centuries, when foreign oppression or internal feuds led the faithful to predict the coming glorious judgment. The "royal" or "king" psalms belong to the category of apocalyptic effusions. It is not necessary to assume that they refer to a ruling king or monarch. The Messianic king warring with the "nations"—another apocalyptic incident—is central in these psalms. The "'Aniyim" and the "'Anawim" are the "meek" as opposed to the "Gewim" and "'Azim" (which readings must often be adopted for "Goyim" and "'Ammim"), the "proud" and "insolent." The former are the (Pharisaic) pious nationalists battling against the proud (Sadducean) violators of God's law; but in their fidelity they behold the coming of the King of Glory, the Messianic Ruler, whose advent will put to flight and shame Israel's foreign and internal foes.

Pilgrim Songs.

The "Songs of Degrees" are pilgrim songs, which were sung by the participants in the processions at the three pilgrim festivals; all other explanations are fanciful. David Ḳimḥi in his commentary quotes the usual interpretation that these songs were sung by the Levites standing on the fifteen steps between the court of the women and that of the Israelites. But he also suggests that they refer to the post-exilic redemption, being sung by those that "ascend" from captivity. In fact, Ḳimḥi often reveals a very clear perception of the psalms of the post-exilic origin.

The text is often corrupt. It contains interpolations, marginal glosses transposed into the body of psalms, quotations not in the original, liturgical glosses, notes, and intentional alterations. Consonantal interchanges abound. Many of the psalms are clearly fragmentary torsos; others, as clearly, are composed of two or more disjointed parts drawn from other psalms without connection or coherence (comp. the modern commentaries, especially those of Duhm and Baethgen; also Grätz, "Psalmen," Introduction). According to Grätz (*l.c.* p. 61), such combinations of two psalms in one was caused by the necessities of the liturgical services. It is not unlikely that some psalms were chanted responsively, part of the Levites singing one verse, and the others answering with the next.

In the synagogues the Psalms were chanted antiphonally, the congregation often repeating after every verse chanted by the precentor the first verse of the psalm in question. "Halleluyah" was the word with which the congregation was invited to take part in this chanting. Hence it originally prefaced the Psalms, not, as in the Masoretic text, coming at the end. At the conclusion of the psalm the "maḳre" or precentor added a doxology ending with ואמרו אמן ("and say ye Amen"), whereupon the congregation replied "Amen, Amen" ("Monatsschrift," 1872, p. 481). The synagogal psalms, according to this, then, are cv., cvi., cvii., cxi., cxii., cxiii., cxiv., cxvi., and cxvii. (the shortest of all psalms), cxviii., cxxxv., cxxxvi., cxlvi.–cl.

Concerning the musical accompaniment less is known. Boys seem to have been added to the men's chorus ('Ar. 13b). Twelve adult Levites constituted the minimum membership of a chorus; nine of these played on the "kinnor," two on the "nebel," and one on the cymbals (*ib.* ii. 3–5). Singing seems to have been the principal feature of their art, the instruments being used by the singers for their self-accompaniment only. The kinnor, according to Josephus, had ten strings and was struck with a plectrum ("Ant." vii. 12, § 3), while the nebel had twelve notes and was played with the fingers. This information is not confirmed by what is known of the "lyra" or "kithara" of the Greeks. Jewish coins display lyres of three strings, and in a single instance one of five strings. Tosef., 'Ar. ii. gives the kinnor seven strings. According to Ps. xcii. 3, there must have been known a ten-stringed instrument. The Jerusalem Talmud agrees with Josephus in assigning the nebel to the class of stringed instruments (Yer. Suk. 55c; 'Ar. 13b). But it seems to have had a membranous attachment or diaphragm to heighten the effect of the strings (Yer. Suk. *l.c.*). The nebel and the "alamot" (I Chron. xv. 20; Ps. xlviii.; Ps. ix., corrected reading) are identical (see Grätz, *l.c.* p. 71). The flute,

Musical Accompaniment.

"ḥalil," was played only on holy days ('Ar. ii. 3). The Hebrew term for choir-master was "menaẓẓeaḥ."

Fifty-seven psalms are designated as מזמור; this is a word denoting "paragraph," hence a new beginning. Thirty psalms are designated as שיר (= "song"), probably indicating that the psalm was actually sung in the Temple. Thirteen psalms are labeled משכיל, the meaning of which word is doubtful (see Hebrew dictionaries and the commentaries). Six psalms are superscribed מכתם—another puzzle—three times with the addition על תשחת, once שושן עדות (lx.), and in lvi. with על יונת רחוקים. Five psalms are called תפלה = "prayer" (xvii., xl., lxxxvi., cii., cxlii.). Two psalms are marked להזכיר = "to remember" (xxxviii., lxx.), the meaning of which is not known. Ps. c. is designated by לתודה = "for thanksgiving," probably indicating its use in the liturgy as a hymn for the thank-offering. Ps. clv. is marked תהלה = "jubilee song or hymn," indicating its content. Ps. lx. has ללמד, probably a dittogram for לדוד = "for David." Ps. lxxxviii. has the heading לענות, which seems to be also a dittogram of the preceding על מחלת. Ps. vii. has another enigmatical caption (see commentaries).

XXXIX

Reform Judaism

REFORM JUDAISM FROM THE POINT OF VIEW OF THE REFORM JEW: By Reform Judaism is denoted that phase of Jewish religious thought which, in the wake of the Mendelssohnian period and in consequence of the efforts made during the fifth decade of the nineteenth century to secure civil and political emancipation, first found expression in doctrine and observance in some of the German synagogues, and was thence transplanted to and developed in the United States of America. The term is not well chosen. It suggests too strongly that the movement culminates in endeavors to recast the external forms of Jewish religious life. Moreover, it is transferred from the terminology of the Protestant Reformation, though in its bearing on the Judaism of the modern Synagogue the term can not be construed as implying that, like Protestantism to the Christianity of the early centuries, Reform Judaism aims at a return to primitive Mosaism; for in that case rabbinical Judaism must have been a departure from the latter.

"Reform" a Misnomer.

The Reform movement in its earlier stages was merely a more or less thoroughly executed attempt to regulate public worship in the direction of beautifying it and rendering it more orderly. With this in view, the length of the services was reduced by omitting certain parts of the prayer-book which, like the "Yeḳum Purḳan" and the "Bameh Madliḳin," were recognized as obsolete; the former being the prayer in behalf of the patriarchs of the Babylonian academies, which had for centuries ceased to exist; the latter, an extract from the mishnaic treatise Shabbat, and thus not a prayer. In addition, the piyyuṭim (see PIYYUṬ), poetical compositions in unintelligible phraseology for the most part, by medieval poets or prose-writers of synagogal hymns, were curtailed. The time thus gained came gradually to be devoted mainly to German chorals and occasional sermons in the vernacular. The rite of CONFIRMATION also was introduced, first in the duchy of Brunswick, at the Jacobson institute. These measures, however, aimed at the esthetic regeneration of the synagogal liturgy rather than at the doctrinal readjustment of the content of Judaism and the consequent modification of its ritual observances.

The movement later took on an altogether different aspect in consequence, on the one hand, of the rise of "Jewish science," the first-fruits of which were the investigations of Zunz, and the advent of young rabbis who, in addition to a thorough training in Talmudic and rabbinical literature, had received an academic education, coming thereby under the spell of German philosophic thought. On the other hand the struggle for the political emancipation of the Jews (see RIESSER, GABRIEL) suggested a revision of the doctrinal enunciations concerning the Messianic nationalism of Judaism. Toward the end of the fourth and at the beginning of the fifth decade of the nineteenth century the yearnings, which up to that time had been rather undefined, for a readjustment of the teachings and practises of Judaism to the new mental and material conditions took on definiteness in the establishment of congregations and societies such as the Temple congregation at Hamburg and the Reform Union in Frankfort-on-the-Main, and in the convening of the rabbinical conferences (see CONFERENCES, RABBINICAL) at Brunswick (1844), Frankfort (1845), and Breslau (1846). These in turn led to controversies (see FRANKEL, ZACHARIAS), while the Jüdische Reformgenossenschaft in Berlin (see HOLDHEIM, SAMUEL) in its program easily outran the more conservative majority of the rabbinical conferences. The movement may be said to have come to a standstill in Germany with the Breslau conference (1846). The Breslau Seminary under Frankel (1854) was instrumental in turning the tide into conservative or, as the party shibboleth phrased it, into "positive historical" channels,

Principles Laid Down in Conferences.

while the governments did their utmost to hinder a liberalization of Judaism.

Arrested in Germany, the movement was carried forward in America. The German immigrants from 1840 to 1850 happened to be to a certain extent composed of pupils of Leopold STEIN and Joseph AUB. These were among the first in New York (Temple Emanu-El), in Baltimore (Har Sinai), and in Cincinnati (B'ne Yeshurun) to insist upon the modernization of the services. The coming of David Einhorn, Samuel Adler, and, later, Samuel Hirsch gave to the Reform cause additional impetus, while even men of more conservative temperament, like Hübsch, Jastrow, and Szold, adopted in the main Reform principles, though in practise they continued along somewhat less radical lines. Isaac M. Wise and Lilienthal, too, cast their influence in favor of Reform. Felsenthal and K. Kohler, and among American-bred rabbis Hirsch, Sale, Philipson, and Shulman may be mentioned among its exponents. The Philadelphia conference (1869) and that at Pittsburg (1885) promulgated the principles which to a certain extent are basic to the practise and teachings of American Reform congregations.

The Center Principle.

The pivot of the opposition between Reform and Conservative Judaism is the conception of Israel's destiny. Jewish Orthodoxy looks upon Palestine not merely as the cradle, but also as the ultimate home, of Judaism. With its possession is connected the possibility of fulfilling the Law, those parts of divine legislation being unavoidably suspended that are conditioned by the existence of the Temple and by the occupation of the Holy Land. Away from Palestine, the Jew is condemned to violate God's will in regard to these. God gave the Law; God decreed also Israel's dispersion. To reconcile this disharmony between the demands of the Law and historically developed actuality, the philosophy of Orthodoxy regards the impossibility of observing the Law as a divine punishment, visited upon Israel on account of its sins. Israel is at the present moment in exile: it has been expelled from its land. The present period is thus one of probation. The length of its duration God alone can know and determine. Israel is doomed to wait patiently in exile, praying and hoping for the coming of the Messiah, who will lead the dispersed back to Palestine. There, under his benign rule, the Temple will rerise, the sacrificial and sacerdotal scheme will again become active, and Israel, once more an independent nation, will be able to observe to the letter the law of God as contained in the Pentateuch. Simultaneously with Israel's redemption, justice and peace will be established among the dwellers on earth, and the prophetic predictions will be realized in all their glories.

At present Israel must maintain itself in a condition of preparedness, as redemption will come to pass in a miraculous way. That its identity may not be endangered, Israel must preserve and even fortify the walls which the Law has erected around it to keep it distinct and separate from the nations. The memories of and yearnings for Palestine must be strengthened even beyond the requirements of the written law. The Law itself must be protected by a "hedge." The ceremonial of the Synagogue, regulated by the Law as understood in the light of rabbinical amplifications and interpretations, is both a memento and a monition of the Palestinian origin and destiny of national Israel, while life under the Law necessarily entails the segregation of Israel from its neighbors.

Relation to Nationalism.

Reform conceives of the destiny of Israel as not bound up in the return to Palestine, and as not involving national political restoration under a Messianic king with the Temple rebuilt and the sacrificial service reinstituted. It is true, many of the commandments of the Torah can not be executed by non-Palestinian Israel. Yet, despite this inability to conform to the Law, Israel is not under sin (the Paulinian view). It is not in exile ("galut"). Its dispersion was a necessary experience in the realization and execution of its Messianic duty. It is not doomed to wait for the miraculous advent of the Davidic Messiah. Israel itself is the Messianic people appointed to spread by its fortitude and loyalty the monotheistic truth over all the earth, to be an example of rectitude to all others. Sacrifices and sacerdotalism as bound up with the national political conception of Israel's destiny are not indispensable elements of the Jewish religion. On the contrary, they have passed away forever with all the privileges and distinctive obligations of an Aaronic priesthood. Every Jew is a priest, one of the holy people and of a priestly community appointed to minister at the ideal altar of humanity. The goal of Jewish history is not a national Messianic state in Palestine, but the realization in society and state of the principles of righteousness as enunciated by the Prophets and sages of old.

Therefore Reform Judaism has (1) relinquished the belief in the coming of a personal Messiah, substituting therefor the doctrine of the Messianic destiny of Israel, which will be fulfilled in a Messianic age of universal justice and peace. (2) Reform Judaism disregards consciously, not merely under compulsion, all Pentateuchal laws referring to sacrifices and the priesthood or to Palestine ("miẓwot ha-teluyot ba-areẓ"). It eliminates from the prayer-book all references to the Messiah, the return to Palestine, and the restoration of the national sacerdotal scheme. It ceases to declare itself to be in exile; for the modern Jew in America, England, France, Germany, or Italy has no cause to feel that the country in which he lives is for him a strange land. Having become an American, a German, etc., the Jew can not pray for himself and his children that he and they may by an act of divine grace be made citizens of another state and land, viz., national Israel in Palestine. (3) Reform Judaism relinquishes the dogma of the RESURRECTION, involved in the Jewish national Messianic hope (see MESSIAH; PHARISEES) that at the final advent of the Messiah all the dead will rise in Palestine, and eliminates from the prayer-book all references to it.

Its Negations.

The foregoing shows that Reform was never inspired by the desire to return to Mosaism. Mosaism certainly presupposes the Levitical institutionalism of Judaism; and it is nomistic, insisting on the eternally binding character and the immutability of the Law. Reform Judaism ignores and declares abrogated many of the laws of Mosaism. Its theory of REVELATION and of the authoritative character of Scripture must of necessity be other than what underlies Orthodox doctrine and practise.

According to Orthodox teaching, God revealed His Law on Mount Sinai to Moses in two forms, (1) the written law ("Torah shebi-ketab"), and (2) the oral law ("Torah shebe-'al peh"). According to Mendelssohn and all rationalists of the "Aufklärung" philosophy, there was no need for the revelation of religion, human reason being competent to evolve, grasp, and construe all religious verities. Judaism is, however, more than a religion. It is a divine legislation, under which the Jew qua Jew must live. Human reason could not have evolved it nor can it now understand it. It is of "superrational," divine origin. It was miraculously revealed to Israel. The Jew need not believe. His religion, like every rational religion, is not a matter of dogma. But the Jew must obey. His loyalty is expressed in deed and observance.

Relation to the Oral Law.

This Mendelssohnian position was undermined, as far as the oral part of revealed legislation was concerned, by the investigations into the historical development of "tradition," or Talmudic literature, brilliantly carried to definite and anti-Mendelssohnian results by Zunz and his disciples. The oral law certainly was the precipitate of historical processes, a development of and beyond Biblical, or even Pentateuchal, Judaism. Judaism, then, was not a fixed quantity, a sum of 613 commandments and prohibitions. The idea of progress, development, historical growth, at the time that the young science of Judaism established the relative as distinguished from the absolute character of Talmudism and tradition, was central in German philosophy, more clearly in the system of Hegel. History was proclaimed as the self-unfolding, self-revelation of God. Revelation was a continuous process; and the history of Judaism displayed God in the continuous act of self-revelation. Judaism itself was under the law of growth, and an illustration thereof. Talmudic legalism certainly was a product of the Talmudic period. It was not originally inherent in Judaism. It must not be accepted as eternally obligatory upon later generations.

Influence of Evolution.

But was Biblical law, perhaps, the original, divinely established norm and form of Judaism, and, as such, binding upon all subsequent generations? If it was, then Reform Judaism, ignoring post-Biblical development and tradition, was identical with Karaism; and, furthermore, its omission of all reference to sacerdotal and sacrificial institutions, though these form an integral part of the Mosaic law and revelation, is in violation of the assumption that Judaism is Law, which Law divinely revealed is the Pentateuch. This was the dilemma with which Reform theologians were confronted. This was an inconsistency which, as long as Judaism and Law were interchangeable and interdependent terms, was insurmountable. To meet it, a distinction was drawn between the moral and the ceremonial laws, though certainly the Torah nowhere indicates such distinction nor discloses or fixes the criteria by which the difference is to be established. God, the Lawgiver, clearly held the moral and the ceremonial to be of equal weight, making both equally obligatory. Analysis of the primitive scheme in connection with the possible violation of the precepts, tends to prove that infractions of certain ceremonial statutes were punished more severely (by "karet" = "excision") than moral lapses.

Nor could the principle be carried out consistently. Reform Judaism retained the Sabbath and the other Biblical holy days, circumcision, and in certain circles the dietary laws. Were these not ceremonial? What imparted to these a higher obligatory character? In this artificial distinction between the moral and the ceremonial content of the divinely revealed law the influence of Kantian moralism is operative. HOLDHEIM, to escape this inconsistency, urged as decisive the distinction between national and religious or universal elements.

National and Universal Elements.

The content of revelation was twofold—national and universal. The former was of temporary obligation, and with the disappearance of state and nation the obligatory character ceased; but the universal religious components are binding upon religious Israel. While this criterion avoided many of the difficulties involved in the distinction between ceremonial and moral, it was not effective in all instances. The sacrificial scheme was religious, as Einhorn remarked when criticizing Holdheim's thesis, and still Reform ignored its obligatory nature. Nor could Judaism be construed as a mere religion, a faith limited by creedal propositions.

Samuel HIRSCH approached the problem from the point of view of the symbolist. With his master Hegel, he regarded history as the divine process of revelation. Against Paul, Hegel, and Kant, and against most of the Reform rabbis, he maintained that Judaism was not law but "Lehre," a body of truths finding expression in Israel through the genius of its prophets, and for the application of which in life and the illustration and exemplifying of which before the whole world Israel was chosen and appointed. This obligation and this appointment descend from father to son, and are imposed at birth. "Torah" does not signify "law," but "Lehre," doctrine. The laws are symbols illustrative of the truths confided to Israel. They are aids to keep alive the Jewish consciousness. As long as symbols are vital and not mechanical they may not be neglected; but when they have fallen into desuetude or are merely retained in mechanical, perfunctory observance, or from fear or superstition, they have lost their value, and they need not be retained. Life and actual observance, not law or custom, decide what rite shall be practised. Between theory and life perfect concord must be established.

Symbolic Views of S. Hirsch.

Yet some symbols have been expressive of the unity of Israel. These (the holy days, the Sabbath) must receive reverent care and fostering attention in the synagogal scheme. Reform is, according to Hirsch, not interested in the abolition of ceremony, but it insists that ceremonies be effective as means of religious culture, that they be observed not as ends unto themselves or with a view to obtaining reward, but as expressions of religious feelings and as means of religious instruction. All ceremonies pointing to Palestine as his national home conflict with the sentiments and hopes of the politically emancipated Jew. Bloody sacrifices are repugnant to modern religious ideas. These national symbols, then, have no longer a place in the cult of the modern Jew. The Sabbath, too, is a symbol. It embodies the deepest truth of Judaism—man's divinity and freedom. It is not conditioned by the notation of the day. If modern Jews could observe the traditional Sabbath, there would be no call to make a change. But they can not and do not. Life and theory are at opposite poles. But the Sabbath is expressive also of the unity of all Israel. All Israel alone could make the change. The misconstruction of Judaism as Law is the thought of the Roman period, and is a clear departure from the broader conceptions of the Prophets.

The foregoing detailed analysis of the positions of the early German Reformers was necessary to understand their attitude with reference to the obligatory character of the Biblical and Pentateuchal laws. The Talmudic amplifications were ignored as being clearly not of divine origin and authority (*e.g.*, second holy days, and many of the SABBATH regulations); but a similar decision was not so easy in the case of the Biblical statutory insistences.

The researches of more recent years in the domain of Biblical literature have enabled the successors of these earlier Reformers to apply to the Bible and Pentateuch the principles applied by their predecessors to rabbinical literature. The Pentateuch is not the work of one period. Pentateuchal legislation also is the slow accretion of centuries. The original content of Judaism does not consist in the Law and its institutions, but in the ethical monotheism of the Prophets. Legalism is, according to this view, originally foreign to Judaism. It is an adaptation of observances found in all religions, and which therefore are not originally or specifically Jewish. The legalism of Ezra had the intention and the effect of separating Israel from the world. This separatism is to-day a hindrance, not a help, to the carrying out of the Jewish mission. The Jew must seek the world in order to make his ethical religion a vital influence therein. The Pentateuchal ordinances are binding upon the Jew in no higher degree than the Talmudic.

Influence of Higher Criticism.

But this new school—commonly designated as the Radical—adopts also, though in a new form, Samuel Hirsch's theory of the symbolic value of the ceremonial element. It invokes the psychological factor as finally decisive. Certain laws and institutions have in course of time, and owing to bitter persecutions, taken on a new significance. They have come to be associated in the Jewish consciousness with Jewish loyalty unto death in the face of apostasy and prejudice and oppression. Circumcision, the Sabbath, and the dietary laws (see Bib. Book of DANIEL) may be said to comprise this class of institutions. The former two, even in Radical congregations and in the life of their individual members, have retained their hold on the religious consciousness. The seventh-day Sabbath, though observed only in theory, is still regarded as the one citadel which must not be reconstructed. It is proclaimed the visible sign of Israel's unity. Congregations that would officially substitute the first day for the seventh as the Sabbath would be called schismatic.

The dietary laws have had their own history in Reform thought. A committee was appointed at the Breslau conference to report on them; but as the conference never again convened, only the suggestions of some of the members appeared in print. The more conservative opinions were in favor of reverting to Biblical practise, recognizing that the rabbinical insistence on a certain mode of slaughtering, and Talmudic interpretations of "ṭerefah," of "meat and milk," etc., are without Biblical warrant (see Wiener, "Die Jüdischen Speisegesetze," pp. 482 *et seq.*). In the United States the Biblical equally with the Talmudic dietary laws have fallen generally into disuse, even in so-called conservative congregations, though no rabbinical conclave or synod ever sanctioned or suggested this. On the principle, fundamental to Jewish Reform, that the national exclusiveness of Judaism is no longer its destiny, these practises, necessarily resulting in Jewish separatism and incorporated into the Levitical scheme to effect Levitical purity, must be looked upon as in one class with all other sacerdotal and Levitically national provisions.

The Dietary Laws.

Reform Judaism withal does not reduce Judaism to a religion of creed, least of all to a religion of salvation, with the prospect of heavenly rewards or life everlasting for the pious believer. In saying that Judaism is a mission to keep alive among men the consciousness of man's godlikeness, Reform Judaism holds that Judaism is imposed on the Jew by birth. It is not accepted by him in a voluntary act of confession. The Jew by his life and example is called to demonstrate the perfectibility—over against the Paulinian dogma of the total depravity—of every human being, and to help to render conditions on earth more and more perfect. Insistence on justice and righteousness are the practical postulate of the Jew's ethical monotheism, which is never a mere belief, but always a vitalizing principle of conduct. This duty of being an exemplar to others, incumbent on the Jew by virtue of his historical descent from prophetic ancestors on whose lips this monotheism was first formulated, at times entails suffering and always requires fortitude; but it is imposed in the certainty that ultimately justice and righteousness will triumph on earth, and all men will learn to know God and live the life which those who know God must live. With this Messianic fulfilment the history of the Jew will attain its goal.

Reform Judaism, then, may be said to advance the following dogmas, using that term, however, not in the Paulinian-evangelical sense:

"Dogmas" of Reform Judaism.

(1) The world and humanity are under the guidance of God, who reveals Himself to man in history as the Supreme Power unto Righteousness, as the Educator and Father of His children, the whole human family. The anthropomorphic character of the theological terminology is fully recognized.

(2) In His grace and wisdom God has appointed Israel to be His witness on earth, laying upon this His priest-people the obligation by its life to lead the world to the recognition of the truth that love and justice and righteousness are the only principles of conduct which can establish peace among men and fill man's life with blissful harmony, besides conferring on man an imperturbable sense of worth and worthiness, independent of accidents of fortune or station.

(3) This election of Israel confers no privilege on the Jew, but imposes greater obligations. Every human being is God's child, called to lead and capable of leading a righteous life.

(4) The dispersion of the Jews and the destruction of the Temple were not acts of providential requital for sins. They were providential devices to

bring Israel nearer unto other children of man. The goal of Israel's history is not national restoration and segregation, but the rise of a more nearly perfect humanity in which Jewish love for God and man shall be universalized. Not a Messiah, but the Messianic age, is the burden of Israel's hope.

(5) Like all Judaism, Reform rejects the doctrine of man's innate sinfulness. The Law—which according to Paul is a means to arouse a consciousness of the futility of man's attempt to conquer sin and is thus expressive of Judaism's content as merely preliminary—is not Judaism's distinctive badge or possession. The Law, often of non-Jewish origin, is the product of time, and is subject to growth and change in the course of time. But Judaism is a body of spiritual and moral truths, and as such independent of legal expression or enactment. CIRCUMCISION is not, like baptism, an indispensable and prerequisite rite of reception. Born of a Jewish mother, the Jew is Jew by birth (see PROSELYTE). As Israel is not now, and is not necessarily destined again to be, a political nation on the soil of Palestine, there are omitted all references not only to Palestine as the only legitimate home of Judaism and to the sacerdotal and sacrificial Temple services and laws, but also to the laws and institutions that are bound up with social conditions no longer extant and not expected to become reactive (in Palestine) in the future. For example, the LEVIRATE and ḤALIẒAH, not being applicable to our times and conditions, are abolished as having lost binding force. The laws regulating marriage and divorce, as developed more especially in Talmudic casuistry, often operate unjustly (see GEṬ) and are, in view of the better provisions in the civil codes of modern nations, amended and in many respects superseded by the law of the land (see MONOGAMY). Woman is no longer deemed to be a minor, but is admitted to full participation in the religious life of the congregation.

As far as possible, Reform Judaism endeavors to preserve the historical continuity with the past, especially in its ritual and synagogal services. The best illustration of this is afforded by Einhorn's prayer-book "'Olat Tamid" (see EINHORN, DAVID). This is based on Zunz's researches into the rise and

Reform Ritual.

development of the Jewish ritual. It omits the MUSAF, as essentially sacrificial. Allusions in the older forms of the prayers to the Messiah are changed into expressions of hope in the Messianic destiny of Israel and of all mankind. For the doctrine of resurrection is substituted that of God's sustaining love. Otherwise, the scheme is maintained as it was in the synagogues of the tannaitic period, the service on Yom ha-Kippurim alone showing departures of greater scope from the traditional pattern, the piyyuṭim being largely replaced by paraphrases of the Psalms illustrative of the Jewish conceptions of sin, repentance, and atonement. The Yom ha-Kippurim itself is treated as typical of the ultimate Messianic fulfilment. The service for the Ninth of Ab ("Tish'ah be-Ab") is especially noteworthy. It is a résumé, in fact, of the Reform construction of Israel's history and Messianic obligations. The Hebrew language is retained in the prayers that are of tannaitic origin—*e.g.*, Shema' with its berakot, and SHEMONEH 'ESREH.

Some minor points resulting from the application of the foregoing principles, in which the practise of the Reform synagogues differs widely from the traditional, should be noticed.

Language of Prayers.

In public and private prayers the use of the vernacular language predominates. For this there is good historical precedent (Yer. Soṭah vii. 1). R. Jose, controverting the prohibition of the use of any language but Hebrew (Soṭah vii. 1, 33a; Yer. Soṭah iii. 1), permits the recitation of the Shema', the Decalogue, the "Tefillah" ("Shemoneh 'Esreh"), and grace after meals in any language understood by the worshiper (comp. Maimonides, "Yad," Ḳeri'at Shema', ii. 10; Shulḥan 'Aruk, Oraḥ Ḥayyim, 62, 2; 102, 4). Einhorn, followed in the main by the Union Prayer-Book (see PRAYER-BOOKS), retains the Hebrew for the mishnaic prayers, and, strange to say, the Aramaic for the ḲADDISH where the original is in the vernacular of its day. The Ḳaddish in America has become a prayer in memory of the dead, though this perversion of its meaning is not countenanced by all. The Reformgenossenschaft of Berlin omitted Hebrew almost entirely; but even in the most radical congregations of America such portions as the Bareku, the Shema', and the Ḳadosh (see Ḳedushshah) are recited in Hebrew. In the reading of the Law the triennial cycle was adopted, though of late most congregations have reverted to the annual one—reading, however, only a small portion of each "parashah," which results in the Torah being read in disjointed fragments. The scheme of the Union Prayer-Book ignores both the annual and the triennial cycle. The "calling up" of the prescribed number of men is omitted, the reader reciting the benedictions before and after and reading the portion without interruption. The trope (see Jew. Encyc. iii. 537b, *s.v.* Cantillation) also has been abandoned.

Ṭallit and tefillin (see Phylacteries) are not worn; neither is the "kittel" (see Sargenes) on the Day of Atonement; nor are the shoes removed on that day. Worship is engaged in with uncovered head. For this latter concession to Occidental custom there seems to have been a precedent in the habits of the Jews in France in the thirteenth century (see Isserles, "Darke Mosheh," on Ṭur Oraḥ Ḥayyim, 282, כמנהג צרפת דקורין בראש מגולה; and "Ha-Manhig," ed. Berlin, p. 15, where the covered head is called the "custom of Spain," from which it is plain that in Provence, the country of Abraham b. Nathan ha-Yarḥi, the author of the "Manhig," the uncovered head was the rule).

Use of Organ.

In Reform synagogues the Organ and mixed choirs are always among the appointments of public worship. In Germany the gallery for women is without curtain or lattice-work to hide its occupants from view; while in America the segregation of the sexes has been abandoned in favor of family pews. Women no longer regard it as a religious duty to clip or to cover up their hair. The Almemar is connected with the Ark.

The observance of the second days of the holy days (see Festivals) has been discontinued, as there is at present no uncertainty concerning the proper day. Minyan is not determined by the presence of ten men. The Dukan of the priests is abolished, since the privileges of priest and Levite are sacerdotal and thus bound up with nationalism.

The priestly benediction is recited by the reader with reading changed from "Aaron and his sons, the priests, Thy holy people" to "Aaron and his sons, the priests of Thy holy people" (from כהנים to כהני). In the understanding of what the proper observance of the Sabbath requires, Reform Judaism rejects the legalism of the rabbinical scheme, with its insistence on 'ERUB, teḥum, and similar legal fictions. Work is interpreted to be "labor for profit," and not merely such work as was undertaken at the construction of the Tabernacle in the desert (see SABBATH). Many of the Reform congregations have introduced supplementary Sunday services, or have set the Friday evening service at an hour later than the "reception of the bride Sabbath" (קבלת שבת), and have changed its character by introducing "lectures." The regular sermon constitutes the principal feature of the Reform service. Reform synagogues are generally called "temples" after the HAMBURG precedent, probably to indicate that they take the place of the temple in Jerusalem, which Orthodoxy looks forward to as the to-be-restored sanctuary.

BIBLIOGRAPHY: D. Einhorn, in *Sinai*, Baltimore and Philadelphia, 1856–61, *passim*; idem, *David Einhorn's Ausgewählte Predigten und Reden*, ed. K. Kohler, New York, 1879; idem, *Ner Tamid* (catechism), Philadelphia, 1865; Samuel Hirsch, *Die Reform im Judenthum*, Leipsic, 1843; *The Jewish Times*, New York, *passim*, especially 1870–72; *The Jewish Reformer*, New York, 1887; *The Reform Advocate*; C. G. Montefiore, *Liberal Judaism*, London, 1904; E. G. Hirsch, *The Originality of Judaism*, in *Hebrew Union College Annual*, Cincinnati, 1904; K. Kohler, *Backwards or Forwards?* New York, 1885.

XL

Right And Righteousness

RIGHT AND RIGHTEOUSNESS: Renderings given in the English versions of the Hebrew root "ẓadaḳ" and its derivatives "ẓaddiḳ," "ẓedeḳ," "ẓedaḳah." The use of "righteous" as a translation for "yashar" (="upright") is less frequent. "Just," "justice," "justify" also occur as equivalents for these Hebrew terms.

The original implications of the root "ẓadaḳ" are involved in doubt. To be "hard," "even," and "straight" (said of roads, for instance) has been suggested as the primitive physical idea. More acceptable is the explanation that the root-notion conveyed is that a thing, man, or even God, is what it, or he, should be, that is, "normal," "fit." That conception may, without much difficulty, be recovered from some of the applications of the terms in the Bible. Weights and measures are called "ẓedeḳ" ("just" or "right"; Deut. xxv. 15; Lev. xix. 36; Job xxxi. 6; Ezek. xlv. 10). Paths are "ẓedeḳ," that is, as they should be, easy to travel (Ps. xxiii. 3). So with offerings, when brought in the proper manner and at the right time (Deut. xxxiii. 19; Ps. iv. 6 [A. V. 5], li. 21 [A. V. 19]). When a king or judge is as he should be he is "just" (Lev. xix. 15; Deut. i. 16; Prov. xxxi. 9). When speech is as it should be it is "truthful" (comp. Ps. lii.). The outcome of the battle being favorable, it is called "ẓedaḳah" (="victory"; Judges v. 11). To justify oneself, or another, is also expressed by the root, as it really means to prove oneself, or another, to be innocent of a charge, or in the right (that is, as one should be; Job ix. 15,

Original Signification.

20; xi. 2; xiii. 18; Isa. xliii. 9; Ps. cxliii. 2). In many of the passages in which the root has this physical implication an ethical element may be discovered. "Right" weights may be also "righteous" weights. The battle may be looked upon as a sort of divine ordeal, and hence the issue may be said to be "righteous" (= "ẓedaḳah"; see Schwally, "Der Heilige Krieg im Alten Israel," p. 8). In the Song of Deborah—one of the oldest literary compositions—this implication is not absent from the word, employed in the plural in connection with YHWH (Judges v. 11). So in its earliest use, among Hebrews, the term "righteousness" seems to have had a moral intention.

In the collection of legal decisions ("mishpaṭim") constituting the Book of the Covenant, "ẓaddiḳ" appears as a juridical, technical term (= "the party [to a suit] that is in the right"; Ex. xxiii. 7). It is noteworthy that the feminine of "ẓaddiḳ" is not found, the verb being used to express the idea in the case of the woman being in the right (Gen. xxxviii. 26); the "hif'il" is used to declare one "not guilty," or as having substantiated his claim (Ex. xxiii. 7; II Sam. xv. 4). The man who makes such a rightful plea is "ẓaddiḳ" (Isa. v. 23; Prov. xvii. 15; *et al.*). In this use, too, a clear ethical note may be detected. To declare him "right" who is in the right is certainly a moral act; the judge who decides in favor of the right is righteous. Even the religious element underlies this use. God is the judge. To have a suit is to seek out ("darash") YHWH (*i.e.*, to inquire of YHWH). The judgment is an ordeal. The winner of the suit, the man found innocent, is by the verdict proved to be righteous in the sight of YHWH.

Use by the Prophets.

But it is in the early prophecies that the ethical aspect of righteousness is forcibly accentuated. Used by Amos in the forensic sense, "righteousness" and "justice" are urged as higher and nobler and more pleasing in the sight of YHWH than ritual religiousness (ii. 6; v. 12, 23). "Social righteousness" alone will save Israel. The fate of the personally guilty and the personally innocent alike is involved in that of the whole people. This social righteousness, then, may be said to be in the eyes of this prophet a religious service.

Hosea marks another step in the evolution of the concept of righteousness. He would have righteousness potentialized by "ḥesed" (love, or mercy). Social justice as a matter merely of outward conduct, and manifest only in public adjustments of institutions and conditions, will not bring about the rejuvenescence of the nation. Inner repentance, spiritual consideration of one's neighbor and brother, yielding love, not mechanical justice alone, are the components of righteousness (vi. 1–4, x. 12).

Isaiah proceeds along the lines indicated by his predecessors. "Justice," or "righteousness," is solicitude for the weak and helpless (i. 16 *et seq.*, 27; x. 2). This righteousness is true religion; Israel is expected to be devoted to it. The moral order of the world is founded in such righteousness, which metes out strict justice (v. 7, xxviii. 17, xxix. 13). This justice, inherent in God's supreme providence, will bring about the salvation of the REMNANT OF ISRAEL (vii. 9). Isaiah looks forward to the coming of a time when Jerusalem, no longer enslaved to mere ritual piety while steeped in injustice, will be called "the fortress of righteousness" (i. 26, Hebr.).

Jeremiah's understanding of righteousness is virtually the same as Isaiah's (see Jer. xxii. 3, which seems to embody his ideas of what it embraces, though the term is not used). He looks forward to the reestablishing of the Davidic kingdom under "a righteous branch," a ruler who will do justice and who will deserve the name "YHWH our Righteousness" (xxiii. 5 *et seq.*, Hebr.). Jeremiah's faith in the righteous character of God's government was sorely put to the test both by his own personal experience and by the conditions prevailing in his own day. Yet he acknowledges that YHWH is in the right ("ẓaddiḳ"), though he can not forego asking why the wicked prosper (xii. 1). YHWH is a "righteous judge," probing the motives of human conduct (xi. 20). In Deut. xvi. 20 the pursuit of righteousness is solemnly inculcated.

"Righteous" Synonymous with "Moral."

"Righteous" in these prophetic passages is synonymous with "moral." He deserves the designation who not only refrains from wrong-doing but is strenuous in his efforts to establish right. To suffer wrong to be done to another is almost equivalent to doing it. Hence the righteous endeavor to see that the weak, the poor, the orphaned, and the widowed secure their rights. The conception that the righteousness of God also involves positive activity in behalf of right, not mere abstinence from wrong-doing, is accentuated. The moral law is so administered that justice will be done.

In the lives of the "righteous" whose names and characters both have been preserved in the national history these qualities were dominant. Noah was "a righteous" man in his generation. He was spared while the wicked perished (Gen. vi. 9, vii. 1). If there had been righteous ones in Sodom they would not have shared the fate of the city. Abraham was warned of the impending catastrophe because it was certain that he would teach his descendants "to do judgment and righteousness"(Gen. xviii. 19, 23–25). Abraham's trust in YHWH is reckoned unto him "for righteousness" (Gen. xv. 6; a statement which, however obscure, certainly does not bear out the construction put on it by Christian theologians, from St. Paul to the present, as little as does Hab. ii. 4—"the righteous shall live by his faith" [Hebr.]).

In Habakkuk "the righteous" has taken on an entirely new meaning. It stands for Israel as represented by the "pious," the "meek," the "poor," the "remnant." Israel will not be disturbed by the seeming falsification of its trust and confidence involved in the actual conditions of the day. For the moment Babylon, the "unrighteous," may be victorious; but ultimately the righteousness of God's government will be manifest in the victory of the "righteous." This application of "righteous" is common in exilic and post-exilic writings (comp. Isa. xxvi. 10). In (Deutero) Isa. xlii. 6 the "servant of YHWH" (Hebr.) is this righteous one; indeed, the "righteousness" of God is manifested in the advent of Cyrus (Isa. xliv. 28). God supports His messengers "with the right hand" of His "righteousness" (Isa. xli. 10)—that is, He will insure their triumph. This "righteousness," which is the victorious purpose of God's providence, is not conditioned or expressed by ritual practises. The contrary is the case. The people who believe that they have done right (Isa. lviii. 2) are told that fasting is inoperative, that justice and love are the contents of righteousness. Righteousness in this sense is the recurring refrain of the second Isaiah's preaching. The remnant of Israel, having suffered, has been purified and purged of its sins. Its triumph, therefore, will establish God's righteousness, for the triumph of the wicked (*i.e.*, Babylon) is unthinkable in view of the moral order of things (Isa. xlvii. 6, li. 1–7, lii. 3–5).

Individualization of Righteousness After the Exile.

With the Exile the individualization of righteousness begins to be recognizable in Hebrew thought. The accountability of man for his conduct is phrased most strongly by writers of this period (Jer. xxxi. 29–30; Ezek. xviii. 2–4). In Ezekiel, a few instances excepted (xvi. 52, xxiii. 45, xlv. 9–10), "righteous" and "righteousness" express the religious relation of individuals to God (xiii. 22, xiv. 14, xviii. 5 *et seq.*). The plural of "ẓedaḳah" (if the text is correct) connotes good deeds proceeding from one's religious character (iii. 20, xviii. 24, xxxiii. 13). The content of this righteousness is preponderatingly ethical, not ritual. The Book of Job approaches the problem of God's righteousness from a new point of view. The suffering of the righteous is its theme as it is that of other Biblical passages (Mal. iii. 15–18; Ps. xxxvii., xxxix., xlix., lxxiii.). That sin and suffering are corresponding terms of one equation is the thesis defended by Job's friends; but Job will not accept it; conscious of his rectitude, he rebels against it. He challenges the Almighty to meet him in a regular judicial proceeding. The book states the problem, but furnishes no answer (see JOB, BOOK OF; OPTIMISM AND PESSIMISM). It must, however, be noted that the terms for righteousness are often used in the Book of Job in a technical, juridical sense, namely, for "being right" (in reference to a pleader). In the other Wisdom books (Proverbs and Ecclesiastes) the "righteous," contrasted with the "wicked," are ethically normal individuals. Righteousness is the supreme moral category. On the whole, the contention of these books is that the righteous are sure to reap rewards while the wicked are as certain to be punished, though Ecclesiastes is not consistent in the exposition of the doctrine of retribution.

In the Book of Psalms "the righteous" more frequently represents a party than individuals—"the meek," "the lowly"; that is, the faithful who, in spite of persecution, cling to God's law. In the Maccabean age these became the "Assidaioi" (the Ḥasidim). Their triumphs are sung and their virtues and faith are extolled. Their righteousness is both social and personal (comp. Ps. vii., xviii., xxv., xxxii., xxxiii., xxxvii., xli., lxiv., xcvii., cvi., cix.; see GODLINESS).

But as the Pharisaic synagogue grew in influence, and legalism struck deeper roots, the righteous came to be identified not with the ideal citizen of Zion pictured in Ps. xv., but with him whose "delight is in the law," described in the prologue to the book—Ps. i. The Law and its observance became an integral part of Jewish righteousness, though by no means to the degree and in the soulless manner assumed by non-Jewish writers, who delight to describe how ritualism and literalism first outweighed mere moral considerations and then ignored them altogether. See NOMISM.

In the Apocrypha.

In the Apocrypha righteousness is ascribed to God as a quality of His judgments and as manifesting itself in the course of human history (II Macc. i. 24–25). As the Righteous Judge He grants victory to the faithful and courageous, whose faith in God's righteousness, in fact, inspires their courage (II Macc. viii. 13). God, as the Righteous Judge, metes out condign punishment to evil-doers (Azariah's prayer, add. to Dan. i.). As evidences of human righteousness the virtues of loyalty to truth and one's oath are adduced (I Macc. vii. 18). The Patriarchs, as sinless, are held to have been perfectly righteous (see Prayer of Manasses). Idolatry and righteousness are represented as incompatible (Ep. Jer. verse 72). In the Wisdom of Solomon (ii.) the skeptics are unmasked as the "unrighteous"; and unrighteousness leads to death (i. 16), while righteousness leads to life. In Ecclus. (Sirach) xxxi. 8 the rich man who has resisted the temptations which beset the getting of wealth is characterized as righteous. It is plain that the man whom Sirach regards as deserving to be called "righteous" is one whose morality is above reproach, whatever may be his loyalty to ritual observances (see *ib.* vi., vii.); and as for the self-righteousness which is imputed to

Judaism it is sufficient to refer to vii. 5 of the same book, where the Hebrew text preserves the technical word "hiẓṭaddeḳ" (to brazenly proclaim oneself as a righteous man).

In the Psalms of Solomon righteousness designates fidelity to the Law (xiv. 2). But this Law demands obedience to the fundamental principles of morality as strenuously as compliance with ritual precepts. The Sadducees are inveighed against as unrighteous. From the vehemence of the denunciations the conclusion has been drawn that in the minds of the Pharisaic authors laxity in ritual piety constituted the essence of wickedness; but the Sadducees' antinational concessions to Rome were much more provocative than their indifference to the ritual. Moreover, it must be remembered that the Psalms of Solomon, like the Gospels, are partizan pamphlets, in which the shortcomings of opponents are exaggerated. Righteousness as interpreted by the Pharisaic synagogue embraced moral considerations as well as ritualistic.

Rabbinical View.

This appears also from the rabbinical sources. Rabbinical theology is never systematic. This must be kept in mind, as well as the fact that many of the rabbinical conclusions are mere homiletic applications of texts, illustrating the exegetical dexterity of their authors rather than a fixed dogma of the Synagogue. This is true of the rabbinical observation that at any given period never less than thirty righteous are found in the world, for whose sake the world escapes destruction (Tan., Wayera, 13, where this conclusion is derived from the gemaṭria of יהיה [= 30]). Another passage has it that one righteous man insures the preservation of the world (Yoma 38b). The righteous are regarded as being inspired by the "holy spirit" (Tan., Wayeḥi, 14, where the context clearly shows that the statement is not dogmatic, but homiletic). The Shekinah rests upon them (Gen. R. lxxxvi.). In fact, before sin entered into the world the Shekinah was permanently dwelling on earth. When Adam lapsed it rose, and it continued to rise to ever greater distances, proportionate always to the increase of sin among men. But it was gradually brought back to earth by the righteousness of Abraham,

Isaac, Jacob, Levi, Kehath, Amram, and Moses (Cant. R. iii. 11). The Patriarchs and the great heroes of Bible days are considered to have been perfectly righteous (Sifre 72b; Yalḳ. i. 94; Gen. R. lxiii., xc.; Meg. 13b; Sanh. 107a; Shab. 56a; *et al.*).

Righteousness is dependent upon man's free choice. All its future conditions are predetermined by God at the very conception of the child, its character alone excepted (Tan., Peḳude). The conquest of the "yeẓer ha-ra'" (*i.e.*, of the inclination toward immorality) marks the righteous (Eccl. R. iv. 15; Gen. R. lxvii.; comp. Yoma 39a). In this contention the ethical implications of the rabbinical interpretation of righteousness are patent. The righteous man is godlike (see GODLINESS); that is, he is desirous of reflecting the attributes of God (Soṭah 14a; Pesiḳ. 57a). The state of sin is not inherited. Men might live in perfect righteousness without "tasting sin" (Eccl. R. i. 8; Shab. 55b). Children are born sinless (Eccl. R. iii. 2; Lev. R. vii.). Abraham, Isaac, and Jacob (Yalḳ. i. 36, 106), and Elijah (Lev. R. xxvii.), among others, are mentioned as having gone through life without yielding to the yeẓer ha-ra'.

Still, most men are not so strong. Hence the race is divided into three categories: (1) "ẓaddiḳim" (the righteous); (2) "benunim" (the indifferent); and (3) "resha'im" (evil-doers). The first and third groups again are divided into "perfect" and "ordinary" righteous and evil-doers ("ẓaddiḳim gemurim," "resha'im gemurim," and mere "ẓaddiḳim" or "resha'im"; Ber. 61b). The first are under the dominion of the "yeẓer ha-ṭob" (the inclination to do good), the third under that of the yeẓer ha-ra'. Class two is now in the first group and anon in the third group. But finally only the first and the third condition are recognized. After death men are judged either as "ẓaddiḳim" or as "resha-'im." The ungodly are not buried with the righteous (Sanh. 47a). The benunim are respited from Rosh ha-Shanah to Yom ha-Kippurim. If they do a good deed in the meantime, they are ranged with the righteous; if they commit an evil deed, they are ranked as ungodly (R. H. 16a). They are like trees that bear no fruit (Tan., Emor, 17).

Three Classes of Men.

The "ẓaddiḳ gamur" is he who, like Abraham, Isaac, Jacob, Moses, Samuel, fulfils the whole Torah from alef to taw (Shab. 55a; comp. Alpha and Omega). Of this order were Michael, Azariah, and Hananiah (Ta'an. 18b). It is not necessarily to be assumed that such truly righteous ones were altogether without blame. They may have committed minor transgressions ("'aberot ḳallot"; Sifre 133a). These are written in the Book of Life on Rosh ha-Shanah (R. H. 16b). They behold the Shekinah in a clear mirror (Suk. 45b). They do not change, while the ordinary ẓaddiḳim are exposed to lapses.

The utterly unrighteous, or the "heavily" unrighteous ("rasha' ḥamur"), are distinct from the "slightly" unrighteous ("rasha' ḳal"; Sanh. 47a). The former receive recompense at once for whatever slight good they may do, but are destined to everlasting perdition. Esau is an example (Gen. R. lxxxii.), as are Balaam (Tan., Balaḳ, 10), those symbolized by the bad figs in Jeremiah's basket (Jer. xxiv.; 'Er. 21b), and others. Yet even a rasha' gamur may repent and appear before his death as a ẓaddiḳ gamur (Ezek. xxxiii. 12; Num. R. x.; Ex. R. xv.).

The Unrighteous.

Man is judged according to the dominant character of his intentions and deeds (Ḳid. 40b). If the majority of them are righteous he is accounted a ẓaddiḳ; but if they are otherwise, or if even a few partake of the nature of gross crimes and immoralities, he is adjudged a rasha' (see Sifre 51b). Far from encouraging self-righteousness, rabbinical theology warns each to regard himself as part good and part bad, and then to determine his own rank by adding to his good deeds (Ḳid. 40a). Intention and the underlying motive are decisive for the quality of an act in a good man, while a good deed done by an ungodly man is reckoned in his favor, whatever may have been its motive (Ḳid. 39b). Yet it is certainly unwarrantable to twist these largely exegetical fancies of the Rabbis into proofs of rigid dogmatic positions. The good act is considered a "miẓwah," a divine command; but still the spiritual element of righteousness is not ignored. Calculations of reward and penalty are declared to be contrary to God's intentions (Deut. R. vi.). The Rabbis assume that reward will be a necessary consequence of a good deed, and punishment that of an evil deed. Yet this causal relation is apprehended as being involved in God's grace (Tan., Ethannen, 3); even Abraham could not do without God's grace (Gen. R. lx.).

This thought underlies also the Talmudic-rabbinical concept of "zekut." "Zakai," a term designating the innocent, or guiltless, the contrary of "ḥayyab," the guilty party in a suit, gradually assumed the meaning of "ẓaddiḳ." The zekut, therefore, primarily, is one's righteousness. But the "righteousness of the fathers" ("zekut abot"), or of a "righteous man," is credited with the effect of helping others and their descendants, though those so benefited have no claim, through their own merit, to the benefit. In strict justice, each should be judged according to his merits. But God's mercy permits man to be judged by the sum total of all the goodness which exists in the world in an age, in a family. As, owing to the righteous, the sum of goodness is sufficient, the less good is granted more than his due. The technical term used in this connection is "ma'aleh 'al" (hif'il of "'alah"), meaning "to tax in favor of" (see Weber, "Jüdische Theologie," pp. 290 *et seq.*; Weber, however, misapprehends the whole matter and twists it into a theological system with a strong note of Pauline dogmatics). The solidarity of the race is basic to the notion, not the idea of God's justice as exacting, measuring, calculating; for God's grace and mercy are involved in the conception ("middat ha-raḥamim").

Idea of "Zekut."

As human righteousness is a reflection of God's, it includes necessarily love for others. This consideration has so strongly influenced the Jewish mind that the word "ẓedaḳah" (righteousness) has assumed the meaning of "alms," "charity." "Gemilut ḥasadim" (philanthropy in its widest sense) is another expression of the righteous man's inner life (Tan., Mishpaṭim, 9, Lev. R. xxvii.; Tan., Emor, 5 [illustrated by Moses]; Tan., Ki Tabo, 1; comp. Eccl. R. vi. 6; Tan., Wayaḳhel, 1).

Identified with Charity.

Why the righteous suffer is one of the problems the Rabbis attempt to solve. The perfectly righteous do not suffer; the less perfect do (Ber. 7a).

Under the law of solidarity the latter often suffer for the sins of others, and therefore save others from suffering (Ex. R. xliii.; Pesiḳ. 154a). Where the nature of suffering is individual, it is assumed to be a punishment for some slight transgression with a view to insure to the righteous a fuller reward in the world to come (Pesiḳ. 161a; Hor. 10b). Or it may be probationary, and as such a signal manifestation of divine favor (Sanh. 101b; Shab. 53b; Ta'an. 11a; Gen. R. xxxiii.). The death of the righteous works atonement for their people (Tan., Aḥare Mot, 7; M. Ḳ. 28a). God allows the righteous man time to repent and to attain his full measure of good deeds before He sends death (Eccl. R. v. 11). The most truly righteous either escape death altogether (*e.g.*, ELIJAH; ENOCH), or it meets them as a kiss imprinted on their lips by God, as with Abraham, Isaac, Jacob, Moses, Aaron, Miriam (B. B. 17a; Yalḳ. i. 42). Death for the righteous is also a release from the struggle with the inclination to do wrong (Gen. R. ix.). Dead, they still live (Ber. 18a). They are like pearls, which retain their preciousness wherever they are (Meg. 15a).

The coming of the righteous into the world is a boon to it; their departure therefrom a loss (Sanh. 113a). The ungodly are sentenced to stay in Gehenna twelve months; then they are released at the intercession of the righteous (Yalḳ. Shim'oni, to Mal. 593). In Gan 'Eden, God will dance with the righteous (Ta'an. 31a); there they will sing God's praise (Ex. R. vii.). Resurrection is reserved for the righteous alone (Gen. R. xiii.; Ta'an. 7a). In "the world to be" the righteous sit with crowns on their heads and delight in the radiancy of the Shekinah (Ber. 17a). They partake of LEVIATHAN (Pesiḳ. 188b; B. B. 74b).

Fate of the Righteous.

Their crowns are those that were worn at Sinai (Sanh. 111b; Shab. 88a). The שְׂבַע שמחות of Ps. xvi. 11 is read שֶׁבַע שמחות ("seven"), and is taken to refer to the seven classes of righteous that enjoy God's glory (Sifre 67a).

The "righteous" are often identified with Israel, and the "ungodly" with the heathen, non-Israelites (Tan., Bemidbar, 19; Lev. R. xiii. 1). But this should not be taken as a general rule. The non-Israelites of whom the Rabbis had knowledge were

Romans, whose cruelty and profligacy made "non-Israelite" and "ungodly" exchangeable terms. Still, righteous ones are found among "the nations" (*e.g.*, Noah, Jethro; see PROSELYTE), and these righteous will have a share in the kingdom to come (Tos. Sanh. xiii.).

Thus righteousness was not a privilege of the Jew; it was rather an obligation. As Judaism does not teach original sin its views on righteousness have no relation to the doctrine of justification (see ATONEMENT). The Jewish prayer-book, the depository of the faith of Israel, contains as a part of the morning liturgy: "Lord of all the worlds, not in reliance upon our righteous deeds do we lay our supplications before Thee, but trusting in Thy manifold mercies." This summarizes the doctrine of the Synagogue upon the subject. Righteousness is a duty which brings no privileges. Self-righteousness is not the key-note of Israel's confession. Simply as descendants of Abraham is it incumbent upon Israel to proclaim the Shema'. The modern Jewish connotation of righteousness carries an ethical (both personal and social), not a liturgical emphasis.

XLI

Sabbath

SABBATH (**שבת**): The seventh day of the week; the day of rest.

——**Biblical Data:** On the completion of His creative work God blessed and hallowed the seventh day as the Sabbath (Gen. ii. 1–3). The Decalogue in Exodus (xx. 8) reverts to this fact as the reason for the commandment to "remember" the Sabbath day to keep it holy. The Sabbath is recognized in the account of the gathering of the manna; a double portion was gathered on the previous day, and the extra supply gathered for consumption on the Sabbath, when no manna descended, did not spoil (xvi. 22–30). The Sabbath is a sign between YHWH and Israel, an everlasting covenant (xxi. 13). Death or excision (xxxi. 14, 15) was the penalty for its profanation by work. An instance of this is afforded by the case of the man who gathered sticks on the Sabbath and was condemned to die by lapidation (Num. xv. 32–36). Work is prohibited, even during harvest-time (Ex. xxxiv. 21), and is declared to be a profanation of the holy Sabbath; and the kindling of fire in the habitations is especially interdicted (Ex. xxxv. 3).

In the DECALOGUE as contained in Deuteronomy (v. 12 *et seq.*) the observance of the Sabbath is again enjoined, but as a day of rest for the servants as well as their masters, in commemoration of Israel's redemption from Egyptian bondage. The Sabbath heads the enumeration of the appointed holy seasons (Lev. xxiii. 3). The SHOWBREAD was changed every Sabbath (Lev. xxiv. 8). The sacrifice ordained for the Sabbath consisted of two he-lambs of the first year, without blemish, and of two-tenths of an ephah of fine flour for a meal-offering, mingled with oil, and "the drink-offering thereof"; these constituted the burnt offering, and were brought in addition to the continual burnt offering (Num. xxviii. 9, 10). The Sabbath is designated also as "Shabbat Shabbaton," as is the Day of Atonement (Lev. xvi. 31), often with the added qualification of "holy unto YHWH" (Ex. xvi. 23, xxxi. 1, xxxv. 2); and it is set apart for a holy convocation (Lev. xxiii. 3).

From II Kings xi. 5 it appears that the royal body-guard was changed every Sabbath. The Sabbath and the day of the New Moon were the favorite occasions for consulting the Prophets (II Kings iv. 23).

Non-Observance by Some in Prophetic Times.

That the Sabbath was either improperly observed or sometimes, perhaps, altogether ignored in the time of the Prophets seems to be evidenced by their writings. Amos castigates those that are impatient for the passing of the Sabbath because it interferes with their usurious business (viii. 5). Isaiah is equally emphatic in condemning his contemporaries for their unworthy celebrations (i. 9). Jeremiah exhorts his people to refrain from carrying burdens on the Sabbath (xvii. 21 *et seq.*). Ezekiel describes the laxness of the fathers, for the purpose of impressing upon his auditors the importance of observing the Sabbath, evidently neglected in his day (xx. 12, 16, 20, 21, 24; xxii. 8; xxiii. 38). In his scheme of reconstruction the hallowing of the Sabbath holds a prominent place (xliv. 24, xlvi. 2, 3). According to him the burnt offering for the Sabbath, provided by the prince (xlv. 17), consisted of six lambs and a ram, with an entire ephah of meal-offering and a "hin" of oil to every ephah (xlvi. 4–5).

Isaiah conditions Israel's triumph on the observance of the Sabbath, which may not be set aside for secular pursuits; its observance should be a delight (lviii. 13, 14). In his vision of Jerusalem's exaltation the prophet predicts that from one Sabbath to another all flesh will come to worship before YHWH (lxvi. 23). The colonists under Nehemiah charged themselves yearly with a third of a shekel to provide, among other things, for the burnt offerings of the

Sabbaths (Neh. x. 32). Nevertheless Nehemiah took them to task for profaning the day (xiii. 16, 17), and to prevent them from continuing to turn it into a market-day he ordered the gates to be closed and kept closed until the end of the Sabbath. This measure, after a while, had the desired effect (x. 19 *et seq.*). Ps. xcii. is entitled "A Psalm or Song for the Sabbath Day." As Hosea (i. 11) threatens the cessation of the Sabbath and other feasts as a punishment to disloyal Israel, so does the author of Lamentations (ii. 6) lament that the Sabbath has come to be forgotten in Zion.

——**In Apocrypha and Pseudepigrapha:** Under the stress of the Syrian persecution, faithful compliance with the strictest interpretation of the Sabbath commandment came to be regarded as a sign of loyalty to God, especially since previously the Sabbath had been habitually desecrated (I Macc. i. 30). Many of the refugees in the mountains, thousands in number, preferred to die rather than violate the Sabbath by hurling stones upon their assailants (I Macc. ii. 29 *et seq.*). This made it necessary for Mattathias to issue an imperative order that the Jews, if attacked, should defend themselves (I Macc. ii. 41). Nevertheless, II Macc. xv. 1 *et seq.* relates that Nicanor planned the destruction of the Jews by attacking them on the Sabbath-day, when he had reason to believe they would not attempt to resist. Though the Jews implored him to honor the "day which had been dignified with holiness by the Heavenly Ruler," he persisted, declaring that he was ruler on earth. His expedition, however, failed. A previous raid against Jerusalem on the Sabbath-day, under Appolonius, had proved successful (II Macc. v. 25, 26).

The Book of Jubilees calls the Sabbath the great sign that work should be done during six days and dropped on the seventh (ii. 17). The chief orders of angels also were bidden to observe the Sabbath with the Lord (ii. 18). In selecting Israel as His chosen people, YHWH purposed to make them a Sabbath-observing people. Eating, drinking, and blessing God are distinguishing features of the Sabbath, besides cessation of work (ii. 21). The

Sabbath was given to Jacob and his seed that they might forever remain "the blessed and holy ones of the first testimony and law," as is the seventh day. Labor thereon entails death, but its defilement leads to violent death (ii. 25, 27). Among the acts prohibited are included preparing food, drawing water, and carrying burdens, however small, out of or into the house, or from one house to another. The Sabbath was hallowed in heaven before it was ordained for earth. Israel alone has the right to observe it (ii. 28–31). Again, in ch. iv., buying and selling, making verbal agreements for future fulfilment, and journeying are mentioned as among the acts prohibited, as well as drawing water, carrying burdens, and marital indulgences. Only work that is necessary for the sacrificial Temple service is permitted. Death shall be the penalty for any one who works, walks any distance, tills his land, kindles a fire, loads a beast of burden, travels on a ship, beats or kills any one, slaughters bird or beast, captures in the chase any living creature, or even fasts or wages war, on the Sabbath.

The archangel Michael instructs Seth (Vita Adæ et Evæ, 43) not to mourn on the seventh day (Kautzsch, "Apokryphen," ii. 528).

——**In Post-Biblical Literature:** Josephus, in the main, follows the Biblical narrative, giving the word "Sabbath" the meaning "rest" ("Ant." i. 1, § 1), and controverting the stupid etymology of the name upheld by Apion, according to whom the Jews were forced to observe the Sabbath by the fact of their being afflicted with bubonic boils known in Egyptian by a word similar to the Hebrew word "sabbath" ("Contra Ap." ii., § 2). Moreover, his descriptions of Sabbath celebration do not differ from the Biblical. That the beginning and end of the Sabbath were announced by trumpet-blasts ("B. J." iv. 9, § 12) is shown by the Mishnah (Suk. v. 5).

In Josephus and the Classical Writers.

Josephus makes much of the spread of Sabbath observance in non-Palestinian cities and among non-Jews ("Contra Ap." ii., § 39; comp. Philo, "De Vita Moysis," ii. 137 [ed. Mangey]). That he does not exaggerate is apparent from the comments of Roman writers on the Jewish Sabbath. Horace, in his "Satires" (i. 9, 69), speaks of "tricesima Sabbata," which certainly does not refer to a Sabbath so numbered by the Jews. Juvenal ("Satires," xiv. 96–106), Persius (v. 179–184), Martial (iv. 4, 7), and Seneca (Augustine, "De Civitate Dei," vi. 11) also refer to the Sabbath. In the Maccabean struggle the observance of the Sabbath came to have special significance as distinguishing the faithful from the half-hearted; but Josephus confirms I Macc. ii. 39–41, where the faithful, under Mattathias, decided to resist if attacked on the Sabbath, and not to permit themselves to be destroyed for the sake of literal obedience to the Sabbath law (comp. "Ant." xii. 6, § 2). He mentions instances in which the Jews were taken advantage of on the Sabbath-day—for example, by Ptolemy Lagi ("Ant." xii. 1; xviii. 9, § 2). Still, according to Josephus, the Jews carried on offensive warfare on the Sabbath ("B. J." ii. 19, § 2). Titus was outwitted by the plea that it was unlawful for Jews to treat of peace on the seventh day (*ib.* iv. 2, § 3). Josephus also publishes decrees exempting Jews from military service on the Sabbath, which exemption gave rise to persecutions under Tiberius ("Ant." xiv. 10, §§ 12 *et seq.*). The Essenes are referred to as very rigorous observers of the Sabbath ("B. J." ii. 8, § 9).

In Philo.

In Philo an element of mysticism dominates the interpretation of the Sabbath: the day was really intended for God, a part of whose divine happiness it is to enjoy perfect rest and peace. "Hence the Sabbath, which means 'rest,' is repeatedly said by Moses to be the Sabbath of God, not of men, for the one entity that rests is God." Divine rest, however, does not mean inactivity, but unlabored energy ("De Cherubim," § 26 [i. 154–155]). "Seven" being "the image of God," the seventh day is a pattern of the duty of philosophizing ("De Decalogo," § 20 [ii. 197]). The purpose of man's life being "to follow God" ("De Migratione Abrahami," § 23 [i. 456]), the commandment was given for man to observe the seventh day, ceasing from work, and devoting it to philosophy, contemplation, and the improvement of character ("De Decalogo," § 20 [ii. 197]). The Sabbath is the most appropriate day for instruction ("De Septenario," § 6 [ii. 282]).

Aristobulus, a predecessor of Philo, wrote a treatise on the Sabbath, fragments of which are extant. Following the Pythagoreans, he enlarges on the marvelous potency of the number "seven," but endeavors, like Philo after him ("De Septenario," §§ 6-7 [ii. 281–284]), to prove the observance of the day to be both reasonable and profitable (Eusebius, "Præparatio Evangelica," xiii. 12, §§ 9-16). He asserts that even Homer and Hesiod observed the Sabbath, citing lines from them and from Linus. According to his understanding, the Sabbath was primarily to be used for searching the Scriptures, fostering the soul's powers, and striving after the knowledge of truth. The Sabbath might be called the first creation of the (higher) light, in which all is revealed (comp. the benedictions preceding the Shema'; Herzfeld, "Gesch. des Volkes Jisrael," p. 478, Nordhausen, 1867).

In the Talmud.

These Alexandrian speculations partake of the nature of haggadic homilies. In those of the Tannaim and Amoraim similar strains are heard. The Sabbath overshadowed every other day (Pesiḳ. R. 23), while Shammai began even on the first day of the week to make provision for the proper observance of the seventh day. It was Hillel who recalled the dignity of other days (Beẓah 16a). The Sabbath is considered to be equivalent to the Abrahamitic covenant (Mek. 62b; Pesiḳ. R. 23; Agadat Bereshit, xvii.). Its observance forestalls the threefold judgment—the Messianic sufferings, the wars of Gog and Magog, and the final day of retribution (Mek. 50b, 51a; comp. Shab. 118a). The privilege of celebrating the three great pilgrim festivals is the reward for faithful Sabbath observance (Mek. *l.c.*). The Sabbath is likened to wholesome spices (Shab. 119a; Gen. R. xi.; Jellinek, "B. H." i. 75). Whosoever keeps the Sabbath holy is protected against temptation to sin (Mek. 50b).

Most characteristic is the dialogue between Rufus and Akiba concerning the two signs of the Covenant—circumcision and the Sabbath (Sanh. 65b; Gen. R. xi.; Pesiḳ. R. 23; Tan., Ki Tissa; Jellinek, "B. H." i. 75). The will of God is alleged to be the sole reason for the day's distinction. As proof that the seventh day is the Sabbath the inability of the necromancer to call a spirit from the River Sambation, and the fact that the grave of Rufus' father sends forth smoke during the six week-days, but ceases to do so on the Sabbath, are adduced. Akiba meets the objection that God violates His own law by sending wind and rain on the Sabbath with the statement that the universe is God's private domain, within which the proprietor is at liberty even on the Sabbath. Moreover, God proved Himself to be a Sabbath observer by interrupting the fall of manna on that day. To observe the Sabbath is regarded as equivalent to having originally instituted it (Mek. 104a, b).

The Sabbath expresses the intimacy between God and Israel; from the days of Creation this relation has existed. Each week-day is associated with another, the first with the second, and so on; but the Sabbath stands alone. In answer to its complaint at being thus neglected, God explained that Israel is its peculiar associate (Beẓah 16a; Gen. R. xi.). Man's face takes on a new luster on the Sabbath. The two great heavenly lights, the sun and the moon, did not begin to lose their original brilliancy until after the first Sabbath (Mek. 69b; Gen. R. xi., xii.). If all Israel were to observe two successive Sabbaths as they should be observed, redemption would ensue at once (Shab. 118b; comp. Yer. Ta'an. 64a); if even one Sabbath were rightly kept the Messiah would appear (Shab. 118b). Simeon ben Yoḥai regarded too much talking as inconsistent with the proper celebration of the day (Yer. Shab. 15b); R. Ze'era reproved his pupils for committing this fault (Shab. 119a, b). Those that observe the Sabbath are ranked with those that give tithes and honor the Law; their rewards are identical (Shab. 119a; Gen. R. xi.; Pesiḳ. R. 23). Two angels, one good, the other evil, accompany every Jew on Sabbath eve from the synagogue to the house. If the Sabbath lamp is found lighted and the table spread, the good angel prays that this may be the case also on the following Sabbath, and the evil angel is compelled to say "Amen" to this; but if no preparations for the Sabbath are seen, the evil angel pronounces a curse, and the good angel is compelled to say "Amen" (Shab. 119b).

The law of the Sabbath is equal to all the other laws and commandments in the Torah (Yer. Ber. 3c; Yer. Ned. 38b; Ex. R. xxv.). The ẓiẓit is intended to be a constant reminder of the Sabbath (Yer. Ber. 3c). "Queen" and "bride" are two typical appellations for the day (Shab. 119a; B. Ḳ. 32a, b; Gen. R. x.); it is the signet on the ring (*ib.*).

Haggadic References.

A special soul ("neshamah yeterah") is given to man on the eve of the Sabbath, and leaves him again at its close (Beẓah 16a; Ta'an. 27b). Simeon ben Laḳish explains the repetition of the Sabbath commandment by relating a parable of a father who sent his son to a merchant with a bottle and some money. The son broke the bottle and lost the money, whereupon the father admonished him to be more careful and gave him another bottle and some more money. Hence comes the use of the word שמור in Deuteronomy ("be careful"; Pesiḳ. R. 23). According to R. Simlai, the "remember" in Ex. xx. 8 indicates the duty of thinking of the Sabbath before, the "observe" in Deut. v. 12 that of keeping it holy after, its advent (Pesiḳ. R. 23). The Sabbath is a precious pearl (Midr. Teh. to Ps. xcii., ed. Buber, p. 201a). The one day which belongs to God is, according to Ps. cxxxix. 16, the Sabbath; according to some it is the Day of Atonement (Pesiḳ. R. 23; Tan., Bemidbar, 20). The superior character of the seventh day is marked by the circumstance that everything connected with it is twofold: *e.g.*, the double portions of manna (Ex. xvi. 22); the two lambs (Num. xxviii. 9); the double menace in Ex. xxxi. 14; the repetition of the Sabbath commandment (Ex. xx. 8 and Deut. v. 12); the double title of Ps. xcii.—"mizmor" and "shir" (Midr. Teh. to Ps. xcii., ed. Buber, p. 201b).

The Sabbath is a foretaste of the world to come (Gen. R. xvii., xliv.; Ber. 57b ["one-sixtieth of the world to come"]). The example of the Creator is cited to teach that all work, however important, should cease as soon as the Sabbath approaches; for God was about to create bodies for the demons whose souls He had fashioned when the Sabbath came and prevented the execution of the intention (Gen. R. vii.). The Patriarchs are said to have kept the Sabbath even before the revelation on Sinai (Gen. R. lxxix.; Tan., Naso, 33 [ed. Buber, p. 22a, b]).

According to the testimony of the Haggadah, the Sabbath was looked upon and observed as a day of joy. Samuel ben Naḥman declared that the Sabbath was intended to be a day of good cheer (Yer. Shab. 15a; Ḥiyya b. Abba in Pes. R. xxiii.). Fasting was forbidden upon it (Ber. 31b), even up to noon (Yer. Ta'an. 67a; Yer. Ned. 40d). Expenses incurred for a proper, joyful Sabbath celebration do not impoverish (Gen. R. xi.); on the contrary, riches are the reward of those that enjoy the Sabbath (Shab. 118a). Hence the special blessing for the Sabbath in Gen. ii. 3, to vouchsafe impunity to the weak for excesses in eating and drinking committed in honor of that day (Bacher, "Ag. Pal. Amor." i. 111). Three meals were considered indispensable (Shab. 118b). Of Ḥanina and Hoshaiah, disciples of R. Johanan, it is reported that they occupied themselves on Friday with the story of creation, which miraculously enabled them to procure a fattened calf for their Sabbath meal (Sanh. 65b, 67b) when they were too poor to prepare properly for the day. Nothing should be eaten on Friday later than the first hour after noon, in order that the Sabbath meal may be better enjoyed (Pes. 99b; Tos. Ber. v. 1; Yer. Pes. 87b). Change of garments was also deemed essential to a proper observance; white Sabbath garments are mentioned in Shab. 25b. Every person should have at least two sets of garments, one for week-days and another for the Sabbath (Yer. Peah 21b); Ruth is referred to as an example (Ruth R. iii. 3; Pes. R. xxxiii.; Shab. 113b). The Jews of Tiberias, who plead their poverty as a reason for not being able to celebrate the day, are advised to make some change in their dress (*ib.*). To this refers also the proverb, "Rather turn thy Sabbath into a profane day [in dress], than be dependent on the assistance of others" (Pes. 112a). The myrtle was used for purposes of decoration on the Sabbath (Shab. 33b). It was noticed with displeasure that Aḥa ben Ḥanina wore mended sandals on the Sabbath (Shab. 114a). The Sabbath was given to instructive sermons and discourses (Yer. Soṭah 16d; Num. R. ix.; Deut. R. v.). To run to the bet ha-midrash on the Sabbath to hear a discourse does not constitute desecration (Ber. 6b). Rain on Friday is not wel-

Dress.

come, as it interferes with Sabbath preparations, while sunshine on the Sabbath is a divine boon to the poor (Ta'an. 8b).

The Haggadah clearly shows that the Sabbath-day was celebrated in a spirit of fervent joyfulness, which was by no means intended to be repressed, and which was not chilled or checked by the halakic construction of the Sabbath commandments. The Sabbath, indeed, was deserving of the designation of "mattanah ṭobah" (a precious gift from on high; Shab. 10b).

——**Critical View:** The origin of the Sabbath, as well as the true meaning of the name, is uncertain. The earliest Biblical passages which mention it (Ex. xx. 10, xxxiv. 21; Deut. v. 14; Amos viii. 5) pre-suppose its previous existence, and analysis of all the references to it in the canon makes it plain that its observance was neither general nor altogether spontaneous in either pre-exilic or post-exilic Israel. It was probably originally connected in some manner with the cult of the moon, as indeed is suggested by the frequent mention of Sabbath and New-Moon festivals in the same sentence (Isa. i. 13; Amos viii. 5; II Kings iv. 23).

Probable Lunar Origin.

The old Semites worshiped the moon and the stars (Hommel, "Der Gestirndienst der Alten Araber"). Nomads and shepherds, they regarded the night as benevolent, the day with its withering heat as malevolent. In this way the moon ("Sinai" = "moon ["sin"] mountain") became central in their pantheon. The moon, however, has four phases in approximately 28 days, and it seemingly comes to a standstill every seven days. Days on which the deity rested were considered taboo, or ill-omened. New work could not be begun, nor unfinished work continued, on such days. The original meaning of "Shabbat" conveys this idea (the derivation from "sheba'" is entirely untenable). If, as was done by Prof. Sayce (in his Hibbert Lectures) and by Jastrow (in "American Journal of Theology," April, 1898), it can be identified in the form "shabbaton" with the "Shabattum" of the Assyrian list of foreign words, which is defined as "um nuḥ libbi" = "day of propitiation" (Jensen, in "Sabbath-School Times," 1892), it is a synonym for "'Aẓeret" and means a day on which one's actions are restricted, because the deity has to be propitiated. If, with Toy (in "Jour. Bib. Lit." xviii. 194), it is assumed that the signification is "rest," or "season of rest" (from the verb "to rest," "to cease [from labor]"; though "divider" and "division of time" are likewise said to have been the original significations; comp. also Barth, "Nominalbildungen," and Lagarde, "Nominalbildung"), the day is so designated because, being taboo, it demands abstinence from work and other occupations. The Sabbath depending, in Israel's nomadic period, upon the observation of the phases of the moon, it could not, according to this view, be a fixed day. When the Israelites settled in the land and became farmers, their new life would have made it desirable that the Sabbath should come at regular intervals, and the desired change would have been made all the more easily as they had abandoned the lunar religion.

Dissociated from the moon, the Sabbath developed into a day of rest for the workers and animals on the farm (Deut. v. 14; Ex. xx. 10). Traces of the old taboo are, however, still found. In Amos viii. 5 it is the fear of evil consequences that keeps the impatient merchants from plying their wicked trade. The multitude of sacrifices (Isa. i. 8; Hosea ii. 11) on Sabbath and New Moon indicates the anxiety on those particular days to propitiate the deity. Closer contact with Assyro-Babylonians from the eighth to the sixth pre-Christian century probably revitalized the older idea of taboo. The assumption that the Hebrews borrowed the institution from the Babylonians, which was first suggested by Lotz ("Quæstiones de Historia Sabbati"), is untenable; but that the Exile strengthened the awe in which the day was held can not be denied. It having become a purely social institution, a day of rest for the farmers, the taboo element in course of time had lost its emphasis. The Assyro-Babylonians may have had similar days of abstinence or propitiation (the 7th, 14th, 19th, 21st, and 28th of the month Elul), and contact with them may have served to lend the Jewish Sabbath a more austere character. The Assyrian calendar seems to disclose an effort to get rid of the movable Sabbath in favor of the fixed. If after the twenty-eighth day two days are intercalated as new-moon days, the 19th day becomes the 49th from the beginning of the next preceding month, as in the Feast of Weeks, in connection with which the emphasis on "complete Sabbaths" ("sheba' Shabbot temimot"; Lev. xxiii. 15) is noteworthy. At all events, in the Priestly Code, Sabbath violation is represented as entailing death (Num. xv. 32-36). The prohibition against kindling fire (Ex. xxxv. 3) probably refers to producing fire by the fire-drill or by rubbing two sticks together; this was the crime of the man put to death according to Num. xv. 32-36, the "meḳoshesh" (see also Beẓah iv. 7), the presence of fire being considered, if the analogy with superstitious practises elsewhere is decisive, a very grave sign of disrespect to the deity.

Assyrian Analogues.

But Hebrew institutions are often in direct antagonism to similar ones among the Assyro-Babylonians. The seventh days in the Babylonian scheme were days of ill omen. The prophets of the Exile laid especial emphasis on the fact that the Sabbath is a day of joy, as did those of the Assyrian period on the futility of the propitiating sacrifices (Isa. i.). The Priestly Code could not neutralize this view. Its rigorous observance found acceptance only among the "Nibdalim" (the Separatists; see Neh. x. 31). Every festival in the Biblical scheme is associated with a historical event. The connection of the Sabbath with the Exodus, in Deut. v. 14-15, was altogether vague; and to supply a more definite relation to an event in Israel's history the Sabbath was declared to have had an important significance in the desert when manna fell (Ex. xvi. 27 *et seq.*). The Decalogue of Exodus supplies a theological reason for the observance of the day; its phraseology reflects that of Gen. ii. 1 *et seq.* Both—this explanation and the story in Genesis—are among the latest additions to the Pentateuch.

BIBLIOGRAPHY: In addition to the abundant literature mentioned in the bibliographies of the Bible dictionaries see Friedrich Bohn, *Der Sabbat im Alten Testament*, Gütersloh, 1893 (the latest contribution; it abounds in parallels for the taboo).

——**Historical and Legal:** A comparison between rabbinical Sabbath legislation and the data of the Bible, Apocrypha, and Pseudepigrapha must establish the fact that the Talmudical conception of what is implied by Sabbath "rest," with the practical determination of what may and what may not be done on that day, is the issue of a long process of development. Even the commandment ("remember") in Exodus presupposes the previous existence of the institution; indeed, tradition assumes that the Sabbath law had been proclaimed at Marah, before the Sinaitic revelation (Rashi on Ex. xv.; Maimonides, "Moreh," iii. 32; Sanh. 56b). The restoration of Sabbath observance in Ezra and Nehemiah's time in no sense transcended the Pentateuchal ordinances. By "no manner of labor" (Ex. xx. 10, Hebr.), as the context shows, were indicated domestic and agricultural occupations (comp. B. Ḳ. v. 7). The special mention of plowing and harvesting, and probably the direct prohibition of kindling fire, the explicit mention of which the Rabbis attempt to explain away (Shab. 70a), suggest that, in the main, field- and household-work were covered by the Biblical idea of labor (Ex. xxxiv. 21, xxxv. 3). Carrying of loads "in and out" can not be held to be an exception (Jer. xvii. 21–22). Probably Jeremiah's censure had reference to carrying to market the yield of field and farm, or the articles manufactured at home (comp. Amos viii. 5). It is just this that Nehemiah deplores (Neh. xiii. 15).

Evolution of Conception of Sabbath Rest.

The Maccabean rebellion marks the beginning of an altogether different conception of the term "labor." The rigorists regarded self-defense, even against a mortal attack, as included in the prohibition (Josephus, "Ant." xii. 6, §§ 2–3). The stricter construction, then, must have been devised among the Ḥasidim, Mattathias representing the broader view. That for a long time the question of what was permitted in this direction on the Sabbath remained open is shown by a comparison of I Macc. ix. 34, 43; II Macc. viii. 26; Josephus, "Ant." xii. 6, § 2; xiii. 1, § 3; 8, § 4; xiv. 10, § 12; xviii. 9, § 2; *idem*, "B. J." ii. 21, § 8; iv. 2, § 3; *idem*, "Contra Ap." i. § 22; Ta'an. 28b, 29a; 'Ar. 11b. Rabbinical law is still busy debating in Shab. vi. 2, 4 whether weapons may be carried on the Sabbath, and what are weapons and what ornaments. Some latitude is allowed soldiers in camp ('Er. i. 10; Dem. iii. 11), and such as had gone forth carrying arms on the Sabbath to wage war were permitted to retain their weapons even when returning on the Sabbath (Yer. Shab. i. 8; 'Er. iv. 3; 15a; Maimonides, "Yad," Melakim, vi. 11, 13).

Freedom to move about is indispensable to military operations; but the interdict against marching, walking, or riding established by the rabbinical law rendered military ventures impossible on the Sabbath. In the time of Josephus this interdict was known. He reports that Jewish soldiers do not march on the Sabbath, their non-Jewish commanders respecting their religious scruples ("Ant." xiv. 10, § 12; xviii. 3, § 5). The "Sabbath way" (see 'Erub), limited to 2,000 ells, is fully recognized in the New Testament (comp. Acts i. 12). The institution of this Sabbath way, or walk, clearly shows a purpose to extend the established limits. There were several calculations by which the limit of distance was arrived at. In the injunction concerning the gathering of manna (Ex. xvi. 29) the phraseology used is, "Let no man go out of his place." But this noun "place" is used also in the law concerning the cities of refuge (Ex. xxi. 13). In Num. xxxv. 26 the "limit" or border of the city is named, while verses 4 and 5 of the same chapter give 2,000 ells as its extent ('Er. 48a). Josh. iii. 4 also is considered, 2,000 ells being the interval that must be maintained between the ark and the people. Whether this distance should be measured in a straight line in one direction, or whether it should be taken from the center of a circle, was open to argument. If the latter, freedom to move within a circle 4,000 ells in diameter would result. This would certainly answer the ordinary needs of the Sabbath walker ('Er. iv. 3, 5, 8; R. H. ii. 5). By another calculation, in which the area of limitation is a square, with each side of 4,000 ells, even greater latitude is arrived at; movement along the border-lines as well as along the diagonal would be free ('Er. iv. 8; see Baneth, "Einleitung zum Traktat Erubin").

Military Exceptions.

In reference to other Sabbath distances, the traditional four ells, so often found in specifications of proportions and quantities, are given as the limit (Yoma i. 2; Suk. i. 10; Ber. iii. 5; B. B. ii. 4, 5, 12). Within the distance of four ells throwing was allowed (Shab. xi. 3, 4). Only so much water might be poured out on the Sabbath as four ells square of ground would absorb ('Er. viii. 9, 10; for other instances see 'Er. i. 2; iv. 1, 5; x. 4, 5). How these four ells should be measured is also a matter of serious inquiry ('Er. iv. 5, 6). Thus the Mishnah preserves the evidence of a constantly active desire to relax the rigor of probably Ḥasidean constructions. For this purpose the legal fiction of the 'erub was resorted to, creating constructively a new residence. Perhaps, originally, huts were built (for instance, the huts, 2,000 paces apart, for those that accompanied the scapegoat on Yom Kippur; Yoma vi. 4; Bohn, "Der Sabbat im Alten Testamente," p. 72, Gütersloh, 1903). Against this 'erub the SADDUCEES (literalists) are reported to have protested ('Er. vi. 1, 2). It is well known that the Samaritans withdrew freedom of movement almost entirely, as did the Essenes ("B. J." ii. 8, § 9). The gloss to R. H. ii. 5 is indicative of the existence of similarly rigorous views among others. At first, in the case of an observation of the new moon on Sabbath, the witnesses were not permitted to move about; but later R. Gamaliel allowed them the freedom of 2,000 ells in every direction. Such laws as the one that he who has exceeded the "teḥum" (Sabbath distance) even by one ell may not reenter point to the same conclusion ('Er. iv. 11). Traveling on a ship was not prohibited, though even in this case the disposition at one time was to require the traveler to remain on the ship three days previous to sailing if the day of departure was the Sabbath, circumstances, of course, necessitating certain exceptions (Shab. 19a; "Sefer ha-Terumah," quoted in "Shibbole ha-Leḳeṭ," ed. Buber, p. 41). A fictitious "shebitah" (acquisition of domicil) helped to remove the rigoristic construction. During the voyage itself it sufficed, even for the stricter interpreters, if the passenger informed the captain of his desire that the ship should lay to on the Sabbath. No responsibility rested upon him

Restricted Freedom of Movement.

if his desire were disregarded. On Sabbath, during the voyage, the Jew might walk the whole length of the ship even if her dimensions exceeded the measure of the Sabbath way (*ib.*). Still, R. Joshua and R. Akiba are remembered as having refrained, while on a voyage, from walking farther than four ells on shipboard on the Sabbath ('Er. iv. 1).

The fact that artificial "gezerot" (apprehensions lest a forbidden act be done) are adduced to explain the so-called "shebutim" (Beẓah v. 2), *i.e.*, acts that ought to be omitted on Sabbath (for instance, climbing a tree or riding on an animal), discloses a purpose to relax the law. It is most probable that at one time the acts classified under this name were not proscribed. Only later practise prohibited them, and when a less strict spirit began again to assert itself, it was found that there was not sufficient warrant for the enforcement of the prohibition.

Restrictions on Riding.

In the case of riding on the Sabbath this evolutionary process is plain. The prohibition appears to have been first promulgated during the Hasmonean period. But riding, especially on asses, was the usual mode of locomotion, and the injunction seems not to have been readily heeded. An instance exists of a court that, desiring to make an example, put an offender to death (Yeb. 90b; Sanh. 46a; Yer. Ḥag. ii. 1). Yet Elisha ben Abuyah is reported to have ridden on horseback within the limits of the Sabbath distance, R. Meïr following to hear him discourse on the Torah until the hoofs of the horse reminded him that he ought to turn back, as he had ridden the full length of the distance permitted (Ḥag. 15a). While the names of riders mentioned in the Talmud are mostly those of apostates, yet the Talmud affords no justification for the prohibition (see Löw, "Gesammelte Schriften," iv. 305 *et seq.*). The Talmud assumes that every living creature carries itself (Shab. 94a); hence the horse or ass does not carry a burden when ridden by a man; and in order to find some basis for the injunction, rabbinical writers allege the apprehension that the rider might cut a switch on the way with which to whip the horse, and thereby become a violator of the Sabbath (Shab. 153b; Maimonides, "Yad," Shabbat, xviii. 16–17; Ṭur Oraḥ

Ḥayyim, 305). It was a rule not to sell or hire animals to non-Jews lest they be deprived of their Sabbath rest. The horse alone was excepted, since it would be used only for riding, which was not in Talmudic law a violation of the Sabbath ('Ab. Zarah i. 6; 15a; Pes. iv. 3).

Against Kindling Fire.

The prohibition against kindling a fire was rigorously and literally observed by the Samaritans (Leopold Wreschner, "Samaritanische Traditionen," p. 15; De Sacy, "Notices et Extraits," xii. 163, 176). The Sadducees, as were later the Karaites, were similarly convinced that light and fire should not be found on Sabbath in the habitations of the faithful (Geiger, "Nachgelassene Schriften," vol. iii.). The purpose of rabbinico-Pharisaic casuistry is to combat this ascetic literalism. Hence its insistence on the lighting of the lamps and its micrologic devices for keeping food warm; it accommodated itself to the rigorism of the literalists only so far as to avoid the creation of an open, flaming fire (Shab. ii., iv.). Marital indulgence on the Sabbath was regarded as a profanation by the Samaritans (De Sacy, *l.c.*). This opinion prevailed also in the earlier rigoristic period of Sabbath legislation. Weddings were not permitted on the Sabbath (Beẓah v. 2). Later casuistry endeavored to find a reason for this prohibition, but the multitude of the explanations advanced—fear of mixing joys; apprehensions that preparation for the wedding-feast might lead to infraction of Sabbath laws; etc.—shows the embarrassment of the later teachers (Ket. i. 1). Except in the case of weddings, which were forbidden, later practise was opposed to that of the Samaritans (Ned. ii. 10, viii. 6).

The Puritan character of the rabbinical Sabbath is shown in the aversion, deducible from some laws, to loud noises (instance Simeon ben Yoḥai's reproof of his mother for loud talking), clapping of hands, striking with a hammer, trumpet-calls, and music (Löw, *l.c.* ii. 355). While to some of the more ascetic rabbis any loud demonstration of joy undoubtedly approached irreverence and impiety, it may be noted that the minor reasons adduced in regard to music (*e.g.*, lest musicians might be tempted to make or repair instruments, or the estimate of music as "labor," not "art" [חכמה]) indicate that ascetic tendencies had but little to do with the prohibition of it. In the later post-Talmudical days non-Jewish musicians were employed on the Sabbath.

But the employment of non-Jews to do what it was not lawful for the Jew to do on the Sabbath presented difficulties. If they were servants they might not work (Ex. xx.). By a legal fiction, however, the presumption was established that in reality the non-Jew worked for himself (see "Shibbole ha-Leḳeṭ," pp. 84 *et seq.*; "Yad," *l.c.* vi.). Among the thirty-nine classes of forbidden acts are also swimming, jumping, dancing, holding court (but comp. Sanh. 88b), performing the ceremony of ḥaliẓah, setting aside as holy, vowing to pay the value of things so set aside, putting under the ban (a beast as devoted to the Temple), and collecting the priest's portion or the tithes (Beẓah v. 2).

Sabbath Work by Gentile for Jew.

The Book of Jubilees reflects the earlier, more rigid conception of the Sabbath. The acts enumerated therein as forbidden are almost identical with those found in the Mishnah. Its temper is evidenced by the fact that it makes death the penalty for violations. Later, flagellation was substituted for the severer penalty.

In the Halakah the observance of the Sabbath, like any other Pentateuchal ordinance or statute, is treated as a legal duty or debt laid upon the Israelite, and the manner and measure in which this duty must be discharged are legally fixed. Undoubtedly, in the case of the Sabbath as in that of other institutions, the Halakah legalized and systematized customs of long standing, endeavoring to connect them with Pentateuchal text and precedent. This systematization resulted in the accentuation of limitations. Under the general precept a number of specific prescriptions were evolved. Again, the principle of "a fence around the Law" led to the enactment of precautionary regulations. Still, rabbinical Sabbath legislation was by no means altogether restrictive. In many instances its effect was to broaden the scope of the Biblical law or its literal interpretation (see 'Erub).

Principle of Halakah.

The subtleties which this legalism engendered are illustrated by the first mishnah in Shabbat, which analyzes the possibilities of Sabbath violation in connection with carrying from one territory into another, or in the passing of alms from the donor within the house to the donee outside it.

Another example is furnished by the following abstract of Maimonides' first chapter of Shabbat. To rest from labor on the Sabbath ("shebitah") is a mandatory commandment. Transgression thereof, however, violates both a positive and a negative precept, as the Pentateuch enjoins rest as well as prohibits work. The penalty for intentional violation by work is excision ("karet"); if there were witnesses to the act and the legal warning ("hatra'ah") had been given, the penalty was stoning. Unintentional desecration entails the bringing of the prescribed sin-offering. The law analyzes and discriminates among the various kinds of acts: some acts are in themselves permissible, though they may involve possible, though not unavoidable, infractions of the Sabbath law. Unless a previous intention was manifest to perform an act in a way that would lead to incidental violation, this latter is not to be taken into account. If, however, the secondary violation is necessarily involved in the usually permissible act, even though no intention to violate the Sabbath may be imputed, the perpetrator is guilty.

The existence of a good motive for doing a thing that is prohibited does not exonerate the doer thereof.

Motive Considered.

For instance, extinguishing a light is forbidden; it is forbidden also to extinguish it for the purpose of economizing oil. The motive, however, is decisive in cases where one act was intended and another of different scope is accidentally performed. Where two men perform one piece of work (*e.g.*, carry a beam) in common, but each alone does less than would render him liable, and it is within the power of either to do it alone, both are exempt. But where the work exceeds the strength of each alone, and it is necessary to do it together, both are guilty. Work which destroys merely ("meḳalḳel") does not entail a penalty; but destruction preliminary to building is forbidden.

With a view to more thoroughly safeguarding the Sabbath against profanation an hour of the previous day ("'ereb Shabbat") was added to it. This was called "adding from the profane to the holy" (Shulḥan 'Aruk, Oraḥ Ḥayyim, 261, 2). The Pentateuchal warrant for this was found in the use of the definite article in Gen. i. 31 (הששי, "the sixth day") or in Ex. xx. 10 (השביעי, "the seventh day"; see Gen. R. ix.; Pesiḳ. R. 23). Indeed, to a certain extent Friday was included in the Sabbath legislation. Everybody was expected to rise very early on that day in order to make the purchases necessary for a worthy celebration of the Sabbath (Shab. 117b; Oraḥ Ḥayyim, 250); the greater the outlay the greater the merit (Yer. Sanh. viii. 2). Personal participation in various preparations for the meals was recommended; indeed, many among the most learned were remembered as having proudly shared in such preparations (Shab. 119a; Ḳid. 41a; Oraḥ Ḥayyim, *l.c.*). According to one of the ten ordinances of Ezra, Jewish women were advised to bake bread early on Friday to supply the poor (B. Ḳ. 82a).

Friday Preparation.

The details of the toilet, such as the dressing of hair and paring of finger-nails, were attended to before the advent of the Sabbath (Shab. 25b, 31a; Sanh. 95a; Beẓah 27b; Oraḥ Ḥayyim, 260). Workaday garments were exchanged for better Sabbath clothes (Shab. 119a; B. Ḳ. 32b; Oraḥ Ḥayyim, 262). While it was still daylight the table was set (Shab. 119a; Oraḥ Ḥayyim, *l.c.*), and it became the custom to cover the table with a white cloth (Tos. Pes. 100b, *s.v.* "She'en"); this was held to be in memory of the manna, as was a certain favorite 'ereb Shabbat pie consisting of two layers of dough between which the meat was placed ("mulai" is the name given by MaHaRIL; Hilkot "Shabbat"). Two loaves of bread, also in allusion to the manna, were to be on the table (Shab. 117a; Ber. 39b; see Ḳiddush). Near dusk the head of the family would inquire: "Have you set aside the tithe, made the 'erub, and separated the ḥallah?" Upon receiving an affirmative answer, he would say: "Then light the lamp" (Oraḥ Ḥayyim, 260).

According to the Mishnah (Shab. i. 3), a tailor should not venture out near dusk with his needle (stuck in his coat); nor a writer of books with his pen; one should not read near the lamp, though children might do so under the supervision of the master. In fact, work was declared unpropitious after "minḥah" (construed to be the "minḥah gedolah," *i.e.*, thirty minutes after noon; Pes. 51b; Oraḥ Ḥayyim, 251). Yet this applied only to work for personal profit; such work as was styled "work of heaven," *i.e.*, work from a religious or some high, altruistic motive, was permitted. Long walks away from one's home on Friday were discountenanced (Oraḥ Ḥayyim, 249). Such work as could not be finished before the beginning of the Sabbath, but would "finish itself" during the Sabbath (as in the case of flax put into an oven to bleach), might be begun near dusk on 'ereb Shabbat (Oraḥ Ḥayyim, 252). So was it lawful to put food intended for the Sabbath where it would stay warm, though under certain conditions and precautions (Shab. 18b, 38a; Tos. *ib.*, s.v. "Shakaḥ Ḳederah"; "Or Zarua'," *s.v.* "'Ereb Shabbat," 9; "Shibbole ha-Leḳeṭ," p. 44 [57]; Oraḥ Ḥayyim, 253, 254, 257-259).

The lighting of the lamp was considered an obligation which had to be discharged before darkness set in (Shab. 25b, 31a; "Yad," Shabbat, v. 1). This duty could be deputed to a non-Jew (Oraḥ Ḥayyim, 261), but so essential was the Sabbath light considered to a joyful celebration that one was advised to beg for the oil if necessary ("Yad," *l.c.*). A benediction was prescribed (Tos. Shab. 25b, *s.v.* "Ḥobah"; R. Tam, in "Sefer ha-Yashar," § 622; "Yad," *l.c.*; Ber. R. xi., lxv.; Pesiḳ. R. 21). Men and women alike were under this obligation, though its discharge generally fell upon the women ("Yad," *l.c.* v. 3). Some rabbis demanded that at least two lamps should be lighted, one to express the "zakor" (remember) of Ex. xx., and the other the "shamor" (observe) of Deut. v. (Shab. 33b). The Sabbath meal might be eaten only where the lamp was burning (Shab. 25b; Tos. *ib.*, s.v. "Hadlaḳah"). Explicit directions are given concerning the material for the wick, the kind of oil that was lawful, the manner of lighting the lamp, and how far one might profit from the light of the Sabbath lamp for reading and other purposes (Shab. ii. 1; "Yad," *l.c.* v.). Later authorities question whether lighting the lamp marked the beginning of the Sabbath rest, or whether Sabbath did not set in until after the prayers had been recited and Ḳiddush performed (see "Tania Rabbati," ed. Warsaw, p. 36a). In Palestine the approach of the Sabbath was announced by six trumpet-

The Sabbath Lamp.

blasts, with an interval after each blast, to give workers a succession of warnings to cease from their labors (Oraḥ Ḥayyim, 256; "Yad," *l.c.* v. 18 *et seq.*).

One of the solicitudes of rabbinical law was to enforce the exceptional character of the Sabbath as a day of rejoicing and good cheer; hence on Friday no sumptuous repast was to be eaten, not even at a wedding, in order that all might anticipate the Sabbath meal with avidity. Some of the pious even went to the length of fasting during Friday in order to whet their appetite (Oraḥ Ḥayyim, 249). For this reason, most of the people being hungry, the service in the synagogue on the eve of Sabbath was shortened; the reader, instead of reciting the tefillah, gave an epitome of it (Ber. 21a, 29a). According to Shab. ii. 1, the "Bameh Madliḳin" was read (see "Sefer ha-Manhig" and "Kol Bo"). Another reason for abbreviating the service was that evil spirits were said to roam about on this evening in greater numbers than on other evenings (comp. Rashi, "Sefer ha-Pardes"; Pes. 112b).

The Mishnah (Shab. vii. 2) enumerates thirty-nine principal classes of prohibited actions, these "abot" (lit. "fathers" or "chief categories") comprehending, when developed casuistically, a large variety of "toledot" (lit. "offspring" or "derivatives"). The number mentioned has been recognized as conventional even by Talmudists, the list as given containing virtual duplications, while certain kinds of work are clearly omitted (Shab. 74a).

The Thirty-nine Prohibited Acts.

The explanation is that whatever was done in the erection of the Tabernacle in the desert was classified as "principal," even if this rendered certain duplications necessary (*ib.*). This number is derived from the phrase אלה הדברים ("These are the words") in Ex. xxxv. 1 (Yer. Shab. 9b; Shab. 70a; Num. R. xviii.; Tan., Ḳoraḥ), the numerical value of אלה being 36; and as "debarim" is plural it must signify at least "two," while the article prefixed indicates that it stands for "three" (36 + 3 = 39). The misreading in Tan., Ḳoraḥ, where מלקות ("beatings") appears for מלאכות ("labors"), discloses the true nature of the number. "Forty," in Hebrew, denotes the extreme number or quantity in the connection in which it is used; for instance, "forty" lashes means the utmost number of lashes that may be inflicted in any given case. Hence, in order to remain within the limit, forty less one was fixed upon as the greatest number of lashes that might be inflicted upon the culprit. The mishnah in regard to the classes of prohibited actions follows the precedent, and borrows the phraseology ("forty, less one") used in regard to flagellation. See SABBATH LAWS.

Maimonides ("Yad," Shabbat, vii.) has the same enumeration, though in different order and with verbal changes, and with the substitution of "ruling [the hide] with lines" for the "salting it" of the Mishnah. According to Driver (Hastings, "Dict. Bible," iv. 320, note †), Margoliouth (in "Expositor," Nov., 1900, pp. 336 *et seq.*) cites, from an unedited Persian manuscript of the eleventh century, a catalogue of thirty-eight forbidden acts containing many variants from the Mishnah. An examination of the thirty-nine discloses that they comprise only the agricultural and industrial occupations as known in the mishnaic period (Löw, "Graphische Requisiten," ii. 28). But these thirty-nine principals expanded into 1,521 (= 39 × 39) derivatives (Yer. Shab. vii. 2); though even before R. Johanan b. Nappaḥa and R. Simeon ben Laḳish, after three and a half years' study of the Sabbath laws, had made this discovery, a mishnah in Ḥagigah (i. 8) had characterized these amplifications as "mountains suspended by a hair."

A few examples may serve to illustrate the method and system of this expansion. The general principle being given that "knots shall not be tied or untied," it was necessary to determine the kinds of knots that were proscribed. This led to the declaration that a camel-driver's or boatman's knot was intended; or a knot that could not be untied with one hand. Knots might be tied by a woman on articles of dress, or in packing articles of food. A pail might be fastened with a band, but not with a rope. Micrological as all this seems at first glance, closer inspection discloses the sound underlying principle that work done on Sabbath to save labor on another day renders guilty. Permanent knots, says R. Judah, are prohibited (Maimonides, "Yad," *l.c.* x., says "professional knots"; comp. Shab. 111a,

Underlying Principle of Preparation.

112b). This is apparent also from the provision that one may not, on the Sabbath, prepare the couch for the following evening (Shab. iii., xv.).

The things that might be saved from a conflagration constituted another solicitude of rabbinical Sabbath legislation. Sacred books, no matter in what language they might be written, might be saved, though on this point, and as to whether the books of Christians, as containing the name of God, were included, some controversies are reported (Shab. xvi. 1, 115a). Non-Jews were invited to help in such cases. Of course, it was not lawful to resort to the usual method of putting out the fire if no life were endangered ("Yad," *l.c.* xii. 3); but indirect means might be resorted to, such as covering with a hide or making a barrier by piling up vessels (Shab. xvi. 5).

But the injunction against carrying received the greatest attention. Territories were classified under four heads ("reshuyot"; Shab. 6a): (1) "Reshut ha-yaḥid": To this belonged an elevation ten spans in height and four by four or more in width; an excavation ten spans deep and four or more in width; a space enclosed by four walls ten spans high and four wide, no matter what its area, if intended for dwelling purposes; a city walled in and with gates shut at night; or covered passages with three enclosures, the fourth being a board; a house and courtyard used for dwelling purposes ("Yad," *l.c.* xiv. 1). (2) "Karmalit": A heap from three to ten spans in height and four by four in width; a corresponding excavation or depression; an area enclosed by four walls three to ten spans in height; a corner adjoining the "reshut ha-rabbim" (the public domain), with three walls on three sides and the public reshut on the fourth (*e.g.*, a covered passage without board or beam on the fourth side). (3) The public domain: Deserts, towns, market-places, and roads at least fifteen cubits wide. (4) "Maḳom paṭur": A free, open space, *i.e.*, a place less than four by four spans in width and three or more spans in height; what is less than three in height is considered the earth, so that thorn-bushes in the public domain, if less than four by four in width, belong to this class ("Yad," *l.c.*). For the effect of the 'Erub see article.

Another consideration involved in this injunction is as to what one may wear abroad on the Sabbath. Arms, certain kinds of sandals, signet-rings in the case of women, plain rings in that of the men (though women were cautioned against wearing these ornaments at all), and many more things in connection with the toilet, were under the ban (see "Yad," *l.c.* xix.). Under certain conditions the head-dress might be considered as a form of building, and therefore prohibited on the Sabbath (Yer. Shab. 12c, where plaiting is regarded as building). Later literature on the toilet for the Sabbath is very extensive, and historically valuable as showing masculine and feminine customs of attire ("Shibbole ha-Leḳeṭ," pp. 38 *et seq.*). It may be noted that in decisions made in the Middle Ages it is assumed that the Jews had at that time no regular reshut ha-rabbim.

Sabbath Garb.

The cautions against wearing jewels and similar ornaments were not inspired by Puritanical moods or views. The Sabbath was always and essentially a day of rejoicing. Hence fasting was forbidden, even for half a day (Ta'an. iii. 7; Yer. Ta'an. 67a; Yer. Ned. 40d; Judith viii. 6). Mourning was interrupted by the Sabbath (M. Ḳ. v. 3).

The technical term for suspensions of the Sabbath is "doḥin et ha-Shabbat" (push aside or set back the Sabbath). For a higher duty, that of observing the Sabbath was held in abeyance. A priest might violate the Sabbath in the discharge of his sacerdotal work at the altar, or while performing the sacrificial rite, or any other function, assigned to him. For "en Shabbat ba-miḳdash" the Sabbath law is not applicable to the service in the Temple (Pes. 65a). Acts necessary for the Passover are not affected by the prohibitions (Pes. vi. 1, 2). The blowing of the shofar is permitted (R. H. iv. 1). A Levite may tie a broken string on his instrument while performing in the Temple ('Er. x. 13). Circumcision also takes precedence of the Sabbath, though whatever preparations for this rite can be completed previously should not be left for the Sabbath (Shab. xviii. 3, xix. 1-3). But whenever there was danger to life, or where a Jewish woman was in the throes of childbirth, the Sabbath law was

Suspensions of the Sabbath.

set aside (Shab. xviii. 3). In the case of one dangerously sick, whatever was ordered by a competent physician might be done regardless of the Sabbath; but it had to be done by pious and prominent Jews, not by non-Jews ("Yad," *l.c.* ii. 1–3). It was forbidden to delay in such a case, for it was intended that man should live by the Law, and not die through it (Yoma 85a, b; Sanh. 74a; 'Ab. Zarah 27b, 54a; Mek., Ki Tissa). Water might be heated and the lamps lighted. In accidents, too, every help might be extended. Some restrictions were placed on the choice of fluids to relieve toothache or of ointments to relieve pain in the loins (Shab. xiv. 4). A sprained member might not have cold water poured over it, but it might be bathed in the usual way (Shab. xxii. 6).

It was permissible to take animals to water, provided they carried no load ("Shibbole ha-Leḳeṭ," p. 74, where it is explained that covers necessary for the comfort of the animal are not considered a load). Water might be drawn into a trough so that an animal might go and drink of its own accord ('Er. 20b). If an animal has fallen into a well, it is provided with food until Sabbath is over, if this is possible; but if it is not, covers, cushions, and mattresses are placed under it so that it may get out without further aid; the pain of the animal is sufficient excuse ("ẓa'ar ba'ale ḥayyim") for this Sabbath violation. But the animal might not be drawn out by men, a precaution taken in those cases where animals had gone astray and had to be driven back into the courtyard ("Yad," *l.c.* xxv. 26; Shab. 128b; B. M. 32b; Ex. xxiii. 5).

In view of the spirit of philanthropy that, as Maimonides constantly asserts ("Yad," *l.c.* ii. 3), underlies the Law, it is difficult to understand the controversies with Jesus attributed to the Pharisees in the New Testament. In Matt. xii. 1, Mark ii. 23, Luke vi. 1, the disciples plucked and rubbed the ears of corn and thus violated a rabbinical Sabbath ordinance ("Yad," *l.c.* viii. 3; Yer. Shab. 10a; Shab. x. 7). But the defense of Jesus assumes that the disciples were in danger of dying of starvation; he charges his critics with having neglected charity. This must imply that they had not provided the Sabbath meals for the poor (Peah viii. 7). Thus he answers their charge with another. For the act of his disciples there was some excuse; for their neglect to provide the Sabbath meals there was none.

In the cases mentioned in Matt. xii. 11 and Luke xiv. 5 the "drawing up" of the animal would be an innovation, but the provision made by the rabbinical law for the comfort and possible escape of the animal is also a violation of the Sabbath. In the instance of the blind man whose sight was restored (John ix. 6) the important point is not the fact that Jesus broke the Sabbath law by kneading (Shab. xxiv. 3), for the provisions in regard to pain in the eyes ("Yad," *l.c.* xxi.; Yer. Shab. xiv.) have no bearing on this case; the point involved is rather the use of magic in the restoration of sight (comp. Shab. 67a; Sanh. 101a). In all cures effected by Jesus this was the matter at issue, not the incidental violation of the Sabbath, which might be justified on the ground that life was in danger.

New Testament Examples.

In John v. 2 *et seq.* the taking up of the bed would constitute the violation. But possibly "bed" here is a misreading for "staff" ("miṭṭah" instead of "maṭṭeh"). A "lame" person may carry his crutch or staff (Oraḥ Ḥayyim, 301). If, moreover, the reading "bed" must be retained, for which there is a strong presumption, another explanation may be advanced. "Take up thy bed" may be a misapprehension of the Aramaic "ṭol we-ẓe," the well-known formula for bidding one depart, "ṭol" being construed as "pick up" (naturally, therefore, "thy couch"), when in reality it means "pick thyself up," or "walk away." Jesus' saying that the "Sabbath was made for man, and not man for the Sabbath" (Mark ii. 27) is a free translation of the Mekilta's comment on Ex. xxxi. 13—"The Sabbath is given over unto you, you are not delivered unto the Sabbath."

A brief description of the Sabbath celebration under the rabbinical system may show that even with all these minute constructions the day was a bringer of unmixed joy. The preparations for the Sabbath having been given in detail in a previous section, they need not be repeated here. At the conclusion of the services in the synagogue with the orphans' "Ḳaddish," the at-

Sabbath Celebration.

tendants hurried to their homes, where upon crossing the threshold they recited the prayer, "Peace be with ye, ye ministering angels," etc. (comp. Shab. 119b, for the reason why the angels were apostrophized). This prayer was preceded by the greeting "Good Shabbat," which was also exchanged on the way with passers-by; it was followed by the recital, on the part of the husband, of Prov. xxxi. 10 *et seq.*, verses laudatory of the good housewife; after which the younger members of the family were blessed by their parents; the elder sons having received this benediction in the synagogue, where the rabbi was wont to bless all the young people of the congregation. Every family had, as a rule, a stranger as its guest, who had been to the synagogue and had been invited to participate in the celebration of the Sabbath. Students ate at the table of their masters (Güdemann, "Gesch." iii. 102). The meal on the eve of Sabbath began with the "Ḳiddush." The meal itself was sumptuous, fish being a favorite dish (Abrahams, "Jewish Life in the Middle Ages," p. 150). The tableware was often of the finest and costliest; there was hardly a family that did not possess its gold or silver drinking-cup for the "Ḳiddush" and an ornamental seven-branched lamp for Friday night (Abrahams, *l.c.* p. 146). After the meal, the Ashkenazim throughout the year, the Sephardim only in winter and summer, sang the "zemirot ha-Shabbat" (idem, *l.c.* pp. 133 *et seq.*). This was followed by a grace containing a special reference to the Sabbath, after which all retired.

On Sabbath the people slept longer than on week-days (Oraḥ Ḥayyim, 281; comp. Ex. xviii. 4, "in the morning," with verse 9, "uba-yom ha-Shabbat," from which the inference is drawn tha on week-days one should rise early in the morning; on Sabbath, when the day is well advanced). After rising and repeating the usual morning prayers, they repaired to the synagogue to recite the "shaḥarit," ending with "ab ha-raḥamim"; after this the Torah roll was taken out and the proper "parashah" read, for which seven men were called up to the pulpit. "Ḳaddish" following, the "mafṭir" was called up, special benedictions were recited, the Torah returned to the ark, and, finally, the "Musaf" pronounced. The services ended, the second Sabbath meal

Sabbath Prayers.

was commenced. Hands were washed and then the blessing was recited over wine and bread. The meal included the "shallet" (dish kept warm overnight in the congregation's oven) and fruit. After this meal "zemirot" were sung, and, grace being said, the next hours were devoted to study or discourses on the Law. Gilds ("ḥebrot") were sometimes organized for this purpose (Abrahams, *l.c.* p. 327). The discourses were often largely attended (see Maimonides' letter in Abrahams, *l.c.* p. 236). The Rabbis regarded the Sabbath as a befitting occasion to exhort their congregations. The "elders" are bidden to do this by a "taḳḳanah" contained in "Ḥuḳḳe ha-Torah" (published by Güdemann, *l.c.* i. 271), especially that the Torah may again come to its own. People of less serious mood would walk about, or be found dancing or gossiping in the yard of the synagogue (Abrahams, *l.c.* p. 381). Music was not regarded as incompatible with the character of the day, and Christian musicians often played gratuitously (see Mordecai on Beẓah v.; MaHaRIL, Hilkot "'Erube Ḥaẓerot").

Chess was a recreation largely indulged in on Sabbath, the figures being made of silver in honor of the day. Some of the rabbis stipulated that no money should change hands at the play (Löw, "Lebensalter," p. 328). The Minḥah service interrupted studies, but this prayer having been concluded, the discussions were resumed (Pirḳe Abot especially was studied in the summer). After Minḥah the third meal, which, however, was much lighter than the others, was served. The Sabbath concluded with the "Habdalah."

The Sabbath was often a refreshing oasis in the desert of persecution. Maimonides ("Moreh," ch. ii. 31) assigns both repose of body and the symbolization of God's existence as the reasons for its institution. Judah ha-Levi, a most scrupulous observer of the Law, while emphasizing the joyful character of the day, doubts that the Sabbath of the Christians and of the Mohammedans is as blessed as that of the Jews ("Cuzari," iii. 5, 9). His Sabbath hymns, as those of Ibn Ezra and of many others, among them being the "Lekah Dodi," attest the justice of Schechter's words concerning the Sabbath ("J. Q. R." iii. 763): "Notwithstanding rabbinical micrology, the

Sabbath was a day of delight, whose coming was looked for with fond anticipations, whose parting was sped with grateful regrets."

In the synagogal services the joyous note alone was heard. In fact, the life of the Jews is ample testimony that the Sabbath under the Law was anything but irksome, gloomy, and fatal to spirituality. Karaitic literalism succeeded in turning the Sabbath into a burden; but rabbinical legalism, with its legal fictions, avoided this. The injunction not to kindle a fire might have worked hardship; but the institution of the Sabbath goy met the exigency, though Meïr Rothenburg and Solomon ben Adret scrupled to avail themselves of this loophole. Even the provisions regulating partnerships with and service of non-Jews with reference to the Sabbath law may be called legal fictions; they are of an order of juridical reasoning which is not foreign to modern English and American courts. Rabbinical law accommodated itself to the demands of life.

XLII

Sabbath And Sunday

SABBATH AND SUNDAY: A brief consideration is desirable as to why and when the keeping of the seventh day as the Sabbath ceased among Christian churches. That Jesus and his disciples kept the seventh day, and without vital departures from Pharisaic usages, is indisputable. The question of Sabbath observance first became acute under Paul, with the rise of the non-Jewish Christian communities. The Petrine, or Judæo-Christian, party insisted on rigid adherence to the Jewish law. It scorned the looser practises of the converts from without Israel. To this Col. ii. 16 *et seq.* has reference; Paul protests against judging the piety of the neophytes "in meat, or in drink, or in respect of a feast-day . . . or a Sabbath-day" (R. V.). He protests with greater bitterness in Gal. iv. 9–11, where observance of days is denounced as a return to the "weak and beggarly elements." In Rom. xiv. 5 *et seq.* it is assumed that whether one day or another is distinguished, or whether all are regarded as equally sacred, is a matter of indifference: every man must decide for himself. Thus while the Petrine partizans continued to assemble for worship on the Sabbath (Acts ii. 1, iii. 1, *et al.*), in non-Jewish Christian circles the first day of the week came to be marked by longer worship than usual and by collections of gifts (I Cor. xvi. 2; comp. Acts xx. 7). The name κυριακὴ ἡμέρα (= "Lord's day") first occurs in Rev. i. 10, where it may mean the day of judgment (see DAY OF THE LORD); it is next found in Ignatius, "Ad Magnesianos" (§ 9). Pliny testifies to the fact that the Christians assembled on "a fixed day" ("stato die"; "Epistolæ," x. 96).

Early Christian Practise.

The author of the "Epistle of Barnabas" adduces the occurrence of the Resurrection on the first day as the reason for the observance of this "true day" (xv.). In the meantime the attitude of the Roman authorities had become intermittently hostile to the Jews; and after the rebellion under Hadrian it became a matter of vital importance for such as were not Jews to avoid exposing themselves to suspicion (Huidekoper, "Judaism at Rome"). The observance of the Sabbath was one of the most noticeable indications of Judaism. Hence, while in the first Christian century more or less regard and tolerance for the Jewish day were shown in Rome, even by non-Jewish Christians, in the second century the contrary became the rule (Justin Martyr, "Dial. cum Tryph." ii., § 28). In the East, however, less opposition was shown to Jewish institutions. Saturday and Sunday both were celebrated by "abstaining from fasting and by standing while praying" (Rheinwald, "Archäologie," § 62). In the West, especially where Roman influence dominated, Saturday was turned into a fast-day (Huidekoper, *ib.* pp. 343-344). The name "Sunday" is used for the first time by Justin Martyr ("Apologies," i. 67) in accommodation to a Roman nomenclature, but with reference to the circumstances that the light was created on the first day (noticed also in the Midrash; Gen. R. iii.: "ten crowns adorned the first day") and that the "light of the world" rose from the night of the grave on the first day of the week. The Christians, accordingly, were obliged to defend themselves against the charge of worshiping the sun (Tertullian, "Apologeticus," xvi.). The celebration of two days (by the Judæo-Christians?) is attested by Eusebius ("Hist. Eccl." iii. 37) and by the "Apostolic Constitutions," which advise the keeping of Saturday as a memorial of the Creation, and of Sunday, the Lord's day, in memory of the Resurrection (ii. 59).

Two Sabbaths Kept in the Second Century.

Originally, then, Sunday and Sabbath were kept sharply distinct. But, like the Jewish Sabbath, Sunday was deemed not merely a holiday, but a holy day, and hence fasting thereon was interdicted (Tertullian, "De Corona Militis," § 3). Ease of mind (*εὐφροσύνη*, which corresponds to "naḥat ruaḥ";

"Epistle of Barnabas," *l.c.*) was the proper condition for the day. One should not kneel at prayer (Irenæus, "Fragm. de Paschate"; "Apostolic Constitutions," *l.c.*); the standing posture, being at first a protest against mourning and ascetic rites (such as were forbidden on the Jewish Sabbath), came to be explained as suggestive of the Resurrection. Tertullian would have all work cease on Sunday as interfering with the proper mental condition, preoccupation and worry being incompatible with joy ("De Oratione," xxiii.).

Down to the sixth century the solicitude of the Church authorities was to prevent what they called the "Judaizing" of the Sunday by the rigorous prohibition of riding, cooking, etc. Even Constantine the Great, when he enacted the first Sunday law in 321, did not refer to Old Testament injunctions, but wished to have the day distinguished and kept sacred merely as the "Sun's day." This first decree was supplemented by orders concerning military exercise, but in general it affected only the courts and the markets (Eusebius, "De Vita Constantini," iv. 18–20, quoted in Herzog-Plitt, "Real-Encyc." xiv. 429). Still, such decrees virtually sanctioned the recognition of Sunday as the sole day of rest, the "Sabbath," and thus consummated the tendency that had been developing in the Christian Church for nearly two centuries to substitute the day of Jesus' resurrection for the Jewish Sabbath. In this way Sunday was given an anti-Jewish significance in accordance with Paul's contention that the Resurrection abrogated completely the old dispensation and the Law.

First Sunday Law, 321.

This aspect of Sunday has been emphasized, and with considerable force, in the discussions more or less continuously provoked in modern Jewry by the increasing neglect of Sabbath observance in the countries where the keeping of Sunday is so strongly established in industrial and social custom that the Jew has been practically compelled to follow the general usage. A few leaders (Holdheim, Samuel Hirsch) proposed to apply to this problem the principles of Reform followed in the readjustment of other religious practises to changed conditions. It is recognized that the Sabbath as the symbol of the full content of Judaism is a fundamental institution; but the argument has been advanced that astronomy discredits the assumption of a universal cosmic seventh day (comp. Judah ha-Levi, "Cuzari," ii. 20); and the notion of God's "resting" on a certain day the beginning and ending of which are determined by terrestrial phenomena, is regarded as tinged with mythology. Six days of labor are prescribed as clearly in the Sabbath law as is one day of rest; both must be religiously observed, which is impossible under prevailing conditions. Furthermore, the phraseology of the commandment does not fix the six days (the definite article is not prefixed to ימים); the definite article before "seventh" implies merely that the day referred to is that following any group of six consecutive days; the phrase "the seventh day" is found also in the Pessah law (Deut. xvi. 8), where it is evident that no fixed day of the week is intended.

Jewish Attitude Toward Sunday.

No obligation should be imposed that is impossible of fulfilment to the majority (B. B. 60b; Maimonides, "Yad," Mamrim, ii. 5). To the Sabbath may be applied Ps. cxix. 126, in the sense often given it (Ber. ix. 5; Yer. Ber. vii. 17; Giṭ. 60a), for now the Sabbath is "remembered," not "observed," just as Pesiḳ. R. 23 asserts is the case with non-Jews. The only consideration to be weighed is the unity of Israel. If all or most Jews were to observe Sabbath on the so-called first day in the manner in which it should be observed, namely, by abstention from work, the difficulty would be met without loss to true religion. This in substance is the contention of Samuel Hirsch and others. Whatever may be the merits of the argument, it has had no practical result. Supplementary Sunday services have been introduced in some congregations, but the facts that Sunday has an anti-Jewish implication and that in the past many allowed themselves to be martyred for the honor of the Sabbath have never failed to arouse both the indifferent and the zealous.

XLIII

Sacrifice

SACRIFICE: The act of offering to a deity for the purpose of doing homage, winning favor, or securing pardon; that which is offered or consecrated. The late generic term for "sacrifice" in Hebrew is קרבן, the verb being הקריב, used in connection with all kinds of sacrifices.

——**Biblical Data:** It is assumed in the Scriptures that the institution of sacrifice is coeval with the race. Abel and Cain are represented as the first among men to sacrifice; and to them are attributed the two chief classes of oblations: namely, the vegetable or bloodless, and the animal or blood-giving (Gen. iv. 3, 4). After the Flood, Noah offered of "every clean beast, and of every clean fowl" (*ib.* viii. 20). The building of altars by the Patriarchs is frequently recorded (*ib.* xii. 7, 8; xiii. 4, 18; xxi. 33; xxvi. 25; xxxiii. 20; xxxv. 7). Abraham offers a sacrifice at which YHWH makes a covenant with him (*ib.* xv.). In the history of Jacob a sacrifice is mentioned as a ratification of a treaty (*ib.* xxxi. 54). He sacrifices also when he leaves Canaan to settle in Egypt (*ib.* xlvi. 1). Abraham had been or believed he had been given the command to sacrifice his son (*ib.* xxii.). These ancient offerings included not only the bloodless kind (*ib.* iv. 3), but also holocausts (*ib.* viii. 20, xxii. 13) and animal thank-offerings (*ib.* xxxi. 54, xlvi. 1).

Place of Sacrifice.

The primitive altar was made of earth (comp. Ex. xx. 24) or of unhewn stones (*ib.* xx. 25; Deut. xxvii. 5), and was located probably on an elevation (see ALTAR; HIGH PLACE). The story in Genesis proceeds on the theory that wherever the opportunity was presented for sacrifice there it was offered (Gen. viii. 20, xxxi. 54; comp. Ex. xxiv. 4). No one fixed place seems to have been selected (Ex. xx. 24, where the Masoretic text, אזכיר = "I will have my 'zeker' [= "remembrance"]," and Geiger's emendation, תזכיר = "Thou wilt place my 'zeker,'" bear out this inference). This freedom to offer sacrifices at any place recurs in the eschatological visions of the Later Prophets (Isa. xix. 19, 21; Zeph. ii. 11; Mal. i. 11; Zech. xiv. 20, 21), thus confirming the thesis of Gunkel ("Schöpfung und Chaos") that the end is always a reproduction of the beginning.

Under Moses, according to the Pentateuch, this freedom to offer sacrifices anywhere and without the ministrations of the appointed sacerdotal agents disappears. The proper place for the oblations was to be "before the door of the tabernacle," where the altar of burnt offerings stood (Ex. xl. 6), and where YHWH met His people (*ib.* xxix. 42; Lev. i. 3; iv. 4; xii. 6; xv. 14, 29; xvi. 7; xvii. 2–6; xix. 21), or simply "before YHWH" (Lev. iii. 1, 7, 12; ix. 2, 4, 5), and later in Jerusalem in the Temple (Deut. xii. 5–7, 11, 12). That this law was not observed the historical books disclose, and the Prophets never cease complaining about its many violations (see HIGH PLACE). The Book of Joshua (xxiv. 14) presumes that while in Egypt the Hebrews had become idolaters. The Biblical records report very little concerning the religious conditions among those held in Egyptian bondage. The supposition, held for a long time, that while in the land of Goshen the Israelites had become adepts in the Egyptian sacrificial cult, lacks confirmation by the Biblical documents. The purpose of the Exodus as given in Ex. viii. 23 (A. V. 25) is to enable the people to sacrifice to their God. But the only sacrifice commanded in Egypt (*ib.* xii.) was that of the paschal lamb (see PASSOVER SACRIFICE). In the account of the Hebrews' migrations in the desert Jethro offers a sacrifice to YHWH; Moses, Aaron, and the elders participating therein (*ib.* xviii. 12). Again, at the conclusion of the revelation on Sinai (*ib.* xxiv. 5), Moses offers up all kinds of sacrifices, sprinkling some of the blood on the altar. At the consecration of the Tabernacle the chiefs of the tribes are said to have offered, in addi-

The Paschal Sacrifice.

tion to vessels of gold and silver, 252 animals (Num. vii. 12–88); and it has been calculated that the public burnt offerings amounted annually to no less than 1,245 victims (Kalish, "Leviticus," p. 20). No less than 50,000 paschal lambs were killed at the Passover celebration of the second year after the Exodus (Num. ix. 1–14).

According to the Book of Joshua, after the conquest of Canaan the Tabernacle was established at Shiloh (Josh. xviii. 1, xix. 51, xxii. 9). During the periods of the Judges and of Samuel it was the central sanctuary (Judges xviii. 31; I Sam. iii. 3, xiv. 3; comp. Jer. vii. 12), where at certain seasons of the year recurring festivals were celebrated and the Hebrews assembled to perform sacrifices and vows (Judges xxi. 12, 19; I Sam. i. 3, 21; ii. 19). But it seems that the people assembled also at Shechem—where was a sanctuary of YHWH (Josh. xxiv. 1, 26)—as well as at Mizpeh in Gilead (Judges xi. 11), at Mizpeh in Benjamin (*ib.* xx. 1), at Gilgal (I Sam. xi. 15, xiii. 8, xv. 21), at Hebron (II Sam. v. 3), at Beth-el, and at Beer-sheba (Amos iv. 4, v. 5, viii. 14). They sacrificed at Bochim and Beth-el (Judges iii. 5, xxi. 4). Private sacrifices, also, in the homes of the families, appear to have been in vogue, *e.g.*, in the house of Jesse in Beth-lehem (I Sam. xx. 6), of Ahithophel at Giloh (II Sam. xv. 12), and of Job (Job i. 5, xlii. 8). Assisting Levites are mentioned (Judges xvii. 4–13). Gideon offered at Ophrah (*ib.* vi. 11–20, 26 *et seq.*); Manoah, at Zorah (*ib.* xiii. 16, 19, 20); Samuel, at Mizpeh, Ramah, Gilgal, and Beth-lehem (I Sam. vii. 9, 10, 17; ix. 12, 13; x. 8; xi. 15; xvi. 25); Saul, at Gilgal (*ib.* xiii. 9 *et seq.*) and during his pursuit of the Philistines (*ib.* xiv. 32–35); David, on the thrashing-floor of Araunah (II Sam. vi. 17, xxiv. 25); Absalom, at Hebron (*ib.* xv. 7–9); Adonijah, near En-rogel (I Kings i. 9); Solomon, "in high places" (*ib.* iii. 2, 3); and Elijah, in his contest with the prophets of Baal, on Mount Carmel (*ib.* xviii.). Naaman took Palestinian soil with him because he desired to offer sacrifice to YHWH in Syria (II Kings v. 17, 19). The Books of Chronicles throw a different light on this period. If their reports are to be accepted, the sacrificial services were conducted throughout in strict conformity with the Mosaic code (I Chron. xv. 26, xxvi. 8-36; II Chron. i. 2-6, ii.

Private Sacrifices.

3, xiii. 11). Enormous numbers of sacrifices are reported in them (II Chron. xv. 11; xxix. 32, 33).

In the Solomonic Temple, Solomon himself (though not a priest) offered three times every year burnt offerings and thank-offerings and incense (I Kings ix. 25); he also built high places. Down to the destruction of the Temple, kings, priests, and even prophets, besides the people, are among the inveterate disregarders of the sacrificial ritual of the Pentateuch, worshiping idols and sacrificing to them; *e.g.*, Jeroboam with his golden calves at Dan and Beth-el (I Kings xii. 28; comp. II Kings xvii. 16), Ahimelech at Nob (I Sam. xxi. 2-10), and even Aaron (Ex. xxxii. 1-6, comp. Neh. ix. 18). BA-AL was worshiped (Hos. ii. 10, 15; II Kings iii. 2; x. 26, 27; xi. 18; Judges vi. 25; Jer. vii. 9, xi. 13, xxxii. 29), as were ASTARTE, BAAL-BERITH, BAAL-PEOR, BAAL-ZEBUB, MOLOCH, and other false gods, in the cult of which not only animal and vegetable but even human sacrifices (see SACRIFICE, CRITICAL VIEW) were important features.

The attitude of the literary prophets toward sacrifice manifests no enthusiasm for sacrificial worship. Hosea declares in the name of YHWH: "I desired mercy, and not sacrifice; and the knowledge of YHWH more than burnt offerings" (Hos. vi. 6; comp. *ib.* viii. 13; ix. 3, 4; xiv. 3). Amos proclaims: "I [YHWH] hate, I despise your feast-days; . . . if you offer me burnt offerings and your bloodless offerings, I will not accept them nor will I regard the thank-offerings of your fat beasts, . . . but let justice flow like water" (Amos v. 21–24, Hebr.; comp. iv. 4, 5). He goes so far as to doubt the existence of sacrificial institutions in the desert (*ib.* v. 25). Isaiah is not less strenuous in rejecting a ritualistic sacrificial cult (Isa. i. 11–17). Jeremiah takes up the burden (Jer. vi. 19, 20; comp. xxxi. 31–33). He, like Amos, in expressing his scorn for the burnt offerings and other slaughtered oblations, takes occasion to deny that the fathers had been commanded concerning these things when they came forth from Egypt (*ib.* vii. 21 *et seq.*). Malachi, a century later, complains of the wrong spirit which is manifest at the sacrifices (Mal. i. 10). Ps. l. emphasizes most beautifully the prophetic conviction that thanksgiv-

Attitude of Prophets.

ing alone is acceptable, as does Ps. lxix. 31, 32. Deutero-Isaiah (xl. 16) suggests the utter inadequacy of sacrifices. "To do justice and judgment is more acceptable to YHWH than sacrifice" is found in I Sam. xv. 22 (Hebr.) as a censure of Saul; and gnomic wisdom is not without similar confession (Prov. xv. 8; xxi. 3, 27; xxviii. 9; Eccl. iv. 17). Some passages assert explicitly that sacrifices are not desired (Ps. xl. 7–9, li. 17–19). Micah's rejection of sacrificial religion has become the classical definition of ethical monotheism (Mic. vi. 6–8). Other Psalms and prophetic utterances, however, deplore the cessation of sacrificial services at the Temple and look forward to their reinstitution (Ps. li. 20, 21; Joel ii. 12, 13; Jer. xxxi. 14; xxxiii. 11, 17, 18). The apocalyptic character of some of these predictions is not disputable, neither is that of Isa. xix. 21, lvi. 7, lx. 7. In Ezekiel's scheme of the restoration, also, the sacrifices receive very generous treatment (Ezek. xl.–xlviii.).

The Mosaic Sacrifices.

The Mosaic sacrificial scheme is for the most part set forth in Leviticus. The sacrifices ordained may be divided into the bloodless and the blood-giving kinds. This division takes into consideration the nature of the offering. But another classification may be made according to the occasion for which the oblation is brought and the sentiments and motives of the offerers. On this basis the sacrifices are divided into: (1) burnt offerings, (2) thank- or praise-offerings, (3) sin- or trespass-offerings, and (4) purificative offerings. Among the thank-offerings might be included the paschal lamb, the offering of the first-born, and the FIRST-FRUITS; in the category of sin-offerings, the jealousy-offering. As a rule, the burnt, the expiatory, and the purificative offerings were animal sacrifices, but in exceptional cases a cereal sin-offering was accepted or prescribed. Thank-offerings might consist either of animal or of vegetable oblations.

Animal sacrifices were generally accompanied by bloodless offerings, and in many cases by a libation of wine or a drink-offering also. Bloodless offerings were, however, brought alone; for instance, that of the showbread and the frankincense offering on the golden altar. Another classification might be (1) voluntary or free-will offerings (private holocausts and thank- or vow-offerings) and (2) compulsory or obligatory offerings (private and public praise-offerings, public holocausts, and others).

The sacrificial animals were required to be of the clean class (Gen. vii. 23; Lev. xi. 47, xiv. 4, xx. 25; Deut. xiv. 11, 20). Still, not all clean animals occur in the specifications of the offerings, for which were demanded mainly cattle from the herd or from the flock; viz., the bullock and the ox, the cow and the calf; the sheep, male or female, and the lamb; the goat, male or female, and the kid. Of fowls, turtle-doves and pigeons were to be offered, but only in exceptional cases as holocausts and sin-offerings; they were not accepted as thank- or praise-offerings nor as a public sacrifice. Fishes were altogether excluded. The bullock formed the burnt offering of the whole people on New Moon and holy days, and for inadvertent transgressions; of the chiefs at the dedication of the Tabernacle; of the Levites at their initiation; and of private individuals in emergencies. It was the sin-offering for the community or the high priest, for the priests when inducted into office, and for the high priest on the Day of Atonement. In cases of peculiar joyfulness it was chosen for the thank-offering. The ram was presented as a holocaust or a thank-offering by the people or by their chiefs, the high priest or ordinary priests, and by the Nazarite, never by an individual layman. It was the ordinary trespass-offering for violation of property rights. The kid was the special animal for sin-offerings. It was permitted also for private burnt offerings and for thank-offerings; but it was never prescribed for public burnt offerings. The lamb was employed for the daily public holocausts, and very commonly for all private offerings of whatever character. The pigeon and turtle-dove served for burnt offerings and sin-offerings in cases of lustrations. They were allowed as private holocausts, and were accepted as sin-offerings from the poorer people and as purification-offerings; but they were excluded as thank-offerings, nor did they form part of the great public or festal sacrifices.

The Materials of Sacrifices.

The bloodless oblations consisted of vegetable products, chief among which were flour (in some cases roasted grains) and wine. Next in importance was oil. As accessories, frankincense and salt were required, the latter being added on nearly all occasions. Leaven and honey were used in a few instances only.

Concerning the qualification of the offerings, the Law ordained that the animals be perfect (Deut. xv. 21, xvii. 1; specified more in detail in Lev. xxii. 18–25), the blind, broken, maimed, ulcerous, scurvied, scabbed, bruised, crushed, and castrated being excluded. This injunction was applied explicitly to burnt (Lev. i. 3; ix. 2, 3; xxiii. 18), thank- (*ib.* iii. 1, 6; xxii. 21), and expiatory offerings (*ib.* iv. 3, 23, 28, 32; v. 15, 18, 25; ix. 2, 3; xiv. 10) and the paschal lamb (Ex. xii. 5). To offer a blemished animal was deemed sacrilegious (Deut. xvii. 1; Mal. i. 6, 7, 8, 9, 13). In most cases a male animal was required; but a female victim was prescribed in a few cases, as, for instance, that of the sin-offering of the ordinary Israelite. In other cases the choice between male and female was left open, *e.g.*, in private thank-offerings and offerings of the firstlings. For pigeons and turtle-doves no particular sex is mentioned.

Qualities of Offerings.

As to the age of the victims, none might be offered prior to the seventh day from birth (Lev. xxii. 27). Mother and young might not be slaughtered on the same day (*ib.* xxii. 28). The first-born males were to be killed within the first year (Deut. xv. 19 *et seq.*). Burnt offerings and sin- and thank-offerings were required to be more than one year old, as was the paschal lamb (Ex. xii. 5, xxix. 38; Lev. ix. 3; xii. 6; xiv. 10; xxiii. 12, 19; Num. vi. 12, 14; vii. 17, 23, 29; xv. 27; xxviii. 3, 9, 11, 19, 27). For doves and pigeons no age was set. Sometimes the sacrifice called for an animal that had neither done any work nor borne any yoke, *e.g.*, the RED HEIFER (Num. xix. 1–10; Deut. xxi. 3, 4). The animal was required to be the lawful property of the sacrificer (II Sam. xxiv. 24; Deut. xxviii. 19; Ezra vi. 9; vii. 17, 22; I Macc. x. 39; II Macc. iii. 3, ix. 16; Josephus, "Ant." xii. 3, § 3).

The ears of corn (Lev. ii. 14) presented as a first-fruits offering were required to be of the earlier and therefore better sort, the grains to be rubbed or beaten out; the flour, as a rule, of the finest quality and from the choicest cereal, wheat. The offering of the wife suspected of adultery was of common barley flour. As to quantity, at least one-tenth part of an ephah or an omer of flour was used. It was mixed with water, and in most cases was left unleavened; it was then made into dough and baked in loaves or thin cakes. The oil had to be pure white olive-oil from the unripe berries squeezed or beaten in a mortar. It was usually poured over the offering or mingled therewith, or it was brushed over the thin cakes. Sometimes, however, the offering was soaked in oil. The frankincense was white and pure. The wine is not described or qualified in the Law. "Shekar" is another liquid mentioned as a libation (Num. xxviii. 7); it must have been an intoxicating fermented liquor, and was prohibited to priests during service and to Nazarites. Salt was used with both the blood-giving and the bloodless sacrifices (Lev. ii. 13); its use is not further described. Leaven and honey were generally excluded, but the former was permitted for the first new bread offered on Pentecost and for the bread and cakes at every praise-offering; the latter, when offered as a first-fruits offering.

Liquid Sacrifices.

Of the necessary preparations the chief was "sanctification" (Joel i. 14; ii. 15, 16; iv. 9; Mic. iii. 5; Neh. iii. 1; Ps. xx.), consisting in bathing, washing, and change of garments, and in conjugal abstinence (Gen. xxxv. 2–4; Ex. xix. 10, 14, 15; xxxiii. 5, 6; Josh. iii. 5, vii. 13). These laws were amplified with reference to the officiating PRIEST (Ex. xxx. 17–21, xl. 30–32).

No particular time of the day is specified for sacrifices, except that the daily holocausts are to be killed "in the morning" and "between the two evenings" (Ex. xvi. 12; xxix. 39, 41; xxx. 8; Num. xxviii. 4).

Times of Sacrifice.

When the gift had been properly prepared, the offerer, whether man or woman, brought (Lev. iv. 4, 14; xii. 6; xiv. 23; xv. 29) it to the place where alone it was lawful to sacrifice—"before YHWH," or "to the door of the tent of meeting," *i.e.*, the court where the altar of burnt offering stood. To offer it elsewhere would have been shedding blood (Lev. xvii. 3–5, 8, 9). The injunction to offer in the proper place is repeated more especially in regard to the individual class of sacrifice (Lev. i. 3; iv. 4, 14; vi. 18; xii. 6; xiii. 2, 8, 12; xv. 29; xix. 21). The victim was killed "on the side of the altar [of holocausts] northward" (Lev. i. 11, iv. 24, vi. 18, vii. 2, xiv. 13). When the offering, if a quadruped, had been brought within the precincts of the sanctuary, and after examination had been found qualified, the offerer laid one hand upon the victim's head (Lev. i. 4; iii. 2, 8, 13; iv. 5, 15). On the scapegoat, the high priest laid both of his hands (*ib.* xvi. 21). This "laying on of hands" ("semikah") might not be performed by a substitute (Aaron and his sons laid hands on the sin- and burnt offerings killed on their own behalf; see Lev. viii. 14, 18). After the imposition of his hand, the offerer at once killed the animal. If presented by the community, the victim was immolated by one of the elders (*ib.* iv. 15). Priests might perform this act for the offering Israelites (II Chron. xxx. 15–17; xxxv. 10, 11), though the priestly function began only with the act of receiving the blood, or, in bloodless offerings, with the taking of a handful to be burned on the altar, while the Israelite himself poured over and mixed the oil. The priests invariably killed the doves or pigeons by wringing off their heads (Lev. i. 15, v. 8).

The Blood.

The utmost care was taken by the priest to receive the blood; it represented the life or soul. None but a circumcised Levite in a proper state of Levitical purity and attired in proper vestments might perform this act; so, too, the sprinkling of the blood was the exclusive privilege of the "priests, the sons of Aaron" (*ib.* i. 5, 11; iii. 2, 8, 13). Moses sprinkled it when Aaron and his sons were inducted; but this was exceptional (*ib.* viii. 15, 19, 23). In holocausts and thank-offerings the blood was sprinkled "round about upon the altar" (*ib.* i. 5, 11; iii. 2, 8, 13). In the sin-offering, the later (*ib.* vii. 2) practise seems to have been to put some of the blood on the horns of the brazen altar, or on those of the golden altar when that was used, or even on parts of the holy edifice (*ib.* iv. 6, 7, 17, 18, 25, 30, 34). The same distinction appears in the case of turtle-doves and pigeons: when burnt offerings, their blood was smeared on the side of the brazen altar (*ib.* viii. 15; xvi. 18, 19); when sin-offerings, it was partly sprinkled on the side of the altar and partly smeared on the base. The animal was then flayed, the skin falling to the priest (*ib.* i. 6, vii. 8). In some SIN-OFFERINGS the skin was burned along with the flesh (*ib.* iv. 11, 12, 20, 21; comp. *ib.* iv. 26, 31, 35). If the entire animal was devoted to the flames, the carcass was "cut into pieces" (*ib.* i. 6, viii. 20). The bowels and legs of the animals used in the burnt offerings were carefully washed (*ib.* i. 9, viii. 21, ix. 14) before they were placed on the altar. Certain offerings or portions thereof had to pass through the ceremony of waving, a rite which is not further described in the Bible (see SACRIFICE, IN RABBINICAL LITERATURE). Another ceremony is mentioned in connection with the waving, viz., the heaving. This ceremony, likewise not further described, was observed with the right shoulder of the thank-offering, after which the part belonged to the priest. The sacrificial rites were completed by the consumption by fire of the sacrifice or those parts destined for God.

Waving and Heaving.

Sacrificial meals were ordained in the cases where some portion of the sacrifice was reserved for the priests or for the offering Israelites. The bloodless oblations of the Israelites, being "most holy," were eaten by the males of the priests alone in the court of the sanctuary (*ib.* vii. 9, 10), those of the priests being consumed by fire on the altar. In other sacrifices other provisions for these meals were made (*ib.* vii. 12–14). The repast was a part of the priest's duties (*ib.* x. 16–18). Public thank-offerings seem to have been given over entirely to the priests (*ib.* xxiii. 20), with the exception of the FAT. In private thank-offerings this was burned on the altar (*ib.* iii. 3–5, 9–11, 14–16; vii. 31), the right shoulder was given to the priest (*ib.* vii. 31–34, x. 14–15), the breast to the Aaronites (*ib.* vii. 31–34), and the remainder was left to the offering Israelite. The priests might eat their portions with their families in any "clean" place (*ib.* x. 14). The offering Israelite in this case had to eat his share within a fixed and limited time (*ib.* vii. 15–18, xix. 5–8), with his family and such guests as Levites and strangers, and always at the town where the sanctuary was (for

penalty and other conditions see *ib.* vii. 19-21; Deut. xii. 6, 7, 11, 12; I Sam. ix. 12, 13, 19). Participation in the meals of idolatrous sacrifices was a fatal offense (Ex. xxxiv. 14, 15; Num. xxv. 1-3; comp. Ps. cvi. 28, 29).

Compound Sacrifices.

The vegetable- and drink-offerings accompanied all the usual holocausts and thank-offerings on ordinary days and Sabbaths, and on festivals (Num. xv. 3) of whatever character (Ex. xxix. 40, 41; Lev. vii. 12, 13; xxiii. 13, 18; Num. xv. 3-9, 14-16; xxviii. 9, 20, 21, 28, 29). The kind of cereal oblation offered varied according to the species of the animals sacrificed, and the amount was increased in proportion to the number of the latter (Lev. xiv. 21; Num. xv. 4, 12; xxviii. 5, 9, 12; xxix. 3, 4, 9, 10, 14, 15). However, a cereal oblation ("minḥah") might under certain circumstances be offered independently, *e.g.*, the SHOWBREAD, the first sheaf of ripe barley on Pesaḥ, the first loaves of leavened bread from new wheat on Pentecost (Lev. xxiii. 16, 17, 20; Num. xxviii. 26), and the sin-offering of the very poor (Lev. v. 11-13). The minḥah with the burnt offerings and thank-offerings was always fine wheaten flour merely mingled with oil; it is not clear whether this minḥah was burned entirely (*ib.* xiv. 20; comp. *ib.* ix. 16, 17). If it was presented alone as a free-will offering or as a votive offering, it might be offered in various forms and with different ceremonies (*ib.* ii. 2; v. 12; vi. 8; vii. 9, 10; also ii.; vi. 12-16; vii. 12-14; xxvii. 10, 11). The mode of libation is not described in the Law; but every holocaust or thank-offering was to be accompanied with a libation of wine, the quantity of which was exactly graduated according to the animal, etc. (Num. xv. 3-11). Water seems to have been used at one time for "pouring out" before YHWH (I Sam. vii. 6; II Sam. xxiii. 16). As to the spices belonging to the sacrifices, four are named in the Torah, BALSAM and FRANKINCENSE being the more important ("stacte, and onycha, and galbanum . . . with pure frankincense," Ex. xxx. 34).

——**In Rabbinical Literature:** The sacrifices treated of in the Law were, according to tradition, the following: (1) the holocaust ("'olah"); (2) the meal-offering ("minḥah"); (3) the sin-offering ("ḥaṭat"); (4) the trespass-offering ("asham")—these four were "holy of holies" ("ḳodesh ha-ḳodashim"); (5) the peace-offerings ("shelamim"), including the thank-offering ("todah") and the voluntary or vow-offering ("nedabah" or "neder"). These shelamim, as well as the sacrifice of the first-born ("bekor") and of the tithe of animals ("ma'aser" and "pesaḥ"), were less holy ("ḳodashim ḳallim"). For the 'olot, only male cattle or fowls might be offered; for the shelamim, all kinds of cattle. The ḥaṭat, too, might consist of fowls, or, in the case of very poor sacrificers, of flour. For the trespass-offering, only the lamb ("kebes") or the ram ("ayil") might be used. Every 'olah, as well as the votive offerings and the free-will shelamim, required an accessory meal-offering and libation ("nesek"). To a todah were added loaves or cakes of baked flour, both leavened and unleavened.

Every sacrifice required sanctification ("ḥakdashah"), and was to be brought into the court of the sanctuary ("haḳrabah"). In the animal offerings the following acts were observed: (1) "semikah" = laying on of the hand (or both hands, according to tradition); (2) "sheḥiṭah" = killing; (3) "ḳabbalah" = gathering (receiving) the blood; (4) "holakah" = carrying the blood to the altar; (5) "zeriḳah" = sprinkling the blood; (6) "haḳṭarah" = consumption by fire. For the sacrifices of lesser holiness the victims might be slaughtered anywhere in the court; for the ḳodesh ha-ḳodashim, at the north side of it only. Zeriḳah, in all cases except the sin-offering, consisted of two distinct acts of sprinkling, in each of which two sides of the altar were reached. In the case of the sin-offering, the blood was as a rule smeared with the fingers on the four horns of the brazen altar, but in some instances (*e.g.*, in the case of the bullock and the goat on Yom ha-Kippurim) it was sprinkled seven times upon the curtain of the Holy of Holies and smeared upon the four horns of the golden altar. Offerings of the latter class were on this account called the "inner"

Acts of Sacrifice.

sin-offerings. The remainder of the blood of these was poured out at the base of the west side of the brazen altar; in other oblations, on the south side.

The haḳṭarah consisted in flaying the carcass and cutting it into pieces, all of which, if it was an 'olah, were burned on the altar; in the case of other offerings only a few prescribed parts, which were called the "emorim," were burned. If an 'olah consisted of a fowl, the acts of offering were as follows: (1) "meleḳah" = wringing the neck so as to sever both the esophagus and the trachea; (2) "miẓẓuy" = the pressing out of the blood against the wall; (3) "haḳṭarah" = burning. When a fowl was sacrificed for a sin-offering the procedure was as follows: (1) "meleḳah" = wringing the neck, but less completely, only one "siman" being severed; (2) "hazzayah" = sprinkling the blood; and (3) the "miẓẓuy."

In the preparation of the meal-offering some differences were observed. Most of such offerings were of the finest wheat flour, the minimum quantity being fixed at an "'issaron" (= one-tenth ephah). One log of oil and a handful of incense were added to every 'issaron. Mention is made of the following minḥot: (1) "minḥat solet," the meal-offering of flour, of which a handful ("ḳomeẓ") was placed on the altar; (2) "me'uppat tanur" = baked in the oven (*i.e.*, consisting either of cakes ["ḥallot"] or wafers ["reḳiḳin"], both of which were broken into pieces before the ḳomeẓ was taken from them); (3) "'al ha-maḥabat" = baked in a flat pan; (4) "'al ha-marḥeshet" = baked in a deep pan; (5) "minḥat ḥabitim" (this consisted of one-tenth ephah of flour mixed with three logs of oil, formed into twelve cakes, and baked in pans, six of which cakes the high priest offered by burning with a half-handful of incense in the morning, and the other six in the evening; Lev. vi. 12 *et seq.*); (6) "minḥat 'omer" (= "second of Passover"; see 'OMER), consisting of one-tenth of an ephah of barley flour, incense, and oil (*ib.* xxiii. 10; comp. *ib.* ii. 14); (7) "minḥat ḥinnuk," the dedication meal-offering (similar to minḥat ḥabitim, with the difference that only one log of oil was used, and the whole was burned at once [*ib.* vi. 13; Maimonides, "Yad," Kele ha-Miḳdash, v. 16; Sifra, Ẓaw, ii. 3; Sifra, ed. War-

Preparation of Minḥah.

saw, 1866, p. 31b; Rashi on Men. 51b; comp. Men. 78a; Hoffmann, "Leviticus," pp. 230 *et seq.*]); (8) "minḥat ḥoṭe," the meal-offering of the very poor, when compelled to offer a "ḳorban 'oleh we-yored"; (9) "minḥat soṭah," the jealousy meal-offering (Num. v. 15); (10) "minḥat nesakim," the meal-offering of the libations (*ib.* xv.).

"Haggashah," the carrying to the "ḳeren ma'arbit deromit" (Lev. vi. 7; Hoffmann, *l.c.* p. 150), the southwest corner of the altar, of the vessel or pan in which the minḥah had been placed, was the first act. The second, in the case of the meal-offering of the priests ("minḥat kohen"), was the burning. In other cases, (1) the "ḳemiẓah" (taking out a handful) followed upon the haggashah, and then ensued (2) the putting of this handful into the dish for the service ("netinat ha-ḳomeẓ bi-keli sharet"), and finally (3) the burning of the ḳomeẓ ("haḳṭarat ḳomeẓ"). At the 'omer- and the jealousy-minḥah (6 and 9 above), "tenufah" (waving) preceded the haggashah.

Haggashah.

Burnt offerings, meal-offerings, and peace-oblations might be offered without specific reason as free-will offerings ("nedabot"); not so sin- and trespass-offerings, which could never be nedabot. A sin-offering might be either "kabua'" (fixed) or a "ḳorban 'oleh we-yored" (*i.e.*, a sacrifice dependent on the material possessions of the sacrificer; the rich bringing a lamb or a goat; the poor, two doves; and the very poor, one-tenth of an ephah of flour). This latter ḳorban was required for the following three sins: (1) "shebu'at ha-'edut" or "shemi'at ḳol" (Lev. v. 1, in reference to testimony which is not offered); (2) "ṭum'at miḳdash we-ḳodashim" (unwittingly rendering unclean the sanctuary and its appurtenances; *ib.* v. 2, 3); and (3) "biṭṭuy sefatayim" (incautious oath; *ib.* v. 5 *et seq.*; Shebu. i. 1, 2). In the last two cases the ḳorban was required only when the transgression was unintentional ("bi-shegagah"); in the first, also when it was intentional ("be-mezid"). The offering of the leper and that of the woman after childbirth were of this order ("Yad," Shegagot, x. 1).

This principle obtained with reference to the fixed sin-offerings: offenses which when committed intentionally entailed excision required a sin-offering when committed inadvertently, except in the case of BLASPHEMY and in that of neglect of CIRCUMCISION or of the Passover sacrifice. The latter two sins, being violations of mandatory injunctions, did not belong to this category of offenses, which included only the transgression of prohibitory injunctions, while in blasphemy no real act is involved ("Yad," *l.c.* i. 2). Of such sin-offerings five kinds were known: (1) "par kohen mashiaḥ" (Lev. iv. 3 *et seq.*), the young bullock for the anointed priest; (2) "par ha-'alem dabar shel ẓibbur" (*ib.* iv. 13 *et seq.*), the young bullock for the inadvertent, unwitting sin of the community; (3) "se'ir 'abodat elilim" (Num. xv. 22 *et seq.*), the goat for idolatry—these three being designated as "penimiyyot" (internal; see above); (4) "se'ir nasi," the he-goat for the prince (Lev. iv. 22 *et seq.*); (5) "ḥaṭṭat yaḥid," the individual sin-offering—these last two being termed "ḥiẓonot" (external; Zeb. 4b, 14a) or, by the Mishnah (Lev. xi. 1), "ne'ekelot" (those that are eaten; "Yad," Ma'ase ha-Ḳorbanot, v. 7–11).

The trespass-offerings ("ashamim") were six in number, and the ram sacrificed for them was required to be worth at least two shekels: (1) "asham me'ilot" (Lev. v. 14 *et seq.*); (2) "asham gezelot" (*ib.* v. 20 *et seq.*; in these two, in addition, "ḳeren we-ḥomesh" [= principal plus one-fifth] had to be paid); (3) "asham taluy," for "suspended" cases, in which it was doubtful whether a prohibition to which the penalty of excision attached had been inadvertently violated (*ib.* v. 17 *et seq.*); (4) "asham shipḥah ḥarufah" (*ib.* xix. 20 *et seq.*); (5) "asham nazir" (Num. vi. 12), the Nazarite's offering; (6) "asham meẓora'" (Lev. xiv. 12), the leper's offering. In (5) and (6) the sacrifice consisted of lambs.

Vegetable Sacrifices.

In reference to the vegetable or unbloody oblations, it may be noticed that the Talmud mentions certain places where the grapes for sacrificial wine were grown (Men. viii. 6), *e.g.*, Kefar Signah. On the strength of Prov. xxiii. 31 and Ps. lxxv. 9 (A. V. 8) some have contended that only red wine was used (but see Bertinoro on Men. viii. 6). Salt was indispensable in all sacrifices, even the wood and the libations being salted before being placed on the altar (Men. 20b, 21b).

While the text of the Pentateuch seems to assume that in the laying on of hands one hand only was employed, rabbinical tradition is to the effect that both were imposed and that with much force (Men. 95a; Ibn Ezra on Lev. v. 4; but Targ. Yer. says the right hand only). This semikah had to be performed personally by the offerer; but in case the latter was an idiot, a minor, deaf, a slave, a woman, blind, or a non-Israelite, the rite was omitted. If two partners owned the animal jointly, they had to impose their hands in succession. Only the Passover sacrifice ("pesaḥ") and those of the first-born and the tithe were exceptions to the rule that individual sacrifices were to include semikah. Communal offerings, except that mentioned in Lev. iv. 13 *et seq.*, and the scapegoat (Lev. xvi. 21), were exempt. In the case of the former the act was performed by the elders; in that of the latter, by the high priest. R. Simon is given as authority for the statement that in the case of the goat offered as a sacrifice for idolatry (Num. xv. 34) the elders were required to perform the laying on of hands (Men. 92a).

The position assumed by the offerer during this ceremony is described in Tosef., Men. x. 12 (comp. Yoma 36a). The victim stood in the northern part of the court, with its face turned to the west; the offerer, in the west with his face likewise to the west. Maimonides asserts that in the case of the ḳodesh ha-ḳodashim the offerer stood in the east looking westward ("Yad," Ma'ase ha-Ḳorbanot, iii. 14). The offerer placed his two hands between the animal's horns and made a confession appropriate to the sacrifice. In the case of a peace-offering, confession would not be appropriate, and in its stead laudatory words were spoken ("Yad," *l.c.* iii. 5). The holakah (by this term is denoted the carrying of the pieces of the dismembered victim [Zeb. 14a, 24a; Men. 10a] as well as the carrying of the blood to the altar) is not mentioned in the Bible as one of the successive acts of the sacrifices. However, as the slaughtering might take place at the altar itself, this act was not absolutely required: it was an "'abodah she-efshar le-baṭṭeah," a ceremony that might be omitted. The blood was collected by a priest in a holy vessel called the "mizraḳ." The holakah, it was generally held, might be performed by priests only, though R. Ḥisda (Zeb. 14a) thinks that laymen were permitted to undertake it.

Where terumah or heaving was prescribed, the part subject to this rite was moved perpendicularly down and up, or up and down. In tenufah or waving the motion was horizontal from left to right or vice versa (Men. v. 6; see Rashi on Ex. xxix. 24). The killing might be done by laymen as well as by priests ("Yad," *l.c.* v. 1 *et seq.*); minute directions concerning the place of its performance were observed ("Yad," *l.c.*; see Ey-zehu Meḳoman, Zeb. v.). In the Second Temple a red line was marked on the altar five ells from the ground below or above which, as the case required, the blood was sprinkled (Mid. iii. 1). Regulations concerning the localities, three in number, where parts of the victim, or the entire carcass under certain eventualities, had to be burned, were prescribed (Zeb. xii. 5).

Terumah.

Under the name "ḥagigah" were known free-will offerings of the shelamim class presented by individuals, mostly at festivals (Ḥag. i. 2, 5).

The defects which in Talmudic law disqualified the victims were minutely described (see "Yad," Issure ha-Mizbeaḥ). While in the Bible the incense consisted of four ingredients, the Rabbis add seven others, making the total number eleven (Ker. 6a; Yoma iii. 11; Yer. Yoma 41d; comp. "Yad," Kele ha-Miḳdash, ii.).

According to the Shammaites, the two lambs of the daily "tamid" (Num. xxviii. 3) indicate by their name that the sacrifices "press down" (כבש), *i.e.*, diminish, the sins of Israel. The Hillelites connect the term with the homonym כבס (= "to wash"), and contend that sacrifices wash Israel clean from sin (Pes. 61b). Johanan ben Zakkai held that what was wrought for Israel by the sacrifices was accomplished for the non-Israelites by philanthropy (B. B. 10b); and when the Temple was destroyed he consoled his disciple Joshua by insisting that good deeds would take the place of the sin-offerings (Ab. R. N. iv.).

Sacrifice in the Haggadah.

The sacrificial scheme was the target at which gnostics and other skeptics shot their arrows. God, it was argued, manifested Himself in this as a strict accountant and judge, but not as the author of the highest goodness and mercy. In refutation, Ben 'Azzai calls attention to the fact that in connection with the sacrifices the only name used to designate God is YHWH, the unique name ("Shem ha-Meyuḥad; Sifra, Wayiḳra, ii. [ed. Weiss, p. 4c], with R. Jose b. Ḥalafta as author; Men. 110a; Sifre, Num. 143). Basing his inference on the phrase "for your pleasure shall ye offer up" (Lev. xxii. 29, Hebr.), Ben 'Azzai insists also that sacrifices were not planned on the theory that, God's will having been done by man, man's will must be done in corresponding measure by God: they were merely expressive of man's delight; and God did not need them (Ps. l. 12, 13; Sifre, *l.c.*; Men. 110a).

Speculating on the exceptions which the minḥah of the sinner and that of the jealousy-offering constitute, in so far as neither oil nor incense is added thereto, Simeon ben Yoḥai points out that the absence of these components indicates that the offering of a sinner may not be adorned (Tos. Soṭah i. 10; Men. 6a; Soṭah 15a; Yer. Soṭah 17d). The name of the 'olah indicates that the sacrifice expiates sinful thoughts ("go up into one's mind"; comp. Job i. 5; Lev. R. vii.; Tan., Lek Leka, ed. Buber, 13; for other comments of similar purport see Bacher, "Ag. Tan." ii. 104). The defense of the Law for having forbidden the participation of non-Israelites in the communal sacrifices while it permitted the acceptance of their free-will offerings (Sifra, Emor, vii. [ed. Weiss, p. 98a]), was not a matter of slight difficulty. A very interesting discussion of the point is found in the appendix to Friedmann's edition of the Pesiḳta Rabbati (p. 192a), in which the non-Jew quotes with very good effect the universalistic verse Mal. i. 11.

To bring peace to all the world is the purpose not merely of the peace-offerings, but of all sacrifices (Sifra, Wayiḳra, xvi. [ed. Weiss, p. 13a]). It is better to avoid sin than to offer sacrifices; but, if offered, they should be presented in a repentant mood, and not merely, as fools offer them, for the purpose of complying with the Law (Ber. 23a). God asked Abraham to offer up Isaac in order to prove to Satan that, even if Abraham had not presented Him with as much as a dove at the feast when Isaac was weaned, he would not refuse to do God's bidding (Sanh. 89b). The sacrificial ordinances prove that God is with the persecuted. Cat-

Functions of the Several Offerings.

tle are chased by lions; goats, by panthers; sheep, by wolves; hence God commanded, "Not them that persecute, but them that are persecuted, offer ye up to me" (Pesiḳ. de R. Kahana 76b; Lev. R. xxvii.). In the prescription that fowls shall be offered with their feathers is contained the hint that a poor man is not to be despised: his offering is to be placed on the altar in full adornment (Lev. R. iii.). That sacrifices are not meant to appease God, Moses learned from His own lips. Moses had become alarmed when bidden to offer to God (Num. xxviii. 2): all the animals of the world would not suffice for such a purpose (Isa. xl. 10). But God allayed his apprehension by ordaining that only two lambs (the tamid) should be brought to him twice every day (Pes. 20a, 61b). Salt, which is indispensable at sacrifices, is symbolic of the moral effect of suffering, which causes sins to be forgiven and which purifies man (Ber. 5a). God does not eat. Why, then, the sacrifices? They increase the offerer's merit (Tan., Emor, ed. Buber, p. 20). The strongest man might drink twice or even ten times the quantity of water contained in the hollow of his hand; but all the waters of the earth can not fill the hollow of God's hand (Isa. xl. 12).

The words in connection with the goat serving for a sin-offering on the New Moon festival "for YHWH" (Num. xxviii. 15) are explained in grossly anthropomorphic application. The goat is a sin-offering for God's transgression committed when He decreased the size of the moon (Sheb. 9a; Ḥul. 60b). The offerings of the sons of Noah were burnt offerings (Yer. Meg. 72b; Gen. R. xxii.; Zeb. 116a). The "illegitimate" sacrifices on high places, *e.g.*, those by Elijah (I Kings xviii. 30 *et seq.*), were exceptions divinely sanctioned (Yer. Ta'an. 65d; Yer. Meg. 72c; Lev. R. xxii.; Midr. Teh. to Ps. xxvii. 5). The seventy bullocks of Sukkot correspond to the seventy nations; the single bullock on the eighth day, to the unique people Israel. God is like that king who, having entertained his guests most lavishly for seven days, commanded his son after their departure to prepare a very plain meal (Suk. 55b; Pes. 143b). Children, when learning the Pentateuch, used to begin with the third

Symbolic Interpretations.

book because they that are pure should first occupy themselves with offerings that are likewise pure (Pes. 60b; Lev. R. vii.). God has taken care not to tax Israel too heavily (hence Lev. i. 10, 14; ii. 1; vi. 13). Indeed, one who offers only a very modest meal-offering is accounted as having offered sacrifices from one end of the world to the other (Mal. i. 11; Lev. R. viii.). By their position, coming after the laws prescribed for the other sacrifices, the peace-offerings are shown to be dessert, as it were (Lev. R. ix.). God provides "from His own" the minḥah of the sin-offering (Lev. R. iii.). The use of the word "adam" ("Adam" = "man"), and not "ish," in Lev. i. 2 leads the offerer to remember that, like Adam, who never robbed or stole, he may offer only what is rightfully his (Lev. R. ii.).

The importance attaching to the sacrificial laws was, as the foregoing anthology of haggadic opinions proves, fully realized by the Rabbis. Unable after the destruction of the Temple to observe these ordinances, they did not hesitate to declare that, in contrast to the sacrificial law which rejected the defective victim, God accepts the broken-hearted (Ps. li. 19; Pes. 158b). With a look to the future restoration, they call attention to the smallness of the desert offerings, while delighting in the glorious prospect of the richer ones to come (Lev. R. vii.). The precept concerning the daily offering is given twice (Ex. xxix. 38–42; Num. xxviii. 1–8), from which repetition is deduced the consolation for Israel in exile, that he who studies these verses is regarded as having offered the sacrifices (Pes. 60b; Lev. R. vii. 3). The same thought is based on "the torah of the sin-offering" and "the torah of the trespass-offering" (Lev. vi. 18, vii. 7; Men. 110a, b). Prayer is better than sacrifice (Ber. 32b; Midr. Shemuel i. 7; Bacher, "Ag. Pal. Amor." ii. 217). Lulab and etrog replace the altar and offering (Suk. 45a, b). Blood lost when one is wounded replaces the blood of the 'olah (Ḥul. 7b). The reading of the "Shema'" and the "Tefillah" and the wearing of phylacteries ("tefillin") are equivalent to the building of the altar (Ber. 15a; comp. Ber. 14b; Midr. Teh. to Ps. i. 2). As the altar is called "table" (Ezek. xlii. 22), the table of the home has the altar's expiatory virtue (Ber. 55a; Men. 97a). This was understood to have reference to "good deeds," such as hospitality shown to the poor (see Ab. R. N. iv.). The humble are rewarded as though they had presented all the offerings prescribed in the Law (Ps. li. 19; Soṭah 5b; Sanh. 43b; Pesiḳta Ḥadashah, in Jellinek, "B. H." vi. 52). Prayer in the synagogue is tantamount to offering a pure oblation (Isa. lxvi. 20; Yer. Ber. 8d). The students engaged everywhere in the study of the Torah are as dear to God as were they who burned incense on the altar (Men. 110a). The precentor ("sheliaḥ ẓibbur") is regarded as officiating at the altar and sacrificing (קרב; see Levy, "Neuhebr. Wörterb." iv. 386b; Yer. Ber. 8b). In the Messianic time all sacrifices except the thank-offering will cease (Pes. 79a; Lev. R. ix., xxvii.). Whoever observes the provisions made for the poor (Lev. xxiii. 22) is regarded as highly as he would have been if during the existence of the Temple he had been faithful in making his oblations (Sifra, Emor, 101c). To entertain a student in one's house is an act of piety as notable as the offering of daily sacrifice (II Kings iv. 9; Ber. 10b). To make a present to a learned man (a rabbi) is like offering the first-fruits (Ket. 105b). Filling the rabbi's cellars with wine is an equivalent to pouring out the libations (Yoma 71a). In their extravagant, apocalyptic fancy, the haggadot even describe a heavenly altar at which the archangel Michael ministers as high priest; but his offerings are the souls of the righteous. In the Messianic time this altar will descend from on high to Jerusalem (Midr. 'Aseret ha-Dibrot; see Tos. Men. 110; comp. another midrash of the same tenor, Num. R. xii.).

Substitutes for Sacrifice.

——**Critical View:** Modern scholars, after Robertson Smith ("Rel. of Sem." 2d ed.) and Wellhausen ("Reste Alt-Arabischen Heidentums"), have abandoned the older views, according to which the sacrificial scheme of the Old Testament was regarded as the outflow of divine wisdom or divine mercy, disciplinary or expiatory in its effects, or as the invention of a man of great genius (Moses), who devised its general and specific provisions as symbols wherewith to teach his people some vital truths. Nor is the sacrificial code the outcome of a spontaneous impulse of the human heart to adore God and placate Him, or to show gratitude to Him. Sacrifices revert to the most primitive forms of religion—ancestral animism and totemism. The sacrifice is a meal offered to the dead member of the family, who meets his own at the feast. As the honored guest, he is entitled to the choicest portions of the meal. From this root-idea, in course of time, all others, easily discovered in the sacrificial rites of various nations, are evolved. The visitor at the feast will reward his own for the hospitality extended. Or it is he that has sent the good things: hence gratitude is his due. Or perhaps he was offended: it is he, therefore, who must be appeased (by expiatory rites). He may do harm: it is well to forestall him (by rites to secure protection or immunity).

Totemistic Interpretation.

The primitive notion of sacrifice is that it is a gift, which is the meaning of the Hebrew word "minḥah." During the period of cannibalism the gift naturally takes the form of human victims, human flesh being the choice article of food during the prevalence of anthropophagism. It is also that which by preference or necessity is placed on the table of the deity. Traces of human sacrifices abound in the Biblical records. The command to Abraham (Gen. xxii.) and the subsequent development of the story indicate that the substitution of animal for human victims was traced to patriarchal example. The BAN ("ḥerem") preserves a certain form of the primitive human sacrifice (Schwally, "Kriegsaltertümer"). The first-born naturally belonged to the deity. Originally he was not ransomed, but immolated; and in the Law the very intensity of the protest against "passing the children through the fire to Moloch" reveals the extent of the practise in Israel. In fact, the sacrifice of a son is specifically recorded in the cases of King MESHA (II Kings iii. 27), of Ahaz (*ib.* xvi. 3; II Chron. xxviii. 3), and of Manasseh (*ib.* xxi. 6). Jeremiah laments bitterly this devouring disgrace (iii. 24, 25); and even Ezekiel (xx. 30, 31) speaks of it as of frequent occurrence. Ps. cvi. 37, 38 confesses that sons and daughters were sacrificed to demons; and in Deutero-Isaiah lvii. 5 allusions to this horrid iniquity recur. If such offerings were made to Moloch, some instances are not suppressed where human life was "devoted" to YHWH. The fate of Jephthah's daughter presents the clearest instance of such immolations (Judges xi. 30, 31, 34–40). That of the seven sons of Saul delivered up by David to the men of Gibeon (II Sam. xxi. 1–14) is another, though the phraseology is less explicit. Other indications, however, point in the same direction. Blood belonged to YHWH; no man might eat it (I Sam. xiv. 32–34; Lev. xvii. 3 *et seq.*). The blood was the soul. When animals were substituted for human victims, blood still remained the portion of the Deity. No subtle theological construction of a philosophy of expiation is required to explain this prominent trait (see S. I. Curtiss, "Primitive Semitic Religion," *passim*). The blood on the lintel (the threshold covenant) at the Passover was proof that that which the Destroyer was seeking—viz., life—had not been withheld. The rite of CIRCUMCISION (Ex. iii. 24) appears to have been originally instituted for the same purpose.

Human Sacrifice.

As at every meal the Deity was supposed to be present and to claim His own, every meal became a sacrifice, and the killing of the animal a sacrificial act (see I Sam. xiv.); and so strong did this feeling remain, even after the lapse of centuries, that when the Second Temple was destroyed, the rigorists abstained from eating meat on the plea that as the sacrifices had been discontinued, all meat was rendered unfit for food (Tos. Soṭah, end; B. B. 60b).

The donative character of the Hebrew sacrifices appears also from the material used, which is always something to eat or drink, the common dietary articles of the Israelites. The phrase "food of God" (Lev. xxi. 6, 8, 17, 21; xxii. 25; Ezek. xliv. 7) proves the use for which such offerings were intended; and Ps. l. 13 also reveals this intention.

Primitive YHWH-religion seems at the very outset not to have favored an elaborate sacrificial ritual. In the desert but little grows. The first of the flock, the spring lamb (see PASSOVER), in all probability, constituted the gift prepared, as was that described in Ex. xii., for the God residing on Sinai in unapproachable (*i.e.*, holy) aloofness. The Canaanites,

Early Stages.

with whom later the Hebrews came in contact, had, as agricultural peoples, a more elaborate and lascivious sacrificial form of worship. From them the Hebrews adopted most of the features of their own priestly scheme, which, even as exhibited in the latest strata of the code, presents some remarkable elements disclosing a non-Hebrew origin (*e.g.*, Azazel, the scapegoat, the red heifer).

This process of adaptation did not proceed without arousing the opposition of the Prophets. They were outspoken in their disapproval of sacrificial religion; and some of them made no concealment of their opinion that the sacrificial rites had no original connection with the worship of YHWH. At all events, the sacrificial ordinances of the Book of the Covenant are simple, as, indeed, the historical glosses of the feasts at Shiloh would lead one to suppose (see SACRIFICE, BIBLICAL DATA). Even Deuteronomy can not be said to have proceeded very far toward a detailed system. The one step taken therein was the centralization of the cult in Jerusalem, with the final official suppression of the HIGH PLACES, and the assignment of rank to the Levitical priests. The freedom to sacrifice thus received a severe check.

In P the system is developed in detail; and comparison with the Holiness Code (H) and with Ezekiel gives some notion of the manner of development. In Deuteronomy the prescribed offerings (firstlings, tithes, etc.) are "ḳodashim" (sacred), in distinction from votive and free-will offerings and from animals slaughtered for food (Deut. xii. 26); victims are taken from the flock and herd ("baḳar"); human sacrifices are inhibited (*ib.* xii. 31); victims must be without blemish (*ib.* xvii. 1); the ritual is given of holocausts and other sacrifices (*ib.* xii. 27), burning of fat, libations (*ib.* xxxii. 38), offerings at feasts (*ib.* xvi. 1 *et seq.*, xxvi.), tithes, priestly dues (*ib.* xii. 17, xiv. 23, xviii.), and firstlings (*ib.* xv. 19 *et seq.*).

H is cognizant of 'olah (Lev. xxii. 18), 'olah and zebaḥ (*ib.* xvii. 8), zibḥe shelamim (*ib.* xvii. 5, xix. 5), todah (*ib.* xxii. 29), neder and nedabah (*ib.* xxii. 18, 21); sacrifices are ḳodashim (*ib.* xxii. 2–15) and are the "food of God" (see above). In addition to the animals in Deuteronomy, "kebes" and "'ez" are enumerated; strict regulations for free-will offerings are elaborated (*ib.* xxii. 23); they must be brought to the holy place (*ib.* xvii. 3, and elsewhere); blood is prohibited as food (*ib.* xvii. 10); the flesh of shelamim must be eaten on the day of the sacrifice or on the following day (*ib.* xix. 5 *et seq.*); that of the todah on the day itself (*ib.* xxii. 29).

Sacrifice According to Ezekiel.

Ezekiel deals almost exclusively with public sacrifices. He names two new species of offerings: ḥaṭṭat and asham. Minḥah is an offering of flour and oil (Ezek. xlvi. 5, 7, 11); a libation is also named (nesek; *ib.* xlv. 17). Birds are not mentioned. The terumah is a tax from which the sacrifices are provided by the prince (*ib.* xlv. 13–17). The morning tamid consists of one lamb, the Sabbath burnt offering, of six lambs and a ram with their appurtenances (*ib.* xlvi. 4 *et seq.*); at the great festivals the prince provides shelamim also. The Levites appear as distinct from the priests (*ib.* xliv. 11; comp. *ib.* xlvi. 2); the flesh is boiled in kitchens in the four corners of the outer court by Temple servants (*ib.* xlvi. 21–24); and so forth (see Ezekiel).

P and Ezekiel do not harmonize as regards every provision. The former reflects conditions actually in force after the Exile. But it is a mistake to suppose that P is entirely new legislation, a copy of Babylonian institutions. The similarity of the sacrificial rites of Israel and Babylonia does not extend beyond some technical terms—which (see Zimmern in Schrader, "K. A. T." 3d ed.), moreover, often had different bearings in the two cults—and such other analogies as may be detected in all sacrificial systems. P represents many old priest-rituals ("torot"), probably in force for centuries at some older shrine or High Place.

Deep *θεολσγούμενα* do not underlie the system; problems of salvation from original sin, restitution, and justification did not enter into the minds of the priests that ministered at the altar in Jerusalem.

——**In Theology:** The critical school contends, and on good grounds (Nowack, "Lehrbuch der Hebräischen Archäologie," ii. 223), that sin-offerings in the technical sense of the word were not recognized before Ezekiel. However, the distinction between "ḳodesh" and "ṭame" is drawn by the Prophets anterior to the Exile; and even in Samuel (I Sam. iii. 14, xxvi. 19; II Sam. xxiv. 25) the notion is expressed that by sacrifice sin may be atoned for ("yitkapper"), though the sacrifices named are meal-, meat-, and burnt offerings. In the question put by Micah's interlocutor, also, the thought is dominant that offerings, even of human life, may protect against the consequences of sin and transgression (Mic. xvi. 6 *et seq.*). That sacrifice had some bearing on sin was not, then, an unknown idea, even if there was no technical term therefor. In the progressive systematization of the sacrificial practises, with a view to placing them more and more under the exclusive control of the priesthood of the central sanctuary, specialization in the nomenclature and assignment of the offerings could not but ensue. Yet, in what sense the specific sin-offerings were credited with atoning power can not be understood without an antecedent knowledge of what constituted sin in the conception of those that first observed the sacrificial cult. "Clean" or "holy" and "unclean" are the two poles; and "holy" implies "set aside for the Deity"; *e.g.*, an object which only the Deity's own may touch, or a precinct into which only the Deity's own may enter. Sin is an act that violates the taboo. As originally the sacrifice was a meal offered to the Deity at which He was to meet His own family (see SACRIFICE, CRITICAL VIEW), only such as were in the proper state of holiness might take part in this "communion service" (see PASSOVER). On the other hand, the Deity Himself would not accept the gift if the taboo was not respected. Contact with persons or things in an "unclean" state violated the taboo. Sin originally connoted a condition which rendered approach to the Deity impossible, and conversely made it impossible for the Deity to approach, to attend the family communion meal. To correct this the sacrifice was offered, *i.e.*, brought near to ("ḳorban," "hiḳrib") the Deity, more especially the blood, which preeminently belonged to God, and that by the priest only. In this connection it must be remembered that slaughtering was primitively a sacrificial rite. Meat was not to be eaten unless the Deity had received His share, viz., the blood. This insistence is the

Expiatory Function of Sacrifice.

motive of the otherwise strange prohibition to slaughter anywhere save at the door of the tent of meeting (Lev. xvii. 3). The presumption was that all belonged to the Deity. Later literature expresses this idea as a spiritual verity (Ps. l. 10–12; I Chron. xxix. 14).

The idea itself is very old. It is dominant in the sacrificial scheme. All animals, as belonging to God, are taboo. Hence at first man is a vegetarian (Gen. ix.). The right to partake of animal food is conditioned on the observance of the blood taboo; by killing an animal one taboo is violated; but if an equivalent one (the blood taboo) is kept inviolate, the sin is condoned. The blood is the animal's life; hence the equation "blood" = "animal." The Deity loses nothing by permitting the slaughtering if the blood is reserved for the altar or covered up (Lev. xvii. 13). This throws light on the primitive implications of the root ("kafar," "kipper"), which has furnished the technical terminology for the Levitical and also for the spiritual doctrine of ATONEMENT.

Connection with Taboo.

Later, as in Assyrian, a signification synonymous with "maḥah" (to wipe off) and a meaning similar to "kisseh" (to cover up), its earlier connotation, were carried by the noun "kofer" (= "ransom"), in the sense of "one for another" ("nefesh taḥat nefesh" = "one life for another life"). The blood (= life), the kofer given to God, was for the life (= animal) taken from God. With this as the starting-point, it is not difficult to understand how, when other taboos had been violated, the sacrifice and the blood came to be looked upon as a "kapparah." The refined sense of the soul's separation from God which is to be offset by another soul (blood) is certainly not inherent in the primitive conception. Moreover, the sin-offering is never presented for grave moral offenses (see above); only such sins as refusal to give testimony, contact with unclean objects, and hasty swearing are enumerated (Lev. v. 1 *et seq.*). That the three sins here specified are of the nature of violated taboos is recognizable. Trial and testimony are ordeals. "Ṭame" is synonymous with broken taboo. "Biṭṭe bi-sefatayim" in all probability refers to "taking the name in vain." Enunciating the "name" was violating the taboo.

In this connection the ceremony of laying on of hands is discovered to be only one of the many symbolic rites, abundant in primitive jurisprudence, whereby acquisition or abandonment of property is expressed. In the case of the sacrifices it implies absolute relinquishment ("manumissio"). The animal reverts thereby to its original owner—God.

This excursus into primitive folk-lore suggests at once the untenable character of the various theological interpretations given to the sacrificial institutions of the Bible. It will not be necessary to explain at length that the expiation of guilt—in any other sense than that given above, though perhaps with a more spiritual scope—is not the leading purpose of the Levitical sacrifices. Purification from physical uncleanness is an important function of sacrifices, but only because "unclean" has a very definite religious meaning (in connection with childbirth or with contact with a dead body, etc.). The consecration of persons and things to holy uses through the sacrifices is not due to some mysterious sacramental element in them; but the profane is changed into holy by coming in contact with what is under all circumstances holy, viz., the blood.

Symbolical Interpretation.

Christian theologians maintain that sacrificial worship was ordained as a twofold means of grace: (1) By permitting penal substitution. The sinner, having forfeited his life, was by a gracious provision permitted to substitute an immaculate victim, whose vicarious death was accepted by God; and this typified another vicarious sacrifice. (2) By recalling to man certain vital truths. This second theory is that of the symbolists, the classical exponent of which in modern times has been Bähr ("Symbolik des Mosaischen Kultus": "the soul placing itself at the disposal of God in order to receive the gift of the true life in sanctification"). The unblemished victim symbolizes the excellence and purity to which the offerer aspires. Other expositions of this kind are found in Oehler ("Theologie des Alten Testament"), Maurice ("The Doctrine of Sacrifice," London, 1879), and Schultz ("American Journal of Theology," 1900). This theology rests on the assumption that God is the direct author of the scheme, and that such analogies as are presented by the sacrificial rites of other nations are either copies of the Jewish rites or dim, imperfect foreshadowings of and gropings after the fuller light; or that Moses with supernatural wisdom devised the scheme to teach the ideas underlying his own laws in contradistinction to the similar legislations of other races.

That the Prophets had risen to a sublime conception of religion must be granted; but this does not necessitate the inference that the primitive basic ideas of sacrifices (a gift to God as one of the clan at the communion meal, taboo, etc.) are not to be detected in the legislation and never were contained therein. The Prophets showed no enthusiasm for the system. Ritual religion always preserves older forms than spiritual religion would or could evolve.

The New Testament doctrine of sacrifice has clearly influenced this theological valuation of the Old Testament laws. The death of Jesus was held to be a sacrifice (Eph. v. 2; Heb. ix. 14). Saving efficacy is imputed to the blood or the cross of Christ (Rom. iii. 25, v. 9; I Cor. x. 16; Rev. i. 5). Jesus is the sin-offering (Rom. viii. 3; Heb. xiii. 11; I Peter iii. 18), the covenant sacrifice (Heb. ii. 17, ix. 12 *et seq.*), the Passover (I Cor. v. 7). In the Epistle to the Hebrews (ix. 28) Jesus is the sin-bearer, the agency of sanctification (*ib.* x. 10); he is also the obedient servant (*ib.* x. 8, 9) and the high priest (*ib.* ix. 11 *et seq.*, 23). Here the precedent is given of treating the Hebrew sacrifices typologically, *i.e.*, as predictive, "expressing a need which they could not satisfy, but which Christ does, and embodying a faith which Christ justifies" (W. P. Paterson, in Hastings, "Dict. Bible," iv. 348b).

Of symbolism many indications are found in the homiletic haggadah (see above): the Tabernacle symbolizes Creation; the ten rods, heaven and earth, etc. (Yalḳ., Ex. 490). Its chief exponent in Jewish literature is Philo, who in his exposition of the sacrifices differs from the Halakah in some details. He ignores the rabbinical prescription of thirty days as the victim's minimum age (Parah i. 4), and he claims that pregnant animals might not be used for the sacrifice, extending thus to all victims a provision mentioned for the Red Heifer (Parah ii. 1). According to him, none but priests

Philo's Symbolism.

were permitted to slaughter the victim (Philo, *ib.* ii. 241). He names only three classes of sacrifices: (1) holocaust (= "'olah"); (2) σωτήριον (= "shelamim"), like the Septuagint; and (3) περὶ ἁμαρτίας (= "ḥaṭṭat"). The "todah" (ἡ λεγομένη τῆς αἰνήσεως) he regards as a subdivision of the 'olah, while the "asham" he ranks with the ḥaṭṭat (*ib.* ii. 246).

Philo devotes a treatise to the victims, the "animals that are fit for sacrifice." God selected the most gentle birds and animals. The perfection of the victims indicates that the offerers should be irreproachable; that the Jews should never bring with them to the altar any weakness or evil passion in the soul, but should endeavor to make it wholly pure and clean; so that God may not turn away with aversion from the sight of it ("De Victimis," § 2). In this way Philo construes every detail of the sacrificial ritual. Withal, he remarks that the "tribunal of God is inaccessible to bribes: it rejects the guilty though they offer daily 100 oxen, and receives the guiltless though they offer no sacrifices at all. God delights in fireless altars round which virtues form the choral dance" ("De Plantatione Noe," § 25 [ed. Mangey, i. 345]). To the eucharist (*i.e.*, thanksgiving) he attaches special importance. This, however, consists not in offerings and sacrifices, but in praises and hymns which the pure and inward mind will chant to inward music (*ib.* § 30 [ed. Mangey, i. 348]). Josephus mentions only two classes of sacrifices: (1) holocaust and (2) χαριστήριον = "eucharistic" = "shelamim" ("Ant." iii. 9, § 1).

The opinion of Maimonides appears to anticipate the views advanced by the most modern investigators. He in the first place refuses to follow the symbolists in finding reason for the details of the various sacrifices. Why a lamb and not a ram was chosen is, he says, an idle inquiry befitting fools, but not the serious-minded ("Moreh," iii., xxxvi.). "Each commandment has necessarily a reason as far as its general character is concerned; but as regards its details it has no ulterior object." These details are devised to be tests of man's obedience. The sacrifices more especially are really not of Jewish origin. As during Moses' time it was the general custom among all men to worship by means of sacrifices and as the Israelites had been brought up in this general mode of religion, God, in order that they might not go from one extreme to the other (from ritualism to a pure religion of righteousness), tolerated the continuance of the sacrifices. As in Maimonides' days prayer, fasting, and the like were serviceable, whereas a prophet preaching the service of God in thought alone, and not in ceremony, would find no hearing, so in the days of Moses the sacrifices were permitted by God in order to blot out the traces of idolatry and to establish the great principle of Judaism—the unity and being of God—without confusing the minds of the people by abolishing what they had been accustomed to (*ib.* iii., xxxii.). The experience of Israel, led not by the shorter way, but by the circuitous route through the land of the Philistines (Ex. xiii. 17), he quotes as typical of the method apparent in the legislation concerning offerings. The sacrificial service is not the primary object of the Law; but supplications, prayers, and the like are. Hence the restriction of the sacrifices to one locality, by which means God kept this particular kind of service within bounds.

Views of Maimonides and Naḥmanides.

Naḥmanides (see his commentary on Lev. i. 9) rejects this view in unsparing words, appealing to the Biblical examples of Abel and Noah, in whose days Egyptian and Chaldean idolatry was unknown, and who were monotheists and not idolaters, but whose offerings furnished a sweet savor for YHWH. If sacrifices must have a meaning, he prefers to see in them a moral symbolism founded on the psychology of conduct. Every act is composed of thought, speech, and execution. So in the sacrifice the offerer must do and speak, while the burning of the kidneys, the seat of thought, refers to the intention.

Abravanel resumes Maimonides' argument and refutes those advanced by Naḥmanides (preface to his commentary on Leviticus). He cites a midrash (Wayiḳra Rabbah xxii. 5; see also Bacher, "Ag. Pal. Amor." ii. 316) to the effect that as the Hebrews had become accustomed to sacrifices (idols) while in Egypt, God, to wean them from idolatry, commanded, while tolerating the sacrifices, that they should be brought to one central sanctuary. This is illustrated by a parable. A king noticed that his son loved to eat forbidden food, as carrion and animals torn to pieces. In order to retain him at his table, he directed that these things should be set before the son at home every day. This induced the prince to forego his evil habits. Hoffmann ("Leviticus," p. 88), speaking of Abravanel, charges him with having altered the text of the midrash, from which, as quoted in the commentary's preface, it would appear that sacrifices are placed in one category with ṭerefah and nebelah. Hoffmann cites another version of the fable, to the effect that on the king's table no forbidden food was found, and that this led to the prince's conversion. But Bacher (*l.c.*) gives Abravanel's version. Rabbi Levi, who is the author of the haggadah, may thus be said to have shared Maimonides' and Abravanel's views. The "Sefer ha-Ḥinnuk" (section "Terumah"), by Aaron ha-Levi of Barcelona, discusses the purpose of the sacrifices. The troubles connected with their proper preparation and with bringing them to the Temple, etc., were planned to arouse the sinner to a sense of his shame. He repeats also the psychological symbolism explained by Naḥmanides ("Sefer ha-Ḥinnuk," ed. Warsaw, pp. 23 *et seq.*).

David Ḳimḥi suggests (see his commentary on Jer. vii. 23) that the sacrifices were never mandatory, but voluntary ("God did not command that they shall offer up ["yaḳribu"], but merely gave contingent orders, 'if a man should offer up' ["adam ki yaḳrib"]").

Judah ha-Levi believes without equivocation in the divine wisdom and origin of the sacrifices. As Israel is the "chosen people" in the midst of whom alone prophets have arisen, as Palestine is the chosen land, and as both Israel and the land therefore are in closest affinity with God, so is Israel on this soil commanded to observe His law, central to which is the sacrificial cult. He spiritualizes the anthropomorphic expressions, contending nevertheless that the sacrifices revealed whether in Israel all was as it should be and all the component members had become united into a well-functioning organism. This was divulged by the divine fire that descended on the offerings ("My fires" = "created by My word" ["ishshai"]; "Cuzari," ii. 26–28).

According to Hoffmann (*l.c.* pp. 88 *et seq.*), the sacrifices are symbols of: (1) man's gratitude to God (illustrated in Abel's minḥah); (2) man's dependence on Him (Noah's offering; blood = life saved); (3) man's absolute obedience (Abraham's 'olah); and (4) man's confidence in God (Jacob's shelamim). They symbolize Israel's election to be, as it were, the camp within which God dwells. This is the only reward for Israel's fidelity: "Ye shall be My people and I will be your God" (see Ha-Levi, "Cuzari," i. 109). As the host of God, Israel must remain pure; and every Israelite must keep himself so as not to be cut off ("nikrat") from his people. Still, sins committed inadvertently are pardonable if man approaches God repentantly. That is the purpose of the sin-offerings. But there is no mortal who sinneth not; hence the Day of Atonement for Israel and all. Sacrifice is called "'abodah" = "service." It is "'abodah sheba-ma'aseh" = "ceremonial service," symbolizing the "'abodah sheba-leb" = "service in the heart," the tefillah prayer.

Views of Hoffmann.

Hoffmann believes in the ultimate reestablishment of the sacrificial cult. The old synagogal prayer-books recognized the sacrificial service as essential; but as it was impossible to bring the offerings prescribed, they were remembered in prayer (Musaf); for their study was as meritorious as their practise (see above). The prayer for the reestablishment of the altar, in which is included the petition "We-Hasheb Et ha-'Abodah"—the "Reẓeh" of the "Shemoneh 'Esreh"—is called the "'Abodah" (Ber. 29b; Shab. 24a; R. H. 12a; Meg. 18a; Soṭah 38b); for the body of the benediction was recited by the priests at the tamidim (Tamid v. 1; Ber. 11b) and by the high priest on the Day of Atonement after reading the Torah (Yoma 68b). Similar petitions for the reestablishment of the "'Abodah" are found in Lev. R. vii., Ex. R. xxxi., and Midr. Teh. to Ps. xvii. Three times every day this or a similar prayer was to be recited. The enforced suspension of the real "'Abodah" was regarded as a punishment for Israel's sins (see the prayer "Mi-Pene Ḥaṭa'enu" in the Musaf for Rosh ha-Shanah).

But the real attitude of rabbinical Judaism on the sacrifices is exhibited in Num. R. xix. A pagan having inquired concerning the Red Heifer, an explanation was tendered by Johanan b. Zakkai, who referred to the analogous treatment of one possessed of an evil spirit. The pupils of the rabbi demurred to that explanation, saying: "Him thou hast driven off with a reed. What answer wilt thou give us?" "By your lives," exclaimed the teacher, "dead bodies do not render unclean, nor does water make clean; but God has decreed 'a statute I have ordained and an institution I have established'; and it is not permitted to transgress the Law." Rabbinical Judaism accepted the law of sacrifices without presuming to understand it. Reform Judaism omits from the prayer-book reference to the sacrifices, sanguinary ceremonies being repugnant to its religious consciousness; it holds that the Jewish doctrine of sin and atonement is not grounded on the sacrificial scheme.

Attitude of Rabbinical Judaism.

BIBLIOGRAPHY: Robertson Smith, *Rel. of Sem.* 2d ed., London, 1894; Morrillier, in *Revue de l'Histoire des Religions*, Paris, 1897-98; Wellhausen, *Reste Arabischen Heidentums*, 2d ed., Berlin, 1897; Tylor, *Primitive Culture*, 3d ed., London, 1891; Zimmern, *Beiträge zur Kenntniss der Babylonischen Religion*, Leipsic, 1896; Frazer, *The Golden Bough*, 2d ed., London, 1900; Smend, *Lehrbuch der Alttestamentlichen Religionsgeschichte*, 2d ed., Freiburg, 1899; Kalisch, *Commentary to Leviticus*, i., London, 1867; Nowack, *Lehrbuch der Hebräischen Archäologie*, Leipsic, 1894; Benzinger, *Arch.* Freiburg, 1894; Volz, *Das Handauflegen*, in Stade's *Zeitschrift*, 1901; Matthes, *Handauflegen*, ib. 1903; Haupt, *Babylonian Elements*, in *Jour. Bib. Lit.*; Hoffmann, *Leviticus*, Berlin, 1905; commentaries on Leviticus by Dillmann and Knobel; Bähr, *Symbolik des Mosaischen Kultus*.

XLIV

Salvation

SALVATION: The usual rendering in the English versions for the Hebrew words ישע, ישועה, תשועה, derivatives of the stem ישע, which in the verb occurs only in the "nif'al" and "hif'il" forms. Other Hebrew terms translated by the corresponding forms of the English "save" and its synonyms are: (1) חיה. This word, meaning in the "ḳal" "to live," acquires in the "pi'el" and "hif'il" the signification "to keep alive," "to save alive" (Gen. xii. 12, xix. 19, xlv. 7; Ex. i. 17, 18; Num. xxii. 33; I Sam. xxvii. 11). Ezekiel employs it to express the condition of the repentant sinner who, having escaped the penalty of sin (death), continues safe in life. (2) הציל = "to deliver" (II Sam. xix. 9; A. V. "save"). (3) מלט, in the "pi'el" (I Sam. xix. 11; II Sam. xix. 5; Job xx. 20). (4) שמר = "to keep," "to spare" (Job ii. 6). (5) גאל = "to redeem" (see GO'EL). (6) פדה = "to release."

Etymological Meanings.

The underlying idea of all these words, save the last two, is help extended and made effective in times of need and danger, and protection from evil. "Padah" means "to free by paying ransom." "Ga'al" denotes the assumption of an obligation incumbent originally on another or in favor of another. "Yasha'" primitively means "to be or make wide." Evil and danger are always regarded as narrowing conditions or effects. From the "narrow" place the sufferer cries out. When help has come he is in a "wide" place (Ps. cxviii. 5). In battle enemies beset, surround, hem in (*ib.* verses 10, 11). Success in the combat relieves and removes the pressure. Hence "yasha'" and its derivatives express "victory." This is the import of the Hebrew in such passages as Judges xv. 12; I Sam. ii. 1, xiv. 45; II Sam. xxii. 51; and Isa. xlix. 8. Combined with "rinnah," the word "yeshu'ah" signifies the jubilant cry of the victors (Ps. cxviii. 15). The passionate appeal "Hoshi'ah-nna" (*ib.* verse 25; = "Hosanna") ought to be rendered "Give victory," a translation all the more assured by the certainty that the psalm is Maccabean. He who leads to victory in battle, therefore, is the "moshia'" = "savior" (*e.g.*, Othniel, in Judges iii. 9; Ehud, *ib.* iii. 15; Gideon, *ib.* vi. 36, 37; and the verb in Judges vii. 3; I Sam. xxv. 26; Ps. xliv. 4; Job xxvi. 2). But, according to the ancient concept, God Himself is the leader in battle ("Ish Milḥamah"; Ex. xv. 3). This throws light on the original bearing of the terms "savior" and "salvation" when applied to the Deity (comp. Isa. xxv. 9, xlv. 20). Language has preserved this notion in the epithet "Elohe yish'enu," which, idiomatically construed, means "our victorious God" (I Chron. xvi. 35; Ps. lxxix. 9; "thy victorious God," Isa. xvii. 10; comp. the similar construction "magen yish'aka" = "thy victorious shield," II Sam. xxii. 36; in the first three passages the A. V. has "God of our salvation" or "God of thy salvation"). Perhaps the king as the head of the army was greeted with the salutation "Hoshi'ah" = "Hosanna," corresponding to המלך לעולם יחיה (II Kings x. 19; Neh. ii. 3). This would appear from II Kings vi. 26, the woman's apostrophe carrying with it all the greater irony if it repeated the usual greeting of respect, and the king's answer being, like that of Naomi (Ruth i. 20, 21), a clever turn of the terminology of the address. This would explain also the greeting extended to Jesus (see HOSANNA) and the Messianic construction of the psalm. He was hailed thereby as "the king."

Hosanna.

From this idea of "victory," those of help in trouble and rescue from evil are logical derivatives; but it is not impossible that even in this secondary usage of the term "salvation" the primary notion of a successful combat is operative. Evils are caused by demons: victory over them results in escape, a grateful help. Thus man is saved from trouble (Ps. xxxiv. 7, Hebr.; Isa. xxxiii. 2; Jer.

xiv. 8, xxx. 7), from enemies (I Sam. iv. 3, vii. 8), from violence ("lion," Ps. xxii. 22; "men of blood," *ib.* lix. 3, Hebr.), from reproach (*ib.* lvii. 4 [A. V. 3]), from death (*ib.* vi. 5, 6), from a great calamity (Jer. xxx. 7), from sin, by paying the ransom ("yifdeh"; Ps. cxxx. 8), and from uncleanness (Ezek. xxxvi. 29).

The great catastrophe in Israel's history was the Exile. The prophetic doctrine concerning the remnant and the restoration readily transformed expressions for "victory" and "help" into technical terms. "Salvation" now connoted the survival (= victory) of the remnant, the return of the "saved" from exile; and God, in this new sense of the preserver of the remnant and the restorer of the new Israel, was recognized and proclaimed as the "savior" (Isa. xliii. 11; xlv. 15, 21; Zech. viii. 7). The prediction of Hosea (xiii. 4) was illustrated in the events that had come to pass, as was the assurance given by another prophet (Jer. xxx. 10, 11). In the happenings of the day Israel had learned that the Holy of Israel was the savior (Isa. xliii. 3, xlix. 26, lx. 16). Babylon had none to save her (*ib.* xlvii. 15).

Post-Exilic Views.

In the Psalms "salvation," by a similar train of thought, expresses the triumph of the "poor" and of the "meek" (Ps. xii. 6). God is the "rock of salvation"; contrary to fickle man, He will not deceive (*ib.* lxii. 3, 7, Hebr.). By God's salvation the poor are lifted up (*ib.* lxix. 30). This salvation will be proclaimed from day to day (*ib.* xcvi. 2; comp. xcviii. 2). God is a stronghold of salvation for His anointed (*ib.* xxviii. 8). Under the scepter of the "anointed king" or MESSIAH this salvation (restoration), with all it implies of happiness, joy, security, splendor of Israel, and universal peace, would be realized. With God's judgment (which also is God's victory [צדק], for a trial is always a combat) God's salvation approaches; and finally salvation is established in Zion for Israel, God's splendor (Isa. xlvi. 13). In this sense, then, the Messiah is a savior; his kingdom, one of salvation.

"Salvation" and "redemption" ("ge'ulah"), as applied in the Messianic conception, are identical.

Relation to Messiah. As God is the "Moshia'," so He is also the "Go'el" (Isa. xliv. 23, xlviii. 20, lii. 9, lxiii. 9; Ps. lxxiv. 2). This savior or redeemer is YHWH (Isa. xliv. 24, xlvii. 4, xlviii. 17, lxiii. 16; Deutero-Isaiah prefers the latter term). The remnant are the "ge'ulim," redeemed of YHWH (Isa. lxii. 12; Ps. cvii. 2). The primary idea underlying the term "ga'al," like that basic to "padah," the derivatives of which are also employed to designate those that are saved for and in this Messianic kingdom (Isa. li. 11; Zech. x. 8; Ps. xxv. 22; cxxx. 7, 8; comp. Isa. i. 27), is related to that of "yasha'" only in so far as both connote an act that results in freedom or ease to its beneficiary. The slave, for instance, might be redeemed from bondage as was Israel (Deut. xiii. 6, xxi. 8; II Sam. vii. 23; Neh. i. 10; Mic. vi. 4). The Exile was a period of captivity. By bringing home the dispersed, God was their redeemer; and in consequence Israel was saved. In ancient Israel the go'el was one upon whom had fallen the obligation to pay the honors due to a deceased kinsman; for with no son born to him a man was deprived of the filial tribute, and his name was in danger of obliteration; therefore it was the duty of the go'el, the next of kin, to raise up his name (see LEVIRATE MARRIAGE).

In case of murder the go'el was the AVENGER OF BLOOD. Thus even in these primitive conceptions the go'el may be said to have been a redeemer, saving men from extinction of name; also saving spirits from restlessly wandering about because deprived of funereal honors, and, in the case of the murdered, because the wrong remained unrequited ("blood for blood"). In no other sense than "avenger" may "go'el" be understood in Job xix. 25 (A. V. "redeemer"). This passage is construed by many theologians as proof of the belief in immortality, and as indicating a presentiment of Paulinian soteriology. The context, even with the corrupt Masoretic text unemendated, refutes this interpretation. The speaker is merely uttering his unshaken belief that the wrongs done him will find their avenger. Emendated the passage would read, "I know my avenger is even now alive, and later will avenge ["yiḳom"] upon [for] my dust." In the next verse "mi-besari" (A. V. "from my flesh") is rightly understood as "away from [outside] my family," the thought being that even if the members of his family ("flesh"; designated also as "skin") prove derelict to their duty, he has seen one, and not a stranger, that will assume the obligation.

The Jewish Messianic doctrine of salvation does not center in personal immortality, nor in the theologized application of the solidarity of the clan. The Jewish savior was not a go'el in the sense that he took upon himself the blood-guiltiness of sin incurred by another. Moreover, the avenger requited murder by killing another and not himself: he did not die for others, but he caused death in behalf of others. The go'el never was the vicarious victim. It was he who demanded blood, but never gave his own as a ransom. In this theology of salvation "go'el" is mistaken for "kofer" (see ATONEMENT). For the later development of the eschatological implications of salvation see ESCHATOLOGY.

XLV

Selah

SELAH (Hebrew, סלה): Term of uncertain etymology and grammatical form and of doubtful meaning. It occurs seventy-one times in thirty-nine of the Psalms, and three times in Hab. iii. It is placed at the end of Ps. iii., ix., xxiv., xlvi., and in most other cases at the end of a verse, the exceptions being Ps. lv. 20, lvii. 4, and Hab. iii. 3, 9. Of the psalms in which it is found, twenty-three belong to the group in which "Elohim" is used to designate God; twenty-eight to that called by Briggs the "director's (למנצח = "choir-leader"; see PSALMS, CRITICAL VIEW) copies"; and twenty to the "Davidic" collection. Again, nine of the twelve Korahite and seven (LXX. eight, including lxxx. 8) of the twelve Asaph psalms have the term. Three psalms with "Selah" are headed "Miktam"; seven, "Maskil"; ten, "Shir"; twenty-six, "Mizmor"; while Habakkuk iii. is superscribed "Tefillah."

That the real significance of this curious term (or combination of letters) was not known even by the ancient versions is evidenced by the variety of renderings given to it. The Septuagint, Symmachus, and Theodotion translate *διάψαλμα*—a word as enigmatical in Greek as is "Selah" in Hebrew. The Hexapla simply transliterates *σελ*. Aquila, Jerome, and the Targum give it the value of "always" (Aquila, *ἀεί*; Jerome, "semper"; Targum, for the most part לעלמין = "in secula" or תדירא = "semper"). Theodotion in Ps. ix. 17 has the translation *ἀεί*; the Quinta gives *εἰς τοὺς αἰῶνας* (לעלמין); and the Sexta, *διαπαντός* (in Ps. xx. 4, *εἰς τέλος*).

Technical Term.

Jacob of Edessa, quoted by Bar Hebræus (on Ps. x. 1), notices that instead of *διάψαλμα* some copies present *αεί* = בכל זבן; and he explains this as referring to the custom of the people of reciting a doxology at the end of paragraphs of the liturgical psalms. In five passages (see Field, Hexapla on Ps. xxxviii. [Hebr. xxxix.] 12) Aquila offers, according to the Hexaplar Syriac, עיניתא = "song," the *ᾆσμα* by which Origen reports Aquila to have replaced the *διάψαλμα* of the Septuagint. According to Hippolytus (De Lagarde, "Novæ Psalterii Græci Editionis Specimen," 10), the Greek term *διάψαλμα* signified a change in rhythm or melody at the places marked by the term, or a change in thought and theme. Against this explanation Baethgen ("Psalmen," p. xv., 1st ed., Göttingen, 1892) urges the circumstance that the enigmatical expression occurs also at the end of psalms. The cogency of this objection would hold if the mark had been inserted by the original writer and not, as is most probable, by a later editor who may have expected the Psalms to be recited in succession without reference to the divisions in the Masoretic text; or if it were an indubitable fact that where in the Hebrew a psalm now ends it ended in the original. Augustin (on Ps. iv. 3) regards *διάψαλμα* as indicating that what follows is not to be joined to the preceding. He suggests also the possibility that the Hebrew "Selah" meant "Fiat" = "Let there be [made]." The Masoretic accentuation always connects "Selah" with the preceding, as though it were part of the text or thought, most likely because it was held to mean "forever." In fact, the vowel-points in סֶלָה seem to indicate a "ḳere" נֶצַח (with "ḳameẓ" on account of ה) = "forever" (see B. Jacob in Stade's "Zeitschrift," xvi. [1896] 129 *et seq.*).

Modern Views.

Nor is there greater unanimity among modern scholars than among the ancient versions. Only on one point is there agreement, namely, that "Selah" has no grammatical connection with the text. It is either a liturgico-musical mark or a sign of another character with a bearing on the reading or the verbal form of the text. As thirty-one of the thirty-nine psalms with the caption "To the choirmaster [למנצח]" present "Selah," the musical value of the mark has been regarded as well assured. In keeping with this it has been assigned to the root סלל, as an imperative that should properly have been vocalized סֹלָּה, "Sollah" (Ewald, "Kritische Grammatik der Hebräischen Sprache," p. 554; König, "Historisch - Kritisches Lehrgebäude der Hebräischen Sprache," ii., part i., p. 539). The meaning of this imperative is given as "Lift up," equivalent to "loud" or "fortissimo," a direction to the accompanying musicians to break in at the place marked with crash of cymbals and blare of trumpets, the orchestra playing an interlude while the singers' voices were hushed. The effect, as far as the singer was concerned, was to mark a pause. This significance, too, has been read into the expression or sign, "Selah" being held to be a variant of "shelah" (שלה = "pause"). But as the interchange of "shin" and "samek" is not usual in Biblical Hebrew, and as the meaning "pause" is clearly inapplicable in the middle of a verse or where a pause would interrupt the sequence of thought, this proposition has met with little favor. Neither has that which proposes to treat it as a loan-word from the Greek *ψάλλε* = "strike the harp," etc.

Grätz ("Kritischer Commentar zu den Psalmen," i. 93 *et seq.*) argues that "Selah" introduces a new paragraph as it were, a transition in thought, and also in some instances a quotation (*e.g.*, Ps. lvii. 8 *et seq.* from cviii. 2 *et seq.*). The fact that the term occurs four times at the end of a psalm would not weigh against this theory. As stated above, the Psalms were meant to be read in sequence, and, moreover, many of them are fragments; indeed, Ps. ix. is reckoned one with Ps. x. in the Septuagint, which omits *διάψαλμα* also at the end of Ps. iii., xxiv., and xlvi. B. Jacob (*l.c.*) concludes (1) that since no etymological explanation is possible, "Selah" signifies a pause in or for the Temple song; and (2) that its meaning was concealed lest the Temple privileges should be obtained by the synagogues or perhaps even by the churches.

Another series of explanations is grounded on the assumption that its signification is liturgical rather

More Liturgical than Musical.

than musical. It marks the place, and is an appeal, for the bystanders to join in with a eulogistic response. Briggs ("Jour. Bib. Lit." 1899, p. 142) accepts the etymology and grammatical explanation given above, *i. e.*, that "Selah" is a cohortative imperative, meaning "Lift up [your benediction]," the eulogy with which psalms or sections of psalms were concluded. One would expect the imperative to be in the plural if the address was to more than one bystander. However, Briggs' explanation indicates the line along which the mystery connected with this term or combination of consonants is to be removed. It has been suspected that "Selah" is an artificial word formed from initials. That is probably the case, though the resolution of the initials usually suggested, סב למעלה השר (= "Return to the beginning, O singer"), has to be abandoned. The renderings in the versions, "'olmin," ἀεί, and the like (= "forever"), if they do not prove that סלה is a corruption for עולם—the word "'olam" standing for the first noun in the benediction—create a strong presumption that the initials of the verse in which "'olam" occurs are hidden in the puzzling word "Selah." Grätz (*l.c.*) shows that in Ps. lv. 20 סלה is a corruption for כלה (or even for כלם), meaning "destroy"; and a similar corruption of the first and third consonants throughout has contrived to make "Selah" the "crux interpretum." If in some instances כלה or כלם (= "destroy") be read and in others כלח, the enigma disappears. "K l ḥ" represents the eulogy "Ki le-'olam ḥasdo" (כי לעולם חסדו), hence the עלמין or ἀεὶ of the versions—a eulogy which is familiar and which is found as such in the Psalms (Ps. c. 5, cvi. 1, cvii. 1, cxviii. 1 *et seq.*; especially cxxxvi.; also I Chron. xvi. 34, 41; II Chron. v. 13, xx. 21). This is confirmed by the fact that just such phrases as כי־טוב, and perhaps ועד עולם, actually do occur in passages where "Selah" might stand equally well and with as little bearing on the context (Ps. lii. 11, 12). In Ps. xxxiv. 11 טוב at the end is certainly superfluous; but it stands where one would expect this very term סלה; and,

Probably a Contracted Form.

therefore, it is not too bold a conjecture to read here כי טוב in the sense of a technical abbreviation of the eulogy. In this connection the midrash on Ps. cxviii. is of importance; quoting Isaiah iii. 10, it commands that after the mention of the righteous the words כי טוב should be added, but that after reference to an evil-doer a curse should be pronounced.

The latter injunction throws light on many passages in which "Selah" has another sense than that noted above, and in which it should be read כלה or כלם (= "Destroy them"), as one word. It is noticeable that the term occurs frequently after a reference to evil-doers (Ps. iv. 3; vii. 6; ix. 21; xxxii. 5; xlix. 14 [xlix. 16 ?]; lii. 5; liv. 5; lvii. 4, 7; lix. 6; lxii. 5; lxvi. 7; lxxxii. 2; lxxxviii. 8; lxxxix. 46, 49; cxl. 6; Hab. iii. [A. V. ii.] 13); and at the mention of these the bystanders break forth into malediction, as they do into benediction at the mention of God's wonderful deeds. Their comment on the recital is "Destroy them," "Make an end of them," or "of the evils," *i.e.*, "Forego" (as in Ps. lxxxviii. 8). "Selah" is thus identical with כלה as twice repeated in Ps. lix. 14 (Hebr.), "Destroy in anger; destroy that they be no more." This very verse ends with "Selah," which, as explained above, is a repetition (but in the mouths of the bystanders) of the passionate outcry כלה (= "Destroy").

Some few passages remain in which סלה seems to fit in neither as a eulogy—*i.e.*, as a corruption of עולם or as an artificial combination of initials making כלה—nor as an imprecation. But even in these the reading כלה (= "Destroy") suggests itself, not indeed as a liturgical response, but as a note to indicate that something in the text should be deleted. This seems to be the case in Ps. lv. 8 (R. V. 7), where verses 8 and 9 virtually conflict; for the desert is the place where storms blow. "Selah" here has the appearance of a sign that the verse, being a quotation from somewhere else and really not belonging to the psalm, should be omitted. The same holds good in Ps. lxxxi. 8, where the third member of the verse is clearly a marginal note explanatory of the preceding. "Selah" after על מי מריבה, "at the waters of Meribah," indicates this fact,

Sometimes Meaning "Delete."

and means כלה (= "Delete"). Another instance of this is Ps. lx. 6, where the words מפני קשט break the connection between verses 6a and 7, and really make no sense. In Hab. iii. (ii.) 3, 9, also, "Selah" points to some defect in the text.

Perhaps the latter use of the term will throw light on the origin of the Greek *διάψαλμα*. It may be connected with the verb *διαψάω* = "to rub away thoroughly," "to erase." At all events some of the versions point to a reading in which כל was visible, *e.g.*, *διαπαντός* (Sexta), while the translation of Aquila according to the Hexaplar Syriac, עוניתא, meaning "responsive, antiphonal song," corroborates the assumption that the benediction or malediction was marked as anticipated in the passage.

"Selah" occurs also in the text of the SHEMONEH 'ESREH. This fact shows that at the time when the text of this prayer was finally fixed, the term had become a familiar one; and as the "Shemoneh 'Esreh" draws its vocabulary largely from the Psalms, the appearance of "Selah" in the prayer is not strange. In the Talmud that word is treated as a synonym of "neẓaḥ" and "wa'ed," all three signifying eternal continuance without interruption ('Er. 54a, אין לו הפסק עולמית). Ḳimḥi connects the term with the verb סלל (= "lift up"), and applies it to the voice, which should be lifted up, or become louder at the places marked by it (commentary on Ps. iii. 2). Ibn Ezra (on Ps. iii. 2) regards it as an equivalent of כן הוא or נכון הדבר, an affirmative corroborative expletive.

XLVI

Servant of God

SERVANT OF GOD: Title of honor given to various persons or groups of persons; namely, Abraham, Isaac, Jacob (Deut. ix. 27; comp. Ps. cv. 6, 42), Moses (Deut. xxxiv. 5; Josh. i. 1; I Chron. vi. 49: II Chron. xxiv. 9; Neh. x. 29; Dan. ix. 11), Joshua (Josh. xxiv. 29; Judges ii. 8), David (Ps. xviii., xxxvi., captions), the Prophets (Jer. vii. 25, xxv. 4, and elsewhere), Isaiah (Isa. xx. 3), Job (Job i. 8, ii. 3, xlii. 8), and even Nebuchadrezzar (Jer. xxv. 9, xxvii. 6, xliii. 10). In the second part of Isaiah, in some passages of Jeremiah, and in Ezekiel the expression occurs with a special significance.

Semitic Use of "Servant."

That devoted worshipers of the Deity were commonly designated as God's servants is attested by the theophorous personal names frequent in all Semitic dialects, and in which one element is some form of the verb "'abad" (עבד) and the other the name of the god (comp. "'Abd Allah"; see Lidzbarski, "Handbuch der Nordsemitischen Epigraphik," pp. 332 *et seq.*). It is in this sense that Abraham, Moses, Job, and Joshua are designated as "the servants" of Yhwh. In the case of Nebuchadrezzar, the meaning is somewhat different. By the prophet the Babylonian king is considered as the instrument of God's plans. To explain why the title was conferred on him it is not necessary to speculate on the possibly monotheistic leanings of this monarch. Nebuchadrezzar in Daniel and Judith is the very prototype of Antiochus Epiphanes, the execrated enemy of God. Nor is the use of the epithet in this connection satisfactorily explained by the theory advanced by Duhm, that Nebuchadrezzar bore the title because during his reign Israel could not very well claim to be YHWH's representative on earth. Unless "'Abdi" in the passages in Jeremiah given above is a scribal corruption—which most probably it is not—Nebuchadrezzar is so designated because he carries out, as would a slave who has no choice, the designs of YHWH (comp. "Ashur shebeṭ appi," Isa. x. 5).

But the epithet represents the whole people or a section of Israel in the following passages: Ezek. xxviii. 25, xxxvii. 25; Jer. xxx. 10, xlvi. 27; Isa. xli. 8; xlii. 19 *et seq.*; xliii. 10; xliv. 1 *et seq.*, 21; xlv. 4; xlviii. 20; it has ceased to be an "epitheton ornans" used to honor and distinguish an individual. This is patent from the use of "Jacob" as a synonymous designation (Ezek. xxviii. 25, xxxvii. 25; Jer. xxx. 10; Isa. xliv. 1, xlv. 4, xlviii. 20). Israel's destiny and duty, rather than its previous conduct, are indicated in this denomination. Israel is God's "chosen one," the equivalent of the expression "servant of YHWH" used by these exilic prophets (Isa. xliii. 20, xlv. 4; comp. *ib.* lxv. 9, 15, 22). "My chosen [ones]" = "My servants" (Sellin, "Studien zur Entstehungsgeschichte der Jüdischen Gemeinde," i. 81). YHWH has "called" and "strengthened" Israel (Isa. xli. 9); therefore it is not abandoned and need not be afraid (*ib.* verse 10). Its enemies shall be confounded (*ib.* verses 11, 12). YHWH has called Israel by its name (*i.e.*, His "servant" or "son"): therefore it belongs to Him; for He has created it and formed it (*ib.* xliii. 1, 2). Through flood and fire it may pass unscathed; for YHWH is with it. He would exchange Egypt, Ethiopia, and Sheba (the richest countries) for Israel. God loves it: it is precious in His eyes (*ib.* verses 3 *et seq.*). YHWH's spirit will be poured out on its seed, and His blessing on its shoots (*ib.* xliv. 3). Israel is, in fact, a witness unto YHWH: as He is one, so Israel is the one unique chosen people (*ib.* xliv. 6, 7, 8, "'Am 'Olam"). As such a servant, predestined to be a light for the nations, Israel is called from the womb (*ib.* xlix. 1–6; but see below). It is for this that Israel will return from exile (Jer. xxx. 10), which was a disciplinary visitation (*ib.* verse 11). Israel, however, does not as yet recog-

Applied to Israel.

nize its own opportunity (Isa. xl. 2). Though Israel has sinned God has not abandoned it (*ib.* xlii. 24), because He has not abdicated (*ib.* xlii. 8). It is for His own sake, not for Israel's, that God has chosen Israel (*ib.* xlviii. 11). In another passage Israel is illed with doubts concerning this (*ib.* lxiii. 15 *et seq.*; probably this is a non-Isaian chapter). At all events, as yet it is blind and deaf, although, inasmuch as it has eyes and ears, it should and might be both an observer and a hearer as behooves one that is "meshullam" and "'ebed YHWH" (*ib.* xlii. 18-20; "meshullam" = "one that has completely given himself over," a synonym of "'ebed," as Mohammed's religion is Islam and he "'Abd Allah," xlii. 18-20). Hence the command "Bring forth the blind people that have eyes, and the deaf that have ears" (*ib.* xliii. 8).

Special Usage in Isaiah.

There are, however, four passages in the Isaian compilation where perhaps the "national" interpretation is not admissible, namely, Isa. xlii. 1-4, xlix. 1-6, l. 4-9, lii. 13-liii. 12. The descriptions in them of the attitude and conduct of the 'ebed YHWH seem to be idealizations of the character of an individual rather than of the whole of Israel. Especially is this true of Isa. lii. 13-liii. 12, the exaltation of the "man of suffering." In this a prophetic anticipatory picture of the MESSIAH has been recognized by both Jewish and Christian tradition. Modern critics read into it the portraits of Jeremiah (so Bunsen), Zerubbabel (Sellin, "Serubbabel," 1898, and Kittel, "Zur Theologie des Altentestaments," 2d ed.: "Jesaja und der Leidende Messias im A. T."), or Sheshbazar (Winckler, "Altorientalische Forschungen," ii. 452-453). Rothstein (and Sellin at present) holds the description to be meant for Jehoiachin (Rothstein, "Die Genealogie des Jehojachin"); while Bertholet ("Zu Jesaja LIII."), dividing the chapters into two distinct "songs," regards the first (Isa. lii. 13-15, liii. 11b-12) as a glorification of a teacher of the Torah; and the second (*ib.* liii. 1-11a) as that of Eleazar (II Macc. vi. 18-31). Duhm also is inclined to separate this description into two distinct "songs" (Duhm, "Das Buch Jesaia," 3d ed., 1902, pp. 355-367); but he declares it to be impossible to assign a definite person as the model. The "man of suffering" is, however, a teacher of the Torah. Even the period when these four 'ebed YHWH songs were written is not determinable save in so far as they are post-exilic—perhaps as late as the days immediately preceding the Maccabean uprising.

It may be noted that these interpretations, according to which the picture is that of a definite individual, were anticipated among Jewish commentators of the Middle Ages. Saadia referred the whole section (Isa. lii. 13–liii. 12) to Jeremiah; and Ibn Ezra finds this view a probable one (see Neubauer and Driver, "The Fifty-third Chapter of Isaiah According to the Jewish Interpreters"). Kraetzschmar ("Der Leidende Gottesknecht"), among moderns, selects Ezekiel for the model on account of Ezek. iv. Cheyne was at one time inclined to associate this 'ebed YHWH with Job ("Jewish Religious Life," p. 162).

Present Conditions of Problem.

Ingenious as these various identifications are, of late years there has been in evidence a decided reversion to the theory that also Israel, or at least a part of the congregation, is idealized in these songs. Budde (in "American Journal of Theology," 1899, pp. 499–540) has successfully met the arguments of Duhm; and other scholars, *e.g.*, Marti (see his commentary on Isaiah), Giesebrecht, and König, are now ranged on his side. This concession must be made: in the four songs, somewhat more strongly than in others where Israel is hailed the servant of YHWH, stress is laid on missionary activity, both within and without Israel, on the part of the servant; furthermore various characteristics are dwelt on that are attributed in a certain group of the Psalms to the "pious." For this reason there is strong presumption that the "poor," the "'anawim" (meek) of the Psalms, are the Israel to which the epithet "'ebed YHWH" and the portrayal of his qualifications refer. Budde reverts to the theory of Rashi, Ibn Ezra, and Ḳimḥi, that the confession in Isa. liii. is uttered by the "nations" referred to in Isa. lii. 15, and that thus Israel is the martyr, with which view Wellhausen, Giesebrecht, Marti, and others agree. If the "remnant" (the "poor") be personified in the "servant," the "We" of the confession may refer to those of Israel that had rejected these "poor" and "meek"; if such an interpretation were to be accepted the exilic date of these idealized personifications would, of course, have to be abandoned. But these "poor" were just such quiet missionaries as are described in Isa. xlii. 1–4. They suffered in the pursuit of their missionary labors (*ib.* l. 4) as well as at the hands of their own fellow Israelites (*ib.* lii., liii.).

BIBLIOGRAPHY: Commentaries on Isaiah; Schian, *Die Ebed-Jahwe-Lieder in Jes. xl.–lxvi.* 1895; Laue, *Die Ebed-Jahwe Lieder in II Theil des Jesaia*, etc., 1898; Füllkrug, *Der Gottesknecht des Deuterojesaia*, 1899; Kraetzschmar, *Der Leidende Gottesknecht*, 1899; J. Ley, *Die Bedeutung des Ebed-Jahwe im 2ten Theile des Propheten Jesaja*, in *Theologische Studien und Kritiken*, 1899; Dalman, *Jes. 53*, etc., 2d ed., 1891; Kosters, in *Theologisch Tijdschrift*, pp. 591 *et seq.*, Leyden, 1896; Cheyne, in *Encyc. Bibl.* iv. 4398–4410, s.v. *Servant of the Lord*.

XLVII

Shemoneh 'Esreh

SHEMONEH 'ESREH: Collection of benedictions forming the second—the SHEMA' being the first—important section of the daily prayers at the morning ("Shaḥarit"), afternoon ("Minḥah"), and evening ("'Arbit") services, as well as of the additional (MUSAF) service on Sabbaths and holy days. Literally, the name means "eighteen"; and its wide use shows that at the time it came into vogue the benedictions ("berakot") comprised in the prayer must have numbered eighteen, though in reality as fixed in the versions recited in the synagogues they number nineteen. As the prayer par excellence, it is designated as the "Tefillah" (prayer), while among the Sephardic Jews it is known as the "'Amidah," *i.e.*, the prayer which the worshiper is commanded to recite standing (see also Zohar, i. 105). The eighteen—now nineteen—benedictions, according to their content and character, are readily grouped as follows: (1) three blessings of praise ("Shebaḥim," Nos. i., ii., iii.); (2) twelve (now thirteen) petitions ("Baḳḳashot," Nos. iv.–xv. [xvi.]), and (3) three concluding ones of thanks ("Hoda'ot," Nos. xvi. [xvii.], xviii., and xix.). The first three and the last three constitute, so to speak, the permanent stock, used at every service; while the middle group varies on Sabbath, New Moons, and holy days from the formula for week-days. The construction of the "Shemoneh 'Esreh" complies with the rabbinical injunction that in every prayer the praises of God must precede private petitions ('Ab. Zarah 6), as the following comment shows: "In the first three [ראשונות]

The Three Groups.

man is like a slave chanting the praise of his master; in the middle sections [אמצעיות] he is a servant petitioning for his compensation from his employer; in the last three [אחרונות] he is the servant who, having received his wages, takes leave of his master" (Ber. 34a).

No. i. of the first group is designated (R. H. iv. 5) as "Abot" = "patriarchs," because the Patriarchs are mentioned, and the love of (or for) them is expressly emphasized therein. Translated, it reads as follows:

"Blessed be Thou, O Lord, our God and God of our fathers, God of Abraham, God of Isaac, and God of Jacob, the great, the mighty, and the fearful God—God Most High—who bestowest goodly kindnesses, and art the Creator ["Ḳoneh," which signifies primarily "Creator" and then "Owner"] of all, and rememberest the love of [or for] the Fathers and bringest a redeemer for their children's children for the sake of [His] Thy name in love. King, Helper, Savior, and Shield; blessed be Thou, Shield of Abraham" (see Dembitz, "Jewish Services in the Synagogue and Home," pp. 112 *et seq.*).

No. ii. has the name "Geburot" (R. H. iv. 5) = "powers," because it addresses God as the "Ba'al Geburot" and recites His powers, *i.e.*, the resurrection of the dead and the sustentation of the living (comp. Gen. R. xiii.). It is called also "Teḥiyyat ha-Metim" = "the resurrection of the dead." Rain is considered as great a manifestation of power as the resurrection of the dead (Ta'an. 2a); hence in winter a line referring to the descent of rain (Ber. 33a) is inserted in this benediction. The eulogy runs as follows:

"Thou art mighty forever, O Lord ["Adonai," not the Tetragrammaton]: Thou resurrectest the dead; art great to save. Sustaining the living in loving-kindness, resurrecting the dead in abundant mercies, Thou supportest the falling, and healest the sick, and settest free the captives, and keepest [fulfillest] Thy [His] faith to them that sleep in the dust. Who is like Thee, master of mighty deeds [= owner of the powers over life and death], and who may be compared unto Thee? King sending death and reviving again and causing salvation to sprout forth, Thou art surely believed to resurrect the dead. Blessed be Thou, O Lord, who revivest the dead."

No. iii. is known as "Ḳedushshat ha-Shem" = "the sanctification of the Name." It is very short, though the variants are numerous (see below). It reads as follows:

"Thou art holy and Thy name is holy, and the holy ones praise Thee every day. Selah. Blessed be Thou, O Lord, the holy God."

At public worship, when the precentor, or, as he is known in Hebrew, the SHELIAḤ ẒIBBUR (messenger or deputy of the congregation), repeats the prayer aloud, the preceding benediction (No. iii.), with the exception of the concluding sentence, "Blessed be Thou," etc., is replaced by the ḲEDUSHSHAH.

In work-day services the Shemoneh 'Esreh continues with Group 2 ("Baḳḳashot"), supplications referring to the needs of Israel (Sifre, Wezot ha-Berakah, ed. Friedmann, p. 142b).

The Intermediate Blessings.

No. iv., known, from its opening words, as "Attah Ḥonen," or, with reference to its content—a petition for understanding—as "Binah" (Meg. 17b), sometimes also as "Birkat Ḥokmah" (on account of the word "ḥokmah," now omitted, which occurred in the first phrase) and as "Birkat ha-Ḥol" = "work-day benediction" (Ber. 33a), reads as follows:

"Thou graciously vouchsafest knowledge to man and teachest mortals understanding: vouchsafe unto us from Thee knowledge, understanding, and intelligence. Blessed be Thou, O Lord, who vouchsafest knowledge."

No. v. is known as "Teshubah" = "return" (Meg. 17b):

"Lead us back, our Father, to Thy Torah; bring us near, our King, to Thy service, and cause us to return in perfect repentance before Thee. Blessed be Thou, O Lord, who acceptest repentance."

No. vi. is the "Seliḥah," the prayer for forgiveness (Meg. 17b):

"Forgive us, our Father, for we have sinned; pardon us, our King, for we have transgressed: for Thou pardonest and forgivest. Blessed be Thou, O Gracious One, who multipliest forgiveness."

No. vii. is styled "Birkat ha-Ge'ullah," the benediction ending with "Go'el" = "Redeemer" (Meg. 17b):

"Look but upon our affliction and fight our fight and redeem us speedily for the sake of Thy name: for Thou art a strong redeemer. Blessed art Thou, O Lord, the Redeemer of Israel."

No. viii. is the "Birkat ha-Ḥolim" ('Ab. Zarah 8a), or "Refu'ah" (Meg. 17b), the prayer for the sick or for recovery:

"Heal us and we shall be healed; help us and we shall be helped: for Thou art our joy. Cause Thou to rise up full healings for all our wounds: for Thou, God King, art a true and merciful physician: blessed be Thou, O Lord, who healest the sick of His people Israel."

No. ix. is the "Birkat ha-Shanim" (Meg. 17b), the petition that the year may be fruitful:

"Bless for us, O Lord our God, this year and all kinds of its yield for [our] good; and shower down [in winter, "dew and rain for"] a blessing upon the face of the earth: fulfil us of Thy bounty and bless this our year that it be as the good years. Blessed be Thou, O Lord, who blessest the years."

No. x. is the benediction in regard to the "Ḳibbuẓ Galuyot," the gathering of the Jews of the Diaspora (Meg. 17b):

"Blow the great trumpet [see SHOFAR] for our liberation, and lift a banner to gather our exiles, and gather us into one body from the four corners of the earth; blessed be Thou, O Lord, who gatherest the dispersed of Thy [His] people Israel."

No. xi. is the "Birkat ha-Din," the petition for justice (Meg. 17b):

"Restore our judges as of yore, and our counselors as in the beginning, and remove from us grief and sighing. Reign Thou over us, O Lord, alone in loving-kindness and mercy, and establish our innocence by the judgment. Blessed be Thou, O Lord the King, who lovest righteousness and justice."

The Birkat ha-Minim.

No. xii. is the "Birkat ha-Minim" or "ha-Ẓadduḳim" (Ber. 28b; Meg. 17b; Yer. Ber. iv.), the prayer against heretics and Sadducees (and traducers, informers, and traitors):

"May no hope be left to the slanderers; but may wickedness perish as in a moment; may all Thine enemies be soon cut off, and do Thou speedily uproot the haughty and shatter and humble them speedily in our days. Blessed be Thou, O Lord, who strikest down enemies and humblest the haughty" (Dembitz, *l.c.* p. 132).

No. xiii. is a prayer in behalf of the "Ẓaddiḳim" = "pious" (Meg. 17b):

"May Thy mercies, O Lord our God, be stirred over the righteous and over the pious and over the elders of Thy people, the House of Israel, and over the remnant of their scribes, and over the righteous proselytes, and over us, and bestow a goodly reward upon them who truly confide in Thy name; and assign us our portion with them forever; and may we not come to shame for that we have trusted in Thee. Blessed be Thou, O Lord, support and reliance for the righteous."

No. xiv. is a prayer in behalf of Jerusalem:

"To Jerusalem Thy city return Thou in mercy and dwell in her midst as Thou hast spoken, and build her speedily in our days as an everlasting structure and soon establish there the throne of David. Blessed be Thou, O Lord, the builder of Jerusalem."

No. xv. begins with "Et Ẓemaḥ Dawid" (Meg. 18a), and is so entitled. It is a prayer for the rise of David's sprout, *i.e.*, the Messianic king. At one time it must have formed part of the preceding benediction (see below). It reads:

"The sprout of David Thy servant speedily cause Thou to sprout up; and his horn do Thou uplift through Thy victorious salvation; for Thy salvation we are hoping every day. Blessed be Thou, O Lord, who causest the horn of salvation to sprout forth."

No. xvi. is denominated simply "Tefillah" = "prayer" (Meg. 18a). It is a supplication that the preceding prayers may be answered:

"Hear our voice, O Lord our God, spare and have mercy on us, and accept in mercy and favor our prayer. For a God that heareth prayers and supplications art Thou. From before Thee, O our King, do not turn us away empty-handed. For Thou hearest the prayer of Thy people Israel in mercy. Blessed be Thou, O Lord, who hearest prayer."

No. xvii. is termed the "'Abodah" = "sacrificial service" (Ber. 29b; Shab. 24a; R. H. 12a; Meg. 18a; Soṭah 38b; Tamid 32b):

"Be pleased, O Lord our God, with Thy people Israel and their prayer, and return [*i.e.*, reestablish] the sacrificial service to the altar of Thy House, and the fire-offerings of Israel and their prayer [offered] in love accept Thou with favor, and may the sacrificial service of Israel Thy people be ever acceptable to Thee. And may our eyes behold Thy merciful return to Zion. Blessed be Thou who restorest Thy [His] Shekinah to Zion."

No. xviii. is the "Hoda'ah" = a "confession" or "thanksgiving" (Meg. 18a; Ber. 29a, 34a; Shab. 24a; Soṭah 68b; see also Articles of Faith):

Concluding Benedictions.

"We acknowledge to Thee, O Lord, that Thou art our God as Thou wast the God of our fathers, forever and ever. Rock of our life, Shield of our help, Thou art immutable from age to age. We thank Thee and utter Thy praise, for our lives that are [delivered over] into Thy hands and for our souls that are entrusted to Thee; and for Thy miracles that are [wrought] with us every day and for Thy marvelously [marvels and] kind deeds that are of every time; evening and morning and noontide. Thou art [the] good, for Thy mercies are endless: Thou art [the] merciful, for Thy kindnesses never are complete: from everlasting we have hoped in Thee. And for all these things may Thy name be blessed and exalted always and forevermore. And all the living will give thanks unto Thee and praise Thy great name in truth, God, our salvation and help. Selah. Blessed be Thou, O Lord, Thy name is good, and to Thee it is meet to give thanks."

After this at public prayer in the morning the priestly blessing is added.

No. xix., however, is a résumé of this blessing. The benediction exists in various forms, the fuller one being used (in the German ritual) in the morning service alone (Meg. 18a), as follows:

"Bestow peace, happiness, and blessing, grace, loving-kindness, and mercy upon us and upon all Israel Thy people: bless us, our Father, even all of us, by the light of Thy countenance, for by this light of Thy countenance Thou gavest us, O Lord our God, the law of life, loving-kindness, and righteousness, and blessing and mercy, life and peace. May it be good in Thine eyes to bless Thy people Israel in every time and at every hour with Thy peace. Blessed be Thou, O Lord, who blessest Thy [His] people Israel with peace."

The shorter form reads thus:

"Mayest Thou bestow much peace upon Thy people Israel forever. For Thou art the immutable King, the Master unto all peace. May it be good in Thine eyes to bless" (and so forth as in the preceding form).

For the Sabbath, the middle supplications are replaced by one, so that the Sabbath "Tefillah" is composed of seven benedictions. This one speaks of the sanctity of the day (Ber. 29a; Yer. Ber. iv. 3). It consists of an introductory portion, which on Sabbath has four different forms for the four services, and another short portion, which is constant:

"Our God and God of our fathers! be pleased with our rest; sanctify us by Thy commandments, give us a share in Thy law, satiate us of Thy bounty, and gladden us in Thy salvation; and cleanse our hearts to serve Thee in truth: let us inherit, O Lord our God, in love and favor, Thy holy Sabbath, and may Israel, who hallows [loves] Thy name, rest thereon. Blessed be Thou, O Lord, who sanctifiest the Sabbath."

On Sabbath-eve after the congregation has read the "Tefillah" silently, the reader repeats aloud the so-called "Me-'En Sheba'," or summary (Ber. 29, 57b; Pes. 104a) of the seven blessings (Shab. 24b; Rashi *ad loc.*). The reason given for this is the fear lest by tarrying too long or alone in the synagogue on the eve of the Sabbath the worshiper may come to harm at the hands of evil spirits. This abstract opens like No. i., using, however, the words "Creator [Owner] of heaven and earth" where No. i. has "Creator of all," and omitting those immediately preceding "bestowest goodly kindnesses." The congregation then continues:

"Shield of the fathers by His word, reviving the dead by His command, the holy God to whom none is like; who causeth His people to rest on His holy Sabbath-day, for in them He took delight to cause them to rest. Before Him we shall worship in reverence and fear. We shall render thanks to His name on every day constantly in the manner of the benedictions. God of the 'acknowledgments,' Lord of 'Peace,' who sanctifieth the Sabbath and blesseth the seventh [day] and causeth the people who are filled with Sabbath delight to rest as a memorial of the work in the beginning [Creation]."

Then the reader concludes with the "Reẓeh," the middle Sabbath eulogy.

On festivals (even when coincident with the Sabbath) this "Sanctification of the Day" is made up of several sections, the first of which is constant and reads as follows:

"Thou hast chosen us from all the nations, hast loved us and wast pleased with us; Thou hast lifted us above all tongues, and hast hallowed us by Thy commandments, and hast brought us, O our King, to Thy service, and hast pronounced over us Thy great and holy name."

Then follows a paragraph naming the special festival and its special character, and, if the Sabbath coincides therewith, it is mentioned before the feast. For Passover the wording is as follows:

Variations on Festivals.

"And Thou hast given us, O Lord our God, in love [Sabbaths for rest,] set times and seasons for joy, [this Sabbath-day, the day of our rest, and] *this day of the Feast of Unleavened Bread, the season of our deliverance*, a holy convocation, a memorial of the exodus from Egypt."

For the other festivals the respective changes in the phrase printed above in italics are the following: "this day of the Feast of Weeks—the day when our Torah was given"; "this day of the Feast of Booths—the day of our gladness"; "this eighth day, the concluding day of the feast—the day of our gladness"; "this Day of Memorial, a day of alarm-sound [shofar-blowing; *i.e.*, on Rosh ha-Shanah]"; "this Day of Atonement for forgiveness and atonement, and to pardon thereon all our iniquities."

On New Moons and on the middle days of Pesaḥ or Sukkot, as well as on the holy days, the "Ya'aleh we-yabo" (= "Rise and come") is inserted in the "'Abodah," the name of the day appearing in each case in its proper place. The Sabbath is never referred to in this prayer, and it forms part of every service save the additional or Musaf:

"Our God and God of our fathers! may the remembrance of ourselves and our fathers, and of Thy anointed servant the son of David, and of Thy holy city Jerusalem, and of all Israel Thy people, *rise and come* [hence the name of the prayer], be seen, heard, etc., before Thee on this day . . . for deliverance, happiness, life, and peace; remember us thereon, O Lord our God, for happiness, visit us for blessings, save us unto life, and with words of help and mercy spare and favor us, show us mercy! Save us, for to Thee our eyes are turned. Thou art the gracious and merciful God and King."

In the final part of the benediction appears an introductory petition on the three joyous festivals:

"Let us receive, O Lord our God, the blessings of Thy appointed times for life and peace, for gladness and joy, wherewith Thou in Thy favor hast promised to bless us." (Then follows the "Reẓeh" [see above], with such variations from the Sabbath formula as: "in gladness and joy" for "in love and favor"; "rejoice" for "rest"; and "Israel and Thy" or "the holy seasons" for "the Sabbath.")

On Rosh ha-Shanah a prayer for the coming of the kingdom of heaven is added at the close of this benediction (for its text see the prayer-books and Dembitz, *l.c.* p. 145). On the Day of Atonement the petition solicits pardon for sins (Dembitz, *l.c.* p. 146). A Habdalah is inserted on Saturday night in the "Sanctification of the Day" when a festival—and this can never happen with the Day of Atonement—falls on a Sunday. The form in use is somewhat longer than that given in the Talmud, where it is called "a pearl" on account of its sentiment (Ber. 33b; Beẓah 17a). Insertions are made in the six constant benedictions on certain occasions, as follows: During the ten days of Teshubah, *i.e.*, the first ten days of Tishri, in No. i., after "in love" is inserted "Remember us for life, O King who delightest in life, and inscribe us into the book of life; for Thy sake, O God of life"; in No. ii., after "salvation to sprout forth," "Who is like Thee, Father of mercies, who rememberest His [Thy] creatures unto life in mercy?"; in No. iii., "holy King," in place of "holy God" at the close; in No. xviii., before the concluding paragraph, "O inscribe for a happy life all the sons of Thy covenant"; in No. xix., before the end, "May we be remembered and inscribed in the book of life, of blessing, of peace, and of good sustenance, we and all Thy people, the whole house of Israel, yea, for happy life and for peace"; and the close (in the German ritual) is changed to "Blessed be Thou, O Lord, who makest peace." In the "Ne'ilah" (concluding) service for the Day of Atonement, "inscribe" is changed to "seal." On the two "solemn days" ("Yamim Nora'im") a petition for the king-

Insertions.

dom of heaven is inserted in No. iii. (see the translation in Dembitz, *l.c.* p. 122), and the concluding phrase of this eulogy also is changed: "Thou art holy, and Thy name is fearful, and there is no God besides Thee, as it is written [Isa. v. 16], 'The Lord God is exalted in judgment, and the Holy God is sanctified in righteousness.' Blessed be Thou, O Lord, the Holy King." In fall and winter, in No. ii., after the words "Thou resurrectest the dead and art great to save" is inserted the words: "Thou causest the wind to blow and the rain to descend." On New Moons and middle days, except in the Musaf, the "Ya'aleh we-yabo" (see above) is inserted in the "'Abodah" before "bring back." On Ḥanukkah and Purim special thanks are inserted in No. xviii. after the words "from everlasting we have hoped in Thee." These narrate the wonderful occurrences which the day recalls. On fast-days, after No. vi. a special supplication is recited, beginning with "Answer us, O Lord, answer us"; and in No. vii., the prayer for the sick, one desirous of remembering a sick person interpolates a brief "Yehi Raẓon" (= "May it be Thy will") to that effect. On the Ninth of Ab in the Minḥah service a supplication is introduced into No. xv. for the consolation of those that mourn for Zion. In No. xvi., as well as in the Minḥah and the silent prayer, the fast-day appeal might be inserted.

The "Hoda'ah" (No. xviii.) has a second version, styled the "Modim de-Rabbanan" and reading as follows:

"We confess this before Thee that Thou art immutable, God our God and the God of our fathers, the God of all flesh. Our Creator, the Creator of all in the beginning: [we offer] benedictions and thanksgivings unto Thy name, the great and holy One, because Thou hast kept us alive and preserved us. Even so do Thou keep us alive and preserve us, and gather together our exiles to Thy holy courts to keep thy statutes and to do Thy will and to serve Thee with a fully devoted heart, for which we render thanks unto Thee. Blessed be the God of the thanksgivings."

As the title suggests, this is an anthology of various thanksgiving prayers composed by the Rabbis (Soṭah 9a). The close is not found in the Talmudical passage cited, nor does it appear in the "Siddur" of Rab Amram or in the formula given by Maimonides and others; but it is taken from Yer. Ber. i. 7. A somewhat different opening, "We confess and bow down and kneel," is preserved in the Roman Maḥzor.

Before the priestly blessing (originally in the morning service, but now in the additional service, and in the Minḥah service on the Ninth of Ab or on any other public fast-day), whenever "the priests" ("kohanim") are expected to recite the priestly blessing (see DUKAN), the leader reads in the "'Abodah":

"May our supplication be pleasing in Thy sight like burnt offering and sacrifice. O Thou Merciful Being, in Thy great mercy restore Thy Shekinah to Zion and the order of service to Jerusalem. May our eyes behold Thy return to Zion in mercy, and there we shall serve Thee in awe, as in the days of old and in former years" (comp. Mal. ii. 2).

He then ends the benediction as usual and reads the "Modim" as well as the introduction to the priestly blessing.

"Our God and God of our fathers, bless us with the blessing which, tripartite in the Torah, was written by the hands of Moses, Thy servant, and was spoken by Aaron and his sons the priests, Thy holy people, as follows [at this point the priests say aloud]: "Blessed be Thou, O Eternal our God, King of the universe, who hast sanctified us with the sacredness of Aaron and hast commanded us in love to bless Thy (His) people Israel."

Thereupon they intone the blessing after the leader, word for word:

"'May the Eternal bless thee and keep thee.
'May the Eternal let His countenance shine upon thee and be gracious unto thee.
'May the Eternal lift up His countenance toward thee and give thee peace.'"

After each section the people usually answer, "Ken yehi raẓon!" (= "May such be [Thy] will!"); but when the kohanim perform this function (on the holy days) those present answer, "Amen." On the morning of the Ninth of Ab the kohanim may not pronounce the blessing, nor may the precentor read it.

The "Shemoneh 'Esreh" is first prayed silently by the congregation and then repeated by the reader aloud. In attitude of body and in the holding of the hands devotion is to be expressed (see Shulḥan 'Aruk, Oraḥ Ḥayyim, 95 *et seq.*). Interruptions are to be strictly avoided (*ib.* 104). In places and situations where there is grave danger of

Mode of Prayer.

interruptions, a shorter form is permissible comprising the first three and the last three benedictions and between them only the "Attah Ḥonen," the petition for understanding (No. iv.; Oraḥ Ḥayyim, 110).

The "Shemoneh 'Esreh" is prefaced by the verse "O Eternal, open my lips, and my mouth shall proclaim Thy praise" (Ps. li. 17; see Ber. 4b). At one time two other Biblical passages (Ps. lxv. 3 and Deut. xxxii. 3) were recited, one before and the other after the verse now retained. But this was considered to break the connection between the "Ge'ullah" (the preceding eulogy, the last in the "Shema'" ending with "Ga'al Yisrael") and the "Tefillah"; and such an interruption was deemed inadmissible, as even an "Amen" was not to be spoken before the words "O Eternal, open my lips," in order that this verse might be considered to belong to the preceding "Ge'ullah" and to form with it a "long Ge'ullah" (גאולה אריכתא; Oraḥ Ḥayyim, 111; and the Ṭur, *l.c.*). A discussion arose among the later "Poseḳim" whether this injunction was applicable to Sabbaths and holy days or only to work-days. In the additional and Minḥah services more verses might be spoken after the "Shema'" and before and after the "Tefillah." The custom has gradually developed of reciting at the conclusion of the latter the supplication with which Mar, the son of Rabina, used to conclude his prayer (Ber. 17a):

"My God, keep my tongue and my lips from speaking deceit, and to them that curse me let me [Hebr. "my soul"] be silent, and me [my soul] be like dust to all. Open my heart in Thy Torah, and after [in] Thy commandments let me [my soul] pursue. As for those that think evil of [against] me speedily thwart their counsel and destroy their plots. Do [this] for Thy name's sake, do this for Thy right hand's sake, do this for the sake of Thy holiness, do this for the sake of Thy Torah. That Thy beloved ones may rejoice, let Thy right hand bring on help [salvation] and answer me. [For the formula here given beginning with "Do this," another one was used expressive of the wish that the Temple might be rebuilt, that the Messiah might come, that God's people might be ransomed, and that His congregation might be gladdened. The angels also were invoked; and the appeal was summed up: "Do it for Thy sake, if not for ours."] May the words of my mouth and the meditations of my heart be acceptable in Thy sight, O Eternal, my rock and my redeemer."

At these words, three steps backward were taken (see Oraḥ Ḥayyim, *l.c.* 123), and then this was recited:

"He who maketh peace in the heights, He will establish peace upon us and upon all Israel, and thereupon say ye 'Amen.'"

Then followed a final phrase praying for the rebuilding of the Temple so that Israel might sacrifice again, to the sweet gratification of God as of yore. The worshiper was bidden to remain at the place whither his three backward steps had brought him for the space of time which would be required for traversing a space of four ells, or, if at public prayer-service, until the precentor, in the loud repetition, intoned the "Ḳedushshah."

The Concluding Section.

In the "Tefillah" for the additional service the constant parts are always retained. On Rosh ha-Shanah there are three middle benedictions (according to R. H. iv. 5; comp. Ta'an. ii. 3 for fast-days): (1) "Fathers"; (2) "Powers"; (3) "Holiness of the Name" with addition of the "Kingdoms"; (4) "Sanctifications of the Day," the shofar being blown; (5) "Remembrances" (with shofar); (6) "Shofarot" (the shofar is blown); (7) "'Abodah"; (8) "Hoda'ot"; (9) Blessings of the kohanim. According to R. Akiba, "Kingdoms," *i.e.*, verses recognizing God as king, must always go with "Blowings"; therefore he rearranges the benedictions as follows: (1), (2), (3) "Holiness"; (4) "Sanctifications" and "Kingdoms" (with blasts of the shofar); (5) "Remembrances," *i.e.*, verses in which God is shown to be mindful of mankind and of Israel (with blasts); (6) "Shofarot," *i.e.*, verses in which the shofar is named literally or figuratively; (7), (8), and (9). On Sabbaths and holy days there is only one middle benediction, an enlarged "Sanctification of the Day." The last part is modified on New Moon. If New Moon falls on a week-day, there is, of course, no "Sanctification of the Day"; but there is a special benediction, the introduction consisting of regrets for the cessation of the sacrifices, and the principal part of it being a petition for the blessing of the New Moon:

"Our God and God of our fathers, renew for us this month for happiness and blessing [Amen], for joy and gladness [Amen], for salvation and comfort [Amen], for provision and sustenance [Amen], for life and peace [Amen], for pardon of sin and forgiveness of transgression [Amen]."

According to the German ritual, when Sabbath and New Moon coincide, the "Sanctification of the Day" is omitted; but a somewhat more impressive prayer is recited, referring to God's creation of the world, His completion thereof on the seventh day, His choice of Israel, and His appointment of Sabbaths for rest and New Moons for atonement; declaring that exile is the punishment for sins of the fathers; and supplicating for the restoration of Israel.

On an ordinary Sabbath the middle benediction, in a labored acrostic composition in the inverted order of the alphabet, recalls the sacrifices ordained for the Sabbath, and petitions for restoration in order that Israel may once more offer the sacrifices as prescribed, the prayer concluding with an exaltation of the Sabbath. In the festival liturgy the request for the restoring of the sacrificial service emphasizes still more the idea that the Exile was caused by "our sins" ("umi-pene ḥaṭa'enu"):

"On account of our sins have we been exiled from our country and removed from our land, and we are no longer able [to go up and appear and] to worship and perform our duty before Thee in the House of Thy choice," etc.

On the three pilgrim festivals another supplication for the rebuilding of the Temple is added to the foregoing, with quotation of the Pentateuchal injunction (Deut. xvi. 16, 17) regarding appearance before God on those days.

The additional for the middle days (the work-days) of Pesaḥ and Sukkot is the same as that for the feasts proper, and is read even on the Sabbath.

The following are some of the more important variants in the different rituals:

Variants in the Rituals.

In No. v. ("Lead us back, our Father," etc.) Saadia, Maimonides, and the Italian Maḥzor read "Lead us back, our Father, to Thy Torah, *through our clinging to Thy commandments*, and bring us near," etc.

The Sephardim shorten the last benediction in the evening and morning services of the Ninth of Ab to this brief phrasing:

"Thou who makest peace, bless Thy people Israel with much strength and peace, for Thou art the Lord of peace. Blessed be Thou, O Eternal, maker of peace."

In No. ix. (the benediction for the year) the words "dew and rain" are inserted during the term from the sixtieth day after the autumnal equinox to Passover. The Sephardic ritual has two distinct versions: one for the season when dew is asked for, and the other when rain is expected. The former has this form:

"Bless us, O our Father, in all the work of our hands, and bless our year with gracious, blessed, and kindly dews: be its outcome life, plenty, and peace as in the good years, for Thou, O Eternal, art good and doest good and blessest the years. Blessed be Thou, O Eternal, who blessest the years."

In the rainy season (in winter) the phraseology is changed to read:

"Bless upon us, O Eternal our God, this year and all kinds of its produce for goodness, and bestow dew and rain for blessing on all the face of the earth; and make abundant the face of the world and fulfil the whole of Thy goodness. Fill our hands with Thy blessings and the richness of the gifts of Thy hands. Preserve and save this year from all evil and from all kinds of destroyers and from all sorts of punishments: and establish for it good hope and as its outcome peace. Spare it and have mercy upon it and all of its harvest and its fruits, and bless it with rains of favor, blessing, and generosity; and let its issue be life, plenty, and peace as in the blessed good years; for Thou, O Eternal" (etc., as in the form given above for the season of the dew).

In No. xiii. the Sephardic ritual introduces before "the elders" the phrase "and on the remnant of Thy people, the house of Israel," while in some editions these words are entirely omitted, and before the conclusion this sentence is inserted: "on Thy great loving-kindness in truth do we rely for support."

No. xiv. among the Sephardim reads:

"[Thou wilt] dwell in the midst of Jerusalem, Thy city, as Thou hast spoken [promised], and the throne of David Thy servant speedily in its midst [Thou wilt] establish, and build it an everlasting building soon in our days. Blessed be Thou, O Eternal, who buildest Jerusalem."

This reading is that of Maimonides, while the Ashkenazim adopted that of Rab Amram.

In No. xvi. God is addressed as "Ab ha-Raḥman" = "the Merciful Father." Before the conclusion is inserted "Be gracious unto us and answer us and hear our prayer, for Thou hearest the prayer of every mouth" (the "'Aruk," under עין, gives this reading: "Full of mercy art Thou. Blessed be Thou who hearest prayer"). In the "Reẓeh" (No. xvii.) the text differs somewhat: "Be pleased . . . with Thy people Israel [as in the German ritual] and to their prayer give heed"—a reading presented by Maimonides also. Furthermore, the word "meherah" (= "speedily") is introduced as qualifying the expected answer to the prayer and the offerings. Amram has this adverb; but MaHaRIL objects to its insertion.

Verbal changes, not materially affecting the meaning, occur also in the "Ya'aleh we-Yabo" (for New Moons, etc.). But before "May our eyes behold" the Sephardim insert "and Thou in Thy great mercy ["wilt" or "dost"] take delight in us and show us favor," while Saadia Gaon adds before the conclusion ("Blessed be," etc.): "and Thou wilt take delight in us as of yore."

Slight verbal modifications are found also in the Sephardic "Hoda'ah"; *e.g.*, "and they [the living] shall praise and bless Thy great name in truth forever; for good [is] the God, our help and our aid, Selah, the God, the Good." Abudarham quotes, "and Thy name be exalted constantly and forever and aye"; while Saadia's version reads: "on account of all, be Thou blessed and exalted; for Thou art the Only One in the universe, and there is none besides Thee." The Roman Maḥzor inserts before "and for all these" the following: "Thou hast not put us to shame, O Eternal our God, and Thou hast not hidden Thy face from us." And so in the final benediction—for which the Sephardim always use the formula beginning with "Sim shalom," never that with "Shalom rab"—among the blessings asked for is included that for "much strength," one not found in the German ritual. Maimonides and Amram likewise do not use the formula beginning with the words "Shalom rab." Following Amram, Saadia, and Maimonides, the Sephardim read: "Torah and life, love and kindness" where the German ritual presents the construct case: "Torah of life and love of kindness."

Moreover, in the Sephardic ritual a number of individual petitions are admitted in various benedictions, which is not the case in the Ashkenazic. In the introduction to the "Sanctification of the Day" (benediction No. iv.) for the Sabbath the Sephardim add on Friday evening lines which the Ashkenazim include only in the additional service (see Dembitz, *l.c.* p. 141). For the middle benediction of the Musaf the Sephardim have a simpler form (*ib.* p. 149). While the Germans quote in the prayer the language of the Pentateuch in reference to the sacrifices, the Sephardim omit it. In praying for the new month the Portuguese ritual adds: "May this month be the last of all our troubles, a beginning of our redemption." (For differences in the Musaf for Sabbath and New Moon see Dembitz, *l.c.* p. 153.)

In the Intermediate Blessings.

In the Vitry Maḥzor's reading the conjunction "waw" is frequently dropped, much to the improvement of the diction. In benediction No. ii. God is addressed as "Maẓmiaḥ Lanu Yeshu'ah," "causing salvation to sprout forth 'for us'"; while in No. iii. the prefixing of the definite article to the adjective gives the context a new significance, viz., not "Thy name is holy," but "Thy name is 'the Holy One.'" In No. iv. the word "ḥokmah" is presented in addition to "binah" and "de'ah," *i.e.*, "understanding, knowledge, wisdom, and reason." In No. vi. the Vitry Maḥzor has "a God good and forgiving art Thou" instead of "pardoning and forgiving," thus conforming with the readings of Amram, Maimonides, and the Roman Maḥzor.

In No. viii. after "our wounds" follows "our sicknesses." In No. x. for "Blow the great shofar" this version reads "Gather us from the four corners of *all* the earth into *our land*," which is found also in the Sephardic ritual and in Amram and Maimonides.

No. xv. is presented as in the Sephardic form (see above), but with the addition:

"And may our prayers be sweet before Thee like the burnt offering and like the sacrifice. O be merciful, in Thy great mercies bring back Thy Shekinah to Zion and rearrange the sacrificial service for Jerusalem, and do Thou in mercy have yearnings for us and be pleased with us. And may our eyes behold Thy return to Zion in mercy as of yore."

So, also, Saadia: "and Thou wilt be pleased with us as of yore." The "Modim" is given in an abbreviated form; and in the last benediction the words "on every day" are inserted before "at all times."

A great variety of readings is preserved in the case of benediction No. iii. In the Roman Maḥzor the phraseology is: "From generation to generation we shall proclaim God King, for He alone is exalted and holy; and Thy praise, O our God, shall not depart from our mouth forever and aye, for a God great and holy art Thou. Blessed be Thou, O Eternal, the holy God." This is also Amram's language; but in Saadia's ritual is presented: "Thou art holy and Thy name is holy, and Thy memorial ["zeker"] is holy, and Thy throne is holy, and the holy ones every day will praise Thee, Selah. Blessed be Thou, God, the Holy One." Maimonides confirms this version, though he omits the words "Thy memorial is holy . . . and Thy throne is holy." In Sifre, Deut. 343 this benediction is quoted as "Holy art Thou and awe-inspiring Thy name," which is the Ashkenazic reading for Rosh ha-Shanah and the Day of Atonement.

No. vii., "Tefillat Ta'anit," the prayer for fast-days (Ta'an. 11b, 13b), has come down in various recensions. In the "'Aruk," under קבל, the reading is as follows:

"Answer us, our Father, answer us in this time and distress of ours, for we are in great trouble. O do not hide Thyself from our supplication, for Thou answerest in time of trouble and tribulation, as it is written, 'and they cried unto YHWH in their need and from their tribulations did He save them.' Blessed be Thou, O Eternal, who answerest in time of trouble."

The formula given by Maimonides differs from this, as it does from those in vogue among the Ashkenazim and the Sephardim respectively, which in turn disagree with each other. Maimonides has this reading:

"Answer us, O our Father, answer us on the fast-day of our affliction, for we are in great distress. Do not hide Thy face from us, and do not shut Thine ear from hearing our petition, and be near unto our cry. Before we call, do Thou answer; we speak, do Thou hear like the word in which it is spoken: 'and it shall be before they will call I shall answer; while still they are speaking I shall hear.' For Thou dost hear the prayer of every mouth. Blessed be Thou, O Eternal, who hearest prayer."

When, however, the reader repeated the prayer aloud, between vii. and viii., on reaching "for Thou dost hear," etc., he substituted "Thou art a God answering in time of trouble, ransoming and saving in all time of trouble and tribulation. Blessed be Thou, O Eternal, who answerest in time of trouble." The Sephardic recension has the following:

"Answer us, O our Father, answer us on this fast-day of affliction; for we are in great distress. Do not turn to our wickedness, and do not hide, O our King, from our supplication. Be, O be, near to our cry before we call unto Thee. Thou, yea Thou, wilt answer; we shall speak, Thou, yea Thou, wilt hear, according to the word which was spoken: 'It shall be before they will call I shall answer; while still they are speaking I shall hear.' For Thou art a God ransoming and helping and answering and showing mercy in all time of trouble and distress."

The German ritual adds: "do not hide Thy face from us"; and again: "May Thy loving-kindness be [shown] to console us."

The petition for healing (No. viii.) appears with altered expressions in the Sephardic ritual, the words for "healing" being the unusual "arukah" and "marpe." Again, "our sicknesses" takes the place of "our sores or wounds." So, also, in Maimonides' ritual, which moreover after the added "and all our pains" has "for a God [omitting "King"] healing, merciful, and trustworthy art Thou."

On the whole the language of the eighteen (nineteen) benedictions is Biblical, and in phraseology is more especially similar to that of the Psalms. The following analysis may indicate the Biblical passages underlying the "Tefillah":

Biblical Sources.

Benediction No. i.: "Blessed be Thou, our God and the God of our fathers, the God of Abraham, Isaac, and Jacob" recalls Ex. iii. 15 (comp. Mek., Bo, 16). "The high God," Gen. xiv. 19. God "great, mighty, and awe-inspiring," Deut. x. 17 (comp. Ber. 33b; Soṭah 69b). "Creator of all," Gen. xiv. 19. "Bringing a redeemer," Isa. lix. 20. "Shield of Abraham," Ps. vii. 11; xviii. 3, 36; lxxxiv. 10; Gen. xv. 1.

No. ii.: "Supportest the falling," Ps. cxlv. 14. "Healest the sick," Ex. xv. 26. "Settest free the captives," Ps. cxlvi. 7. "Keepest his faith" = "keepeth truth forever," *ib.* cxlvi. 6 (comp. Dan. xii. 2). "Killing and reviving," I Sam. ii. 6.

No. iii.: "Thou art holy," Ps. xxii. 4. "The holy ones," *ib.* xvi. 3. "[They shall] praise Thee" = sing the "Hallel" phrase, which is a technical Psalm term and hence followed by SELAH.

No. iv.: "Thou graciously vouchsafest" is a typical Psalm idiom, the corresponding verb occurring perhaps more than 100 times in the psalter. "Understanding," Isa. xxix. 23; Jer. iii. 15; Ps. xciv. 10.

No. v.: "Repentance," Isa. vi. 10, 13; lv. 7.

No. vi.: "Pardon," *ib.* lv. 7.

No. vii.: "Behold our distress," Ps. ix. 14, xxv. 18, cix. 153. "Fight our fight," *ib.* xxxv. 1, xliii. 1, lxxiv. 22. "And redeem us," *ib.* cix. 154 (comp. Lam. iii. 58).

No. viii.: "Heal," Jer. xvii. 14 (comp. *ib.* xxx. 17). Maimonides' reading, "all of our sicknesses," is based on Ps. ciii. 3.

No. ix.: Compare *ib.* lxv. 5, 12; ciii. 5; Jer. xxxi. 14.

No. x.: "Gather our exiles," Isa. xi. 12, xxvii. 13, xliii. 5, xlv. 20, lx. 9; Jer. li. 27; Deut. xxx. 4; Mic. iv. 6; Ps. cxlvii. 2.

No. xi.: "Reestablish our judges," Isa. i. 26. "In loving-kindness and mercy," Hos. ii. 21. "King who lovest righteousness and justice," Ps. xxxiii. 5, xcix. 4; Isa. lxi. 8 (comp. also Isa. xxxv. 10, li. 11; Ps. cxlvi. 10).

No. xii.: The expression "zedim" is a very familiar one of almost technical significance in the "Psalms of the poor" (for other expressions compare Ps. lxxxi. 15; Isa. xxv. 5).

No. xiii.: For some of the words of this benediction compare Jer. xxxi. 20; Isa. lxiii. 15; Ps. xxii. 6, xxv. 2, lxxi. 5, cxliii. 8; Eccl. vi. 9.

No. xiv.: Zech. viii. 3; Ps. cxlvii. 2, lxxxix. 36–37, cxxii. 5.

No. xv.: Hos. iii. 5; Isa. lvi. 7; Ps. l. 23, cxii. 9; Gen. xlix. 18; Ps. lxxxix. 4, 18, 21, 26; xxv. 5; Ezek. xxix. 21, xxxiv. 23; Ps. cxxxii. 17; Jer. xxiii. 5, xxxiii. 15; Ps. cxxxii. 10.

No. xvi.: Ps. lxv. 3.

No. xvii.: Mic. iv. 11.

No. xviii.: I Chron. xxix. 13; II Sam. xxii. 36; Ps. lxxix. 13; Lam. iii. 22; Ps. xxxviii. 6 (on the strength of which was printed the emendation "Ha-Mufḳadot" for the "Ha-Peḳudot"); Jer. x. 6.

No. xix.: Ps. xxix. 10; Num. vi. 27; Mic. vi. 8; Ps. cix. 165, cxxv. 5.

While in the main the language is Biblical, yet some use is made of mishnaic words; for example, "teshubah," as denoting "repentance," and the hif'il

Mishnaic Phraseology. "hasheb" have a synonym, "we-haḥazir" (in No. v.), in which sense the root is not found in Biblical Hebrew. The expression "meḥal" (vocalized "meḥol") is altogether mishnaic (Yoma vii. 1; Ket. 17a; Ber. 28a; Shab. 30a; Ta'an. 20b; Sanh. 107a). "Nissim," for "wonders," "miracles," has a significance which the Biblical word "nes" does not possess (Ab. v.; Ber. ix. 1; Niddah 31a). So also the term "sha'ah," an adaptation from the Aramaic, occurs as the equivalent of the Hebrew "rega'" = "moment" (secondarily, "hour"). "Peleṭat soferim" is a rabbinical designation (Meg. Ta'an. xii.; Yer. Ta'an. 66a), while "ḥerut" = "freedom" is another late Hebrew term. "Gere ha-ẓedeḳ" is the late technical term for PROSELYTES.

The language of the "Tefillah" would thus point to the mishnaic period, both before and after the destruction of the Temple, as the probable time of its composition and compilation. That the Mishnah fails to record the text or to give other definite and coherent directions concerning the prayer except sporadically, indicates that when the Mishnah was finally compiled the benedictions were so well known that it was unnecessary to prescribe their text and content (Maimonides on Men. iv.1b, quoted by Elbogen, "Gesch. des Achtzehngebetes"), although the aversion to making prayer a matter of rigor and fixed formula may perhaps have had a part in the neglect of the Mishnah. That this aversion continued keen down to a comparatively late period is evidenced by the protests of R. Eliezer (Ber. 28a) and R. Simeon ben Yoḥai (Ab. ii. 13). R. Jose held that one should include something new in one's prayer every day (Yer. Ber. 8b), a principle said to have been carried into practise by R. Eleazar and R. Abbahu (*ib.*). Prayer was not to be read as one would read a letter (*ib.*).

While the Mishnah seems to have known the general content and sequence of the benedictions, much latitude prevailed as regards personal deviations in phraseology, at all events; so that men's learning or the reverse could be judged by the manner in which they worded the benedictions (Tos. to Ber. i. 7).

Prayers were not reduced to writing (Shab. 115b; Yer. Shab. 15c). Not until the times of the Masseket Soferim were written prayer-manuals in existence (see Zunz, "Ritus," p. 11). Hence the necessity of resorting to mnemonic verses in order to prevent too much variety—a method employed even by very late authorities. For instance, the "Ṭur" gives the verse Isa. vi. 3, containing fourteen words, as a reminder that benediction No. iii. contains the same number of words. For No. iv., Ex. xxviii. 3 is the reminder that only seventeen words (excluding "ḥokmah") are admissible. The number of words in No. v., namely, fifteen, is recalled by the similar number of words in Isa. lv. 7 or *ib.* vi. 13, which proves the correctness of the German text.

Preserved by Memory.

The "Kol Bo" states that No. vii. has eighteen words, as has the verse Ex. xvi. 25; and this would justify the insertion of the word "Na" (נא), which appears in some versions. The "Roḳeaḥ," however, reports only seventeen words, as in the German version. No. viii. has twenty-seven words, corresponding to the same number in Ex. xvi. 26 or in the verse concerning circumcision (Gen. xvii.), or to the twenty-seven letters of Prov. iv. 22 or Ps. ciii. 3. This list of correspondences in the number of words or letters, invoked by the very late authorities to settle disputed readings, might be extended, as such analogy is assigned to almost every benediction (see Baer's commentary in his "Seder 'Abodat Israel," pp. 89 *et seq.*).

The earlier Talmudic teachers resorted to similar aids in order to fix the number of the benedictions contained in the "Tefillah." The choice of eighteen is certainly a mere accident; for at one time the collection contained less, and at another more, than that number. The fact that such mnemonic verses came into vogue suggests that originally the number of the benedictions was not definitely fixed; while the popularity of the verses fixing the number as eighteen is probably caused by the continued designation of the prayer as the "Shemoneh 'Esreh," though it now has nineteen benedictions (according to "J. Q. R." xiv. 585, the Yemen "Siddur" has the superscription "Nineteen Benedictions"). Eighteen corresponds to the eighteen times God's name is men-

Choice of the Number Eighteen.

tioned in Ps. xxix. (Yer. Ber. 8a, above; Lev. R. i.), which psalm, nevertheless, seems to indicate the number of benedictions as nineteen (see Elbogen, *l.c.*; "Monatsschrift," 1902, p. 353). Another mnemonic reference, based upon the number of times the names of the three Patriarchs occur together in the Pentateuch (Gen. R. lxix.), is resorted to, and points to the fact that at one time seventeen benedictions only were counted.

Other bases of computations of the number eighteen are: (1) the eighteen times God's name is referred to in the "Shema'"; (2) the eighteen great hollows in the spinal column (Ber. 28b); (3) the eighteen psalms at the beginning of the Book of Psalms (i.-ii. being really only i.; Yer. Ber. iv.); (4) the eighteen "commands" which are in the pericope "Peḳude" (Ex. xxxviii. 21 *et seq.*); (5) the eighteen names of YHWH in Miriam's song by the sea (Ex. xv.). These mnemonic references suggest the fact that originally the number was not eighteen; otherwise the pains taken to associate this number with other eighteens would be inexplicable.

The Talmud names Simeon ha-Paḳoli as the editor of the collection in the academy of R. Gamaliel II.

History of the Prayer.

at Jabneh (Ber. 28b). But this can not mean that the benedictions were unknown before that date; for in other passages the "Shemoneh 'Esreh" is traced to the "first wise men" (חכמים הראשונים; Sifre, Deut. 343), and again to "120 elders and among these a number of prophets" (Meg. 17b). This latter opinion harmonizes with the usual assumption that the "men of the Great Synagogue" arranged and instituted the prayer services (Ber. 33a). In order to remove the discrepancies between the latter and the former assignment of editorship, the Talmud takes refuge in the explanation that the prayers had fallen into disuse, and that Gamaliel reinstituted them (Meg. 18a).

The historical kernel in these conflicting reports seems to be the indubitable fact that the benedictions date from the earliest days of the Pharisaic Synagogue. They were at first spontaneous outgrowths of the efforts to establish the Pharisaic Synagogue in opposition to, or at least in correspondence with, the Sadducean Temple service. This is apparent from the haggadic endeavor to connect the stated times of prayer with the sacrificial routine of the Temple, the morning and the afternoon "Tefillah" recalling the constant offerings (Ber. 26b; Gen. R. lxviii.), while for the evening "Tefillah" recourse was had to artificial comparison with the sacrificial portions consumed on the altar during the night. In certain other homilies the fixation of the day's periods for the three "Tefillot" is represented as being in harmony with the daily course of the sun (Gen. R. lxviii.; R. Samuel bar Naḥman, in Yer. Ber. iv.). Again, the Patriarchs are credited with having devised this tripartite scheme (Ber. 26b; Abraham = morning; Isaac = afternoon; Jacob = evening). Dan. vi. 11 is the proof that this system of praying three times a day was recognized in the Maccabean era. Gradually both the hours for the "Tefillah" and the formulas thereof acquired greater regularity, though much uncertainty as to content, sequence, and phraseology continued to prevail. R. Gamaliel II. undertook finally both to fix definitely the public service and to regulate private devotion. He directed Simeon ha-Paḳoli to edit the benedictions—probably in the order they had already acquired—and made it a duty, incumbent on every one, to recite the prayer three times daily. Under Gamaliel, also, another paragraph, directed against the traitors in the household of Israel, was added, thus making the number eighteen (Ber. iv. 3; see Grätz, "Gesch." 3d ed., iv. 30 *et seq.*).

Edited by Gamaliel II.

Old material is thus preserved in the eighteen benedictions as arranged and edited by the school of Gamaliel II. The primitive form of most of them was undoubtedly much simpler. J. Derenbourg (in "R. E. J." xiv. 26 *et seq.*) makes two facts appear plausible:

(1) While recited in the Temple, the original conclusion of benedictions was "Blessed be Thou, O Eternal, God of Israel from eternity to eternity" (Ber. ix. 5; Geiger, in "Kerem Ḥemed," v. 102; *idem*, "Lehr- und Lesebuch zur Sprache der Mischnah," ii. 2; "He-Ḥaluẓ," vii. 88), emphasizing the "other eternity or world" denied by heretics. From this is derived the usual designation of God as "King of the

world," not found, strange to say, in the eighteen benedictions—a circumstance that attracted the attention of the Rabbis (Ber. 29a). This omission might indicate that the bulk of the benedictions received something like their present form under the supremacy of the Romans, who did not tolerate the declaration "God is king." More likely is the explanation that the omission was for the purpose of avoiding the misconstruction that God ruled only over this world. In the Rosh ha-Shanah prayer the thought of God's rulership is all the more strongly emphasized; and this fact suggests that the Rosh ha-Shanah interpolations are posterior to the controversies with the Jewish heretics and the Romans, but not to the time when Christianity's Messianic theology had to be answered by affirmations of the Jewish teaching that God alone is king. The word מלך, wherever found in the text, is a later insertion. So also is the phrase באהבה = "in love," which also carries an anti-Pauline point (see Epistle of Paul to the Romans).

(2) In the middle, non-constant benedictions (Nos. iv.-xvi.) there is a uniform structure; namely, they contain two parallel stichoi and a third preceding the "Blessed be" of the "sealing" (as the Rabbis call it) of the benediction; for example, in No. iv. are: (1) "Thou graciously vouchsafest knowledge to man" = (2) "and teachest mortals understanding"; and (3) "Vouchsafe unto us from Thee knowledge, understanding, and intelligence." By this test the later enlargements are easily separated from the original stock.

In the "sealing" formula, too, later amplifications are found. It was always composed of two words and no more, as in Nos. vii., ix., xiv., and xvi. of the present text; so No. vi. originally read המרבה לסלוח; No. viii., רופא חולים; and the others similarly.

The Abstracts.

The abstracts of the benedictions (Ber. 29a) which R. Joshua (*ib.* 28b) recommended, and Rab and Samuel explained, so that the last-named has come to be considered as the author of a résumé of this kind (*ib.* 29a), indicate that primarily the longer eulogies were at least not popular. Abaye (4th cent.) found the fondness for these abstracts so strong that he pronounced a curse upon those who should use them (*ib.*). In the time of R. Akiba the knowledge of the eighteen benedictions was not yet universal; for he advised that one who was familiar with the prayer should recite it, and that one who was not might discharge his duty by reciting a résumé (*ib.* 28b). In dangerous places a very brief formula was, according to R. Joshua, substituted: "Help, O Eternal, Thy people, the remnant of Israel. May their needs at all the partings of the roads be before Thee. Blessed be Thou, O Lord, who hearest prayer" (Ber. iv. 3). The following brief prayer, attributed to R. Eliezer, is for use in places where wild animals and robbers may be prowling about: "Thy will be done in heaven above, and bestow ease of mind upon them that fear Thee [on earth] below, and what is good in Thine eyes execute. Blessed be Thou, O Eternal, who hearest prayer" (*ib.* 29b). R. Joshua recommended this formula: "Hear the cry of Thy people Israel, and do speedily according to their petition. Blessed be Thou, O Eternal, who hearest prayer." R. Eliezer, the son of R. Zadok, virtually repeated the preceding, with merely the substitution of a synonym for "cry." Others used this form: "The needs of Thy people Israel are many, and their knowledge is scarce [limited]. May it be a pleasure from before Thee, O Eternal, our God, to vouchsafe unto each sufficiency of sustenance and to each and every one enough to satisfy his wants. Blessed be Thou, O Eternal, who hearest prayer" (*ib.*). This last form came to be officially favored (*ib.*).

That, even after the "Tefillah" had been fixed as containing eighteen (nineteen) benedictions, the tendency to enlarge and embellish their content remained strong, may be inferred from the admonition not to exaggerate further God's praises (Meg. 18a); or, as R. Johanan has it: "Whoever exaggerates the laudations of the Holy One—praised be He!—will be uprooted from the world" (*ib.*). R. Ḥanina took occasion to reprove very severely a reader who added attribute to attribute while addressing the Deity. If the "men of the Great Synagogue" had not inserted the qualifications "great, mighty, and awe-inspiring," none would dare repeat them (Meg. 25a; Ber. 33b; see AGNOSTICISM). Provisions were made to silence readers who should indulge their fancy by introducing innovations (Ber. 33b), especially such as were regarded with suspicion as evincing heretical leanings.

The abstracts, however, throw light on what may have been the number of the benedictions before Gamaliel fixed it at eighteen by addition of the petition for the punishment of traitors ("wela-malshinim"). The Babylonian Talmud has preserved one version; Yerushalmi, another (or two: a longer and a briefer form, of which the fragments have been combined; see J. Derenbourg in "R. E. J." xiv. 32).

These abstracts, known as the "Habinenu" from their first word, were intended to replace benedictions Nos. iv.–xvi. The Babylonian text reads as follows:

"Give us understanding, O Eternal, our God, to know Thy ways, and circumcise our hearts to fear Thee; and do Thou pardon us that we may be redeemed. And remove from us bodily pain; and fatten us with the fertility of Thy land; and our dispersed ones from the four corners of the earth do Thou gather together; and they that go astray against the knowledge of Thee shall be judged; and upon the evil-doers do Thou lift up Thy hand; but may the righteous rejoice in the building of Thy city, and in the refounding of Thy Temple, and in the sprouting up of a horn unto David Thy servant, and in the preparing of a light for Jesse's son, Thy Messiah. Before we call Thou wilt answer. Blessed be Thou, O Eternal, who hearest prayer" (Ber. 29a).

An examination of the phraseology establishes the concordance of this abstract and the "Shemoneh 'Esreh" as in the prayer-books.

The Palestinian text (Yer. Ber. iv.) reveals the contraction of two blessings into one. "Give us understanding, O Eternal, our God [= No. iv.], and be pleased with our repentance [= v.]; pardon us, O our Redeemer [vi.–vii.], and heal our sick [= viii.], bless our years with dews of blessing [ix.]; for the dispersed Thou wilt gather [x.], they who err against Thee to be [will be] judged [xi.]; but upon the evil-doers thou wilt lay Thy hand [xii.], and they who trust in Thee will rejoice [xiii.] in the rebuilding of Thy city and in the restoration of Thy sanctuary [xiv.]. Before we call Thou wilt answer [xvi.]. Blessed be Thou, O Eternal, who answerest prayer." From this it appears that No. xv. ("the sprout of David") is omitted; it was not regarded as an independent benediction, but formed part of the one preceding. According to this, seventeen was the number of benedictions without the

"Birkat ha-Ẓadduḳim." That this was the case originally is evidenced by other facts. In Yer. Ber. iv. 5, R. H. iv. 6, Midr. Teh. to Ps. xxix. (ed. Buber, p. 232), and Midr. Shemu'el R. xxvi. the "sealing" of benediction No. xiv. is quoted as "Blessed be Thou, O Eternal, the God of David, and the builder of Jerusalem," indicating that Nos. xiv. and xv. formed only one benediction. In support of this is the notation of what now is No. xvi. as No. xv. (Yer. Ber. ii. 4; Gen. R. xlix.). Again: (1) In Yer. Ber. ii. 4, iv. 3, and Ta'an. ii. 2, the Tosef., Ber. iii. 25 is quoted as reporting the inclusion of the "David" benediction in that concerning the rebuilding of Jerusalem. (2) In the account by Yer. Ber. 4d of the order in which the benedictions follow each other, the benediction concerning David is not mentioned. (3) In many of Ḳalir's compositions—still used in the Italian ritual—for Purim, Hosha'na Rabbah, the Seventeenth of Tammuz, and the Tenth of Ṭebet, in which he follows the sequence of the "Tefillah," this No. xv. is not found (Rapoport, in "Bikkure ha-'Ittim," x., notes 28, 33). Additional indications that Nos. xiv. and xv. were originally one are found in "Halakot Gedolot" (Ber. vi.), "Sefer ha-Eshkol" ("Tefillah," etc., ed. Auerbach, p. 20), and Midr. Leḳaḥ Ṭob on Deut. iii. 23.

The Fifteenth Benediction.

But in Babylon this contraction was deemed improper. The question, put into the mouth of David (Sanh. 107a), why God is called the God of Abraham but not the God of David, suggests the elimination of "Elohe Dawid" from benediction No. xiv. In Babylon Nos. xiv. and xv. were counted as two distinct blessings. But this division seems to have been later than the introduction of the prayer against the traitors by Gamaliel (see Pes. 107a, 117b; Tan., Wayera [ed. Buber, p. 42]: "in Babel they recite nineteen"), though Rapoport ("'Erek Millin," p. 228b), Müller ("Ḥillufim," p. 47), and others hold, to the contrary, that the contraction (in Palestine) of Nos. xiv. and xv. was a contrivance to retain the traditional number eighteen, which had been enlarged by the addition of one under Gamaliel II. Which of the two views is the more plausible it is difficult to decide.

At all events, the sequence in the existing arrangement is logical. The midrashic explanation connects it with events in the lives of the Patriarchs. When Abraham was saved the angels recited the "Blessed be Thou . . . shield of Abraham" (No. i.; Pirḳe R. El. xxvii.); when Isaac was saved by the substitution of the ram they chanted ". . . reviving the dead" (No. ii.; Pirḳe R. El. xxxi.); when Jacob touched the gate of heaven they intoned ". . . the holy God" (No. iii.; Pirḳe R. El. xxxv.); and when Pharaoh raised Joseph to the dignity of viceroy and Gabriel came to teach him the seventy languages, the angels recited ". . . vouchsafing knowledge" (No. iv.; comp. Pirḳe R. El. ix., where Moses calls forth the benediction by receiving the knowledge of God's ineffable name). No. v. was spoken over Reuben and Bilhah (or when Manasseh the king repented; *ib.* xliii.). No. vi. refers to Judah and Tamar; No. vii. to Israel's deliverance from Egypt; No. viii. was first sung at Abraham's recovery, through Raphael's treatment, from the pain of circumcision; No. ix. refers to Isaac's planting and plowing; No. x. to Jacob's reunion with his family in Egypt; No. xi. to Israel's receiving the Law ("Mishpaṭim"); No. xii. to Egypt's undoing in the Red Sea; No. xiii. to Joseph's tender closing of Jacob's eyes; No. xiv. to Solomon's building of the Temple; No. xv. to Israel's salvation at the Red Sea; No. xvi. to Israel's distress and ever-present help; No. xvii. to the establishment of the Tabernacle ("Shekinah"); No. xviii. to Solomon's bringing the Ark into the inner sanctuary; No. xix. to the Israelites' conquest of the land after which they had peace.

Haggadic Explanation of Sequence.

Why No. iv. follows upon No. iii. is explained in Meg. 17b by a reference to Isa. xxix. 23; why the "Teshubah" immediately succeeds the "Binah," by a reference to Isa. vi. 10. Again, upon the "Teshubah," repentance, follows the "Seliḥah," pardon, in keeping with Isa. lv. 7. The "Ge'ullah," redemption, should be the seventh benediction (Meg. 17b) because redemption will take place on the seventh day, or rather, as stated by the "Cuzari" and the "Ṭur," because the result of forgiveness is redemption. No. viii. treats of healing because the eighth day is for circumcision (Meg. 17b). No. x. follows No. ix. so as to harmonize with Ezek. xxxvi. 8 (Meg. 17b). As soon as the dispersed (No. x.) are gathered, judgment (No. xi.) will be visited on the evil-doers as stated in Isa. i. 26 (Meg. 17b); and when this has taken place all treason (No. xii.) will cease (Ber. 28b; Meg. 17b; Yer. Ber. iv.). As the traitors are mentioned, the righteous (No. xiii.) naturally are suggested: and their triumph is assured by the downfall of the wicked (Ps. lxx. 11; Meg. *l.c.*). The immediate outcome of this triumph is the resurrection of Jerusalem (No. xiv.; Ps. cxxii. 6; Meg. *l.c.*) and the reenthronement of David's house (No. xv.; Hos. iii. 5; Isa. lvi. 7; Ps. l. 23; Meg. 18a). The connection between the last benediction and the priestly blessing is established (Meg. 18a) by Num. vi. 27 and Ps. xxix. 11.

The Age of the Concluding Benedictions.

The last three benedictions seem to be the oldest of the collection. The names of Nos. xvii. and xviii. ("'Abodah" and "Hoda'ah") occur in the liturgy for the high priest for the Day of Atonement as described in the Mishnah (Yoma vii. 1). It goes without saying that parts of the present text of No. xvii. could not have been used before the destruction of the Temple. But in Yer. Yoma 44b is given a concluding formula almost identical with that now used on holy days when the blessing is recited by the kohanim (שאותך ניראו ונעבוד; in Yer. Soṭah 22a, and in the commentary of R. Hananeel on Yoma *l.c.*, the reading is: שאותך לבדך ביראה נעבוד), while in the "Hoda'ah" the ending is almost as now, הטוב לך להודות = "Thou, the one to whom it is good to give thanks." The last three and the first three blessings were included in the daily prayer of the priests (Tamid iv., v. 1; see Grätz, *l.c.* 2d ed., ii. 187, note 4). Zunz ("G. V." 2d ed., p. 380) would assign these to the days of the high priest Simeon. These six are also mentioned by name in an old mishnah (R. H. iv. 5). This would support the assumption that the motive of the early Synagogue was anti-sacerdotal. The very prayers used in the Temple service by the high priest in the most solemn function were taken over into the Synagogue with the implication that this "'Abodah" was as effective as was the sacerdotal ritual. The function of blessing the people the Pharisees would not and could not arrogate unto themselves. Instead they adopted or composed the "Sim Shalom," known as the "Birkat Kohanim" (priestly blessing), and therefore equivalent to the "lifting up of the priest's hands" (for these terms see Maimonides and RaBaD on Tamid v. 1; and Ta'an. iv. 1; Tamid vii. 2; Ber. v. 4). The affinity, noticed by Loeb (in "R. E. J." xix. 17), of the "Shemoneh 'Esreh" with the "psalms of the poor" is in keeping with the Pharisaic-Ḥasidic emphasis of the benedictions. The "pious and poor" of the Psalms were the ideal types which the Pharisees sought to imitate. The palpable emphasis of No. ii. on the resurrection (hence one of its names, "Teḥiyyat ha-Metim"; Ber. v. 2; Ta'an. 2a) confirms this theory. The expressions used in this blessing are Biblical (see Loeb in "R. E. J." xix.). The doctrine of the resurrection is intimately connected with Pharisaic nationalism. The anti-Sadducean protest in this benediction is evident.

The "Psalms of the Poor."

Of the middle benedictions, No. ix., the blessing for the year, discloses a situation such as prevailed before the disruption of the state, when agriculture was the chief occupation of the Jews. It must for this reason be credited with being one of the oldest parts of the "Tefillah." Nos. iv. and xvi. are not specific in content. The latter is a good summary of the petitions (comp. that of the high priest in Yoma 70a and Yer. Yoma 44b), while No. iv., more than any other, is characteristic of a religion in which understanding is considered essential to piety. The importance of this petition was recognized at an early date. R. Judah ha-Nasi desired to have it used on the Sabbath as well as on week-days (Yer. Ber. v. 2: "if no understanding, whence prayer?"). This passion for knowledge also was characteristic of Pharisaism. The prayer for the sick may perhaps likewise be assigned among the older portions (see Elbogen, *l.c.* p. 341).

In its earlier composition, then, the "Tefillah" seems to have comprised Nos. i., ii., iii., iv., viii., xiv., xvii., xviii., and xix. The other benedictions are altogether of a national content. None of them may be assigned to a date before the Maccabean era, while for many a later one is suggested by the content. But the prayer found in Ecclus. (Sirach) xxxvi. should be kept in mind, as it proves that prayers for Jerusalem, and even for the Temple, were not unusual while both were still standing. The original meaning of the prayer against enemies is perhaps also apparent in this chapter:

Verse 1. "Save us, God of all, and lift up Thy fear upon all the nations."

Verse 2. "Swing on high the hand against the strange people and let them behold Thy might."

Verse 3. "As before their eyes Thou wert proved the Holy One in us, so before our eyes be Thou glorified in them."

Verse 4. "And they shall know as we do know that there is no God besides Thee."

Verse 5. "Renew signs and repeat miraculous deeds. Lift up in glory hand and right arm."

Verse 6. "Summon wrath and pour out glowing anger. Hurl back the adversary and humiliate the enemy."

Verse 7. "Gather all the tribes of Jacob and do Thou cause them to inherit as of old."

Verse 8. "Make glad the people called by Thy name, Israel Thou namedst the first-born."

Verse 9. "Have mercy on Thy holy city, Jerusalem, the place of Thy dwelling."

Verse 10. "Fill Zion with Thy splendor and with Thy glory Thy Temple."

Verse 11. "Hear the prayer of Thy servants like the blessing of Aaron upon Thy people."

This has the appearance of being an epitome of the "Tefillah" as known in the days of Ben Sira.

Verse 1: "God of all" recalls benediction No. i., while 1b is the key-note of the prayer for Rosh ha-Shanah.

Analogies in Sirach.

Verse 2 contains the word גבורות = benediction No. ii.

Verse 3 is a summary of the "Ḳedushshah" = benediction No. iii.

Verse 4 explains the knowledge asked for in No. iv.

Verse 6 accounts for the petition against the enemy, No. xii.

Verse 7 is the prayer for the exiles, No. x.

Verse 8 is the content of the prayer in behalf of the pious, No. xiii.

Verse 9 is the prayer for Jerusalem, No. xiv.

Verse 10 recalls No. xvii.

Verse 11 is clearly related to both Nos. xvi. and xix.

Another line begins "Hasten the end-time," which may, by its Messianic implication, suggest benediction No. xv. ("the sprout of David").

If this construction of Ben Sira's prayer is admissible, many of the benedictions must be assigned to the Maccabean era, though most scholars have regarded them as posterior to the destruction of the Temple. The verse marked 5, indeed, seems to be a commentary on benediction No. xi. It begins with the word חדש, and thus suggests the verse: "Lead us back to Thee and we shall return, renew our days as of yore" (Lam. v. 21, Hebr.). Instead of for the "judges," Ben Sira prays for the reestablishment of God's "judgments," in open allusion to the Exodus (Ex. xii. 12; Num. xxxiii. 4; Ezek. xxv. 11, from which verse he borrows the name "Moab" as a designation of the enemy in the prayer). It is probable that the reading of No. xi. as now given is a later reconstruction of a petition with the implications of the Ecclesiasticus paraphrase. This explanation will obviate the many objections raised against the current opinions; *e.g.*, that under Roman or other foreign rule the Jews would hardly have been permitted to cast reflections on the courts of their masters. The Maccabean period seems to furnish adequate background for the national petitions, though the experiences of the Roman war and the subsequent disasters may have heightened the coloring in many details.

The history of the petition against enemies may serve to illustrate the development of the several component parts of the "Tefillah" in keeping with provocations and changed conditions. The verses of Ecclesiasticus make it certain that the Syrian oppressors were the first against whom this outcry of the poor, oppressed victims of tyranny was directed. As the Syrians were aided by the apostates, the "zedim," these were also embraced in the imprecatory appeal. The prayer was in fact designated even in later days as ברכה למכניע זדים, a petition to humiliate the arrogant ("zedim"; Yer. Ber. ii. 3, iv. 2). A century later the Sadducees furnished the type, hence it came to be designated as the "Birkat ha-Ẓadduḳim" (but "Ẓadduḳim" may in this connection be merely a euphemism for "Minim"; Yer. Ber. iv. 3; Ber. 28b). Under Gamaliel II. it was invoked against heretics, traitors, and traducers: the "minim" and the "posh'im," or, as Maimonides reads, the APIḲORESIM (see also his commentary on Sanh. x. 1, and "Yad,"

Petition Against Enemies.

Teshubah, iii. 6–8). The latter were the freethinkers; the former, the Judæo-Christians. These had brought much trouble into the camp of faithful Israel; they disputed with the Rabbis; even R. Gamaliel had often to controvert them (see "He-Ḥaluẓ," vii. 81 *et seq.*); they involved the Jews in difficulties with the Roman government (Tosef., Ḥul. ii. 24); they denounced the Jews to the authorities (hence "minim" and המסורות, R. H. 18a; Tos. to Sanh. xiii.; 'Olam R. iii.; comp. Joël, "Blicke in die Religionsgeschichte," i. 33 *et seq.*; Gutmann, in "Monatsschrift," 1898, p. 344).

R. Gamaliel revitalized the prayer originally directed against the Syrians and their sympathizers (so also Loeb, Weiss, and Hoffmann; Elbogen [*l.c.* p. 357] rejects this view in favor of the assumption that the original composition of the prayer was due to Gamaliel), his purpose being to test those suspected of being minim (Tan., Wayiḳra, ed. Buber, p. 2a; Yer. Ber. v. 4). The editorship is ascribed to Samuel the Younger (Ber. 28a), who, however, is reported to have forgotten its form the very next year. According to Yer. Ber. v. 3 he merely omitted some part of the prayer; and, as he was not under suspicion of heresy, the omission was overlooked.

The above account seems to suggest that this "new" (revised) addition to the benedictions was not admitted at once and without some opposition. The prayer has undergone since the days of Gamaliel many textual changes, as the variety of versions extant evidences. "Kol Bo" gives the number of the words contained therein as thirty-two, which agrees with none of the extant recensions. The prayer furnished the traducers of Judaism and the Jews a ready weapon of attack (*e.g.*, Wagenseil; see "Sefer Niẓẓaḥon," p. 348). In the Maḥzor of Salonica it begins with the word "La-meshummadim" (see Oraḥ Ḥayyim, 118), as it does in the Roman Maḥzor (see also "Kesef Mishneh, Tefillah," at the beginning of ii.). "Meshummad" designates a Jew who apostatizes (Ramban on Ex. xii. 43 gives an incorrect identification, as does Parḥon, *s.v.* שגע) or is lax in his religious duties ('Er. 69a; Ḥul. 5a; Sanh. 27a; Hor. 11a; Targ. Onḳ.

Modifications in "Birkat ha-Minim."

to Ex. xii. 43; Mek., Bo, 15; Giṭ. 45a, in the uncensored editions; the censored have "Mumar"). The prayer is not inspired, however, by hatred toward non-Jews; nevertheless, in order to obviate hostile misconstructions, the text was modified. Originally the opening words were "La-zedim ula-minim," and the conclusion had "maknia' zedim" (see "Sefer ha-Eshkol" and "Shibbole ha-Leḳeṭ"). The change of the beginning into "La-meshummadim" is old (Zunz, "G. V." 2d ed., p. 380). Another emendation was "We-la-posh'im" (*idem*, "Ritus," p. 39), which readily gave way to the colorless "We-la-malshinim" (in the German ritual among others). For "minim" was substituted the expression "all doers of iniquity"; but the Sephardim retained "minim," while Maimonides has "Epicureans." In the older versions the continuation is: "and all the enemies of Thy people," or, in Amram Gaon's "Siddur," "all our enemies"; but this is modified in the German and Roman into "and they all," while Maimonides omits the clause altogether. Finally, there was mention of the "kingdom of arrogance" ("zadon") = the Roman empire. For this Amram presents "the doers of 'zadon,'" which at last was turned into "zedim," thus reverting to the earliest expression. The conclusion is either "who breakest the enemies" (Midr. Teh.) or "humiliates the arrogant" (Amram); in the former phrase Saadia and Maimonides replace the noun "enemies" by "evil-doers."

According to Zunz, the seventh benediction looks like a duplication and is superfluous: at all events it is misplaced. There is some probability that it originally formed part of the liturgy for the fast-days, when 18 + 6 benedictions constituted the "Tefillah" (Ta'an. ii. 2); for in specifying the additional benedictions the Mishnah enumerates seven, not six (*ib.* ii. 4). The first of the seven enumerated is identical with the one contained in the "Shemoneh 'Esreh" as No. vii. Most likely when Israel's distress became constant this petition for help was gradually made a part of the daily liturgy.

As the prevailing use of the plural shows, the "Shemoneh 'Esreh" was first intended as a prayer in behalf of the congregation, which listened in silence and at certain points bowed with the reader (Tos. to Ber. i. 9). By joining the precentor in reading aloud, one became notorious (*ib.*).

Method of Recital.

At the conclusion of every benediction the congregants, while in the Temple, said "Amen," probably because the Tetragrammaton was pronounced; the response was "Blessed be the name; the glory of His kingdom [endureth] forever and aye" (Tos. to Ber. vii. 22; Ta'an. 16b). Gradually, after R. Gamaliel, it came to be the custom that every man softly read the "Tefillah" for himself, instead of merely listening to the reader's recitation of it; only for one not familiar enough (שאינו בקי) with the prayer was the older practise held permissible. Then, in order to give the reader time to go over the "Tefillah" first for himself, silent praying by all was allowed to precede the audible recitation by the reader (see Soṭah 40a; Yer. Ber. i. 8). In Babylon this became the rule, but in Palestine the "Tefillah" was read aloud by the congregation (Müller, "Ḥillufim," No. 43; Zunz, "Ritus," p. 83). Formerly the reader would not ascend (or descend to) the rostrum before beginning the loud (second) recital (Elbogen, *l.c.* p. 431). Familiarity with the contents and reverential recital of the benedictions was insisted on in a reader (Bacher, in "J. Q. R." xiv. 586), that those who were ignorant might by listening to him discharge their duty. Maimonides abrogated the repetition of the "Tefillah" (Zunz, *l.c.* p. 55) for the congregation at Cairo, though not in his "Yad" (see "Yad," Tefillin, ix. 2 *et seq.*). In the evening service, attendance at which was by some not regarded as obligatory (Weiss, "Dor," ii. 76; Ber. 27b), the "Tefillah" was not repeated aloud; and as a rule only eighteen Biblical verses, to take the place of the eighteen benedictions, were read (see L. Loew in "Monatsschrift," 1884, pp. 112 *et seq.*; "Shibbole ha-Leḳeṭ," ed. Buber, p. 21; SeMaG, command No. 19).

According to "Shibbole ha-Leḳeṭ" (ed. Buber, p. 9), some prefaced the "Tefillah" by the verse Ps. lxv. 3, while in Constantine "Wehu Raḥum" was recited as an introduction (Zunz, "Ritus," p. 52). At the end, after Mar bar Rabina's "My God keep my tongue" (Ber. 17a), during the Middle Ages was added "do on account of Thy name," etc.; then to this, Ps. xix. 15; and, still later, the phrase "He who established peace," etc. ("Shibbole ha-Leḳeṭ," p. 18). In the Roman ritual the "Elohai Neẓor" (Ber. 17a) is missing (Zunz, *l.c.* p. 79).

In the Reform liturgies, in benediction No. i. "go'el" is changed to "ge'ullah" (redemption). In No. ii. the resurrection is replaced by "sustaining in life the whole" and by "redeeming the soul of His servants from death." The prayers for Jerusalem, for the reestablishment of the sacrifices, and for the coming of the Messiah are omitted, as is also the petition against the enemies of Israel (comp. "Protokolle der Zweiten Rabbinerversammlung," pp. 104 *et seq.*, Frankfort-on-the-Main, 1845).

BIBLIOGRAPHY: Zunz, *G. V.* 1st ed., pp. 367–369; Delitzsch, *Zur Geschichte der Jüdischen Poesie*, 1836, pp. 191–193; Herzfeld, *Gesch. des Volkes Israel*, iii. 200–204; Bickell, *Messe und Pascha*, 1872, pp. 65, 66, 71–73; Hamburger, *R. B. T.* ii. 1092–1099; Enoch, *Das Achtzehngebet nach Sprache*, 1886; Derenbourg, in *R. E. J.* xiv. (1887) 26–32; Loeb, *Les Dix-huit Bénédictions*, in *R. E. J.* xix. (1889) 137–166; Lévi, *Les Dix-huit Bénédictions*, in *R. E. J.* xxxii. (1896) 161–178; xxxiii. (1896) 142 *et seq.*; Gaster, *Targum zu Shemoneh Esreh*, in *Monatsschrift*, xxxix. 79–90; Gollancz, in *Kohut Memorial Volume*, pp. 186–197, Berlin, 1897; Schürer, *Gesch.* 3d ed., ii. 460 *et seq.*; Elbogen, *Die Gesch. des Achtzehngebets*, in *Monatsschrift*, 1902.

XLVIII

Son Of God

SON OF GOD: Term applied to an angel or demigod, one of the mythological beings whose exploits are described in Gen. vi. 2–4, and whose ill conduct was among the causes of the FLOOD; to a judge or ruler (Ps. lxxxii. 6, "children of the Most High"; in many passages "gods" and "judges" seem to be equations; comp. Ex. xxi. 6 [R. V., margin] and xxii. 8, 9); and to the real or ideal king over Israel (II Sam. vii. 14, with reference to David and his dynasty; comp. Ps. lxxxix. 27, 28). "Sons of God" and "children of God" are applied also to Israel as a people (comp. Ex. iv. 22 and Hos. xi. 1) and to all members of the human race.

Yet the term by no means carries the idea of physical descent from, and essential unity with, God the Father. The Hebrew idiom conveys nothing further than a simple expression of godlikeness (see GODLINESS). In fact, the term "son of God" is rarely used in Jewish literature in the sense of "Messiah." Though in Sukkah 52a the words of Ps. ii. 7, 8 are put into the mouth of Messiah, son of David, he himself is not called "son of God." The more familiar epithet is "King Messiah," based partly on this psalm (Gen. R. xliv.). In the Targum the בן of Ps. lxxx. 16 is rendered מלכא משיחא (= "King Messiah"), while Ps. ii. 7 is paraphrased in a manner that removes the anthropomorphism of the Hebrew: "Thou art beloved unto me, like a son unto a father, pure as on the day when I created thee."

The Apocrypha and Pseudepigrapha contain a few passages in which the title "son of God" is given to the Messiah (see Enoch, cv. 2; IV Esdras vii. 28–29; xiii. 32, 37, 52; xiv. 9); but the title belongs also to any one whose piety has placed him in a filial relation to God (see Wisdom ii. 13, 16, 18; v. 5, where "the sons of God" are identical with "the saints"; comp. Ecclus. [Sirach] iv. 10). It is through such personal relations that the individual becomes conscious of God's fatherhood, and gradually in Hellenistic and rabbinical literature "sonship to God" was ascribed first to every Israelite and then to every member of the human race (Abot iii. 15, v. 20; Ber. v. 1; see ABBA). The God-childship of man has been especially accentuated in modern Jewish theology, in sharp contradistinction to the Christian God-sonship of Jesus. The application of the term "son of God" to the Messiah rests chiefly on Ps. ii. 7, and the other Messianic passages quoted above.

The Pious as Sons of God.

The phrase "the only begotten son" (John iii. 16) is merely another rendering for "the beloved son." The Septuagint translates יחידך ("thine only son") of Gen. xxii. 2 by "thy beloved son." But in this translation there is apparent a special use of the root יחד, of frequent occurrence in rabbinical literature, as a synonym of בחר ("choose," "elect"; see Bacher, "Die Aelteste Terminologie der Jüdischen Schriftauslegung," *s.v.*); the "only begotten" thus reverts to the attribute of the "servant" who is the "chosen" one.

It has been noted that the Gospel of John and the First Epistle of John have given the term a metaphysical and dogmatic significance. Undoubtedly the Alexandrian Logos concept has had a formative and dominant influence on the presentation of the doctrine of Jesus' sonship in the Johannean writings. The Logos in Philo is designated as the "son of God"; the Logos is the first-born; God is the father of the Logos ("De Agricultura Noe," § 12 [ed. Mangey, i. 308]; "De Profugis," § 20 [ed. Mangey, i. 562]). In all probability these terms, while implying the distinct personality of the Logos, carry only a figurative meaning. The Torah also is said to be God's "daughter" (Lev. R. xx.).

At all events, the data of the Synoptic Gospels show that Jesus never styled himself the son of God in a sense other than that in which the righteous might call themselves "sons" or "children" of God.

The parable of the faithless husbandmen and the vineyard (Mark xii. 1 *et seq.*) certainly does not bear out the assumption that Jesus described himself as the "son of God" in a specific theological sense. The parable recalls the numerous "son" stories in the Midrash, in which "son" is employed just as it is here, and generally in similar contrast to servants. If these considerations create a strong presumption in favor of the view that the original gospel did not contain the title, the other Synoptics do not veil the fact that all men are destined to be God's children (Matt. v. 45; Luke vi. 35). The term is applied in Matt. v. 9 to the peacemakers. God is referred to as the "Father" of the disciples in Matt. x. 29, xxiii. 9, and Luke xii. 32. Several parables illustrate this thought (Luke xv. 11 *et seq.* and Matt. xxi. 28 *et seq.*). Much has been made of the distinction said to appear in the pronouns connected with "Father," "our" and "your" appearing when the disciples are addressed, while "my" is exclusively reserved to express the relation with Jesus, and then, too, without the further qualification "who art [or "is"] in heaven" (see Dalman, "Worte Jesu," pp. 157, 230). But in the Aramaic this distinction is certainly not pronounced enough to warrant the conclusion that a different degree or kind of sonship is conveyed by the singular pronoun from what would be expressed by the plural. In the Aramaic the pronoun would not appear at all, "Abba" indiscriminately serving for the apostrophe both in the prayer of a single individual and in the prayer of several.

The title occurs with a distinct theological significance in Rev. ii. 18 and xxii. 13, as it does in the Pauline documents (Rom. i. 3, 4; viii. 3, 4, 32 [Jesus is God's ἴδιος, *i.e.*, own son]; and in Heb. i. 2, 3, 6; v. 5, 8). These writings indicate that the rise of the dogma was subsequent to the decades marked by the ministry of Jesus and his immediate disciples.

XLIX

Son Of Man

SON OF MAN: The rendering for the Hebrew "ben adam," applied to mankind in general, as opposed to and distinct from non-human relationship; expressing also the larger, unlimited implications of humanity as differentiated from limited (*e.g.*, national) forms and aspects of human life. Thus, contrasted with the "sons of God" ("bene Elohim") are the "daughters of man" ("benot ha-adam"), women taken by the former, non-human or superhuman, beings as wives (Gen. vi. 2 *et seq.*). As expressing difference from God, the term occurs in the blessing of Balaam: "God is not a man, that he should lie; neither the son of man, that he should repent" (Num. xxiii. 19). Similarly, David appealing to Saul puts YHWH over and against the children of men (I Sam. xxvi. 19). The punishment of God, also, is contrasted with that of the "children of men," the former being much more severe, as appears from the promise solemnly given to David (II Sam. vii. 14). God alone knows the heart of the "children of man" (II Chron. vi. 29 *et seq.*). In the prayer in which this thought is expressed, "man" is used in distinction to the "people of Israel"; indeed, "children of men" appears to mark a contrast to "children of Israel" in the Song of Moses (Deut. xxxii. 8, R. V.).

In Contrast to Deity.

"Son of man" is a common term in the Psalms, used to accentuate the difference between God and human beings. As in Ps. viii. 4 (A. V. 5), the phrase implies "mortality," "impotence," "transientness," as against the omnipotence and eternality of God. YHWH looks down from His throne in heaven upon the "children," or "sons," of "man" (Ps. xi. 4, xxxiii. 13). The faithful fail among them (Ps. xii. 2 [A. V. 1]); the seed of YHWH's enemies will not abide among the "children of men" (Ps. xxi. 10). "Children of men" is thus equivalent to "mankind" (Ps. xxxvi. 8 [A. V. 7], lxvi. 5).

"Sons of men," or "children of men," designates also the slanderers and evil-doers in contrast to the righteous, that is, Israel (Ps. lvii. 5 [A. V. 4], lviii. 2 [A. V. 1]). It occurs most frequently, however, as a synonym for "mankind," "the human race" (Ps. xc. 3, cvii. 8, cxv. 16, cxlv. 12); it has this sense also in the passage in which wisdom is said to delight with the "sons of men" (Prov. viii. 31). Job (xvi. 21) employs the expression in the passionate plea for his rights while he is contending against God and against his neighbors. But Bildad insists that the "son of man," who is a mere worm, can not be justified with God (Job xxv. 4–6). In the same spirit the prophet (Isa. li. 12) censures Israel for being afraid of "the son of man which shall be made as grass" when YHWH is their Comforter; but in Isa. lvi. 2-3 the Sabbath is extolled as making the "son of man" (i.e., any man, regardless of birth) blessed; indeed, God has His eyes "open upon all the ways of the sons of men: to give every one according to his ways" (Jer. xxxii. 19).

The meaning of the term as employed in these passages admits of no doubt; it connotes in most cases the mortality of man, his dependence upon God, while in only a few it serves to differentiate the rest of the human race from Israel.

In Ezekiel the term occurs in YHWH's communications as the prevailing form of address to the prophet (ii. 1; iii. 1, 4, 10, 17; iv. 1 *et al.*; in all about 90 times). It has been held that it conveyed the special idea that a wide chasm stood between God, the speaker, and the prophet so addressed, but that it implied at the same time that Ezekiel was considered to be the ideal man. This view must be abandoned as unwarranted. The term "ben adam" is merely a cumbersome but solemn and formal substitute for the personal

In Ezekiel, Daniel, and Enoch.

pronoun, such substitution being due, perhaps, to the influence of Assyro-Babylonian usage (see Delitzsch, "Wörterbuch," *s.v.* "Amelu"; comp. "zir amiluti" in the Babylonian myth concerning Adapa).

Similarly in Aramaic, "son of man" is the usual designation for "man," and occurs in the inscriptions in Syriac, Mandaic, Talmudic, and other dialects (see Nathanael Schmidt in Cheyne and Black, "Encyc. Bibl." iv. 4707–4708). In Dan. vii. 13, the passage in which it occurs in Biblical Aramaic, it certainly connotes a "human being." Many see a Messianic significance in this verse, but in all probability the reference is to an angel with a human appearance, perhaps Michael.

"Son of man" is found in the Book of ENOCH, but never in the original discourses. It occurs, however, in the Noachian interpolations (lx. 10, lxxi. 14), in which it has clearly no other meaning than "man," if, indeed, Charles' explanation ("Book of Enoch," p. 16), that the interpolator misused the term, as he does all other technical terms, is untenable. In that part of the Book of Enoch known as the "Similitudes" it is met with in the technical sense of a supernatural Messiah and judge of the world (xlvi. 2, xlviii. 2, lxx. 27); universal dominion and preexistence are predicated of him (xlviii. 2, lxvii. 6). He sits on God's throne (xlv. 3, li. 3), which is His own throne. Though Charles does not admit it, these passages betray Christian redaction and emendation. Among Jews the term "son of man" was not used as the specific title of the Messiah. The New Testament expression ὁ υἱὸς τοῦ ἀνθρώπου is a translation of the Aramaic "bar nasha," and as such could have been understood only as the substitute for a personal pronoun, or as emphasizing the human qualities of those to whom it is applied. That the term does not appear in any of the epistles ascribed to Paul is significant. Psalm viii. 5—7 is quoted in Heb. ii. 6 as referring to Jesus, but outside the Gospels, Acts vii. 56 is the only verse in the New Testament in which the title is employed; and here it may be a free translation of the Aramaic for "a man," or it may have been adopted from Luke xxii. 69.

In the Gospels the title occurs eighty-one times. Most of the recent writers (among them being H. Lietzmann) have come to the conclusion that Jesus,

In the New Testament.

speaking Aramaic, could never have designated himself as the "son of man" in a Messianic, mystic sense, because the Aramaic term never implied this meaning. Greek translators coined the phrase, which then led, under the influence of Dan. vii. 13 and the Logos gospel, to the theological construction of the title which is basic to the Christology of the Church. To this construction reference is made in Abbahu's controversial saying in Ta'an. 65b. Indeed, examination of many of the passages shows that in the mouth of Jesus the term was an equivalent for the personal pronoun "I."

L

Tables Of The Law

TABLES OF THE LAW: Tablets containing the Ten Commandments.—**Biblical Data**: Moses, bidden to go up to God on the mountain to receive "tables of stone, and a law ["Torah"], and commandments ["miẓwot"]" (Ex. xxiv. 12, R. V.), is given "two tables of testimony, tables of stone, written with the finger of God" (*ib.* xxxi. 18) "on both their sides" (*ib.* xxxii. 15), "the work of God" (*ib.* xxxii. 16). Descending from the mount with these two tables, Moses, beholding the iniquity of the golden calf (see Calf, Golden), cast them "out of his hands and brake them" (*ib.* xxxii. 19). Later he was ordered by God to hew two tables of stone like unto the first; and on these God wrote the words that had been written on the original tablets (*ib.* xxxiv. 1-4), that is to say, the words of the covenant, the Ten Commandments (*ib.* xxxiv. 28). These new tables also are designated "the two tables of the testimony" (*ib.* xxxiv. 29). According to I Kings viii. 9, these tables of stone were put by Moses into the Ark at Horeb (*ib.* xxv. 10 *et seq.*), and were still in it when the Solomonic Temple was dedicated.

——**In Rabbinical Literature**: The two tables furnish copious suggestions for amplifications and analogies. According to R. Berechiah, the tables were six handbreadths in length. In their delivery to Moses two handbreadths were held in the grasp of the Almighty, two constituted the distance between God and Moses, and two were seized by Moses (Ex. R. xxviii.). The number of the tables, two, corresponds to the natural coupling of pairs, such as bridegroom and bride, heaven and earth, this world and the world to come. By the circumstance that "luḥot" is written defectively without "waw," לחת, not לחות, the fact is indicated that the two tablets were perfectly equal (*ib.* xli.). The splendor of Moses' face (Ex. xxxiv. 30) was derived from the part of the tables that was between God and himself (*ib.* xlvii.). The first tables were given to Moses without effort on his part; the second, only after forty days of self-humiliation and privations (*ib.*). The angels objected to the writing of the second set by Moses on the ground that he might claim to be the author of the tables or might even go so far as to change their text and content; but God trusted him implicitly (with reference to Num. xii. 17; Ex. R. *l.c.*). Moses was commanded to write the second set, just as a royal husband who had written a matrimonial pact with his wife might, upon discovering that she had violated it, pardon her, but would most likely require her to draw up the second agreement (Deut. R. iii.; Ex. R. *l.c.*; Tan., Ki Tissa, ed. Buber, p. 117a). The word חרות in Ex. xxxii. 16 must be pointed חירות ("free"), indicating that death, earthly governments, and pain had no power over the Israelites, who accepted the tables (Lev. R. xviii.; Pirḳe R. El. xlvi.).

Why Two Tables.

Moses had in his tent a block of sapphire, created for the very purpose, from which he hewed the second set of tables (Pirḳe R. El. *l.c.*). The tables had a weight of 40 seah (Tan., *l.c.* p. 117b). Indeed, from the sale of the chips made in the course of the dressing of the block, Moses became rich (Ned. 38a). This sapphire was of a nature that admitted of the tables being rolled up (Ex. R. viii.; Cant. R. v. 14). The fact that the tables were of stone is emphasized as indicating that stoning was the punishment for infractions of the laws written thereon (Tan., *l.c.*, ed. Stettin, p. 158a). The letters of the inscription were 613 in number, suggesting the 613 COMMANDMENTS (Num. R. xviii.). Moses having thrown away the first set, it was only fair that he should provide the second (Deut. R. iii.). The sapphire from which Moses hewed the

Moses' Block of Sapphire.

tables had been quarried from the solar disk (Cant. R. v. 14).

As to the arrangement of the words, rabbinical opinions differ: according to some, five commandments were inscribed on one table and five on the other; according to others, each table contained the complete DECALOGUE (Cant. R. v. 14). Moses was able to carry the heavy tables because God helped him; but when God saw that the people were worshiping the GOLDEN CALF, He withdrew His support; and this compelled Moses to cast the tables away. According to another version, the letters supported themselves as well as the stone in which they were encased; but, learning of Israel's lapse from grace, they flew back to heaven, and thus Moses was left, too feeble to carry the heavy burden. Again, the account is varied to introduce a struggle between God and Moses, or between Moses and the letters, Moses doing his utmost to save the tables from falling (Yer. Ta'an. iv.).

The Breaking of the Tables.

After all, it was well that the first tables were not delivered to Israel; for, having been written by the finger of God, they would have brought about the annihilation of every creature on account of their intense brightness (Tan., *l.c.*). As the first set had been given after loud proclamation and amid great pomp, the EVIL EYE had control over the tables; therefore the second set was given quietly to teach the lesson of humility (*ib.*). The seventy elders, indeed, endeavored to prevent Moses from breaking the tables; but in the struggle Moses prevailed. He, knowing their contents, would not deliver them to the faithless Israelites lest he should entail punishment on them; but when the letters flew away Moses was forced to drop the tables. When Moses broke the tables God was wroth with him: "Hadst thou worried and labored to produce them, thou wouldest have been more careful"; therefore Moses was commanded to hew the second set, which was given on the Day of Atonement, in the afternoon (Yalḳ., Ex. 392). According to some, Moses did not cast away the first set until God had encouraged him, saying, "May thy strength increase because thou brakest the tables" (Ab. R. N. ii. 3; Yalḳ., Ex. 363, 740). The instrument by which the inscription was traced was God's third finger (Pirke R. El. xlviii.). Moses broke the first set on the 17th of Tammuz (*ib.* xlvi.).

The tables were not of earthly but of celestial origin. The stone had been in existence from the very beginning of time, and the writing, too, had been extant equally long (*ib.*). The letters "mem" (final) and "samek" were miraculously supported in the stone, indicating "Meṭaṭron" and "Sandalfon" (comp. "Yalḳuṭ Ḥadash," p. 121a). In cabalistic expositions the numerical values of the text or of single words are utilized very extensively to indicate mystic and occult suggestions. The Divine Name, for instance, is by this method alleged to be found in the tables in varied combinations (see, for examples, *ib.* s.v. לוחות).

In the Cabala.

Both the second set and the fragments of the first were deposited in the Ark (Ber. 14b); and in connection with this the expression "fragments of the tables" came to be used to designate a learned man who in consequence of old age or infirmity had forgotten his learning, but to whom respect was nevertheless due. Similarly the phrase "the tables of the covenant" (לוחות הברית) was employed to paraphrase "the heart of Rabbi" (Yer. Kil. ix. 32b, above).

——**Critical View**: In the account of the tables of the Law two historical reminiscences have been combined (1) that in olden times laws and other public documents were written on stone; and (2) that a stone of some sort served as a tribal or national palladium, and was transported from place to place (in times of war more particularly) in a box specially made for it (comp. ARK OF THE COVENANT).

Tables of laws would naturally be set up in conspicuous places, and not, as in the case of those mentioned in Exodus, hidden away where none could see them. A "holy" stone, however, would thus be screened from vulgar eyes; for a profane gaze to rest upon it meant sure death for the perpetrator of the insufferable transgression. The early references to the Ark in Samuel make no mention of the tables which, according to the later theory, were contained therein. Furthermore, tradition is uncertain concerning the text of the inscription engraved on the tables (see DECALOGUE). This uncertainty probably gave rise, on the one hand, to the explanation that an older set of tables had been broken, and, on the other, to confusion with the invisible fetish hidden away in the chest. If none had seen the tables, there is small wonder that there was no agreement concerning the inscription. Furthermore, the dimensions of the ARK make it very improbable that two tables of the kind presupposed could be stored away therein. Significant as referring to tables of stone is Jeremiah's simile of "tables of the heart" (Jer. xxxi. 32).

LI

Theocracy

THEOCRACY (Greek, Θεοκρατία): System of state organization and government in which God is recognized as the ruler in whose name authority is exercised by His chosen agents, the Priests or the Prophets. The word in its technical meaning seems to have been first used by Josephus, to describe the peculiar nature of the Jewish government as devised under divine direction by Moses: "Our legislator . . . ordained our government to be what, by a strained expression, may be termed a theocracy, by ascribing the authority and the power to God" ("Contra Ap." ii., § 17).

Derived from Josephus.

The term expresses most succinctly the conception of the Old Testament historiographers, and more especially that of the books which are written from a priestly-Levitical point of view (*e.g.*, Chronicles, the Levitical code P). Basic to the notion is the relation of Israel to God as His peculiar people (comp. Ex. xix. 5), which therefore is to constitute "a kingdom of priests and an holy nation" (*ib.* xix. 6). By redeeming Israel from Egyptian bondage God has acquired this people for Himself (*ib.* xv. 16). The wonderful manifestations of divine power at the Red Sea proclaim God the Ruler forever (*ib.* xv. 18). Moses is only God's man, bringing the people's concerns before YHWH (*ib.* xviii. 19), and communicating to the people God's will. Gideon rejects the proffered crown on the plea that God alone should rule over Israel (Judges viii. 22 *et seq.*). The desire of the people for a king is regarded as equivalent to the rejection of YHWH (I Sam. viii. 7). Even after the kingdom is established God is said to go before the king (II Sam. v. 24). Therefore, down to their least details all legal, political, and social provisions are essentially religious, as the direct outflow of God's regal and supreme will; and the Torah as God's word is the ultimate revelation of the divine King's commands, and the basic law of the nation. Even the retribution meted out to criminals and their detection are the immediate concern of God (Lev. xx. 3, 5–6, xxiv. 12; xx. 20; Num. v. 12 *et seq.*; Josh. vii. 16).

The visible king—originally not known and recognized in Israel—is seated on God's throne (I Chron. xxix. 23; comp. *ib.* xxviii. 5). His authority is derived from that of the real ruler, God: hence the prophet's prerogative to dethrone even the king (comp. SAMUEL; see I Sam. xv. 26, xvi. 1 *et seq.*; I Kings xi. 29, xiv. 10, xvi. 1 *et seq.*, xxi. 21). The king represents before the people the reflected majesty of God (Ps. xlv. 7). The king's enemies are God's enemies (Ps. ii. 1 *et seq.*, xxi. 10): hence the Messianic visions are organically interwoven with the restoration of the kingdom in the dynasty of David (see MESSIAH). But the rerise of this theocratic kingdom in Israel will coincide with the acknowledgment of God as the ruler over the whole earth (see 'ALENU; ROSH HA-SHANAH; SHOFAR).

Relation Between Heavenly and Earthly Ruler.

It is certain that in antiquity every people felt itself to be under the direct tutelage and government of its ancestral god: all government in ancient days was theocratic; and the conception that Israel is bound to be loyal to YHWH is not exceptional. In the stories relating to the rise and fall of Saul's family and the choice of David, later antipathies and sympathies of the prophetic party come to light (see SAMUEL; SAUL). The theocratic idea, in the sense that it postulates the supreme authority of the Torah with the effect of making Israel a holy nation, is the final development of the Levitical-sacerdotal program culminating in P, and carried out under Ezra and Nehemiah, leading at the same time to the recasting of antecedent history along the lines of this sacerdotal program.

An original theocratic republicanism of Israel can not be admitted. The tribal organization of Israel was none other than that obtaining among its cognates. The restrictions placed upon royal authority (Deut. xvii. 14–20) by the Deuteronomist reflect on the practises prevailing at court, as the strictures placed on the lips of Samuel (I Sam. viii. 6 *et seq.*) describe actual conditions that prevailed in pre-Deuteronomic times and that were, of course, condemned by the Prophets. The hereditary kingdom was probably an adopted foreign (Canaanitish) institution; the Israelitish tribes, jealous of their independence, being ruled by elders (sheiks) or judges, possibly by elective monarchs. But even these sheiks were only in so far agents of theocracy as the "oracles" of the tribal deity were consulted and obeyed. The dominance of the Law is as clearly recognized in Islam as it ever was in post-exilic Judaism. In fact, Islam is even to-day a theocracy (comp. Juynboll, "Handleiding der Mohammedaansch Wetenschap," Leyden, 1903).

Index

Aaron, 173, 180, 237, 244, 301, 315, 325, 336, 373, 375
Aaron ben Elijah, 57, 93, 206
Aaron ha Levi, 403
Aaronites, 381
Abaye, 445
Abba-Mari ben Moses, 18, 34
Abba, Saul, 31
Abbahu, 441, 464
Abel, 158, 160, 372, 402, 404
Abiathar, 236, 244
Ablution, 61
Abodah, 404, 426, 428, 430-431, 433, 450-451
Abot, 423
Abraham, 81-82, 143, 173, 184, 207, 216, 270, 300, 329, 332-337, 372, 389, 393, 404, 417, 439, 444, 448-449
Abraham ben David of Posquieres, 206
Abraham ben Nathan ha Yarhi, 324
Abravanel, Isaac, 21, 32, 35, 95, 108, 273, 402-403
Absalom, 374
Absolute, 96, 178, 187, 200
Absolute Mind, 224
Absolute Religion, 225, 227
Abstemiousness, 39, 41
Abstract, 197
Abtalion, 30, 281
Abudarham, 436
Accidents, 363
Acrostic, 298, 434
Actions, 34
Adam, 49, 56, 63, 97, 148-160, 167-169, 171-173, 207, 281, 300, 332, 391
Adiadene (Family), 277
Adler, Samuel, 313
"Adon 'Olam", 90
Adonai, 14
Adonay, 250
Adonijah, 374
Adultery, 116, 128, 130, 146, 147, 379
Agression, 263
Agnosticism, 9-14, 54, 193, 207, 446
Agriculture, 451
Aha ben Hanina, 346
Ahaz, 234
Ahijah, 259
Ahimelech, 375
Ahithopel, 374
Ahura-mazda, 138
Air, 58
Akiba, 31, 61, 119, 223, 254, 278, 281, 290, 343-344, 353, 433, 446
Al-Ghazzali, 100, 103, 105, 196
Albalag, Isaac, 95
Albargeloni, Abraham Bar Hiyya, 95
Albo, Joseph, 13, 15-22, 34-35, 37, 96, 100, 102-103, 108, 132, 205, 272, 294
Alcimus, 306-307
Alenu, 194
Alexandria, 17, 32, 50, 52, 91, 264, 343, 459,
Alfarabi, 196
Alfonso X, 285
Al-Kindi, 196
All, 12, 54, 149
All doers of Iniquity, 455
All-good, 148
All-spirit, 269
Allegorical, 134, 271
Almemar, 324
Alms, 335
Altar, 211, 229, 234, 372, 391-392, 396, 398, 401, 404
Alter (ego), 25
Altruism, 23-25, 358
Amen, 309, 344, 431-432, 456
Amidah, 422
Ammi, 173
Ammon, 285
Amon, 234
Amoraim, 31, 265, 289, 343
Amos, 124-125, 212, 260-262, 267, 327, 339, 348, 375
Amran, 333, 430, 435-438, 455
Anafim, 20
Anan, 196
Anawim, 420
Ancestor-Worship, 163
Ancient People, 83

Angel of Death, 173
Angels, 81, 96-97, 159, 166-168, 269, 340, 344, 449, 458, 463, 466
Angeology, 48
Anger, 80, 118, 272
Angro-mainyush, 138
Animal elements, 149
Animal sacrifice, 375, 394
Animals, 86, 88, 348, 377-378, 383, 390, 394, 398-399, 401, 403, 446
Animism, 163-164, 209, 393
Annual Cycle, 324
Anointed King, 408
Anointed Priest, 237
Anthropology, 170
Anthropomorphism, 12, 14, 53, 87, 160, 163, 178, 180, 184, 189, 206, 213, 298, 321, 390, 403, 458
Anthropopathaism, 12, 53, 182, 184, 203, 206, 213
Anthropophagism, 393
Antiochus Epiphanes, 417
Antoninus (Emperor), 280
Apikoresim, 453
Apion, 51, 341
Apocalyptic, 307-308, 376
Apocalyptic Visions, 87
Apocrypha, 172, 179, 217, 288, 331, 340, 350, 459
Apostasy, 320
Apostates, 101, 453-454
Apostles, 281
Apostles' Creed, 26
Appetites, 39—40, 149
Appolonius, 340
Aquila, 411—412, 416
Aquinas, Thomas, 252
Arab, 94, 96, 208, 285
Arabian, 92
Arabic, 15, 17, 33, 52, 58, 94, 288
Arama, Isaac, 34
Aramaic, 323, 441, 460, 463—464
Araunah, 374
Arch Angel, 341, 392
Archelaus, 237
Architect of the World, 192
Aristeas, 181, 183
Aristobulus, 181, 183, 237, 343
Aristotle, 92, 95, 103-105, 270, 293
Aristotelians, 15, 17, 103, 196, 271, 293
Ark, 211, 324, 365, 449, 465, 468—469
Artapanus, 181
Articles of Faith, 16—18, 26—38, 194, 206
Artificer, 181
Arts, 162
Aruk, 437—438
Asa, 234
Asaph, 296, 300, 304—305, 411
Asceticism, 39—45, 148, 150
Ascetics, 39—40, 370
Asham, 383, 386, 396, 401
Ash'ariya, 195, 293
Asher ben Jehiel, 35
Ashkenasim, 365, 434—439, 455
Ashre, 300
Askesis, 39
Asketerion, 39
Assidaioi, 331
Assyria, 262, 347—349, 398, 463
Astarte, 155, 375
Astruc-Levi, 15
Atavism, 162
Athanasian, 26
Atheism, 10, 46—54, 174
Atom, 197
Atomist, 94
Atonement, 237, 241, 246, 323, 336, 397—398, 404—405, 410, 428
"Attah honen", 424, 432
Attitude, 297
Attributes, 206—207, 333
Aub, Joseph, 313
Aufklarungsphilosophie, 135, 150, 316
Augustin, 412
AUTHOR, 54, 155, 174
Autocracy, 24
Autumnal Equinox, 435
Avenger of Blood, 409—410
Averroes (Ibn Roshd), 103, 196
Avicenna, 196
Azael, 166, 168
Azariah, 334
Azazel, 167, 395
Az
Azeret, 348

Baal, 155, 231, 258, 374—375, 423
Baal—Berith, 375
Baal—Peor, 375
Baal—Zebob, 375
Babylon, 267, 329, 408, 448, 456
Babylonian, 85—88, 311, 348—349, 396, 417, 447
Bacher, 266,459
Back, S., 16
Baethgen, 412
Bahr, 399
Bahya, 269
Bahya ben Joseph, 249
Bahya Ibn Pakuda, 33, 58, 95, 132, 201—202
Baidawi, 97
Balaam, 268, 334, 461
Balsam, 382
Bamah, 228—230, 232—235
Ban, 393
Baptism, 28, 286, 322
Baptize, 283
Barbarity, 120
Bareku, 324
Bar Hebracus, 412
Baring—Gould, J., 170

Barley, 382, 384
Bartolocci, 190
Baruk, 254
Bashyatzi, Elijah, 36
Battle, 407
Beasts, 158
Beer—Sheba, 374
Beginning, 85
"Behinat ha-dat, 35
Being, 13, 24, 174, 402
Bekor, 383
Belief, 27, 28
Ben Adam, 461—462
Ben Asai, Simon (Azzai), 31, 63, 388—389
Ben Jeroham, 196
Benays, 62
Bene Elohim, 461
Benediction, 44, 61, 365, 404, 414, 416, 422—437, 439, 441—445, 449—454, 456
Benot, 461
Benevolence, 147
Ben Sira, 302, 452—453
Benunim, 333
Berakot, 422
Berenhiah, 465
Bertholet, 275, 419
Bet Din, 283—284
Beth-el, 374—375
Bethlehem, 374
Bible, 29, 36, 42, 58, 60, 79, 81, 83, 87, 94, 142, 148, 163, 171—172, 174, 176, 179—180, 186, 195, 198, 208, 213, 227, 248, 263, 265, 274, 289, 291, 319, 326, 381, 387, 393, 399, 432, 439—440, 451, 456
Bible hero, 281
Biblical Hebrew, 288, 441
Biblical Law, 316—317, 319
Bildad, 462
Bile, 58
Bilhah, 449
Binah, 449
Biology, 170
Birds, 88, 396, 401
Birkat ha-Din, 425
Birkat ha-'Ge 'ullah, 424
Birkat ha-holim, 424
Birkat ha-Minim, 425
Birkat ha-Snanim, 425
Birkat ha-Zaddukim, 448, 453
Birkat Kohanim, 451
Bi-sex, 56
Blasphemy, 62, 111, 386
Blemish, 378, 395
Blessed, 462
Blessings, 365, 427, 433, 451
Blind, 419
Blood, 58, 237, 380, 394, 396—400, 404
Bochim, 374
Body, 33,40, 56—58, 118—119, 149, 152
Body in Jewish Theology, 55—59
Book of the Covenant, 327, 395
Book of Enoch, 463
Book of Jubilees, 340, 355
Book of Life, 334
Books, 361
Bousset, 221—222
Box (Ark), 468
Brahman, 226
Bread, 357, 359
Breath, 80
Breslau Conference, 312, 320
Bride, 466
Bridegroom, 466
Briggs, 411, 414
Brother, 217, 279
Brotherly Love, 221
Buddha, Gautama, 40
Budde, 420
Buddhism, 23, 40, 226, 252
Bullock, 377, 383, 386, 390
Burning, 384
Burnt-offerings, 376, 380, 382, 385, 390, 397
Butler, 24

Cabal, 468
Cabala, 35, 44, 91, 139, 186, 206
Cabalists, 168
Cain, 143, 158, 160, 167, 372
Cakes, 379
Canaan, 86, 115, 164, 211, 231—233, 248, 279, 372, 374, 472
Canaanites, 44, 394
Cannibalism, 393
Canon, 42, 141—142, 213, 221, 257, 306
Capital Punishment, 109, 118
Captives, 115, 439
Captivity, 409
Cardinal Tenets, 26—27, 35
Carnal Lust, 172
Carrying the Blood, 383
Catechism, 35, 59, 90, 133, 273, 294
"Catechismas", 256
Categorical Imperative, 152
Cattle, 377, 383, 389
Causality, 106
Causation, 11
Celestial Bodies, 88
Celibacy, 40, 44
Central Conference of American Rabbis, 35, 38, 286
Cereal, 379
Cereal-oblation, 382
Cereal-offering, 376
Ceremonial Law, 317
Ceremonies, 102, 155, 226, 318
Chaldeans, 52, 79, 116, 138—139, 262—263, 402
Charity, 156, 219—220, 363
Chaste, 267
Chastity, 40, 146
Chazars, 285

Chess, 366
Cheyne, 420
Children of God, 215—217
Chinese Religion, 226
Choice, 153
Choirmaster, 411
Chosen, 418
Chosen Agents, 174
Chosen People, 143, 146
Christian, 186, 196, 250, 276, 329, 366, 368, 370, 399, 419, 445, 459
Christian Doctrine, 17, 199
Christian Dogma, 18, 101, 151, 286
Christian Musicians, 366
Christianity, 26, 31, 40, 134, 150—152, 226—227, 279, 311
Christians, 99, 104, 285
Christology of the Church, 464
Chronicles, 295
Church, 27, 186, 253, 413
Cicero, 252, 277
Circumcision, 28, 131, 275—276, 278, 280, 282—283, 286, 317, 322, 362, 386, 394, 442, 449—450
Civilization, 162
Clan, 410
Clean, 397
Clean Animals, 377
Cleanliness, 41
Climatic Conditions, 83
Collins, Anthony, 135
Colors, 97
Commandment, 60—78, 106, 342, 350, 434, 465
Commentary, 402—403
Communion, 270, 400
Common Sense, 135
Community of Saints, 152
Comparative Religion, 227
Compassion, 79—82, 177, 188
Comte, Auguste, 10, 23—24
Conception, 158
Conduct, 19, 151, 270, 402
Confession, 26, 387, 426
Confidence, 404
Confirmation, 35, 312
Covenant, 24, 27—28, 143, 210, 263, 330, 400, 429, 465, 468
Covet, 133
Cow, 377
Creation, 20, 24, 30, 33, 36, 89—99, 103, 107, 108, 121, 150, 158, 159—160, 203, 224, 252, 254, 256, 290, 344, 369, 400, 434
CREATOR, 36, 54—56, 58, 87, 91—92, 121, 131, 148, 152, 155, 174, 178—179, 181, 183, 193, 197—198, 202, 206, 255, 345, 427
Creed, 22, 155, 320
Crescas, Hasdai, 15, 17, 20—21, 29, 34, 53, 96, 100—108, 205—206, 256, 273
Cripples, 57
Cross, 109—110, 400
Crown, 336, 470
Crown of hair, 44
Crucifixion, 109—113, 122
Cruel, 81
Cruelty, 114—120
Cult, 395—396, 403—404
Cultural Conditions, 83
Cumberland, 24
Curse, 160, 415
"Cuzari", 28, 33, 93, 95, 203, 254—255, 270, 292, 366, 403, 449
Cymbals, 413
Cyrus, 329

Dahri, 53
"Dalalat Al-Ha 'irin", 205
Dan, 375, 463
Danger, 406
Danger to life, 362
Daniel, 127, 187, 192, 417
Darkness, 85, 121—123, 139
Darwin, Charles, 162
Daughters of Man, 461
David, 31, 244, 259, 296, 300, 302, 304—306, 374, 394, 417, 426, 447—448, 450, 458, 461, 471
David ben Samuel Estella, 34
David ben Yom-Tob ibn Bilia, 34
Davidic Psalms, 411
Day of Atonement, 41, 324, 345, 377, 404, 429, 450, 467
Day of the LORD, 124—127
Dead, 57, 81, 119, 219, 223, 237
Deaf, 419
Death, 31, 56, 58, 107, 159—160, 169—170, 173, 176, 178, 333, 336, 406, 410, 457
Deathlessness, 169—170
Decalogue, 30, 32, 47, 187, 323, 338, 349, 467, 469
Decalogue in Jewish Theology, 128—133
Decay, 93
Deceit, 147
Deed, 151
Deformed, 58
Degeneration, 162
Deism, 53, 134—137
Deities, 105
Deity, 13, 31, 41, 49, 89, 164, 347, 372, 393—394, 397—398, 407, 417, 446, 472
Delight, 151
Delitzsch, Franz, 84, 210
Demented, 267
Demetrius, 181
Demigod, 458
Demon, 160
Demonology, 48
Dependence, 404
Depravity, 40

Derenbourg, J., 444
Desert, 43, 193, 391, 394
Destiny, 149
Destroy, 415
Destroyer, 394
Determinism, 152
Deutero-Isaiah, 276, 376, 393
Deuteronomic Law, 233
Deuteronomist, 472
Deuteronomy, 262, 330, 345, 395
Devil, 97
Devotion, 27
Dew, 435
Dhunuwas, 285
Dialectic, 224, 227
Diaspora, 425
Didactic Psalms, 297, 303
Diderot, Denis, 135
Dietary Laws, 41, 317, 320
Dignity, 54, 88, 149
Dillmann, 84
Dio Cassius, 277
Director's Psalms, 411
Discipline, 153
Dishonesty, 261
Dispersed, 409
Dissection, 57
Distress, 440
Divided, 97
Divine, 33, 227
Divine Attributes, 195, 198, 203, 206—207
Divine Being, 182, 272
Divine Creation, 90
Divine Element, 163
Divine Energy, 175
Divine Guidance, 19
Divine Light, 270
Divine Mercy, 392
Divine Mind, 224
Divine Plan, 163
Divine Powers, 185, 200
Divine Purpose, 154, 163—164
Divine Spirit, 225, 271, 273
Divine Truth, 164
Divine Will, 63, 200—201
Divine Wisdom, 269, 392, 403
Divining, 257
Divorce, 322
Dogma, 27—29, 96, 316, 459—460
Dogmatism, 30
Domitian (Emperor), 277—278
Donolo, 58
Doom, 262
Doves, 378, 380, 389
Doxology, 303—304, 309, 412
Dragon, 87
Dreams, 271, 273
Drink-offering, 382
Driver, 360, 420
Drummond, 91—92
Drusius, 251
Dry earth, 87
Dualism, 94, 103, 138—139, 199
DuBois, Raymond, 54
Duhm, 420
Dukan, 324, 431
Duran, Simon, 18, 22, 34
Dust, 55—56, 59
Duties, 102, 133
"Duties of the Heart", 201
Duty, 134, 140, 152, 155—156, 164, 444

Ear of corn, 378
Earth, 56, 58, 86—88, 97, 99, 167, 400, 466
Ebed YHWH, 419—420
Ecclesiastes, 52, 174, 253, 302, 330
Ecclesiasticus, 452—453
Economic Doctrine, 156
Economic Life, 156—157
Economic Man, 24
Eden, 158, 160, 169, 171
Edict, 444
Edom, 285
Efficiency, 184
Effulgent Light, 270
Egg idea, 86
Ego, 12, 25
Egoism, 23—25
Egotism, 151
Egypt, 267, 278, 285, 341, 372—373, 375, 402, 418, 449
Egyptians, 50, 85, 90, 115, 402, 470
Ehad, 186—187
Eighteen Benedictions, 30, 422, 439, 443—446, 456
Einhorn, David, 35, 38, 59, 273, 286, 313, 317, 322—323
Eisenmenger, 190
Elders, 472
Eleazar, 244—245, 419, 441
Eleazar ben Pedat, 280
Elegies, 296—297
Elements, 58
Eleven Degrees in Prophecy, 272
Eli, 236
Eliezer, 284, 441, 446
Eliezer ben Azariah, 278
Eliezer ben Hyrcanus, 282
Eliezer ben Nathan of Mayence, 32
Elijah, 126, 233, 235, 258—259, 266, 274, 333, 390
Elisha, 258
Elisha ben Abuyah, 353
Elohe Dawid, 448
Elohim, 82, 87, 411
El-Shaddai, 210
Emanation, 94, 199
Emotionalism, 155
Employer, 423
"Emunah Ramhah", 33, 204, 292
"Emunot we-De'ot", 292

Encyclopedists, 24
Enemy, 114, 452, 455, 457, 471
English moralists, 24
Enoch, 143, 168, 463
En-Rogel, 374
Environment, 153, 265
Ephod, 211, 229, 237
Epicureans, 30, 49—50, 293, 455
"Epistle to the Hebrews", 400
'Erub, 61, 352
Esau, 334
Eschatological, 87, 122, 373, 410
Essence, 190
Essenic, 172—173
Essnes, 44, 294, 342, 352
Esther, 42, 51, 61
Eternal, 94, 136, 148, 178, 254, 436, 447—448
Eternal Elements, 94, 103
Eternal Light, 181, 416
Eternal Order, 179
Eternity, 34, 53, 95, 180, 184, 200, 294, 461
Ethan, 296
Ethical, 207
Ethical Monotheism, 156—157, 163—164, 207, 319, 321, 376
Ethical Religion, 319
Ethics, 23—24, 140—157, 162, 222
Ethiopia, 262, 418
Etrog, 391
Etymology, 411
Etzemah Dawid, 426
Eucharist, 401
Euclid, 402
Eulogy, 414—415, 423
Eusebius, 369
Eve, 158—161, 169, 172—173, 281
Everlasting, 175, 180
Evil, 23, 40, 134, 138—139, 148, 150—151, 155, 166, 170, 176, 178, 182, 184—185, 199, 212, 220, 252, 254—256, 266, 291—292, 294, 401, 406
Evil Demons, 407
Evil Doer, 290, 331, 415, 447, 450, 455, 462
Evil Eye, 467
Evil spirits, 122, 405, 427
Evolution, 53—54, 84, 154, 162—165, 227, 316
Ewald, 229
Excision, 356
Execution, 402
Exile, 48, 213, 236, 245, 276, 315, 330, 348, 391, 397, 408—409, 418, 420—421, 434, 472
Existence, 18, 21, 34, 91, 162, 205
Exodus, 181, 210, 330, 349, 373, 453, 468
Experience, 14
Expiation, 397, 399
External Light, 181
External Universe, 182
Extramundane, 187, 189
Eye for eye, 114
Eyes, 81
"EZ HAYYIM", 93
"EZ SHATUL", 21
Ezekiel, 126, 233, 244, 265, 330, 339, 376, 393, 395—396, 406, 417, 420, 462
Ezekielus, 181
Ezra, 245, 254, 276, 300, 319, 350, 357, 471

Fagius, 251
Faith, 28, 33, 101, 103
Fall of Angels, 166—168
Fall of Man, 163—164, 169—173
Falling, 439
False Gods, 375
False Prophet, 266
Falsehood, 147
Family, 133, 410
Fashion, 262
Fast-days, 430, 437—438, 455
Fasting, 40, 42—43, 176, 329, 346, 369, 402
Fat, 283, 381, 395
Fatalism, 203—204, 292
Fatalists, 293
Father, 174, 213, 458, 460
Fathers, 433
Fear, 227, 281
Feast of Booths, 428
Feast of Weeks, 428
Feelings, 220
Felsenthal, Bernard, 286, 313
Festivals, 128, 324, 374, 382, 428—429, 434
Fetishism, 40, 163
Fidelity, 147
Fight, 440
Fig leaves, 158, 171
Final Judgement, 36, 97
Finite Mind, 225
Fire, 58, 418
Firmament, 180
First, 175, 203
First born, 376, 383, 393
First Cause, 95, 105, 174, 184, 204
First Epistle of John, 459
First-Fruits, 302, 376, 379, 392
First Man, 170
First Temple, 267
Firstlings, 395
Fiscus Judaicus, 282
Fish, 97, 365, 377
Five Religious Truths, 134
Flagellation, 110, 238, 355
Flesh, 40, 55, 62
Flood, 85, 167, 172, 372, 418, 458
Flour, 378—379, 383—384
Flour oil, 396
Folk-lore, 399
Folk-poetry, 83
Food, 394

Food of God, 394—395
Fools, 267
Forbidden Acts, 355
Forbidden Fruit, 158
Fore-Know, 181
Foreknowledge, 181
Foreordain, 181
Forespeaker, 257
Forgive, 119
Forgiveness, 424, 449
Form, 92—93, 95
Forty Less One, 360
Fowl, 158, 376, 383, 390
Fragments of the Tables, 468
Frankel, Zacharias, 312
Frankincense, 376, 378—379, 382
Frankfurt Conference, 312
Free Being, 94
Free Determination, 94
Free Will, 34, 94, 105, 108, 143, 152—153, 199, 292
Free will-offering, 377, 382, 388—389, 395
Freedom, 93, 154, 204, 253, 256, 409
Freedom of Action, 39
Freethinker, 134—135, 195, 454
French Revolution, 24
Friday, 97, 357
Frivolity, 147, 262
Fruit, 169—170
Fruitful, 425
Funeral, 41
Future, 265

Ga'al, 409
Gabriel, 98, 449
Gad, 259
Galatin, Peter, 251
Galut, 314
Gamaliel, 187, 278, 352, 447—448, 454, 456
Gamaliel II, 443—444, 448, 453
Garden of Eden, 158, 160, 169, 171
Garments, 237
Gathering the Blood, 383
Gautama Buddha, 40
Geburot, 423
Gedeliah ben Solomon Lipschitz, 21
Gehenna, 99, 336
Genealogies, 83
Genealogy, 237
Genebrad, 22
Generation to Generation, 438
Genesis, 56, 86—91, 121, 143, 169—170, 215, 252, 372, 458
Genius, 165, 263, 392
Gentiles, 125
Geology, 88
Ger, 274, 276, 279—280
German, 436—437
German Ritual, 434, 439, 455
Gersonides (Ralbag), 95—96, 103, 107, 273
Ge'ullah, 432, 449, 457
Ge'ulim, 409
Gibeon, 394
Gideon, 374, 470
Giesebrecht, 420
Gift, 271, 393
Gilead, 374
Gilgal, 374
Giloh, 374
Giver, 155
Gluttony, 147
Gnomic, 376
Gnostic, 9, 91, 139, 186, 388
Goat, 377, 383, 386—387, 390
GOD, 9—14, 18—19, 28, 30, 32—34, 36, 39, 46—47, 50, 53—55, 60—61, 79—81, 87—98, 103, 105—107, 128—129, 133—139, 142—143, 146—149, 152, 154—156, 158—159, 166—167, 169, **174—214**, 224—227, 236, 252—254, 256, 260—263, 265—266, 268—269, 271, 275, 280, 285, 288—294, 298—299, 313, 316—317, 321, 326, 329—331, 333—336, 338, 340, 342—345, 361, 381, 388—391, 393—394, 409, 411, 417—419, 422—423, 433—434, 436, 439, 442—443, 446—449, 458—462, 465, 467, 470—471
God, children of, 215—217
God-Concept, 186, 196
God-Consciousness, 227
God-Idea, 186, 207, 209, 213, 227
God of Israel, 248
Godhead, 53
Godlike, 333
Godlikeness, 143, 320, 458
Godliness, 150, 218—220, 458
God (Living), 198, 203
God's Daughter, 459
God's Image, 227
God's Kiss, 173
God's Law, 191
God's Will, 203
God's Word, 471
Go'e
Goethe, 162
Gog, 343
Golden Alter, 376, 380
Golden Calf, 82, 173—174, 465, 467
Golden Calves, 375
Golden Rule, 31, 221—223
Golem, 56
Good, 40, 44, 92, 106, 139, 150—151, 155, 178, 180, 184, 199, 212, 220, 252, 254—256, 265, 293—294, 334, 436
Good deeds, 388, 392
Goodness, 150, 154
Goshen, 373
Gospels, 332, 459, 463—464
Government, 33, 470
Governor, 179, 183
Grace, 12, 181, 220, 399

Grain, 379
Grapes, 386
Gratification, 151
Gratz (Graetz), 14, 16, 18, 203, 276, 278—279, 281, 301, 308, 413—414
Great Synagogue, 192, 443, 446
Greed, 147, 261
Greek, 46, 48, 50—51, 55, 90, 92, 181, 195—196, 276, 295, 416, 464
Greek Religion, 226
Grief, 272
Gunkel, 84, 373

"H"-Code, 244, 395
ha-Adam, 461
Habakkak, 31, 125, 263, 329
Habdalah, 366, 429
Habinenu, 447
Hadassi, Judah ben Elijah, 36
Hadrian, 42, 282—283, 369
Hadrianic Rebellion, 283
Haeckel, Ernst, 162
Haggadah, 346—347, 388, 400, 403, 444
Haggadic, 345, 391—392, 449
Haggadist, 188, 190
Haggai, 245
Haggashah, 385
Hagigah, 388
Hagiographa, 295
Hair, 41
Ha—konen, 236, 244
Haktarah, 383—384
Halakah, 31, 284, 355, 400
"Halakot Gedolot", 63
Ha-Levi, Aaron, 403
Ha-Levi, Judah, 28, 33, 92, 95
Ha-Levi
Ha-Levi Zechariah, 100
Half-Converts, 278—279
Halizah, 322
Hallel, 61
Halleluyah, 309
Hamburg Conference, 312
Hammurabi, 116
Hanancel, 450
Hananel ben Hushiel, 34
Ha-Nasi, Judah, 57
Hanging, 109
Hanina, 346, 446
Hanina Bar Hama, 280
Hanukkah, 61, 302, 430
Happiness, 23—24, 54, 135, 150, 169—170, 252, 408
Harith Ibn 'Amar, 285
Harmony, 54, 152
Harnack, 281
Harut, 168
Hasid, 218
Hasidean, 352
Hasidic, 451
Hasidim, 44, 350
Hasmoneans, 22, 246, 306—307, 353
Ha-tat, 383
Hatraah, 356
Hatred, 256
Hattat, 396, 401
Hazzayah, 384
Heal, 440
Healing, 439, 449
Heart, 159
Heathen, 280
Heaven, 86, 88, 97, 167, 400, 462, 466
Heavenly Bodies, 86, 108
Heaving, 381, 388
Hebrew Language, 323, 406—407, 412—413, 424, 441, 458, 461
Hebrew Sacrifices, 400
Hebrews, 83—84, 88, 116, 119, 160, 171, 231 257, 373—374, 395, 402
Hedonism, 150—151
Hedonistic, 23—24
Hegel, 207, 224—227, 316, 318
Hellenistic, 181, 459
Help, 407—408
Heman, 296, 300
Henetheism, 141, 163—164, 212
Heraclitas, 162
Herbert, Lord (Edward) of Cherbury, 134
Hereafter, 106, 253
Heredity, 153
Herem, 393
Heresies, 27
Heresy, 454
Heretical Teaching, 29
Heretics, 49, 104, 425, 444—445, 447, 453
Herod, 237, 277
Hesiod, 343
Heterodoxy, 20
Hexapla, 411
Hexaplar Syriac, 416
Hezekiah, 234
High Place, 228—235, 375, 390, 395—396
High Priest, 236—247, 377, 387, 392, 400, 404, 450
Higher will, 269
Higher world, 56
Hilgenfeld, 221—222
Hilkiah, 244
Hillel, 25, 31, 44, 90, 221, 253, 277, 343
Hillelites, 388
Him, 13, 143
Himyarite Empire, 285
Hippolytus, 412
Hirsch, Emil G., 313
Hirsch, Samson Raphael, 226
Hirsch, Samuel, 133, 172, 207, 225, 227, 256, 313, 318—319, 370—371
His Purposes, 174
Hisda, 387
Historic People, 149
History, 54, 145, 163, 175, 212, 224—225

Hobbs, Thomas, 134
"Hobat Ha-Lebabot", 33, 58, 95, 201, 294
Hoda'ah, 426, 436, 450
Ho-Da'ot, 433
Hoffman, 403—404
Holakah, 283, 383, 387
Holdheim, Samuel, 136, 317—318, 370
Holiness, 28—29, 143, 148, 151, 157, 164, 212, 227, 232
Holiness Code, 244, 395
Holiness Laws, 222
Holiness of
Holocaust, 373—377—379, 382—383, 395, 401
Holtzmann, O. 275
Holy, 176—177, 203, 213, 284, 397, 399, 408
Holy Days, 422, 432—433, 450
Holy Land, 313
Holy Nation, 471
Holy of Holies, 383
Holy People, 146, 471
Holy Place, 396
Holy Spirit, 266
Holy Vessel, 387
Homer, 343
Homiletics, 400
Homilie, 444
Honey, 378—379
Honor, 240, 281
Horace, 277
Hospitality, 146
Hosanna, 407
Hosea, 171, 212, 261—262, 328, 375, 408
Hoshaiah, 346
Hosha'na Rabbab, 448
Host of God, 404
Host of Heaven, 248—249
Hubsch, 313
Human Being, 463
Human Conduct, 153
Human Elements, 146—147
Human Race, 458—459
Human Sacrifices, 375, 394
Humanitarianism, 213
Humanity, 35, 143, 461
Humble, 392
Humility, 218—220, 467
Huppot, 159
Hutcheson, 24, 150
Huxley, Thomas, 9, 162
Hymns, 296, 401
Hyrcanus, John, 277

"I" Psalms, 302—303
Iblis, 97
Ibn Daud, Abraham, 33, 204, 255, 271, 292—293
Ibn Ezra, Abraham, 32, 48, 63, 89, 366, 387, 416, 420
Ibn Gabirol, Solomon, 58, 64, 94, 199—201, 269
Ibn-Roshd (Averroes), 103, 196
Ibn Sakawai, 196
Ibn-Sina, 103, 196
Iceberg, 97
Idea, 226
Idolatry, 28, 31, 34, 62, 146, 164, 194, 279, 331, 382, 387, 402
Idols, 375, 402
"Ikkarim", 15—17, 20, 22, 102, 132, 294
Imagination, 271—272
Immanent, 207
Immolation, 393—394
Immortal, 264
Immortality, 18, 103, 107, 135, 155, 167, 253, 409—410
Immutability, 34, 187, 194
Impenitence, 182
Imperishable, 180
Impious, 182
Impotence, 461
Incarnation, 18, 199
Incense, 384, 388, 392
Incest, 31, 62
Inclination, 151
Incorporeal, 184, 197, 206
Incorporeality, 18, 21, 33, 133, 175
Individual, 151
Industrial Customs, 370
Industrial Life, 156
Ineffable Appellation, 14, 250
Infinitude, 200
Informer, 425
Inner eye, 270
Innocence, 169—170
Injunctions, 31, 136, 434
Injury, 285
Inscribe us into the Book of Life, 429
Inspiration, 267, 269
Institutions, 157
Intellect, 19, 271, 273, 294
Intemperance, 147
Intuitionalists, 151
Invisible God, 51
Isaac, 173, 333—334, 336, 389, 417, 439, 444, 449
Isaac ben Moses, 272
Isaac ben Sheshet (Ribash), 100
Isaiah, 31, 41, 47, 125, 212, 262, 265—267, 328, 339, 375, 417
Ish, 158
Ishmael ben Elisha, 61
Ishshah, 158, 160
Isit, 160
Islam, 26—27, 196, 207, 292, 472
Israel, 28, 35, 41, 48, 54, 81—82, 125, 142—143, 149, 157, 163—165, 171, 173—174, 177, 181, 186, 192—193, 208, 212—213, 215—216, 225, 233, 254—255, 258, 260, 263, 267—268, 270—271, 276, 280—281,

Israel (continued)
285, 287—290, 301—302, 313—314, 317, 319, 321—323, 329, 336—338, 340—341, 344, 371, 388, 390—391, 393, 396, 402—404, 409, 418—421, 424, 433—435, 444, 446, 449, 454—455, 457—458, 462, 470—472
Israel Worship, 177
Israeli, Isaac ben Suleiman, 58
Israelite, 299, 380—381, 401, 459, 466—467
Istar, 167
Italian Ritual, 448
Itureans, 277

Jaabez, Joseph, 34
Jacob, 173, 184, 275, 279, 302, 333—334, 336, 372, 404, 417—418, 439, 444, 449
Jacob ben Samuel Koppelman ben Bunem, 21
Jacob Ibn Habib, 102
Jacoby of Edessa, 412
Jahvistic, 87
Jastrow, 313, 347
Jeduthun, 300
Jehoiachin, 419
Jehoiada, 244
Jehoshaphat, 234
Jehovah, 250—251
Jellinek, 278
Jephthan, 394
Jeremiah, 47, 86, 192, 213, 263, 328, 339, 350, 375, 393, 417—420, 469
Jeroboam, 47, 234, 259, 375
Jerome, 295, 411
Jerusalem, 36, 71, 240, 262, 267, 277—278, 328, 339, 373, 392, 395—396, 425, 435, 448, 450, 452, 457
Jesse, 374
Jesus, 43, 111, 221, 363—364, 368, 370, 400, 407, 459—460, 463—464
Jethro, 280—281, 373
Jew, 33
Jewish, 286, 400, 419, 459
Jewish Consciousness, 320
Jewish Customs, 275
Jewish Mission, 319
Jewish Morality, 278
Jewish Penal Code, 109
Job, 86—87, 121—122, 147, 161, 171, 215, 253, 281, 295—296, 330, 374, 417, 420, 462
Joel, 267
Joel, M., 17, 100, 108
Johanan, 188, 280, 346, 446
Johanan ben Zakkai, 388, 405
John, 459
Jonah, 276
Jose, 286, 323, 441
Jose ben Judah, 284
Joseph, 449
Joseph ben Jacob ibn Zaddik, 255, 271
Joseph of Couchy, 78
Josephus, 29, 109—110, 116, 237—238, 243, 246, 274—275, 277, 294, 306, 309, 341—342, 350—351, 401, 490
Joshua, 245, 388, 417
Joshua (Rabbi), 278, 282, 286, 353, 445—446
Joshua Ben Hananiah, 281
Joshua ben Levi, 300—301
Josiah, 233—234
Joy, 148, 364, 370, 408
Jubilee, 280
Judaeo-Christian, 172, 186, 368, 454
Judah, 449
Judah (Rabbi), 360
Judah Ha-Levi, 203—204, 254—255, 270, 292, 366, 403
Judah ha-Nasi, 451
Judaism, 12, 14, 20—21, 23—24, 26, 31, 33, 41, 135, 141, 150—151, 152—156, 163—165, 172, 186, 196, 207, 217—218, 221, 226—227, 252—253, 256, 276—281, 285, 311—313, 316—317, 321—322, 332, 337, 369, 402, 454, 472
Judge, 174, 178, 258, 463
Judgement, 33, 36, 262, 450
Judges, 472
Judith, 417
Jupiter, 155
Jurisprudence, 399
Just, 218—220
Justice, 12, 28—29, 82, 147, 156—157, 174, 181, 263, 297, 315, 321, 329, 425
Justin Martyr, 369
Juvenal, 277, 342

Kabbalah, 383
Kabbel, 280
Kabod, 191
Kaddish, 323, 364—365
Kadosh, 164, 324
Kahira, Simeon, 63—64
Kaktarah, 384
Kalam, 195—196
"Kalimat" As-Shadat", 26
Kalir, 448
Kant, Immanuel, 10—11, 54, 151—152, 162, 206—207, 317—318
Kapparah, 398
Karaism, 17, 194, 317
Karite, 196, 354
Karaites, 17, 33, 36, 52, 57, 96, 133
Karaitic, 367
Karet, 356
Kedushshah, 424, 433
Kedushshay ha-Shem, 423
Kenites, 285
"Ketubim", 295

Kibbuz Galuyot, 425
Kid, 377
Kiddush, 358, 365
Kidneys, 402
Killing, 383, 394, 410
Kimhi, David, 308, 403, 416, 420
Kindling Fire, 356
Kindness, 147
King, 458, 471
Kingdom, 472, 433
Kingdom of God, 152
Kingdom of Heaven, 429
Kings, 339, 375
"Kitab La-Amanat wal-I'tikadat, 196
"Kittel", 324
Knowledge, 13, 19, 25, 28, 106, 196, 451
Kodashim, 395
Kodesh, 212, 396
Kodesh ha-Kodashim, 387
Kodosh, 212
Kofer, 410
Kohanim, 431, 433, 450
Kohler, Kaufmann, 313
"Kol Bo", 442, 454
König, 420
Korahite Psalms, 411
Korah, 296, 300, 304—305
Koran, 52, 96, 168, 195
Korban, 385
Kraetzschmar, 420
Krauss, S., 281
"Kuh", 97

Labor, 87
Lamarck, 162
Lamb, 345, 383, 388, 390, 394, 396—397, 401
"Lamed Auctoris," 305
Land-Grabbing, 262
Language, 162, 267
Lapidation, 109, 111, 338
Last, 175, 203
Law, 21, 28, 43, 80, 143, 148, 191, 226—227, 254—255, 278—279, 285, 313—314, 331, 363, 370, 378—379, 382, 389, 393, 402—403, 405, 465, 472
Law of God, 191
Laying On of Hands, 380, 383, 387, 399
Leaven, 378—379
Leavened Bread, 382
Legal, 471
Legal Fictions, 367
"Legends of Old Testament Characters," 170
"Lehre," 226, 318
Leibnitz, Gottfried Wilhelm, 27, 252
Leo X (Pope), 251
Leper, 385—386
Leprosy, 284
Levi Ben Gershon, 205, 273, 294
Levirate, 240, 322
Levirate Marriage, 409
Levite, 61, 230, 301—302, 308—309, 324, 362, 374, 377, 380, 396
Levitical, 246, 315, 320, 395, 398—399, 470—471
Levitical Code, 41, 56—57, 61
Levitical Law, 233
Leviticus, 376
Lex Talionis, 114, 118
Libation, 27, 230, 379, 382—383, 392, 395—396
Liberty, 254, 263, 292
Life, 13, 40, 83, 149, 150, 164, 178, 263
Light, 88, 121, 139
Lilienthal, 313
Lintel, 394
Linus, 343
Lions, 290, 390
Literary Prophecy, 259—260
Liturgy, 26, 30, 32, 138, 150, 155, 282, 290—291, 412—414, 434, 450, 455
Living God, 178—179, 198, 203
Locke, John, 134
Loeb, 451
Logic, 224
Logical Idealism, 224
Logos, 183, 185, 459, 464
LORD, 29
Lord's Prayer, 188
Love, 106—107, 146, 155, 157, 176—177, 212, 329
Low, L., 28, 35, 135
Lower World, 56
Loyalty, 146, 147, 263
Lucifer, 166
Luke, 460, 463
Lulab, 391
Lulab, 391
Lust, 159
Luxury, 262
Lying, 147

Maccabean, 29, 50, 236, 246, 342, 350, 407, 420, 444, 452—453
Maccabees, 179, 181, 306—308
"Magen Abot," 18
Magi, 99
Magog, 343
Maharil, 436
Mahzor, 431—434
Mahzor of Salonica, 454
Mai, Clauidus, 22
Maimon, 206
Maimonides, Moses, 13—14, 16—21, 34—35, 37, 50, 53, 57, 64, 89—90, 92—93, 95, 102—108, 119, 132, 138, 205—207, 237—238, 240, 255—256, 271—273, 279—280, 293—294, 323, 350—351, 356, 360, 363,

Maimonides, Moses, (continued)
366, 387, 401—403, 430, 434—441, 451
453, 455—456
Malachi, 126, 375
Malediction, 416
Man, 39, 55, 86, 88, 97, 148, 152, 155, 158, 164, 167, 187, 203, 227, 252—254, 256, 265, 269, 463
Man of Suffering, 420
Manasseh, 233—234, 393, 449
Mandaic, 463
Mandatory Laws, 60, 64, 76
Manicheans, 139
Mankind, 461, 463
Manna, 43, 344—345, 349, 351, 357
Manoah, 374
Manumisso, 399
Manumitted Slave, 287
Mar, 432
Mar bar Rabina, 456
Marduk, 86
Margoliouth, 360
Marriage, 159, 240, 268, 281, 322
Marti, 420
Marial, 342
Martin, Raymond, 251
Martyr, 420
Marut, 168
Masha, 170
Mashyana, 170
Masorah, 301
Masoretic, 309, 409, 412
Masseket Soferim, 442
Master, 423
Mas'udi, 97
Material Elements, 153
Materialism, 54
Maternal Love, 24
Mattathias of Saragossa, 100
Matter, 92, 96, 103, 181, 255, 293
Matthew, 223, 278, 460
Mattathias, 340, 342, 350
Maurice, 399
Maybaum, 273
Meal, 394
Meal-offering, 383—385, 391, 393
Meat, 394—397
Meat-offering, 397
Medical Science, 15
Medieval, 186
Medieval Jewish Philosophy, 16
Medieval Transmundane, 186
Medium, 269
Meek, 408, 420—421
Me-'en Sheba, 427
Mehal, 441
Meier, 181
Meir, 254, 281, 353
"Mekor Hayyim," 94, 199
Melchizedak, 300
Melchizedak, 300
Melekah, 384
Meliorism, 150
Melkarth, 155
Memra, 183, 189
Men, 99, 461
Mendelssohn, Moses, 28—29, 135, 252, 311, 316
Mental Condition, 370
Mental Perfection, 272
Merciful Father, 435
Mercy, 146—147, 174, 178, 181, 218—220, 297
Meret, 219
Mesha, 228, 393
Meshummad, 454
Mesita, 228
Messiah, 18, 21, 34, 36, 93, 99, 113, 141, 284, 314—315, 322—323, 408, 419, 457—459, 463
Messianic, 18—19, 33, 35, 107—108, 112, 125, 149, 152, 157, 245—246, 252, 254, 256, 289, 312, 314—315, 321—323, 343, 392, 407—410, 445, 459, 464, 471
Messianic King, 426
Metaphor, 198
Metaphysics, 224, 256, 459
Metatron, 167
Mezvzah, 61
Mezuzot, 281
Micah, 218, 376, 397
Michael, 97, 341, 392, 463
Micah, 31, 125
Midrash, 90, 139, 160, 189, 267, 275, 281, 369, 402—403, 415, 449, 460
"Milhamot Adonai," 294
Militarism, 363
Mind, 33, 54, 149, 163, 184, 224—225
Minhah, 366, 382—383, 385, 389, 391, 393, 396, 404, 422, 430—432
Minhot, 384
Minim, 186, 453—455
Minyan, 324
Miracles, 33, 93, 107, 163, 268—269, 272, 285
Miriam, 336, 443
Mishnah, 30, 135, 286, 323, 341, 352, 355, 357, 360, 386, 440—441, 450, 455
Mishnah Law, 359
Mission, 225
Missionary, 27, 420—421
.uF
Mizrak, 387
Mizwah, 60—62, 334
Mizwot, 465
Mizzuy, 384
Mneominic, 442-443
Moab, 285
Moabites, 231
Modesty, 219
Modim, 194, 431

Mohammedan, 13, 17—18, 26, 33, 51—52, 93, 96—98, 104, 119, 194, 366
Molech, 233
Molo, Apollonius, 51
Moloch, 375, 393—394
Monarch, 472
Monastery, 39—40
Monday, 97
Monogamy, 161
Monolatry, 163, 209
Monotheism, 28, 50, 86—87, 141—142, 163—165, 207, 210, 276, 278
Monotheistic, 417
Monotheists, 402
Montanists, 40
Moon, 99, 208, 248
Moral, 136, 140, 155
Moralists, 150—151
Moral Action, 150—151
Moral Conduct, 151
Moral Cosmos, 149
Moral Destiny, 155
Moral Freedom, 153
Moral Holiness, 164
Moral Law, 149—150, 152, 164, 317, 329
Moral Liberty, 252
Moral Life, 24, 152, 154—155
Moral Offenses, 398
Moral Order, 149
Moral Perfection, 272
Moral Power, 54
Moral Purpose, 154—155
Moral Value, 151
Moralism, 135
Morality, 24, 135, 143, 154—155, 221
Morals, 402
"Moreh," 293
"Moreh Nebukim," 205
Mortal, 264
Mortality, 461
Mosaic, 374, 376
Mosaic Law, 21, 40, 91, 118, 317
Mosaism, 30, 311, 315
Moses, 21, 34, 36, 50, 52, 61, 63, 82, 93, 103, 129, 132, 134, 173, 180, 190, 192, 207, 210, 219, 258, 265—267, 270, 272, 280, 290, 296, 299—300, 306, 316, 335—336, 342, 373, 390, 392, 400—402, 417, 449, 461, 465—468, 470
Moses ben Jacob of Couchy, 64, 77
Moses ben Maimon, 205
Moses, I.S., 286
Moses Taku, 206
Moslems, 99
Most High, 179, 458
Mosques, 99
Motazilites, 53, 195—196, 293
Motekallamin, 33, 94, 195, 202
Motion, 93
Motives, 151, 153
Mountains, 96—97
Mt. Carmel, 374
Mountain God, 231
Mountains, 179
Mourning, 370
Muller, 448
Munk, 16
Munolatry, 164
Munolatry, 164
Murder, 31
Musaf, 35, 323, 365, 404, 422, 428, 430, 437
Music, 362, 366, 401, 412—414
Musical Instruments, 309—310
Mutilations, 41, 57, 115, 118
Mutualism, 25
Mystics, 44

Naamah, 167, 374
Nahum, 125
Nahawandi, 196
Nahmanides, 34, 63—64, 76—77, 89, 95, 132, 402—403
Nahum of Gimzu, 254
Nakedness, 158
Name, 409
Name, The, 13
Naomi, 281, 407
Nathan, 259
"Natin," 287
National, 453
National Conditions, 83
National Elements, 317
National Law, 471
National Legalism, 135, 148
Nationalism, 314, 451
Nationality, 27
Nations, 390
Natural, 227, 271
Natural Law, 106, 134, 227
Natural Religions, 226
Natural Selection, 162
Natural Theology, 135
Nature, 174—175, 227
Nature-Worship, 41, 163
Nazarites, 43, 61, 377, 379
Nazirs, 43
Nebelah, 403
Nebi'im, 43
Nebuchadnezzar, 48, 417—418
Necessity, 181
Nedabah, 383
Neder, 383
Needy, 147, 223
Nefilim, 166
Nehemiah, 245, 339—340, 350, 471
Ne'ilah, 429
Neophyte, 27
Neoplatonic, 196
"Ner Tamid," 273
Nero, 280

Nestorians, 195
New Moons, 301, 339, 422, 428, 430, 433—434
New Testament, 110—111, 166, 222, 246, 274—275, 306, 351, 363—364, 400, 463
"Nibdalim," 369
Nicanor, 340
Nicene, 26
Nicolaus Cusanus, 252
Nietzche, 24, 155, 176
Nikrat, 404
Nineteen Benedictions, 422, 439
Ninth of AB, 323, 430—431, 434
Nirvana, 23
Nissim, 441
Nissim ben Reuben (Ran), 100
Noachian, 279, 463
Noah, 27, 62, 143, 167, 172, 207, 329, 372, 390, 402, 404
Nob, 375
Noldeke, 160
Non-Jew, 223, 278—279, 288, 341, 367—368, 455
Non Jewish Prophets, 268
Nudity, 169, 171

Obadiah, 267
Obedience, 146, 404
Oblations, 373, 378, 392
Oceans, 179
Oehler, 399
Offerings, 376
"Ohel Ya'akob," 21
Oil, 378, 384
'Olah, 383—384, 395, 401, 404
'Olam, 414
"Olam Katôn," 271
"Olat Tamid," 35, 286, 322—323
Old Testament, 171, 183, 231, 263, 370, 392, 400, 470
Olive-Oil, 379
'Olot, 383
Omer, 384
Omnipotence, 154, 198, 204, 292, 461
Omnipotent, 88, 93, 105, 106, 179—180, 185
Omnipresent, 49, 178—179, 182—185, 189—190
Omniscience, 105—106, 199
Omniscient, 178, 185
One and Indivisible, 13—14
One Day of Rest, 371
One God, 275
Oprah, 374
Optimism, 140, 150
Optimism and Pessimism, 252—256
"Or Adoni," 15, 102
Orabuena, Joseph, 101
"Oracula Sibyllina," 180
Oral Law, 316
Ordinances, 60
Organ, 324
Oriental Religions, 226
"Origin of Species," 162
Original Sin, 40, 256, 396
Orphan, 80
Orthodox Judaism, 313, 315—316
Orthodoxy, 20, 103—104, 227
Other Worldliness, 23, 108
Overman, 24, 155
Ox, 377

"P" Code, 244, 275, 396-396, 471
Pagan, 277-278, 404
Palestine, 86-87, 270-271, 274-275, 277, 290, 313-315, 318, 322, 358, 403, 448, 456
Palestinian Talmud, 447
Paley, 24
Palladium, 468
Pandora, 160
Pan-Monotheism, 207
Pantheism, 52, 95, 201, 207
Panthers, 390
Parable, 460
Paradise, 99, 160, 170
Pardon, 440, 449
Pascal Lamb, 373, 376, 378
Passion, 39-40, 185, 270
Passover, 362, 371, 373-374, 382, 384, 386, 394, 397, 400, 428, 434-435
Patriarchs, 143, 235, 331, 333, 345, 372, 423, 443-444, 449
Patriotism, 263
Paul, 9, 21, 226, 318, 321-322, 335, 368, 445, 463
Paulinian Soteriology, 409
Pause, 413
Peace, 147, 223, 266, 315, 321, 365, 389, 408, 427, 449
Peace-Oblations, 385
Peace Offerings, 383, 387, 389
Penal, 399
Penini, Jedaiah, 35
Penitent, 167
Pentateuch, 28, 39, 43, 63, 80-81, 84, 129, 146, 191, 244, 287, 301, 303-304, 306, 315, 317, 319, 349-350, 355-357, 373, 375, 387, 390, 434, 437, 443
Pentateuchal Laws, 315, 319
Pentecost, 379, 382
People, 270, 458, 471
Perfection, 21, 40, 93, 134, 170, 205
Persecution, 253
Persian, 360
Persius, 342
Personal Identity, 12
Personality, 150, 156, 184
Pessimism, 40, 44, 140, 150
Petition, 422
Pharoah, 449

Pharisaic, 222, 246, 278, 331-332, 368
Phariseeism, 227
Pharisees, 29, 277, 294, 303, 307, 363, 443, 451
Phenicians, 84, 86
Philanthropy, 335, 363, 388
Philipson, 313
Philistine, 258, 374, 402
Philo, 12, 17, 30-32, 52, 55, 62, 82, 90-92, 117, 119, 128-129, 133, 138-139, 160, 172, 183-185, 253, 264, 274-276, 291, 342-343, 400-401, 459
Philosopher, 197
Philosophical Literature, 90
Philosophy of History, 224
Philosophy of Religion, 225
Phocylides, 181
Phylacteries, 324, 391
Piety, 134, 267, 392, 451
Pigeon, 377-378, 380
Pilate, Pontius, 113
Pilgrim Festivals, 434
Pilgrim Songs, 308
Pious, 181, 359, 363, 420, 425, 451, 459
Pity, 79, 81, 147, 156
Piyyutim, 312, 323
Plague, 122, 262
Plants, 86, 88
Plato, 92, 139, 252, 264
Platonic Idea, 90-91
Pleasure, 151, 172
Pliny, 51, 368
Plotinus, 199
Political, 471
Political Life, 156
Ploybius, 46
Polygamy, 240
Polytheism, 87, 142, 163, 209, 275
Polytheistic, 208, 215, 249, 278
Poor, 80-81, 261, 390, 392, 408, 420-421, 451
Portuguese, 437
Posh'Im, 453
Posidonius, 51
Positive Religion, 225-226
Positivists, 163
Positivity, 292
Possession, 24-25
Post-Exilic, 29
Posterity, 172
Poverty, 40, 156
Power, 13, 24-25, 177, 263
Powers, 423, 433
Praise, 192, 422
Praise-Offerings, 376
Praises, 401
Prayer, 220, 268, 282, 391-392, 402, 404, 422, 426, 429, 441, 443-444, 446, 448, 451, 454, 456, 460-461
Prayer Book, 32, 34, 59, 193, 311, 315, 337, 404, 447
Prayer-Manuals, 442
Preacher, 260
Precentor, 392, 424
Pre-Destination, 292
Prediction, 265
Pre-Existence, 463
Prescience, 12, 154, 195, 204, 294
Pressing Out Blood, 384
Pride, 147, 218, 220
Priest, 258, 315, 362, 397
Priest-People, 146, 321
Priest-Rituals, 396
Priesthood, 27, 148, 233
Priestly Benediction, 325
Priestly Blessing, 426, 431, 450-451
Priestly Code, 84, 141, 234, 244, 349
Priestly Community, 315
Priestly Law, 470
Priests, 13, 41, 134, 230, 234, 324, 375, 377, 379-381, 385, 387, 395-396, 400, 404, 431, 450, 470
Primeval Egg, 85
Primeval Olean, 88
Primitive Religion, 46, 83
Premudane, 36
Principles, 15, 136
Probability, 268
Probation, 280
Profanation, 133, 356
Profane, 399
Prohibition, 31, 63, 398
Prohibitory Laws, 60, 69-75, 77-78
"Prologus Galeatus," 295
Property, 25, 155-156, 268
Prophecy, 34, 105-106, 165, 266, 273
Prophetic, 164
Prophetic Doctrine, 124
Prophets, 21, 28-29, 34, 41, 47, 50, 52, 79-80, 89, 99, 106, 117, 119, 141, 146-147, 164, 171, 174, 177, 184, 201, 207, 212-213, 222, 233-234, 257, 294, 315, 318-319, 339, 373, 375, 395-396, 400, 402, 408, 417-418, 443, 462, 470-472
Prophets and Prophecy, 257-273
Proselyte, 27, 35, 62, 274-287, 441
Protestant Reformation, 311
Proverb, 330
Proverbs, 86, 296
Providence, 29, 34, 50, 105, 135, 181, 188, 262-263, 288-294
Psalms, 29, 48, 86-87, 89, 147, 174, 186, 213, 253, 295-310, 323, 330-332, 376, 407-408, 411-416, 420, 439, 443, 451, 458, 461, 463
Pseudepigraph, 172
Pseudepigraph A, 172, 340, 350, 459
Pseudo-epigraphic, 90
Pseudo-Messiah, 101
Psychology, 402
Ptetrine Party, 368
Public Sacrifices, 396

Punishment, 33, 82, 106, 149, 151, 158, 263, 266, 467
Purification, 237, 282, 399
Purificative Offerings, 376
Purim, 61, 430, 448
Puritan, 354
Purity, 33, 155, 269
Purpose, 162-163
Purposes, 54, 106-107, 148
Pythagoreans, 343

Quietism, 150
Quinta, 411
Quirinius, 237

Rab, 299, 445
Rabad, 451
Rabbinic Literature, 383
Rabbinical Authorities, 283
Rabbinical Code, 39
Rabbinical Conferences, 312
Rabbinical Court, 283
Rabbinical Judaism, 405
Rabbinical Law, 359, 367, 383
Rabbinical Literature, 299, 312, 459
Rabbinical Prayers, 430
Rabbinical Theology, 332
Rabbinites, 17, 36
Rabbis, 281, 335, 454
Rabina, 432
Race, 27, 83
Radical Reform, 319
Rahab, 267, 280
Rahmana, 81
Rain, 290, 423, 435
Ralbag (Gersonides), 95-96, 103, 107, 204-205
Ram, 377, 383, 386, 396, 401, 449
Ramah, 374
Raphael, 449
Rapoport, 448
Rashi, 420
Rational, 172, 268
Rationalists, 39
Rea, 222
Reality, 292
Reason, 135, 268
Recant, 284
Red Heifer, 378, 395, 400, 405
Red Sea, 187, 449, 470
Redeem, 440
Redeemer, 409, 424
Redemption, 314, 449, 457
Reform Judaism, 59, 136, 163, 165, 225, 311—325, 405, 457
Reform Temples, 325
Rehoboam, 234
Religion, 27, 88, 140, 155, 162, 164, 222, 400, 402, 471
Religion of Beauty, 226
Religion of Fantasy, 226
Religion of Good, 226
Religion of Intellect, 226
Religion of Inwardness, 226
Religion of Light, 226
Religion of Pain, 226
Religion of Pessimism, 252
Religion of Sublimity, 226
"Religions—Philosophic Der Juden," 227
Remember us for Life, 429
Remembrances, 433
Remnant, 408-409, 420, 435, 446
Remnant of Israel, 328
Rénan, 84, 165, 208
Repent, 404
Repentance, 297, 328, 440, 447
Repentant, 389
Repugnance, 151
"Reshaím, 333
Resignation, 150
Response, 414
Restitution, 396
Restoration, 408
Resurrection, 21, 29-30, 33-34, 36, 53, 57, 59, 193, 315, 336, 369-370, 423, 450-451, 457
Retribution, 18, 21, 28, 30, 33-34, 36, 134-135, 253-254, 343, 471
Return, 424
Reuben, 449
Revealed Commandments, 268
Revealed Religions, 19-20, 105
Revelation, 18, 21, 28, 33-34, 103, 106-107, 134-135, 164-165, 224-225, 254-255, 258, 262-263, 265, 269, 285, 315-316, 471
Revenge, 142
Reverence, 146, 176
Reward, 33, 106-107, 149, 151, 334-335, 404
Rezeh, 428
Rhythm, 412
Rib, 158-159
Ribash, Isaac ben Sheshet, 100
Rich, 265
Riches, 218
Right, 135, 149-150, 156, 181, 225
Right and Righteousness, 326—337
Righteous, 218, 261, 290, 292, 327, 392, 415, 450, 462
Rights, 133, 140
Righteousness, 27, 29, 33, 80, 146—148, 152, 155, 176-177, 218, 321, 402
Rites, 237, 400
Ritual, 146, 439, 451
Ritual Religion, 400
Ritualism, 402
Rituals, 396
Robbers, 446

Robbery, 62
Robe, 237
Rock of Salvation, 408
"Rokeah," 442
Roman, 237, 277-278, 285, 319, 332, 337, 342, 369, 431, 445, 453—455
Roman Empire, 277, 455
Roman History, 277
Roman Law, 109—113, 117, 119
Roman Mahzor, 436, 454
Roman Religion, 226
Roman Ritual, 457
Roots, 20
"Rosh Amanah," 35
Rosh Ha Shanah, 291, 333, 428-429, 433, 445
Rothenburg, Meir, 367
Rothstein, 419
Rousseau, Jean Jacques, 24, 135
Royal Authority, 472
Rufus, 343-344
Ruler, 155, 178, 470
Ruler of the World, 174
Ruth, 275-276, 280-281, 295

Saadia ben Joseph, 13, 32-33, 58, 64, 94, 132-133, 139, 196—199, 254, 268-269, 292, 420, 434, 436, 438, 455
Sabbath, 42, 49, 87, 112, 133, 238, 279, 281, 283, 317—320, 325, 338—367, 396, 422, 427-428, 432-434, 436, 451, 462
Sabbath Accidents, 363
Sabbath and Sunday, 368-371
Sabbath Celebration, 364-365
Sabbath Conflagration, 361
Sabbath Friday Preparation, 357
Sabbath Garb, 362
Sabbath Goy, 367
Sabbath Grace, 365
Sabbath Lamp, 61, 358, 365
Sabbath Meal, 358
Sabbath Prayers, 365
Sabbath JRiding, 353
Sabbath Sick, 363
Sabbath Study, 366
Sabbath Suspensions, 362
Sabbath Walking, 351-353
Sabbath Work, 356
Sacerdotal, 177, 213, 246, 303, 314, 317, 320, 322, 373, 450-451, 471
Sacred Books, 361
Sacred-Offerings, 395
Sacrifice, 27-28, 41, 46, 61, 115, 230, 235, 237, 270, 282, 298, 314, 322, 338, 348, 372-405, 433-434, 457
Sacrifice Materials, 377
Sacrifice Substitutes, 392
Sacrificial, 404
Sacrificial Religion, 395
Sacrificial Service, 426
Saducean, 451
Saducees, 29, 294, 303, 307, 332, 352, 354, 425, 443, 453
Saint, 40, 152
Sale, 313
Salt, 378, 386, 390
Salvation, 177, 320, 396, 406-410
Samael, 159, 168
Samaritans, 352, 354
Samhazi, 166-168
Samuel, 235, 257-258, 334, 374, 397, 445, 468, 471-472
Samuel Ben Nahman, 346
Samuel The Younger, 454
Sanctification, 379, 383, 399, 400, 423, 428-429, 434, 436
Sanctifications, 433
Sanctuary, 240, 244
Sanguinary Ceremonies, 405
Sanhedrin, 111-112, 238, 240, 246
Sapphire, 466
Sarcedotal, 41, 141, 164, 177
Satan, 159, 166, 389
Saturday, 369
Saul, 374, 376, 394, 461, 471
Savior, 407, 409-410
Sayce, (Prof.), 347
Scape-Goat, 352, 380, 387, 395
Schecter, Solomon, 35, 91, 131, 222, 366
Schlesinger, Ludwig, 16, 22
Scholastic, 154
Schopenhauer, 156, 252
Schultz, 399
Schürer, 275
Science, 88
Scribes, 284
Scripture, 271, 288-289, 343
Sea, 93, 97
Second Temple, 278, 302, 306, 388, 394
Security, 408
Seduction, 167
Seductive, 167
Seer, 257-258, 263, 270
"Sefer Emunotwe-De'ot," 196
"Sefer Hegyon ha-Nefesh," 95
"Sefer Mizwot ha-Gadol," 64
"Sefer Yezirah," 58
Segan, 240
Selah, 411-416, 436, 438-439
Self, 156
Self-assertion, 25
Self-consciousness, 12, 14, 54, 225
Self-creation, 95
Self-determination, 106
Self-effacement, 25
Self-existent, 180
Self-obliteration, 23
Self-realization, 23, 25
Selfishness, 148-149
Selihah, 424, 449

Sellin, 419
Semikah, 380, 383, 387
Semitic, 86
Semitic Dialect, 417
Seneca, 109, 288, 342
Sennacherib, 262, 285
Sensationists, 12, 139
Senses, 58
Sensual, 197
Sensuous, 172, 189
Sephardic, 295, 422, 435-439, 455
Sephardim, 35, 365, 434, 437
Septaugint, 180, 274, 295-296, 304, 401, 411-412, 459
Seraiah, 244
Sermon on the Mount, 221
Serpent, 158-160, 170-173, 290
Servant, 400, 417, 420, 423, 460
Servant of God, 417-421
Service, 24, 155-156, 404
Seth, 158, 160, 341
Seven Noachian Injunctions, 279
Seventeenth of Tammuz, 448
Seventh Day, 368, 434
Seventy Elders, 467
Seventy Languages, 449
Sexta, 411
Sha'ah, 441
Shabbat, 347, 356
Shaftesbury, 24, 150
Shaharit, 422
Shahrastani, 195
Shallet, 366
Shalom, 223, 436
Shame, 169, 220
Shammai, 90, 253, 277, 343
Shammaites, 388
Sheba, 418
Shebitah, 356
Shechem, 374
Sheep, 377, 390
Shehitah, 383
Sheiks, 472
Shekar, 379
Shekinah, 172, 189, 277, 332, 334, 449
Shelamim, 401, 404
Sheliah Zibbur, 392, 424
Shema, 30, 32, 61, 105, 128-129, 186-187, 206, 286, 323-324, 337, 391, 422, 432, 443
Shemaiah, 281
Shemoneh-'Esreh, 30, 283, 291, 300, 323, 416, 422-457
Sheshbazar, 419
"Shibbole ha-Leket," 456
Shilol, 374, 395
Ship Travel, 352-353
Shofar, 82, 362, 428, 433
"Sharashim," 20
Showbread, 338, 376, 382
Shulman, 313
Sick, 81, 363, 424, 439, 451
Sickness, 439
Sidereal, 248
Siegfried, 92
Sigfried, 221
Silent Prayer, 430-431, 456
Sim Shalom, 436, 451
Simeon, 227, 450
Simeon ben Eleazer, 173, 279-280
Simeon Ben Lakish, 285, 345
Simeon Ben Yohai, 282, 354, 389, 441
Simeon ha-Pakoli, 443-444
Simile, 271
"Similitudes," 463
Simlai, 31, 63, 345
Simon, 179
Simon, Rabbi, 387
Simon ben Asai (Azzai), 31, 63, 388-389
Simon ben Eleazar, 63
Sin, 33, 40-41, 134, 148, 150, 166-167, 169-172, 177, 212, 237, 254, 260-261, 321-322, 388-390, 397, 404-406, 419, 429, 434
Sin-Bearer, 400
Sin-Offering, 356, 376, 381-383, 385-386, 390-391, 396, 404
Sinai, 34, 61, 128, 173-174, 187, 210, 266, 285, 316, 336, 345, 373, 394
Sinner, 43, 176, 289, 399, 403, 406
Sirach, 30
Six-days, 91
Six Days of Labor, 371
Six Hundred Thirteen (613) Commandments, 31, 35, 63, 131-132, 316, 466
Skepticism, 47-48
Sky, 56, 97
Slander, 220
Slanderer, 462
Slaughtering, 397
Slave, 109, 287, 409, 418, 423
Slavery, 156
"Slavonic Enoch," 90, 99
Smith, Adam, 24
Smith, Robert, 392
Smith, Robertson, 42
Smith, W. R., 160, 231
Social, 471
Social Justice, 328
Social Righteousness, 327
Society, 25, 162
Socinians, 134
Socrates, 46, 288
Sodom, 143, 329
Solomon, 181, 183, 186, 236, 244-245, 259, 296, 300, 306, 331-332, 374-375, 449
Solomon ben Adret, 367
Solomonic (Temple), 465
Son, 460
Son of God, 458-460, 461
Son of Man, 461-464
Soncino, 21

Sonship, 459
Soothsayers, 273
Soothsaying, 271
Sorrow, 79
Soul, 33, 56-58, 99, 107, 149, 152-153, 194, 255, 269, 398, 401
Souls, 392
Space, 155
Speech, 95, 402
Spencer, Herbert, 10, 24, 154, 162, 209
Spices, 382
Spies, 282
Spinal Column, 443
Spinoza, Baruch, 53, 100, 108
Spirit, 44, 56, 224, 264
Spirit of God, 175
Spiritual, 150-151
Spiritual Individuality, 226
Spiritual Religion, 400
Spirituality, 34, 263
Splendor, 408
Sprinkling the Blood, 384
Stars, 88, 99, 208, 248
State, 34
Statistics, 153
Stein, Leopold, 313
Sterner, Max, 24
Steward, 156
Stoics, 182
Stone, 468
Stoning, 356
Stranger, 80, 118, 276, 410
Strong, 25, 146, 156
Student, 392
Study, 392
Sub-consciousness, 11
Sub-deities, 91
Submission, 150
Suffer, 199
Suffering, 170, 253-254, 256, 390
Suicide, 153
Sukkot, 301, 390, 428, 434
Summum Bonum, 23, 142-143, 149
Sun, 99, 208, 248, 369, 444
Sunday, 97, 368, 429
Sunday Law, 370
Super corporeal, 197
Supernatural, 33, 271, 463
Superstitious, 281
Supplications, 402
Supramundane, 186-187, 189, 196
Supremacy, 24
Supreme, 262
Supreme Being, 174
Supreme Judge, 174, 225
Supreme Will, 471
Survival, 408
Swearing, 398
Symbolic, 319
Symbolism, 14, 400, 402-403
Symbolist, 318, 399, 401
Symbols, 155, 225-226, 390, 392, 404
Symmachus, 411
Sympathy, 25
Synagogue, 40, 89, 186, 189, 193, 195, 253-254, 309, 325, 367, 392, 404, 413, 422, 443, 450
Synoptic, 460
Syria, 374
Syriac, 463
Syrian, 340, 453-454
Syrian Religion, 226
Szold, 313

Tabernacle, 267, 325, 359, 373-374, 377, 400, 449
Table, 391
Table of the Law, 465—469
Tables of the Heart, 469
Tables of Stone, 465
Taboo, 347-348, 397-398, 400
Tabri, 21, 105
Tacitus, 51, 109, 277
Talent, 24, 25, 156-157
Tallit, 324
Talmud, 45, 49, 56, 58, 90, 93, 97, 100, 139, 163, 173, 186, 192-193, 254, 265, 268, 274, 289, 291, 301, 309, 312, 316, 319-320, 322, 350, 353, 355, 359, 386, 388, 416, 429-430, 442-443, 447, 463
Tam, Rabbi, 358
Tamar, 449
Tamid, 396
Tamidim, 404
Tannaim, 265, 277, 289, 343
Tannaitic, 323
Targum, 411, 458
Targumim, 180, 189
Targumic, 183
Tax, 396
Teaching, 28
Tebilah, 282
Tefillah, 323, 359, 391, 404, 422, 426-427, 432-433, 439, 441-442, 444, 446, 448, 451—453, 455-456
Tefillin, 61, 324, 391
Te-Hiyyatha-Metim, 423, 451
Teleological, 162-163, 254-255
Temper, 119
Temperament, 270
Temple, The, 36, 99, 112, 190, 235, 267, 282, 307-308, 313, 322, 362, 373, 375-376, 388, 391, 413, 433-434, 441, 443-444, 449-450, 452-453, 456
Ten Commandments, 63, 130-131, 465
Ten Rods, 400
Ten Words, 32, 130
Tent of Meeting, 61, 398
Tenth of Tebet, 448
Tents, 229

Tenufah, 388
Teraphim, 211, 229
Terefah, 403
Tertullian, 109, 370
Terumah, 388, 396
Teshubah, 424, 429, 440, 449
Testimony, 398
Tetragrammaton, 250, 456
Thank-Offering, 376, 382-383, 392
Thanks, 422
Thanksgiving, 375-376, 401, 426
Thanksgiving Prayer, 430
Theism, 10, 52, 54, 163
Theistic, 47, 54
Theme, 412
Theocracy, 141, 470-472
Theodicy, 175, 253—255, 294
Theodotion, 411
Theogonies, 83, 87
Theophany, 122
Theophorous Name, 417
Theosophy, 30, 201
Thirteen Articles, 34, 37
Thirteen Attributes of God, 34, 90
Thirteen Attributes of Compassion, 79
Thirteen Theories of Creation, 94
Thought, 13, 402, 412
Throne, 463
Thummim, 107, 237, 267
Thursday, 97
Tiamat, 85-86
Tiberius, 342
Time, 93, 95, 149, 155-156, 196, 200
Tindal, 135
Tish'ah be-Ab, 323
Tithe, 357, 383, 387, 395
Titus, 48
Tobias, 221, 307
Tobit, 221-222, 254
Todah, 383, 396, 401
Toland, John, 134
Torah, 28, 43, 56, 60, 81, 90, 104, 106—108, 129, 131, 133, 173, 191-192, 218-219, 222-223, 258, 268, 280, 284, 296, 299, 314, 317-318, 324, 345, 353, 365-366, 382, 392, 404, 419-420, 428, 436, 459, 465, 471
Torot, 396
Tosef, 387
Totemism, 163-164, 393
Toy, 348
Tradition, 107, 165
Traducer, 425, 453
Training, 272
Traitor, 425, 444, 450, 453
Transcendence, 186, 191
Transcendent, 183, 185
Transcendental, 189, 207, 226-227, 254
Transgression, 62, 397
Transientness, 461
Transmundane, 186
"Tratado," 101
Treason, 450
Treasure, 156-157
Tree, 159
Tree of Knowledge, 98
Tree of Life, 169
Trees, 97-98, 109
Trespass-Offering, 276, 283, 286
Tribal, 472
Tribal Conditions, 83, 142
Tribal Gods, 210
Tribe, 46
Tribes, 472
Triennial Cycle, 301, 324
Trinitarianism, 199
Trinity, 134
Tripartite, 444
Trope, 324
Trumpets, 413
Truth, 19-20, 147, 181, 192, 256, 268, 399
Tuch, 170
Tuesday, 97
"Tur," 449
Turtle-Dove, 377-378, 380
Twelve Tribes, 237
Twenty-one Attributes of Wisdom, 182
Twigs, 20
Tyranny, 453

Ultimate Reality, 54
Unbegotten, 184
Unchangeable, 175
Unchastity, 31
Unclean, 399
"Union Prayerbook," 323-324
Unity, 21, 28, 33-34, 105, 133, 178, 180-181, 186-187, 189, 195, 197, 201-202, 206, 210, 226, 318, 320, 371, 402
Universal, 163, 260, 262-263
Universal Dominion, 463
Universal Elements, 317
Universal Fellowship, 44
Universal Peace, 408
Universal Matter, 95
Universal Principle, 20, 136, 147
Universalism, 141
Universe, 36, 88, 150, 155, 256
Unknowable God, 14
Unrighteousness, 334
Urijah, 244
Urim, 107, 237, 267
Utilitarianism, 150-151

Vanity, 253
Vegetable-Oblation, 386
Vegetable-Offering, 382
Vegetable Sacrifices, 375
Vegetarian, 171, 398

Vegetarianism, 86
Vegetation, 87
Vernacular Prayers, 323
Vicarious, 410
Vicarious Sacrifices, 399
Victory, 407-408
Violence, 218
Virtue, 39, 134-135, 140, 156
Vitrymahzor, 437
Voltaire, 24, 135
Votive-offering, 395
Vow-offering, 483
Vows, 80

Warakah ibn-Naufal, 285
Warfare, 342
Water, 55, 85, 87-88, 96-97, 382
Waving, 381, 388
Weak, 25, 146, 156, 176
Weakness, 25
Wealth, 147, 156, 281
Weber, 57, 187-188, 190-191, 335
Wednesday, 97
Week-day, 433, 451
Wellhausen, 392, 420
Wheat, 379, 382, 384
Who Is Like Unto Thee, 429
Wicked, 180, 253, 265, 450
Wickedness, 40
Widow, 80
Wife, 159
Will, 13, 91, 94-95, 151, 153-154, 200, 269
Will-Power, 153
Wind, 85
Wine, 43, 160, 378-379, 382, 386, 392
Winter, 423, 435
Wisdom, 12, 91, 93, 179, 182-183, 227, 256, 265, 273, 400, 403
Wisdom Books, 29, 141, 147, 213
Wisdom of God, 179
Wise, 201
Wise, Isaac M., 32, 133, 286, 313
Wise Man, 267, 272
Wolf, 252
Wolff, 150
Wolves, 390
Woman, 158, 167, 172, 322
Women, 81, 99, 149, 277
Word, 183
Work-Days, 432
World, 87, 149, 224, 466
World to Come, 466
Worship, 34, 50, 134, 155, 174, 177, 211, 225, 248, 261, 275, 395, 399, 424
Wrath, 80
Wringing of the Neck, 384
Written Prophecy, 260, 266
Wrong, 149-150, 154

Ya'Aleh We-Yabo, 428
Yehi Razon, 430
"Yesodatha-Maskil, 34
"Yezer Ha-ra," 333
YHWH, 28-29, 43, 47, 50, 54, 79, 82, 124, 126-127, 158, 164, 167, 170-171, 174,183, 186, 188,191, 208, 210-213, 215-216, 218-219, 231—233, 237, 248—250, 258—264, 275, 280, 299, 304-305, 327-328, 338—340, 372—376, 379, 382, 389, 394-395, 402, 409, 417-418, 420, 443, 461—462, 470-471
"Yigdal," 35, 90
Yima, 170
Yitkapper, 397
Yom Ha-Kippurim, 323, 333, 352, 383, 428-429

Zaddik, 218
Zaddikim, 333, 335, 425
Zadok, 236, 244-245, 446
Zechariah, 245
Zedakah, 326, 330, 335
Zedim, 453
Zeira, 42
"Zekut," 335
Zeller, 138
Zemirot, 366
Zerubbabel, 246, 419
Zion, 408, 430
Zizit, 345
Zohar, 168
Zoroastrianism, 170, 226
Zunz, Leopold, 312, 316, 322, 455

13

SO